# HUMANITY

## THIRD EDITION

THIRD EDITION

# HUMANITY

## AN INTRODUCTION TO CULTURAL ANTHROPOLOGY

 **JAMES PEOPLES**
Ohio Wesleyan University

 **GARRICK BAILEY**
University of Tulsa

**WEST PUBLISHING COMPANY**
MINNEAPOLIS / ST. PAUL     NEW YORK     LOS ANGELES     SAN FRANCISCO

## WEST'S COMMITMENT TO THE ENVIRONMENT

In 1906, West Publishing Company began recycling materials left over from the production of books. This began a tradition of efficient and responsible use of resources. Today, up to 95% of our legal books and 70% of our college texts and school texts are printed on recycled, acid-free stock. West also recycles nearly 22 million pounds of scrap paper annually—the equivalent of 181,717 trees. Since the 1960s, West has devised ways to capture and recycle waste inks, solvents, oils, and vapors created in the printing process. We also recycle plastics of all kinds, wood, glass, corrugated cardboard, and batteries, and have eliminated the use of Styrofoam book packaging. We at West are proud of the longevity and the scope of our commitment to the environment.

Copyeditor:            Barbara Hodgson
Composition:           Carlisle Communications, Ltd.
Artwork:               Patti Isaacs/Parrot Graphics
Text Design:           K. M. Weber
Cover Design:          K. M. Weber
Cover Image:           Henning Christoph / Black Star
Production, Prepress, Printing and Binding by West Publishing Company.

Library of Congress Cataloging-in-Publication Data

Peoples, James G.
    Humanity : an introduction to cultural anthropology / James Peoples, Garrick Bailey. — 3rd ed.
        p.   cm.
    Includes bibliographical references and index.
    ISBN 0–314—02875—7
    1. Ethnology.   I. Bailey, Garrick Alan.   II. Title
GN316.P384   1994
306—dc20                                    ∞   93-34740
                                                CIP

# PHOTO CREDITS

## Chapter 1

2, © BIOS (A. Compost)/Peter Arnold, Inc. 4, Woodfin Camp & Assoc. 5 (top), Anthro-Photo File. 5 (bottom), Courtesy of Michael Whalen. 6 (top), Reuters/Bettman. 6 (bottom), Anthro-Photo File. 7, Anthro-Photo File. 10, © David R. Frazier Photolibrary. 12, Anthro-Photo File. 13, © Tony Stone Worldwide/Dan Bosler. 15 (UL), Reuters/Bettman. 15 (UR), Reuters/Bettman. 15 (LL), © Mireille Vautier/Woodfin Camp & Assoc. 15 (LR), Reuters/Bettman.

## Chapter 2

18, Tony Stone Worldwide. 20, Courtesy of Garrick Bailey. 21, © Bruno J. Zehnder/Peter Arnold, Inc. 22, © Bradley Smith. 23, © David R. Frazier Photolibrary. 24, Anthro-Photo File. 27 (all), Courtesy of Garrick Bailey. 28, © David R. Frazier Photolibrary. 30, © Sylvia Howe/Anthro-Photo File. 35 (top), Duke University Library/Photo Researchers. 35 (bottom), © Mary Evans Picture Library/Photo Researchers. 36. © Crandall/The Image Works. 38, Bradley Smith.

## Chapter 3

40, © Chester Higgins Jr./Photo Researchers. 42, © David R. Frazier Photolibrary. 44, Bradley Smith. 46, © Erika Stone 1992/Peter Arnold, Inc. 48, © Lynn Lennon 1986/Photo Researchers. 49, © David R. Frazier Photolibrary. 51, Anthro-Photo File. 54, © Spencer Grant/Photo Researchers. 57, © Paul N. Patmore.

## Chapter 4

62, © Sara Steck. 64, © Kal Muller 1989/Woodfin Camp & Assoc. 66 (UL), Courtesy of Garrick Bailey. 66 (LR), The Bettman Archive. 67, Culver Pictures, Inc. 69, © Penny Tweedie/Woodfin Camp & Assoc. 71(UL), Courtesy of Donald O. Henry. 71 (UR), Image Works. 73, Historical Pictures Service. 76, © David R. Frazier Photolibrary. 78, © David R. Frazier Photolibrary. 82, Courtesy of Lamont Lindstrom.

## Chapter 5

36, Anthro-Photo File. 88, Courtesy of Garrick Bailey. 89, © Jeff Greenberg/Photo Researchers. 95, The Bettman Archive. 97,

## Chapter 6

102, Photo Researchers. 104, FPG International. 108, Tony Stone Worldwide. 109, Tony Stone Worldwide. 110 (UR), Anthro-Photo File. 110 (LL), Anthro-Photo File. 113 , Courtesy of Garrick Bailey. 118, Historical Pictures Service. 120, Historical Pictures Service.

## Chapter 7

130, Anthro-Photo File. 131, © Stephen J. Krasemann/Peter Arnold Inc. 134 (UL), Anthro-Photo File. 134 (UR), © Bill O'Connor/Peter Arnold, Inc. 134 (MR), Chip & Rosa Maria Peterson. 134 (LL), © Jeffrey L. Rotman/Peter Arnold, Inc. 134 (LR), Anthro-Photo File. 136, Richard Weiss/Peter Arnold, Inc. 137, © Bradley Smith. 139 (UL), Anthro-Photo File. 139 (UR), Anthro-Photo File. 141, Anthro-Photo File. 142, Anthro-Photo File. 143, Anthro-Photo File. 146, Anthro-Photo File.

Photo credits continue following index.

*For Roberta, Deborah, and Matthew*

# CONTENTS IN BRIEF

# CONTENTS

# PART II
# THEORIES AND METHODS OF CULTURAL ANTHROPOLOGY    62

## CHAPTER 4
## THE DEVELOPMENT OF ANTHROPOLOGICAL THOUGHT    64

## CHAPTER 5
## METHODS OF INVESTIGATION    86

# PART III
# DIVERSITY    102

## CHAPTER 6
## THE WORLD SINCE 1500    104

## CHAPTER 7
## ADAPTATION: FORAGING    130

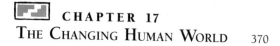

# PREFACE

*Humanity* is designed as a textbook for introductory courses in cultural anthropology. More than any other scholarly discipline, anthropology studies and tries to explain the rich cultural diversity of the world's peoples. We try to convey to students and other readers the value of discovering and understanding this diversity. We also want to encourage readers to develop appreciation and respect for cultural variety, an attitude that has increasing relevance in the modern world.

As with textbooks in other disciplines, we first introduce the key concepts, perspectives, methods, and theoretical ideas of anthropology, which are the main subject of parts 1 and 2. The main contribution of anthropology to the understanding of humankind is its documentation of the remarkable diversity of the world's cultures. Accordingly, the description and analysis of this diversity in part 3 takes up most of the book. Anthropological insights on the modern world form the main focus of Part 4, which discusses the interdependence of the world's peoples and nations, ethnic conflicts, population growth, hunger, and the survival of indigenous peoples and cultures.

## Changes in the Third Edition

There are numerous major changes in this edition, beginning with a substantial rewriting of Chapter 1. Applied anthropology now appears as a fifth subfield. A separate section describes how modern cultural anthropologists increasingly study industrial societies, a point that was not given due weight in previous editions. The revisions to other chapters are most conveniently summarized part by part.

In Part 1, Chapter 2 is greatly revised. The concept of culture is redefined to bring it more in line with common usage. The phrase *sociocultural system* has been dropped altogether and we now use the term *culture* throughout the book. The conceptual distinction between cultural knowledge and behavior is retained, however. The discussion of the relation between human biology and culture, which formerly appeared in Chapter 3, has been greatly reduced and now forms the concluding section of chapter 2. Chapter 3 (formerly 4) is reorganized, thanks to the suggestions of reviewers.

In Part 2, Chapter 4 (theory) is somewhat condensed, in line with reviewers' comments that too much detail was included in the previous edition. Large portions of Chapter 5 (methods) are rewritten and the description of historical methods is shortened.

We agree with the comments of many reviewers that the coverage of cultural diversity in Part 3 can usefully begin with a brief chapter (6, in this edition) discussing the impact of European expansion after 1500 on the preindustrial world. Hopefully, this chapter will drive home the point that no contemporary culture has escaped the consequences of the changes in the last half millenium. Chapters 7, 8, 9, 13, and 15 are much the same as in the second edition, although there have been rewordings (such as !Kung and Inuit) and some material is deleted. All other chapters in Part 3 contain substantial deletions, additions, or revisions. Material on explanations of the incest taboo in Chapter 10 (family and marriage) is deleted and some of the sections are reorganized. In Chapter 11 (kinship) double descent and Sudanese terminology are deleted; bilateral kinship is redefined to make it more technically correct; there is a new section on cognatic descent; and new examples are used. Chapter 12 now contains a section on the cultural construction of gender. In Chapter 14 (inequality) statistical data on the distribution of income and wealth in the United States are updated. Chapter 16 (personality, life cycle) is shorter due to a general streamlining and the deletion of one ethnographic example of initiation rites.

More than in previous editions, the four chapters in Part 4 form an integrated unit focused around anthropological insights on the modern world. Chapter 17 discusses the major features of the modern global system, including economic interdependence, international migration, and the creation of political boundaries often at variance with preexisting ethnic divisions. Chapter 18 (ethnicity) is revised to reflect recent ethnic conflicts in the former Soviet Union and eastern Europe. Some statistical data in chapter 19 are updated and new material on sustainable agriculture is included. Finally, introductory material in the Epilogue is changed to shift its focus further towards humanitarian concerns.

Many design and pedagogical features also are new. Most maps, tables, and other figures are revised or updated. There are two new boxes and over a hundred new illustrations, most in color. We have retained the convention of boldfacing key terms in the chapter text, and all key terms are again defined in the glossary for easy reference. As before, each chapter concludes with a summary and list of key terms, and most chapters contain several new suggested readings. Once again, to help keep student attention focused on the material discussed, we have assembled references at the end of the book, organized by chapter and by major heading. To give full credit to the scholars whose ethnographies and theoretical ideas are discussed, we have worked their names into the text wherever possible.

# ACKNOWLEDGMENTS

We are indebted to those scholars and colleagues who reviewed the second edition of *Humanity* and whose comments proved so helpful in developing the third. West Publishing Company had the text reviewed by thirteen anthropologists, both users and non-users. These include: Donald Brown (Oklahoma State), Norbert Dannhaeuser (Texas A&M), William Davis (University of California, Davis), Robert Kelly (Louisville), Karen Larson (Gustavus Adolphus), Nancy B. Leis (Central Michigan), Henry Lundsgaarde (Kansas), Margo L. Matwychuk (Victoria), Barbara J. Michael (Alabama), Mattison Mines (University of California, Santa Barbara), Donald K. Pollock (SUNY Buffalo), Dianne Smith (Santa Rosa), and Michael B. Whiteford (Iowa State). The suggestions for rethinking, rewriting, additions, and deletions of these reviewers were very helpful. All of them will recognize at least some of their handiwork in the revisions.

Our personal friends and colleagues lent moral support as well as contributed their expertise. J.P. thanks his Ohio Wesleyan department mates—Ted Cohen, Mary Howard, and Jan Smith—for their oft-needed encouragement. G.B. thanks his Tulsa colleagues Pat Blessing, Annette Fromm, Don Henry, Monty Lindstrom, Peter Stromberg, and Michael Whalen for their comments. Both of us are grateful to Don Brown and John Wilson. William Davis tried to straighten us out in the previous edition on the difference between bilateral kinship and cognatic descent; this time we took his advice. Once again, Nancy Leis contributed her valuable knowledge and experience to *Humanity*.

Several people wrote to us directly or to the publisher with their unsolicited (but welcome) comments and suggestions. We thank Paul Winther and Thomas Stevenson for doing so. Douglas Hayward and Judith Lingenfelter may find part of their objections to Chapter 16 eliminated. Shirley Fedorak provided us with a list of typos, misprints, and numerous other suggestions, almost all of which we have incorporated. We especially thank her for what must have been many hours of her time. Thanks also to Doug Raybeck for his encouragement and to Henry Rutz for his support over the years.

Once again, various editors at West were attentive to our preferences and tolerant of our tardiness. Our new editor and friend Bob Jucha proved as competent and caring as was Tom LaMarre (no longer our editor but still our friend). Development Editor Diane Colwyn oversaw the reviews and put the comments together in a maximally useful form. We also thank Production Editor Cliff Kallemeyn and Copyeditor Barbara Hodgson for producing the book and making our English readable.

Garrick's spouse Roberta was as patient as always. Jim's family, wife Deborah and son Matthew, helped maintain his motivation.

# HUMANITY

**THIRD EDITION**

**CHAPTER 1**

# THE STUDY OF HUMANITY

*Anthropologists are interested in the full range of human diversity. These men are from the Asmat culture of New Guinea.*

**CONTENTS**

Where did the human species come from? How have we changed over time, both biologically and culturally? Is there a common human nature and, if so, what is it like? In what ways do humans who live in various times and places differ? How can we explain why cultures vary in their economic systems, religious beliefs, family relations, and artistic styles? Such questions are the concern of anthropology, the study of humanity.

Anthropologists are interested in almost everything about people. We want to know when and where the human species originated, how and why we evolved into our present form, and the ways in which this biological evolution continues to affect us today. Anthropologists want to know about the technological, economic, political, and intellectual development of humanity. We want to know the extent to which different human populations vary in their biological and social characteristics and to understand why these differences exist.

Anthropologists try to explain why people in some places believe that sickness is caused by dead ancestors, whereas others claim that tarantulas throw magical darts into their bodies, and still others tell you that the spirits of evil humans leave their bodies at night and seek out the internal organs of their victims, which they devour from the inside out. We want to understand the rules that you know unconsciously that instruct you when to bow your head and speak reverently, when to sound smart, when to act dumb, and when to cuss like a sailor. Anthropologists are interested in why Americans eat beef but devout Hindus do not, and in why some New Guinea people periodically engorge themselves with pork but some Middle Easterners regard pig flesh as unclean. We want to know why Balinese are fascinated by cock fights, Spaniards by bull fights, Thais by fish fights, and North Americans by people fights. In short, anthropologists are liable to be curious about practically everything human: our evolution, our genes, our bodies, our emotions, our behaviors, and our thoughts.

If you already have the impression that anthropology is a broad field and that anthropologists have quite diverse interests, you are correct. In fact, it is commonly said that the distinguishing characteristic of anthropology—the thing that makes it different from the many other fields that also include people as their subject matter—is its broad scope. A good way to emphasize this broad scope is to say that anthropologists are interested in *all* human beings—whether living or dead, Asian or African or European—and that they are interested in many different *aspects* of humans, including their skin color, family lives, political systems, tools, personality types, and languages. No place or time is too remote to escape the anthropologist's notice. No dimension of humankind, from genes to art styles, is outside the anthropologist's attention.

## SUBFIELDS OF ANTHROPOLOGY

Anthropology, then, is a diverse field. No individual anthropologist can master the whole range of subjects encompassed by the whole discipline. For practical reasons, almost all modern anthropologists specialize in one of five principal subfields. Physical (or biological) anthropology is concerned mainly with the evolutionary origins and physical diversity of the human species. Archaeology focuses on the technological and cultural development of human societies over long time periods. The subdiscipline known as cultural anthropology describes and analyzes contemporary and historically recent societies, trying to understand how and why the world's cultures are so diverse. Anthropological linguistics deals with human languages and their relations to cultures. Finally, applied anthropology uses anthropological concepts, methods, and theories to try to solve contemporary human problems. Anthropology is even more complicated than this fivefold division implies because each of these subfields is in turn divided into several specializations. Although cultural anthropology is the primary subject of this book, a brief look at the other subfields is essential to understand the whole discipline.

## Physical Anthropology

**Physical** (also called **biological**) **anthropology** is concerned with such topics as the biological evolution of the human species, the anatomy and behavior of monkeys and apes, and the physical variations between different human populations. As these subjects indicate, physical anthropology is closely related to the natural sciences in its goals and methods.

An important goal of physical anthropology is to understand how and why the human species evolved from prehuman, ape-like ancestors. Scholars who investigate human biological evolution are known as **paleoanthropologists**. Over decades of tedious searching for fossils and meticulous excavations and laboratory studies, paleoanthropologists have reconstructed the history of how humans evolved anatomically. The fossil record is incomplete and can be interpreted in many ways. But the outlines of human evolution are becoming clear. Most scholars agree that the evolutionary line leading to modern humans split from those leading to modern African apes (chimpanzees and gorillas) around five million years ago. It also appears that the only human species alive today, *Homo sapiens,* came into existence surprisingly recently, probably around 100,000 years ago. New discoveries may alter our current understandings, just as they have done in the past.

**Primatologists**, another kind of biological anthropologist, specialize in the evolution, anatomy, social behavior, and adaptation of primates, the taxonomic order to which humans belong. By conducting field studies of how living primates forage, mate, move around in their environment, and interact socially, primatologists hope to shed light on the forces that affected early human populations. Detailed studies of ground-dwelling monkeys and apes (such as gorillas, chimpanzees, and baboons) have been especially fruitful. Research has shown that the social behavior of many primate species is astoundingly complex.

Yet another type of biological anthropologist is interested in how and why human populations vary physically. All humans are members of a single species, and one of the basic tenets of anthropology is that the physical similarities between the world's peoples far outweigh the differences. Nonetheless, the residents of different continents were once more isolated from one another than they are today, and during this separation they evolved differences in overall body and facial form, height, skin color, blood chemistry, and other genetically determined features. Anthropologists who study **human variation** seek to measure and explain the differences and similarities among the world's peoples in these and other physical characteristics.

Sometimes law enforcement agencies call on **forensic anthropologists** to help identify and analyze human

*Paleoanthropologists use physical remains to investigate the biological evolution of humanity.*

4

Barbara Smuts, a primatologist shown here with a baboon troop, studies monkeys and apes in their natural habitats.

skeletal remains. Forensic anthropologists aid in determining the age, gender, and height and other characteristics of crime or accident victims. For example, in the 1980s the newly elected government of Argentina hired Clyde Snow, a forensic anthropologist, to help identify the people killed by death squads between 1976 and 1983, the years of military rule.

## Archaeology

**Archaeology** is the investigation of the human past by excavating and analyzing physical remains. Because it investigates the ways in which human life has changed over the centuries and millennia, archaeology has much in common with history. It differs, however, in its methods and, to some extent, its goals. Modern archaeology usually is divided into two major kinds of studies: prehistoric and historic.

**Prehistoric archaeology** is the investigation of ancient cultures—those that never kept written records of their activities, customs, and beliefs. Although prehistoric peoples lacked writing, evidence of their activities exists in the form of the tools, pottery, ornaments, bones, plant pollen, charcoal, and other materials they left behind, in or on the ground. Through meticulous excavation and laboratory analysis of these material remains, prehistoric archaeologists reconstruct the way people lived in ancient times and trace how human cultures have changed over the centuries. In fact, research conducted by prehistoric archaeologists provides our only source of information about how people lived before the development of writing.

To learn about the more recent past, historians use written materials such as diaries, letters, land records, newspapers, and tax collection documents. Written

records provide useful data, but they typically are fragmentary and provide information only on specific subjects and subgroups within a society. The growing field of **historic archaeology** supplements written materials by excavations of houses, stores, plantations, factories, and other historic structures. Historic archaeologists often uncover hard data on living conditions and other topics lacking in written accounts. One interesting application of historic archaeology is the study of what America's trash tells us about contemporary American life. Since the 1970s William Rathje of the University of Arizona has managed the Garbage Project, which analyzes the stuff people throw out. This study has provided insight into waste management policies and American consumer

An archaeological field crew under the direction of Michael Whalen excavates a site in the American Southwest. Prehistoric archaeologists attempt to reconstruct the past by careful and systematic excavation of the material remains of prehistoric peoples.

Excavations conducted by historic archaeologists provide data that complements written records of historic peoples. This excavation confirmed the presence of a Roman amphitheatre beneath the modern city of London. Gladiators fought here two thousand years ago.

habits; the study of America's garbage shows, for instance, that many households drink more beer than they claim when they respond to surveys.

## Cultural Anthropology

**Cultural anthropology** (also called **ethnology**) is the study of contemporary and historically recent human societies and cultures. As its name suggests, the main

Traditionally ethnographers travelled to far-away places and studied exotic peoples. Here Harvard anthropologist David Mayberry-Lewis sits with the Xavante of the Brazilian Amazon.

focus of this subfield is culture—the customs and beliefs of some human group (the concept of culture is discussed at length in chapter 2). Ethnologists are especially fascinated by the great variety of the world's peoples and cultures, and describing and attempting to understand and explain this cultural diversity is one of their major objectives. Making the public aware and tolerant of the cultural differences that exist within humanity is another mission of ethnology.

To do their research and collect their data, ethnologists conduct **fieldwork** among human communities. Fieldwork ordinarily involves moving into the community under study and communicating in the local language and living in close contact with the people. Intimate interaction with the members of a community provides ethnologists with firsthand experiences that yield insights that could not be gained in any other way. For this reason many cultural anthropologists believe that the fieldwork experience is the hallmark of their discipline—the single most important feature that distinguishes it from other human sciences such as sociology, psychology, economics, and political science. Fieldworkers usually report the findings of their research in books or scholarly journals, where they are available to the general public. A written account of how a single human population lives is called an **ethnography** (which means "writing about a people").

Cultural anthropology is the largest of the subfields. Of the doctoral degrees (Ph.D.s) in anthropology awarded in the United States between 1972 and 1990, about one-half were in cultural anthropology, about one-fourth in archaeology, one-eighth in physical anthropology, and the remainder in linguistic anthropology or some other specialization.

## Anthropological Linguistics

Defined as the study of human language, linguistics is a field all its own, existing as a separate discipline from anthropology. Linguists describe and analyze the sound patterns and combinations, words, meanings, and sentence structures of human languages. As seen in chapter 3, language has some amazing properties, and the fact that humans are able to learn and use language at all is truly remarkable.

Language interests anthropologists for several reasons. For one thing the ability to communicate complex messages with great efficiency may be the most important capability of humans that makes us different from

*Cultural anthropologists usually collect data on contemporary peoples by living with them, often in much the same way as the people themselves. Here fieldworker Richard Lee socializes with the !Kung, a southern Africa people who until recently lived by hunting and gathering.*

primates and other animals; certainly our ability to speak is a key factor in our evolutionary success. Cultural anthropologists, especially, are interested in language because of how the language and culture of a people affect each other. The subfield of **anthropological linguistics** is most concerned with the complex relations between language and other aspects of human behavior and thought. For example, anthropological linguists are interested in how language is used in various social contexts: What style of speech must one use with people of high status? What does the way people attach labels to their natural environment tell us about the way they perceive that environment? We return to these and other topics in anthropological linguistics in chapter 3.

## Applied Anthropology

In the past almost all professional anthropologists spent their careers in some form of educational institution, most commonly in colleges and universities and in museums. Today hundreds of anthropologists hold full-time positions that allow them to apply their expertise in governmental agencies, nonprofit groups, private

corporations, and international bodies. Many more make their living as consultants to such organizations and institutions. These institutions and organizations employ anthropologists because they believe that people trained in the discipline will help them in problem solving. In recognition of the growth of noneducational employment opportunities, the American Anthropological Association (the professional organization of anthropologists) officially recognizes **applied anthropology** as a separate subfield.

Applied anthropologists work for a wide range of organizations. A few examples illustrate the ways in which anthropologists contribute to the alleviation of human problems. *Medical anthropologists* investigate the interrelations between human health, nutrition, and cultural beliefs and practices. Because the transmission of pathogenic organisms is affected by peoples' dietary, sanitary, sexual, and other habits, medical anthropologists work with epidemiologists to identify cultural practices that affect the spread of diseases. By studying a community's beliefs about the causes and treatments of illness, they may give advice that helps hospitals and agencies to deliver health care services more effectively to people in need. *Economic* and *development anthropologists* are employed by or consult for institutions involved in Third World development, including the U.S. Agency for International Development, the Asian Development Bank, the Rockefeller Foundation, and the World Bank. One of their major roles is to provide information on local communities that help agencies to adapt development projects to local conditions and local needs. *Educational anthropologists* work in programs for bilingual education and conduct detailed observations of interactions in classrooms to advise on how to improve learning. Anthropologists work for several organizations whose purpose is to help indigenous people around the world fight plans and projects that would relocate them, violate their sovereignty, or harm their rights to resources. Increasingly, anthropologists are employed by corporations, where they work on problems ranging from the interactions of humans and machines to the training of executives engaged in international business to be sensitive to the cultures of their potential customers, clients, and partners (see Box 1.1 for other examples).

In these and many other ways the concepts, methods, and theories of anthropology are being applied to practical issues. Anthropological involvements in policy-making and problem solving are likely to expand in the future, as the interdependency between the world's geographical regions and peoples increases.

## NEW YORK

As a graduate student in anthropology, Patricia Sachs went to great lengths to understand the economic role of women and children in Nigeria. She spent the summer of 1977 in the ancient city of Kano, living in a white-washed mud house. She ate the local specialties of spicy, deep-fried beans and rice smothered in hot sauce. She even tried to learn to spin cotton so she could sit alongside Nigerian women and gain insights into how they saw their work.

Now Sachs has turned her anthropologist's skills to study another culture full of distinctive rituals: the local phone company. These days, she spends her time in the Manhattan offices of New York Telephone Co., chronicling—and trying to relieve—some of the unexpected problems technology creates for union workers and their managers.

Sachs is one of a growing number of anthropologists who are offering their services to the business world. These researchers use their techniques of painstaking observation and patient interviews in the field to understand how people work together. But these corporate anthropologists are not just passive observers. They are helping companies redesign work practices to improve teamwork and efficiency.

Xerox Corp., which many think offers contemporary corporate anthropologists the sort of opportunity Samoa offered Margaret Mead, hired its first anthropologist in the mid 1970s to help the computer scientists think about how paper flows through a real-life office. These days, a half dozen Xerox anthropologists tackle issues from how Xerox engineers should design prod-

# BOX 1.1

## ANTHROPOLOGY, INC.: THE SCIENTISTS OF CULTURE HELP BUSINESS DISCERN CORPORATE RITES AND WRONGS

By Elizabeth Corcoran,
SPECIAL TO *THE WASHINGTON POST*

ucts to how those products should look to customers.

General Motors Corp. managers lean on staff anthropologist Elizabeth K. Briody to help puzzle through vexing personnel issues, such as why promising young executives have been reluctant to do overseas stints.

The federal government is also turning to anthropologists to understand how changes in policy may affect the rhythms of local communities. The National Oceanic and Atmospheric Administration, for example, is paying some anthropologists to study how local communities adapt to new fishing regulations—in hopes of smoothing some of the problems such changes can cause.

The World Bank, meanwhile, is using anthropologists in developing nations to try to reduce the trauma experienced by communities forced to resettle to make room for a new dam or other development project.

## THE WATCHERS

Why anthropologists? What do they offer that the legions of management consultants, marketing experts and Peter Drucker wannabees already scrambling for business do not?

The answer, enthusiasts say, is simple: Anthropologists listen.

"We've been trained to watch," said Marietta L. Baba, a professor of anthropology at Wayne State University in Detroit. "We don't come around with a battery of instruments or a grid that we map problems onto," she said. Instead, anthropologists try to get an inside peek at how people in a group interact or how they get a job done.

"Anthropology is interested in finding all the hidden jewels in an organization," said Eleanor Wynn, an anthropologist based outside of Portland, Ore., who consults for high-technology companies. It's about making things that people take for granted in doing their jobs more obvious, Wynn said.

Like most other anthropologists practicing their craft in business and government, Wynn did not intend to devote herself to unraveling the mysteries of corporate rites. She had planned to spend the summer of 1976 in Peru, but wound up at the Xerox Palo Alto Research Center (PARC) in California instead.

"Really, it was like going to deepest, darkest New Guinea," she recalled. "What goes on in an R&D computer lab, well, it was one of the strangest things I'd ever seen." She was even baffled by the scientists' jokes, all punctuated with mathematical innuendos. "I didn't speak the language. It took awhile."

*continued on next page*

Over time, Wynn learned how things that seem obvious to researchers on the ground floor can be invisible to managers above. In the late 1970s, she spent some time watching a group of Xerox trainers and educators learn to use a novel system called the Star workstation, a forerunner to the personal computer. In her report, Wynn noted that the Star was handy because professionals like the trainers could compose their thoughts on the computer and then, with some help, swiftly print out high-quality documents.

The observations seemed so obvious they were almost not worth noting. Then the management blew up. "The guy I wrote this for was incensed," Wynn recalled. "Professionals weren't suppose to type their own stuff."

## THE ROGAINE RESEARCH

Where market research groups traditionally rely on dry, aggregate data to spot trends, anthropologists trot out to the field and chat up the locals. After Upjohn Co. introduced the hair-growing drug Rogaine, managers wanted to learn more about how niche groups—call them subcultures—felt about losing their hair. They called Baba, the Michigan anthropology professor.

With a colleague, Baba interviewed groups of Navajo Indians in Arizona, Mexican Americans in San Diego, the Amish in Pennsylvania, punk rockers in the East Village in New York City and women in Dallas. Their findings: Everyone worries about losing hair—but for very different reasons.

To keep with their traditions, for instance, Amish women pull their hair back tightly in a bun—so tightly that many suffer hair loss at an early age. "Do they care? Yes!" Baba said. "They didn't want people staring at them."

In contrast, people in the East Village often sport spiked, vividly colored hair precisely so they can stand out from the crowd, she added. Losing hair means losing some of the freedom to rebel.

Although Baba was not promoting Rogaine as she interviewed her subjects and is getting ready to publish her findings, Upjohn can make good use of the information. Therein lies the ethical dilemma for anthropologists: What to do with the information they elicit from their research?

"There's little point to doing anthropology, aside from artistic and intellectual merit, unless the people studied can derive some benefit from it," asserted William L. Partridge, a senior anthropologist at the World Bank.

Such ethical concerns nonetheless point up another way that anthropologists differ from business consultants. Business consultants often recommend that companies consolidate jobs—and cut staff in the process. That is where most anthropologists, including Sachs at New York Telephone, draw the line.

"I'm not going to make a recommendation that some people lose their jobs," she said. "I think my greater responsibility is to reveal what's going on, to show the intelligence that's already there."

## TENSION IN THE FIELD

Even so, "business still doesn't sit well with most anthropologists," Baba conceded. "There is real tension between academic and applied anthropologists in the value of problem solving," said GM's Briody. "It's too bad. It seems there's room for all kinds of work."

The controversy has deep historical roots. From the 1930s through World War II, anthropologists regularly crossed the corporate threshold. Anthropologist W. Lloyd Warner played a pivotal role in the classic studies on worker productivity carried out at Western's Electric Co.'s Chicago-based Hawthorne Works. Others worked to boost manufacturing productivity, especially during the war.

In the 1960s, however, the U.S. military tried to tap anthropologists for information on political movements in developing countries, Baba notes. In an uproar, the profession rewrote its ethics code, banning any work that could not be published. Cooperating with companies consequently became taboo.

These days, the number of practicing anthropologist is still small. Even at Xerox, the scientists continue to see themselves as a tiny band of early explorers. "There are still a lot of battles to be waged to show the value of what we're doing," said Lucy Suchman, a scientist at Xerox PARC.

But the numbers are growing. Baba estimates that at least a third of the new PhDs this year—about 100 people altogether—will venture into the bureaucracies of American companies and government. By the turn of the decade, she said she expects the number of practicing anthropologists to reach 3,000. ✦

SOURCE: The Washington Post, February 21, 1993. Copyright Elizabeth Corcoran 1993. Reprinted by permission.

## ▛▟ CULTURAL ANTHROPOLOGY TODAY

As the overview of the five subdisciplines indicates, anthropology is indeed a broad field. One or another kind of anthropologist studies human biology, prehistory, language and its relations to culture, and contemporary human ways of life. Even by itself cultural anthropology—the main subject of this text—is enormously broad, for modern ethnological fieldworkers study human communities from all parts of the world, from the mountains of Tibet to the deserts of the American Southwest, from the streets of Calcutta to the plains of East Africa.

In the popular imagination, cultural anthropological fieldworkers go to far-off places and study exotic peoples or "natives." Except for the stereotypes about the "natives," this image was reasonably accurate until the 1970s. Until then ethnology differed from sociology and other disciplines that studied living peoples and cultures mainly by the kinds of cultures studied. Cultural anthropologists mainly focused on small-scale, non-Western, preindustrial, subsistence-oriented cultures, whereas sociological studies mainly dealt with large Euro-American, industrial, money-and-market countries. Cultural anthropologists themselves often sought out pristine, untouched tribal cultures to study because living among the "primitives" brought prestige and fame in the discipline.

All this has changed. Modern ethnologists may be found studying American factory workers, Swedish churches, Chicago motorcycle gangs, Canadian medical clinics, British witches' covens, and Appalachian towns. There are many reasons for this shift of emphasis. One reason is the realization by anthropologists that their concepts and fieldwork methods could yield insights about their own nations that other disciplines have missed. Another is that increasing numbers of anthropologists have become interested in using their discipline's concepts and methods to solve real-world problems. At any rate, the boundaries between cultural anthropology and other disciplines (especially sociology) are much less firm than they were even a few decades ago. Most ethnological fieldwork, however, still occurs in relatively small communities (on the order of a few hundred to a few thousand) where the researcher can participate firsthand in the lives of the people. More than any other single factor, the fieldwork experience distinguishes cultural anthropology from other disciplines concerned with humankind.

In many ways modern cultural anthropology overlaps with numerous other disciplines that study people. For example, a fieldworker may be especially interested in the agriculture, leadership patterns, legal system, or art of a culture or region. He or she will, therefore, want to be acquainted with the work of economists, agronomists, political scientists, and artists or art historians—disciplines that have made some particular dimensions

*Increasingly, cultural anthropologists are studying their own society as well as peoples of other continents.*

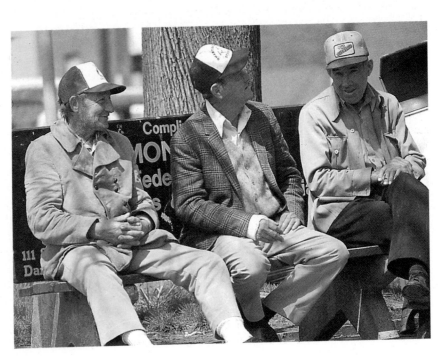

of human life their specialization. Likewise, an ethnologist who specializes in some geographical region (such as West Africa, China, or Brazil) will read the works of historians, sociologists, novelists, and political scientists who also have written about the region. Cultural anthropologists regularly study subjects that are the specializations of other disciplines, as is nicely illustrated by anthropological specializations in such areas as ethnomusicology, ethnopoetics, ethnobotany, and ethnolinguistics. (Here's an amusing and at least half-true general principle: Any subject can be made into a subject for ethnological research by prefixing it with "ethno.") Cultural anthropology thus cuts across many disciplines, encompassing many of the subjects that other scholars consider their special province—law, religion, literature, music, and so on.

## ANTHROPOLOGICAL PERSPECTIVES

Because cultural anthropologists study many of the same kinds of things studied by other scholars, obviously it is not *what* they study that makes the field distinct. Most ethnologists believe that the main difference between their discipline and other social sciences and humanities lies not so much in the kinds of subjects they investigate as in the approach they take to studying humanity. We believe it is important that cultures and communities be studied holistically, comparatively, and relativistically. Because it is these perspectives as much as anything else that makes cultural anthropology distinctive, they need to be introduced.

### Holism

To study a subject "holistically" is to attempt to understand all the factors that influence it and to interpret it in the context of all those factors. With respect to studies of human cultures and societies, the **holistic perspective** means that no single aspect of a community can be understood unless its relations to other aspects of the community's total way of life are explored. Holism requires, for example, that a fieldworker studying the rituals of a people must investigate how those rituals are influenced by the people's family life, economic forces, political leadership, relationships between the sexes, and a host of other factors. The attempt to understand and interpret a community's customs, beliefs, values, and so forth holistically is one reason why ethnographic fieldwork takes so much time and involves close contact with people. An adequate description of rituals themselves is difficult enough, but the holistic perspective requires that the fieldworker also try to place the rituals in the total context of people's lives.

Taken literally, a holistic understanding of a people's customs and beliefs is probably not possible because of the complexity of human societies. But cultural anthropologists have learned that various aspects of human life do affect one another. To ignore the interrelations between these aspects—language, religion, art, economy, family, and the rest—results in serious distortions and misunderstandings. Therefore, a holistic account is a goal most fieldworkers strive for, although it may be impossible to achieve. Although more complicated than this, the essence of the holistic perspective may be stated fairly simply: *Look for connections and interrelations between things, and try to understand parts in the context of the whole.*

### Comparativism

As we have already seen, in the early decades of its existence ethnological research focused mainly on non-Western peoples, many of whom thought and acted quite differently from the citizens of the anthropologist's own (usually European or North American) nation. Anthropologists soon learned that the ideas and concepts that applied to their own societies often did not apply to those of other peoples, whose cultural traditions were vastly different. They learned, for example, to mistrust the claims put forth by French scholars about human nature when the only humans these scholars had ever encountered lived in Western Europe.

More than the members of any other discipline, anthropologists are aware of the enormous diversity of the world's cultures. This diversity means that any general theories or ideas scholars might have about humans—about human nature, sexuality, warfare, gender relationships, and so on—must take into account information from a wide range of societies. In other words, general theoretical ideas about humans or human societies or cultures must be tested from a **comparative perspective**. The ways of life of people in different times and places are far too diverse for any theory to be accepted until it has been tested in a range of human populations. Some ways in which these tests are conducted are covered in chapter 5. For now, we may state the comparative perspective as: *Generalizations about humans must take the full range of cultural diversity into account.*

*Anthropologists emphasize the need to compare a wide variety of cultures before drawing conclusions. Generalizations about humanity that did not include peoples such as these Yąnomamö, shown preparing a tapir for eating, would likely be erroneous.*

## Relativism

Fundamentally, the perspective known as **cultural relativism** means that no culture is inherently superior or inferior to any other. The reason anthropologists adopt this perspective is that concepts such as "superiority" require judgments about the relative worthiness of behaviors, beliefs, and other characteristics of a culture. Such judgments are inevitably rooted in one's values, and one's values, by and large, depend on the culture in which one was raised. (You may think, incidentally, that surely there are universally valid standards for judging and evaluating cultures. Perhaps you are right; the trouble is, people don't agree on what they are!)

To see why approaching the study of cultures relativistically is important, we may contrast cultural relativism with **ethnocentrism**. Ethnocentrism is the belief that the moral standards, manners, attitudes, and so forth of one's own culture are superior to those of other cultures. Most people are ethnocentric, and *a certain degree* of ethnocentrism probably is essential if people are to be content with their lives and if their culture is to persist. Mild ethnocentrism—meaning that people hold certain values dear but don't insist that everyone else hold and live by those values—is unobjectionable to ethnologists. But extreme ethnocentrism—meaning that

people believe that their values are the only correct ones and that all people everywhere should be judged by how closely they live up to those values—breeds attitudes and behaviors of intolerance that are anathema to cultural anthropology.

Ethnocentric attitudes are detrimental to the objectivity of ethnographic fieldworkers. However difficult in practice, anthropologists should try not to evaluate the behavior of the people being studied according to the standards of the fieldworker's own culture. Ethnocentrism should also be avoided in comparative work. Nineteenth-century anthropologists, who mainly were interested in the evolution of culture, ranked cultures into a series of stages and tried to show how lower stages of culture developed into higher ones. Most often at the top of their hypothetical ladder of progress was the culture of the West. This was because their comparisons of cultures used ethnocentric standards: They decided whether a particular culture belonged to a lower or higher stage by deciding how closely that culture resembled their own.

Like the holistic and comparative perspectives, the essential point of cultural relativism may be stated simply: *In studying another culture do not evaluate the behavior of its members by the standards and values of your own culture.*

## THE VALUE OF ANTHROPOLOGY

What insights does the discipline of anthropology offer about humanity? What is the value of the information anthropologists have gathered about the past and present of humankind? We have already seen that applied anthropologists help in planning and implementing programs, and in future chapters we look further at how anthropological research contributes to the solution of human problems. For now, we want to note some of the more general insights of the field.

First, because of its broad scope, anthropology gives us the information we need to understand the biological, technological, and cultural development of humanity over long time spans. Most of the reliable data now available about human biological evolution, prehistoric cultures, and non-Western peoples were collected by anthropologists. Because much of this knowledge has become part of our cultural heritage, where it is recorded in textbooks and taught in schools, it is easy to forget that someone had to discover and interpret these facts. For example, only in the late nineteenth century did most scientists accept that people are related to apes, and only in the late twentieth century did the closeness of this relation become apparent.

But anthropology has contributed more than just a plethora of factual material to our understanding of the human condition. Concepts first developed or worked out by anthropologists have been incorporated into the thinking of millions of people. For example, in this chapter we have used the term *culture*—a concept that we assume our readers are aware of and a word that commonly is used in everyday life. You may not be aware that the scientific meaning of this word, as used in the phrase "Japanese culture," is not very old. Into the nineteenth century, people did not fully understand the importance of the distinction between a people's culture (the learned beliefs and habits that made them distinctive) and their biological makeup (their physical characteristics). Patterns of acting, thinking, and feeling often were thought to be rooted in a group's biological constitution. For example, because there often were readily observable differences in the physical appearances of various races, it was thought that these physical differences accounted for differences in beliefs and habits as well. In other words, differences that we now know are caused largely or entirely by learning and cultural upbringing were confused with differences caused by biological inheritance. Early-twentieth-century anthropologists such as Franz Boas, Alfred Kroeber, and Ruth Benedict marshaled empirical evidence showing that race and culture are independent of each other. As this example shows, anthropologists have already contributed to our understanding of the human condition, although most people are not aware of these contributions.

Another value of anthropology (ethnology, especially) is that it teaches us the importance of understanding and appreciating cultural diversity; that is, it urges us not to be ethnocentric in our attitudes toward other peoples. The orientation known as cultural relativism is not only important to the objectivity of ethnologists but also one of the main lessons anthropology offers to the general public. Mutual toleration and understanding between the world's peoples is increasingly important in this era of global travel and international migration. To be sure, if everyone in the world became less ethnocentric, the world's problems would not be solved. But a relativistic outlook on cultural differences might help to alleviate some of the prejudices, misunderstandings, interethnic conflicts, and outright racism that continues to victimize so many people in all continents.

A related point is that anthropology can help people to avoid some of the miscommunication and misunder-standings that commonly arise when people from different parts of the world interact with one another. As we shall see in future chapters, our upbringing in a particular culture influences us in subtle ways of which we are not aware. For instance, Canadians know how to interpret one another's actions on the basis of speech styles or body language, but these cues do not necessarily mean the same thing to people from different cultures. A Canadian salesperson selling products in Turkey may wonder why her host will not cut the chitchat and get down to business, whereas the Turk can't figure out why the visitor thinks that they can do business before they have become better acquainted. A North American trying to exude self-confidence in his dealings with a Latin American may instead come across as arrogant or egotistical. Anthropology teaches people to be aware of and sensitive to cultural differences—peoples' actions may not mean what we take them to mean, and much misunderstanding can be avoided by simply becoming aware of cultural differences and taking them into account in our dealings with other people.

Finally, by its insistence that humankind be studied from a comparative perspective, anthropology helps us to better understand our own individual lives and our

*Cultural anthropology can help members of different cultures to understand and appreciate each other's outlooks and ways of doing things. Such cross-cultural understanding can be helpful to individuals and companies engaged in international business.*

own societies. In materially wealthy, industrialized nations, dissatisfaction with one's own life is commonplace. In the United States, New Agers move to Sedona, Arizona, in search of harmonic convergences, whereas in England magicians meet in the evenings to inscribe sacred circles into which they step to call on supernatural powers. What attracts people to these beliefs? Even well-to-do Americans who seem to have it all often sense that something is missing in their personal lives. Have modern folk lost something in their quest for affluence? Is there part of our humanness that we have given up?

Racial prejudice, extreme economic inequalities, high rates of crime, and family violence plague many of our nations, and we may wonder whether problems such as these afflict human societies everywhere. As we write this chapter, David Koresh and 85 of his Branch Davidian followers have burned to death in Waco, Texas; Muslims, Croatians, and Serbs are dying because of ethnic violence in the region of Eastern Europe that used to be Yugoslavia; a car bomb at the World Trade Center in New York City killed several people; neo-Nazis in Germany are beating up Turkish workers and other people of foreign descent; members of the Islamic and Hindu faiths are fighting on the streets of Bombay; severe hunger and starvation afflict millions in African nations, such as Somalia and Sudan; and in Florida an opponent of abortion shot and killed a physician in front of a medical clinic. How can we understand such events? Will people ever be able to live in harmony, or is humanity forever destined to live with hatred and violence? Are large numbers of people doomed to lives of sickness, poverty, and hunger? We as anthropologists do not know the answers, but we do have contributions to make to such matters, as discussed in part 4 of this book.

## SUMMARY

Defined as the study of humanity, anthropology differs from other disciplines in the social sciences and humanities primarily because of its broad scope. The field as a whole is concerned with all human beings of the past and present, living at all levels of technological development. Anthropology is also interested in all aspects of humanity: biology, language, technology, art, politics, religion, and all other dimensions of human ways of living.

As a practical necessity, however, anthropologists must specialize. Traditionally, the field is divided into five subdisciplines. Physical anthropology studies the biological dimensions of human beings, including our biological evolution, the physical variations between contemporary populations, and the biology and behavior of nonhuman primates. Archaeology uses the material remains of prehistoric and historic cultures to investigate the past, focusing on the long-term technological and social changes that occurred in particular regions of the world. Cultural anthropology, or ethnology, is concerned with the social and cultural life of contemporary and historically recent human societies. By conducting fieldwork in various human communities and describing their findings in ethnographies, cultural anthropologists contribute to the scientific understanding of cultural diversity and to making the general public more aware and tolerant of cultural differences. Anthropological linguistics studies language, concentrating on nonwritten languages and investigating the interrelations between language and other elements of a people's way of life. Finally, applied anthropology uses the concepts, methods, and theories of the discipline of anthropology to solve real-world problems in such areas as health, development, education, and the survival of indigenous cultures.

Until around 1970 cultural anthropology (the main subject of this text) concentrated on human cultures that are popularly known as "tribal," "premodern," or "preindustrial." This is not as true today, when anthropologists often do their research in the complex urbanized and industrialized nations of the developed world. It is increasingly difficult to distinguish ethnology from the kindred discipline of sociology. However, firsthand, extended fieldwork in villages or relatively small towns or neighborhoods continue to be a hallmark of cultural anthropology.

Cultural anthropologists are different from other scholars who study living people not so much by what they study as by their approach to their studies. There are three main characteristics of this approach. Holism

*Although there are no simple solutions to the multitude of troubles confronting the modern world, anthropology does offer insights on famine, racism, ethnic and sectarian violence, and other problems. Clockwise from upper left: hunger in Somalia;* *neo-Nazis in Leipzig, Germany; Hindus demonstrating against Muslims in India; makeshift housing of urban poor in Lima, Peru.*

is the attempt to discern and investigate the interrelations between the customs and beliefs of a particular society. The comparative perspective means that any attempt to understand humanity or to explain cultures or behaviors must include information from a wide range of human ways of life, for anthropologists have learned that most customs and beliefs are products of cultural tradition and social environment, rather than of a universal human nature. The perspective known as cultural relativism refers to fieldworkers' efforts to understand people's behaviors on their own terms, not those of the anthropologist's own culture. It requires that anthropologists avoid being ethnocentric in their research, for each people's way of life has its own history, its own values, and its own standards of morality and decency.

Anthropology has practical value in the modern world, and it is not as esoteric as many people think. Only anthropology allows us to see the development of human biology and culture over long time spans. Most of the knowledge we have about human evolution, prehistoric populations, and modern tribal societies was discovered by anthropologists. Early anthropologists were instrumental in popularizing the concept of culture and in showing that cultural differences are not caused by racial differences. The value of inculcating understanding and tolerance between citizens of different nations is another practical lesson of anthropology, one that is increasingly important as the economies of the world become more interdependent and as the development of weaponry makes the consequences of international misunderstanding more serious. The information that ethnographers have collected about alternative ways of being human allows us to judge the benefits against the costs of industrialization and progress. The comparative perspective of anthropology helps us to see which elements of our societies are amenable to change and what the consequences of these changes might be. Finally, specific anthropologists apply their expertise directly to the solution of medical, economic, social, environmental, and other problems.

## KEY TERMS

physical (biological) anthropology
paleoanthropologists
primatologists
human variation
forensic anthropologists
archaeology
prehistoric archaeology
historic archaeology
cultural anthropology (ethnology)
fieldwork
ethnography
anthropological linguistics
applied anthropology
holistic perspective
comparative perspective
cultural relativism
ethnocentrism

## SUGGESTED READINGS

Fagan, Brian M. *The Journey from Eden: The Peopling of Our World.* London: Thames and Hudson, 1990.
   *A history of the spread of the human species from our African homeland into all the continents of the earth.*

Fagan, Brian M. *People of the Earth: An Introduction to World Prehistory.* 7th ed. New York: Harper Collins, 1992.
   *An overview of what archaeologists have learned about prehistoric humans and about the development of technology, agriculture, and civilization in various parts of the world,*

Farb, Peter. *Word Play: What Happens When People Talk.* New York: Knopf, 1974.
   *A highly readable introduction to language and how it is used in social life.*

Fromkin, Victoria, and Robert Rodman. *An Introduction to Language.* 5th ed. San Diego: Harcourt Brace Jovanovich, 1993.
   *Witty and thorough introduction to linguistics.*

Jurmain, Robert, Harry Nelson, and William A. Turnbaugh. *Understanding Physical Anthropology and Archaeology.* 4th ed. St. Paul, Minn.: West, 1990.
   *A thorough textbook covering human genetics, racial classification, primate taxonomy and behavior, and human biological and sociocultural evolution.*

Renfrew, Colin, and Paul Bahn. *Archaeology: Theories, Methods, and Practice.* London: Thames and Hudson, 1991.

> *A lengthy and detailed yet very readable introduction to archaeological methods, focusing especially on how prehistorians use artifacts to draw conclusions about the past.*

Wenke, Robert J. *Patterns in Prehistory: Humankind's First Three Million Years.* 3rd ed. New York: Oxford, 1990.

> *Covers the same ground as Fagan's text, but more thoroughly and technically.*

**The following ethnographies are excellent for introducing the ways of life of various people around the world. All are highly readable.**

Balikci, Asen, *The Netsilik Eskimo.* Garden City, N.Y.: Natural History Press, 1970.

> *A well-rounded description of an Eskimo people.*

Chagnon, Napoleon A. *Yanomamö: The Last Days of Eden.* San Diego, Harcourt Brace Jovanovich, 1992.

> *A readable ethnography of an Amazonian people who are threatened by the incursions of missionaries, miners, tourists, and other outsiders.*

Fernea, Elizabeth. *Guests of the Sheik.* Garden City, N.Y.: Anchor, 1969.

> *A writer, journalist, and academician's account of her experiences in an Iraqi village with her anthropologist husband.*

Kluckhohn, Clyde, and Dorothea Leigton. *The Navaho.* Garden City, N.Y.: Anchor, 1962.

> *A classic account of the most well studied Native American tribe.*

Kraybill, Donald B. *The Puzzles of Amish Life.* Intercourse, Penn.: Good Books, 1990.

> *Focusses on how the Amish of Lancaster county, Pennsylvania, have maintained intact communities and their values by selectively using modern technologies.*

Service, Elman. *Profiles in Ethnology.* New York: Harper & Row, 1978.

> *One of the best resources for one who wishes a short comparative overview of the way of life of diverse peoples. Contains short sketches of the life of twenty-three societies found on all continents.*

Shostak, Marjorie. *Nisa: The Life and Words of a !Kung Woman.* New York: Vintage, 1983.

> *An outstanding biographical account of a San woman.*

Thomas, Elizabeth Marshall. *The Harmless People.* 2nd ed. New York: Vintage, 1989.

> *A wonderfully written account of the customs and beliefs of the San (formerly called "Bushmen") of southern Africa.*

Turnbull, Colin. *The Forest People.* New York: Simon & Schuster, 1962.

> *A readable and sympathetic ethnography about the traditional culture of the BaMbuti pygmies of the African rain forest.*

Ward, Martha C. *Nest in the Wind.* Prospect Heights, Ill.: Waveland, 1989.

> *A delightful account of a fieldworker's experiences and difficulties on a tropical Pacific island.*

# PART I

## HUMANITY, CULTURE, AND LANGUAGE

The human species differs physically from other animals in many ways: Our legs and feet are adapted to walk upright, we have hands with fingers that perform a phenomenal variety of functions, and our brains are large in proportion to our body size. Cultural anthropologists are most interested in two other ways humanity is unique: our reliance on culture for our survival and our ability to use language to communicate incredibly complex messages. In the two chapters in part 1 we discuss culture and language. We also consider some of the ways in which these two uniquely human phenomena are related.

# CHAPTER 2

# CULTURE

Biologically all humans are quite similar, but the world's peoples differ greatly from one another in their cultures. These are Guatemalan musicians.

## CONTENTS

▼▼▼▼▼▼▼▼▼▼▼▼▼▼▼▼▼▼▼▼▼▼▼

Although many people use the word *culture* in everyday life, most of us do not think much about the term. Sometimes we use it in the sense of cultural events, such as symphonies and art exhibitions. Sometimes we even think of culture as something that some people have more of than others, as if how much culture someone has depends on their social class, education, or upbringing.

Anthropologists use the concept of culture in quite a different way. In this chapter we consider the anthropological definition of culture. We also discuss how cultural differences are related to the biological and physical differences between human groups.

## WHAT IS CULTURE?

Anthropologists have defined the term *culture* in literally hundreds of ways. Many modern conceptions of culture are based on the work of E. B. Tylor, one of the founders of anthropology. In 1871 Tylor defined culture as "that complex whole which includes knowledge, belief, art, morals, law, customs, and any other capabilities and habits acquired by man as a member of society." Notice how this definition includes almost everything about a people—their thoughts about the world, their beliefs about how people should live, their actions, and all other "capabilities and habits" that they acquire while growing up in a particular society or other group.

The essential elements of Tylor's definition are still with us. Today, too, culture usually is defined as the whole way of life of some group of people. When we speak of Chinese culture, for example, we usually mean practically everything about how the Chinese people live—their family life, religion, values, economy, government, and so forth. The word *culture* often is intended to emphasize the unique or distinctive aspects of a people's customs and beliefs. How the Chinese think and act differ in some ways from how the French, Iranians, Americans, and Japanese think and act, and the phrase *Chinese culture* nicely calls attention

*As this photo of a Buddhist wedding ceremony in Japan illustrates, members of different cultures do things in different ways.*

to the overall differences between the Chinese and other peoples.

A later definition of culture was that of Ralph Linton, who in 1940 defined culture as "the sum total of knowledge, attitudes, and habitual behavior patterns shared and transmitted by the members of a particular society." Linton's definition rightly calls attention to two of the major characteristics of culture: It is shared by some group of people, and it is learned (transmitted) while growing up among this group.

Notice that what Linton called knowledge and attitudes exist in the minds of people—knowledge and attitudes are mental phenomena. Anthropologists cannot observe knowledge, attitudes, and other kinds of mental phenomena directly, although we can learn what people are thinking and feeling indirectly by asking questions or observing what they do in certain familiar situations.

In contrast, the habitual behavior patterns of Linton's definition are directly observable. Behavior patterns refer to how most people act when they are in various situations. How people habitually act is greatly influenced by the particular knowledge and attitudes they learned while they were growing up in their society. But Linton's definition separated people's actions (or habitual behaviors) from their thoughts and feelings (or knowledge and attitudes).

Most modern cultural anthropologists agree that it is important to distinguish between these two components of culture, which often are called the *mental* and *behavioral* components. The mental components of culture include all the knowledge and information about the world and their society that children learn while growing up. Some examples of this knowledge and information are the skills of how to make and use tools and other material objects; attitudes about family, friends, enemies, and other people; notions about right and wrong (morality); ideas about appropriate dress, hygiene, and personal ornamentation; conceptions about females and males and their proper roles; beliefs about the supernatural; rules about sexual activity; the values they have; and their perceptions of the world and other people. This list could be expanded indefinitely to encompass all the specific knowledge that people acquire because they were born into and live among some group. In this book the phrase **cultural knowledge** refers to the information, skills, attitudes, notions, ideas, conceptions, beliefs, rules, values, perceptions, and other mental phenomena of culture. The terms *knowledge, beliefs,* and *ideas* are also used to mean the same thing.

In contrast, the behavioral components of culture include all the things that people regularly do, or the way they habitually act. As the terms *regularly* and *habitually* imply, people in the same culture adopt similar behaviors when they are in similar situations. It usually is these behavioral regularities and habits that anthropologists are most interested in. We call them **patterns of behavior**, meaning how most people act when they are in certain situations (e.g., in church, on the job, at a wedding or funeral, at a convention, in a classroom). Because people are born into and live most of their lives in organized social groups, relationships with other people are enormously important in all cultures. Anthropologists pay special heed to the regularities and patterning of these social relationships, including how family members and other relatives typically relate to one another, how males and females usually interact, how political leaders deal with subordinates, how shamans and priests perform their roles, and so forth. In this book we use the terms *behavior patterns, behavior,* and *actions* synonymously to mean what the members of a culture typically do in particular situations.

*Economic organization is just one of the multitude of ways in which societies differ. In Haiti, many people earn most of their cash by selling produce in marketplaces such as this one.*

Although we distinguish between the mental and the behavioral components of culture, the two are closely related and profoundly affect each other. To emphasize the interconnections and relations between the various elements that make up an entire culture, we speak of **cultural integration**. This means that the various elements of culture fit together in a more or less coherent way. Stated differently, cultural integration means that the parts of culture are mutually interdependent. The phrase *cultural system* is used to emphasize the integration of culture.

## A FORMAL DEFINITION OF CULTURE

The concept of culture is so important to cultural anthropologists that it is useful to have a formal definition of the term:

> *Culture* is the socially transmitted knowledge and behavior shared by some group of people.

This definition is used partly because it is easy to break up into sections that can be discussed separately.

### Socially Transmitted . . .

To say that culture is socially transmitted is to say that it is learned from the other members of one's group in the process of growing up in or living among that group. This seems obvious, but it has certain implications that are not immediately apparent. These implications can best be seen by distinguishing between two kinds of learning.

The first kind, found among many different animals, is called **trial-and-error learning**. In this type an animal learns by trying out a behavior to see whether it will work—that is, bring an adequate reward. If it is not rewarding, another behavior is tried and so on until some behavior works, after which it is repeated. By trial-and-error any animal—from snails to humans—can acquire behaviors that work or are adaptive in its environment. But the erroneous trials are costly because they require time and energy that could be spent in behaviors that are rewarding. Learning would be more efficient if there were a way to avoid the erroneous trials.

The advantage of the other type of learning is that it eliminates the costly trials and, therefore, is more efficient. It is called **social learning** because an individual learns by imitating or communicating with other individuals who have already learned something and, thus,

During enculturation, children learn the cultural knowledge of the society or other group into which they happen to have been born. This American father is teaching his son to interpret maps.

benefits from their experience. The knowledge that some people have acquired about what is rewarding in some situation is socially transmitted to other people. In human groups social learning is more important than trial-and-error learning. For example, once you have learned that some food is good to eat, I do not have to learn about this food on my own but can profit from your experience.

Social learning thus saves each person the costs of trial-and-error learning. But it does more than this. The knowledge that a whole generation has acquired from its experience can be passed on to the next generation. In turn this knowledge is transmitted to a third generation, then to a fourth, and so on. This means that current generations live largely off the cultural knowledge they have learned from previous generations. Think of the enormous implications of social learning! For instance, whatever technological improvements one generation has made can be transmitted to future generations. (Formal education in schools and universities is partly an attempt to teach younger generations what previous generations have thought and learned—or think they have learned—about the world.)

The transmission of culture from one generation to the next by means of social learning is called **enculturation**. Enculturation happens mainly during childhood, as part of the normal process of growing up in a given society.

## . . . Knowledge . . .

By *knowledge* anthropologists do not mean that a culture's beliefs, ideas, conceptions, and so forth are true, in some absolute or objective sense. What matters about cultural knowledge is not its correctness by some objective standard of truth. Rather, what is most important is that

✦ people share enough knowledge that they are capable of behaving in ways that are acceptable and meaningful to others, so that they do not constantly misunderstand one another; and that
✦ cultural knowledge results in behavior that works at least well enough to allow the people to survive and reproduce themselves and their culture.

To state these two points in a few words, cultural knowledge must lead to behavior that is meaningful to others and adaptive to the natural environment. Cultural knowledge is considered in more detail in the next section.

## . . . and Behavior . . .

The behavior of the individual members of a culture is quite variable. In part, people act differently because of the distinctions their culture makes between males and females, old and young, rich and poor, plumbers and attorneys, and so forth. For instance, behavior appropriate for women may not be suitable for men, and vice versa. Besides the distinctions a culture makes between kinds of people are those it makes between kinds of situations or social contexts: A woman acts differently depending on whether she is interacting with her husband, her daughter, her priest, her employee, a clerk, and so forth. Added to this complexity is the fact that each person is unique: One woman's relationship with her husband is not exactly the same as that of another's, even within the same culture.

Despite such complications and complexities, there usually are behavioral regularities or patterns. If, for instance, you were to visit the Yąnomamö, an Amazonian rain forest people, you might be shocked by some of the things they do. By our standards of normal, the Yąnomamö—called "The Fierce People" by ethnographer Napoleon Chagnon—are abnormally demanding and aggressive. Slight insults meet with violent responses. Quarreling men may duel by engaging in a chest-pounding contest, during which they often put rocks in their hands and take turns beating one another

*By most people's standards the Yąnomamö are aggressive. Here combatants take sides in a club fight.*

across the chest. Serious quarrels call for clubs, with which men bash one another on the head; a Yąnomamö man often shaves the top of his head to reveal the scars left from his many club fights. When the members of one village visit another for a feast, an event that supposedly is a manifestation of friendly relations between them, they are on the lookout for treachery because their hosts are liable to attack and kill them. Husbands beat their wives' heads with clubs, and the wives compare scars among themselves. Fathers encourage their sons to strike them (and anyone else) by teasing and goading, all the while praising the child for his fierceness.

If, on the other hand, you were to visit the Semai, a people of Malaysia, you would be surprised at their refusal to express anger and hostility. Indeed, you might find them *too* docile. One adult should never strike another—"Suppose he hit you back?" they ask. With this attitude toward violence, murder is nonexistent or extremely rare—so rare in fact that there are no penalties for it. The Semai seldom hit their children—"How would you feel if he or she died?" they ask. When children misbehave the worst physical punishment they receive is a pinch on the cheek or a pat on the hand. Ethnographer Robert Dentan suggests one reason for the nonviolence of the Semai: Children are so seldom exposed to physical punishment that when they grow up they have an exaggerated impression of the effects of violence.

A Yąnomamö and a Semai react to similar situations in different ways, with different behaviors. If one

Yąnomamö demands something of another—as they often do—and the demand is refused, the asker is likely to fly into a rage and make threats and may resort to violence. If a Semai fails to grant the request of another, the person who is refused may experience a psychological state Semai call *punan*. Punan might be translated as "accident proneness" because the Semai think that to make someone unhappy by frustrating their desires increases that person's chances of having an accident. So (and this is perfectly logical given their beliefs) if you ask me for something and I refuse your request, I have committed an offense against you that could result in your becoming accidentally injured. You, being the victim of the punan caused by my affront, have the right to demand compensation from me.

Yąnomamö and Semai belong to different cultures, so their behavioral responses to similar situations are not the same. No doubt, most Americans would react in yet another way to comparable situations. The general points are that (1) the behavior of people is greatly affected by the culture they learned during enculturation and (2) behaviors of different individuals in a single culture tend to follow common patterns.

## . . . Shared by Some Group of People

By definition, culture consists of *collective* knowledge and behavior. People are part of a common cultural tradition because they share similar knowledge and exhibit similar behavior that they socially learned during enculturation. Culture is a collective phenomena—it is shared by some group of people.

"Shared by some group of people" is deliberately imprecise. The group that shares a common cultural tradition may be enormously large, as illustrated by the phrases European culture and African culture. Although we use these phrases whenever we want to emphasize differences between the peoples of Africa and those of Europe, the so-called groups to which they refer are so large and diverse that the phrase African culture is almost meaningless. At the other extreme, the group that is said to share a common culture may be small. Some Pacific islands, for instance, have only a few hundred inhabitants, yet the people speak a unique language and have distinct customs and beliefs. The phrase Western culture also illustrates the problem with defining the word shared: Most of the continents of Europe and North America, large parts of South America, and Australia are lived in by members of "Western culture," which here refers to people whose customs

and beliefs can be traced back historically to Western Europe.

What, then, does it mean to say that culture is shared? It usually means at least one of two things. First, people who share a culture are capable of communicating and interacting with one another without serious misunderstanding and without the necessity of constantly explaining what their behavior means. Second, people share a common **cultural identity**, meaning that they recognize themselves and their cultural tradition as distinctive from other people and other cultural traditions. The phrase Western culture is meaningless according to the first criterion, since Americans and the French cannot easily communicate and interact. But Western culture is meaningful according to the second criterion, because Americans and the French do recognize the distinctiveness of their cultural heritage from that of, say, Japan or China.

The people who share a common culture often are part of the same **society**, or a territorially distinct population whose members speak the same language and who share a feeling of common identity relative to other societies. Sometimes the identification of a cultural tradition with a single society is convenient because it allows us to use phrases like "the culture of French society" and "the culture of Chinese society." Societies and cultures, however, are not necessarily coterminous. For example, we usually think of a modern nation-state as a single society. Yet, as anyone who pays attention to news reports knows, many cultural groups and identities are represented in most of the nations of the modern world.

These identities usually are based on some combination of racial type, national origin, and native language. The distinctions between such **ethnic groups** may be strong and enduring, even though they live within a single nation and theoretically are subject to the same laws and government. Despite the old myth of the "melting pot," numerous ethnic identities exist in the modern United States, including Hispanics, African-Americans, Jews, whites, and various Asian-Americans and Native Americans (see Figure 2.1). Members of ethnic groups consider themselves to be different from one another even though they live within the same national boundaries. Indeed, ethnic distinctions and rivalries are one cause of the violent conflict that has recently split nations apart, an important subject to which we return in chapter 17.

A single country may be said to contain many cultures if it has many ethnic groups living within its national boundaries. Other types of differences also

## FIGURE 2.1
**Distribution of Selected Ethnic Groups in the United States, 1980**

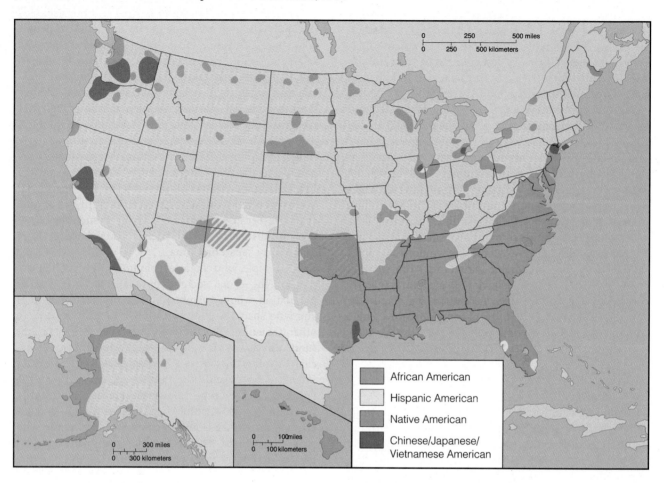

exist within modern nations. The term **subculture** refers to minor differences in life-style and values that exist within a nation even though its citizens see themselves as basically alike. Among American whites the southern, northern, and midwestern sections of the country differ in some ways, so we speak of regional subcultures. Subcultural variation may also be based on religion (Protestants versus Catholics), occupation (working class versus professionals), class (preparatory school students versus public school students), and other factors. The term subculture also often is applied to communities that live separately from the larger society and tightly control their relations with outsiders, such as the Amish and the Hutterites. Other scholars consider Amish and Hutterite communities sufficiently different from those of other Americans that they constitute

entirely separate cultures. Whether one applies the term culture or subculture to some group within a larger society depends partly on one's interests at the moment.

## CULTURAL KNOWLEDGE

As we have seen, cultural knowledge includes a people's ideas, beliefs, attitudes, assumptions about the world, and other mental phenomena. In this section we identify and discuss five specific components of cultural knowledge: norms, values, collective understandings, classifications of reality, and world views. These five elements are not necessarily more important than other kinds of cultural knowledge, but they do require some discussion because they are not entirely commonsensical.

Most modern nations are pluralistic. Shown here are a few of the subcultures represented in only one American city—Cleveland, Ohio. Clockwise from upper left: Americans of German ancestry dance at German American Day; a folk drama is performed annually in the Hungarian community; at the St. Vladimir Ukranian Orthodox Church, dances are held on Easter Monday; Hispanics sing at the Feast Day of St. John the Baptist; Palm Sunday is celebrated by children of Slovenian extraction at St. Vitus Church.

*Because the members of a culture share knowledge of norms, like these Chinese men they know how to act in various situations.*

## Norms

A **norm** is a shared ideal (or rule) about how people ought to act in certain situations, or about how particular people should act toward particular other people. The emphasis here is on the words *ideal, rule, ought,* and *should.* To say that norms exist, it is not necessary for everyone to follow them all the time; indeed, some norms are violated with great regularity. *Norm* implies, rather, that (1) there is widespread agreement that people ought to adhere to certain standards of behavior, (2) other people judge the behavior of a person according to how closely it adheres to those standards, and (3) people who repeatedly fail to follow the standards face some kind of negative reaction from other members of the group. We are able to make collective judgments about someone's personal morality because we share common norms. The ethical codes of some professions, such as medicine and law, are essentially norms that have been debated on by some authority and then formalized. A law is a special kind of norm, one that is formulated and enforced by a governmental authority.

Sometimes it seems to people that norms are irrational rules that stifle their creativity or keep them from doing what they want for no good reason. People may believe that some norms about proper conduct are confining, such as norms about how to dress correctly for special occasions, or about when and to whom we must give gifts, or about fulfilling familial obligations, or about when to have sex. But in fact, norms are quite useful to us. It is mainly because we acquire norms during enculturation that we know how to behave toward others and that we have expectations about how others should act toward us. For example, when you enter a roomful of strangers at a party, you are somewhat uncertain about how to act. But everyone knows how to go about getting acquainted in your cultural tradition, so you soon are introducing yourself and shaking hands and asking the other guests how they make their living or what they are studying or—under some circumstances—finding out whether they are married, single, available, or willing. Here and in many other cases in everyday life norms are not thought to be constraining but serve as useful instructions on how to do something in such a way that others know what you are doing and accept your actions as normal.

## Values

**Values** consist of a people's beliefs about the kinds of goals or way of life that is desirable for themselves and their society as a whole. Values have profound, although partly unconscious, effects on people's behavior. The aims we pursue, as well as our more general ideas about "the good life," are influenced by the values of the culture into which we happen to have been born. Values also are critical to the maintenance of culture as a whole because they represent the standards that people believe are essential to continuing their way of life. It is useful to think of values as providing the ultimate standards that people believe must be upheld under practically all circumstances. An excellent example of how values provide ultimate standards is the American emphasis on certain rights of individuals as embodied in the Bill of Rights in the Constitution. No matter how much some Americans hate what the press prints, what the right or left wing says, or being approached by Hari Krishnas in airports, few of them believe that unpopular newspapers or organizations should be suppressed, so long as they do not engage in or advocate violence. Freedom of the press, of speech, and of religion are ultimate standards that take precedence over the opinions and interests of the moment. People may be deeply attached emotionally to some of their values and, under certain circumstances, are prepared to sacrifice their lives for them.

## Collective Understandings

Members of a culture usually know how to interpret one another's behavior. Our understanding of what some behavior means allows us to interact with one another without the constant need to explain what we are doing. Such **collective understandings** seem to be among the most unconscious of all components of culture. It is possible to talk about and explain to a stranger the norms and values of one's own cultural tradition and to give reasons why we think people ought to act in certain ways or why we think certain standards are important to uphold. We cannot, however, explain why a wink or a tone of voice or certain gestures mean what they do; we "just know" what meaning they convey but cannot say why they mean this rather than something else, or even how we know their meanings.

The feeling that we "just know" what things mean—that they are common knowledge—is attributable to an enormously important characteristic of much cultural knowledge. Most things and behaviors carry meanings that have no obvious and necessary relation to their physical properties; that is, their meanings are arbitrary. *Arbitrary* in this context means that there are no inherent qualities in the object or action itself that lead some human population to attribute one meaning to it, rather than some other meaning. The meaning exists only because of shared conventions and collective understandings.

Words provide a good example of how the meaning of something is conventional and arbitrary. In English the word for a certain kind of large animal is *horse,* but in Spanish it is *caballo,* in German it is *pferd,* in Arabic it is *hisanun,* in French it is *cheval,* and so on for other languages. There is nothing about the animal itself that makes one of these words better than others to stand for it. The relation between the word and the animal it represents is based entirely on people's agreement about the meaning of the word.

Like words, objects and actions whose meaning is arbitrary and conventional are called symbols. A **symbol** is a thing or behavior that stands for something else or that carries a meaning that is not inherent in its physical properties. The twitch of an eyelid muscle that causes a momentary closing of the eye, which we call a wink, carries a flirtatious significance in some cultural tradi-

tions and is meaningless in others. The shared meaning of an upraised middle finger can result in a brawl in a few societies, but the same movement in other parts of the world elicits no reaction. For the Ndembu people of Zambia the white secretions of a certain sacred tree carry connotations of womanhood, fertility, nourishment, and sexual maturity, although to most other people in the world it is merely tree sap. For the Christian the cross arouses deep emotions of reverence, but for many other people it stands for oppression and imperialism. All these objects and actions are examples of symbols.

## Classifications of Reality

The members of a cultural tradition share ideas of what kinds of things and people exist. They have similar **classifications of reality,** meaning that the human and natural environments are divided up according to common principles.

For example, people everywhere recognize a category of people who are related to them biologically—their relatives, as we call them. But the principles by which certain kinds of relatives are placed into cultural categories vary between different kinds of kinship systems. Thus, English speakers think of the sisters of both our mother and our father as a single kind of relative, and we call them by the same kinship term, *aunt*. But there are some cultural traditions in which the sister of one's mother is considered to be one kind of relative and the sister of one's father a different kind, and each is called by a separate kinship term. As we shall see in chapter 11, these various ways of classifying kin into different categories or kinds of relatives are related fairly consistently to other characteristics of a people's kinship system. The general point for now is that people of different cultural traditions have different ideas about social life, and the way they conceive of their societies as divided up into kinds of people varies.

The same applies to the way a people classify their natural environment. Cultural knowledge not only provides the categories by which we classify kinds of people but also categories by which plants, animals, phases of the moon, seasonal changes, and other natural phenomena are classified into kinds. The way people classify the things in their natural environment both affects and is affected by how they relate to it.

For example, on the island of Mindoro in the Philippines live a people known as the Hanunóo. These people grow most of their food by a method called *shifting cultivation.* This method, described further in chapter 8, involves farming a plot for one or two years, abandoning it for a number of years until some of the natural vegetation has regrown and it has recovered its potential to yield a crop, and then replanting it. It, therefore, is useful for the Hanunóo to be able to tell when a plot they abandoned some years previously has recovered enough to make it worthwhile to replant it. They judge this by the quantity and kind of natural vegetation that has recolonized the plot. The need to assess the degree of readiness of a plot for recultivation has led the Hanunóo to develop an extremely complex classification of the plants found in their habitat. They are able to identify more than 1,600 "kinds" of plants, which exceeds by more than 400 the number of species that a scientific botanist would distinguish.

Which classification is right, that of the Hanunóo or that of the botanist? Both. The point is not that the Hanunóo are right and the botanist wrong, or vice versa. Rather, the botanist uses one set of criteria to decide whether two individual plants belong to the same kind, and these criteria have been adopted because they have proved useful to science. The Hanunóo use a different set of criteria that, over the course of many generations, they have developed for their specific needs. The criteria by which various realms of nature are carved up and assigned to categories are important components of cultural knowledge because they influence the way a people perceive the natural world.

They also influence how a people use the resources that occur in their environments. Plants and animals are classified not just into various kinds but also into various categories of usefulness. Members of different cultural traditions perceive nature in different ways, and what one people consider a resource is not necessarily a resource for another people. For example, Muslims and Orthodox Jews consider pork unclean and traditional Hindus refuse to consume the flesh of cattle, their sacred animal. The fact that a given animal or plant is edible does not mean that people *consider* it edible (had any boiled dog or roasted beetle larvae lately?). The same principle applies to resources other than food. For example, the gold and silver metals that led Europeans to conquer the Americas were not valued to the same extent by most North American Indians.

Taking this one step further, people of different cultures differ in their beliefs about the kinds of things that do and do not exist. For instance, some peoples believe that some individuals (called witches) use malevolent supernatural powers to harm their enemies. Traditional Navajo believe that witches can and do

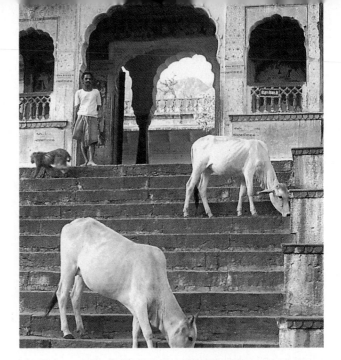

All cultures prohibit the eating of some potentially edible foods, often for religious reasons. Strict Hindus, for instance, will not eat the flesh of cattle.

change themselves into wolves, bears, and other animals. The Tukano of the Bolivian rain forest think that a spirit of the forest controls the game animals they depend on for meat. So a Tukano group's shaman periodically makes a supernatural visit to the abode of the forest spirit. He promises to magically kill a certain number of humans and to send their souls to the forest spirit in return for the spirit's releasing the animals so the hunters can find game. As a final example, in cultures that practice ancestor worship, the family group that gathers for the rituals genuinely believes that the ghosts of their deceased relatives partake of the food and other offerings made to them. In sum, not only do different cultures classify objective reality in different ways but they differ on what reality *is;* one culture's reality may not be the same reality as that of another culture.

## World Views

The **world view** of a people is the way they perceive and interpret reality and events, including their images of themselves and how they relate to the world around them. World views are affected by how people classify the social and natural world, which we have just discussed. But world views include more than just the way people and nature are carved up by a culture. People have opinions about the nature of the cosmos and how they fit into it. All systems of cultural knowledge distinguish physical bodies from spiritual souls and have beliefs about what happens to the latter after the former dies. People have ideas about the meaning of human existence: how we were put on earth, who put us here, and why. They have a notion of what evil is, where it comes from, why it sometimes happens to good people, and how it can be combated. They have beliefs about what supernatural powers or beings are like, what they can do for (or to!) people, and how people can worship or control them. Everywhere we find myths and legends about the origins of living things, objects, and customs.

These examples of various aspects of world view all come from religion. But it is important not to confuse world view and religion and especially not to think that religion and world view are synonymous. Although religious beliefs do influence the world view of a people, cultural traditions vary in aspects of world view that we do not ordinarily think of as religious.

For instance, the way a people view their place in nature is part of their world view: Do they see themselves as the masters and conquerors of nature, or as living in harmony with natural forces? The way people view themselves and other people is part of their world view. Do they see themselves, as many human groups do, as the only true human beings, and all others as essentially animals? Or do they see their way of life as one among many equally human but different ways of life? Most modern scientists share a similar world view: They believe that all things and events in the universe have natural, discoverable causes that we can know through logic supported by certain procedures of observation and experimentation.

A people's conception of time and space is also part of their world view. Westerners are so used to thinking of time in arbitrary units—for our seconds, minutes, and hours are not natural segments of time—that we forget that other people do not share our ideas of how important these units are. North Americans frown on "wasting time" and "living in the past" because our "period" in this world is "limited," so it is important to "make the most of our time here" by—among other things—eating "fast foods." This view of time as a resource that, like money, can be spent wisely or foolishly is not present in many other cultural traditions. Similar considerations apply to space. In a North American house unused space—that is, areas in which little activity occurs or

that are not filled up to the culturally appropriate degree with our possessions—is "wasted" space.

To a large extent, such views of time and space are understandable, given other dimensions of the American way of life. They are connected to various American values, such as progress and the work ethic. They also are connected to certain economic conditions not found in many other places in the world. We must pay, and pay dearly, for the space of earth enclosed by the walls of our dwellings; in general, the larger the space, the more we pay; so unused space truly is wasted space because we have paid for something we are not using. If, on the other hand, spaces of earth are freely available to all who want to use them, the notion of wasting space is less likely to be strong. The same applies to time. We can waste it because it is possible for us to use every bit of it in some way. Time not spent sleeping, eating, and maintaining our bodies can be spent earning money or enjoying the things that money allows us to possess or participating in social activities that we barely can "find the time for." If, on the other hand, we were to stop working whenever we satisfy our bodily needs, as was once common among humanity, we would find ourselves with "time on our hands," and the view of time as a resource that can be wasted and used wisely or foolishly would be less developed.

In summary, cultural knowledge includes shared, socially transmitted norms, values, meanings, categories for classifying reality, and world views. Certainly by now you can appreciate that much of what you consider common knowledge, or just plain common sense, is in fact socially learned and, hence, cultural knowledge.

## ▞▞ CULTURAL KNOWLEDGE AND BEHAVIOR

We have seen that most cultural anthropologists distinguish between the mental and the behavioral components of culture. Having just discussed some of the main elements of cultural knowledge—the mental components—we can now look at how these ideas and beliefs are related to behavior.

A simplistic view might see cultural knowledge as providing rules or instructions for behavior that tell people how to act in specific situations and how to relate to other people. We might imagine, for example, that there are cultural rules that instruct people how to plan and carry out a wedding, how to get resources from their environment, how to settle a quarrel, and how to act toward their mothers-in-law. For the most part, a culture's ideas and beliefs tell people how to act, according to this approach. In all societies there are individuals who do not act according to the rules, but such deviants usually are brought back into conformity, or eliminated or ostracized. To state this view somewhat baldly: The mental components of our culture instruct us how to behave, and we usually behave this way; if we deviate, other members of the group punish us. This approach emphasizes how the normative components of cultural knowledge—the *oughts* and *ideals*—affect behavior.

Certainly, the view above applies to some behaviors, but most modern ethnologists reject it as a general approach because it is way too simple. Cultural knowledge consists of far more than just instructions for behavior. It consists of values, that provide only rough and sometimes conflicting guidelines for behavior. It includes shared classifications of reality and world views; these certainly influence behavior but only indirectly (by affecting how we perceive the world) rather than directly (as instructions). Finally, cultural knowledge includes attitudes, shared understandings, and other kinds of ideas and beliefs that affect how people act but not in the same way as rules. The effects of these and other mental components of culture on behavior are too subtle and complex to think of them as rules or instructions.

At any rate, even when a culture's rules provide highly detailed behavioral instructions—and sometimes they do—people are not robots. People usually have some leeway to choose between alternative courses of action. In their everyday lives most people do not blindly follow their culture's "dictates" but plan, calculate, weigh alternatives, and make decisions. They think ahead (sometimes at least!) and consider the possible benefits and consequences of alternative actions before they act. In deciding how best to approach the relation between knowledge and behavior, we must take into account people's ability to think ahead, plan, and choose.

One way to do this is to realize that formulating plans and making choices are mental processes, and therefore, they rely on and work within the existing framework of cultural knowledge. Deciding how to behave involves at least the following procedures: deciding on one's goals (or ends); determining the resources (or means) available to acquire these goals; considering which specific actions are likely to be most effective; calculating the relative costs (in resources) and benefits (rewards) of these alternative actions; and, finally, choosing between these alternative behaviors.

Cultural knowledge affects every step of this choice-making process. Norms, for instance, force individuals to take into account how others are likely to react to their behavior. Values affect the goals that people have and help prevent them from acting in ways that infringe on the rights of others. Choices are affected by the existing cultural categories of people and things, world views, and the chooser's anticipations of how others will interpret the meaning of his or her actions. We can see how important cultural knowledge is when people choose between alternative behaviors: It affects goals, perceptions of resources, availability of means, relative weighting of costs and benefits, and so on. So important is the effect of cultural knowledge on decisions that one influential anthropologist has defined culture itself as "standards for deciding what is, . . . what can be, . . . how one feels about it, . . . what to do about it, and . . . how to go about doing it" (Goodenough 1961, 552).

Following this line of reasoning we can say that one important way in which the cultural knowledge shared by a people affects their behavior is by its profound influences on the choices they make about what to do in various situations. Another way of stating the same thing is to say that cultural knowledge supplies "boundaries" for the behavior of individuals. Speaking metaphorically, culture draws the lines that behavior usually does not cross, meaning that it determines which behaviors are likely to be proper or acceptable or understandable to others. Within these boundaries people are free to choose between alternative actions. Most people do not violate the boundaries of their culture because they believe in the moral rightness of norms, because they fear negative reactions from others, or because doing so would involve actions that others might misinterpret.

We saw earlier that although behavior varies a great deal between individuals, patterns of behavior that characterize a culture usually are identifiable. One reason for the existence of these patterns is that people share the cultural knowledge that limits their options, so they make similar choices when they face similar circumstances.

Why is the distinction between knowledge and behavior important? One reason is that people's ideas and beliefs do not always predict behavior very well. We cannot necessarily say what someone will do in a given situation even though we know what other people expect the person to do and even though cultural requirements (norms) are fairly clear. Thus many industrialized societies have an explicit norm that the only thing an employer should take into account in deciding who to hire for some job is the relative qualifications of applicants. There is little doubt that this norm frequently is violated; it may even be violated more often than it is followed. Even norms that are powerful (in the sense that violations are considered serious breaches of morality and usually are punished if detected) are not honored. For example, the norm against adultery is widely accepted and powerful; yet in the United States in the 1980s almost one-half of the married population committed adultery.

The same thing applies to the relation between values and behavior. Equality of opportunity for all is a cherished value of North Americans; society should be set up so that all people can do as well for themselves as their abilities and energies allow. Yet there is no doubt that some people have a head start in life's competition, and others must possess truly unusual talent or ambition to "make it" because of their ethnicity or impoverished background. Such distinctions between the ideal and the actual—between the "oughts" and the "ares" of a society—make it essential not to confuse culture with behavior.

Norms and values are not always consistent and so may not provide clear guidelines for behavior. (You should not lie, but sometimes a small lie is necessary to preserve a relation or avoid hurt feelings, or is so useful to you personally that you violate this rather weak norm.) In situations in which pursuing one worthwhile goal or upholding one value conflicts with pursuing another goal or value, individuals must choose between them. (Most North Americans simultaneously believe in the work ethic, in materialism, and in what recent political leaders call family values. But jobs and career pursuits necessarily detract from the time we devote to our spouses, children, and parents, so we must decide how to allocate our time between activities that are all culturally defined as worthwhile.) Violations of rules and standards for behavior often are rationalized by believing that the person harmed by one's actions deserved it because of his or her own past violations. (You might justify stealing from your employer because you are underpaid.) Finally, people receive contradictory messages about acceptable behavior. Sometimes the official norms that are supposed to serve as models for behavior are contradicted by messages and models people receive from their friends' actions or from the popular media. (Adultery is wrong, but we gain the impression from television and movies that it is common and almost to be expected.)

Thus far we have considered the effects of knowledge on behavior. In the long term at least the behavior that people exhibit affects the mental components of their culture. This often happens because there is an incon-

sistency between existing norms, values, and so forth and what many people actually are doing. There was a time in Medieval Europe when usury—the earning of interest from loans—was considered to violate the teachings in the Bible and was prohibited by the Catholic Church. To make money off of money without being excommunicated, Catholics lent such large sums that the borrower could not possibly repay when the loans came due. They then charged damages for failure to pay. Technically, the norms of Catholic interpretations of the scriptures were not violated, and money could always be borrowed from Jews because their Torah contained no such restrictions. Later, with the Protestant Reformation and the beginnings of capitalism, the norms against usury became so burdensome even to Catholics that they disappeared. This specific example shows how sometimes it is in people's interest to find ways of getting around inconvenient norms to escape punishment or negative reactions from others. If enough people (and especially powerful people) are motivated to avoid the norm, and if economic conditions continue to change, the norm itself eventually may disappear. The general point is that behavior affects knowledge as well as vice versa. This is not surprising: We know that norms, values, world views, and other ideas change, and this change often originates from the fact that people find alternative behaviors beneficial.

## BIOLOGY AND CULTURE

An important question for the holistic discipline of anthropology is: How are human biology and human culture related? Within a single society or ethnic group the relations between the *physical* traits that people inherit genetically and the *cultural* system that they socially learn while growing up are quite complex. Psychologists, human biologists, and scholars do not agree on the nature of the relations. Although we cannot go into this issue in any depth, it is necessary to discuss one topic: Are the cultural differences between groups of humans caused by the genetic and biological differences between them? Rephrased so that the full implications of the question are apparent: Is there any correlation between types of cultures and human physical forms (or races, as they usually are called)? For instance, are the cultures of Africans, Native Americans, Europeans, and various Asian peoples different because of the physical differences between them?

Before the twentieth century it was widely thought that the physical differences between groups of people explained differences in how groups thought and felt and behaved. That is, many people believed that racial differences partly accounted for differences in culture. According to this notion, now called **biological determinism**, cultural differences have a biological basis, meaning that groups of people differ in how they think and feel and act because they differ in their innate biological makeup.

Biological determinism can be a convenient "theory" of what makes groups of people different from one another, especially if it is combined with ethnocentric attitudes about the superiority of one's own culture. If French or English culture is superior to African or Native American culture, then it must be because the French or English are superior biologically to Africans or Native Americans (it is obvious how so-called innate intelligence would be brought into such opinions). Colonial rule, the expropriation of land and other resources, slavery, forced labor, and other practices could be and were justified by the idea that groups of people differed in their customs and beliefs because of their physical differences.

Almost all modern ethnologists reject biological determinism. We believe that the racial or other physical differences between human populations do not cause differences in cultural knowledge and behavior. The diverse cultures of Africa did not and do not differ from the cultures of Europe, Asia, or the Americas because Africans, Europeans, Asians, and Native Americans differ biologically. Nor do the cultures of different ethnic groups within a modern nation differ because these ethnic groups differ physically: African-Americans, Euro-Americans, and Asian-Americans do not differ in their beliefs and behaviors because of their different genetic makeup. Nor do they differ significantly in their mental or physical abilities or talents because of genetic differences (see Box 2.1 for an example of this point).

To claim that physical differences do not account for cultural differences might seem like a sweeping overgeneralization. Certainly, the claim that racial or other physical differences have little or nothing to do with explaining cultural differences is difficult to prove. But although it cannot be "proven"—little in the complex existence of human beings can—this claim is based on good evidence, some of which is familiar to most people. Consider the following three facts.

◆ Members of any race or physical type are equally capable of learning any culture. For instance, the United States now contains people whose biological ancestors came from all parts of the world. Yet modern-day African-, Chinese-, Indian-, Irish-, Hispanic-, and Italian-Americans have far more in common in their thoughts and actions than any of them have in common with the peoples of their ancestral homelands. Indeed, many members of these groups have been assimilated and are culturally indistinguishable from other American citizens.

◆ An enormous range of cultural diversity occurs among the members of a single race. The cultures of Africa, the Americas, Asia, the Pacific, and Europe were and are quite diverse—far too much cultural diversity is found within a single race than can be accounted for biologically.

◆ Hugely different cultural systems succeed one another in time within the same race and indeed within the same society. Cultures can and regularly do undergo vast changes within a single human generation; these changes cannot be due to genetic changes in the population, which usually take many generations to be noticeable.

Because of these and other kinds of evidence, most cultural anthropologists feel justified in reaching the following conclusion: Physical (including racial) differences between human populations are largely irrelevant for explaining the cultural differences between them. This means that if we want to explain the differences between the Kikuyu culture of east Africa and the Chinese culture of east Asia, we should largely ignore the physical and genetic differences between the Kikuyu and the Chinese. We might argue that differences in the Kikuyu and Chinese natural environment, technology, and history make their cultures different. But for the most part we ignore the physical differences between them.

As one can infer from the discussion above, cultural anthropologists strongly oppose biological determinist notions. In fact, in the early decades of the twentieth century some anthropologists, such as Franz Boas, fought such ideas by marshaling evidence that—to state the point simply—culture is not determined by race.

This does not mean that biological factors are irrelevant in the study of culture. Human beings have physiological needs and biological imperatives just like other animals. Food, water, shelter, and the like are necessary to sustain life. Sexual activity is pleasurable for its own sake as well as necessary for reproduction. And no human group or society can persist unless its members effectively nurture and enculturate their children. To survive and persist over many generations, all

*Biological determinism is an idea that is often used to justify exploitation and the dominance of one group over another. Slavery in the American south (above) and the English colonization of parts of Africa (below) often were rationalized by the claim that some races are innately inferior.*

groups must provide their members with behavioral ways of meeting these biological needs and imperatives; those that have failed to do so are no longer around.

Can we add anything to the obvious point that much of any people's behavior must be oriented to the satisfaction of their physiological needs? Does the shared genetic heritage of the human species have any other effects on cultures? Many anthropologists believe that it does: The biological makeup that all humans share appears to limit the forms culture can take.

Evidence for this is the existence of **cultural universals**, or elements that can be found in all known human societies. Some cultural universals are obvious because they are requirements for long-term survival in a species that relies on material technology for survival and lives in highly organized social groups. Such universals include tools, shelter, methods of communication, patterns of cooperation used in acquiring food and other essential resources, ways of teaching children, and so forth. There is no great mystery about why all human groups have such things.

An interesting exploration of the notion that racial differences cause differences in behavior and performance is the overrepresentation of black Americans in the nation's three most popular spectator sports: baseball, football, and basketball. In 1993, two-thirds of National Football League players are black, and over three-fourths of players in the National Basketball Association are black. In the early 1980s, one-fourth of major league baseball players were black; in 1993, only one-sixth are black, but another one-sixth are Latino. A high percentage of boxers and track and field athletes also are black. Because only 14 percent of Americans are black, African-American men are doing exceptionally well in these sports—certainly better overall than whites. Why?

One possible reason is biological factors. There may be something about the bone structure, stamina, strength, coordination, or size of blacks that makes them better natural athletes than whites. If so, then blacks do so well in these sports because they have greater natural talents than whites. Less skilled athletes are eliminated as they pass through increasing levels of competition in high school and college, so that by the time one has made it as a pro, only the very best are left. The fact that so many of these are African-Americans must mean that the best blacks are better endowed biologically for sports than the best whites.

Sensible as this argument seems, it does not show that the overrepresentation of blacks in American sports is explained entirely or even to any significant degree by biological factors. First, notice that African-Americans are successful in only a few sports. Why are there so few black figure skaters, tennis players, gymnasts, skiers, swimmers, divers, and golfers? Whatever biological factors make blacks so successful at

*BOX 2.1*

# ARE AFRICAN-AMERICANS NATURAL ATHLETES?

baseball, basketball, football, boxing, and track and field would be expected to carry over into other athletic competition. Yet blacks are underrepresented in these sports.

Second, notice that hardly anyone uses physical differences to explain why people of different nationalities perform well or poorly at particular sports. Physical factors do not explain why Germans do so well in swimming; Canadians in ice hockey; Swiss in skiing; Russians in gymnastics; Brazilians, Italians, or Argentinians in soccer; British in cricket; Taiwanese, Koreans, and Japanese in the martial arts; or Cubans in boxing. Minnesota and Maine produce more hockey players than Florida and Texas—is this because of biological differences between residents of northern and southern states?

Third, notice that there was a period when various immigrants into the United States were overrepresented in sports. Boxing today is dominated by blacks and Hispanics. How many of us know that other ethnic groups once dominated this sport? Large numbers of Irish came to the United States in the late nineteenth century after the potato famine in their homeland. In the first two decades of the twentieth century most of the great boxers were of Irish extraction. Later Jews and Italians ar-rived in large numbers, and from the 1920s through the 1930s Jews and Italians did well in boxing. An observer during the early decades of the twentieth century might have concluded that Irish, Jews, and Italians were naturally well equipped for fighting, based on their dominance of professional boxing. But this statement sounds silly today because most descendants of these immigrants are so assimilated that we do not think of them as different from other whites.

For these and other reasons (see Edwards 1971 and 1973) there is no solid evidence that blacks dominate certain kinds of professional athletics because on average they are better natural athletes than whites. Then why do blacks perform so well? Part of the reason is the past and present racial discrimination experienced by blacks who pursue other lucrative careers. Sports offer young African-Americans the opportunity to become rich and famous in a country in which they have few other chances to make it really big. So they work harder at sports than at other things, since it offers them their best opportunity. In addition, young blacks have plenty of role models. Talented and highly visible men who have escaped the poverty of the inner cities by means of sports are bound to serve as examples for other blacks.

But the existence of opportunities in sports and athletic role models cannot

*continued on next page*

alone explain why African-Americans do so well in certain sports. Before there can be viable role models, a fair number of blacks must already have done well in college and pro sports. Why should they have done so well in such large numbers if not because of biological factors? And before they could have done well, they must have had the opportunity to participate. Why should they have had such opportunities when they have been denied equal opportunity in so many other professions? Is there anything special about sports that would lure blacks into it over other potential careers? Specifically, is there anything about sports that would make it especially likely for African-Americans to be able to overcome the effects of poverty, poor education, and racial prejudice that hamper their achievement in other careers?

At root, racial prejudice means that a person is evaluated negatively because of his or her perceived membership in racial category. For individual African-Americans, it means that they are not evaluated on the basis of their merits and abilities because so many whites' perceptions of blacks' merits and abilities are clouded by whites' prejudices. Members of an ethnic or racial minority can overcome prejudice by pursuing careers in which their performance can be evaluated easily and objectively, so that to some degree their performance overcomes the perceptual barrier of prejudice. In sports, statistics are kept that identify the better players in a relatively objective way. Batting average, rushing yardage, points per game, speed for the 100 meters, number of knockouts—such objective numbers allow fans, coaches, owners, and other players to judge individual performance accurately. Many fans in Brooklyn, and many fellow major league players, did not like it when Jackie Robinson broke the "color barrier" in major league baseball in 1947. But his ability was obvious from his record.

There are other special features of sports that explain why African-Americans are better able to overcome prejudice in athletics than in most other occupations. Teams are small groups, so the presence or absence of even one star player can make the difference between success and failure. The skills necessary for success are so rare than owners compete for the best talent. Any owner or coach who refused to hire or play a skilled black player would be at a competitive disadvantage with those teams who did not discriminate. For the same reason, white players are less likely to reveal overtly any prejudice they may harbor, since the success of the whole team (and their prestige and next year's contract) may be affected. Blacks, therefore, experience less overt prejudice from their co-workers (teammates).

Further, teams are organized in such a way that cooperation takes precedence over competition. More than in most other occupations, the success of an athlete is not achieved at the expense of his co-workers because success does not lead to promotion to a position of authority. White teammates, therefore, do not have to worry about taking orders from successful blacks, since all team members are subject equally to the authority of coaches or managers. And, significantly, there are few blacks in managerial roles in which they would be making important decisions and issuing commands because this would threaten whites. The one exception, college and professional basketball, has such a high percentage of black players that black coaches are giving orders to mostly black teams.

In sum, African-Americans suffer from less overt prejudice and discrimination in athletics than in most other lucrative careers, so they are more attracted to and more likely to succeed in such careers. They experience less discrimination because their abilities can be objectively measured and compared, because their bosses and teammates recognize that they need their skills to succeed, and because getting ahead need not be at the expense of someone else on the team. So it is the special nature of sports and of athletic competition and not biology that explains why African-Americans have done relatively well in sports.

This analysis also explains why blacks are overrepresented only in certain sports, which the natural-athlete explanation does not do. The sports in which blacks do well are cheap sports, meaning that free public facilities are available and equipment is inexpensive and durable. This contrasts with sports like golf and skiing, which require high expenses. With the exception of boxing, the sports in which blacks do well do not require expensive private coaching to acquire professional status (unlike gymnastics and tennis).

Although the claim that African-Americans are naturally better athletes than whites seems to be antiracist and even pro-black, a subtle form of racism is involved. For example, whites who do well at basketball are sometimes said to have worked hard and to be "thinking players," whereas blacks are said to have great "instincts" and to be "natural athletes." Implicitly, to claim that blacks are physically superior is to deny them equal intellectual abilities. Finally, and more important, to use black biology as the explanation for superior athletic performance results in channeling the energies of black youngsters into sports careers for which they are held to be naturally suited. But only a tiny fraction succeed in these careers; for most African-Americans, sports offer a false hope. ✦

SOURCE: Blalock (1962), Coakley (1978), Edwards (1971, 1973), Figler (1981), Kahn (1991) USA Today, July 9, 1993.

*A division of labor based partly on sex is universal among the world's cultures. These Arawak women are weaving floor mats.*

Other cultural universals are not so obvious; they do not seem to be necessary for the survival of individuals or groups, but they are nonetheless present everywhere. Among these are ways of assigning tasks and roles according to age, gender, and skill; prohibitions on sexual relationships between certain kinds of relatives; organized ways of sharing and exchanging goods; games, sports, or other kinds of recreational activities; beliefs about supernatural powers and rituals that are used to communicate with and influence them; decorative arts; ways of classifying various kinds of relatives into social categories; customary ways of handling the dead and expressing grief; myths; and rites of passage that ceremonially recognize the movement of people through certain stages of life.

More elements found in all cultures could be listed, but our point is made: All human cultures share certain characteristics whose universal existence cannot be explained simply by the fact that they are necessary for short- or long-term survival. The very existence of such cultural universals suggests that the human genetic endowment limits the forms that culture can take. It may be impossible for a human culture to exist that has no rules about sexual intercourse with relatives, no religion of any kind, no play or recreation or decorative art, no recognition of kinship ties beyond the immediate family, and no sharing or exchanging of goods.

There may be an inborn genetic or biological basis for sexual rules, religion, play, kinship, and other cultural universals precisely because they *are* universal. Yet the precise forms that these and other universal elements take vary from culture to culture. For instance, all human societies have beliefs about the supernatural (religion), but the nature of these beliefs varies enormously among cultures, as seen in chapter 15. Likewise, people in all societies keep track of their family and kinship relationships, but they do so in a wide variety of ways, as documented in chapters 10 and 11. Part 3 describes and analyzes the different and diverse ways in which cultures meet their material needs, organize their exchanges, trace their relatives, and believe in the supernatural.

## SUMMARY

Culture is the key concept of the field of ethnology. The term has been defined in hundreds of ways but usually refers to the whole way of life of some society or group.

To describe and analyze culture it is useful to distinguish between its mental and behavioral components, or between cultural knowledge and patterns of behavior. Culture is defined in this book as the socially transmitted knowledge and behavior shared by some group of people. The term group may refer to an entire society, an ethnic group, or a subculture, depending on the context of the discussion.

Culture is socially learned, meaning that it can be transmitted from one group or individual to another. Enculturation is the transmission of culture to new generations. Cultural knowledge is not true in any objective sense, but it must at least allow a society to persist in its environment and must enable people to interact appropriately and meaningfully.

Cultural knowledge has many components, some of which are norms, values, collective understandings (including the common understanding of the meanings of symbols), classifications of reality, and world views. Because these and other components of cultural knowledge are products of social learning—not inborn—we must learn them during enculturation, no matter how natural or commonsensical they seem.

A simplistic view would hold that cultural knowledge determines the behavior of the individuals who share that knowledge. But cultural ideas and beliefs serve as more than just rules or instructions for behavior. A more useful and realistic view sees cultural knowledge as affecting the choices people make about how to act in particular situations. Cultural knowledge limits and influences behavior but does not determine it in great detail because people are not robots. In the long term at least behavioral changes themselves can lead to changes in norms, values, and other kinds of cultural knowledge.

Biological determinism holds that the culture of a human population derives in part from biological or racial factors, so that biological or racial differences help to explain cultural differences between human groups. This idea is rejected by nearly all modern ethnologists, who consider the biological differences between groups irrelevant in explaining cultural differences between them. The shared biological endowment of the human species, however, certainly does affect culture, since how people meet their biologically given needs is reflected in their culture. The existence of nonobvious cultural universals also suggests that the shared genetic heritage of all humanity strongly affects the kinds of cultures that are possible in the human species.

## KEY TERMS

| | |
|---|---|
| cultural knowledge | subculture |
| patterns of behavior | norm |
| cultural integration | values |
| culture | collective understandings |
| trial-and-error learning | symbol |
| social learning | classifications of reality |
| enculturation | world view |
| cultural identity | biological determinism |
| society | cultural universals |
| ethnic groups | |

## SUGGESTED READINGS

Barclay, Harold B. *Culture: The Human Way.* Calgary: Western Publishers, 1986.

*A brief book about culture, its characteristics, its components, and the forces that change it.*

Barrett, Richard A. *Culture and Conduct.* Belmont, Calif.: Wadsworth, 1984.

*In addition to serving as a short text, this book summarizes many issues in contemporary anthropology.*

Brown, Donald E. *Human Universals.* New York: McGraw-Hill, 1991.

*An up-to-date description and analysis of cultural universals.*

Gamst, Frederick, and Edward Norbeck. *Ideas of Culture: Sources and uses.* New York: Holt, Rinehart and Winston, 1976.

*A collection of articles arranged according to approaches taken by their authors.*

Geertz, Clifford. *The Interpretation of Cultures.* New York: Basic, 1973.

*Collected articles by a leading American anthropologist. Two articles are especially well known: "Thick Description: Towards an Interpretive Theory of Culture" and "The Impact of the Concept of Culture on the Concept of Man."*

Gould, Steven Jay. *The Mismeasure of Man.* New York: W. W. Norton, 1981.

*Summarizes nineteenth- and early-twentieth-century attempts by scientists to prove the inferiority of some races and nationalities by measuring their skulls. Informative, yet highly readable, this book shows the errors in the assumptions of biological determinism, including the notion that intelligence is genetically determined.*

Lewontin, R. C., Steven Rose, and Leon J. Kamin. *Not in Our Genes: Biology, Ideology, and Human Nature.* New York: Pantheon, 1984.

*An argument against biological determinism, this book analyzes the social roots of the idea that differences between individuals, sexes, and races can be explained genetically.*

## CHAPTER 3

# LANGUAGE

*The ability to speak is one of the main abilities that sets humans apart from other animals.*

## CONTENTS

Language may be the single most important human capability that makes our species distinct from other animals. Certainly, many of the unique properties of human minds—perhaps even the very capacity to think abstractly—are closely related to our ability to speak and understand complex and precise messages. That we ordinarily communicate with one another so well without consciously thinking about it is surely one of the most remarkable facts about humanity—although one that most of us take for granted.

We begin this chapter with a brief discussion of some of the features of language that distinguish it from communication systems in other animals. We next show how people communicate by combining sounds into words and words into sentences. Finally, we discuss how language is related to various aspects of culture and how the act of speech itself is culturally conditioned.

## SOME PROPERTIES OF LANGUAGE

Language is a specialized and extremely complex form of communication. Communication occurs when two things happen. First, one organism perceives through its senses some attribute or result of the action of another, such as a physical feature, a movement, a sound, an odor, or a touch. Second, the receiving organism decodes (understands) the attribute or action, usually showing a visible reaction to it. The information communicated from the sender to the recipient is known as the *message*. In human languages, before the development of writing, messages usually were communicated through speech. Knowing a language implies mastery of the rules by which messages can be spoken (put into words) and understood.

We can introduce language by describing some of its key properties. In 1960, Charles Hockett identified thirteen features shared by all human languages. We describe only the five that most sharply distinguish language from other systems of communication.

### Multimedia Potential

All communication occurs by means of messages passed through some medium. When someone shouts "Fire!" a distinctive pattern of sound waves is created in the air. These waves strike the eardrums of those present. If they know what this particular pattern of sound waves means (i.e., if they understand the English language), they will respond to the message. In this case, sound is the medium through which words, as well as cries, growls, barks, and purrs, are transmitted. Similarly, light is the medium through which gestures are transmitted, and chemicals are the medium through which communication by means of the sense of smell occurs.

Unlike most other ways of communicating, language has **multimedia potential**, meaning that messages communicated with language can be transmitted through several media. Ordinarily, language messages are spoken (the medium is sound), but they may also be written or signed with movements of the hand (the medium is, respectively, marks on an object or light). Humans can even send language messages through touch (the medium is nerve signals; Helen Keller, blind and deaf, communicated this way).

The property that allows the messages of language to be transmitted through several media also allows the messages to be stored and later retrieved and transmitted, as the reading of this book illustrates. We can understand the message "I love you" whether it is spoken, written, or signed, assuming we know the language—that is, how to interpret the sounds, marks, or gestures made by the speaker, writer, or signer.

### Arbitrariness/Conventionality

The fact that humans are able to learn to transmit messages through several media is related to another fundamental characteristic of human language known as **arbitrariness**.

Language relies on arbitrary symbols. Consider what happens when children learn the words used by their community. During his or her first and second years of life, a child masters many words that refer to objects (*ball*), people (*mama*), qualities (*blue, hot*), commands (*no, go to sleep*—her parents hope she learns these two early!), actions (*eat, run*), emotions (*love*), and so forth. The specific words that stand for these objects, people, qualities, commands, actions, and emotions have no inherent relation to the things themselves. The child must learn to match up words with what they stand for, which is to say that the child must learn the meanings that speakers assign to words. The feelings aroused by the sounds that make up "I love you" to an English speaker are also aroused by "*Te amo*" to a Spanish speaker, although the sounds that communicate the message are completely different.

To say that linguistic messages are communicated by means of arbitrary symbols is to say that understanding is based entirely on conventions shared by both the sender and the recipient of the message. Analogously, it is because of shared conventions that one drives on the left side of the road in Britain and on the right side in North America. So long as drivers know and agree to abide by the convention, either side works as well as the other.

## Discrete and Recombinable Elements

All languages are made up of discrete units or elements that are combined in different ways to communicate different messages. We can introduce the discreteness and recombinability of these elements by noticing that an alphabet is possible because of this property. In writing, the letters of an alphabet are strung together to symbolize words. What do these letters stand for?

Originally, they symbolized discrete sounds—each letter represented a single recognizable sound, which was produced in a similar way in all the words in which it appeared. For example, the letter *b* appears in *bat, able, mob,* and *textbook,* and so does the sound we write as *b* in our alphabet. The same applies to all other letters in an alphabet.

(Incidentally, in the English alphabet, most single letters no longer represent a single sound. The letter *a,* for example, is pronounced differently in the words *act, father, warden, assume,* and *nature.* The same is true for other letters that represent English vowels. Some single sounds in English are rendered in spelling as two letters, such as *th, ou,* and the *gh* in *rough.* Why does the spelling English now uses for certain words not reflect the way these words are pronounced? Basically, because the way words are spelled became standardized after the invention of the printing press, but the pronunciation of many English sounds has changed since then.)

Alphabets are possible because words are composed of discrete sounds. These sounds can be seen as the building blocks of language. By themselves, most of the sounds of a language carry no meaning: The three English sounds in the word *cat,* for example, are meaningless when pronounced by themselves. But by combining this limited number of sounds in different ways, words are formed, and words do communicate meanings. Thus, the same three sounds in *cat* can be put together in different sequences to form the words *act* and *tack.* Words, then, are composed of sound combinations that have recognized, conventional meanings in

*The ability to send and receive complex messages by means of language is unique to humans.*

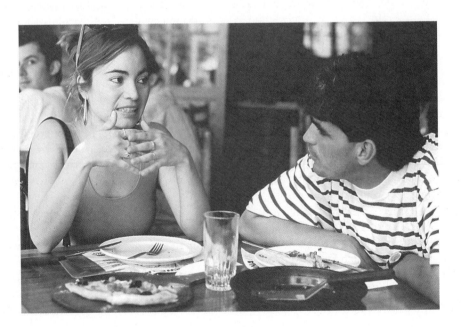

a speech community. And all languages use a small number of sounds to make a large number of words.

Sounds are not the only units of language that people recombine when speaking with one another. Words are combined according to the rules of the language to convey the quite complex messages carried by sentences. Sentences carry a message "greater than" the words that make them up. (This is seen clearly by contrasting the meaning of the following sentences composed of the same five words: This dog bit a man. This man bit a dog.) By mastering their language's words and their meanings, and its rules for combining words into sentences, speakers and hearers can send and receive messages of great complexity with amazing precision (e.g., "In the basket of apples on your left, hand me the reddest one on the bottom.").

Because language is composed of these **recombinable elements**, it is the most precise and complete system of communication known, as seen in the next important property of language.

## Productivity

Also known as *creativity*, **productivity** refers to a speaker's ability to create totally novel sentences (and to a hearer's ability to comprehend them). Consider the following sentence: "A garden spider ate the mayfly on my shoulder." Neither you nor I have previously heard this precise message; indeed, it is unlikely that it has ever been sent until now. Yet I formulated the sentence without consciously thinking about how to put the words together; and you understand it well enough to wonder why I allowed bugs on my body, even though you may not know what garden spiders or mayflies are.

Productivity means that a language's finite number of words can be combined into an infinite number of meaningful sentences. The sentences are meaningful because the speaker and hearer know what each word means individually and the rules by which they may be meaningfully combined. The amazing thing is that individuals are not consciously aware of their knowledge of these rules, although they routinely apply them each time they speak and hear.

## Displacement

**Displacement** refers to our ability to talk about objects, people, things, and events that are remote in time and space. Language has this property because of the symbolic nature of words and sentences, which means that things do not have to be visible to communicate about them. We can discuss someone who is not immediately present because the symbols of language call that person to mind, allowing us to picture and think about him or her. We can speculate about the future because although its events have not happened and may never happen, our language has symbols that stand for future time and more symbols that allow us to form a mental image of events that are only possible. We can learn about events (such as the French Revolution, worldwide depressions, and world wars) that happened long ago. Displacement makes it possible for us to talk about things that do not even exist, such as goblins, ghosts, and ghouls; indeed, we can give these imaginary things detailed characteristics in our mind's eye, although our real eyes have never seen them. Because of displacement, we can tell one another stories about things that never happened, and thus create myths, folklore, and literature. Because of the displacement property, people can learn of events remote from them in space, such as the collapse of the Soviet Union, ethnic cleansing in Bosnia, sectarian violence in India, and riots in Los Angeles. Much of culture depends on this important property of language.

## GRAMMAR

When we learn a language, we master the sounds used in that language, how the sounds can be combined into words, the meanings of words and idiomatic expressions, and the rules that govern how words are combined to form sentences. The elements (sounds, words) and the rules for combining these elements make up the total system of linguistic knowledge called a **grammar**. The term *grammar* refers to all the knowledge shared by those who are able to speak and understand a language: what sounds occur, how they may be properly combined into sequences that carry meaning, how words may be formed out of these sequences, and how new sentences may be constructed by stringing words together according to precise rules. The grammatical knowledge we share gives us the ability to speak to and understand one another—it is the basis of our linguistic *competence*. Knowledge of grammar underlies our speech, or linguistic *performance*—what we actually say, when we say it, and how we say it.

Grammatical knowledge is *unconscious*, meaning that those who share a language cannot verbalize the nature of the knowledge that allows them to speak and comprehend one another. It also is *intuitive*, meaning that speaking and understanding are second nature—we ordinarily do not need to think long and hard about how to transform the message we want to communicate into a sentence, or how to decode a sentence we hear into a message.

This scientific, technical use of *grammar* differs from the common use of the term. In everyday speech we judge people partly on the basis of whether we consider their grammar proper. In the United States there are several dialects, or regional variants of English. One, called *Standard American English* (SAE)—the dialect we usually hear in the national news media—is culturally accepted as most correct. Other dialects, especially those spoken by many African-Americans and by southern or Appalachian whites, are looked down on by many of those whose dialect is SAE.

But we need to realize that there is no such thing as superior and inferior dialects (or languages) *in the linguistic sense*. That is, each language, and each dialect, is equally capable of serving as a vehicle for communicating the messages its speakers need to send and receive. So long as a person successfully communicates, there is no such thing as "bad grammar," or people who "don't know proper grammar." The exchange of messages

MERLE: I ain't got no shoes.

PEARL: I ain't got none neither.

is perfectly good English—to members of certain subcultures who speak one English dialect. So long as

speakers communicate their intended meaning to hearers, then the words they use or the way they construct their sentences is as valid as any other. The evaluations we make of someone else's grammar or overall style of speech, then, are cultural evaluations. Culturally, people define some dialects as more correct than others. But if the history of the United States had been different, some other dialect of American English might have become standard, and the sentences

AMY: I have no shoes.

DONALD: Nor do I.

might have become one of our cultural markers of ignorance or lack of sophistication.

This point is so important that it is worth saying another way. Many languages are not uniform but have variations based on region, class, ethnicity, or some other difference between people. These variations in the grammar of a single language are called **dialects**. The speakers of a language or dialect share a complete knowledge of its grammar. When linguists try to discover this grammar, they call what they are investigating a *descriptive* grammar: They are trying to describe completely and objectively the elements and rules that underlie communication in some particular language or dialect. The descriptive grammar a linguist would write of Black English would differ slightly from that of SAE. But a linguist would never describe the differences

The residents of Appalachia speak one of many English dialects, each of which is equally grammatical in the linguistic sense.

between the two dialects in terms of relative superiority, since each dialect is capable of conveying the same messages.

In contrast, when some speakers of SAE label black or southern dialects as substandard English, they are basing their judgments on their cultural assumptions about the relative correctness of dialects. But this judgment is entirely *cultural. Linguistically,* all languages and all dialects work as well as others, meaning that all languages and all dialects have equal ability to communicate the messages their speakers need to send and receive.

With this point about the relativity of all languages and dialects in mind, we can discuss three areas of the study of grammar. The first, known as **phonology**, deals with the sounds of a language and how they are patterned into a consistent system. The second, called **morphology**, deals with how sounds are put together to form words and other sound sequences that carry meaning. The third field of study, **syntax**, deals with the unconscious rules of a language that the speakers use to string together a series of words to create a sentence or other utterance that conveys a complex meaning.

## Phonology

As we have seen, any act of speech can be broken down into a string of sounds. The sounds of a language, together with the way these sounds occur in regular, consistent patterns, make up the *phonological system* of the language.

For example, when you hear the word *debt,* you hear a sequence of sounds that you have learned to associate with a certain meaning. You do not consciously think, and may even be unable to recognize, that *debt* consists of three distinguishable sounds, /d/, /E/, and /t/. (The slash marks / / denote sounds recognized as distinctive in a single language.) In fact, if someone asked you, "How many sounds are there in 'debt'?" you might say "Four" because you would confuse the sounds in *debt* with its number of letters in English spelling.

But you do know what the three sounds in *debt* are, although you might not know that you know. You know because you recognize that the word *pet* is a different word from *debt,* although only its initial sound, /p/, is different. You know because you recognize *debt* and *date* as different words, although they differ only in their second sound. And you know because you recognize the profound contrast in meaning between *debt* and *dead,* although this difference is caused by a single sound at the end of the two words. If English speakers did not know, at an unconscious level, that *debt* must be pronounced /dEt/, rather than /pEt/, /dayt/, or /dEd/, they would mispronounce it, and their listeners would be unable to distinguish *debt* from these other words. Conversely, if a hearer did not know that /dEt/ is different from /pEt/, she or he might expect to receive a cat or dog when the speaker said, "I'm repaying my debt to you."

The particular sounds that the speakers of a language recognize as distinct from other sounds are called the **phonemes** of the language. Phonemes are the atoms or minimal bits of a language that make a difference in the meanings of its words. For example, we can break up the word *brought* into four phonemes: /b/, /r/, /O/, and /t/. The substitution of any other phoneme for any of the phonemes in the word *brought* would either change the word into another word (e.g., *bright,* in which a different vowel sound, /ay/, is substituted for /O/) or make it unintelligible (e.g., *blought* or *broughk*).

Languages have different phonemes, and various languages' phonological systems are patterned differently. This means that languages recognize and distinguish between sounds based on different sound qualities, and that each language has its own logic and consistency in making these distinctions.

As an example of the patterning of the phonological system of one language, compare two phonemes of English: /b/ and /p/. The phoneme /b/ appears in *boy, able, probation,* and *flab.* It is made by putting the lips together and then releasing them while making a slight vibration with the vocal cords. The phoneme /p/ appears in *pat, approach, mop,* and *example.* We make the /p/ sound the same way as /b/, except that we do not vibrate our vocal cords.

You can hear the vibration of your vocal cords in /b/ by placing your hands over your ears while saying the word *bat* slowly and listening for a slight buzz during the pronunciation of /b/. This buzz is the sound your vocal cords make when your lungs force air through them while they are constricted, or tightened, and brought nearly into contact with one another. All sounds in which the vocal cords vibrate are called *voiced.* Examples of other voiced consonants in English are /d/, /z/, and /j/ (/j/ is the first and last sound in *judge*). All vowel sounds also are voiced in English.

Now place your hands over your ears while saying the word *pat.* You will not hear a buzz during the pronunciation of /p/. This is because your vocal cords are completely open, so the flow of air from your lungs is unimpeded and no buzzy sound is created. All sounds in which the vocal cords are open, so that their vibration does not contribute to the sound, are called *voiceless*. Other voiceless phonemes in English are /t/, /s/, and /č/ (/č/ is the first and last sound in *church*).

The only difference between *bat* and *pat* is this first sound, and the significant difference between the sounds /b/ and /p/ is that the vocal cords vibrate during /b/ but are open during /p/. Stated technically, the only difference between the two phonemes is that /b/ is voiced, whereas /p/ is voiceless.

We discussed these two English phonemes in some detail to make a general point: Our understanding of words is based on our shared ability to hear *distinctions* between their constituent sounds and to recognize these distinctions as *significant*. People who speak English have no difficulty hearing the distinctions between the first sounds of *bill* and *pill*, although they do not consciously know what qualities make these sounds different. We also recognize the distinctions between the two sounds as significant—that is, as making a difference in the meanings of the words in which they appear. If the difference between /b/ and /p/ were not significant, we would not recognize any difference between words that differ only in these sounds—*pill* and *bill* would have the same meaning and hence would be the same word! Further, the one sound that makes *bill* and *pill* different itself differs only in whether it is voiceless (/p/) or voiced (/b/). Now, if *pill* and *bill* have different meanings, but the only difference between them is whether the initial sound is voiceless or voiced, then it must be the voiceless/voiced distinction that makes the words different.

In fact, the voiced/voiceless distinction matters for all English consonants. The distinctions that speakers make between phonemes tend to be consistent across phonemes of a language. In other words, the features of sounds that the speakers of a language recognize as significant are *patterned*. If a distinction (e.g., voiced/ voiceless) is recognized for some sounds, the same distinction tends to be recognized for other sounds that differ in the same way. Thus, English speakers recognize the differences between /f/ and /v/ (as in *feel* versus *veal*), between /s/ and /z/ (as in *peace* versus *peas*), between /k/ and /g/ (as in *curl* versus *girl*), and between other consonants that differ only in whether they are voiced or voiceless.

## Some Variations in Phonology

So what? All we have done is put into words what every speaker of English unconsciously and intuitively knows: that we detect the difference between sounds such as /t/ and /d/, and /f/ and /v/, and that we recognize this difference as significant. Can't everyone in the world hear this difference, and doesn't everyone recognize this difference as significant?

No, they can't and don't. Although it may seem incredible to those who speak English, there are a great many languages in which sounds that differ only in whether they are voiced or voiceless are not recognized as different sounds. In fact, the speakers of one of these languages may not be able to hear the difference between sounds that differ only in whether they are voiced or voiceless. For instance, in Kosraen, a Micronesian language, the distinctions between the sounds /t/ and /d/, /p/ and /b/, and /k/ and /g/ make no difference in meaning. So the two alternative pronunciations of the following words make no difference in meaning to Kosraens:

*k∅p* and *g∅p* mean "satiated," "full from eating"
*t n* and *d n* mean "color"
*p k* and *b k* mean "sand"

*As they grow up, children master the sounds, words, and permissible word combinations of the language of their community.*

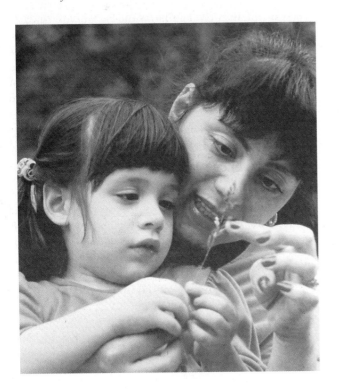

It is as if English-speaking people made no distinction between *cot* and *got,* between *tan* and *dan*, and between *pig* and *big*. This does not mean that Kosraen ears are not as sensitive as Canadian, Australian, or English ears; it certainly does not mean that Kosraen is an inferior language to English. It means only that the Kosraen and English languages do not recognize the same distinctions in similar sounds as making a difference in the meanings of words. In English, /k/ and /g/ are different phonemes; in Kosraen, they are alternative ways of pronouncing the same phoneme.

So differences between sounds that are meaningful in one language's phonological system do not always have meaning in another's. Conversely, one language may recognize distinctions between similar sounds that the speakers of another language do not detect. For example, we have referred to the English phoneme /p/ as if it is always pronounced the same way. In fact, we use two pronunciations for /p/, depending on the sounds around it. Consider the words *pit* and *spit*. You might think that the only difference between the two is the sound /s/. If so, you are wrong. The /p/ in *pit* is followed by a short puff of air (called *aspiration*) between it and the vowel; the /p/ in *pit* is said to be aspirated. The /p/ in *spit* is not followed by such a puff; it is unaspirated. (You cannot hear this difference, but you may be able to feel it: Put your hand immediately in front of your mouth while saying the two words, and you may feel the aspiration after the /p/ in *pit,* but not after *spit*.)

Surely such a slight difference cannot matter, but in many languages it does. In Thai, for example, /p/ and /pʰ/ (the ʰ stands for aspiration) are separate phonemes, which means that those who speak Thai detect the difference between many aspirated and unaspirated sounds and recognize it as changing the meaning of many words. This is seen in the following Thai words:

| | |
|---|---|
| *paa* "forest" | *pʰaa* "to split" |
| *tam* "to pound" | *tʰam* "to do" |
| *kat* "to bite" | *kʰat* "to interrupt" |

Note that a difference in sound that is nearly inaudible to a speaker of English changes the meanings of the paired Thai words just listed. Hindi, the language spoken by many Asian Indians, also recognizes the difference between aspirated and unaspirated sounds.

One of the most interesting ways in which languages differ in their phonological systems is the way the pitch of the voice is used to convey meaning. (The pitch of a voice depends on how fast the vocal cords vibrate: The higher the frequency of vibration, the higher the pitch of the voice.) English speakers use pitch to convey different meanings, as you can see by contrasting the following sentences:

She went to class.

She went to class?

The first statement is turned into a question by altering the pitch of the voice: in the question, the pitch rises with the word *class*. Now contrast these sentences:

What did Mary hit, a ball?

What, did Mary hit a ball?

Here, pitch is used together with slight pauses to convey questions with a different sense. Parents also use high pitch—often together with loudness—to scold their children. Consider the following statements by one mother to her son:

"You're playing with the ball in the house, Matthew." (IMPLICATION: "how cute!")

"YOU'RE PLAYING WITH THE BALL IN THE HOUSE, MATTHEW." (IMPLICATION: "which I've told you a zillion times not to do!")

Matthew may respond to the second sentence—the scold—with:

"I never get to do anything!"

Assuming, as is likely, that Matthew whines when he says this, he also uses pitch to show his displeasure.

Speakers of English use the changing pitch of their voices over the whole sentence to communicate a message; that is, the voice pitch falls or rises mainly from word to word, rather than within a word. There are many other languages in which a high, medium, or low pitch used within an individual word, or even in a syllable, changes the fundamental meaning of the word.

Languages in which the pitch (or tone) with which a word is said (or changes in the voice pitch during its pronunciation) affects the meaning of a word are known as **tone languages.** Tone languages occur in Africa and southeastern and eastern Asia. Chinese, Thai, Burmese, and Vietnamese are all tone languages, which is why they have a musical quality to ears accustomed to English. As an example of how pitch can affect meaning, consider these words from Nupe, an African tone language:

*bá* (high tone) means "to be sour"

*bā* (mid tone) means "to cut"

*bà* (low tone) means "to count"

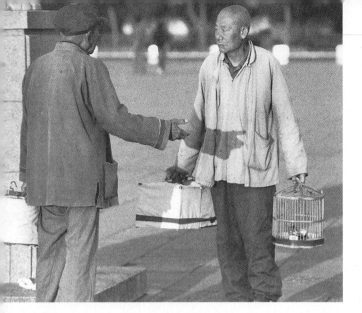

Languages vary in the use of voice pitch to convey meaning. In tone languages, such as that spoken by these Chinese, voice pitch affects the basic meaning of words.

Here, whether the two phonemes in *ba* are pronounced with a high, mid, or low tone changes their meaning. The same principle can apply to syllables within a word—how the pitch of the voice changes between the syllables alters the meaning. This is exemplified by the following Thai words:

*nâa* (tone of voice falls on second vowel) means "face"

*năa* (tone of voice rises on second vowel) means "thick"

Because the tone with which a word is pronounced, or changes in the tone within the word, can change its meaning, the pitch of the voice is a kind of phoneme in tone languages. It has the same effect as adding /s/ in front of the English word *pot*, which totally alters its meaning to *spot*.

## Morphology

Morphology is the study of meaningful sound sequences and the rules by which they are formed. In the preceding section we used *word* to refer to any sequence of phonemes that carries meaning to speakers and hearers. Any language contains a finite number of words, matched to one or more meanings, and its total inventory of words is called its **lexicon**. In morphology we need a more precise concept than *word*. To see why, ask yourself if you know the meaning of the following sound sequences, none of which qualifies as a word:

| un | ed |
|------|------|
| pre | s |
| non | ing |
| anti | ist |

You do, of course, recognize these sound sequences. Those in the first column are prefixes, which change the meaning of certain words when placed before them. Those in the second column are suffixes, which alter a word's meaning when they follow the word.

Sound sequences such as these are "detachable" from particular words. Take the words *art* and *novel*, for example. By adding the suffix *-ist* to these words, we make new words meaning something like "a person who creates art" or "one who writes novels." That *-ist* has a similar meaning whenever it is attached to other words is shown by the made-up word *crim*; you don't know what this word means, but by adding *-ist* to it, you instantly know that a *crimist* is "a person who crims." We need a concept that will include prefixes and suffixes such as *uni-*, *-ing*, *-ly*, and so forth to analyze such compound words and their meanings.

Any sequence of phonemes that carries meaning is known as a **morpheme**. There are two kinds of morphemes in all languages. **Free morphemes** are any morphemes that can stand alone as words, for example, type, walk, woman, establish. **Bound morphemes** are morphemes that are attached to free morphemes to modify their meanings in predictable ways, for example, *dis-*, *bi-*, *-er*, *-ly*. Thus, by adding suffixes to the example free morphemes, we get:

| typist | typed | typing |
|-------------|---------------|-------------|
| walked | walking | walks |
| womanly | womanhood | womanish |
| established | establishment | establishes |

Both prefixes and suffixes—which in English are the two kinds of bound morphemes—can be attached to a free morpheme to change its meaning, as shown in the following examples:

| desire | desirable | undesirable |
|----------|------------|--------------|
| excuse | excusable | inexcusably |
| possible | impossible | impossibility |
| health | healthy | unhealthful |
| complete | completely | incompletely |

Note that both free and bound morphemes carry meaning (although the meaning depends on the context in which they are used), unlike most phonemes such as /l/,

/g/, /n/, and so on. Just as phonemes are the minimal units of sound, morphemes are the minimal units of meaning of a language. Thus, we cannot break down the free morphemes *friend, possible, man,* or *run* into any smaller unit that carries meaning. Nor can we break down the bound morphemes *non-, -ish, -able,* or *tri-* into any smaller units and still have them mean anything in English.

There is no doubt that the speakers of a language learn its rules for forming compound words by combining free and bound morphemes. That is, people learn how to make new compound words by applying a rule of compound-word formation, not by learning each compound word separately.

For instance, take the English rule for forming a plural noun from a singular noun. It can be done by adding the bound morpheme /z/, thus: *beads, apples, colors, eggs.* (Incidentally, /z/ represents one of only a few cases in English in which a phoneme is also a morpheme. When used as a bound morpheme at the end of a noun, /z/ usually carries the meaning "more than one"). Children learn the morphological rule for plural formation at an early age, but it takes them a while longer to learn the many exceptions to the rule. They apply the rule consistently to all words, saying "childs," "mans," "foots," "mouses," and so on.

The same is true for the English rule for forming the past tense of a verb. Generally, the bound morpheme /d/ is added as a suffix to the verb, as in *formed, bored, loaded,* and *included.* Again, children learn this rule for past-tense formation early, and they apply it consistently. We hear children say "goed," "runned," "bringed," and "doed."

Thus, one of the many things people unconsciously know when they know a language is its rules for changing the meaning of free morphemes by the addition of bound morphemes. We do not have to learn *tree* and *trees* as separate words. We need only apply a general morphological rule (i.e., add /z/ as a suffix to make a noun plural) to *tree,* or to many other nouns.

## Syntax

*Syntax* refers to the unconscious rules that instruct speakers of a language how to combine words into meaningful sentences and listeners how to decode the string of words into a message. Each speaker-hearer of a language has a knowledge of syntactic rules and knows intuitively whether a particular sentence is said in a grammatical way. Yet, just as with phonology and mor-

phology, untrained individuals are unable to describe (verbalize) these rules, although they apply them each time they speak or listen, and although they can tell when some particular utterance violates the rules.

As anyone who has tried to master a foreign language knows, languages vary in their syntactical rules. To give a brief impression of the range of this variability, consider these short sentences from four languages:

ENGLISH: You are a beautiful person.

SPANISH: *Usted es una persona bonita.*
(You are a person beautiful.)

TANNESE: *Ik iema amasan.*
(You person good/beautiful.)

KOSRAEN: *Mwet kato se pa kom.*
(Person beautiful one equals you.)

As these simple sentences demonstrate, one way in which the syntax of languages varies is in the permissible order of morphemes. But this is by no means the only way. The Spanish example used the formal word *usted* for *you,* but it would also be possible to use the informal *tú.* Which form of *you* a speaker used would depend on whom she was addressing and the precise kind of message she wanted to convey. In English and Spanish, to speak grammatically it was necessary to use some form of the verb *to be.* In this sentence, *are* is the

*Although the conversation of these Chilean women cannot be understand by those who do not know Spanish, many linguists believe all human languages share certain fundamental elements.*

correct form. Most English speakers would consider "You is a beautiful person" to be ungrammatical, although "He is a beautiful person" is acceptable. In contrast, Spanish has no different form of *to be* that needs to be used in this context: *es* is used regardless of whether the subject is *you* or *he*. Tannese lacks the verb *to be* altogether: It is simply understood that *amasan* refers to *ik*. Kosraen also has no verb *to be,* but one must use *pa* (meaning roughly "equal to" or "equivalent to") when two noun phrases (*you* and *beautiful person*) are being equated. If a Kosraen wanted to communicate "You are beautiful," he would say merely *Kom kato,* omitting the *pa* that is required in "You are a beautiful person."

To sum up, the speakers of a language possess detailed unconscious knowledge that provides them with rules for combining words and other morphemes into meaningful sentences. Languages differ in these syntactic rules. We already have seen that languages also differ in their sound inventories, in which features of sound they consider significant, in their rules for combining sounds into morphemes, and in their rules for forming words out of free and bound morphemes. Do these facts together mean that human languages have little in common? Is all this diversity in phonology, morphology, and syntax unlimited?

## UNIVERSAL GRAMMAR

The answer to the questions just posed is no, according to most modern linguists. Despite their variability—which we have merely introduced—all human languages share many important features. All include both vowels and consonants among their phonemes. Every language has a way to discuss events that occurred in the past, a way to form negations, ask questions, make requests, give commands, express emotions, and so forth. Similar syntactical categories (or parts of speech, such as nouns, verbs, adverbs, and adjectives) occur in all languages. The speakers of all languages can discuss not just events, people, qualities, things, and actions but also abstract concepts similar to our notions of good and evil, souls, spirits, love, and beauty.

These and other universals suggest that languages are not as different as they initially appear to be. Is there other evidence that human languages share certain universal rules? Indeed, there is. It comes from an unexpected source: children.

Parents know the joy of experiencing their children's language learning. We try to coax them into saying their

first word, which happens at about one year of age. We anxiously wait for them to put several words together, which most are able to do consistently at around two years. Some of us wonder about the best way to teach them to speak. We may compete with our friends to see whose child will advance fastest, believing that rapid learning of language is correlated with high intelligence.

Yet we do not teach language to our children, at least not in the sense that schools teach them to write, read, do arithmetic, memorize dates, and recite poetry. Adults cannot possibly teach children the rules of a language the way a third-grade teacher teaches them multiplication tables, for adults do not consciously know the rules themselves. An English-speaking person cannot teach a child who does not already know the English language grammatical rules such as "the adjective goes before the noun," that "/z/ after a noun means 'more than one,'" that "voiced stops are unaspirated," that "a sentence consists of a noun phrase plus a verb phrase," and so on.

Further, even if we could agree on what *intelligence* means, the ability of children to learn language seems to have no relation to it. By the time they are four or five, most normal children have a complete knowledge of the grammar of the language to which they have been exposed. They can formulate sentences as well as any adult, although they continue to add vocabulary for many more years. A child who has been regularly exposed to two or more languages soon learns to distinguish them when speaking and seldom confuses their phonology, morphology, or syntax.

Children do learn language, but they do not do so in the same way they learn most other things—by imitation and memorization. At an early age they use language productively, uttering and comprehending sentences they have never heard. They do not merely copy adult models of speech. Children of English-speaking parents are most unlikely ever to have heard sentences like

Want other one spoon.
Oh, nobody don't like me.
I goed to the store.
You hurted me.

So where do children learn the grammar that produces such utterances, since they did not hear similar sentences from adults? Apparently, speech like this is characteristic of a certain period of language acquisition, during which a child is able to put together multiword sentences that express complex and comprehensible meanings but has not yet mastered the grammar used by adults.

*Children learn to speak the language of their society by hearing adults talk. These Fijian women are doing just that. As the children listen, they are acquiring an unconscious knowledge of the grammar of Fijian.*

This and other evidence suggests that children master the language of their community by successive approximation: At different stages of language learning, children deduce a set of grammatical rules from the speech around them, which they use to form novel sentences. (We say "deduced" because no adult could have told the child these rules; the child must figure them out from the evidence of adult speech.) The grammar of one stage is superseded as a child moves into the next stage, acquiring a closer and closer approximation of adult grammar.

Finally, and significantly, there seems to be little variation in the speed with which children who are exposed to different languages learn to speak. It might seem that some languages would be harder for children to learn—certainly some languages are more difficult to master than others for adults who already know one language. Yet children around the world show little variation in the rate at which they develop linguistic competence.

In short, normal children

✦ learn language without formal instruction because no one is capable of teaching them which of all possible phonemes their language uses, or the rules for how these phonemes can be combined into meaningful morphemes and sentences.
✦ learn language in a remarkably short period of time that varies surprisingly little from language to language.
✦ learn language almost regardless of how well they perform other mental tasks.
✦ learn language by deduction rather than by imitation and memorization.

The ability of children to learn language in this way is truly astounding. As we have already tried to make clear, the knowledge of the grammar of any language is incredibly complex. Children under the age of five, however, learn it routinely, easily, and at nearly the same rate everywhere. How is this possible?

It would seem to be possible only if all children are born with a knowledge of *human language*. Noam Chomsky, probably the world's most influential linguist, was asked, "How could anyone possibly learn enough about the English language to possess the rich and exotic grammatical knowledge that we all seem to possess by the time we are five or six years old?" Chomsky replied:

The knowledge is built in. You and I can learn English, as well as any other language, with all its richness because we are designed to learn languages based upon a common set of principles, which we may call universal grammar . . . [which is] the sum total of all the immutable principles that heredity builds into the language organ. The principles cover grammar, speech sounds, and meaning. Put differently, universal grammar is the inherited genetic endowment that makes it possible for us to speak and learn human languages. (Gliedman 1985, 371)

Notice that Chomsky is not merely claiming that children are born with the capacity to learn language. Rather, he and many other linguists claim that there is an inborn human language, which consists of a set of grammatical rules—**universal grammar**—that do not have to be learned and that guide children's discovery and mastery of the grammar to which they are exposed at the proper time in their lives. Children are born with a genetically programmed plan to discover and replicate the elements and rules of the specific language spoken around them. We do not know what this plan looks like, but it or something like it seems necessary to account for the speed and ease with which children around the world master their native languages.

# ⌧ LANGUAGE AND CULTURE

Although linguists debate the nature (and even the existence) of a universal grammar, it does seem likely that some sort of universal grammatical knowledge is inborn in children. What implication might this have for the study of culture? There are several possibilities, only one of which we can discuss here: the possibility that all or part of cultural knowledge is organized in the same way as linguistic knowledge, that is, as the grammar of language.

Certainly, it is plausible (which does not mean it is correct) to assume that the human mind organizes cultural and grammatical knowledge in much the same way. Notice that grammar consists of unconscious rules or principles by which the messages that speakers want to transmit are transformed into the speech that hearers can understand. Likewise, much of cultural knowledge consists of the rules and principles that provide individuals with the information they need to know how to behave in meaningful and appropriate ways.

Along these same lines, cultural knowledge underlies behavior in much the same way that grammatical knowledge underlies speech. Grammar greatly influences how people say what they want to say because serious violations of grammatical rules lead to miscommunication. But grammar does not determine what the speakers of a language say to one another. People decide what messages they want to communicate based on the situation in which they find themselves, what goals they seek, whom they are addressing, and many other factors. Analogously, many factors influence a person's nonverbal behavior besides the cultural knowledge he or she shares with others. Grammar and culture underlie and constrain—yet do not determine—speech and nonverbal behavior.

## Language and Cultural Classifications of Reality

Such analogies between language and culture can easily be pressed too far. What would be the linguistic analogue of "values" or "attitudes," for example? Language, however, has provided a useful model for the analysis of at least one component of cultural knowledge; specifically, the phonological system of language has been helpful in analyzing how various cultures organize their classifications of reality (see chapter 2). Such analysis first became popular among cultural anthropologists in the 1960s, when the specialization known as *cognitive* *anthropology* or *ethnoscience* was developed. Cognitive anthropologists often study how various cultures build up their classifications of reality by perceiving the objective natural and social world in different ways. Language has provided a useful model for describing and analyzing this component of cultural knowledge. In particular, a culture's classification of reality may be organized into consistent patterns much like those of the phonological system of a language.

To glimpse the organization of these patterns, we return for a moment to phonology. As we have seen, English recognizes the difference between voiced and voiceless consonants as significant. On the other hand, many other languages do not recognize this distinction between sounds, for the meaning of a word in these languages is not affected by whether certain of its consonants are voiced or voiceless. The distinctions between the same sounds are objectively present in all languages, but they are not necessarily perceived and made significant.

Now recall that one difference between cultures is how they classify reality into categories of objects, people, and events. This is done by perceiving or not perceiving different features of things and by recognizing or not recognizing these differences as important (just as the speakers of a language do or do not perceive or recognize differences between sounds). On the basis of these perceptions and recognitions of contrasts and similarities between things, humans define categories of reality. We classify specific objects, people, natural phenomena, and so forth into one or another category, depending on which of their many features we notice and view as significant. And members of different cultural traditions do not necessarily base their categories on the same contrasts and similarities (just as speakers of different languages do not distinguish phonemes based on the same contrasts and similarities; recall, for example, that aspiration is not a difference that matters in English phonology, although it is the only difference between some phonemes in Hindi and Thai).

An example sheds light on how the "cognitive categories" of a people can be built up in much the same way as elements of language. Take three kinds of livestock: cattle, horses, and swine. How do North American farmers categorize and classify these animals? Consider the following list:

| CATTLE | HORSES | SWINE |
|--------|--------|-------|
| cow | mare | sow |
| bull | stallion | boar |
| steer | gelding | barrow |
| heifer | filly | gilt |
| calf | colt | shoat |

(Unless you have a farming background, you will not recognize some of these terms. Farmers need to discuss cattle, horses, and swine more than do suburban or city folk, so they use a rich lexicon to talk about livestock.) Note that the same features are used to contrast the different categories of cattle, horses, and swine. *Cow* and *bull* contrast in the same way as *mare-stallion* and *sow-boar*: the first is female; the second, male. There is a special term for each kind of male animal that has been neutered: *steer, gelding,* and *barrow*. And there are separate terms for female and male immature animals: *heifer-calf, filly-colt,* and *gilt-shoat*. Each kind of livestock then is divided into categories based on gender (female, male, neutered male) and age (adult, immature). And each category can be described by the features that distinguish it in the farmers' classification of livestock: a *filly* is an "immature female horse," a *barrow* is a "mature castrated male swine," and so on.

These are the features of animals that farmers find important enough to make the basis of their classification of livestock. Notice that this classification rests on contrasts and similarities between *selected* characteristics of the animals—just as the speakers of a language recognize only *some* features of sounds as significant. Notice also that the classification is patterned: the same contrasts and similarities (gender, age) are used to distinguish kinds of cattle, horses, and swine. Similarly, the phonological rules of a language are patterned: if a feature (e.g., voicing) of one class of sound (e.g., stop) is recognized as significant for one member of the class, it tends to be recognized as significant for other members of the class as well.

As this example shows, the way a people culturally classify things is built up out of selected features of the things, and these same features are the basis for distinguishing between other, similar things. This subsystem of culture appears to be organized much like the knowledge speakers have of their language's phonology: Potential differences and similarities between things are perceived as significant, and cultural conceptions of reality are constructed from these selected differences and similarities. This makes sense because a people classify reality, at least in part, by assigning labels (words) to things, and it is hard to imagine any other criteria for placing things under one or another label besides the patterned recognition of differences and similarities between them. So phonological patterns have provided useful models for describing and analyzing cultural classifications of reality.

Another important issue is the nature of the relation between the language a particular people speak and their culture. The two are connected in some way. How?

On the one hand, a people's language mirrors (reflects) their way of life. People assign names or labels to some objects, qualities, and actions rather than others; they have ways of discussing the specific social relationships that are important to them; they may develop a specialized vocabulary or speech style to use in religious rituals or social ceremonies; and so on. How the culture of a people affects their language is one topic to be discussed.

On the other hand, some scholars have argued that language does not merely reflect culture but also helps to create it. Specifically, they argue that the language people speak influences the way they perceive reality, and hence shapes their world view.

In the next two subsections, we discuss both of the above topics: first, how the language of a people reflects certain aspects of their way of life and, second, the possibility that language is a creative force in culture, shaping how people perceive the world and entire world views.

## Language as a Mirror of Culture

Many elements of a language reflect the way of life of those who speak it. For example, a complex lexicon develops around things that are especially important to some group of people, as we saw with the farmers' classification of livestock. This makes it easier for them to communicate effectively about the social relations, actions, natural phenomena, and other subjects that matter most to them.

Examples of how vocabulary reflects peoples' needs to communicate about certain subjects are found among individuals of different subcultural, occupational, and gender categories in North American society. Take automobile tools, for example. A professional mechanic can identify hundreds of kinds of tools; the Saturday-afternoon home mechanic can identify perhaps several dozen; and the rest of us don't know a ring compressor from a hub puller, or a compression tester from a feeler gauge. Numerous other examples could be cited to show that a language's lexicon responds to the needs of people to discuss certain topics easily.

But not all specialized vocabularies are developed entirely to meet an objective need of the members of some group to converse easily or precisely among themselves. Specialized vocabularies also serve as status markers for professions and other groups. Lawyers speak "legalese" only partly because they need to make fine distinctions between points of law that are obscure to the rest of us. Legalese is a secret—as well as a

*Occupational groups sometimes have terms and concepts that make it easier for their members to converse and that protect their position in society. The legal profession is a familiar example.*

specialized—vocabulary. Entry into the select group of attorneys depends in part on mastery of an esoteric vocabulary with all its nuances. And it does not hurt the profession as a whole that the general population cannot understand bills of sale or many other contracts written by attorneys. Many of us feel compelled to pay for the specialized knowledge of an attorney to interpret important documents.

In a similar manner, we are familiar with "bureaucratese," a special vocabulary bureaucrats use to put us off (or down). Sometimes unfamiliar words are used to *avoid* communicating information, to obscure messages intentionally, to direct questioners to someone else, or simply to say go away. (But we shouldn't be too hard on bureaucrats, for, as we shall see, we all routinely use language for similar purposes.)

In sum, in a diverse and complex society, occupational or other kinds of groups may develop specialized speech to facilitate communication, to mark themselves off from everyone else, to help ensure the continuation of their privileges and rewards, and so on. This is probably familiar, but what about differences *between* whole languages, spoken by members of *different* cultures? Similar ideas apply. To understand them, the concept of **semantic domain** is useful. A semantic domain is a set of words that belong to a more inclusive class. For example, *chair, table, ottoman,* and *china cabinet* belong to the semantic domain of "furniture." "Color" is another semantic domain, with members such as *violet, red,* and *yellow.*

Semantic domains typically have a hierarchical structure, meaning that they have several levels of inclusive-

ness. For instance, two colors the English language distinguishes can be further broken down:

| BLUE | GREEN |
| --- | --- |
| aqua | kelly |
| sky | mint |
| royal | forest |
| navy | avocado |
| teal | lime |

We divide the semantic domain of color into specific colors (e.g., blue, green), each of which in turn is divided into "kinds of blue" and "kinds of green," and even into—for some of us—"shades of sky blue" or "tones of forest green."

By now you can see where this discussion is headed: Different languages spoken by members of different cultures vary in the semantic domains they identify, in how finely they carve up these domains, and in how they make distinctions between different members of a domain. Some of these differences are rather obvious. For instance, the semantic domain of "fish" is unlikely to be as elaborate among desert dwellers as among coastal or riverine peoples. Tropical lowland peoples are not likely to have the semantic domain we call "snow" in their native language, whereas some Arctic peoples discuss it so much that they have an elaborate vocabulary to facilitate communication about snow conditions. Further, the degree to which some semantic domain has a multilevel hierarchical structure depends on the importance of the objects or actions in peoples' lives: island, coastal, or riverine people dependent on fish are likely to have many categories and subcategories of aquatic life, fishing methods, and flood and tide stages, for instance. Can we go beyond such fairly obvious statements?

For some domains we can. There are some things or qualities that seem to be "natural domains," meaning that the differences between their members seem to be obvious to anyone. In fact, they seem to be inherent in the things themselves. We therefore would expect that people everywhere would carve up these domains in similar ways. For instance, color is an inherent (natural) quality of things, which can be measured by instruments that determine the wavelength of light reflected from an object. Surely anyone can recognize that blue and green are different colors, and surely this recognition is reflected in separate terms for the two colors! Likewise, biological kinship is a natural relationship, in the sense that who an infant's parents are determines who will and will not be his or her closest genetic relatives. What human cannot recognize that his or her aunts and uncles are fundamentally different kinds of relatives than parents?

Although blue and green are objectively different colors, and aunts are objectively different relatives from mothers, people are not obliged to recognize these differences and make them culturally significant. The semantic domains of color and relatives are in fact divided up differently by different cultures, and these divisions are not self-evident.

The domain of "relatives" or "kinfolk" is an excellent example of how members of different cultural traditions divide up an apparently natural domain according to different principles. Because we return to this subject in chapter 11, here we want only to show that different cultures do not in fact make the same distinctions between relatives as we do; that is, the way relatives are culturally classified is variable.

Consider the relatives that English-speaking people call *aunt, first cousin,* and *brother.* An aunt is a sister of your mother or father; a first cousin is a child of any of your aunts and uncles; and a brother is a male child of your parents. These individuals are all biologically related to you differently, so you place them in different categories and call them by different terms.

But notice that other distinctions are possible that you do not recognize as distinctions and that are not reflected in the kinship lexicon of English. Your aunts are not related to you in the same way: One is the sister of your mother, one the sister of your father. Why not recognize this distinction between them by giving them different terms? Similarly, your first cousins could be subdivided into finer categories and given special terms, such as *child of my father's sister, child of my mother's brother,* and so on. And since we distinguish most other categories of relatives by their gender (e.g., brother versus sister, aunt versus uncle), why does gender not matter for any of our cousins?

We know it is possible to divide up the domain of relatives differently because other cultures do not identify the same categories of relatives as speakers of English. People in many societies, for instance, call their mother's sister by one term and their father's sister by another term (although we collapse both into one term, *aunt*). It is also common for a people to distinguish between the children of their father's sister and their father's brother, calling the first by a term we translate as "cousin," the second by the same term as they use for their own brothers and sisters! (These various ways of carving up relatives, by the way, are not haphazard. Anthropologists have discovered that these terminolog-

ical systems are related to other aspects of a people's way of life, as we discuss in chapter 11.) So the ways people divide up members (specific kinds of kin) of the seemingly "natural domain" of biological relatives is not the same the world over.

The same applies to color, our other example. Brent Berlin and Paul Kay found great diversity in color terms among various human populations. Some had only two terms for, roughly, "light" and "dark." Others had terms for other wavelengths of the color spectrum, which, however, do not always translate neatly as our words *red, blue, green,* and so forth. This does not mean that members of other cultural traditions are unable to see differences between what we call, for example, "green" and "yellow." It does mean that any differences they perceive are not linguistically encoded, presumably because people do not need to communicate precise information about colors.

A fascinating, and unexpected, result of these investigations about differences in color lexicons is that color terminology seems to have a regular evolutionary development. New colors are incorporated into the color lexicon in the same order everywhere. If a language has terms for only two colors, they will be *light* and *dark.* If a language has only three colors, the third will be *red,* although the term does not correspond to our *red,* since it may also include our *orange* and *pink.* Languages that have four primary color terms add either *green* or *yellow.* Languages with five terms add either *green* or *yellow,* depending on which they already had. If there is a sixth term, it refers approximately to our *blue.* Our *brown* is the seventh term, assuming there is a seventh term in the language. Only a few languages have more than seven primary terms, and they always add *pink, orange,* and *purple.*

Other examples could be cited, but the overall point is clear. Cultures divide up the world differently, forming different categories and classifications of natural and social reality out of the objective properties of things. These differences are reflected in the language of the bearers of the culture.

## Language and World Views

There is another possible relation between a people's way of life and their language. As we have just seen, some elements of a language mirror the lifeway of its speakers. Is this relation also reversed? Does language predispose its speakers to perceive the world in certain ways?

Language could shape perceptions and world views both by its lexicon and by its syntax. Any language's lexicon assigns labels to only certain things, qualities, and actions. It is easy to see how this might encourage people to perceive the real world selectively. For instance, as we grow up, we learn that some plants are "trees." So we come to think of *tree* as a real thing, although there are so many kinds of trees that there is no necessary reason to collapse all this variety into a single label. But we might perceive the plants our language calls *trees* as more similar than do people who speak a language that makes finer distinctions between these plants.

As for syntax, it might force people to communicate about time, space, relations between individuals and between people and nature, and so forth in a certain kind of way. Potentially, this constraint on the way people must speak to be understood by others can shape their views of what the world is like.

The idea that language influences the perceptions and thought patterns of those who speak it, and thus conditions their world view, is known as the **Whorf-Sapir hypothesis**, after two anthropological linguists who proposed it. One of the most widely quoted of all anthropological passages is Edward Sapir's point, written in 1929:

[Language] powerfully conditions all our thinking about social problems and processes. Human beings do not live in the objective world alone, nor alone in the world of social activity as ordinarily understood but are very much at the mercy of the particular language which has become the medium of expression for their society. . . . The fact of the matter is that the "real world" is to a large extent unconsciously built up on the language habits of the group. . . . The worlds in which different societies live are distinct worlds, not merely the same world with different labels attached. (Sapir 1964, 68–69)

Sapir and Benjamin Whorf believed that language helps define the world view of its speakers. It does so, in part, by providing labels for certain kinds of phenomena (things, qualities, and actions), which different languages define according to different criteria. Some phenomena are therefore made easier to think about than others. The attributes that define them as different from other, similar things become more important than other attributes. So the lexicon of our language provides a filter that biases our perceptions. It digs grooves in which our thought patterns tend to roll along.

But the Whorf-Sapir hypothesis is subtler than this. In the 1930s and 1940s, Whorf suggested that language conditions a people's conceptions of time and space.

Whorf noted that English encourages its speakers to think about time in spatial metaphors (e.g., "a long time" and "a long distance"), although time cannot really be "long" or "short" in the same sense as distance. Also, English-speaking people talk about units of time using the same concepts with which we talk about numbers of objects (e.g., "four days" and "four apples"), although it is possible to see four objects at once but not four units of time. Finally, English-speaking people classify events by when they occurred: those that have happened, those that are happening, and those that will happen.

Because they share a certain kind of language, however, the Native American Hopi must speak about time and events differently. With no tenses exactly equivalent to our past, present, and future and no way to express time in terms of spatial metaphors, Hopi speak of events as continuously unfolding, rather than happening in so many days or weeks. Whorf argued that the Hopi language led the Hopi people into a different perception of the passage of time.

What shall we make of the Whorf-Saphir hypothesis? None of us as individuals creates the labels our language assigns to reality, nor do we create the way our grammar constrains the way we talk about time and space. We must adhere to certain rules if we are to be understood. Surely this necessity biases our perceptions to some degree. It is, therefore, likely that language does affect ways of perceiving, thinking about, classifying, and acting in the world. To some degree, language then does "create" views of reality. The question is, how much? More precisely, how important is language as opposed to other things that also influence perceptions and views of reality?

Although intriguing, the Whorf-Sapir hypothesis is not widely accepted, for several reasons. First, if a language greatly shapes the way its speakers perceive and think about the world, then we would expect a people's world view to change only at a rate roughly comparable to the rate at which their language changes. Yet there is no doubt that world views are capable of changing much more rapidly than language. How else can we explain the fact that the English language has changed little in the past 150 years compared with the dramatic alteration in the world views of most speakers of English? How else can we explain the spread of religious traditions such as Islam and Christianity out of their original linguistic homes among people with enormously diverse languages? (This is not to suggest that these traditions have remained unchanged as they diffused.)

Second, if language strongly conditions perceptions, thought patterns, and entire world views, we should find that the speakers of languages that have a common ancestor show marked cultural similarities. More precisely, we would expect to find the cultural similarities between speakers of related languages to be consistently greater than the cultural similarities between speakers of languages that are less closely related. Sometimes we do find this; unfortunately, we often do not.

For these and other reasons, the Whorf-Sapir hypothesis is not highly regarded today by most scholars. But research on this intriguing idea is continuing, and future results may show some unexpected effects of language on perception, cognition, and world views.

*Speech can be used to emphasize the relative social rank of individuals. These two Colombian men seem to be social equals.*

## SOCIAL USES OF SPEECH

During enculturation, humans learn how to communicate and how to act appropriately in given social situations. They learn that different situations require different verbal and nonverbal behavior, for how one speaks and acts varies with whom one is addressing, who else is present, and the overall situation in which the interaction is occurring.

To speak appropriately, people must take the total context into account. First, they must know the various situations, or social scenes, of their culture: which are solemn, which are celebrations, which are formal and informal, which are argumentative, and so on. Cultural knowledge includes knowing how to alter one's total (including verbal) behavior to fit these situations. Second, individuals must recognize the kinds of interactions they are expected to have with others toward whom they have particular relations: Should they act lovingly, jokingly, contemptuously, or respectfully and deferentially toward someone else? Cultural knowledge thus also includes knowing how to act (including how to speak) toward others with whom an individual has relations of certain kinds.

These two elements—the particular situation and the specific individuals who are parties to the interaction—make up the *context* of verbal and nonverbal behavior. Enough linguists have become interested in such topics that a special field of study has been devoted to them: **sociolinguistics**, the study of how speech behavior is affected by cultural factors, especially by the social context.

How the speech of the parties to a social interaction reveals and reinforces the nature of their relationship is seen clearly by terms of address. In some parts of the United States, unless instructed otherwise, Americans usually address those of higher social rank with a respect term followed by the last name (e.g., Dr. Smith or Mr. Jones). Those with higher rank are more likely to address those with lower rank by their first name, or even by their last name used alone (e.g., "You were in charge of that, weren't you, Smith?") This nonreciprocal use of address terms often not only expresses a social inequality; it also reinforces it each time the individuals address each other. When address terms are used reciprocally—when both individuals call each other by their first names, for example—their relation is likely to be more equal. "Call me by my first name" often carries a meaning beyond mere instruction.

Spanish-speaking people have a similar understanding with polite address terms such as *Don* or *Señora*. They also have to choose between two words for *you*: the formal (*usted*) versus informal (*tú*). *Tú* is used between occupants of certain statuses, such as between intimate friends and relatives and to address children. In parts of Latin America, the informal *tú* is also a marker of rank, used by landlords, officials, and some employers toward their tenants, subordinates, servants, and employees. Here the fact that a social subordinate uses *usted* with a higher-ranking person, while the latter uses "*tú*," symbolizes and reinforces the social differences between them.

Speech style and habits depend on status and rank in other ways. For example, there use to be greater differences between the speech of men and women in North America than there are today. Because of their enculturated fear of being considered unladylike, women were less likely to use profanity, at least in public. Men, likewise, were expected to avoid profanity in the presence of women, to avoid offending the ladies. Certain words were (and to some extent still are) regarded as more appropriate for women's use than men's, such as *charming, adorable,* and *lovely.* More emphasis was placed on women using "good grammar" than on men doing so. Even minor differences in sentence construction existed between the genders. Women were more likely to show uncertainty and desire for approval and permission. When her husband asked, "What time is dinner?" a wife often responded with, "Is six o'clock all right?" Linguist Robin Lakoff suggests that such "half-declarative" sentences indicate a lack of self-confidence and an unwillingness to state an opinion, which are related to the cultural value on women being (overtly) submissive to men. (Box 3.1 discusses gender bias in English.)

Other cultures exhibit customs in speech behavior with which most English-speaking people are unfamiliar. Here are a few examples:

✦ Some languages accentuate the difference between the sexes far more than English does. In languages such as Gros Ventre (of the northeastern United States) and Yukaghir (of northeastern Asia) men and women pronounced certain phonemes differently, which led to differences in the pronunciation of the words in which these phonemes appeared. In Yana, an extinct language spoken by a people who formerly lived in northern California, many words had two pronunciations, one used by men and one by women. In a few languages, the vocabularies of men and women differ, with men using one word for something and women quite a different word. In a language spoken by the Carib, who formerly inhabited the West Indies, the vocabularies of men and women differed so much that early European explorers claimed (mistakenly) that the sexes spoke different languages! In many languages, the speech of the sexes differs in other respects, such as the degree of forcefulness of their speech, the degree to which they avoid confrontational speech, and the tone of voice.

✦ In parts of Polynesia and Micronesia there use to be a special language, sometimes called a *respect language,* with which common people had to address members of the noble class. On some islands this was much more than a difference in speech style because different words were used. Often there were severe penalties for commoners who erred in addressing a noble.

✦ On the Indonesian island of Java, there are distinct "levels" of speech, involving different pronouns, suffixes, and words. A speaker must choose between the three levels—plain, more elegant, and most elegant. The speech style the parties to the interaction use depends on their relative rank and on their degree of familiarity with one another. In choosing which style to use with a specific person, a Javanese thus communicates more than the message encoded in the utterance. He or she also imparts information about the quality of their relationship. Accordingly, changes in the relationship between two individuals are accompanied by changes in speech style.

✦ In Japanese, a complicated set of rules (called *honorifics*) governs the degree of formality and politeness people normally use to show respect to those of higher social position. For instance, verbs and personal pronouns have several alternative forms that speakers must choose between in addressing others. The main determinant of which forms are used is the relative status of the parties. One form of the verb is used when the speaker is of higher status than the listener, another form when the two are of roughly equal status, and yet another when the speaker is a social inferior. Women, who to some extent even today are considered "beneath" men, would generally be obliged to address men with honorific verb forms that symbolically express the superiority of the addressee. The same applies to personal pronouns (*I, you*), different forms of which are used to reflect the relative status of the parties. In fact, when a social superior is addressing an inferior, he or she often does not use the pronoun *I* as a self-reference but refers to his or her status relative to the person being addressed. For instance, a teacher says to a student, "Look at teacher" instead of "Look at me"; a father says to his son, "Listen to father" instead of "Listen to me"; and so forth. Reciprocally, one usually does not use the pronoun *you* with one of higher status but replaces it with a term denoting the superior's social position. This yields sentences like: "What would teacher like me to do next?" and "Would father like me to visit?" Confused foreigners trying to learn the subtleties of Japanese speech etiquette usually are advised to use the honorific forms to avoid giving offense unintentionally. (Fortunately for the rest of us, most Japanese are tolerant of our inability to master the nuances of their honorifics!)

✦ All societies have customs of taboo, meaning that some behavior is prohibited for religious reasons or because it is culturally regarded as immoral, improper, or offensive. It is fairly common to find taboos applied to language: Some words cannot be uttered by certain people. For instance, the Yanomamö Indians of the Venezuelan rain forest have a custom known as *name taboo*. It is an insult to utter the names of important people and of deceased relatives in the presence of their living kinfolk. So the Yạnomamö use names such as "toenail of sloth" or "whisker of howler monkey" for people, so that when the person dies they will not have to watch their language so closely. Other name taboos are enforced only against specific individuals. Among the Zulu of southern Africa, for example, a woman was once forbidden to use the name of her husband's father or any of his brothers, under possible penalty of death.

Most modern societies have stringent word taboos prohibiting the use of certain kinds of profanity in newspapers, magazines, and radio and television. People are paid to guard against taboo violations—we call them *censors.* Curiously, many popular TV shows now leave no doubt about what goes on in bedrooms, but to say "screw"—much less the other word—is prohibited. Figurative ass kicking—violence—has long been portrayed on prime time. Yet to say "kick your ass" is tabooed.

So speech is influenced by social context, including the culturally defined situations in which it is used and the individuals who are engaged in conversation. But there is still more to speaking: It also is a strategy, or a behavioral means by which individuals get what they want out of others. It is, as social scientists say, part of our "presentation of self." By speaking in a certain way, we communicate the image of ourselves we want others to see.

In everyday life we want to present ourselves properly, meaning that we want someone else—a potential employer, a suitor, a pastor or priest, a co-worker, even a parent—to gain a favorable impression of us. Our speech habits, or our speech style, are an important part of our presentation of ourselves to others (as are the ways we dress, sit, stand, walk, comb our hair, and do many other things). Almost without knowing it, we adjust our speech style and mannerisms to fit the context by our use and avoidance of certain words, by our enunciation, by the degree of formality of our speech, by whether we try to hide or accentuate our regional accents or dialect, and so forth.

When we play this "language game," we attempt to use our speech habits to manipulate the ways others see us. Most politicians have mastered the art of creating favorable impressions of themselves through their public speeches. This is done, as we know, by telling particular audiences what they want to hear without, at the same time, alienating other audiences (i.e., voters) who are not present. We often are critical of our elected officials for this wishy-washiness, but in fact we all alter our speech style in our efforts to present favorable impressions of ourselves.

We said early in this chapter that language is composed of arbitrary symbols that convey conventional meanings. We can now add that the act of speaking itself is symbolic in another way. Recall that any behavior (including speech habits such as word choice, overall style, conformity to cultural notions of proper syntax, mannerisms, and so on) has a symbolic component if it stands for something else. Our speech habits are symbolic in this sense. Like the clothes we wear, the foods we eat, and the cars we drive, the way we speak is part of the way we represent ourselves to others. Because we know that others will read meanings into our speech habits, we can adjust our style of speaking and, to some extent, control the implicit messages we communicate about ourselves. In other words, we change our speech habits from situation to situation, context to context, when it is to our advantage to do so.

## SUMMARY

Language is the single most important capability of humans that distinguishes us from other animals. Five properties of language make it different from other systems of communication: its multimedia potential; its reliance on the conventional, shared understanding of arbitrary symbols; the fact that it is composed of elements (sounds, words) that can be combined into different sequences that convey different meanings; the fact that its speakers regularly and unconsciously use these recombinable elements creatively to send an infinite number of messages; and the fact that it allows humans to communicate about things remote in time and space.

Grammar refers to the elements of language and the rules for how these elements can be combined to form an infinite number of meaningful sentences. Grammatical knowledge is enormously complex, yet it is both unconscious and intuitive. Linguists divide the study of language into several fields, including phonology, morphology, and syntax.

Phonology is the study of the sounds and sound patterns of language. The basic meaningful sounds are called *phonemes*. Languages differ in the phonemes they recognize as distinctive and significant. Only some of the sounds humans are able to make with their vocal tract are recognized by any given language. Qualities or features of sounds that the speakers of one language recognize as significant—that is, as making a difference in the meanings of words in which they appear—vary from language to language. Languages also vary in the way they use the pitch of the voice to convey meanings, as shown by tone languages.

Morphology studies meaningful sound sequences and the rules by which they are formed. Any sequence of phonemes that conveys a standardized meaning is a morpheme. Free morphemes can stand alone as meaningful sequences, whereas bound morphemes are not used alone but are attached to free morphemes during speech. When people learn a language they learn its free and bound morphemes and their meanings. They also learn the rules by which bound morphemes can be attached to free morphemes.

Syntax refers to the unconscious rules that tell speakers how to combine words into meaningful sentences. Although languages vary in their syntax, most modern linguists believe that this variation is limited—that all languages are variations of a single basic design, or universal grammar, that underlies apparent diversity. Research on how children learn language seems to support this conclusion.

Cultural anthropologists have turned to linguistics as a source of ideas and models that might have value in the description and analysis of culture. Cognitive anthropologists propose that cultural classifications of reality are built up and organized in the same way as language.

The culture of a people is related to their language. Some aspects of language, particularly lexicon, reflect the cultural importance of subjects, people, objects, and natural phenomena. The need to converse easily about some subject leads to the elaboration of semantic domains connected to the subject, as seen in the domain of color. In other domains, such as relatives, anthropologists have discovered surprising diversity in how various peoples divide kin into kinds and give them different labels according to different principles.

Some anthropologists have argued that the language a people speak predisposes them to see the world in a certain way by shaping their perceptions of reality. This idea, known as the *Whorf-Sapir hypothesis,* argues that the lexicon of a language influences perceptions by leading its speakers to filter out certain objective properties of reality in favor of other properties. Syntax can also affect perception, and even world view, by forcing people to talk about time and space in a certain way if they are to be understood. The Whorf-Sapir hypothesis is not highly regarded by most modern scholars, although there has been a recent revival of interest in it.

Sociolinguistics is the study of how speech is influenced by cultural factors, including culturally defined contexts and situations, the goals of the speaker, the presence of other parties, and so forth. Speech can be used in subtle ways to mark differences in rank and status, as between ethnic groups, classes, and males and females. Because it is part of the way we present ourselves to others, control of the way we speak is one way we influence how others perceive us.

# Key Terms

| | |
|---|---|
| multimedia potential | phonemes |
| arbitrariness (conventionality) | tone languages |
| recombinable elements | lexicon |
| productivity | morpheme |
| displacement | free morpheme |
| grammar | bound morpheme |
| dialects | universal grammar |
| phonology | semantic domain |
| morphology | Whorf-Sapir hypothesis |
| syntax | sociolinguistics |

# Suggested Readings

Escholz, Paul, Alfred Rosa, and Virginia Clark, eds. *Language Awareness.* 5th ed., New York: St. Martin's Press, 1990.
> Thirty-six short articles dealing with various elements of English-language use. Contains sections on political speech, advertising language, jargon, prejudice, and taboos.

Farb, Peter. *Word Play.* New York: Knopf, 1974.
> Readable, enjoyable introduction to anthropological linguistics.

Frank, Francine, and Frank Anshen. *Language and the Sexes.* Albany, N.Y.: SUNY Press, 1983.
> How linguistic patterns and speech reflect and contribute to sexist attitudes. Contains an appendix on nonsexist language for speech and writing.

Fromkin, Victoria, and Robert Rodman. *An Introduction to Language.* 4th ed., New York: Harcourt Brace Jovanovich College Publishing, 1988.
> Excellent textbook, thorough in its coverage, readily understandable, with many excellent examples.

Hymes, Dell, ed. *Language in Culture and Society: A Reader in Linguistics and Anthropology.* New York: Harper & Row, 1964.
> Nearly seventy articles, many of them classics, on the subject of language and culture and the social uses of language.

Tannen, Deborah. *You Just Don't Understand: Women and Men in Conversation.* New York: Ballantine, 1991.

Tannen, Deborah. *That's Not What I Meant!: How Conversational Style Makes or Breaks Your Relations with Others.* New York: William Morrow, 1986.
> These two popular books by linguist Tannen show how conversational speech affects relationships, both negatively and positively.

Trudgill, Peter. *Sociolinguistics: An Introduction to Language and Society.* Middlesex, England: Penguin, 1983.
> Excellent short book that summarizes sociolinguistic research on distinctions of class, ethnicity, and gender. Also has chapters on how speech varies with context and on the use of speech in everyday social interaction.

# PART II

# THEORIES AND METHODS OF CULTURAL ANTHROPOLOGY

Any academic discipline has theoretical ideas that guide its general ways of thinking about its subject matter. Since anthropology became a separate field of study in the nineteenth century, the kinds of questions it has asked about humankind and its diverse cultures have changed, as have the theoretical approaches taken to answer these questions. One goal of this part is to show how anthropological thinking about human cultures has altered over the decades. Another is to discuss some of the ways that contemporary ethnologists approach the study of culture and cultures. Chapter 4 is concerned with such issues.

Just as scholars ask certain kinds of questions, so do they develop methods that allow them to investigate these questions empirically. Modern cultural anthropologists usually conduct fieldwork among a particular people to acquire data or information about that people's culture. Ethnologists also are interested in the comparative analysis of cultures, and a fairly sophisticated set of cross-cultural methods have been developed to conduct comparative work. Chapter 5 discusses such methods and the problems encountered in implementing them.

## CHAPTER 4

# THE DEVELOPMENT OF ANTHROPOLOGICAL THOUGHT

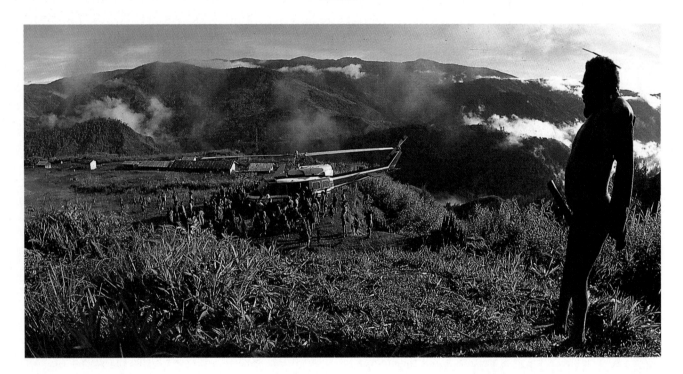

*Anthropology emerged in the nineteenth century as a consequence of the encounters of Westerners with the rest of the world. The way ethnologists approach and analyze cultures has changed dramatically in the past century.*

**CONTENTS**

The way anthropologists approach the study of humanity has undergone many changes since the discipline originated in the nineteenth century. Some ideas held by most scholars a century ago have been discarded today; others are still with us. In this chapter, we discuss some of the important scholars and schools of thought that shaped the way modern anthropologists approach their studies. For each approach, we emphasize its assumptions, its basic questions, its errors, and its contributions to the theoretical ideas of modern anthropology.

## THEORETICAL ORIENTATIONS

We shall use the term *theory* in this and future chapters, but be aware that this term is used rather loosely in the social sciences. In the physical sciences, a theory is a precise (often mathematical) statement about how some kinds of phenomena are related to other kinds of phenomena. Physical theories are constructed in such a way that experimentation can determine with a high degree of confidence whether phenomena are in fact related in the way the theory specifies.

In the social sciences, theories seldom are stated with mathematical precision and are not tested through experimentation. For these and other reasons, we prefer the more encompassing phrase *theoretical orientation* to the term *theory*. A theoretical orientation refers to the questions asked and to the concepts, assumptions, and methods used by a scholar or school of thought—more like an "approach" or a "way of thinking" about humankind than like the physicist's theory. Theoretical orientations guide research by asking questions and suggesting ways to answer them, but they cannot be shown definitively to be right or wrong by seeing how well they "fit the facts." Rather, they are judged by their usefulness: Do they ask fruitful questions? Do their methods give reliable results? Do their concepts and assumptions take us very far in understanding human culture in general and/or particular cultures? A given theoretical orientation suggests that some elements of human cultures are more important than others, and so scholars who work from different orientations often focus on completely different subjects, as we shall see.

## NINETEENTH-CENTURY ORIGINS

As a separate field of scholarly study, anthropology arose in the nineteenth century. There is little point in trying to pin down exactly when and where anthropology originated. We can learn more by showing why interest in human cultural variability became especially strong in the 1800s.

Early in the nineteenth century, at several places in England and France, crude axe-like stone tools were found in association with extinct mammals. Influenced by the Judeo-Christian world view, many claimed that Satan had buried the stones in the earth to cause confusion and doubt. But others concluded (correctly) that the early, "prehistoric" inhabitants of Europe had once used stone tools and lived at the same time as extinct animals. For them, the problem was understanding the significance of the remains for human history. How, and how long ago, did these ancient people live?

Meanwhile, several centuries worth of written records had accumulated about the strange—to European eyes—ways of life of people of other lands. Beginning in the 1500s, Europeans increasingly came into contact with folk who differed from themselves in physical appearance, language, beliefs, and habits. European explorers, priests, fortune hunters, scientists, and other travelers reported on the customs and beliefs found among the inhabitants of the Americas, Africa, Asia, and the Pacific Islands. Who were these people (if in fact they were people at all)? How could they believe such fantastic things and engage in such "savage" practices? How were they related to Europeans and other "civilized" people? For that matter, how were they related to one another?

Answers to such questions varied, but again most were within the range of permissible interpretations of the Bible. Some intellectuals concluded that "primitives" were so different from Europeans that God must have made them separately from civilized man, during some creation event not mentioned in Genesis, and placed them on other continents. Others argued that they did in fact come from the same ancestor as ourselves. But then the problem was explaining (within the biblical

In part, anthropology arose out of curiosity about the residents of other continents that Europeans encountered in the fifteenth through the nineteenth century. The Englishman James Cook explored the northwest coast of North America in the late 1700s. The caption on this lithograph from his voyage reads: "A Savage of Prince Williams Sound on the North West Coast of America."

be only a few thousand years old. New geological theories demolished this estimate and established that the earth has existed for many millions of years. The other was the belief that divine creation accounted for all life on earth. A new biological theory showed how the history and diversity of life were caused by naturalistic, rather than supernaturalistic, forces. These and other changes in the way scientists interpreted the world contributed to the beginnings and growth of anthropology.

First, let us consider geology. In 1795, James Hutton proposed that the physical features of the earth were formed by gradual processes, such as erosion of rock caused by winds and waves, and slow deposition of sediments in the bottom of ancient seas and lakes. These natural forces operated so slowly that they were scarcely noticeable in a human lifetime, but over many thousands of years their effects accumulated. Mountains, sediments, and other geological features result from the actions over long time spans of imperceptible natural

Early interpretations of non-Western peoples were generally consistent with the biblical account of creation, illustrated in the painting "Expulsion from the Garden", by Ramon de Mur.

world view of possible events) how they became separated from us and how they came to have such depraved customs and false beliefs. Were they modern-day remnants of one of Israel's lost tribes? Could they be descendants of Noah's son Ham?

Until the early 1800s the dominant interpretation of these exotic peoples was that they had fallen from a previous higher state of civilization. Living without knowledge of the Creator, their ancestors had fallen under the influence of Satan. (Today this notion is known as *degenerationism*—the idea that contemporary "primitives" are descendants of peoples who had once been more advanced, but lost knowledge of the teachings of God, knowledge that all of humankind once possessed.) Most intellectuals who bothered to wonder about the "savage" residents of other continents agreed with this interpretation.

Thus, the customs and beliefs of other peoples were interpreted in terms of the biblical account of human history. Two elements of this account lost credibility among most scientists in the nineteenth century. One was the age of the earth, which generally was believed to processes; thus, major changes result from the cumulative effects of a multitude of minor changes. In the 1830s, Charles Lyell popularized this **uniformitarian theory**. He amassed evidence that the processes responsible for the formation of the earth occur at steady ("uniform") and gradual rates. If uniformitarianism was correct, this meant that the earth must be incredibly old—millions of years rather than the few thousands of years previously believed.

These ideas about the history of the earth influenced the ideas of biologist Charles Darwin about the history of life. In turn, Darwin's ideas about the history of life influenced, and continue to influence, anthropology's ideas about humanity.

Darwin's *Origin of Species* appeared in 1859. Darwin presented evidence that natural species have changed, or "evolved," over long time spans. He also argued that radically new forms of life develop out of existing species. The reason we do not observe this transformation of one life form into another is simply that human lifetimes are too short for the slow changes to be perceptible to our senses. Darwin gave much evidence in support of this view of the history of life. One form of

*Charles Darwin's theory of evolution influenced anthropology as well as biology. It suggested to some that preindustrial lifeways could be arranged into a sequence of progressive stages.*

evidence is the great diversity of domesticated animals and plants produced by intentional breeding. In each generation, breeders select for breeding those individual animals and plants that have the characteristics their human masters find desirable. Given enough time, new varieties are produced by this selection, although in each generation the differences are scarcely noticeable.

Darwin proposed a mechanism by which these changes occur. He noted that organisms compete with one another over space, mates, food, and other things needed for survival and reproduction. Those individuals who are most successful in this competition have the greatest chance of reproducing. The characteristics that give them greater success are passed along to their offspring. In each generation, organisms encounter "natural" conditions that "select" for those individuals best able to compete, avoid being eaten, resist diseases and parasites, find and hold mates, and so on. Darwin called this process **natural selection**. He realized that it would favor the survival and reproduction of those organisms that are "most fit," or better adapted to the conditions of their environments.

Because of natural selection, each generation is slightly different from the previous generation. Over hundreds or thousands of generations, one form of life evolves into one or more other forms. The present diversity of life is explained partly by the fact that environments vary from place to place and time to time. For example, some individual members of a species periodically move into new environments, where their offspring encounter new conditions that make new characteristics useful. They gradually change into new varieties and, eventually, into new species. Two or more new forms of life can arise out of a single "parent" species by this process of adaptation.

Darwin's theory had many implications for the study of humanity (aside from the obvious one—that humanity itself had evolved out of other life forms). First, it was a theory that *explained* the diversity of species by a purely natural process. Like the movements of the moon, the history of life was subject to natural laws. No creation or supernatural intervention was required to account for the origins of species. This is the main reason Darwin's theory was (and is) so strongly resisted by many fundamentalist religious leaders.

In addition, Darwin's ideas seemed to many to support the idea of overall progress in the history of life. This progress resulted mainly from competition. It came from the struggle for survival, in which "higher," "more complex" forms appeared successively. (Note, however, that many modern biologists prefer to speak merely of *diversification* or *change,* terms that carry fewer value judgments than *progress.*) In the fossil record, it was possible to see complex forms evolving out of simpler forms, to observe the evolutionary "stages" through which present-day organisms changed into their modern forms.

Most important to the development of anthropological thought, evolution provided a concept that suggested how the "natives" of other continents were related to one another, to the early residents of Europe who left behind those mysterious artifacts, and to Western civilization itself. The answer seemed to be that the prehistoric residents of Europe had not progressed to our level of technological, social, and moral advancement. They were still living in the "early stages" of evolution. What were these stages like? What were the customs and beliefs of these extinct people? It was impossible to know very much about them from the tools buried in the earth, for in those days scientists could infer little about the religion, marriage, and so forth of long-dead peoples from artifacts alone.

But there was a way to find out more about how ancient humans lived: by studying the customs and beliefs of those curious Indians, Africans, Polynesians, and other "primitives," who still retained many characteristics of the early stages of humankind's evolution. The thinking at the time was as follows: We can use the reports on these people to reconstruct the stages through which our own civilization passed in its progress toward the pinnacle of human achievement, that is, nineteenth-century Western civilization. To do so, we need to study these people scientifically, using our knowledge of them to advance our understanding of our own past. They are not "degenerated" folk whose barbaric customs prove that they have come under the iron grip of the Devil. They are, rather, merely undeveloped—their minds have not yet attained the level of scientific understanding of the world, their technology is still primitive and simple, their morals and manners remain rude, and so forth. By comparing them to one another and to Western civilization, we can reconstruct the sequence of stages through which our own civilization passed.

Such is the intellectual climate that gave rise to anthropology. To trace the development of humankind, scholars thought that they had to study the nearest thing they could get to the ancient ancestors of civilization— surviving "primitive" ways of life. Anthropology had its beginnings as the discipline that described and explained the sequence of stages through which humanity progressed along its long road to civilization.

# UNILINEAL EVOLUTION

The theory that nineteenth-century anthropologists developed to account for cultural development is known as **unilineal evolution.** Unilineal evolutionists believed that all human ways of life pass through a similar sequence of stages, or grades, as they evolve. These stages explained why various peoples around the world differ in their ways of life: Different peoples are representative of different grades of development. The concept of stages also accounted for why some customs and beliefs were scattered around the world among people who could not have had any contact with one another: Regardless of their location in space, two or more peoples with similar cultures had developed up to the same stage. Favored names for the stages were savagery, barbarism, and civilization.

So if we want to know why the Iroquois of North America had different habits from the native peoples of Australia, the answer, according to unilineal evolutionists, is that the Australians were arrested in their development at the stage of savagery, whereas the Iroquois had progressed into barbarism. If we want to find out how the earliest humans lived, we should study the surviving representatives of the stage of savagery, such as the Australians. If we want to know what the immediate ancestors of civilized folk were like, we must examine the representatives of barbarism who have persisted into modern times, such as the Iroquois.

Unilineal evolutionists differed in the criteria they used to define the stages of progress. One influential scheme was that of Lewis Henry Morgan, a lawyer from New York State. In *Ancient Society,* published in 1877, Morgan identified seven stages:

   I. Lower Savagery
  II. Middle Savagery
 III. Upper Savagery
 IV. Lower Barbarism
  V. Middle Barbarism
 VI. Upper Barbarism
VII. Civilization

Morgan defined these stages by what he called "inventions and discoveries" (today we would call them "technological and economic innovations"). For example, middle savages had fire but lacked the bow and arrow; upper savages had invented the bow and arrow but still lacked pottery; lower barbarians had discovered pottery but did not know about the domestication of animals and plants; middle barbarians kept animals and grew their own food but had no knowledge of smelting metals; and upper barbarians had advanced enough to use iron but had no alphabet and hence no writing. Only the representatives of the final stage, civilization, were literate.

Unilineal evolutionists defined their stages on the basis of relative complexity. Just as the evolution of forms of life proceeded in an orderly manner from relatively simple to increasingly complex, so did the evolution of cultural forms. The stages could be ranked in an orderly sequence, with the simplest stages at the bottom and the most complex at the top. Various peoples then could be fitted into the sequence, as appropriate to their relative level of progress.

Unilineal evolutionists believed that they had "discovered" the stages through which cultural systems develop. They did so by comparing the reports on non-Western peoples around the world written by explorers, missionaries, colonial administrators, traders, and other untrained and frequently biased observers. By comparing and contrasting these accounts, they decided whether the customs and beliefs of one people were more or less complex than those of another people, and hence whether people A belonged to a higher stage than people B. Later scholars correctly objected to the ethnocentrism of this method. But the unilineal evolutionists did recognize that human ways of life had to be compared if any "laws of progress" were to be discovered. As discussed in chapter 1, this comparative perspective on humanity became an enduring hallmark of anthropological thought.

The unilineal evolutionists believed that different people are at different levels of development because some peoples' ways of life have changed, whereas others' have altered little over many centuries. What made some ways of life change at faster rates than others? What is the "engine" that powers progress? Unilineal evolutionists were unclear about this. Morgan seemed to believe that technological and economic discoveries provided the impetus for progress into a higher stage. And once a new technology was invented, other aspects of a peoples' way of life had to undergo change as well. For example, some Lower Barbarians developed into Middle Barbarians once they learned to grow crops. This discovery led to progress in their property institutions, family and marriage relations, and systems of government. So as new inventions and discoveries occur, other aspects of culture are "pulled" into a new stage of progress as well. Notice that this notion implies a holistic perspective: Things do not change piecemeal, but changes in one element lead to changes in other

Unilineal evolutionists placed cultures into a sequence of stages of development, with peoples such as the Australian aborigines at the bottom of the ladder of progress. Later anthropologists correctly pointed out the ethnocentrism of their stages.

elements. Morgan realized that cultural systems are *integrated*, as we would say today.

Other scholars believed that progress occurred mainly because people gradually improved their abilities to reason from evidence. From long experience a few peoples managed to rid their minds of erroneous beliefs, and their improved ability to reason propelled them into a new stage. For example, in *Primitive Culture*, published in 1871, E. B. Tylor investigated the origins and development of religion. He proposed that religion had passed through three stages. The earliest was *animism*, defined as the belief that the world is populated by spiritual beings such as ghosts, souls, and demons. How can we explain the origins of such beliefs?

Tylor believed that people everywhere sought explanations for things and events. Two questions puzzled primitive peoples: (1) What is the difference between a live body and a dead one? (2) What is the origin of things seen in dreams, trances, and visions? Early cultures reasoned (falsely but nonetheless logically) that (1) living people have a spiritual essence—a soul—that leaves the body and thus causes death, and (2) the things people see in their dreams and fantasies are real, not the products of their imaginations. Souls must live on after death, since sometimes people see dead people in dreams and visions. Early peoples eventually viewed the whole world as inhabited by supernatural beings. Later some of the beings became elevated to a higher position than others, to become gods of the sun, moon, sky, earth, and so forth. The next stage of religion—*polytheism*—was thus born. Finally, one god acquired dominance over all the others; the others became "false gods," and the final stage—*monotheism*, Westerners' belief—came into existence. Religion thus originated from intellectual puzzlement, and it evolved as people gradually learned to reason correctly from evidence, according to Tylor.

From today's perspective, the unilineal evolutionists were mistaken about many things. But they did make several enduring contributions to anthropological thought. They helped to establish two important perspectives of anthropology: holism and comparativism. (Relativism—the third perspective of anthropology—did not come into vogue until the early twentieth century.) Unilineal evolutionists also had great faith that the application of scientific methods and reasoning would lead to the discovery of natural laws that govern humanity's development. The "history of mankind is part and parcel of the history of nature, . . . our thoughts, wills, and actions accord with laws as definite as those which govern the motion of waves, the combinations of acids and bases, and the growth of plants and animals," wrote E.B. Tylor (1871, 2). Many later anthropologists were not so sure about the existence of "laws of culture"; but the search for general causes of cultural differences and for law-like regularity in cultural change remains a strong current in much modern anthropological research.

## DIFFUSIONISM (CA. 1900–1930)

The unilineal evolutionists described many similarities between peoples who lived in widely scattered regions of the earth. For example, numerous peoples from various continents were reported to practice worship of the sun. Why should tribes living far away from one another share such striking similarities in customs? There seemed to be two alternative answers. First, the custom had spread from one place to another through either movement of or contact between peoples. Migration or **diffusion** (the spread of customs and beliefs through contact between peoples and subsequent imitation of one people by another) thus might account for the widespread distribution of some cultural element. Second, the various peoples that practice the custom had "thought it up" independently, on their own. This second alternative, called **independent invention**, is a possibility because of the assumption that human minds everywhere work the same way. Because various peoples often encounter similar circumstances and problems, then naturally the same customs and solutions will

occur again and again among assorted peoples who have never had contact with one another. If similar cultural elements occurred among widely scattered peoples, then unilineal evolutionists usually explained the similarities as due to independent invention rather than diffusion.

Around the turn of the century, many scholars in Europe doubted that people—at least "primitive people"—were sufficiently innovative to have independently invented most of their own customs. Instead, they argued that most cultural "traits" (as they came to be known) originated among only a few societies, from whence they diffused outward to less innovative peoples. For instance, in this view if you want to explain why the Crow have clans, you must consider the history of their contact with other Indians from whom they "borrowed" the idea of clans. This meant also that most similarities between peoples resulted from diffusion, rather than from independent invention. These scholars became known as **diffusionists**.

For example, two English diffusionists in the early twentieth century, W. R. Rivers and Elliot Smith, held that most of the "more advanced" elements of human cultures arose in ancient Egypt. They were most impressed by the fact that architectural styles and megalithic constructions greatly resembling the Egyptian pyramids also occurred among certain North American Indians, such as the Maya and Aztec civilizations of Central America. It seemed to them unlikely that the Indians discovered such advanced architectural skills on their own. They never satisfactorily solved the problem of how the Egyptians managed to cross the Atlantic Ocean to plant the idea of pyramids into the "less developed minds" of the American Indians.

Although it is well established that cultural elements are transmitted from place to place, diffusionism leaves numerous questions unanswered. First, examples abound of peoples who have been in contact with one another for decades or even centuries, yet each people often retain their own distinctive way of life. Diffusion is not an inevitable result of contact between peoples. Under what conditions will a people adopt cultural traits of another people with whom they have been in contact? Little attention was given to this fundamental question by the diffusionists.

Second, diffusionists made little effort to account for why traits arose in the first place. Even granting that diffusion accounts for the current geographic distribution of a trait, its origination among a particular people at a particular time still must be explained.

Third, there is a subtle kind of cultural prejudice, or even racism, in the diffusionist assumption that there

*On the left is an early Egyptian stepped pyramid. On the right is a similar-looking "pyramid" from Palenque, of the Maya civilization of Mexico. On the basis of such apparent similarities, some diffusionists mistakenly believed that "higher" architectural forms, and indeed all of civilization, had diffused from Egypt to the rest of the world.*

are human populations who acquired the bulk of their customs and beliefs from more "advanced" peoples. The evidence is overwhelming that many of the world's people "progressed" into higher "stages"—whatever those terms may mean—whenever conditions were ripe, quite without the help of ancient Egyptians or any other higher civilizations.

# HISTORICAL PARTICULARISM (CA. 1900–1940)

In the early twentieth century, another approach developed in the United States. Known as **historical particularism**, it arose as a reaction to the unilineal evolutionary sequences of the late 1800s. Historical particularism assumes that each culture is the product of the many things that affected it in the past. Because each people have their own "particular history," every way of life is, in many ways, unique.

Such an emphasis on the differences between peoples has two implications. First, the search for general laws that explain cultures and why they change may be futile. If each culture is unique, how can we generalize? How, in fact, can we even compare them meaningfully? Second, we must make every effort to free ourselves from our own culture's moral standards and assumptions when we study another way of life. This is because these assumptions and standards may not apply elsewhere in the human world. We must, therefore, study each way of life on its own terms, rather than imposing our culture's

judgments (e.g., "progress") on it; that is, we must adopt a *relativistic* perspective toward other ways of life.

More than anyone else, American anthropologist Franz Boas formulated this approach. Around the turn of the century, Boas concluded that the developmental sequences of the unilineal evolutionists were ethnocentric, speculative, and based on unproven assumptions. Let's look briefly at his objections and at the alternative he offered.

As we have seen, unilineal evolutionists defined their stages on the basis of relative complexity. But what does "complex" mean? We *might* agree that some peoples possess simpler tools than others: propelling a projectile (spear) with human arms may be simpler than with a bow (arrow), which in turn is simpler than with barrels and gunpowder (bullets). But what do we mean by "simple" in the context of religious beliefs? In what respect is animism "simpler" than monotheism? The same applies to many other aspects of human life: What does it mean to claim that one marriage or family form, or one way of holding property, is more complex than another? Boas realized that these things are merely different from people to people. One is not more simple, nor does one represent "progress" over the other, at least by any objective criterion.

If there is no objective way to judge the relative complexity of institutions, then how did the unilineal evolutionists develop their stages? Boas saw that the stages were defined using ethnocentric assumptions. Take our own marriage form, for instance: one woman married to one man who is not her close relative. Call this marriage "complex." Imagine its opposite: several women married to several men, with all the marital partners being close relatives. Call this marriage "simple." Then search through reports on hundreds of Indian, African, and Asian peoples, looking for marriage forms that fall somewhere between the forms labeled simple and complex (e.g., one woman married to several men who are brothers). Arrange the intermediate forms into a sequence of stages, in order of how closely they resemble Western marriage. You then have defined "grades of progress" and have assigned particular peoples to one or another grade.

But these grades exist only on paper. Boas saw that the unilineal evolutionists had not "discovered" developmental stages; they had made them up. Indeed, only by assuming that the Western marriage form is the end point of evolution can the stages be ranked in order of increasing complexity. In other words, ethnocentric assumptions underlaid the arranging of ways of life into a sequence of progress. If the stages themselves are invalid, then the notion that all cultures pass through them on their road to civilization is invalid as well. Cultural evolution, therefore, is not unilineal. Cultures change along many narrow paths, not one wide road. Further, the direction in which any one culture changes depends on its own characteristics and on the external influences that affect it.

Boas believed that anthropologists must rid themselves of all such speculative schemes of progress, for only by doing so can they rid their minds of preconceived ideas and assumptions. Accompanying Boas' call for "less speculation" was his demand for "more facts." One reason the unilineal evolutionists had been led astray was that they had little firsthand knowledge of the peoples they so readily placed into the slots of their theory. They had only read reports written by other observers, who themselves were mostly untrained and ethnocentric. (One notable exception to this generalization is Lewis Henry Morgan, whose ethnography of the Iroquois is still an important source of information on these people.) Boas was scornful of such "armchair theorizing." He believed that to understand another way of life, one must have the familiarity that can only come with long personal experience with it. Therefore, Boas contended that anthropologists need to leave their armchairs and immerse themselves in the direct observation of other societies. They need to do fieldwork among a people, to experience their customs and understand their beliefs from an insider's perspective, before engaging in idle speculation about "how all cultures develop."

Two benefits would follow from more firsthand experience with other cultural traditions. First, many cultures were already disappearing at a rapid rate (especially in North America, where Boas did his own work). Boas believed it was the duty of anthropology to record their traditional ways of life before they were gone forever. Many anthropologists trained by Boas did fieldwork on Native Americans. Second, Boas believed that in his day the immediate need of the infant science of anthropology was more data. He stressed the need to know more about specific other cultures and their particular histories before speculating further about laws that supposedly apply universally. Boas approached science *inductively*: He believed that—insofar as possible—facts should be gathered without the preconceived notions that, he felt, always lead to bias in observation. Anthropologists should construct theories to account for the facts only after obtaining an unbiased record of the facts.

How can we obtain such an unbiased account? By approaching the study of another cultural tradition relativistically, we can come close to objectivity. Thinking relativistically, as we have seen, means not judging other peoples' religions by our own religious beliefs, nor their morality by our own moral codes, nor the overall worth of their way of life by our standards of worthiness. The relativistic approach requires a temporary suspension of the beliefs, morality, and value standards of the anthropologist's own culture. It requires that we judge the customs and beliefs of people by their own standards. In this way we might avoid the mistake of the unilineal evolutionists: "grading" (with both meanings) other peoples by how closely they approximate us. More than any other single individual, Boas imparted into anthropology the doctrine of cultural relativism, which he believed was essential for scientific detachment and objectivity.

Boas was enormously influential. He trained most of the best-known American anthropologists of the twentieth century, including Margaret Mead, Ruth Benedict, Alfred Kroeber, and Robert Lowie. Most of his objections to unilineal evolutionism still seem valid. The evolutionists' stages were indeed ethnocentric and speculative; it seems certain today that all peoples do not pass through the same unilineal sequence of development. More fieldwork was indeed urgently needed in the early twentieth century, and today fieldwork is part of the professional training of most cultural anthropologists. By and large, it is still carried out in a relativistic manner—although modern fieldworkers recognize that it is impossible to work without preconceptions.

*Franz Boas is best known for his insistence on relativistic studies of other peoples and for his research on Native Americans.*

Another of Boas' enduring contributions was summarized in chapter 2; he and his students promulgated the idea that biological and racial differences between human populations do not explain the cultural differences between them. Historical particularism thus almost eliminated biological differences as a potential explanation for cultural differences—at least, it did so in anthropology!

From a modern perspective, historical particularism has shortcomings of its own. Consider the claim that each culture is unique. Certainly, if differences between cultures are what we are interested in, we can find them, and we can then go on to prove that no two cultures are identical. Certainly, too, each society has its own past, and the precise events that shaped its history happened nowhere else. So, *to some extent,* no culture is like any other, and no line of historical development is duplicated anywhere else; but also, *to some extent,* there are similarities between human ways of living. Historical particularists tended to overlook the similarities and to neglect the study of factors that might explain them. The interest of American anthropologists returned to similarities—and to evolution—in the 1940s. Meanwhile, another theoretical orientation developed in Great Britain.

## FUNCTIONALISM (CA. 1920–1950)

At about the same time that historical particularism dominated American anthropology, an alternative approach was popular in Great Britain. Its basic tenet was that the cultural characteristics of a people should be explained by the useful functions they perform for the well-being of individuals or society as a whole.

Two varieties of **functionalism** developed in Britain during the early decades of the twentieth century: **biopsychological functionalism** and **structural functionalism**.

### Biopsychological Functionalism

Biopsychological functionalism is associated most strongly with Bronislaw Malinowski, a man well known to all anthropologists because of his magnificent ethnographies of the Trobriand Islanders of the Pacific. Malinowski believed that cultural features exist to meet certain biological and psychological needs of humans. These needs, or "basic imperatives," are nutrition, reproduction, shelter from the elements and from enemies, and health (or maintenance of the body in good condition). The primary function of culture is to fulfill these requirements for survival and well-being. The basic imperatives themselves are essentially constant across all populations, but the cultural mechanisms a people develop to fulfill them vary from place to place and time to time.

Humans do not meet their needs in isolation from other humans. They organize cooperative groups to meet their basic imperatives more effectively. They develop institutions to give their need-serving activities regularity and predictability. People, therefore, must maintain the groups and institutions that serve their biopsychological needs: The behavior of group members must be regulated, roles must be doled out to individuals, access to natural resources must be assigned, and so forth. Malinowski called these "derived needs"—in essence, the needs of groups and institutions to be maintained and perpetuated over time.

Finally, Malinowski argued that a people will adhere to the requirements of their groups and institutions only if they become committed to the norms and standards that guide behavior. This commitment is achieved through creating emotional attachment to the whole way of life. For example, attachment is achieved by enculturating individuals to value their way of life in its own right and by providing symbolic acts and objects that lend meaning and purpose to human life. Thus, other elements of the cultural system, notably values and religion, are explained by their functions in creating sentimental attachment to the whole way of life.

For anthropological thought, one important thing about Malinowski's approach is that it considers individuals as the starting point for explanation. Directly or indirectly, all cultural elements function to meet the biopsychological needs of individuals. The main problem with such an approach is that, *by themselves,* individual needs provide no explanation for why cultures *differ* in the way they meet basic imperatives. Why do different peoples fulfill their needs in different ways? For example, unless we know why some peoples satisfy their nutritional needs by eating beef, whereas others refuse to consume cattle flesh even though they are hungry, we have not explained a population's food-getting behavior. To generalize this point: Human biological and psychological needs are relatively constant across societies and, therefore, cannot by themselves explain cultural variation.

## Structural Functionalism

The second variety of functionalism that arose in Great Britain takes the needs of society, not the needs of individuals, as its starting point. Its adherents became known as *structural functionalists,* because they believed that the function of some particular cultural element is the contribution it makes to the persistence of social structure. *Social structure* refers to the enduring pattern of relationships between individuals and groups.

The leading proponent of structural functionalism was A. R. Radcliffe-Brown, who imagined that human societies are in some ways like living organisms. Organisms are composed of cells and organs that perform essential functions that maintain the body. Living things have a bodily structure: Each organ plays a role in maintaining the whole body, and the functions of one organ complement the functions of others. We study the physiology of the organism—or how the organism stays alive through its life process—by analyzing how all its parts work together to maintain the body as a living whole.

For Radcliffe-Brown, the functions of the various parts of a cultural system are analogous to the functions of the body's various organs—to maintain the whole "social body." If a social body is to be maintained, the relationships between the individuals and groups that are its parts must be orderly and predictable. The parts must perform their functions adequately, just as with real organisms. If some relations cause conflict, this conflict must be regulated in some way. And if some part fails to work properly (analogous to disease), compensating mechanisms must correct the malfunction and restore its essential activities on behalf of the whole.

Structural functionalists believed that the normal state of human societies is *equilibrium,* or the steady state of orderly relations between individuals and groups. After a disturbance, societies ordinarily return to equilibrium. Many puzzling customs were explained by their functions in maintaining this steady state, partly by regulating any potential conflict that might disturb it.

For example, Radcliffe-Brown noted that in any society there are certain social relationships in which conflict is especially likely to occur. To minimize this conflict, and the disruption in equilibrium that accompanies it, societies have developed norms of how the occupants of certain statuses ought to relate to one another. One such norm is obligatory *avoidance:* The individuals are obliged to avoid direct contact or communication with one another; in some cases, they are forbidden to even look at one another. Obligatory avoidance sometimes occurs between individuals and their parents-in-law, a relationship often fraught with conflict over the husband or wife or over the children of the marriage. Another widespread norm is *joking relationships,* in which one individual is permitted to poke fun at another with whom he or she has a certain relation. Brothers-in-law quite often are expected to joke with one another. This is because, Radcliffe-Brown argued, their relationship contains contradictory elements: They are united by their common interest in the wife-sister and her children, yet they are divided because they usually belong to different kinship groups that may be in conflict with one another. By giving a definite form to the brother-in-law relationship, the norm of joking resolves the contradictory aspects of the relation between these statuses and reduces the potential conflict between the individuals involved. Both obligatory avoidance and joking relationships function to reduce conflict between the occupants of statuses who are especially likely to have reasons to quarrel with one another.

More than any previous approach, structural functionalism emphasized that the various customs and beliefs of a people form an integrated system. Parts cannot be understood in isolation from each other or from the whole system because each has definite relations to the others and each has its function to perform on behalf of the social body. (Incidentally, structural functionalists disliked the diffusionist term *trait* because it implies that cultural elements are sufficiently independent from one another that they can be transmitted freely from people to people.) By emphasizing the integration of culture, structural functionalism strengthened the holistic perspective of anthropological thought.

Despite this contribution, the structural functionalists failed to answer many questions adequately. First, because of their emphasis on steady states, they did not produce an adequate theory of why cultures change. Such a theory is certainly a reasonable requirement of any approach because change occurs everywhere at varying rates.

Second, most structural functionalists treated widespread conflict as an abnormal state: If individuals and groups regularly quarreled or fought with one another, structural functionalists believed that something had gone wrong with the mechanisms that restored equilibrium. Most anthropologists of today recognize that conflict is a normal condition of almost all peoples. Divergent interests, competition over resources (or desirable social roles, or mates), disagreement over how group activities should be carried out, and violation of the culturally legitimate rights of others are all sources of conflict that exist to varying degrees among all peoples. We would like to know the conditions under which dispute, feud, and outright warfare are most likely to occur in human societies; but structural functionalism, by and large, only tells us how these conflicts are regulated and resolved, not why they occur to different degrees among different peoples.

## ▰▰ LATER EVOLUTIONARY APPROACHES (CA. 1940–1960S)

In the United States the historical particularists' attack on the unilineal evolutionists led to the virtual abandonment of studies of cultural evolution for almost forty years. The particularists did indeed demolish the notion that all cultures pass through a single sequence of stages but one need not adhere to a one-line view of progress to study cultural evolution.

In the 1940s two new evolutionary approaches emerged, both of which influenced contemporary anthropology. One is known as **general evolution**. The other is called **specific evolution**.

### General Evolution

General evolution was first championed by Leslie White, who did most of his important writings between the 1940s and 1960s. White agreed with the nineteenth-century evolutionists' claim that there was an overall direction to cultural change. He argued that cultural evolution was propelled forward by technological advances—by what Morgan had called "inventions and discoveries." The major purpose of technology, he contended, is to capture the energy locked up in the environment of a people. White, therefore, proposed that levels of cultural evolution be defined by energy capture and use: Systems in which more energy is captured and used per person per year are more evolved, according to his view.

White went further. As technology advances and more energy becomes available to a people, other changes in their way of life necessarily occur as well. Their family forms, economic organization, and political structures change to enable people to use the new technology effectively. Finally, to strengthen and reinforce the new social relations, groups, and organizing principles created by technological advances, ideas and beliefs eventually changed as well. New classifications of the natural and social world, norms of behavior, values, world views, symbolic systems, and so forth (which we call *cultural knowledge*) developed. Technology thus is the "prime mover" of change and the "prime determinant" of other cultural dimensions of human life. (White adapted these ideas from Karl Marx, whom we discuss later.)

As evidence of his theory, White noted that throughout the *general* course of human history, major changes in technology were soon followed by changes in other elements of the cultural system. Until about 10,000 years ago, all peoples lived in small bands and ate only wild plants and animals. After certain peoples began to cultivate crops and keep domesticated animals—that is, after a new source of food was developed—they settled down into larger and relatively permanent villages. As the food-growing methods improved, more food energy could be produced on a given area of land, which meant that more people could be supported in a region. Villages gradually grew, until people eventually began living in cities; and grand architectural styles, writing, specialization of labor, paved roads, large-scale political organization—in a word, civilization—developed. These changes occurred in only a few areas of the world: ancient Mesopotamia, the Nile valley, the Indus valley,

*Leslie White defined general stages of cultural evolution based on technological criteria. The industrial economy that produces these aircraft captures large quantities of energy and useful materials from its environment, which in White's theory makes it highly evolved.*

eastern China, Central America, and the western highlands of South America. Other peoples remained relatively undeveloped and continued to live by hunting and gathering of wild foods or by simple cultivation.

These technological conditions continued, essentially unchanged, for several thousand years. Cultures could not evolve further, according to White, until some fundamental technological innovation led to the discovery of a new source of energy to thrust development onward. Beginning in the late eighteenth century and continuing into the present, the industrial revolution unleashed this new source of energy: first steam, then fossil fuels and electricity, and most recently the power of the atom. This latest revolution in technology gave rise to modern, industrial society, with its huge cities, social class divisions, occupational specializations, political parties, and other characteristics of the nineteenth and twentieth centuries.

More than anyone else, White made studies of cultural evolution once again acceptable. He managed to avoid most of the errors of the unilineal evolutionists, such as excessive ethnocentrism in defining the "stages" of evolution. However, many modern scholars believe that he overemphasized the importance of technological

innovations as the main causal force in cultural change. Another problem is that White was interested mainly in tracing the broad outlines of cultural evolution. For instance, he was interested in the origin of human civilization, meaning the new form of culture with the general set of cultural features known as *civilization*. He was much less interested in origins of particular civilizations, meaning how and why particular civilizations arose in certain times and places. This is why his approach to cultural evolution is called *general:* It is more useful in explaining broad, general trends than in accounting for specific cultures whose people live in specific environments. This is one of its major weaknesses, according to many modern ethnologists.

## Specific Evolution

Taking off from this criticism, Julian Steward, a contemporary of White, developed another evolutionary approach. Steward noted that White's grand theory, although useful for some purposes, revealed little about specific peoples. He agreed with White that technology is an important influence on how human populations *in general* live, but he thought that White paid insufficient attention to the influence of the local environment on the way *specific* populations live. If we want to explain why *a* people live the way they do in a particular place and time, we must understand how technology and environment interact to influence their cultural system, said Steward.

In the 1930s and 1940s, Steward proposed an approach that has become known as specific, or multilineal, evolution. Two key concepts underlie his approach. The first is *adaptation,* or the relations between humans and their natural environments. Many aspects of a people's way of life are greatly influenced by their need to exploit the environment for food and other materials. The way a population adapts is determined by the environment itself and by the technology the people have developed to exploit it.

Like White, Steward divided cultures into parts, some of which are more important than others. He called one part the *culture core,* or those aspects of a people's whole way of life that allow them to exploit nature effectively. Culture core—which is Steward's second key concept—includes cultural features such as technology, patterns of settlement, ways of dividing up tasks, groups that cooperate in exploiting resources, and methods of regulating access to land. Steward believed that technology and environment together determine the core elements of a people's way of life. Other elements of their culture are far less influenced by how they relate to their environment, such as legends, dances, art styles, and folklore. He applied the term *secondary features* to those cultural elements that are largely irrelevant for adaptation.

Despite their differences, White and Steward agreed that many aspects of cultural systems are related (directly or indirectly) to the need of all populations to exploit nature. They believed that a people's needs for food, water, shelter, fuel, and other material things took precedence over, and to some extent determined, other aspects of their way of life.

One contrast between the two men was the relative emphasis they gave to the influence of technology and local environments. Whereas White argued that technological improvements powered cultural changes through the centuries, Steward argued that local environments also greatly influenced particular cultures in specific places and times. As you might guess, the two approaches are complementary, not contradictory. Humans can only apply technology to the raw materials available in the environments in which they live; yet any population's ability to exploit an environment varies with the technology to which it has access. Technology and environment interact; neither exerts its impact in isolation from the other.

The intellectual heirs of each school we have discussed so far are well represented in modern anthropological thought. Contemporary theorizing is enormously diverse—far too diverse to summarize here. However, a great many contemporary anthropologists can be "fit into" one of two general theoretical orientations, which we shall call *materialism* and *idealism*.

## ◼ MODERN MATERIALIST APPROACHES

Modern anthropology includes several varieties of **materialism.** Although they differ greatly, they share a common theme: The way a human population acquires life-sustaining materials and energy from its environment is the most important influence on other aspects of its way of life. The harnessing of nature's resources influences the patterned relations individuals have with one another, the kinds of groups they form, and, ultimately, norms, attitudes, values, categories, world views, and other kinds of cultural knowledge.

Two influential modern varieties of materialism are historical materialism and cultural materialism. Historical materialism traces its roots to the nineteenth-century writings of Karl Marx. Cultural materialism, which also owes much to Marx, is similar to general and specific evolution. We now look briefly at each variety.

### Historical Materialism

Although best known as the "father of communism," Karl Marx was also a brilliant theorist who influenced the thinking of future scholars about humankind. Marx proposed a theory—called **historical materialism**—that he thought explained history by peoples' striving to meet their material needs and wants. His theory is much more complex than we can summarize here, but its basic tenets can be presented simply.

Marx believed that two important forces determine a human way of life and, indeed, all of human history. First is the *mode of production,* which consists of the "forces," "relations," and "means" of production. The *forces of production* include, essentially, the technology used in the process of production. To use the productive forces, people form *relations of production* with one another. For example, in societies in which the forces of production are relatively undeveloped, tasks are assigned on the basis of age and gender, so that individuals work on tasks they can do best. Land and other resources are owned communally by the group, which cooperates in work and shares the products among all members on the basis of need. Everyone has access to all the tools and resources he or she needs to survive. Conflict is minimal because communal control over resources leads to an emphasis on cooperative labor and sharing of products.

But people everywhere seek to master nature, according to Marx, and in some places this striving results in the development of the forces of production. These developments make labor and land more productive, but the benefits of this productivity are not equally distributed to all. Once the productive forces have developed enough to allow workers to produce a great surplus over their needs, a few people manage to acquire ownership over the *means of production*—that is, over land, resources, tools, and other things used in production. Society then becomes divided into two classes: those who own the means of production and those who are forced to work for the owners. The interests of the two classes are always opposed: The owners make their living by exploiting the nonowners, whereas nonowners resist the exploitation.

The opposing interests of the classes lead to conflict between them. This class conflict results from

*Historical materialists hold that courts and other aspects of legal systems protect the private property and other privileges of the wealthy and powerful classes in society.*

exploitation, which is made possible by one class's control over the means of production. Class conflicts are the second important force in human history because they lead to revolutions. Revolutions create new relations of production and new classes, which create new forms of exploitation and inevitable conflicts, which breed new revolutions. This process, in which one mode of production and its class system breed conflicts, which produce a new mode and a new class system, Marx called the "dialectic." The struggle between classes for control over the means of production (and over the material rewards of such control) thus drives change in human history.

The owners of the means of production attempt to protect their privileged position by forestalling the threat of revolution. They use some of their wealth to control laws and government, which become instruments to protect their property rights and maintain law and order. The ruling class also controls the religious ideas of society, and it uses this control over religion to reinforce its own wealth and power—by, for example, offering heavenly rewards for earthly submission to authority or for placid acceptance of one's worldly poverty.

Marx lived in the nineteenth century, and we have learned much about humanity since his day. Few anthropologists—including those who call themselves Marxians—accept his theory in total. (Remember that the preceding description is greatly simplified.) But like Marx, modern Marxians believe that conflict between classes is the major source of change in human ways of life. When they study a particular society, Marxians often focus on questions such as, What groups control productive resources? To what extent do they use this control to exploit others? How do existing ideas and beliefs reinforce and justify class relations? How are prevalent patterns of conflict influenced by the class structure? Marxian anthropologists often investigate colonialism, for colonial situations create periods of rapid change in which new classes arise and achieve control over the production process.

Modern Marxians agree also that control over the means of production is a major influence on the legal and political system and on the religious beliefs of a society. They view laws not as rules that benefit everyone in society equally but as enforced edicts that protect the property and privilege of the wealthy. They view governments not as impartial "dispensers of justice" and "protectors of the public welfare" but as formal social groups that "dispense" the wishes of the wealthy and "protect" the interests of the ruling class. Also, they agree with Marx's view of religion as a set of ideas that increases conformity with the status quo and submission to authority.

## Cultural Materialism

Another modern variety of materialism is called **cultural materialism.** Cultural materialists believe that the way a people exploit nature using their tools and technical knowledge is the most important aspect of their cultural system. In this respect, they agree with White and Steward; however, they recognize the influence of more than just technology and overall environment on human cultures. The density of the human population in a region greatly affects the way a people can exploit its resources. For example, with dense populations, some ways of acquiring life-sustaining materials are not viable. The presence of other human populations with whom a people trade, fight, or have other kinds of relations likewise affects a way of life. If a people are engaged in warfare with their neighbors, then they must adapt themselves to the military threat, which will affect the ways in which they exploit their own territory.

Cultural materialists also recognize a *feedback* relationship between people and their environment; that is, as they interact with nature, people change it, and this change "feeds back" to affect the people themselves. For instance, as people exploit a resource, they often deplete its supply to themselves and to future generations. They must then work harder to acquire the resource in the future, or develop a new method of acquiring it, or switch to an alternative resource. Other cultural changes accompany these changes in adaptation.

Following this line of argument, one leading cultural materialist, Marvin Harris, proposes that many important changes in human cultures result from a process known as *intensification*. Although human societies develop various ways of limiting their population growth, over the long term the population in a region increases. As population grows, people overexploit resources, which leads to degradation of their natural environment. This forces them to use their environment more "intensively": They turn to resources they previously ignored, which requires them to expend more labor in acquiring energy and materials, which leads them to develop new technologies to harvest and process resources. As human numbers continue to increase, the environment continues to deteriorate because of overexploitation, so people must continue to intensify their use of it. Both population growth and intensification lead to new social relations and organizations, which develop to facilitate the new ways of exploiting nature. In turn, new social arrangements require new world views, values, and norms to reinforce them.

Notice how similar this line of reasoning is to both White's and Marx's: Exploitation of nature (adaptation and production, using technology) lies at the base of human cultures; social relations, groups (including classes), and other social arrangements develop to facilitate the acquisition of resources; and the mental components of human life exist to provide ideational support for social arrangements.

## MODERN IDEALIST APPROACHES

A great many (possibly most) modern cultural anthropologists do not accept any variety of materialist explanation. They believe that materialism gives insufficient attention to the causal influence of what is most unique about humanity: our minds and ideas. We next consider contemporary approaches that emphasize the importance of culturally determined perceptions and classifications of the world. A good way to introduce these approaches is to contrast them with materialism.

### Materialism Versus Idealism

Much controversy in contemporary anthropology revolves around the relative influence of material conditions versus mental perceptions on human life. As we have seen, materialists emphasize the *objective conditions* under which people live. They believe that the need to exploit nature is a hard reality that no people can escape.

Other scholars question whether this reality has much significance in determining the specific way in which any given people live. They believe that the way a people *subjectively perceive* their material conditions is as important as the objective reality of the conditions. This approach often is called **idealism**. It holds that the ideas of a people are more than reflections of and justifications for the way they acquire resources or for the exploitation of one class by another. Cultural perceptions and classifications of reality have a life of their own. They affect, and are affected by, material forces.

As we have seen, materialists assume that the needs and wants of people for shelter, nutrition, fuel, items of wealth, and so forth take priority over other satisfying things. They take priority in the sense that the human desire for material satisfactions is more important than other needs and wants. The desire for "nonmaterial satisfactions"—such as for emotionally rewarding social relations, intellectually satisfying views of reality, or a meaningful as well as a prosperous existence—are less important or are acted on only after material needs and wants are met.

Idealists, in contrast, place more emphasis on what goes on in human minds than on what goes into human stomachs. Idealists assume that humans require more than material satisfactions for contentment, and even for survival. Like all life forms, we do have bodily needs for food, water, and so forth. But idealists hold that humans do not live by wheat and meat (or rice and fish) alone: we need social relationships, symbols, satisfying world views, ultimate values, a sense of belonging, and so forth to lend meaning to our lives.

Idealists also believe that materialists are mistaken when they take resources as a natural and given condition of the environment—as a hard fact of nature. Idealists think that resources are always culturally defined: Hindus do not consume their cattle, Muslims and Orthodox Jews refuse pork, Americans shun dog and horse flesh, and so on. All these animals are perfectly edible and available, yet members of many cultures refuse to consume them because of religious or other cultural beliefs. (For an example of the contrast in how materialists and idealists explain a specific food prohibition, see Box 4.1.)

This also implies that the materialists' belief that the local environment, population size and density, and technology interact to determine the basic organization

Members of the Jewish and Islamic faiths regard the flesh of the pig as unclean and unfit for human consumption. In Judaism two of the books of Moses—Leviticus (chapter 11) and Deuteronomy (chapter 14)—provide a long list of mammals, birds, fishes, and insects whose consumption was forbidden to the ancient Israelites. Among the list of forbidden animals was the pig. The prophet Muhammad also forbad the eating of pork in the Koran, the holy writings of members of the Muslim faith. Why?

Several explanations have been offered. Here we concentrate on only two, one idealist and one materialist. We do need to note, however, that one popular explanation for the prohibition is inadequate. It holds that pork that is not cooked thoroughly transmits a disease (trichinosis) to people, so both religions forbid the eating of pork to avoid this danger to human health. But this explanation is inadequate: Pork is such an excellent source of protein that both Moses and Muhammad should have merely admonished their followers to cook it well. Forbidding its consumption altogether is unnecessary. Besides, pork is consumed avidly by other peoples, especially in Asia and Oceania. These people are not free from the danger of trichinosis, so the health explanation alone cannot explain why Jews and Muslims abhor pig flesh—

## BOX 4.1

## THE CASE OF THE UNCLEAN PIG

otherwise, Asians and Pacific Islanders would loathe it as well.

In her book *Purity and Danger,* Mary Douglas proposed an idealist explanation for the prohibition on eating pork among the ancient Israelites. (She says nothing explicitly about the Islamic taboo on pig flesh.) Douglas begins her analysis by asking: What do humans everywhere consider "dirty"? Dirt is simply anything that is out of place—that is not where it belongs—according to local cultural ideas. For instance, when we say "my house is dirty," we do not just mean that soil is on our floors. We also mean that our clothes are in the living room, our books are on the kitchen table, and our dishes are in front of the TV—rather than, respectively, in the closet, on the shelf, or in the dishwasher where they should be. Dirt is "matter out of place," Douglas (1966, 48) believes. Her idea is exemplified by "dirty dishes"; you've just eaten what was on your plate (it was "food" a few minutes ago), but now that you've finished eating, the dishes are

unclean ("food" has become "dirt"). So something is considered dirt because it contradicts people's cultural ideas about where things properly belong. This means that dirt implies (1) a notion of where things should be (an order) and (2) something out of place (a violation of the order).

The preceding notion of dirt refers to things regarded as *physically* unhygienic or disgusting. But the same logic can apply to things regarded as *spiritually* unclean or unholy. Any culture includes a classification of animals and other things in nature. Humans always classify things by putting them into distinguishable conceptual categories—into "mental boxes." But no matter how a culture classifies things, some things fall in between the categories: They do not belong clearly to any existing category but are unclear, ambiguous, or anomalous. Douglas believes that members of a culture regard these anomalous things as supernaturally unclean, unholy, polluting, or defiling because they fail to conform to existing classifications of reality. They are permanently "out of place" because they have no category in the existing cultural classifications.

What does all this have to do with pigs? Douglas argued that all the prohibited animals share one characteristic that led the children of Israel to regard

*continued on next page*

of society is wrong. If only some of the raw materials objectively present in nature are subjectively perceived and culturally defined as resources, then culture itself helps to determine the social arrangements that organize the exploitation of nature. Idealists believe that cultural knowledge does not just reflect and support the organization of society but also shapes this organization.

Idealists also argue that the material needs of a people impose only broad limits on their actions because these

needs can be satisfied in a multitude of ways. No human population adapts to its environment in a historical vacuum. That is, any people carry their long history with them into their habitats. This history influences not only how they define *resource* but also which of the many possible ways of exploiting nature they will adopt. The particular way in which any population satisfies its material wants depends on its unique history and on its specific cultural tradition, according to idealists.

them as unclean: They violated the Israelites' cultural conceptions of the order of creation. Their classification of the natural world is given in Genesis, where God created animals with certain characteristics to soar in the sky (birds with feathers), to swim in the water (fish with scales and fins), and to walk, hop, or jump on the land (creatures with four feet). But some animals did not conform fully to their category for they had anomalous characteristics. These animals were declared to be unholy and unfit for eating. For example, terrestrial animals that moved by "swarming upon the earth" were unclean (Leviticus 11:41–42), since they did not move around by walking, hopping, or jumping.

As for the pig itself, it was considered unclean because it, too, failed to conform to any existing class, according to Douglas. The biblical text specified that clean, edible animals to the Israelites should chew the cud and have cloven hoofs; so domesticated animals such as cattle, sheep, and goats were edible. Although they do have cloven hoofs, pigs do not chew the cud; therefore, they were anomalous in the order of creation and were considered unclean and bad to eat. In this idealist explanation, the pig was unclean because it failed to fit into a particular cultural classification of reality—or so Mary Douglas argued.

Contrast this idealist explanation with the materialist explanation offered by Marvin Harris. Harris argues that people accept or reject ideas or behaviors on the basis of cost-benefit ratios. That is, before a cultural element will be found among a population, its material benefits must exceed its costs. Pigs yield returns (in calories and protein), but they also are costly (in time and energy required to feed and breed them). Because cost-benefit ratios can change over time, what once was useful often becomes harmful. Harris thinks that religious prohibitions are most likely to be applied to foods that once were useful but have become expensive in material cost-benefit ratios. A supernaturally based food prohibition serves to reduce the eating of things that previously were beneficial.

Applying this logic, Harris argues that swine have biological requirements that made them a poor animal for the inhabitants of the ancient Middle East to raise for food. Wild pigs are creatures of woodland habitats. This means that they cannot tolerate high heat well and that they thrive best when foraging on the forest floor. Because of human agricultural activity, the formerly extensive forests of the eastern Mediterranean shrank dramatically beginning about 7,000 years ago. As the forests declined, grasslands expanded, and the pig lost both the shade and the food of the forest. This meant that favorable habitats for pigs were rare by the time Leviticus and Deuteronomy were written. It was still *possible* to keep pigs, but their food habits are so similar to those of humans that they became competitors with people. This changed environment made pigs too costly to raise, although pork was formerly important in the diet of most Middle Eastern peoples.

Further, unlike cattle, goats, and sheep, pigs are useful to humans only as food. Pigs do not pull plows or provide milk, wool, or hide. Their flesh alone is valuable to people. Because cattle, goats, and sheep thrived in the changed environment and could be used to pull plows and provide milk, clothing, and fertilizer as well as meat, there was no material benefit in continuing to raise pigs. It became "forbidden flesh" because it had an unfavorable cost-benefit ratio.

In sum, Douglas argues that the pig's physical features violated the Israelite cultural classification of reality. Harris argues that the pig's physical requirements violated their material interests. There is no better example of the contrast between idealist and materialist analyses than the case of the unclean ("unclear" or "unuseful"?) pig. ◆

SOURCES: Douglas (1966), Harris (1977).

---

Many idealists regard the materialists' effort to reduce ideas to mere reflections or justifications of material conditions as little more than Western ethnocentrism. Because Western culture places such a high value on material welfare and consumption, materialists mistakenly see "primitive economic men" everywhere else, idealists claim.

In contemporary anthropology there are two major varieties of idealist thought. One, called **structuralism**, emphasizes the universal pattern of human thinking. Structuralists believe that underneath the apparent diversity of human cultures lies the human mind, which unconsciously manipulates ideas, themes, symbols, and relationships. The other popular variety of idealism is known as **interpretive anthropology**. Unlike structuralists, interpretive anthropologists emphasize cultural diversity and in fact argue that the aim of cultural anthropology itself is to document and interpret the

*Melanesians make pigs the focus of much of their cultural as well as material existence. These men from the island of Tanna, Vanuatu, are preparing a pig for a feast. Muslims and Jews, on the other hand, consider pork to be unclean and unfit for consumption (see Box 4.1).*

unconsciously oppose it to something else with which it contrasts in some respect. The mind imposes a logical order on natural and social phenomena by opposing certain qualities to other qualities. Such binary oppositions are not real or objective characteristics of reality; actual objects and qualities in the real world grade into one another. But because the mind thinks in dual contrasts, it makes reality intelligible by breaking it up into pairs of opposites, then rearranging the opposites into a pattern. This structure of thought, which is common to all humanity, underlies culture, for culture results from the unconscious activity of the mind, according to Lévi-Strauss.

Notice the similarity between these ideas and the way linguists analyze language (chapter 3). Indeed, the inspiration for structuralism came from linguistics: Just as a grammar selectively recognizes and makes patterns, structures, and meanings from distinctions between sounds and morphemes, so does the mind impose patterns, structures, and meanings on phenomena of all kinds. Further, like Noam Chomsky's universal grammar, which underlies a linguistic diversity that is only superficial, Lévi-Strauss believes that cultural diversity is more apparent than real. In many of his (quite complex) empirical studies of myth he tries to show that some myths are merely transformations of other myths, the same themes rearranged in new ways.

## Interpretive Anthropology

Anthropologists have always been interested in the cultural differences found between different societies and other groups. As much as any other single characteristic, this fascination with cultural diversity distinguishes modern ethnology from other social sciences and humanities. Indeed, many anthropologists go to the field in search of The Other, meaning in search of a way of life that contrasts to their own. Through such a search they hope to better understand not only the particular culture in which they are living but themselves and the totality of the human condition as well.

Following in this tradition, many modern cultural anthropologists are much more interested in describing and interpreting particular cultures than they are in attempting to explain and make generalizations. They believe that the essence of anthropology is the effort to immerse oneself deeply into another culture and, through such immersion, to come to an understanding of it on its own terms.

various ways as "being human." We conclude this chapter with an overview of these two varieties of idealism.

## Structuralism

Structuralism is one of the most controversial approaches of contemporary anthropological thought. Originating in France from the writings of Claude Lévi-Strauss, structuralism also is popular among English-speaking anthropologists. The term *structure* as used by Lévi-Strauss should not be confused with Radcliffe-Brown's "social structure." Whereas social structure refers to the pattern of social relations between individuals and groups, Lévi-Strauss is concerned with the structure of the human mind. His goal is to show how the structure of the mind unconsciously rearranges available ideas, themes, symbols, and objects into patterns, and thus creates culture itself.

What is this structure like? How does the human mind work? Lévi-Strauss believes that our thought is patterned in dual contrasts—the mind works by "binary oppositions." When we think about something, we

This orientation is known as *interpretive anthropology*. Interpretive anthropologists emphasize the uniqueness and individuality of each human culture. Every culture has its own ways of doing things, its own world view, its own values, and so forth. This uniqueness makes comparisons between different cultures misleading, at best. And since science usually attempts to generalize through making comparisons between phenomena, it follows that anthropology is more of a humanistic discipline than a scientific one. It has more in common with literature and art than with biology or psychology, according to the interpretive approach.

For interpretive anthropologists, all social behavior has a symbolic component, in the sense that participants constantly must behave in ways that others will understand. All social interaction, therefore, is symbolic and meaningful. Meanings exist only by virtue of common agreement among the parties to the interaction— whether the interaction is making conversation, making change in a store, making bumpers in an auto factory, or making time at a party. Neither participant can tell an observer how he or she knows what the other participant "means" by this or that behavior. Yet the participants consistently behave in ways that others understand, and they consistently interpret the behavior of others correctly.

The job of the anthropologist is not to explain elements of a culture but to explicate one element through others. That is, the anthropologist shows how one thing in a cultural system makes sense in terms of other things in the same system because interpretation *is* seeing how things make sense when understood in their context. (Analogously, a dictionary explicates the meanings of words in terms of other words. Only if one knows the meaning of many words in the dictionary can one use it to decipher the meaning of unknown words.) We seek to understand a people's way of life as they understand it. In the words of one interpretivist, Clifford Geertz, we seek to grasp "the native's point of view," "to figure out what the devil they think they are up to" (Geertz 1983, 58).

According to many interpretive anthropologists, the search for generalized explanations of human ways of life is futile. So many factors contributed to the formation of a culture, and these factors interacted in such complex and unpredictable ways that we must concentrate on understanding the unique elements of each way of life. In this respect, interpretive anthropologists share the assumptions of historical particularism more than any other body of thought we have discussed.

 ## EITHER/OR?

There are other theoretical orientations in modern anthropology. The leading debate today, however, is probably between materialists and idealists, which is why we chose to organize our discussion of modern thought around this theme.

No one has been able to resolve this issue—certainly not the authors of this textbook! Here we simply note that material forces such as technology, available raw materials, and population densities certainly influence all cultures. The question is, How much? More precisely, How important are material forces as opposed to other kinds of forces?

Most modern materialists are careful not to imply that material forces determine everything else in detail. They claim that technology, environment, and so forth determine other elements in a general way. They also insist that the determination is *probabilistic* rather than absolute; that is, more often than not, material conditions broadly determine social arrangements, which in turn broadly determine values, norms, world views, symbols, and other elements of cultural knowledge. (As you might guess, idealists respond that terms such as *probabilistic* and *broadly determine* water down materialist theory so much that hardly any theoretical power is left.)

The argument is not likely to end in any of our lifetimes. For this book, a sensible solution is to find a way of looking at the problem that avoids the either/or dilemma.

One way of doing this is to recognize (as Steward did) that different elements of a culture are influenced to different degrees by material conditions. Certainly, the way an economy is organized is greatly influenced by the local environment, by technology, and by the size and density of the human population. But the way a people resolve their disputes, raise their children, perform their rituals, or act toward their fathers-in-law is less influenced by material conditions or is influenced by them only indirectly. The legends they recite, the specific natural objects they use as religious symbols, or the way they decorate their bodies may have little to do with material conditions. Such elements of a cultural system may be only loosely tied to material forces and to desires for material things. If so, we cannot account for them without considering people's desires for a meaningful existence, for an emotionally gratifying social life, for an intellectually satisfying world view, and so forth.

# SUMMARY

This chapter discusses some of the past and present schools of thought in cultural anthropology. Today, as in the past, anthropological research is guided by a variety of theoretical orientations—questions, concepts, assumptions, and methods used to study particular cultures or humanity in general.

Anthropology originated as a separate academic discipline in the late nineteenth century. Colonialism brought people of European ancestry into increasing contact with the native inhabitants of Africa, Asia, the Americas, and the Pacific. The changing intellectual climate associated with the rise of uniformitarianism in geology and evolution in biology provided theories that led scholars to try to explain scientifically the customs and beliefs of people of other continents. Evolution was the key. These scholars' argument was that because such people remain at an early stage of cultural evolution, they are survivors of the precursors of modern civilization. By studying their ways of life, one could learn how Europeans had progressed out of rude beginnings. Late-nineteenth-century anthropologists such as Tylor and Morgan developed the approach known as *unilineal evolutionism* to describe and account for the progress of humanity into civilization.

Diffusionists of the early twentieth century questioned that independent invention accounted for the wide geographic distribution of similar cultural "traits." They believed that diffusion accounted for cultural similarities among even widely scattered peoples. But the mechanism by which people such as the ancient Egyptians transmitted their "advanced" cultural traits to Native Americans or to other, more "primitive" cultures remains unclear, and many people believe that there is an implicit prejudice or even racism to diffusionist ideas.

In the United States the historical particularist Boas noticed the inconsistencies and invalid assumptions in the work of the unilineal evolutionists. Notions such as "progress" and "complexity" involved value judgments and had little objective meaning. A strong empiricist and inductivist, Boas believed that Tylor and Morgan engaged in too much speculative theorizing, and that only after more objective descriptions were available should anthropologists begin to talk about "laws of progress." His demands for more data had a lasting influence, leading to an emphasis on fieldwork as part of professional training and to the adoption of a relativistic outlook on members of other cultural traditions. On the other hand, Boas's view that each way of life is unique because it is the product of its own unique history led to an overemphasis on cultural differences to the neglect of similarities, in the opinion of many.

In Great Britain the functional orientation was popular between about 1920 and 1950. Biopsychological functionalists, notably Malinowski, argued that the purpose of any culture is to meet the bodily, emotional, social, and cognitive needs of people. Structural functionalists such as Radcliffe-Brown assumed that cultural elements function to maintain a social structure in equilibrium and to maintain orderly relations between individuals and groups. Functionalists strengthened the holistic perspective of anthropology; but modern scholars believe that the approach cannot handle change well and gives an inadequate explanation for disputes, wars, feuds, and other conflicts.

In North America new evolutionary approaches gained popularity in the 1940s. White's general evolution proposed that cultural evolution is powered by technological changes. As new sources of energy are discovered, changes in economy, family life, and political organization occur; and these in turn lead to changes in values, norms, world views, and other elements of cultural knowledge. White thus saw technological progress as the prime mover of change and technology as the prime determinant of everything else. Steward's specific evolution looked to adaptation to the natural environment as the major influence on the core elements of a culture. Both White and Steward thought that how and how well a people exploit nature are the most important influences on other aspects of their way of life.

Many contemporary theoretical orientations fall into one of two overall approaches: materialism and idealism. Materialists agree that the way a people acquire energy and materials from nature is the main determinant of their culture. Historical materialism goes back to Marx, who argued that the development of the forces of production lead to changes in the relations of production and to unequal access to the means of production. Societies become divided into classes: those who own the means of production and those who are forced to work for the owners. Class conflicts result from exploitation, revolutions follow and institute new relations of production, and so on in a dialectical process. Cultural materialists believe that the necessity to organize labor for production leads societies to develop certain kinds of groupings and power relations, which then are reinforced and justified by certain kinds of ideas and beliefs.

Idealists believe that ideas affect as well as are affected by the material conditions of life; that humans seek meanings and social, emotional, and cognitive gratification as well as food; that resources themselves are culturally defined; that material forces impose only broad limits on a people's way of life; and that materialism is ethnocentric. Lévi-Strauss's structuralism argues that the universal properties of the human mind underlie culture and produce its many variants. Interpretive anthropologists glory in the cultural diversity of humanity and largely give up attempts to explain this diversity in favor of gaining an understanding of particular ways of life.

## KEY TERMS

| | |
|---|---|
| uniformitarian theory | structural functionalism |
| natural selection | general evolution |
| unilineal evolution | specific evolution |
| diffusion | materialism |
| independent invention | historical materialism |
| diffusionists | cultural materialism |
| historical particularism | idealism |
| functionalism | structuralism |
| biopsychological functionalism | interpretive anthropology |

## SUGGESTED READINGS

A number of large volumes are available that provide detailed histories of the development of anthropological thought, including these:

Harris, Marvin. *The Rise of Anthropological Theory*. New York: Crowell, 1968.

Hatch, Elvin. *Theories of Man and Culture*. New York: Columbia, 1973.

Honigman, John J. *The Development of Anthropological Ideas*. Homewood, Ill.: Dorsey Press, 1976.

Voget, Fred. *A History of Ethnology*. New York: Holt, Rinehart and Winston, 1975.

A comprehensive reader in the history of anthropological theory, featuring original works by key figures, is:

Bohannan, Paul, and Mark Glazer. *High Points in Anthropology*. 2nd edition. New York: Knopf, 1988.

Several works are helpful to those who want a fuller understanding of the contemporary split between materialists and idealists:

Geertz, Clifford. *The Interpretation of Cultures*. New York: Basic Books, 1973.
> *Assorted works by an idealist and interpretivist. Good place to start to understand this approach.*

———. *Negara: The Theatre State in Nineteenth-Century Bali*. Princeton: Princeton University Press, 1980.
> *Empirical, interpretive study.*

Harris, Marvin. *Cannibals and Kings*. New York: Random, 1977.
> *Intensification hypothesis of cultural evolution is explained and illustrated. Easy reading; excellent example of cultural materialist thought.*

———. *Cultural Materialism: The Struggle for a Science of Culture*. New York: Vintage, 1980.
> *Title speaks for itself. Lays out theoretical principles of this approach and defends it from rival approaches, including dialectical materialism, structuralism, and idealism.*

Kurzeil, Edith. *The Age of Structuralism: Lévi–Strauss to Foucault*. New York: Columbia University Press, 1980.
> *An overview of French structural thought. Structuralism had its start in France and has been enormously influential in that country in many fields.*

Lévi-Strauss, Claude. *Structural Anthropology*. New York: Doubleday, 1963.

———. *Totemism*. Boston: Beacon, 1963.

———. *The Savage Mind*. Chicago: University of Chicago Press, 1966.
> *Three books considered to be the basic works of the most famous structuralist.*

Sahlins, Marshall. *Culture and Practical Reason*. Chicago: University of Chicago Press, 1976.
> *Essentially structuralist in orientation. Difficult going for beginners, but this book has become a bit of a manifesto for idealists in anthropology.*

**CHAPTER 5**

# Methods of Investigation

*Anthropological field research emphasizes direct contact with the people being studied. Here Richard Lee converses with a group of San.*

**CONTENTS**

Any science has a set of methods that its practitioners use to explore the reality they investigate. In cultural anthropology, our primary interest is in human ways of life—particularly the cultural differences and similarities that exist among the world's peoples. Over the decades, anthropologists have developed certain methods of investigating human cultures. These methods are described in this chapter.

Anthropological methods of investigation fall into two broad categories. The first is **ethnographic methods,** which involve the collection and analysis of descriptive data from a single society or several closely related societies. The end product of ethnographic research is either a case study describing the cultural system of some people (e.g., the way of life of the Cheyenne) or a descriptive account of some aspect of a people's cultural system (such as the Cheyenne religion). The second category is **comparative methods,** which involve attempts to test hypotheses about relations between certain aspects of cultural systems by using comparative ethnographic data from a number of societies. The product of comparative research usually is a monograph or article that tries to generalize about causal relations between cultural phenomena.

So anthropological research has two purposes: (1) the collecting and recording of new data about specific people (ethnography) and (2) the expansion of our theoretical understanding of human cultural systems in general through comparative analysis. We first discuss the methods used to describe a single people and then summarize how anthropologists use descriptive accounts to test hypotheses.

## ETHNOGRAPHIC METHODS

There are two sources of cultural data about a particular people: the living members of the society and written accounts or other records about that group of people. The collection of cultural data by studying and interviewing living members of a society is called **ethnographic fieldwork.** The study of a people's culture using written accounts and other records is termed **ethnohistoric research.**

### Ethnographic Fieldwork

Ethnographic fieldwork involves the direct collection of cultural data from living individuals. It requires that the researcher live with or close to the people being studied so that he or she can interact with them on a day-to-day basis for a long period, usually a year or more. Not infrequently the anthropologist has to learn the group's language and adjust his behavior to their social norms. By its very nature, fieldwork fosters a close personal relationship between the researcher and the members of the society being studied. This social closeness distinguishes anthropologists from other social scientists.

Fieldwork has always been the primary method used by anthropologists to collect cultural data. Over the past century the objective of fieldwork has changed and with it, the data-gathering techniques used by anthropologists. Today a number of techniques are used in the course of any research project.

**Interviewing** is the most basic method of collecting cultural data. The anthropologist asks questions and elicits answers from members of the society being studied. Interviews may be structured or unstructured. A *structured interview* consists of a limited number of specific questions. It may take the form of a questionnaire that the researcher fills in as the questions are answered. This type of interview is best suited for collecting general quantitative data about the group. For example, most research begins with a census of the community: the number of people in each family, their ages and relationships, and basic economic information about the family. In this manner a demographic and an economic profile of the group can be constructed. Structured interviews are also used to create genealogies. Most research requires a clear knowledge of how everyone in the group is related to one another. Genealogies are important in understanding the social and economic behavior of individuals beyond the immediate family. There are, however, limits to the utility of structured interviews.

In *unstructured interviews* the researcher asks open-ended questions, hoping that the interviewee will elaborate on the answers. The questions may be general, about family life, marriage, a particular religious ritual, or economic activity. Most cultural data are collected through unstructured interviews. In these interviews the researcher learns the cultural explanations for information collected in the structured interviews.

Although the source of most cultural data, interviewing has severe limitations. The problem usually is not with the answers given by the members of the group, but rather with the questions asked by the researcher. What is relevant or irrelevant to the proper understanding of a particular cultural phenomenon depends on the culture of the individuals involved. Initially, the researcher does not understand the cultural context of the data and thus does not know what questions need to be asked and answered. The early stages of a research project often are characterized by "shotgun" questioning as the anthropologist seeks to learn enough about the culture to ask the right questions. Through interviewing, a researcher can gain a good basic knowledge of a culture's major structural features. However, no matter how knowledgeable and willing the interviewees might be, verbal descriptions in themselves are incomplete and do not enable the researcher to gain an in-depth knowledge of the people or an understanding of the true dynamics of their culture.

To understand the limitations of interviewing, ask yourself this question: If an anthropologist from another culture asked you to describe a baseball game, what would you tell her? How complete would your description be? Chances are, if you are an avid fan, you could relate enough information for her to gain a basic understanding of the game. You could tell her how many players there are on each side and explain the basic rules about balls, strikes, runs, errors, and innings. From memory alone, it is highly unlikely that you would explain eveything that might occur during a game. What you probably would give the researcher is an idealized model of a baseball game. Certain facts would be left untold, not because you were hiding them but because they are so commonplace or unusual that they are not part of your consciousness concerning the game. The same is true of other peoples and their description of their own cultural phenomena. Interviews alone can give the researcher only a simplified overview of a particular cultural phenomenon, an idealized model.

If a researcher wants to truly understand baseball, he cannot simply talk to someone about it; he needs to at least see a game. In fact, the researcher should observe several games and discuss what occurred with a knowledgeable person. It would be even better for the researcher to participate, at least in a minor way, in a game. Only by combining interviewing with observing and participating can one begin to understand the rules and dynamics of the game. So it is with the study of any cultural phenomenon.

During the late nineteenth and early twentieth centuries, anthropologists relied primarily on interviews alone to collect cultural data. This technique was well suited to the anthropological objectives of that time. Early American anthropologists were concerned with collecting general cultural information about Native American groups. These groups had already been placed on reservations, and their economies and cultures had drastically changed. Anthropologists wanted to record the earlier Native American life-styles before all knowledge

*Among the earliest anthropological field researchers and writers was Francis LaFlesche (1857–1932), an Omaha Indian from Nebraska.*

of the pre-reservation period was lost. The only way the aboriginal culture of these peoples could be studied was by interviewing individuals who had grown to adulthood before the reservations were created. In a relatively short period, anthropologists were able to collect, and thus preserve, a vast body of general descriptive data on Native American culture.

In the 1920s the interest of anthropologists began to shift from just describing the general culture of a society to attempting to understand the basic dynamics of cultural systems. In other words, anthropologists wanted to see how these systems worked and how their parts fit together. A leader in this change was Bronislaw Malinowski, mentioned earlier in the discussion of functionalism, who popularized a new data-collection technique called **participant observation.** Anthropologists no longer merely recorded and analyzed people's statements. To a greater or lesser extent, they took up residence with the people they were studying and began trying to learn about the culture by observing people in their daily lives and participating in their daily activities.

Participant observation often has been misinterpreted, even by some anthropologists who have taken it too literally. It does not mean becoming a full participant in the activities of the people—in other words, "going native." The emphasis of this technique is more on observation than on participation. Participant observation usually does require that one live in the community, for only by doing so can one observe and record the behavior of individuals as they go about their daily work, visit their friends, interact with their relatives, participate in rituals, and so on. These observations of behavior serve to generate new questions concerning the people. Why does a man share food with some families but not with others? Why do some men wear a particular type of hat or headdress? Does a particular color of clothing have any meaning? Some behaviors have significance, whereas other behaviors do not. For example, variations in types of headdress worn by individuals may be merely the result of personal preferences, or it may reflect status differences. The color of clothing may or may not have special significance. In American society black symbolizes mourning, but in other societies covering one's body with white clay symbolizes the same emotion. Participant observation allows the researcher to collect more detailed data than does interviewing alone, and thus it makes possible a deeper understanding of interrelations between cultural phenomena.

Firsthand observations of the members of a society also allow the researcher to see how people diverge from

*Through participant observation, fieldworkers try to gain a deeper understanding of the lifeways of their hosts, as in the case of this anthropologists working in Guanajuato, Mexico.*

the culturally defined, idealized model of behavior. An incident that occurred while Malinowski was working in the Trobriand Islands illustrates the divergence between cultural norms—the way people say they ought to behave—and the way they actually behave. One day Malinowski heard a commotion in the village and discovered that a young boy in a neighboring village had committed suicide by climbing a palm tree and flinging himself onto the beach. In his earlier questioning of the islanders, Malinowski had been told that sexual relations between a man and his mother's sister's daughters were prohibited. On inquiring into the suicide of the young boy, he found that the boy had been sexually involved with his mother's sister's daughter and that in fact such incestuous relationships were not rare. So long as such liaisons were not mentioned in public, they were ignored. In this particular case the girl's rejected boyfriend had become angry and publicly exposed the transgression. Although everyone in the village already knew of this incestuous relationship, by making it public the exboyfriend exposed his rival to ridicule, thus causing him to commit suicide. It is doubtful that such behavior could have been discovered only by interviewing indivduals.

## Problems in Field Research

Every fieldwork experience is, to some extent, unique. Specific problems differ, depending on the individual characteristics of the researcher, the nature of the community, and the particular questions being studied. There are, however, several difficulties that, to varying degrees, affect virtually every field-research situation: (1) stereotyping, (2) defining the fieldworker's role in the community and developing rapport, and (3) identifying and interviewing consultants.

STEREOTYPING.     When we think of **stereotypes**— the preconceived generalizations concerning a particular group of people—we usually think only of their effects on the perceptions of one party to a relationship. Anthropologists ask themselves how they can overcome their own stereotypes and cultural biases about the people they study. Stereotyping, however, is a two-way street. Every society has stereotypes concerning members of other societies and of ethnic and racial groups. Thus, although the goal is for an anthropologist to put aside his or her personal stereotypes sufficiently to research the cultural system of another people with some degree of objectivity, those with whom the ethnographer will be living and working will not have shelved their stereotypes. Most anthropologists are of European ancestry, yet most subjects of anthropological research are non-European peoples. Even if a particular anthropologist is of Asian, African, or Native American ancestry, a similar problem exists because anthropologists seldom belong to the local community they study and thus are outsiders. As a result, an anthropologist who enters another community must contend with local stereotypes about the ethnic group with which he or she is identified.

In the case of anthropologists of European ancestry, the local stereotyping about their ethnic group has most frequently been derived from contact with only a limited range of individuals, such as missionaries, soldiers, colonial officials, and government bureaucrats. Regardless of the nature and intensity of this contact, most non-Western peoples have a well-developed idea about the expected behavior of such individuals. The tendency of local people to fit the ethnographer into one of their stereotypical categories can at times prove a burden for fieldworkers. The behavior of anthropologists seldom conforms to the model that the local people have developed. Previous contacts with Europeans and Euro–Americans often have been structured in such a manner as to place the "native" in the position of social inferior. Thus, an anthropologist attempting to gain social acceptance in such a society typically is met with suspicion and not infrequently with hostility. The types of questions anthropologists ask about behavior and beliefs

frequently arouse suspicions further and elicit guarded answers. Why does he or she want to know about our family structure, our political organization, our ritual secrets? What is this person going to do with this information? While the anthropologist is trying to understand the community, its members are attempting to understand what the anthropologist is doing. Depending on the nature of previous contacts, some types of questions may provoke more suspicion than others. For example, a minority or tribal group involved in some illegal or illicit activity—such as smuggling, poaching, or growing drugs—may wonder if the anthropologist will inform government authorities. Members of groups that have been more exposed to Western culture usually assume that the ethnographer's objective is to make money and that researchers become wealthy by publishing books.

In other cases, members of the community may be aware that Europeans and Euro–Americans do not approve of or believe in certain types of behavior, and few people will disclose information on topics they think will be met with disapproval or scorn. This reticence is particularly evident in certain types of religious beliefs and practices. As a result of extensive activities of Christian missionaries, most non-Western peoples are well aware that Westerners usually deny the validity of witchcraft and the existence of wereanimals. Members of societies with these beliefs usually are hesitant about discussing such subjects with people who they perceive do not believe in them. They understandably are reluctant to talk openly about an uncle who they believe can turn himself into a deer or a snake with someone who will probably view it as ridiculous. Likewise, they probably would not say that their father had been killed by a witch if they thought that the outsider did not believe in witchcraft.

DEVELOPING A ROLE AND RAPPORT.     Often against a background of suspicion, distrust, and, in some cases, fear, an anthropologist has to develop a status in the society that gives him rapport with local people. Rapport in this sense means acceptance to the degree that a working relationship is possible, although ethnographers are rarely, if ever, totally accepted by the people among whom they work. However, over a period of time most anthropologists succeed in gaining some degree of trust and friendship, at least with a few members of the group.

The particular role or roles that an anthropologist eventually defines for herself within the society vary greatly with the circumstances of the particular situation. Depending on the amount and nature of research funding, the anthropologist may be an important economic resource, paying wages to interpreters and assistants or distributing desirable goods as gifts. Anthropologists with a car or truck frequently find themselves providing needed transportation for members of the community. Ethnographers may also provide comic relief by asking silly questions, behaving in a funny manner, making childlike errors in speaking the language, and generally being amusing to have around. They may be a source of information about the outside world, disclosing information to which local people would not otherwise have access. Sometimes community members are as curious about the anthropologist's society as he is about their society. Or the anthropologist may just be considered a harmless nuisance. During the course of research, the typical fieldworker at one time or another adopts all these roles plus many others.

## IDENTIFYING AND INTERVIEWING CONSULTANTS.
Ethnographers learn a good deal about a people simply by living among them and participating in many of their activities. This rather casual, informal participant observation provides a good feel for the general tone of life. For instance, it allows fieldworkers to report that village life seems "relaxed," that the people are "outwardly polite," that they "show respect for authority," and so on.

But for most purposes, observation and participation alone are insufficient. We do not just want to know what they are doing, but why they are doing it. Because certain realms of culture are not observable (e.g., religious beliefs, myths, stories, and social values), the researcher has to interview members of the group.

An individual who supplies the ethnographer with information is called a **consultant** or **informant**. Field research involves the help of many consultants, who sometimes are paid for their services. Just as no one individual is equally well informed about every aspect of our own cultural system, so no one person in another society is equally knowledgeable about every aspect of his or her society's way of life. Women are more knowledgeable than men concerning certain things and vice versa. Shamans and priests know more about religious rituals than other people. The elderly members of the community usually are most knowledgeable about myths, stories, and histories. Thus the anthropologist has to attempt to identify and interview those people who are the most knowledgeable about the particular subjects she is interested in. Individuals whom the local community considers to be expert in some particular area, and whom the ethnographer spends much time with, are known as **key consultants** or **key informants**.

A number of factors affect the quality and accuracy of the data collected through interviewing. The people being studied seldom understand fully what the anthropologist is trying to accomplish. In some instances, especially among minority populations, there may be a deliberate attempt to deceive the researcher. For example, collecting livestock-ownership data on the Navajo reservation can at times prove difficult. The total number of livestock on the reservation is controlled by the tribe, and each stockowner has a permit that allows him to keep a certain number of animals. Because some people keep more stock than their permits allow, they are reluctant to disclose the actual number in their herds. There is also the problem of humorous deception. The Osage men wear a deer tail roach on their heads during dances. During a dance an Osage was overheard telling an inquisitive visitor that these roaches were made of horse tails, and that a young Osage male proved his manhood by cutting the hair for his roach from the tail of the meanest horse he could find. In this case, the Osage was simply having fun at the expense of a visitor, but anthropologists also encounter this problem. To get around these and other difficulties, anthropologists try to interview a number of individuals separately about specific points to gain several independent verifications.

Some societies prohibit the relating of certain kinds of cultural knowledge to outsiders. The Pueblos of the Rio Grande Valley of New Mexico are extremely secretive about their non-Christian religious beliefs and rituals. Non-Indians are not allowed to witness these ceremonies, and members of these pueblos are prohibited from talking about them to non-Indians.

Other kinds of cultural barriers also make it difficult to collect certain types of data. For example, collecting genealogies is not always as easy as it might seem because in many societies it is customary not to speak the names of the dead. Among the Yanomamö of Venezuela and Brazil, not only is it taboo to speak the names of the dead, but it is considered discourteous to speak the names of prominent living men, for whom kinship terms are used when possible. When ethnographer Napoleon Chagnon persisted in his attempts to collect genealogies, the Yanomamö responded by inventing a series of fictitious names for individuals, living and dead, as well as creating fictitious genealogical relationships. Only after five months of intensive research did he discover the hoax. When he mentioned some of the names he had collected during a visit to a neighboring village, the people responded with "uncontrollable laughter" because his informants had made up names such as "hairy rectum" and "eagle shit" to avoid speaking real names.

## Fieldwork as a Rite of Passage

Fieldwork is important to cultural anthropologists not just because it is the major source of our data on human cultures but because it is a key aspect of the education of the anthropologist. It is one thing to read ethnographies about other ways of life, but it is something quite different to live among and interact with individuals from another cultural tradition every day for a year or more. As we have seen, the anthropologist usually lives in the native community, submerging himself in the social life of the people, living in native dwellings, eating local foods, learning the language, and participating as fully as an outsider is allowed in daily activities. Living as social minorities, usually for the first time in their lives, anthropologists depend on the goodwill of people whose norms and values they neither totally understand nor accept. Under these conditions, the participant observer has to adjust his activities to fit the cultural ideas and behavior patterns of the people. This modification of the fieldworker's own behavior is one— necessary—part of learning about the community. Fieldworkers usually work alone and are socially and physically vulnerable to members of the community. During the course of their research, anthropologists will violate, or at least be perceived as violating, some of the societal norms of behavior. Such incidents may destroy the rapport gained with some key consultants or result in the researcher's being ostracized. In serious cases, the fieldworker may find himself the target of physical violence.

When in the field, except on rare occasions, the anthropologist is there as the uninvited guest of the community. Regardless of how researchers may rationalize their work as being for the long-term good of the community or humanity, they are basically there to serve their own needs and interests, not those of the community. If a serious problem develops between the anthropologist and members of the community, the fieldworker must bear the primary responsibility and blame (see Box 5.1).

The fieldwork experience tests and taxes the attitude of cultural relativity that anthropologists teach in their classrooms. It is easy to discuss the concept of relativity in a university setting, but it is more difficult to apply this concept to one's own situation. Regardless of which society it is, certain cultural aspects will offend one's own cultural norms and values. Fieldworkers are regularly exposed to certain attitudes and behaviors that are unacceptable in their own society. For example, according to the anthropologist's own cultural standards, some local people might "abuse" certain family members or certain powerful leaders might "exploit" lower-ranking members of the society. As the fieldworker develops friendships, this "abuse" or "exploitation" frequently becomes personalized. Under what circumstances, if ever, an anthropologist should attempt to intervene and impose her cultural standards on the members of another society poses a real and personal dilemma. In theory, such intervention is never permissible, but in real-life situations the answer is not always so clear.

Many people experience a kind of psychological trauma when surrounded by people speaking a language they cannot fully understand and speak only imperfectly, eating foods that are strange, seeing architecture that is alien, and observing people using gestures and behaving in ways they either do not comprehend or do not approve. The strange sounds, smells, tastes, sights, and behaviors result in the disorientation of many fieldworkers. Out of their normal cultural context, they do not understand what is happening around them yet realize that their own actions often are being misunderstood. The symptoms of this **culture shock** are psychological and sometimes even physiological: paranoia, anxiety, a longing for the folks back home, nausea, hypochondria, and, frequently, diarrhea.

The attempts by ethnographers to maintain their relativistic perspective and objectivity in their daily interactions with members of the other society usually compound the normal trauma of culture shock. Socially isolated and unable to release their frustrations and anxieties through conversations with sympathetic others, they often have to cope with their psychological difficulties alone.

For many anthropologists much of their time in the field is extremely traumatic, and as a result, most anthropologists view fieldwork as a rite of passage. More than any other aspect of their training, fieldwork transforms the individual from a student of anthropology into a professional anthropologist. Although many overemphasize the importance of fieldwork in the training of anthropologists, it is undeniably a significant educational experience. Most individuals return from their fieldwork with a different perspective on themselves and

Most of the societies and communities that modern anthropologists work among are ethnic minority peoples within larger nation-states. Even when they are not social minorities, they can still be damaged individually or as groups by information collected by anthropologists. Thus it is ethically imperative that research findings not be "misused." In 1971 the Council of the American Anthropological Association adopted the "Principles of Professional Responsibility." This statement was amended in November 1976, and in 1989 additional revisions were proposed. The proposed revisions contain six parts; the following is only part I, the portion that addresses the question of fieldwork ethics.

I. **Responsibility to peoples whose lives and cultures anthropologists study.** Anthropologists' first responsibility is to those whose lives and cultures they study. Should conflicts of interest arise, the interests of these people take precedence over other considerations. Anthropologists must do everything in their power to protect the dignity and privacy of the people with whom they work, conduct research or perform other professional activities. Their physical, social and emotional safety and welfare are the professional concerns of the anthropologists who have worked among them.

A. *The rights, interests, safety, and sensitivities of those who entrust information to anthropologists must be safeguarded.*

1. The right of those providing information to anthropologists either to remain anonymous or to receive recognition is to be respected and defended. It is the responsibility of anthropologists to make

## BOX 5.1

## ETHICS AND ANTHROPOLOGICAL RESEARCH

every effort to determine the preferences of those providing information and to comply with their wishes.

a. It should be made clear to anyone providing information that despite the anthropologist's best intentions and efforts anonymity may be compromised or recognition fail to materialize.

2. Anthropologists should not reveal the identity of groups or persons whose anonymity is protected through the use of pseudonyms.

3. The aims of all their professional activities should be clearly communicated by anthropologists to those among whom they work.

4. Anthropologists must not exploit individuals or groups for personal gain. They should give fair return for the help and services they receive. They must recognize their debt to the societies in which they work and their obligation to reciprocate in appropriate ways.

5. Anthropologists have an ongoing obligation to assess both the positive and negative consequences of their activities and the publications re-

sulting from those activities. They should inform individuals and groups likely to be affected of any consequences relevant to them that they anticipate. In any case, however, their work must not violate these principles of professional responsibility. If they anticipate the possibility that such violations might occur they should take steps, including, if necessary, discontinuance of work, to avoid such outcomes.

6. Whether they are engaged in academic or nonacademic research, anthropologists must be candid about their professional identities. If the results of their activities are not to be made public, this should be made clear to all concerned from the outset.

7. Anthropologists must take into account and, where relevant, make explicit the extent to which their own personal and cultural values affect their professional activities. They must also recognize and deal candidly and judiciously with the effects that the often conflicting demands and values of employers, sponsors, host governments and research publications may have upon their work.

The principal point of this statement is that anthropologists must take all reasonable care to see that their research does no harm to the individuals and groups that provide them with information. ◆

SOURCE: Reproduced by permission of the American Anthropological Association from *Anthropological Newsletter*, 30:8, November 1989. Not for sale or further reproduction.

their own culture. Fieldwork thus often teaches us as much about ourselves as about those we are supposed to be studying.

## Ethnohistory

The study of past cultural systems through the use of written records is called **ethnohistory**. Since the late nineteenth century, anthropologists have used written materials in their studies, but the importance of this research has become widely recognized only since the 1970s. The growing interest in ethnohistory has come with the realization that non-Western societies have changed far more dramatically over the past few hundred years than had previously been thought.

Like historians who study their society's past, ethnohistorians make use of such materials as published books and articles, newspapers, archival documents, diaries, journals, maps, drawings, and photographs. Not surprisingly, many scholars treat history and ethnohistory as if they were synonymous. There are, however, critical—yet frequently overlooked—differences that distinguish ethnohistory from history.

◆ An ethnohistorian is primarily interested in reconstructing the cultural system of the people. The actual historical events themselves are of interest only because they cast light on the cultural system or changes in the system.

◆ Historical events have little significance outside the cultural context of the peoples involved. Ethnohistorians study nonliterate peoples. Thus, whereas historians can use accounts recorded by members of the society being studied, ethnohistorians have to use accounts recorded by members of other, literate societies. As a result, the problem of interpreting accounts usually is more difficult for the ethnohistorian than for the historian.

The varying interpretations of historical events are most evident in events that involved the members of two or more distinct cultural groups. In his 1981 study, *Historical Metaphors and Mythical Realities,* Marshall Sahlins illustrates how differently the Hawaiians and the English interpreted such an event. Captain James Cook was in command of the first European expedition to discover the Hawaiian Islands. Having never seen Europeans or their technology before, the Hawaiians, not surprisingly, thought that these British sailors in their large and powerful ships were somehow divine and that Captain Cook must have been a god—the question was, what god?

Lono was a mythical god-king whom the Hawaiians believed periodically returned to the islands and ruled in human form, usurping power from the earthly kings who were representatives of the rival god Ku. Several earlier Hawaiian kings had been identified as Lono ruling on earth. Every year, during a period called *Makahiki,* a series of rituals were dedicated to Lono. Lono symbolically returned to the islands at the beginning of Makahiki, at which time the priests of Lono took control of the temples from the priests of Ku. During the four lunar months that followed, the priests of Lono were in charge of rituals. Makahiki ended with Lono being symbolically sacrificed and returning to the sky. With Lono gone, control returned to the king and the priests of Ku, the earthly representatives of Ku.

As Cook sailed among the islands, the timing and direction of his movements coincidentally corresponded with the mythological movements of the god-king Lono. His arrival took place at the start of Makahiki, and he set sail from the islands at the end of Makahiki. The Hawaiians thus identified Cook as the personification of Lono, and the interpretation was further strengthened when Cook announced during his departure that he would return the next year.

Soon after departing, Cook had problems with his ship's mast and had to return to land for repairs. Cook's untimely return was ominously interpreted by the king and priests of Ku as Lono returning to claim earthly powers. Not surprisingly, the Hawaiian priests had him killed and viewed the killing as the ritual sacrifice of the rival god-king Lono, which they symbolically reenacted every year. In contrast, the English felt that the Hawaiians viciously murdered Cook for no justifiable reason. Although an extreme case, this example illustrates the need for historical events to be interpreted within their proper cultural context. We could not understand the "murder" of Cook without being aware of how the Hawaiians interpreted his presence and his actions on the basis of their beliefs.

In ethnohistorical research the anthropologist has to use and analyze accounts of people who, not being members of the society, had at best only an imperfect understanding of the cultural context of the data they were recording. As a result, the ethnohistorian faces two major problems: (1) discerning whether the accounts are factually accurate, a problem that they share with historians, and (2) determining how the participants interpreted the events.

The problem of interpretation raises an additional question about the validity of particular reports. Not only do we have to ask about the accuracy of the account, but we also have to ask how knowledgeable the

*Cook's death has been the subject of numerous romanticized paintings, such as J. Zoffany's "The death of Captain Cook at Hawaii, 1779".*

recorder was about the cultural context of the events. Ethnohistorians use certain criteria to evaluate the potential validity of an account. How long did the individual live among these people? Did the observer speak the language? What was the role of the individual? Soldiers, missionaries, traders, and government officials have different views, biases, and access to information.

The difficulty with ethnohistory is that no hard-and-fast rules can be used in evaluating these data. The longer an individual lived among members of a particular society and the better she spoke the language, the more reliable the account should be; however, this rule cannot be automatically assumed. In some cases, the writer may have had little interest in the people among whom she was living, perhaps because the contacts were only related to a job. This attitude is evident in the accounts of many traders and government officials. In other cases, the account may be self-serving, with the individuals attempting to enhance their careers. Thus sometimes soldiers and government officials falsified their official reports. Ethnocentrism is still another factor. Missionary accounts, in particular, often demonstrate overt bias against local customs and beliefs; one has to remember that an individual becomes a missionary because he is an avid believer. However, some of the most objective accounts of other societies were written by well-educated missionaries, who often were scholars themselves.

Thus, in ethnohistoric research, there is no simple way to evaluate a particular document or account. At best, a single event may be recorded in several independent accounts that can each be used to verify the accuracy and interpretation of the others. Unfortunately, multiple observations are the exception, not the rule.

A final limitation on the use of ethnohistoric materials is that seldom are all aspects of a particular society evenly reported. For example, data on economic activities may be the most abundant, whereas information on religious ceremonies and beliefs may be absent or limited. As a result, ethnographic studies based on ethnohistoric research lack the depth and balance of those gleaned from research with living individuals. Despite its problems and limitations, ethnohistoric research provides us with the only clues we have to the past of many societies as well as the key to a vast store of cultural data hitherto untapped.

## ETHNOLOGICAL METHODS

So far we have discussed only how anthropologists collect cultural data on peoples, past and present, using fieldwork and historical materials. We have some cultural data available on more than 1,200 societies. As shown in the following chapters, anthropologists have used these data to demonstrate a wide range of cultural variability among human populations. However, we are not merely interested in describing particular cultural systems and the range of variability in these systems. We are also interested in attempting to explain why these differences exist. In other words, anthropologists want to make generalizations concerning cultural systems, and thus explain why differences exist between peoples. Generalizations cannot be made based on the study of a single society; we need methods by which many societies can be compared in a systematic way. There are two major forms of multisystem comparisons: cross-cultural comparisons and controlled historical comparisons. The objective in both types of comparative studies is to test hypotheses.

## Cross-Cultural Comparisons

The most frequently used comparative method is **cross-cultural comparison**. In this method, hypotheses are tested by examining the statistical correlations between particular cultural variables, using synchronic data drawn from a number of societies. Historical changes in the societies examined are ignored; the societies are compared at whatever period they were studied. This research method involves three steps. First, the researcher must state the idea as a hypothesis—that is, state it in such a way that it can be supported or not supported ("tested") by data drawn from a large number of human populations. Second, the ethnologist chooses a sample of societies (usually randomly) and studies the ethnographies that describe their way of life. Third, the data collected from these ethnographies are then classified and grouped in such a manner that the correlations between variables may be shown statistically. What the ethnographer is attempting to find is the pattern of association: Do two or more cultural variables consistently occur together or not? In most cases, these tasks are far more difficult than they may sound.

To illustrate how the cross-cultural method is used to test an hypothesis, we shall examine the relations between sorcery and legal systems within a group of societies. Sorcery is discussed in some detail in chapter 15. Here it is sufficient for you to know that sorcery is the belief that certain people (sorcerers) have power, either supernatural or magical, to cause harm to others. Some anthropologists believe that sorcery serves as a means of social control in societies that lack a formalized legal apparatus—courts, police, and so forth—to punish wrongdoers. They argue that people will be reluctant to cause trouble if they believe that a victim of their trouble-making has the ability to use supernatural power to retaliate against them. Overall, societies without a formal legal system should have a greater need for a mechanism such as sorcery to control behavior. So if

the hypothesis that sorcery is a mechanism for social control is correct, we ought to find that sorcery is more likely to be important in societies without formal means of punishment than in societies with a specialized legal system.

To see if this hypothesis is true across a variety of societies, we use the cross-cultural method. We determine for many societies (1) the relative degree of importance of sorcery and (2) whether the society has a formal apparatus for punishing wrongdoing. We make a table in which all the possible combinations of the two cultural elements are recorded:

| SORCERY | SPECIALIZED LEGAL APPARATUS | |
| --- | --- | --- |
| | Absent | Present |
| Important | A | B |
| Unimportant | C | D |

In the cells of the table we record the number of societies in which the four possible combinations are found. If the hypothesis is supported, we should find that cells A and D contain the greatest number of societies. If the hypothesis is not supported, we should find that the distribution of societies in the cells is random, or that cells B and C contain the greatest number of societies, or some other distribution.

In 1950, Beatrice Whiting conducted such a study by surveying the ethnographic literature for fifty societies. Her results were as follows (Whiting 1950, 87):

| SORCERY | SPECIALIZED LEGAL APPARATUS | |
| --- | --- | --- |
| | Absent | Present |
| Important | 30 | 5 |
| Unimportant | 3 | 12 |

On the basis of this comparison, we might conclude that the hypothesis is supported, since most of the societies fall into the cells predicted by our hypothesis. We would not worry about the eight societies (the "exceptions") that appear in cells B and C. The hypothesis did not claim that social control was the *only* function of sorcery, so the importance of sorcery in the five societies in cell B might be explained by some other factor. Nor did we claim that sorcery was the *only* way that societies lacking a specialized legal apparatus had to control their members, so the three societies in cell C might have developed some alternative means of social control. (Although outside the scope of this text, statistical tests are available that show how confident a researcher can be that such associations did not occur by chance.)

Some confusions are caused by cross-cultural tabulations such as this. One of the most common is to mistake correlation for causation: Simply because two cultural elements (X and Y) usually are found together does not mean that one (X) has caused the other (Y). Y could have caused X, or both X and Y could have been caused by some third element, W. In the preceding example, it was assumed that the absence of formal legal punishments "caused" many societies to need some other social control mechanism and that sorcery became important to meet this need. On the basis of the data in the table, we might also conclude that societies in which sorcery is important have little need for a formal legal apparatus, so they fail to develop one.

To acquire the data needed to test her hypothesis, Whiting read through ethnographic information on all fifty societies in her sample. This approach suffers from several disadvantages. It is so time-consuming that only a small number of societies can be included in the sample. There is also the problem of bias by the researcher, who must decide, for example, whether sorcery should be considered "important" or "unimportant" among some people. Borderline cases might get lumped into the category that supports the researcher's hypothesis.

Thanks largely to a lifetime of work by George Murdock, another method is available to modern researchers that partially overcomes these two problems (although it has troubles of its own, to be discussed shortly). In the *Ethnographic Atlas,* Murdock and his associates have summarized information on more than 1,200 societies in the form of coded tables. For each cultural system there are codes that show its form of kinship, marriage, economy, religion, political organization, division of labor, and so forth. Contemporary cross-cultural researchers no longer need to search through ethnographies for information relevant to their investigations; rather, they use the information already coded and analyze the results by using a computer. This reduces the bias of the researcher, for whoever coded the information on a particular society had no knowledge of the hypothesis under investigation. It also allows a larger number of societies to be included in a sample because the data can be retrieved far more quickly.

Using cross-cultural methods to see if some specific hypothesis applies to a large number of societies is thus easier today than ever before, but some difficulties still exist. One seems to be inherent in the method itself, which dissects whole cultures into parts ("variables" as we called them) and assigns a value (or "state") to each part. In the preceding example, the variables were sorcery, which had two states (important, unimportant),

and specialized legal apparatus, which also had two states (present, absent). To test the hypothesis that the states of these two cultural elements are consistently related, we ignored everything else about them. We also ignored everything else about the societies in the sample, such as their family systems and their economies.

A more familiar example makes the point clearly. One element of cultural systems is the number of gods in whom people believe. For purposes of some specific hypothesis, the possible states of this variable might be monotheism (belief in one god), polytheism (belief in many gods), and no gods. Any researcher who included modern North America in the sample would probably consider our primary religion—Christianity—as monotheistic. Most of the Middle East also would be considered monotheistic. The problem is, can North American monotheism be considered equivalent to the Middle Eastern monotheisms? If we consider them the same, we ignore the differences between the worship of the

*Christianity, Judaism, and Islam all are monotheistic and have common historical roots. But Christians and Jews would not pray by prostrating themselves toward Mecca, as this Muslim man from New Delhi, India, is doing. Should cross-cultural researchers consider them one kind of religion or not?*

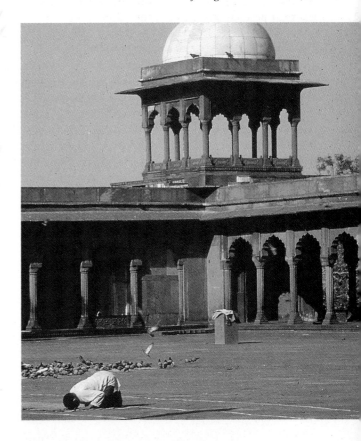

Christian God, the Jewish Yahweh, and the Islamic Allah. When we lump these three varieties of monotheism together into a single kind of religion, we distort them to some degree.

Cross-cultural studies examine data ahistorically, or without reference to time. In other words, the cultural system of a particular society is treated as timeless or unchanging. Thus in cross-cultural studies and the *Ethnographic Atlas*, there is "a" cultural system coded for the Cheyenne: Cheyenne cultural system circa 1850. However, the cultural system of a society is never stable but constantly changing (in chapter 6 we discuss this process). For example, today the Cheyennes live in houses, drive cars and trucks, and participate in a wage-money economy. In 1850 the Cheyennes lived in hide-covered tepees, rode horses, and hunted buffalo. In 1650 the Cheyennes lived in permanent earth lodge villages, traveled by foot or canoe, and depended on farming and hunting for their subsistence. Although the Cheyenne cultural systems have continuity, all aspects of their culture changed, to some degree, over the period just described. Thus, in reality, there is no stable Cheyenne culture, but an ever-changing system. The synchronic studies used in cross-cultural research create an artificial picture of the cultural system of a society.

## Controlled Historical Comparisons

Only in the past decade or two have anthropologists attempted systematic diachronic analyses of cultural data. Such studies are called **controlled historical comparisons.** Unlike cross-cultural studies, controlled historical comparisons use changes in particular groupings of societies over time to define general cultural patterning and test hypotheses. Controlled historical comparisons, like cross-cultural studies, usually are extremely complex. We illustrate this method by a simple example.

As we discuss in chapter 11, people organize their family lives in various ways. Two common ways are matrilineal descent and patrilineal descent. In matrilineal societies, family group membership is inherited through your mother; you belong to your mother's family. In patrilineal societies, group membership is inherited through your father; you belong to your father's family. Anthropologists have long attempted to explain why some societies are matrilineal and others patrilineal. Cross-cultural research has shown that a relation exists between matrilineality and patrilineality and the relative economic importance of males and

females in the society. However, cross-cultural studies can only show us correlations between descent and other synchronic aspects of their cultural system. For example, these studies can tell us what types of economic systems are most frequently found with matrilineal or patrilineal societies. Cross-cultural studies cannot measure the long-term effects of external changes on matrilineal or patrilineal societies. Is matrilineality or patrilineality more adaptive in some situations than in others? If so, what types of situations favor matrilineal societies, and what types of situations favor patrilineal societies? To examine this question, we must turn to controlled historical comparisons.

Michael Allen (1984) has asserted that matrilineal societies in the Pacific appear to be more successful in adapting to European contact than are patrilineal societies. Is there a way to test Allen's assertion? First, we must restructure this statement as a testable hypothesis. What do we mean by success? The term *success* is rather subjective and cannot be directly measured. Thus we have to convert this term into some measurable quantity. One quantifiable measure of the success of a particular system is the relative ability of a society to maintain or expand its population over time. Thus our hypothesis would be that given the same degree of disruptive external pressures, matrilineal societies maintain their population levels better over time than patrilineal societies. Now we need to find a group of matrilineal societies and patrilineal societies that experienced a comparable intensity of external contact over a period of time and compare their relative populations at the beginning and end of the period. If Allen is correct, the matrilineal societies should have a relatively higher population at the end of the period than the patrilineal societies.

The farming Native American tribes of the eastern United States present an almost ideal case for testing Allen's assertion. They had similar cultural systems, except that some were matrilineal and others were patrilineal. Their collective histories of contact with Europeans were also basically the same. During the historical period, all these societies suffered the effects of epidemic diseases, warfare (with Europeans as well as intertribal), severe territorial dislocation, political domination, and social discrimination.

Now the problem is determining an appropriate time frame to examine and finding comparable population data. One problem with ethnohistoric research is that the researcher is forced to use the data available in the records. It is not until about 1775 that sufficient population data are available in missionary, military, and explorer accounts to estimate the populations of all these tribes with any accuracy. In 1910 the U.S. Bureau of the Census conducted a special Native American census, which was the first truly comprehensive census of Native American societies in the United States. Thus the time frame we will use is from 1775 to 1910. Using ethnographic data, we can then classify particular societies as either matrilineal or patrilineal and determine their populations for the beginning and end of this period:

|  | 1775 | 1910 | PERCENT |
| --- | --- | --- | --- |
| Matrilineal societies | 88,590 | 82,714 | 93 |
| Patrilineal societies | 36,400 | 13,463 | 37 |
| Totals | 124,990 | 96,177 | 77 |

From this table we can see that during this 135-year period, the matrilineal societies declined by only about 7 percent of their total population, whereas patrilineal societies lost 63 percent of their population. Thus if maintenance of population is a measure of a society's success, then matrilineal societies in the eastern United States were more successful than patrilineal societies.

As is the case with all comparative studies, findings such as these raise more questions than they answer. Are these population figures and the historical experience of these societies truly comparable? If they are comparable, is the significant factor differences in descent form, or is it some other cultural factor we have not considered? We need to add at this point that not all matrilineal societies in this study were equally successful in maintaining their population levels and that a few patrilineal societies studied increased in population during this period. Thus there is room for argument. If, in the final analysis, however, we decide that our findings are valid and that matrilineal societies are, under certain conditions, more adaptive than patrilineal societies, we still cannot directly say why.

Cross-cultural comparisons and controlled historical comparisons give us distinctly different measures of cultural phenomena. They address different types of questions and test different types of hypotheses. Thus they are complementary, not competitive, methodologies.

Some anthropologists (especially idealists—see chapter 4) believe that both kinds of comparative studies distort each cultural system in the sample so much that the whole method is invalid. They believe that human ways of life are too complex to be broken down into neat variables or elements that take on a small number of states or values. They also think that ripping each element out of the particular context in which it is embedded robs it of its significance because each element acquires its meaning only in its local historical and cultural context. They therefore argue that comparisons of elements across cultural systems are at least misleading and, possibly, always invalid.

Despite these and other problems, comparative methods are the only practical means available for determining whether a hypothesis is valid among human cultural systems. Those who use these methods are aware of the difficulties, yet they believe that the advantage of being able to process information on large numbers of societies outweighs the problems.

## SUMMARY

Anthropological methods fall into two overall categories. Ethnographic methods involve the collection of information on a specific cultural system, whereas comparative methods are used to test hypotheses or to investigate theoretical ideas by comparing information on numerous cultural systems. The basic aims of ethnographic methods are descriptive, whereas comparative investigations aim to determine whether some hypothesis or theoretical idea is supported by the accumulated data on human cultures.

The kinds of methods used by anthropologists depend on whether they are investigating a contemporary or a past way of life. Research into the past usually involves ethnohistory (perusal of written documents). This method requires considerable interpretation by the researcher. Sometimes those who wrote the documents used in ethnohistoric reconstructions misinterpreted events because of their cultural backgrounds and ethnocentrism. The contents of documents often are affected by the private interests of their authors.

Fieldwork is the primary method of acquiring data about living people. Fieldworkers usually live among those they study for at least a year, conducting formal interviews and surveys and engaging in participant observation. Although the difficulties of conducting fieldwork vary with the personality and gender of the fieldworker and with the people and specific topic being studied, three problems are common. Fieldworkers must not only fight against their own ethnocentrism and tendencies to stereotype those they study, but they must also overcome the stereotypes local people have developed about foreigners. It often is difficult to establish a rapport with local people because they may have had no previous experience with the kinds of questions fieldworkers ask. Identifying reliable informants and finding people willing to participate in intensive surveys may pose a serious problem. Sometimes people deliberately deceive the anthropologist, because they mistrust his motives, do not want certain facts to become public, or are culturally forbidden to give away secrets of their religion. Today fieldwork is viewed as an essential part of the graduate education of anthropologists and almost a prerequisite for professionalism. It is, in some respects, a rite of passage.

Comparative methods involve ways of systematically and reliably comparing massive amounts of information collected by previous ethnographers. The use of comparative methods presents many difficulties, including stating the research hypothesis in such a way that it is testable, reliably defining and measuring the variables of interest for many societies, deciding whether similar cultural elements from two or more societies are the "same" or "different," and contending with unintentional researcher bias. The results of comparative studies can be difficult to interpret. Correlation often is confused with causation. Many anthropologists (especially idealists) believe that all comparative methods are invalid because they rip cultural elements out of the context that gives them meaning. They therefore inevitably distort the variables they claim to measure objectively, according to some. Despite such difficulties, comparative methods are the only way to test hypotheses and investigate theories in a large sample of societies.

# KEY TERMS

ethnographic methods
comparative methods
ethnographic fieldwork
ethnohistoric research
interviewing
participant observation
stereotypes
consultant (informant)

key consultant (key informant)
culture shock
ethnohistory
cross-cultural comparison
controlled historical comparisons

# SUGGESTED READINGS

Works that deal with research methods and problems include:

Agar, Michael. *The Professional Stranger: An Informal Introduction to Ethnography.* New York: Academic, 1980.
> *Quite good for the beginning student. Tells how ethnographers do their work, with lots of examples taken from the author's own field experiences.*

Martin. Calvin ed. *The American Indian and the Problem of History.* New York: Oxford University Press. 1987.
> *In this edited work, anthropologists, historians, and Native Americans discuss the problems in trying to objectively interpret the culture history of Indian America. This is a critical book for any ethnohistorian studying Native American culture.*

Obeyesekere, Gananath *The Apotheosis of Captain Cook: European Mythmaking in the Pacific.* Princeton, N. J.: Princeton University Press 1992.
> *In part, this study attacks Marshall Sahlin's interpretation of the Cook murder (discussed in the chapter), accusing him of Eurocentric bias. Obeyesekere shows the difficulty in attempting to objectively analyze historical documents.*

Pelto, Perti J., and H. Gretal. *Anthropological Research: The Structure of Inquiry.* Cambridge: Cambridge University Press, 1978.
> *Emphasizes importance of quantification and measurement in fieldwork.*

Spradley, James P. *The Ethnographic Interview.* New York: Holt, Rinehart and Winston, 1979.

————. *Participant Observation.* New York: Holt, Rinehart and Winston, 1980.
> *Two books that complement each other, one focusing on structured interviewing of informants, the other on detailed observation.*

A number of books deal with the actual experiences of ethnographers in the field. They are valuable for conveying the feeling of fieldwork, of problems ethnographers encounter, of relating to local people, and so forth.

Briggs, Jean. *Never in Anger: Portrait of an Eskimo Family.* Cambridge, Mass.: Harvard University Press, 1970.
> *A personal account of life with an Eskimo family.*

Dumont, Jean-Paul. The Headman and I. Prospect Heights, Ill.: Waveland Press, 1992.
> *Account of a fieldworker's relationships with the Panare people of the Venezuelan Amazon.*

Fernea, Elizabeth. *A Street in Marrakech.* New York: Doubleday/Anchor, 1969.
> *Journalist-author provides a lively account of her life among women in Morocco.*

Freilich, Morris, ed. *Marginal Natives: Anthropologists at Work.* New York: Harper and Row, 1970.
> *Ten anthropologists discuss the problems of fieldwork.*

Golde, Peggy, ed. *Women in the Field: Anthropological Experiences.* Chicago: Aldine, 1970.

    *Twelve female ethnographers discuss special difficulties they encountered because of their gender.*

Hayano, David M. Road Through the Rain Forest. Prospect Heights, Ill.: Waveland Press, 1990.

    *Describes the fieldwork experiences of Hayano and his wife among the Awa, a people of the highlands of Papua New Guinea.*

Maybury-Lewis, David. *The Savage and the Innocent.* Boston: Beacon, 1968.

    *A description of the author's fieldwork in the central Brazilian rain forest.*

Powdermaker, Hortense. *Stranger and Friend: The Way of an Anthropologist.* New York: Norton, 1966.

    *Autobiographical work, with a description of the author's fieldwork experiences in four sociocultural settings, including Hollywood.*

Rabinow, Paul. *Reflections on Fieldwork in Morocco.* Berkeley: University of California Press, 1977.

    *An interesting discussion of the author's experiences in Morocco.*

Ward, Martha C. Nest in the Wind. Prospect Heights, Ill.: Waveland Press, 1989.

    *Wonderfully readable account of Ward's personal experiences and fieldwork difficulties on Pohnpei island of Micronesia.*

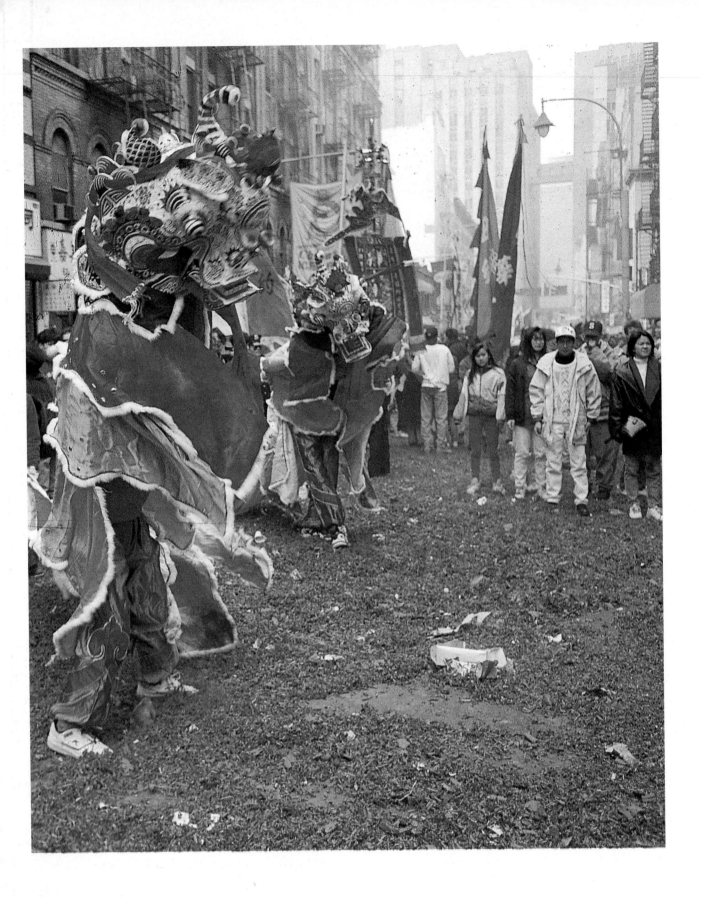

# PART III

## DIVERSITY

Perhaps the major contribution of cultural anthropology to the understanding of humanity is its documentation of the remarkable diversity of the world's cultures. It is important to realize that cultural diversity exists not only between different peoples but that cultures change over time as well. No culture is the same today as it was 100 years ago, let alone 400 or 500 years in the past. Because cultural diversity has both temporal and spatial dimensions, to understand how and why cultures vary we ideally have to control both dimensions. Unfortunately, our historical time depth for the cultures of most of the world's peoples and regions is extremely shallow and fragmentary.

We begin this part with a chapter discussing the broad patterns of change that have occurred in the world since 1500. After this overview, we examine the range of diversity in particular aspects of cultures—adaptation, economy, family life, political organization, religion, and so forth.

In the discussions of these ten chapters, time is ignored—that is, we pay little attention to how particular cultures have changed. In most cases, when we discuss the culture of a particular people, the discussion applies either to the time when the culture was studied, or to the earliest period for which reliable information is available. For example, when describing the economic structure of the Inca empire, we speak of the early sixteenth century; the information given about the political and legal system of the Cheyenne applies to the mid-nineteenth century; and the data on the adaptation of the !Kung of southern Africa refer to the mid-twentieth century. Few of the peoples discussed live exactly today as they are described in the text, for significant changes in the ways of life of every people have occurred. Many of these changes, and how anthropology is useful in understanding them, are described in Part Four.

## CHAPTER 6

# THE WORLD SINCE 1500

## CONTENTS

When we who are the products of the urban-industrial world look at a small farming village in China or India, learn about the Masai herding cattle on the plains of Africa, or watch a movie about Pygmy hunters of the Ituri forest, we think of these peoples as being unchanged for centuries, if not millennia. In their actions, dress, and technology other people may differ greatly from us, and we think that they have yet to be affected by the massive changes taking place in the world. Without questioning, we assume that they have a "pristine" or untouched "traditional culture." In reality, no people are caught in a cultural time warp. The culture of a people is a highly dynamic and always changing system, even though to urban-industrial peoples these changes may not appear great.

In this chapter we examine the processes by which culture changes and then look at the broad patterns of change that have occurred among the peoples of the world over the past 500 years. The voyage of Columbus to the Americas in 1492 initiated a period of unparalleled change in the world. No group of people, no matter how geographically isolated, has escaped these changes.

## CULTURE CHANGE

Since the late nineteenth century, anthropologists have been aware that culture is never stable—that it is in constant change. Although the process of culture change has been extensively studied by anthropologists, here we only briefly discuss how and why a system changes over time. There are two main processes by which a culture changes: *innovation* and *diffusion*.

An **innovation** may be anything—from new religious beliefs to a technological change—that is internally generated by members of the society. People are constantly changing what they do and how they do it. In most cases these are minor and imperceptible unconscious changes. In the telling of a myth a person may delete some part while elaborating another. Individuals may wear their hair differently or paint their faces with a new design. In a sense we are all innovators, and sometimes these innovations are adopted by others and become part of the culture and collective behavior of the group. Still other innovations are intentional, as when an individual has an idea about how to do something better or more efficiently. Most innovations consist of the recombining of two or more existing ideas or objects to produce something new. This factor is evident in technology, since most technological advancements are the result of such recombinations. In North American society Fulton took a paddle wheel, a steam engine, and a boat and put them together to create a steamboat. Still later several individuals succeeded in powering a wagon by the use of a gasoline internal combustion engine, and thus the automobile was born.

**Diffusion** is a second way in which new elements are introduced into a culture. Diffusion consists of "borrowing" or adopting a cultural trait from another society. Any category of customs, beliefs, or objects, from religious beliefs and practices to technology, may be diffused from one people to another. The adoption of new traits requires that these traits be integrated into the existing culture of the recipient population. In many cases the form may remain the same while the meaning and function of the trait change.

Why a group of people adopts or rejects a particular new custom or belief is extraordinarily complex. As a rule, people are receptive to new traits that either enhance their economic well-being or their social survival. Thus farming peoples often are receptive to new crops that complement their existing crops and new technology that increases their harvest. Societies involved in warfare readily accept more advanced military technology. Still other factors stimulate changes in culture. Political and economic domination usually result in the forced introduction of new traits from the dominant society as it restructures the culture of dependent peoples to meet new needs and objectives. The displacement and relocation of a people into a different natural environment generate changes in the existing culture. Demographic changes—rapid increases or decreases in population—and their associated changes in relative population densities also necessitate changes in the culture.

## HISTORY AND ANTHROPOLOGY

Frederick Maitland, a historian, commented during the late nineteenth century that anthropology had to be history or it was nothing. Although few, if any, anthropologists would totally agree with Maitland, they have for some time realized that history has played an important role in shaping culture. Until recently anthropologists have treated non-Western societies as if they have been static. The importance of change among these peoples was either ignored or minimized. During the early part of this century, ethnographers wrote descriptions of nineteenth-century culture using the "ethnographic present," indicative of the "timeless" or static concept of these societies. If any changes had taken place, they were seen as very recent.

Only during the past two decades have anthropologists begun to see the magnitude of the changes that have occurred among even the most technologically unsophisticated peoples over the past few hundred years. Virtually every group of people in the world, no matter how geographically isolated, has directly or indirectly had its culture altered to some degree as a result of European expansion and industrialization. In turn, the Europeans were also changed by borrowing and adopting ideas and technology from other peoples. There is not now, nor has there been for several hundred years, a truly pristine society. Not only has the way of life of every people changed, but many societies have become extinct during this period, and numerous new socially and culturally distinct populations have come into existence.

## THE WORLD BEFORE 1500

Keeping in mind how and why changes occur in cultures, we can now briefly outline world history over the past 500 years. In this summary we have two objectives: (1) to provide the reader with some idea of the magnitude and pervasiveness of change, and (2) to demonstrate the main patterns and directions of change.

The world has experienced phenomenal changes over the past 500 years. Foremost among these changes have been the technological advancements and the harnessing of new sources of energy: coal, petroleum, electricity, and nuclear power. Associated with these advancements has been an explosion in the human population of the earth—from only about 500 to 600 million in A.D. 1500 to more than 5 billion today. Not only has the population of the world grown, but there have been major intraregional and interregional population shifts. In the period since 1500, profound cultural changes have affected virtually all peoples in the world.

The key cause of these changes has been the economic and political expansion of European populations that began toward the end of the fifteenth century and has served as the major catalyst for these changes. To understand world cultural history during this period, we have to trace the history of European expansion and determine how and when it affected the various regions and peoples of the world.

European expansion took place in two rather distinct stages. The first stage can be called the *mercantile phase.* During this period European traders brought most of the continents of the world into direct trade contact with one another. Some migration and colonization and limited political conquest occurred during the mercantile phase, which began during the 1490s and lasted until the latter half of the eighteenth century. The second stage, called the *industrial phase,* encompassed the period when European peoples politically conquered almost every region of the world and established a global economic system that they dominated.

Before A.D. 1500 the major world regions were relatively isolated from one another. Most contact was limited to societies that occupied adjacent territories. Trade was minimal, and long-distance trade that existed between Europe and China or Africa seldom involved direct exchange between members of those societies. Trade was managed by intervening groups whose members acted as middlemen. Thus, although Europeans were aware of the existence of places like China, India, and Ethiopia, their knowledge was extremely limited and seldom based on firsthand accounts. Although innovations in technology and cultural institutions did diffuse from one center to another, diffusion was slow because direct contact was lacking.

Although the terms *Old World* and *New World* are ethnocentric, this distinction is useful from a cultural-historical perspective. The Old World—Europe, Africa, and Asia—did form a unit within which trade and contact, however tenuous and limited, allowed for the spread of technology and institutions. The *New World* is a term usually applied only to the Americas, but it could be applied just as well to Australia and most of Oceania because both of these regions were outside this exchange network before 1500. Thus before European expansion the world consisted of two broad geographical regions with peoples who had for much of their history developed technologies and lifeways in isolation from one another.

To better understand the changes that were to occur, we need first to see what the peoples of the world were like before 1500. For this purpose it is best to think of cultures not in terms of individual groups but rather in terms of culture regions. A cultural region is a geographical area of peoples who share a common cultural heritage. Various factors, such as physical types, language, and even religion, may be used to define this "common" heritage. By common we do not mean identical; in fact, there can be rather dramatic cultural differences between peoples in the same region. Also, the boundaries between adjacent regions seldom are well defined and are not necessarily stable over time. Culture regions frequently are separated by transition zones that are occupied by peoples who do not clearly belong in either region. Boundaries of culture region can shift over time because of the migrations of people or

the spread of particular cultural institutions. With these limitations in mind, let us look at and define the major culture regions of the world before 1500 (see Figure 6.1). Because the peoples of Europe were the main catalyst for change, we begin with them.

European peoples occupied most of the region between the Ural Mountains, the Atlantic Ocean, the Mediterrean Sea, and the Arctic Circle. Thus the boundaries of the European culture region in 1492 were about the same as those of the European continent. Compared with other regions, the European culture region had a relatively modest population. In 1450, immediately after a plague that had sharply reduced the population, only about 55 million people occupied the region. By 1500 the population had recovered, but it still numbered only about 65 million. In terms of language and cultural institutions, Europe was a relatively homogeneous region. Most European peoples spoke languages that belonged to one of four branches of the Indo-European language family: Germanic, Slavic, Celtic, or Romance. In religion, its peoples were Christians, although di-

**FIGURE 6.1**
**World Culture Regions (ca. 1500)**

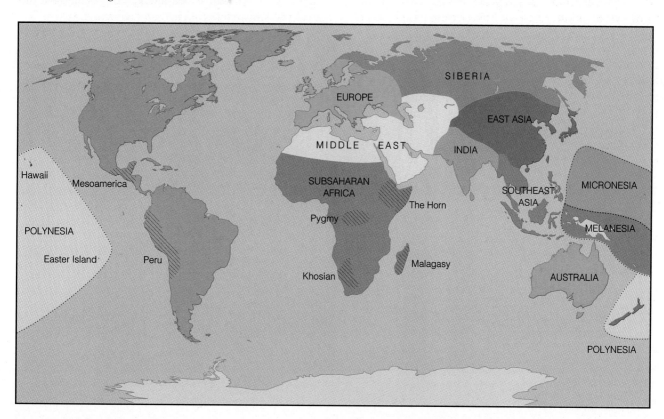

vided into Catholic, Eastern Orthodox, and Protestants. The vast majority of European peoples lived in small farm villages or coastal fishing villages. Along the coasts and major rivers were numerous small towns and cities occupied by artisans and merchants. The relative cultural homogeneity of Europe was, in large part, the result of a common religion and a well-developed internal maritime and riverine trade network that connected the towns and cities.

Politically, Europe was fragmented into numerous small states, most of which were governed by heriditary rulers. Of the soon-to-be colonial powers, France, with perhaps 15 million people, was the largest in population. England (the British Isles) had a population of only about 5 million, whereas Spain had 6.5 million, Portugal 1.25 million, and the Netherlands less than 1 million.

Asia was the most technologically and politically developed portion of the Old World. There were three main culture regions in Asia: the Middle East, South Asia, and the Far East.

The Islamic religion gave the peoples of the Middle East their distinctive culture and serves to define the region. Reaching from the steppes of central Asia, the Middle East encompassed southwestern Asia and northern Africa. Islam carried with it not only the distinctive "Arabic" writing system, architecture, and art forms but also a set of social rules derived from the Koran. Beneath this veneer of commonality, significant differences ex-

isted in the region's peoples. Arabic, Turkic, and Indo-European languages were spoken. In life-style they ranged from nomadic herders of cattle, camels, sheep, goats, and horses to settled village farmers, maritime traders, and urban artisans, scholars, and merchants. In 1500 the region had a population of between 30 and 45 million.

Politically, most of the peoples in the region were, or would soon be, under the centralized control of the rapidly expanding, Turkish-dominated Ottoman Empire. Not only would most Arabic-speaking peoples soon be brought under the control of the Turks, but the Ottoman Empire would expand at the expense of European peoples. In the sixteenth and seventeenth centuries Turkish armies would conquer the Greeks and many southern Slavic-speaking peoples in the Balkans. Thus Greece and the Balkans were politically incorporated into the Middle East. Turkish domination resulted in many of these peoples being converted to the Islamic religion and put a Middle Eastern cultural imprint on the peoples of the Balkans, blurring the boundary between the Middle East and Europe in this area.

India, also commonly called South Asia, consisted of what is today Pakistan, India, Bangladesh, Sri Lanka, and Nepal. Although most people were Hindus and the Hindu religion, with its art and caste system, gave the region its distinctive character, there were also substantial numbers of Muslims, Buddhists, and Sikhs. Linguis-

*Today as in the past, a multitude of languages and traditions exist in South Asia, making it one of the most heterogenous regions of the world.*

*The civilization of ancient China was unrivalled in riches, power, and size. As this photo of the Imperial Palace in the Forbidden City of modern Beijing suggests, at the height of their empire Chinese emperors were among the most powerful men in the world*

tic, religious, and cultural differences cut across the population, creating a bewildering array of more than 200 distinct ethnic groups. Although there were large cities, where artisans and merchants lived, most people were farmers in small villages. With a population of about 100 million in 1500, the region was then, as it is today, the most densely inhabited major region of the world.

In 1500, India was not—nor had it ever been—politically unified. Politically, the region was highly fragmented. The north was ruled by the Moguls, Muslim conquest states with large politically dominated Hindu populations. The rest of the region was divided into numerous small kingdoms and principalities with hereditary rulers.

East Asia included most of modern China, Korea, and Japan. With a population between 100 and 150 million, it was the single most populous region in the world. East Asia was also the most culturally homogeneous of the regions. There were only three main languages and ethnic groups: Chinese, Korean, and Japanese. These peoples shared a common writing system, art, architecture, and cultural heritage derived from

ancient Chinese culture. Although most people were farmers, there were numerous large cities, and in terms of technology and artisanship China led the world in 1500. Political organization in East Asia was far more centralized than in other regions. With a population of about 100 million, China was the most populous unified country in the world.

Southeast Asia included the modern countries of Burma, Thailand, Laos, Vietnam, Cambodia, Malaysia, Indonesia, and the Philippines. Although the total population of Southeast Asia in 1500 was only about 30 to 40 million, it was divided into several hundred distinct ethnic groups, each with its own language. Because this region was at the crossroads of Asia, its people had at different times before 1500 come under the varying influences of Indian, Middle Eastern, and Far Eastern peoples but had managed to retain their distinctiveness. Some of the region's peoples had become Buddhists, others Muslims or Hindus, and still others stayed with their own religions. The same mix of Middle East, South Asia, Far East, and local traditions was evident in their art, architecture, writing systems, and cultural institutions. All the major cultural traditions of Asia came together in Southeast Asia but none truly dominated. Thus the farming and fishing peoples of the region demonstrated a bewildering array of cultural variability. In 1500 the region was fragmented into numerous small kingdoms and politically autonomous local ethnic groups.

In northern Asia, in the subarctic forest (taiga) and tundra, were the Siberian peoples, who lived as nomadic hunters, fishers, and herders of reindeer. Lacking cities, agriculture, and writing systems, these peoples were, in terms of technology, the least developed of the Asian peoples. Numbering at most 1 million, they lived in widely scattered camps across this vast inhospitable region. Most groups had their own ethnic religions, and politically, they seldom were organized beyond the small local group.

South of the Sahara desert were the peoples of sub-Saharan, or black, Africa. Although the vast grasslands of the Sudan and eastern Africa were occupied by cattle-herding peoples, the majority of sub-Saharan Africans were settled village farmers. Some of the peoples on the Sahara's fringe and along the coasts had been converted to Islam before 1500, but most Africans were adherents of so-called tribal religions. States and even

*The Khoisan peoples of southern Africa were foragers who occupied the deserts and dry grasslands.*

*People who speak one of the Niger-Congo languages had spread over most of sub-Saharan Africa by the eighteenth century. Most were farming people, and many lived in highly organized states with an hereditary elite.*

multiethnic empires existed in some areas. The Songhai Empire occupied much of the Sudan, reaching from the mouth of the Gambia river eastward to the bend of the Niger. Further east, around Lake Chad, was the Kanem-Bornu Empire. To the south were smaller states, such as Oyo and Benin. Near the mouth of the Congo river was the Kongo Kingdom, and to the southwest were the states of Monomatapa and Luba. Along the east coast were the Omani or Arab city-states, such as Kilwa and Zanzibar. Little is known about the areas of Africa between these centers at this early time, but in general the region was politically fragmented into hundreds of small local groups, some headed by hereditary rulers and others not. For its physical size, sub-Saharan Africa had a relatively small population in 1500, probably between 35 and 60 million. In contrast to Europe, the Middle East, the Far East, and India, there were few true cities. Along the Niger there were Gao and the great city of Tombouctou, but otherwise, cities were rare. Neither were skilled artisans and traders as common.

There were four distinct and important smaller groupings of peoples in sub-Saharan Africa that need to be mentioned. In the jungle of the Congo basin were the nomadic hunting peoples known as the Pygmies. Physically distinct from their farming neighbors, they lived in small groups attached to village farmers, whose language they spoke. In the Kalahari desert of southwestern Africa were the Khoisan. These nomadic herders and hunters and gatherers were physically and linguistically distinct from adjacent farming and herding peoples. The Horn of Africa, modern Ethiopia and Somalia, was an area in which sub-Saharan Africa and the Middle East overlapped. Physically, these people were more closely tied to sub-Saharan Africa, but culturally they were strongly influenced by the Middle East. In religion, they were about equally divided between Ethiopian Christians and Muslims, with even a small Jewish population. The Malagasy of the island of Madagascar showed physically and culturally a mixture African and Southeast Asian peoples, whereas linguistically,

they were related to the people of Southeast Asia (see Figure 6.2).

All the major population and cultural centers of the Old World were connected by a weakly developed trade network. The Mediterranean Sea, a major center of maritime trade, connected the port cities of southern Europe and the Middle East. Traders sailed through the Straits of Gibraltar to the Atlantic coastal ports of western Europe and into the Baltic Sea to the coastal ports of northern Europe. From the Islamic ports in North Africa, caravans crossed the Sahara to the cities of the Sudan. From the cities of Tombouctou, Gao, and others gold, slaves, ivory, ostrich feathers, cola nuts, and

**FIGURE 6.2**
**Major States and Regions of Europe, Asia, and Africa (ca. 1500)**

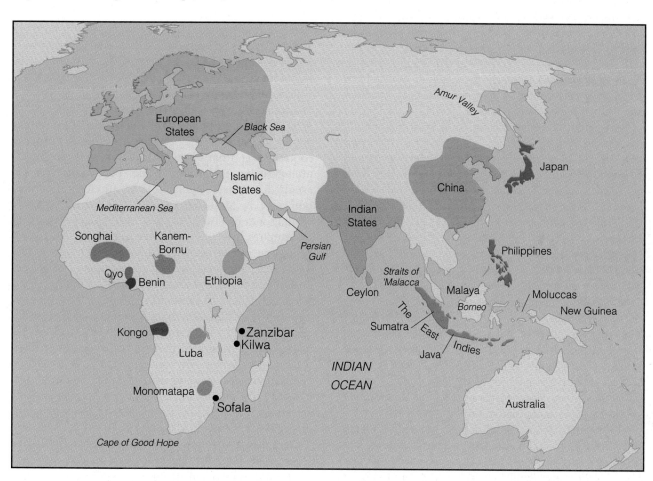

hides flowed northward. The specific nature of the goods that flowed south is not well known, but iron was an important trade item. The most significant cultural trait that flowed south was the Islamic religion. Most of the Sudanic states were Muslim, and during the fourteenth century Tombouctou had emerged as a major center of Islamic learning.

At the eastern end of the Mediterranean were Islamic ports from which caravans carried goods east. The longest and most important of these routes was the Silk Road, which linked Mediterranean ports with China. As its name implied, the most important item carried west over this route was silk, and western European gold and silver flowed to China in exchange. Other caravan trails linked the Mediterranean ports with cities on the Persian Gulf, from which other maritime traders, primarily Arabs, sailed to India, the East Indies, and even China. Cotton textiles from India as well as highly valued spices were traded west by this land-and-sea route, and gold and silver flowed eastward in exchange. The Islamic religion had also spread by this route and by the twelfth century had found converts as far away as the East Indies.

Along the eastern coast of Africa, Islamic traders from Oman had established trading ports such as Zanzibar and Kilwa, some dating from as early as the eighth century. From these ports Islam found converts among the coastal African societies. Omani traders marketed East African gold, iron ore, camel-hair cloth, slaves, and ivory in India and as far east as China (see Figure 6.2).

Within Asia itself, an active maritime trade existed between China, India, Southeast Asia, and the islands of the East Indies. Of subsequent strategic interest to Europeans was that much of this trade had to pass through the Straits of Malacca, a long and relatively narrow body of water separating the Malay Peninsula (Malaya) from the island of Sumatra (Indonesia).

Before 1492 both the Americas and Oceania were outside this network of trade and cultural exchange. The Americas were unknown to the peoples of the Old World. Although the westernmost portion of Oceania, primarily New Guinea and Australia, had some sporadic contact with a few peoples of the East Indies, on the whole the societies of Oceania were as unknown to Old World societies as the natives of the Americas.

The peoples of the Americas had originally entered the continent as simple foraging societies migrating out of Siberia over a land bridge that connected Asia and North America during the late ice age. After entering the Americas 10,000 to 20,000 years ago, these peoples became isolated from the Old World. The isolation persisted, and they developed cultural traditions that were uninfluenced by changes in the Old World. In some respects Native American cultural development surpassed that of the Old World, but in a few critical areas it lagged behind. Although some Native Americans had learned to work silver, gold, and copper, and, in the Andes, some bronze, on the whole metallurgy was still in its infancy in the Americas. The impressive temples, buildings, and fortifications of Mesoamerica and Peru were constructed by societies with stone-tool technologies and without wheeled vehicles.

The most important contribution of Native Americans was the domestication of food plants. In Mesoamerica and Peru they successfully domesticated a wide range of crops: corn, potatoes, pineapples, papayas, tomatoes, avocados, peanuts, sweet potatoes, and cacao, as well as numerous varieties of beans and squash. As a result, at the time of European contact many Native American societies were, to some degree, dependent on agriculture for their subsistence. Hunting and gathering peoples were found primarily in those portions of northern North America and southern South America that were not well suited for cultivation with a preindustrial technology.

Because so many of their peoples were agricultural and had a relatively stable food supply, the Americas had a relatively large population. Recent estimates of the population of the Americas at the time of European contact range from 80 to 120 million, with about 100 million being the average. This population was not evenly distributed. The main concentrations of population were in Mesoamerica and Peru, where intensive farming was practiced. In these regions large multiethnic empires, such as the Aztec and Inca, had arisen. According to one estimate, Mexico, which was mostly under Aztec domination, had a population of more than 25 million. Some estimates of the Inca Empire set the figure as high as 12 million. Adjacent to these empires were other, smaller, well-organized states; in Mexico, for example, the Tarascans, the Zapotec, and the city-states of the Maya surrounded the Aztecs. Beyond Mesoamerica and Peru, the two centers of Native American civilization, most farming societies were organized only at a chiefdom or tribal level, and the remaining foraging societies were politically organized as tribes or as simple or composite bands (see chapter 13).

Oceania was composed of the islands of the Pacific Ocean, and Oceanian peoples were divided into four main geographical and cultural areas. Micronesia consisted of the predominantly small coral atolls of the western Pacific. The Polynesian triangle encompassed

*The peoples of the Mesoamerica developed their own distinctive cultural traditions.*

the islands from New Zealand in the southwest to Hawaii in the north and to Easter Island in the southeast. Melanesia included New Guinea and the large island groups as far east as Fiji. Australia included both Australia and the large island of Tasmania. The inhabitants of Micronesia, Polynesia, and Melanesia were basically stone-age farming and fishing peoples. On the Polynesian and Micronesian islands, societies were organized at the chiefdom level. In contrast, the peoples of Australia and Tasmania were among the least technologically advanced peoples in the world, and they depended solely on foraging for their subsistence.

## THE WORLD SINCE 1500

With the "discovery" of the Americas by Christopher Columbus in 1492 and Vasco da Gama's successful voyage to India in 1498, the age of European expansion began.

### Initial Expansion of Europe

In population and technological achievement, Europe was not the most developed region of the world during the fifteenth century. Asia had a total population four to five times that of Europe, and in overall technology Asia was ahead of Europe. Compared with the states of Asia, European countries were small. The populations of such soon-to-be-imperial powers as England, Portugal, Spain, and the Netherlands were insignificant in comparison with those of China or the Mogul (Islamic) states of India. Even the Aztec Empire in the Americas may have

had a population equal to the total of these four European countries. The major advantage of the European societies was in military technology. Guns, crossbows, iron weapons, armor, and horses gave them significant advantages over the stone-tool military technologies of the peoples of the Americas and Oceania. To a lesser degree, they also enjoyed a military advantage over most peoples of Africa. The same was not true in Asia: On land, European armies enjoyed no technological advantage. Only in naval warfare were the Europeans technologically superior to the Asian states. These factors influenced European expansionist policies during the early period and caused the history of contact with Asia, Africa, the Americas, and Oceania to differ significantly. With some exceptions, principally in the Americas, the expansion of Europe during the sixteenth, seventeenth, and eighteenth centuries consisted of the development of maritime mercantile empires, as opposed to actual overseas colonies and territorial empires.

Because European contact took such different forms from one region to the next, it is necessary to examine the history of contact region by region.

**CONQUEST OF THE AMERICAS.** In 1492, Columbus found a new world inhabited by numerous people, who still had only an advanced stone-tool technology. Initially, the Spaniards were disappointed in their new discoveries because they failed to find the immense treasures of the Indies they were expecting. On the island of Hispaniola, where they first settled, there were some gold deposits, but most Spanish settlers quickly turned their attention to the development of sugarcane plantations and cattle ranches.

During the first quarter century after its discovery, the New World attracted only a few thousand Spaniards, but they quickly spread over the major islands of the West Indies: Cuba, Jamaica, and Puerto Rico. In 1513, Balboa crossed the narrow Isthmus of Panama and set foot on the shores of the Pacific. In 1519, Hernando Cortez landed on the coast of Mexico and by 1521 had completed the conquest of Tenochtitlán, the capital of the Aztec Empire. Cortez sent gold and silver back to Spain in quantities beyond belief. The discovery of such vast treasures encouraged the migration of others to search for still more wealth and plunder. Between 1532 and 1534 a military expedition led by Francisco Pizarro conquered the Inca Empire and took the wealth of Peru for Spain. By the late 1500s, Spanish expeditions had explored much of the Americas, from the lower Mississippi valley to the southern Andes and the Amazon valley, and had located and conquered every major Native American state. In little more than half a century the Spaniards had conquered the richest and most populous portions of the Americas: the West Indies, Mesoamerica, and Peru. More than half the native population of the Americas had fallen under Spanish political domination.

The Treaty of Tordesillas, signed in 1494, divided the non-Christian world between Spain and Portugal. The easternmost part of South America, Brazil, fell into the Portuguese portion. Although Portugal's area lacked rich gold and silver deposits, the coastal regions of Brazil were well suited for sugarcane plantations. Starting in 1500, Portuguese settlers began colonizing Brazil, and by 1550 small settlements were scattered along most of the coast.

The Spanish and Portuguese were able to conquer and occupy large portions of the Americas in a surprisingly short time. As the Spanish demonstrated in their conquests of the Aztecs and Incas, their military superiority was so pronounced that small armies numbering in the hundreds were able to vanquish well-organized native armies whose troops numbered in the thousands. Small groups of European troops could move about with near impunity throughout the length of the Americas. Only the lack of manpower limited Spanish and Portuguese expansion and kept them from subjugating all of the Americas. The populations of Spain and Portugal were relatively small, and there were never enough troops or civilians to control such a vast and populous region. Although the conquests of Mexico and Peru stimulated Spanish migration to the New World, the number of immigrants remained relatively small, averaging between 1,000 and 2,000 a year during the 1500s.

The main period of conquest and territorial expansion had virtually ended by 1600, and Spanish settlers turned their attention to exploitation of the West Indies, Mesoamerica, and Peru, where they developed silver and gold mines, ranches, and plantations. The Portuguese contented themselves with coastal Brazil and worked to expand their plantations.

The cultural impact of the Spanish and Portuguese was most pronounced in those regions directly under their control. Existing native political organization was either replaced or modified and integrated into a colonial government. European technology was introduced—iron tools, plows, cattle, horses, sheep, and so forth—as the existing economic systems were altered or destroyed to meet European needs. Indian labor was used in the mines and on the plantations and ranches that were developed. Missionaries flooded the Americas seeking converts, and they razed temples and other overt signs of the old religions and religious practices. Temples were replaced by Christian churches. In some regions, such as Mexico and Peru, native peoples managed to maintain their languages and Indian social and ethnic identity, but even these societies were given a veneer of Christian customs and beliefs. Even Native American peoples beyond direct European control were affected. Old World crops, domesticated animals, and metal tools in limited numbers were diffused to these autonomous peoples. In some regions the introduction of European items had revolutionary effects. The horse in particular revolutionized many native societies. On the Great Plains of North America the adoption of the horse resulted in a cultural florescence, and a whole new way of life evolved (see Box 6.1). The adoption of the horse had an equally profound effect on native life on the Gran Chaco and pampas of South America.

As important as these material elements were in altering Native American culture, they were not the only causes of change. Old World diseases such as smallpox, measles, influenza, bubonic plague, diphtheria, typhus, cholera, malaria, and scarlet fever were the most pervasive agents of change introduced by early Europeans. Isolated as they had been, the peoples of the Americas had no natural immunities to these diseases. Because they frequently spread well in advance of European contact, it is impossible to estimate with any exactness the size of the native populations before that contact. The massive population decline caused by European diseases is best documented in regions under direct Spanish and Portugese control. Father Bartolome de las Casas reported that there were 1,100,000 Indians fourteen years of age or older on Hispaniola in 1496. Even

To the white American public, no group of Indians typifies what Native American life was like more than the Plains Indians: the Cheyenne, the Dakota, the Crow, and Comanche. Thanks in large part to Hollywood, these tipi-dwelling, buffalo-hunting, horse-mounted warriors of the grass-lands have come to represent the very essence of "Indianness." When we visualize Indian ways of life of the past, we picture Red Cloud, Black Kettle, Sitting Bull, or some other plains leader dressed in beaded buckskin clothing, wearing a feather "war bonnet," and seated on a horse. What we fail to realize is that Plains Indians in particular, and American Indians in general as we view them, were in large part a product of European contact.

Horses were the primary means of transportation and as such were an integral part of nineteenth-century Plains Indian culture. The modern horse was not native to the Americas but was first brought by the Spanish. It was not until the late 1600s and early 1700s that horses in any numbers became available to the tribes of the Great Plains.

Before horses were available, the open grasslands of the Great Plains held little attraction for American Indians. Not only were bison difficult to hunt for people on foot and armed with only a bow and arrow or spear, but transporting of game any distance over the vast grasslands was physically arduous. Whether food or other material goods, all the possessions of these people had to be carried either on their own backs or those of their dogs. For these reasons, the Plains were inhabited year round by only widely scattered small bands of nomadic foragers. People probably depended more on the collecting of wild food plants than on the vast herds of bison for subsistence. Compared with the farming peoples who lived along the eastern and south-

BOX 6.1

# THE WHITE MAN AND THE PLAINS INDIANS

western margins of the plains, the Plains tribes were materially impoverished and militarily weak. Thus, not surprisingly, before acquiring horses, only a few tribes lived the nomadic life on the plains: the Comanche, Kiowa, Shoshone, a few groups of Apache, possibly the Blackfoot, and a few other, smaller tribes. Many of the major tribes later associated with the plains were still farming people.

The horse truly revolutionized life among the Plains tribes. The horse drastically altered the economic base and changed the life-style of these peoples. On horseback a hunter armed with bow and arrow could find and kill enough bison within a few months to feed his family for the year. Not only could he kill larger numbers of game animals, but he could pack the meat onto horses and readily transport it vast distances. Horses also allowed for the transporting of increased quantities of material goods. Tipis increased in size, and clothing and other material items became increasingly abundant and elaborate in decoration. For the first time these widely scattered groups could gather together in large camps, sometimes numbering in the thousands, for at least a portion of the year. In short, the horse quickly elevated the Plains tribes to relative prosperity.

The horse also sharply altered the relationship between these peoples and the neighboring farming tribes. The once relatively inoffensive nomads were now transformed into aggressive predatory raiders. The Plains tribes were now capable of quickly assem-

bling large parties of horse-mounted warriors who could raid the sedentary farming villages with impunity. The military balance of power had shifted.

In the decades immediately after the acquisition of the horse, the original Plains tribes flourished. Attacks on the neighboring farming peoples had a devastating effect, and many villages were abandoned. It was not long, however, before many cultivators saw both the economic and the military advantages derived from being horse-mounted nomadic bison hunters. The Cheyenne and some of the Dakota abandoned the life of settled farmers and moved westward to the Plains to become nomadic tipi-dwelling bison hunters themselves. As they moved onto the Plains, they came to challenge directly the original Plains tribes for dominance over critical hunting resources, which intensified warfare. As a result, warfare and the warrior tradition became an integral part of Plains Indian values, social organization, and behavior.

The Plains Indian culture as we think of it emerged during the first half of the nineteenth century. Given the diverse origins of the various Plains tribes, they developed a remarkably homogeneous way of life within a short period: elaborately equipped tipis, beaded (with European trade beads) clothing, sign language for communication, the Sun Dance, and the emphasis on the male's role as a warrior. It was not until the latter half of the nineteenth century that Euro-Americans seriously challenged the Plains Indians for control of the Great Plains, 300 years after they had first begun acquiring horses. Because the Plains peoples were the last major group of tribes to resist Euro-American dominance militarily, it is not surprising that we mistakenly think of them as the "essence of Indianness." ◆

SOURCES: Ewers (1955), Lowie (1954), and Oliver (1962).

the most conservative estimate of the Indian population for the island is 100,000. Regardless of the original population figure, we do know that the native population underwent rapid decline and that by 1535 there were only 500 Indians left on Hispaniola. By the 1550s the Taino and Ciguayo Indians were extinct. Similar declines were reported on the other major islands of the Caribbean: Cuba, Puerto Rico, and Jamaica. In Mexico the decline was also severe but not as devastating. One study places the contact population at 25,200,000 in 1519, with a decline to 16,800,000 by 1532, 2,650,000 by 1568, and 1,075,000 by 1605. Although these estimates are open to question, there is no doubt that Native American societies suffered severe population declines after European contact.

Disease was the major factor in the population decline, but other factors also contributed. As the native populations under their control decreased, the Europeans faced a shortage of available laborers. One answer to this problem was to "recruit" new labor by raiding other Native American groups for slaves. Thus peoples who were not under direct Spanish or Portuguese control suffered heavy losses from slave raiders during the sixteenth and seventeenth centuries. During the first half of the sixteenth century more than 200,000 Indian slaves were taken from Nicaragua and sold in the West Indies. Similar decreases in population caused by slave raiders were common in coastal regions and interior areas beyond European political control. Enslavement of Native Americans proved to be only a stopgap measure because these new recruits also died off rapidly from European diseases. New sources of human labor had to be found to fill the expanding vacuum.

Awareness of the rapid and dramatic decline in Native American population is critical to understanding the history of the Americas during the past 500 years. If the Native American societies had maintained their populations, there is little doubt that they would have eventually been able to absorb the relatively small numbers of Europeans who initially conquered them. The history of the Americas could have been similar to the histories of European contact with Africa and Asia, which we discuss later in this chapter. This decline created a vacuum that was filled by the massive resettling of Old World peoples in the Americas. Neither Spain nor Portugal sent sufficient emigrants to offset the declining Native American population and meet the increasing labor demands of their American colonies. Another source of labor had to be found. This was the genesis of the African slave trade. As early as the 1490s, African slaves had been sent to the island of Hispaniola. During the 1500s and 1600s ever-increasing numbers of African slaves were sent to the Spanish and Portuguese colonies. By the eighteenth century there were more individuals of African ancestry than of European ancestry in these colonies.

During the late sixteenth and early seventeenth centuries other European powers—England, France, and the Netherlands—began contesting Spanish and Portuguese dominance of the Americas. For the most part, these countries occupied portions of the Americas outside the limits of Spanish and Portuguese control. There were some exceptions. The French, English, and Dutch were able to gain control over some of the small islands in the West Indies, but the major region of occupation by these European powers became the Atlantic Coast of North America. During the early 1600s the French, English, and Dutch were able to successfully establish colonies along this coast. The Native American populations in this region had already suffered the devastating effects of Old World diseases, and were of little interest to northern Europeans as a source of labor. Unlike the Spanish and Portuguese to the south, these settlers were primarily interested in the land the Indians occupied, and they considered Native Americans to be a hindrance and danger to their settlements, not an economic resource. As these northern European settlers pushed their frontiers into the interior, Native American populations were evicted and forced west. Although there was some enslavement of Native Americans by these colonists, it was not as significant as in the Spanish and Portuguese colonies. Native American slaves usually were sold or traded in the West Indies for African slaves; few were kept in mainland North America. As early as 1619, English colonists in Virginia were purchasing African slaves. The number of African slaves in the French, English, and Dutch West Indies and in English North America steadily increased during the 1600s and 1700s, paralleling the pattern in the Spanish and Portuguese colonies.

Although Native Americans seldom were enslaved in the northern European colonies, their labor was used indirectly. Unlike the Spanish and Portuguese, the French, English, and Dutch quickly established trading networks in the interior regions, exchanging cloth, metal tools, guns, and other items of European manufacture for hides and furs. By the mid-1700s most of the Native American societies in North America were in regular commercial contact with these Europeans and dependent on this fur trade. By the end of the eighteenth century virtually every Native American society had been affected by European expansion. Many had already become extinct. Others were under the direct political and economic control of European colonial governments. Even those societies that had been able to retain their autonomy had seen their populations sharply reduced through disease or warfare and their life-styles changed by the introduction of European material goods and technology. No "pristine" societies were left in the New World.

## SUB-SAHARAN AFRICA.

The Portuguese were the first Europeans to establish contact with African societies south of the Sahara. Portuguese explorers first made contact with sub-Saharan Africans in 1444 and 1445 when their ships made landfall at Cape Verde and the mouth of the Senegal River. Trade quickly followed, and Portuguese explorer-traders steadily expanded farther south down the west coast of Africa. In the 1470s they reached the Gold Coast and found the area so rich in gold that in 1482 they erected a fort at Elmina to protect their trading interest. This fortification was the first of a series of coastal forts that they established to exclude other European powers from the region. By 1488, Portuguese explorers had reached the Cape of Good Hope, the southern extremity of the African continent. Between 1497 and 1499, Vasco da Gama successfully sailed to India and back by way of the Cape. By the beginning of the fifteenth century the Portuguese had established the basis for a trading empire that stretched down the western coast of Africa, up the east coast, and all the way to Asia. The problem confronting the Portuguese was strengthening and maintaining their hold against European and Islamic rivals. Trading ports were created along the African coast not only to acquire gold and ivory but also to serve as way stations for ships bound to and from Asia. The major Portuguese centers in Africa became what are today Angola (on the west coast) and Mozambique (on the east coast).

In 1482 the Portuguese discovered one of the largest states in Africa, the Kongo kingdom, near the mouth of the Congo. The Portuguese developed friendly relations with the Kongo, and in 1490 missionaries and various artisans were sent to the Kongo. The missionaries soon converted the king and many of the people, and the capital of the kingdom was rebuilt on a European model and renamed Sao Salvador. Many younger Kongo were voluntarily sent to Portugal for formal education.

In 1505 the Portuguese attacked, looted, and virtually destroyed the Omani city of Kilwa. Shortly afterward they occupied the Kilwa port town of Sofala, which became their main base in Mozambique. From this base they usurped the trade with the Monomatapa Empire formerly held by Kilwa.

Although gold and ivory were the primary trade items, early Portuguese traders dealt in other commodities as well: slaves, sea lion oil, hides, cotton cloth, and beeswax. Slaves eventually emerged as the most valuable trade item of the African coast, and this factor led other European countries to challenge Portuguese control.

Slavery and the slave trade existed in portions of Europe before European expansion. On the Iberian Peninsula in Spain and Portugal, slavery knew no racial or religious boundaries: slaves could be black or white, Christian, Jewish, or Muslim. However, the number of slaves in Europe was limited, and African slaves were transported by the Spanish to Hispaniola in the 1490s. During the early 1500s the market for African slaves in the New World expanded rapidly, not only in the Spanish colonies but also in the Portuguese colony of Brazil.

The magnitude of the African slave trade cannot be determined with any exactness. We know that the slave trade grew steadily during the sixteenth and seventeenth centuries, reached its zenith during the last decades of the eighteenth century, and ended about 1870. Estimates of the number of African slaves shipped to the Americas range from about 10 million to about 50 million, but the actual number was probably closer to the 10 million estimate. Likewise, estimates of the number of slaves taken to the Americas during particular centuries vary: estimates for the sixteenth century range from 250,000 to 900,000; for the seventeenth century from 1,341,000 to 2,750,000; and for the eighteenth and nineteenth centuries from 6 million to 11 million.

The Portuguese became the first major traders of African slaves in the Americas. In the earliest period of the trade, slaves were individuals who were already being held as slaves by Africans. However, the number of such people was limited, and as the demand for slaves increased the Portuguese turned to other methods—in particular raiding—to acquire them. The expanding demand for slaves changed the relationship of the Portuguese with African societies. The kings of Kongo allowed their subjects to trade slaves to the Portuguese, but they refused to permit them to raid for additional slaves for the trade. As a result, in 1575 the Portuguese mercenaries and African "allies" began systematically to stage slave raids throughout much of central Africa. Finally, in 1660 the Portuguese virtually destroyed the Kongo kingdom in a short war.

In Mozambique the Portuguese also increased their control over trade. Trading posts were built along the

*The African slave trade was a direct result of labor shortages in the Americas.*

Zambezi River, which led to war with the Monomatapa Empire and the subsequent disintegration of that power. In 1629 the king of Monomatapa declared himself a vassal of the king of Portugal.

In the late 1500s the English and French began competing for a share of the African slave trade by marketing slaves in the Spanish colonies. During the early 1600s, with the establishment of French, English, and Dutch colonies in the West Indies, even more traders attempted to tap this lucrative trade. French, English, Dutch, Swedes, and Danes obtained slaves along the west coast of Africa. For the most part, these new traders concentrated on West Africa, where they established their own fortified trading stations and drove the Portuguese out of many posts. The French, English, and Dutch were not just challenging the Portuguese in Africa; they were also competing for the Asian trade. To reach Asia, they also had to circumnavigate Africa, and they needed ports. In 1652 the Dutch East India Company established a colony of Dutch farmers at the Cape of Good Hope to supply their ships.

By the late 1700s the French, English, Dutch, Portuguese, and Spanish controlled ports scattered along the western coast and much of the eastern coast of Africa. Most of these posts were manned by only a handful of Europeans. Actual European settlements were few and small; the main settlements were the Portuguese colonies in Angola and Mozambique, and the Dutch colony at the Cape. Few Europeans had ever penetrated the interior, and little was known of the inland peoples of Africa. Yet at the same time the European presence in Africa had produced far-reaching effects on the lives of all Africans through the slave trade and through the introduction of New World food crops.

Slaves were acquired through raiding and warfare, usually in exchange for guns supplied by the Europeans. In Africa the gun trade and the slave trade were inextricably linked. By the early eighteenth century about 180,000 guns were being traded annually, and by the end of the century that figure had climbed to between 300,000 and 400,000.

The slave-for-gun trade shifted trade networks and disrupted the existing balance of power among the African societies. Some groups, primarily coastal peoples in contact with Europeans, faced the choice of becoming slave raiders and acquiring guns or falling victim to those who opted for raiding. As slave-related warfare escalated, new states sprang up, and there was a concurrent decline in many older states.

In West Africa there was a decline in the power and influence of the old states of Sudan. The Songhai Empire disintegrated, and Kanem-Bornu weakened considerably. At the same time, along the coast of West Africa many small kingdoms and city-states—such as Oyo, Aboney, Ashanti, and Benin—were undergoing rapid expansion that was traceable to the slave traffic. In west-central Africa the Kongo kingdom refused to be involved in the slave trade and disintegrated because the Portuguese supported and encouraged the development of slave-raiding states. Lunda was the largest and most important of these new states.

At the same time that Africa was undergoing this dramatic escalation in warfare, New World crops brought to the continent by Europeans dramatically changed African farming. During the early 1500s the Portuguese introduced corn, manioc, sweet potatoes, pineapples, peanuts, papayas, and some lesser crops. The introduction of these new crops, particularly corn and manioc, greatly increased the productivity of farming in Africa. In the savannas and grasslands, corn produced higher yields than native cereal crops, and in the tropical forest regions manioc was superior to existing starchy crops. In portions of West Africa, central Angola, and the northern and southern extremes of the Congo basin, as well as in portions of eastern Africa, corn became the dominant staple in the diet. Manioc, which was not introduced in portions of the Congo basin until the late 1800s, spread more slowly than corn. Few details are known about exactly how these New World crops affected African populations. Some researchers have suggested that the introduction of corn resulted in a population explosion that minimized the demographic impact of the slave trade. It is also clear that corn and manioc allowed for the expansion of populations into regions that had hitherto been only sparsely occupied.

Thus, on the one hand, the Europeans' quest for slaves had caused an escalation in warfare that had resulted in major losses in population and significant restructuring of African political power. However, the Europeans also introduced new crops that increased and expanded African farming. Although we cannot describe exactly what happened, we can say with certainty that the population of Africa underwent major changes. Basil Davidson (1969, 235) provides an excellent summary of the situation in Africa at the end of the eighteenth century: "By 1800 or soon after there were few regions where many polities, large or small, old or new, had not clearly felt and reacted to strong pressures of transition. Widely varying in form and power though it certainly was, the impact of change had been constantly and pervasively at work."

EUROPEANS IN ASIA.    The Portuguese were the first Europeans to reach Asia by sea: In 1498, Vasco da Gama landed on the coast of India. The Europeans soon learned that Asia offered a situation quite different from what confronted them in the Americas and Africa. The population of Asia far surpassed that of Europe, and Asia was divided into numerous highly developed and militarily powerful states. In almost every aspect of technology, Asian peoples were equal to if not more advanced than Europeans. In economic terms Asia was a self-sufficient region with only limited interest in outside trade. Although Asia offered such desirable goods as silk, cotton textiles, spices, coffee, tea, porcelain, and so forth for trade, the Europeans had little to offer Asia in exchange other than gold and silver bullion. The Europeans had only one major advantage over Asia: in naval warfare European technology was superior to that of Asia.

Da Gama encountered difficulty trading Portuguese goods in India, but he managed to trade his cargo and returned home to make a fantastic profit. From the outset the Portuguese realized that the only significant role they could play in the Asian trade was as middlemen in the inter-Asian trade, particularly between the Far East (China) and India. In 1509 they defeated the Egyptian fleet and effectively wrested control of the Indian Ocean trade from Islamic traders. Although they were militarily inferior to the Asians on land, the Portuguese were able, by entering into agreements with local rulers, to establish a series of fortified trading ports along the coast of southern and eastern Asia: Diu (India) in 1509; Goa (India), 1510; Malacca (Malaya), 1511; Colombo (Ceylon), 1518; and Macao (China), 1557. Asian goods flowed through these ports and others to European markets in exchange for silver and gold coming from the Americas. This trade was extremely limited; during the 1500s the Portuguese trade between Europe and Asia averaged only ten ships annually. Of greater economic importance was the fact that an ever-increasing percentage of the lucrative trade between Asian peoples themselves was being carried by Portuguese merchant ships.

The same treaty that gave Portugal a portion of the Americas (Brazil) gave Spain a portion of Asia (the Philippines). In 1564 the Spanish founded Manila (Philippines). Unlike the Portuguese trade that flowed westward around Africa, the Spanish ships (called *Manila Galleons*) sailed between Manila and Acapulco, Mexico. From Acapulco goods were transported over land to Vera Cruz, and from there shipped to Spain.

It was not until after 1600 that other European powers began to compete for the trade with Asia. The earliest of these new competitors was the Dutch, who in 1602 organized the Dutch East India Company. By 1605 they had established themselves in a portion of the Moluccas, despite Portuguese opposition. In 1619 they established a base at Batavia (modern Jakarta) on the island of Java. Between 1638 and 1658 they were able to dislodge the Portuguese from Ceylon, and in 1641 they seized Malacca from the Portuguese. With fewer ships and less capital, the English were at a disadvantage relative to the Dutch during the first half of the seventeenth century. Early English attempts to establish trading bases in Asia failed. Their first success came in India (Madras) in 1639. By 1665 they had Bombay, and in 1691, Calcutta. The French were also establishing bases in India during the late 1600s at Chandarnagar and Pondicherry.

While western European maritime powers were active on the southern and eastern coasts of Asia, Russia was expanding by land across northern Asia. Ivan the Terrible fused the Russians into a single centralized state during the 1550s, which allowed them to challenge the powerful Tartar groups to the east. Russian frontier people, the Cossacks, were able to sweep eastward quickly and conquer the small nomadic tribal groups of Siberia. By 1637 the Russians had reached Okhotsk, on the Pacific Coast of Asia. In the 1640s they invaded the Chinese settlements in the Amur valley, only to be defeated by the Chinese Imperial Army in the 1650s. In 1689 Russia and China signed a treaty that permitted trade: the Russians exchanged gold and furs for Chinese tea.

On the whole, the initial European influence on Asian society was not significant. European territorial holdings and populations under direct control were small, usually little more than port cities. The regions most strongly affected by Europeans were the Philippines and the areas in the Indies under Dutch political control. But such regions constituted only a small portion of Asia. Europeans had little effect on Asian economic life; they were little more than a small parasitic group attached to an Asian economic system. The most significant influence on the Asian economy during this period was the introduction of New World crops, the most important of which were corn and sweet potatoes.

OCEANIA.    Oceania was the region of the world least affected by the rise of European mercantilism. In 1520, Ferdinand Magellan crossed the Pacific from east to west and in the process discovered some of the islands. Starting in 1565, the Manila Galleon annually sailed between Acapulco and Manila. The galleons stopped only at Guam; other islands were either avoided or unknown to Spanish navigators, who held to the same course for 250 years. As a result, only Guam came under European domination and had any significant direct European contact.

European expansion indirectly exerted an influence on other Oceanic peoples during this period. By some unknown means, the sweet potato, a Native American crop, was introduced into Melanesia sometime during this period. Capable of being grown at a higher altitude than yams, the sweet potato made possible the growth of native populations in the highlands of New Guinea.

Although Europeans had limited effects on Micronesia (mainly Guam) and Melanesia, Polynesia and Australia appear to have experienced no significant contact with Europeans and few indirect cultural influences during this period.

## The World and the Industrial Revolution

The industrial revolution began during the waning decades of the eighteenth century with the production of machine-woven cotton textiles in England. By the early nineteenth century the industrial revolution included the production of steel and was spreading to other European countries and the former English colonies in North America, now the United States. The industrial revolution dramatically changed the relationship between European peoples and the other peoples of the world. The technological advances that were associated with industrialization rapidly elevated European peoples to a position of almost absolute military, political, and economic dominance in the world.

*The development of textile mills in England was the first stage of the industrial revolution.*

As a result, European peoples redrew the political map of the world and restructured the world economy to meet the needs of their new industrial economy. This new European economic system required overseas sources of raw materials as well as markets for finished goods. Technological advancements resulted in the construction of larger and faster ships, which meant that maritime commerce was no longer limited to high-cost luxury goods. Sharply lower shipping costs made possible the transportation of massive shipments of basic foodstuffs and raw materials on a global scale. The development of railroads opened the interiors of the continents by lowering the cost of transporting goods to the coastal ports.

During the sixteenth, seventeenth, and eighteenth centuries global trade and cultural exchange had developed. In the nineteenth century there was the incipient evolution of a global economy based on regional economic specialization and the production of commodities for export. As in the earlier period, the effects of this change varied from one portion of the world to another.

THE AMERICAS.    The Americas were the first region to experience this changed relationship because the Americas were more closely tied politically and economically to Europe. Just as the industrial revolution was beginning in Europe, a political revolution was starting in the Americas. From the English-speaking colonies this revolution spread to the Spanish-speaking portions of the Americas. By the third decade of the nineteenth century most areas of mainland America were independent of European political domination. These independence movements did not change the status of Native Americans because the new countries were dominated by Euro-Americans or, in the case of Haiti, African-Americans.

Although these new countries had achieved political independence, they maintained economic ties to Europe; and these countries quickly became the major sources of raw materials as well as markets for industrializing Europe. The West Indies and the United States supplied cotton for the textile mills of England, and the Americas—both the English- and the Spanish-speaking countries—served as the earliest major market for finished cotton textiles. The expanding European market for raw materials stimulated economic development and territorial expansion of Euro-American and African-American settlements throughout the Americas. This extraordinary economic development and expansion was made possible by an increased relocation of Old World peoples, in particular African slaves. With the initial emphasis of the industrial revolution on the production of plantation crops, such as cotton and sugar, the African slave trade escalated to unprecedented proportions. Of the estimated 10 million plus African slaves brought to the Americas, the vast majority were relocated between 1750 and 1850.

As industrial centers developed in the northeastern United States and as mining, grain farming, and ranching expanded throughout the Americas during the nineteenth century, the need for inefficient slave labor declined. In 1833 slavery was abolished in the British West Indies, and by the 1880s slavery had been abolished throughout the Americas. As the importation of African slaves declined, the migration of Europeans to the Americas increased. In 1835 there were about 18.6 million individuals of European ancestry in the Americas compared with 9.8 million people of African ancestry. By 1935 the population of Euro-Americans had jumped to 172 million, whereas the number of African-Americans had risen to only 36.5 million.

In 1775 the area of Euro-American and African-American settlement in North America was, for the most part, limited to the region east of the Appalachian Mountains. Within a century, however, the territorial limits of these settlements had been pushed across the continent to the Pacific Ocean. During the period of expansion, Native American populations had been quickly defeated militarily and confined to small reservations. A similar pattern of territorial expansion occurred in South America. The grasslands of Argentina had initially attracted few European settlers. In 1880 the territorial limits of Euro-American settlements were about the same as they had been in 1590. In the late 1800s, however, Euro-American ranchers swept through the pampas and Patagonia, virtually eliminating the Indian population. By the early 1900s autonomous or semiautonomous Native American societies were found only in the Amazon basin and in a few scattered and isolated pockets in other portions of the Americas.

SUB-SAHARAN AFRICA.    The initial impact of European industrialization on Africa was an intensification of the slave trade. During the mid-nineteenth century, as the slave trade declined, European economic interest in Africa changed. Africa had potential as both a supplier of raw materials for industrial Europe and a market for finished goods. This economic potential could not be realized under existing conditions because the slave trade and resulting warfare had destroyed the political stability of the entire region. If the economic potential of Africa was to be realized, political stability had to be reestablished, transportation systems developed, and the economies restructured to meet European needs. These goals were accomplished through direct military and political intervention by European countries, primarily England, France, Germany, Belgium, and Portugal, who proceeded unilaterally to divide up the peoples and resources of Africa. As late as 1879, European powers claimed only small portions of Africa. The Portuguese had the coastal areas of Angola, Mozambique, and Guinea. The British had Cape Colony, Lagos, Gold Coast, Sierra Leone, and Gambia. The French had only Gabon, Senegal, and a few coastal ports. Twenty years later, virtually all of sub-Saharan Africa, with the exception of Liberia and Ethiopia, was under direct European rule.

With Africa divided, the European countries concentrated on bringing the peoples of their new territories under political control and economic domination. Colonial administrations supported by European soldiers and native troops soon established their authority. With some exceptions, the imposition of colonial control was accomplished with relatively little bloodshed. In German Southwest Africa, however, the Herero War, which lasted from 1904 to 1906, cost the lives of about 100,000 Africans; and in German East Africa wars between 1905 and 1906 claimed between 75,000 and 125,000 lives.

As colonial authority was established, the usual policy was to institute a tax system. Taxation of native populations served a dual purpose. The revenues generated were frequently sufficient to cover the cost of the colonial administration and troops. In addition, native populations were forced either to produce marketable exports or to work for European-owned plantations or mines to raise the money for taxes. Thus taxation forced Africans into the European economic network.

Although exploitation of native populations characterized all European colonies in Africa, it reached its height in the Congo basin. In 1885, King Leopold of Belgium claimed the Congo as "Crown lands" and organized it as the Congo Free State. He then sold concessions to companies, which received sole rights to all land and labor within given tracts. These companies then were able to ruthlessly exploit the resources and native populations within their concessions. Africans were forced to work for the companies, and any resistance was crushed. Murder and mutilation were common. Between 1885 and 1908, when protests from other European powers caused the Belgian government to assume control, as many as 8 million Africans were killed, or about half the total population of the Congo.

By the early part of the twentieth century the authority of Europeans had been established throughout black Africa. The economy of the region was being developed and integrated into the European system. Gold, silver, copper, diamonds, palm oil, rubber, cacao, and other raw materials were flowing back to Europe, while Africa became an expanding market for European manufactured goods. Few Europeans immigrated to Africa, except to South Africa, although black Africa had been divided into European colonies. In most regions the presence of Europeans was limited to a handful of government administrators, soldiers, missionaries, and entrepreneurs.

ASIA.    The basic pattern of European political and economic expansion in Asia was similar to that of Africa. However, the magnitude of the population and the presence of an already highly developed economic system tempered much of the European impact. The industrial revolution had resulted in major advances in European military technology, which shifted the balance of power in favor of the Europeans. For the first time they could successfully challenge even the largest and most powerful Asian states. This change became evident during the mid-1800s. China had successfully resisted making trade concessions to European powers. In the Opium War (1839–1842) with England, and in a second war with England and France between 1856 and 1858, China saw its navy and army badly defeated and was forced to make humiliating land and trading concessions. During the late 1700s and early 1800s the British East India Company steadily expanded its territorial control in India through manipulation of internal political rivalries and limited localized wars. The crushing of the Sepoy Mutiny (1857–1858) ended any question about English political dominance of India.

By the end of the nineteenth century most of Asia had been brought under the control of European colonial governments. England had India, Burma, Malaya, Sarawak, Hong Kong, and Ceylon. The French held Indochina, and the Dutch had extended their control over the Dutch East Indies. Although still politically independent, China, Nepal, Afghanistan, Thailand, Persia (Iran), and most of the Middle Eastern countries were so strongly dominated by various European powers that some historians have called them *semicolonial regions.* Japan stood alone as the only Asian state that truly retained its autonomy.

During the late nineteenth century, as European political control spread over Asia, the economy of the area was steadily modified by various means to meet the needs of industrial Europe. Although Europeans owned and operated plantations, mines, and various industries in some areas, the principal instruments for changing the existing economies were taxes and duties. Taxation encouraged the production of cash crops for export, whereas import and export duties encouraged the production of some goods and commodities and discouraged the production of others. Native industries that would directly compete with European goods were discouraged.

The degree to which the local economy was changed differed greatly from region to region. In some regions there were large-scale developments for the production of critical cash crops, and massive relocations of populations to supply labor often were associated with these developments. Such changes were most characteristic of, but not limited to, territories within the British Empire. Ceylon became a tea-producing colony, whereas Malaya focused on rubber, Burma on rice, and Bengal (India) on jute (hemp for rope). To increase production, additional labor frequently was needed. Indians and Chinese were recruited to work on the rubber plantations in Malaya. Tamil speakers from southern India provided the labor on the tea plantations of Ceylon. Rubber, tea, and hemp flowed to Europe, and Indian immigrants in Burma increased rice production ninefold, a surplus that was in turn shipped to India, Malaya, Ceylon, and other plantation regions within the empire to feed the workers.

These comprehensive changes in the political and economic life of Asia were accomplished despite the relatively small number of Europeans present in Asia.

For example, in India during the mid-1920s, Europeans numbered only about 200,000 administrators, soldiers, and civilians, as opposed to a native population of about 320 million—a ratio of 1:1,500.

OCEANIA.     During the latter half of the eighteenth century French, Russian, and English naval expeditions explored the Pacific, charting and describing the major islands and island groups. These men were soon followed by merchants, colonists, and whalers. In one way the history of Oceania during the nineteenth century parallels the history of the Americas during the first three centuries after European discovery. The total population of Melanesia, Micronesia, Polynesia, and Australia was estimated at several million at the time of contact. Disease and warfare quickly reduced the population of much of Oceania during the nineteenth century.

In 1785 the English established a penal colony at Botany Bay in Australia and laid the foundation for the Europeanization of portions of Oceania. The pattern of white settlement expansion in Australia, Tasmania, and New Zealand during this period closely followed that of European settlement and occupation of the United States and Canada. The initially small colony of Europeans grew through continued migrations of European settlers. Native populations declined because of disease and warfare, whereas European settlements expanded, occupying an ever-increasing portion of the land. Surviving native populations were eventually limited to small reserve areas. Numbering about 5,000 at the time of contact, the Tasmanians were extinct within fifty years. During the nineteenth century the population of native Australians declined from about 300,000 to only 60,000. Tasmania and Australia had become European regions. In New Zealand the native Maori were only slightly more successful in resisting. Numbering only about 100,000 in 1800, by the 1840s the surviving 40,000 Maori were a minority population confined on small reserves.

Aside from Tasmania and Australia, Polynesia (including New Zealand) was the region most affected by Europeans. During the nineteenth century the indigenous population of these islands declined from 1,100,000 to only 180,000. The causes varied significantly from one island group to another. Easter Island was depopulated by Peruvian slave raiders who raided the island in 1842, taking about 1,000 slaves and killing numerous others. Fifteen of these slaves, who were suffering from smallpox, eventually were returned home; this had a deadly effect on the remaining islanders. Among a population that had formerly numbered between 4,000 and 7,000, decline set in, until only 111 Easter Islanders were left by the late nineteenth century. Captain Cook in 1779 estimated the native population of Hawaii at between 300,000 and 400,000. By 1857 only 70,000 native Hawaiians remained. Missionary-entrepreneurs from the United States were able to secure lands for plantations, and as the native population declined, they began importing laborers from Asia to work the fields. This influx of Europeans and Asians reduced the native Hawaiians to a minority population before the end of the nineteenth century. There were major exceptions to these patterns. Although the native populations of Samoa and Tonga declined, there was no significant influx of Europeans, and the native populations of these islands eventually recovered.

The islands of Micronesia also suffered from a population drop during the nineteenth century, declining from about 200,000 to about 83,000. However, these small, scattered islands had little to attract large numbers of Europeans. For the most part, Europeans contented themselves with asserting their political dominance and claiming these islands as possessions. Micronesians were mostly left on their own.

The pattern of contact differed significantly from island to island in Melanesia. Although the Germans, English, and Dutch politically divided New Guinea and established plantations along the coast, the indigenous population of the island was too vast to be displaced by Europeans. The same was not true in Fiji and New Caledonia. The native population of Fiji decreased from 300,000 to 85,000, and New Caledonia's native population declined from 100,000 to a low of 27,000. In Fiji, English entrepreneurs secured land for sugar plantations and began importing laborers from India, until by the twentieth century the Indians constituted a majority of the population. Mineral wealth attracted European settlers to New Caledonia, which came under French administration. By the twentieth century the population of the island was about equally native and nonnative.

## European Impact on World Cultural Systems

By the start of the twentieth century, European political and economic domination of the world was complete. The four decades from the turn of the century until the start of World War II were, for the relationship between European peoples and non-Western peoples, a period of stability and consolidation.

At this point we need to pause and evaluate what had happened to the world's people during the preceding four and one-half centuries of European expansion. The demographic and cultural changes in the world's population had been profound. Not only had the total world population grown dramatically, but there had also been major dislocations and movements of peoples, the most important of which were the migrations of European peoples (see Fig. 6.3). The cultures of all peoples had changed, some extensively. What had been the combined effect of demographic shifts and cultural change?

In no region are the demographic and cultural changes wrought by European expansion more apparent than in the Americas. In terms of people and cultural traditions, by the early twentieth century the Americas bore little resemblance to the Americas in 1492. Native American peoples had declined dramatically in numbers and had been evicted from most of their lands. Many once numerous Native American peoples had vanished. The Massachusetts, Erie, and Illinois of the United States; the Taino peoples of the West Indies; the Tupinamba of coastal Brazil; and the Ona and Yahgan of Tierra del Fuego, to name a few, were no more. Intact communities of Native American peoples survived only in the more isolated and undesirable regions. Although still different from neighboring peoples, their cultures had been drastically altered by contact. Most of the American land mass was occupied by European peoples, African peoples, or highly Europeanized mixed-blood descendants of Native Americans (see Figure 6.4).

Thus three new culture regions had evolved in the hemisphere by the turn of the twentieth century: Anglo-America, Latin America, and African America. Except in the Amazon, the Native American culture region had been reduced to a few discontiguous, widely scattered areas where surviving indigenous peoples had managed to retain separate social identities and cultural distinctiveness. Of these survivors, all but a handful of native groups had lost their political autonomy and were economically dependent on neighboring Latin-American or Anglo-American peoples by 1900. Anglo America consisted of English-speaking peoples of North America, the West Indies, and small portions of Central and South America. Although the vast majority of Anglo-American peoples were European in ancestry, a substantial minority of African peoples were also found

**FIGURE 6.3**
**European Migration and Areas Settled by Europeans** Major routes and destinations of European migrants.

FIGURE 6.4
Peoples of the Americas

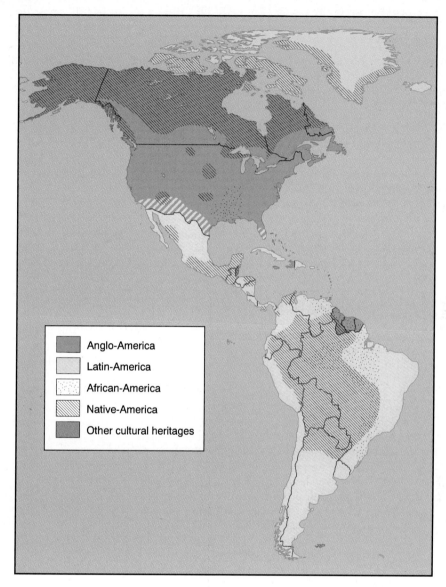

in Anglo America. Although the European population of Anglo America had been drawn from all parts of Europe, most were Protestants, and cultural traditions drawn from northern and western Europe were dominant. Latin America consisted of the Spanish- and Portuguese-speaking peoples of Central and South America and the West Indies. Regional cultural diversity was far more pronounced in Latin America than in Anglo America. In some regions the population was predominantly European. In other regions the population was predominantly African or Native American. In most areas, however, most of the population was of mixed ancestry. In terms of culture Latin-American peoples shared a common veneer of southern European culture traditions that overlay varying mixtures of Native American, African, and other European traditions. Thus there was

BOX 6.2

## THE GULLAHS AND THE BLACK SEMINOLES

The Gullah people of the Sea Islands and adjacent coastal areas of South Carolina and Georgia are culturally the most distinctive African-American population in the United States. In their language and culture Gullahs have preserved more of their African heritage than other groups. The Gullah language is a creole language based on English but with many words drawn from several West African languages. Historically, it is related to Krio, a language still spoken today in Sierra Leone. African cultural traits permeate many aspects of Gullah culture. In addition to their personal names, individuals have African nicknames, or what they call *basket names*. Some of these names are African personal names: Bala, Salifu, Jah, Fatu, and Jilo. Other names come from African clan names: Kalawa, Koroma, and Marah. Still other names are derived from Sierra Leonean tribal groups: Limba, Susu, Kissi, and Kono. The Gullahs have retained the African storytelling tradition, drawing on African folktales for many of their own stories. The Brer Rabbit stories, immortalized by Joel Chandler Harris in his collections of "Uncle Remus" tales, are the best known of the Gullah stories. Animal tricksters such as Brer Rabbit are a common theme in African storytelling.

Other aspects of Gullah culture also demonstrate their African heritage.

Burial customs, such as drumming to announce a death, stopping the funeral party at the cemetery gate to ask the ancestral spirits for permission to enter, breaking bottles and dishes on the grave so that no one else in the family will die, and leaving food on the veranda for the spirit of the deceased, are directly traceable to African practices. Until the early part of this century many aspects of Gullah material culture were African in origin; for example, their basketwork, wooden mortars and pestles for processing rice, carved wooden grave markers and walking sticks, calabash containers, and indigo-dyed cotton blankets. Their rice-based diet and the ways they prepared food strongly reflected their West African heritage. This list is just a sampling of African cultural traits of the Gullahs. A unique set of historical circumstance allowed them to retain more of their African heritage than other African- American peoples in the United States.

During the early part of the 1700s, English plantation owners in South Carolina and Georgia discovered that the low-lying tropical islands and coastal areas were ideally suited for the cultivation of rice. Lacking any firsthand knowledge of rice cultivation, these planters began importing large numbers of slaves from the rice-growing areas of West Africa, notably the region around Sierra Leone. In essence these plantation owners transplanted both rice-growing peoples and technology from the west coast of Africa to the coastal region of the southern English colonies.

Fevers and other tropical diseases were prevalent along the low-lying tropical coast and islands. Plantation owners tried to avoid the area, preferring to live inland, where these diseases were not as common. Thus most plantation owners lived for only part of the year on their coastal plantations. The actual running of the plantations was left to a few white managers and trusted slaves, who worked as foremen or "drivers." This arrangement greatly limited direct contact between Europeans and Gullahs. In many ways their life on the Sea Islands was like their life in Africa. They grew the same crops and used the same technology and material items. Although the ancestors of

*continued on next page*

significant regional variability in Latin America. Overlapping Latin America and Anglo America was African America, those regions whose peoples were primarily African in ancestry. Although they were strongly influenced by the more dominant Latin-American or Anglo-American cultural traditions, African-American peoples also reflected, to varying degrees, their African cultural heritage. Thus in the Americas a whole new series of cultural traditions had emerged by the early twentieth century derived from various mixtures of European,

African, and Native American traits and with them a whole new set of ethnic identities had developed— Canadian, American, Mexican, Peruvian, Argentinian, Haitian, Meti, Garifuna (Black Caribs), and Gullah (see Box 6.2) to name only some.

There were also migrations of European peoples to Asia, Africa, and Oceania; Russian settlers followed the armies of the czar across southern Siberia. There was a continuous band of settlers all the way to the Pacific Ocean. The European culture region had expanded at the Gullahs were drawn from various African groups such as the Mende, Temmne, Limba, and others, all had similar cultural systems and spoke Krio as a trade language. Because there was no need to learn English, Krio became the language of the group, and the cultural traditions of the different groups blended easily together to create a "new" people. When and how they acquired the name *Gullah* is not known. The social isolation of the Gullah people in these coastal areas continued until well after the turn of the twentieth century.

During the late 1700s many Gullah people escaping from the plantations found refuge in the swamps and forests of what was then Spanish Florida. There they formed small free settlements and survived by growing rice and corn and by hunting. At about the same time, small groups of refugee Creek Indians began moving south and settling in Florida. These Creek splinter groups eventually became known as the *Seminoles*. Friendly relations developed between the free Gullahs and their more numerous Seminole neighbors. The free Gullahs eventually adopted much of the Seminole clothing styles and material culture and even the language, although they never stopped speaking Gullah as well. In turn the Seminoles learned rice cultivation and technology from the Gullahs. Although

they kept their separate identities and communities, the evergrowing presence of their common enemy, the Americans, forged a close alliance between the two peoples. Readily distinguishable from other African-Americans and closely associated with the Seminoles, the free Gullahs came to be known as the *Black Seminoles*.

In 1819 the United States acquired Florida from Spain and in 1830 initiated a plan to relocate Native Americans from the east to new areas west of the Mississippi River. The original plan of the federal government was to move the Seminole Indians west and force the Black Seminoles into slavery. The Seminoles and Black Seminoles joined forces in resisting the plan, and in 1835 war broke out. The war proved to be far longer and costlier than the government had anticipated. It lasted six years, cost the lives of 1,500 American soldiers, and resulted in the capture or surrender of only some of the Seminoles and Black Seminoles. By the end of the war it had become clear that the Black Seminoles were far too dangerous to be allowed to come into contact with other African-Americans. Thus the Black Seminoles were sent west with the other Seminoles to live in the Indian Territory.

In the 1850s a small group of Black Seminoles broke away, left the Indian Territory, and made their way to Mex-

ico. In northern Mexico they were hired as mercenaries by the government to fight Comanche and Apache raiders. The Black Seminole community attracted runaway slaves from Texas plantations, and the population grew.

After the Civil War the Comanches became a major problem on the plains of Texas. In 1870 the U.S. Cavalry invited the Black Seminoles in Mexico to come to Texas and join the army. Many did, and a cavalry unit known as the *Seminole Negro Indian Scouts* was formed. For valor in their battles with the Comanches, three of these "scouts" were awarded the Congressional Medal of Honor.

Today there are four Gullah-derived groups in the United States and Mexico. The largest, the Gullahs, is in coastal South Carolina and Georgia. Although their exact numbers are not known, about 100,000 Gullah speakers still live in the community. The Black Seminoles, who still live among the Seminoles in Oklahoma, number about 2,000. At Brackettville, Texas, in a small community known as the *scouts*, live the descendants of the cavalry scouts. Finally, at Nacimiento, in the Mexican state of Coahuilla, there is a small community of people called the *Mascogos*. ◆

*SOURCES:* Opala (1987) and Bateman (1990)

the expense of Siberian peoples until by the nineteenth century, it stretched from the Atlantic to the Pacific (see Figure 6.3).

In Oceania, English settlers in Australia and New Zealand repeated what had occurred in North America. The indigenous peoples were defeated and evicted from most of the land and replaced by Europeans. By the end of the nineteenth century culturally these were "European" countries. In South Africa the descendants of early Dutch settlers had evolved into the Boers, a new

social identity, with its own distinctive language and culture.

Some African-American peoples returned to Africa. In West Africa repatriated African-Americans, known as the Libero-Americans, existed as a culturally distinct English-speaking people living among and politically dominating the indigenous African peoples of Liberia.

Although the movements of Europeans and Africans before 1900 were the most significant, some Asian peoples also migrated during this early period. Large numbers of Indian peoples settled in many areas of the British Empire—Malaya, Trinidad, Guyana, Fiji, East Africa, and South Africa. Chinese immigrants established communities in Hawaii, Malaya, Sarawak, French Indochina, the Dutch East Indies, and even the United States, Canada, and Mexico. This is just a small sampling of the new social identities that were being created and the new cultural systems that were evolving.

Thus European expansion generated a wide range of social and cultural changes. By the early twentieth century many of the peoples who had existed in 1492 were gone. Although many peoples had vanished, the vast changes that took place, together with massive migrations, resulted in the creation of still other new cultural traditions and social identities. In many respects the peoples of the world were more socially and culturally differentiated and complex at the turn of the twentieth century than they were on the day Columbus arrived in the Americas.

Only against this background of pervasive change can the material presented in the following chapters be properly understood. The information we present in the chapters on economic systems, on family and kinship, on law and political systems, and so forth has been drawn from different peoples at different times. Using cultural information dating from the sixteenth century through the twentieth century we have constructed a composite picture of the diversity in human culture. While reading these chapters it is important to keep in mind that most of the descriptions of specific cultures apply to earlier periods in their culture history. Thus a specific cultural practice or institution may or may not still exist among the particular people described in one of the examples.

## Summary

In this chapter we have outlined worldwide cultural history since 1500, touching on only a few aspects of a complex subject. The purpose of this is to show the magnitude and pervasiveness of the recent historical changes that underlie existing cultural systems.

Worldwide history over the past 500 years falls into three major time categories. First, the discovery of the Americas by Columbus in 1492 initiated a period of rapid change, in that contact allowed for the transferring of Old World technologies, food crops, domesticated animals, diseases, and people to the New World and vice versa. Although the region most profoundly affected during this period was the Americas, the effects of these changes were global. By the end of this period in the late 1700s the cultural system of virtually every society in the world had been either directly or indirectly affected.

Next, with the advent of the industrial revolution the nature of European contact with non-Western peoples changed from trade to colonialism and political domination. During the nineteenth century European political domination spread throughout Africa, Asia, and Oceania, until by 1900 it was complete. Colonial powers restructured the economies of their possessions to meet European needs.

There are no "pristine" cultural systems among the peoples of the world, nor have there been for some centuries. For social identities and cultural systems the past 500 years have been extremely volatile. Anthropologists are only now beginning to research intensively and gain some appreciation of the magnitude of the changes that have occurred. Virtually every society in the world has experienced major changes in its culture, some more dramatically than others. In addition to the changes within preexisting societies, numerous societies that existed in 1492 have become extinct and a host of "new" social identities and associated cultural systems have developed. Although most prevalent in the Americas with the emergence of numerous new mixed African-American, Euro-American, and Native American societies, this phenomenon has also taken place on a lesser scale in other regions. Thus the old view of non-Western societies and culture as unchanging is no longer adequate. The past and present culture of any society is understandable and explainable only within the context of its history.

# Suggested Readings

There are numerous excellent historical studies of world history since 1500. The following list includes only studies of more general interest.

Abu-Lughod, Janet L. *Before European Hegemony. The World System A.D. 1250–1350*. New York: Oxford University Press, 1989.

> *An excellent introduction to the economy and trade of Europe, the Middle East, India, the Far East, and Southeast Asia just before European expansion.*

Crosby, Alfred W. *The Columbian Exchange*. Westport, Conn.: Greenwood, 1972.

> *An important and readable study by a historian, showing some of the major cultural and demographic effects of contact between the Old World and the New World. The study emphasizes the exchange of food plants, animals, and diseases.*

Crosby, Alfred. *Ecological Imperialism: The Biological Expansion of Europe, 900–1900*. Cambridge: Cambridge University Press, 1986.

> *A companion work to his earlier study, Crosby shows that European expansion was not just of people but of plants and animals as well.*

Levenson, Jay A., ed. *Circa 1492: Art in the Age of Exploration*. New Haven/Washington: Yale University Press/National Gallery of Art, 1992.

> *This book provides an excellent visual impression of world cultures on the eve of European expansion.*

Mintz, Sidney W. *Sweetness and Power*. New York: Penguin, 1986.

> *An interesting study examining the effect of sugar and its production on the course of world history.*

Stavrianos, L. S. *The World since 1500: A Global History*. 4th ed. Englewood Cliffs, N.J.: Prentice-Hall, 1982.

> *A history textbook that is the best and most readable general description available of world history over the past 500 years.*

Wolf, Eric. *Europe and the People without History*. Berkeley: University of California Press, 1982.

> *A study that should become one of the great classics in anthropology, this is the first attempt by an anthropologist to describe and analyze global history since 1400.*

In recent decades a host of studies have considered historical changes within the cultural systems of particular societies or regions of the world. The following studies are recommended.

Ewers, John. *The Horse in Blackfoot Indian Culture*. Smithsonian Institution, Bureau of American Ethnology Bulletin no. 159. Washington, D.C.: U.S. Government Printing Office, 1955.

> *The best and most complete study of the effects of the horse on an American Indian society.*

Hemming, John. *Red Gold: The Conquest of the Brazilian Indians, 1500–1760*. Cambridge, Mass.: Harvard University Press, 1978.

> *Few books so well illustrate the destruction of Native American peoples as this study of European settlement of Brazil.*

Kelly, Raymond. *The Nuer Conquest*. Ann Arbor: University of Michigan Press, 1985.

> *An important study of the Nuer from a historical perspective that challenges many of the earlier ahistorical explanations for the development of Nuer cultural institutions.*

Klien, Martin A., ed. *Peasants in Africa: Historical and Contemporary Perspectives*. Sage Series on African Modernization and Development, vol. 4. Beverly Hills, Calif.: Sage, 1980.

> *A group of essays in which some of the effects of colonialism on native African populations are discussed and analyzed.*

Leacock, Eleanor, and Nancy Lurie, eds. *North American Indians in Historical Perspective*. New York: Random House, 1971.

> *A collection of fourteen essays on various North American Indian societies that directly challenges the static notion of American Indian culture.*

Rosaldo, Renato. *Ilongot Headhunting, 1883–1974: A Study in Society and History*. Stanford: Stanford University Press, 1980.

> *An excellent cultural historical study of the Ilongot of the Philippines.*

Sahlins, Marshall. *Islands of History*. Chicago: University of Chicago Press, 1985.

> *An important but not very readable theoretical study of historical anthropology in which the author analyzes a series of historical events in Hawaii, Fiji, and New Zealand. The focus of the study is how native populations interpreted and responded to events of European contact.*

Schieffelin, Edward, and Robert Crittenden, eds. *Like People You See in a Dream: First Contact in Six Papuan Societies*. Stanford: Stanford University Press, 1991.

> *In this edited work the nature and effects of the first contact with Europeans on six New Guinean peoples are examined. With this contact in the 1930s one could say that the period of expansion had come to an end.*

White, Richard. *The Roots of Dependency: Subsistence, Environment, and Social Change among the Choctaws, Pawnees, and Navajos*. Lincoln: University of Nebraska Press, 1983.

> *A study by a historian who, by using a dependence model, examines the effects of white contact on three Native American societies.*

Wolf, Eric. *Sons of the Shaking Earth*. Chicago: University of Chicago Press, 1959.

> *A very readable sociocultural history of Mexico and Guatemala from prehistoric times to the present.*

## CHAPTER 7

# ADAPTATION: FORAGING

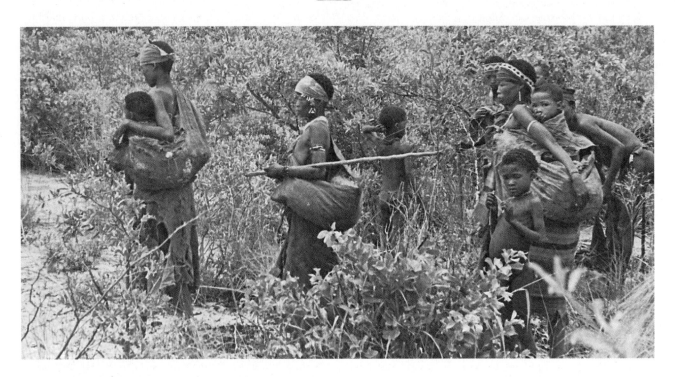

*Adaptation refers to the ways organisms relate to their environment. Foragers are people who acquire their food from gathering wild plants and hunting wild animals. These !Kung women and children are gathering wild plants.*

**CONTENTS**

Like any other animal, humans must acquire resources from their natural environment if they are to survive and persist. Food getting is an essential part of this process, and various human populations have developed diverse ways of exploiting their environments for food. In this chapter, we first introduce some useful concepts that help us to understand the technical and organizational factors involved in acquiring food and other necessities of existence. We also describe the earliest and most enduring adaptation of humanity—foraging, or the exploitation of wild plants and animals. In chapter 8, we discuss the adaptation that has nourished most of humankind for the past several thousand years—domestication, or the intentional breeding and care of plants and animals that have been selected for their usefulness to people.

## ADAPTATION

The process by which an organism develops physiological and behavioral characteristics that allow it to survive and reproduce is called **adaptation**. A useful way to think about adaptation is that the environment (or *habitat,* the place where an organism lives) poses certain problems that living things must solve if they are to survive and reproduce; adaptation is coping with these problems. Because environments are constantly changing, organisms are constantly adapting; adaptation is then an ongoing process, not a steady state.

Natural selection (see chapter 4) is the most important mechanism by which nonhuman organisms adapt. Ordinarily, natural selection favors the survival and reproduction of those individual organisms that have inherited traits that allow them to cope most effectively with conditions of their local environment. Human populations likewise adapt to the environment through genetic/biological changes. For instance, diseases spare those who are most resistant, so over many generations populations who suffer from some disease will become more resistant to it. As in other living things, natural selection works on our bodies to fashion physiological adaptations to viruses, bacteria, and other pathogenic organisms; to local climate; and to other environmental factors.

Humankind differs from other animals in an important way: We adapt to environmental conditions primarily by means of technologies, behavioral patterns, and cultural knowledge, not mainly by alterations in our anatomy or physiology. If the climate becomes colder, or if a people migrate into a colder area, they cope mainly by lighting fires, constructing shelters, and making clothing, not mainly by evolving physiological adaptations to cold. Humans hunt animals by making weapons and learning techniques of cooperative stalking and killing, not mainly by evolving the ability to run faster than our game. Technology (including both the material

*People adapt to cold climates and other unfavorable environmental conditions more by clothing and shelter than by biological and physiological changes.*

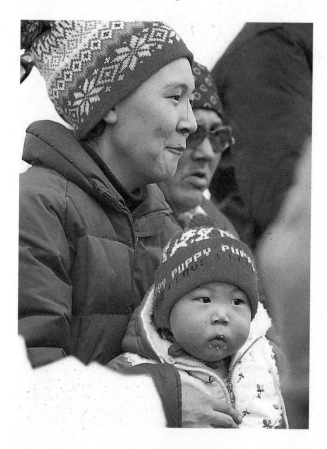

tools themselves and the socially learned skills of making and using them) and social organization allow us to adapt to a wide range of habitats without undergoing major alterations in our genetic endowment.

Any human population must adjust to three kinds of forces in the environment. The first is the nonliving—or *abiotic*—environment, which includes temperature, precipitation, terrain, water, and so forth. The second is the living—or *biotic*—environment, including the nature, distribution, and abundance of plants and animals that people eat or that affect them in other ways. The third is the human environment, or the presence of other human populations with whom a population competes, fights, trades, or has other kinds of relations. Human cultures are adapted to all of these external forces. But as we shall discuss, most populations do not simply respond to their environment; they also interact with it, modifying it to suit their needs and desires.

**FIGURE 7.1A**
**Distribution of Major Biomes in the Western Hemisphere**

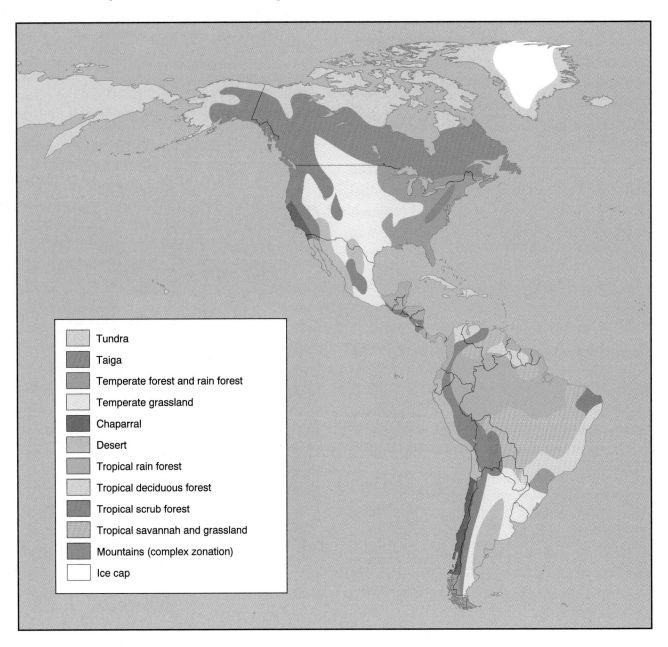

Tundra
Taiga
Temperate forest and rain forest
Temperate grassland
Chaparral
Desert
Tropical rain forest
Tropical deciduous forest
Tropical scrub forest
Tropical savannah and grassland
Mountains (complex zonation)
Ice cap

## ◼◼ BIOMES

The ways people adapt to their habitat are affected by its biotic and abiotic characteristics. In understanding human adaptations, it therefore is useful to have a broad knowledge of the types of terrestrial environments that occur on the earth. Ecologists divide the earth into several biological regions, or **biomes**. A biome is a large geographical region with similar climatic, edaphic (soil), and vegetational characteristics. Generally speaking, annual precipitation, temperature, and incident solar radiation determine the kind of soil and vegetation found in a biome. In turn, these climatic and vegetational features broadly determine the kinds and abundance of fauna (animals) that occur.

The map in Figure 7.1 shows the global distribution of biomes. (We discuss the characteristics of each biome

**FIGURE 7.1B**
**Distribution of Major Biomes in the Eastern Hemisphere**

Humans have colonized and successfully adapted to all the earth's biomes. Clockwise from upper left; southeast Asian women winnowing wheat (mountains); Inuits carving up a whale (tundra); gauchos riding on the pampas near Buenos Aires, Argentina (temperate grassland); Efe pygmies collecting honey in central Africa (tropical rain forest); Bedouin woman with tent (desert).

that are most relevant for human adaptation to it as we go along in this chapter and the next.) Ecological conditions within each biome are not perfectly uniform, and the boundaries between biomes are not as sharp as they appear in Figure 7.1. Biomes nonetheless provide a convenient classification of the earth's plant and animal communities for purposes of this text.

Some of the ways the ecological characteristics of a biome limit the methods a human population can use to exploit it are obvious: it is hard to farm deserts unless you irrigate, and it is tougher to raise cattle or sheep in a tropical forest than in a grassland or savannah. Other limitations on human adaptation imposed by a habitat are subtler. For example, there are places where it is possible to farm, but low and unreliable rainfall make it risky; so people combine farming with keeping domestic animals (chapter 8).

## PRODUCTION

The acquisition of energy and materials from an environment is one of the most important ways people interact with nature. The activities through which the energy and raw materials available in a local habitat are exploited by people are called **production.** Productive activities transform nature's raw materials into things that satisfy people's material wants. Production thus takes something that is in the environment (a resource) and makes it into something that people can use (a good or product). Productive activities are essential to the persistence of any individual human being and of any population. Indeed, some anthropologists—those who follow the materialist (see chapter 4) theoretical orientation—think that production is so essential that many other features of a people's cultural system are determined by it.

### Factors of Production

Productive activities ordinarily bring together three components. In producing a good, people apply (1) their own time and energy and (2) available technology to (3) the resources available in their habitat. These three **factors of production** may be brought together in various ways to produce a good humans can use to satisfy their material needs and wants.

Another word for the human time and energy required to produce something is *labor* or *work.* As individuals working alone or in cooperative groups,

people must expend the energy of their muscles to produce a consumable product.

*Technology,* the second factor of production, has two components. The first is the physical objects themselves, the tools. Some tools reduce the amount of human time and energy needed to produce goods, and thus save labor (e.g., hoes). Others allow more goods or a greater variety of goods to be produced from a given area of land (e.g., fertilizer). Still other tools allow people to produce goods that human labor alone could not provide (e.g., an axe used to chop and split large trees). The second component of technology is that part of cultural knowledge that people bring to bear in exploiting their environments: how to make and use tools, how to define and recognize resources, the places and seasons where plants and animals are to be found, how to manage resources for long-term conservation, and so forth. This kind of cultural knowledge often is incredibly complex and detailed, among preindustrial peoples as well as ourselves.

Labor and technology work on or with *resources,* the third factor of production. A peoples' habitat influences the kinds of resources that are available, their abundance, their distribution in time and space, and so forth. Different biomes, for instance, offer different resources. However, the resources available to a human population do not depend *solely* on their environment. The raw materials present in a habitat are not always recognized and defined as resources. Coal, oil, wind, and geothermal energy were not resources until the technology became available to use them. Likewise, resources, as well as permissible uses of them, are influenced by cultural ideas people have inherited from previous generations (Box 7.1 discusses an example of the cultural definition of resource use). Thus, habitat, material technology, and cultural ideas and beliefs all interact in determining the resources available to a people.

### Organization of Production

In satisfying their material wants and needs, people expend their own labor, use tools and skills, and exploit resources. In theory, nothing more is required to obtain life-sustaining and want-satisfying energy and materials from an environment. Stranded on his island, Robinson Crusoe survived. But real individuals and real societies do not live in social isolation: They may have to worry about whether the products of their labor can be exchanged for the products of someone else's labor, or about other individuals or groups who would like to

In traditional India the slaughter of cattle for eating is forbidden by teachings of the Hindu religion. To Westerners, this religious prohibition on the consumption of beef appears to be an example of inefficient or even irrational resource use: Indians allegedly "would starve rather than eat their sacred cows." This opinion arises partly from the observations of visitors, who see cattle roaming around unharmed in towns and countrysides even while beggars and many farmers are malnourished. It certainly looks like India has too many cattle!

The Hindu prohibition does not mean, however, that cattle are economically useless, that not eating them is irrational, or even that the country is overrun with nonproducing cattle. In India, cattle serve as resources in ways other than as a source of animal flesh. Harnessed to the plow, they help farmers prepare their fields for planting. Their excrement, spread over the farmer's fields, serves as useful fertilizer. When allowed to dry and taken to the family hearth to burn, cattle dung also serves as cooking fuel. Although their yield is low compared with cattle bred

*Foreign observers who see cattle roaming around unharmed in the towns and countryside of India, while beggars and many farmers are malnourished, conclude that the Hindu religion makes these animals economically useless. Such conclusions are erroneous.*

BOX 7.1

# WHO IS WORSHIPPING THE SACRED COW?

especially for their milk, Indian cattle also provide dairy products. Cattle thus provide traction, fertilizer, fuel, and dairy products. It is easy for Westerners to overlook some of these other uses because we use fuel-powered tractors for plowing, manufactured chemicals for fertilizing, and natural gas and electricity for cooking. Because of their religious beliefs, Hindus do not use cattle primarily as a food resource in the same way as do North Americans, but this does not mean that their uses are irrational.

At any rate, before North Americans condemn Hindus for not making efficient use of their sacred animal, we should examine the way we raise and feed our own cattle and other livestock. As discussed in the next chapter, domesticated animals are used most efficiently as human food when they convert vegetation that humans cannot eat into meat, milk, and other high-quality proteins that humans can digest. It is not efficient to feed livestock vegetable foods that people can consume because most of the vegetables' food value is lost to the animals' metabolism.

Yet our North American economic system encourages farmers to devote much of their land to the production of animal feed. In the United States in 1975, more than 90 percent of the vegetable protein suitable for human consumption was fed to livestock. For every five pounds of vegetable protein consumed by livestock, only one pound of animal products (meat, milk, and eggs) was returned to humans. Stated differently, Americans could have eaten about the same amount of protein using only roughly one-fifth the amount of land simply by consuming the food directly rather than converting it into animal products. Food specialist Frances Moore Lappé emphasizes the point:

Of the 145 million tons of grain and soy fed to our beef cattle, poultry, and hogs in 1979, only 21 tons were returned to us in meat, poultry, and eggs. *The rest, about 124 million tons of grain and soybeans, became inaccessible to human consumption. . . .* To put this enormous quantity in some perspective, consider that 120 million tons is worth over $20 billion. If cooked, it is the equivalent of 1 cup of grain for every single human being on earth every day for a year. (Lappé 1982, 69, 71)

Using agricultural land to grow grains or other crops to feed to cattle, poultry, or hogs is thus a poor use of our continent's agricultural resources. You don't have to go all the way to India to see food resources used inefficiently; you need look no farther than your own dinner plate. ✦

SOURCES: Harris (1977, 1985), Lappé (1982), Pimentel et al. (1975).

have access to the resources they are using, or about who is to perform what kinds of tasks. Production, in other words, is universally an *organized social activity:* Individuals know what to do and what to expect others to do; they know who to work with and how; they know when and where to work so that they do not violate the rights of others. The organization of production has three important components: the **division of labor**, **patterns of cooperation**, and **rights of access**.

**DIVISION OF LABOR.**     To say that labor is divided is to say simply that different kinds of tasks (specific productive activities) are assigned to different categories or groups of people. Gender and age are universal bases for the division of labor, and in most societies differences in skill and knowledge also are an important basis for assigning tasks to individuals. One advantage the division of labor offers humanity is that, in theory, productive activities can be assigned to those individuals best suited, or at least well suited, to perform them.

**PATTERNS OF COOPERATION.**     Accompanying the division of labor, and closely related to it, are patterns of cooperation in production. Most kinds of productive activity involve some kind of cooperation: People combine their labor with that of other people because this allows them to produce more goods with a given amount of labor.

**RIGHTS OF ACCESS.**     Another aspect of the organization of production is assigning (to individuals and groups) rights of access to resources. This is roughly what we call *property rights*. Generally, a given area of land or territory, or a specific resource of a territory, is allocated to some group. Members of this group are allowed to exploit the territory's resources; others are prohibited from doing so or may do so only with permission.

There is great cross-cultural variability in the way rights of access to resources are assigned. Anthropologists distinguish *ownership rights* from *use rights* and *group rights* from *individual rights*. In preindustrial populations ownership of territory and resources is frequently vested in a group—most often a kinship (e.g., family) or residential (e.g., village) group. Individual members of the group have the right (*use right*) to exploit the resources of the area, but they must do so without violating the other members' culturally legitimate rights over the territory's resources. The rights of

*Organized cooperation makes it possible for people to perform many tasks that individuals could not accomplish alone, as these Haitians recognize.*

individuals are always limited by the rights of others in the group. This is true even in our own private-property system. No individual is free to do anything he or she wants to with his or her land, house, auto, or lawn mower because some actions taken with these possessions would violate our cultural conceptions of the legitimate rights of others.

In sum, the organization of production includes who will do what and when, who will cooperate with (or take orders from) whom and how, and who has rights of access over which areas and resources. We can see that production requires the three factors of production—labor, technology, and land—plus organization. We can see also that organization is essential; without it labor and technology would be less efficient and competition and conflict over access to resources would disrupt production.

We now have a good conceptual background with which to discuss the major ways that various peoples wrest a living from their environment. In the remainder of this chapter we discuss the foraging adaptation and its influence on human cultures. In the next chapter we consider domestication and its effects on human ways of life.

FORAGERS

Foragers, also called hunter-gatherers, are peoples who make little or no effort to control the natural resources that provide their subsistence. For the most part, they live by collecting (gathering) the wild plants and hunting (and sometimes fishing) for the wild animals that occur naturally in their habitats. Hunter-gatherers have great interest to scientist and layperson alike. For one thing, *Homo sapiens*—modern humanity—has existed as a species for between 200,000 and 300,000 years. Recent evidence indicates that our ancestors diverged from the evolutionary line leading to modern African apes at least 5 million years ago. Yet there is no evidence of cultivation or animal domestication anywhere on earth until around 10,000 years ago. Humanity thus has spent only a tiny proportion of its entire history cultivating foodstuffs and keeping domestic animals; for the rest of the past, humans lived by foraging. Presumably, then, what ethnographers have learned about hunter-gatherers who survived into the twentieth century can tell us something important about how our prehistoric ancestors lived. Another reason for studying foragers is that they provide a good opportunity to investigate how the cultures of humans who live especially close to nature are influenced by their habitat. Further, as we shall see, fieldworkers have uncovered some surprising facts about many hunter-gatherers—how adequately they are nourished, how long and hard they work, and so forth. This information allows us to judge what the human species might have gained and lost as a result of agriculture, civilization, and—most recently—industrialization.

Until around 10,000 years ago all human populations lived by hunting and gathering. As methods of cultivating plants and herding animals developed in a few regions, agricultural and herding peoples began to increase in numbers and expand geographically. Over the millennia this increase and expansion pushed foragers into habitats that cultivators and herders found relatively useless or were unable to exploit effectively. As a result, when Europeans encountered non-Western peoples in the sixteenth and seventeenth centuries, most foragers were located in environments that are too cold or arid to support cultivation with preindustrial technologies (Figure 7.2). By the twentieth century, foragers were found in only a few tropical rain forests, deserts or dry savannas, tundras, and boreal forest biomes.

How does their adaptation affect other elements of the way of life of hunter-gatherers? In particular, how is production organized, and how does this organization affect the cultures of foragers?

## Foraging and Culture

Foragers are diverse in the wild foods they exploit and in their cultures. There is an enormous difference between the Indians of the northwest coast of North America, who lived quite a sedentary existence in sizable settlements, and the Shoshone, who roamed the Great Basin in tiny bands or even individual families. Despite the dangers of overgeneralization, we can identify cultural features that are widespread—but by no means universal—among foraging populations. Many of these characteristics are related to how hunter-gatherers organize themselves to exploit their habitats efficiently.

**DIVISION OF LABOR BY AGE AND GENDER.** The division of labor among foragers is largely organized along the lines of age and gender, although special knowledge and unusual skill also serve as a basis for assigning tasks. Among the great majority of foraging peoples, men do the bulk of the hunting of animals and women most of the gathering of plants. It is not unusual for either sex to lend a hand with the activities of the other. For example, among the BaMbuti of the tropical forest of Zaire, the women and children help the men with hunting by driving the game into nets. But in general, hunting is men's work.

**SEASONAL MOBILITY.** Most foragers are seasonally mobile. None of the earth's biomes offer the same kinds and quantities of resources year round. At the least, there are seasonal differences in precipitation; outside the tropics there usually are marked seasonal variations in temperature as well. Ordinarily, game animals are available in some places and not others at different seasons, and nuts and fruits tend to be available only at certain times of the year.

Foragers migrate to where food or water is most plentiful, or easiest to acquire, during a given season. For example, the Hadza people of Tanzania lived in an arid region with a marked distinction between wet and dry seasons. In rainy months the Hadza dispersed around the many temporary water holes that formed, living from the wild plants and animals in the immediate vicinity. At another time of the year, when these

*Among foraging peoples, most commonly women gather plant foods while men do the hunting. Here !Kung women gather*

*plants (left), while men provide meat to the camp with their hunting (right).*

**FIGURE 7.2**
**Principal Regions of Foragers at Time of First Contact with Europeans**

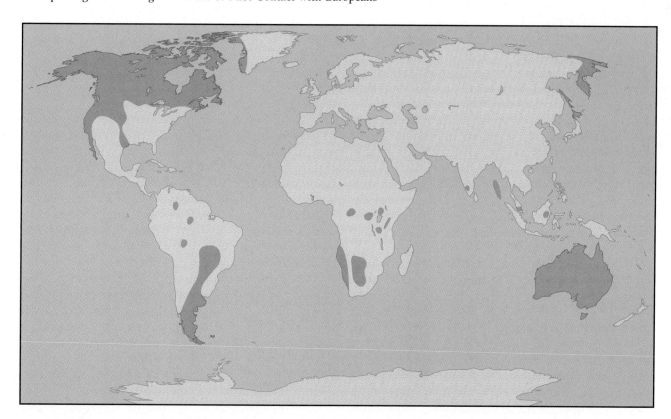

ponds evaporated, they congregated into camps clustered around the few relatively permanent water sources.

## CONGREGATION AND DISPERSAL.

Among most foragers seasonal mobility is accompanied by the concentration and dispersal of groups. Not only do people move around, but sometimes they aggregate into relatively large settlements, only to split up again into small camps at another time of the year. This concentration-dispersal pattern follows the availability of wild animal and plant foods.

A good example of this pattern is provided by the Cheyenne, a Native American people of the Great Plains. After the horse diffused into the Great Plains, the Cheyenne lived mainly from hunting the gigantic herds of bison that once grazed the grasses of central North America. Spring and early summer are the times of greatest precipitation on the plains. During this time of the year the native grasses grew luxuriant, and the bison congregated in herds of thousands to graze it. As the summer wore on, the land became drier and the grass patchier. As their forage declined, the bison broke into smaller herds, which persisted until the next spring. The Cheyenne followed the seasonal congregation and dispersal of their principal game animal. From June until late summer the Cheyenne lived as a single tribe in an enormous camp, from which mounted men hunted the bison herds cooperatively. But as the bison split up so did the Cheyenne, for it was too difficult for the whole tribe to camp together when their major food was dispersed over a large area. So from roughly late summer until the next June, the Cheyenne split up into many small camps. This was not only a more efficient organization for hunting bison, but the dispersal of camps over a wide area also provided the Cheyenne horses with more abundant winter pasture. This also provided the people with heat to withstand the harsh winters because in this nearly treeless biome dried dung was the major source of fuel for fires.

In the highest latitudes of the northern hemisphere, other hunter-gatherers live. In what is now called Alaska, Canada, and Greenland, hunting and fishing provided most of the peoples' food supply, and plant foods were relatively unimportant. The diverse peoples of these latitudes are popularly known as *Eskimo*, but many members of these cultures today prefer to be called *Inuit* because the term *Eskimo* has derogatory connotations. Before their contact with the larger world, the various Inuit cultures differed in many ways. In the early 1960s an anthropologist named Asen Balikci studied the adaptation of one Inuit people of Canada, known as the Netsilik. The Netsilik, who lived mainly by hunting caribou and sea mammals and fishing around north Hudson Bay, illustrate how the size of foraging groups varies with the seasonal abundance and distribution of important food resources.

It is a testament to their technological ingenuity that the Netsilik were able to survive in this environment, one of the harshest on earth for human habitation. The tundra is nearly treeless, for no roots can penetrate the permafrost layer, and all water is locked up in ice for about nine months of the year. The Netsilik adapted to the shortage of wood by constructing their houses from snow and ice in the winter and their tents from sealskin in the summer. In the winter igloos, carved soapstone lamps were filled with liquefied seal blubber and lit; as the blubber burned it provided all the heat and light the occupants required. Wet feet would be deadly, but the Netsilik discovered that sealskin is waterproof and makes warm and dry boots. Sealskin also could be made into a cover for the frame of the kayak used for hunting caribou as they crossed inland waters in the summer. Clothing was sewn by women from the prepared skin of the caribou. Needles and thread for the job came from the wing bones of certain birds and the sinew of caribou. Harpoons and other weapons for the hunt were made from bone or, preferably, the harder antler of a caribou. Skins, bones and antlers, soapstone, and snow and ice—these were the main raw materials with which the people manufactured the complex technology that allowed them to survive in the tundra.

Like other Inuit groups across North America and Greenland, the Netsilik are unusual among foragers because they depended almost totally on animals for their food. Other than the berries that ripened in late summer, animal flesh provided practically all their diet. Their principal summer game were caribou, musk oxen, and salmon; they relied on stored meat and sea mammals the rest of the year. The way these animals were distributed seasonally influenced the way the Netsilik organized themselves to hunt them.

To go after seals and other marine mammals effectively, the Netsilik grouped together in large camps from about January to May. After the ocean bays iced over in the fall, the people moved onto the ice to cooperate in seal hunting. The minimum size of the midwinter camp was set by the seals' habit of living under the ice. Being mammals, seals must breathe air, and to do so they keep open several breathing holes through the ice. The hunters took advantage of this fact during winter sealing.

*The Inuit (popularly known as Eskimo) inhabited one of the earth's harshest environments. Marine mammals were an important source of food. Here a whale is butchered.*

Once their dogs had sniffed out the breathing holes, a man was stationed at each. It was necessary for him to remain still because significant motion would alert the seal. Another of the many ingenious devices of the Netsilik detected the presence of a seal at the hole. A bit of down was glued with frozen saliva to a tiny piece of antler and placed over the hole. When the down fluttered from the seal's breath, the hunter struck with his barbed harpoon and pulled the animal onto the ice, where its carcass was split up among the camp's families. To maximize the chances of a capture, it was necessary to have enough men in the camp to cover all of a seal's breathing holes. This required about fifteen hunters, together with their wives and children; hence a winter settlement typically contained fifty to sixty people camped on the ice.

When summer (and the migrating waterfowl, salmon, and caribou) arrived the winter camps gradually split up into smaller groups that contained only a few families. By July most of the ice and snow were gone, and salmon began their annual run; the Netsilik trapped them in stone dams and speared them with multipronged spears. In late August and September the caribou gather in huge herds for their annual migration south. The Netsilik dug knife-lined pits along caribou routes; shot them using bows and arrows; or stampeded them into traps or into rivers, where they were speared from kayaks. In the fall the men fished through the thin ice of rivers, or in some areas they hunted musk oxen. Mostly the people lived off stored meat acquired during the caribou hunt, and the women prepared the winter clothing from their hides. By December it was time to begin the movement

onto the iced-over bays for seal hunting, for which a larger group again became the most efficient cooperative unit.

**BANDS.** Another common characteristic of foragers is the relatively small size of the group that lives in and exploits a territory. Most hunter-gatherers live in groups of less than fifty. As we have seen, these groups, which anthropologists usually call **bands**, typically fluctuate in size according to the seasonal distribution and abundance of critical resources such as food or water.

The Western Shoshone, for instance, lived in the arid habitat of the American Great Basin, which is now Nevada, western Utah, and eastern Oregon. Until the nineteenth century (when most of their territory was taken by white ranchers) the Shoshone got their meat from deer, antelope, and small mammals such as rabbits. Plant foods included roots and seasonally available seeds, berries, pine nuts, and other wild products. For most of the year the Shoshone roamed the dry valleys and slopes of the Great Basin in tiny bands consisting of a few nuclear families, or even single families. Bands occasionally would gather for cooperative hunting of antelopes and rabbits, which they would drive into corrals and nets. But a more permanent aggregation of families was difficult because a local environment did not have enough resources to support large numbers of people for more than a few days.

The Shoshone harvested one critical plant food, which became available in the fall and in most years was capable of supporting many families throughout the winter. Each year, around October, the cones of the piñon trees on the high mountains would ripen and produce large, nourishing pine nuts. During their wanderings in late summer Shoshone families noticed which specific mountain areas seemed to have the most promising pine nut harvest. They would arrange their travels to arrive at these productive areas in the fall. Ten to twenty families would camp in the same region, harvesting and storing pine nuts. During favorable (i.e., rainy) years the pine nut harvest would support these large camps throughout most of the winter. Spring would find the families splitting up again, to renew the pattern of dispersal into tiny bands until the next fall. No family or band had exclusive access to any particular territory in any season. Rights of access to resources were essentially on the basis of first come, first served, here meaning that whichever group arrived at an area first would be free to harvest its plants and animals.

The small band size is best seen as an organizational adaptation to foraging. Over a period of days or weeks (depending mainly on the environment and its resources) bands exhaust the wild resources of a given area and must move into a fresh (actually a "recovered") environment. All else equal, the larger the band, the faster it uses up the wild plants and animals of an area and, hence, the more frequently it must relocate. One reason for the small size of bands, then, is that smaller groups do not need to move as often as larger groups.

So most hunting and gathering bands are small, although their number typically varies seasonally according to resource availability. Among most foragers, the composition of bands is also flexible—individuals or families are not attached permanently to any band or to any territory but have many options about where to live and whom to live with.

The !Kung of southern Africa offer a good illustration of the band organization and its flexibility. The !Kung live in what is now southeast Angola, northeast Namibia, and northwest Botswana. With respect to their diet, health, labor, productivity, and population, the !Kung are certainly the most thoroughly studied of all surviving foraging populations.

The environment of the !Kung is an arid tropical savanna, which in the south grades into the Kalahari desert. In aboriginal times the !Kung exploited this habitat entirely by foraging. They gathered more than 100 species of plants and hunted more than 50 animal species, including mammals, birds, reptiles, and insects. Wild plant foods consisted of nuts, fruits, berries, melons, roots, and greenery. The main source of plant food

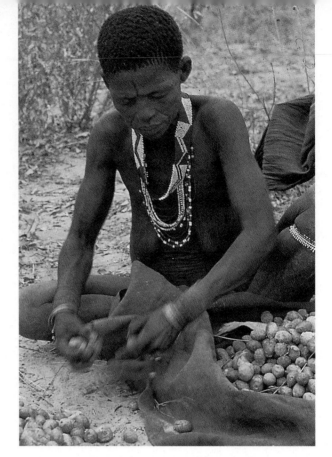

*This woman is bagging mongongo nuts, an important and nourishing food to the !Kung.*

was the mongongo nut, which ripens around April (autumn in the Southern Hemisphere) and provided roughly half of the food calories consumed. As among most foragers, women did most of the gathering and men most of the hunting.

Because their habitat received so little rainfall and then only seasonally, the availability of water greatly influenced the rhythm of !Kung life. From about April to October there was little precipitation, and practically no rain fell between June and September. During this dry season, water for people and animals was available only at a few permanent water holes, around which bands congregated into relatively large settlements of between twenty and fifty individuals. Between November and March—the summer months and wet season—temporary water holes formed, and the bands split up to exploit the wild resources around them. But rainfall in this part of the world is not reliable, neither from year to year nor from place to place. In some years up to forty inches of rain falls during the wet season; in other years as little as six inches. Drought occurred in about two out of every five years. Precipitation also was erratic and unpredictable geographically; one area frequently received severe thunderstorms, whereas twenty miles away no rain fell.

These characteristics of their abiotic environment—its aridity, seasonality, and marked temporal and geographic variability in precipitation—influenced the band organization of the !Kung. Because the distribution of wild foods and water was determined by rainfall, the annual cycle of congregation and dispersal of !Kung bands followed the seasonal distinction between wet and dry. During the wet months the bands were spread out among the temporary water holes in camps numbering about ten to thirty. When the bands first moved to a "fresh" water hole, wild resources were relatively plentiful; game was abundant and nuts, melons, roots, greens, and other plant foods were easily available. But the longer a band remained around a water hole, the more the surrounding resources became exhausted. The men had to roam farther afield in their hunting, and the women had to travel longer distances in their plant collecting. After several weeks a camp reached the point at which its members judged that the costs of continu-

ing to forage in the area were not bringing adequate returns in food. They then moved to a new wet-season camp. One ethnographer, Richard Lee, succinctly notes that the !Kung "typically occupy a camp for a period of weeks or months and eat their way out of it" (Lee 1969, 60).

As the dry season approached, !Kung bands made their way back to the area around one of the permanent water holes. These settlements, larger than the wet-season camps, commonly numbered between twenty and fifty and often even more. By the end of the dry season the supply of mongongo nuts and other preferred plant foods was exhausted and the people ate the less tasty bitter melons, roots, and gum. This was considered a relatively hard time of the year, and the !Kung waited in anticipation of the November rains, when they could again disperse into the smaller wet-season camps.

Another feature of !Kung bands also is affected by the geographical and annual variation in precipitation. Foraging bands typically do not constitute tightly knit, closed, and territorial social groups. The !Kung are no exception. In such an arid environment it might be thought that each band would jealously defend its rights of access to its scarce wild resources. In fact, the !Kung

*!Kung camps were temporary settlements. Their bands moved to a new foraging area once the time and energy needed to gather edible plants and hunt game became excessive.*

had only a comparatively loose and vague notion of "ownership" of a water hole and its associated land and wild resources: A few people returned to the same territory year after year and so others came to think of them as the owners of the area. But this does not mean that only these "owners" had rights of access to it. By merely asking permission, anyone with a kinship relation to one of the owners had the right to live in and exploit the water and food resources of an area. Because the !Kung trace their kinship ties bilaterally—that is, through both sides of their family (see chapter 11)—each !Kung family had a multitude of options about where and with whom they would live. And the composition of a !Kung band fluctuated radically because each band received visiting relatives many times a year.

This social pattern again makes sense as an adaptation. The territory to which I share rights of "ownership" may have lush resources this year, but precipitation varies so much from year to year and from place to place that I may be forced to abandon it temporarily in the future. By accepting my relatives this year I help to ensure myself of being accepted by them in possible later hard times. The flexibility in the composition of camps thus allows the resident population of a territory to adjust its size to the resources available in the area in any given year.

To sum up, most foraging peoples exhibit certain cultural features that organize their adaptation:

◆ a high degree of mobility, especially from season to season;
◆ congregation and dispersal of groups, at least on a seasonal basis; and
◆ settlements consisting of small bands with varying size and flexible composition.

The foragers whose adaptation we have described could have developed other forms of organization to exploit their environments. For instance, the !Kung could perhaps have spent the entire year camped around the permanent water holes and still have *survived* in their habitat; but this would have meant additional travel time to the seasonally lush resources around the wet-season water holes. It would have meant additional time and energy spent in the food quest. It would, in other words, have been a less efficient way to adapt to their habitat, given the technology available to them.

As mentioned earlier, the foraging adaptation is diverse. Not all hunter-gatherers fit the generalized description just presented because not all were highly mobile and lived in small bands that fluctuated in size.

In some parts of the earth, habitats were sufficiently rich and constant in resources that foragers lived in large, sedentary villages. This was especially true if a people had the knowledge of food preservation technology. By preserving and storing food when it is most abundant, a population can artificially even out natural fluctuations in resources, and sometimes this allows them to adopt a sedentary existence.

The Native Americans of the Northwest Coast (from roughly northern California into the Alaskan panhandle) lived in such a resource-rich habitat. Settled mainly on offshore islands and along riverbanks, tribes such as the Kwakiutl, Tlingit, Bella Coola, Haida, Coast Salish, and Tsimshian exploited a wide variety of wild but fairly reliable plant and animal foods. Chief among the latter were fish (notably salmon), whose annual fall spawning migrations through the estuaries and up the rivers provided the people with an abundant source of food. Each fall the Northwest Coast peoples captured the fish in fish dams and nets and by other methods and smoked, dried, and preserved them for the rest of the year.

The abundance of fish and other resources, together with the knowledge of methods of preserving them, produced some cultural features that are somewhat unusual among foraging peoples. Northwest Coast tribes were settled in fairly well defined territories, which they defended against intruders who attempted to violate their exclusive access. Their elaborately decorated plank houses were built to last a long time, although some villages moved to a different location for part of the year to exploit seasonally available resources. Unlike most foragers, the Northwest Coast cultures developed significant differences between social ranks. In some tribes certain members held formal, hereditary titles that gave them high esteem and authority over others. Rank differences were validated (and to some extent created) by the famous potlatch, a large-scale competitive exchange of blankets, large copper sheets, canoes, carved wooden boxes, and other wealth objects between kin groups. Whereas most foragers are unspecialized (meaning that gender and age are the main basis for the division of labor), Northwest Coast tribes featured some degree of specialization—artists, craftspeople, and weavers produced beautiful stylized carvings, totem poles, wooden boxes, blankets, and other objects.

The unusual productivity of their habitat, together with their own technological ingenuity and knowledge of their environment, allowed the Northwest Coast peoples to develop a culture that in many respects—

settlement permanence and size, vigorous defense of territorial resources, elaborate social ranking, semispecialization, and so forth—is more characteristic of cultivators than of foragers. The reasons that the Northwest Coast tribes were different are complex and controversial. Many scholars believe that the reliability and abundance of natural resources led to the possibility of producing and accumulating sizable surpluses over immediate needs and to different patterns of organized cooperation and intergroup conflict. In turn, these resulted in the previously described cultural features usually found among cultivators.

## Original Affluent Society?

In most of this discussion we have used the past tense to reflect that only a handful of populations still acquire much of their food from foraging. In the past several centuries, but especially since the expansion of Western peoples and their way of life in the past two or three centuries, foragers have been forced out of regions that cultivators, herders, and industrialized peoples find easily exploitable. In some cases they have been killed off intentionally. In others, introduced diseases have so decimated their numbers that foragers are now assimilated into other ways of life. We should not conclude from these facts that foraging is an inferior mode of adaptation (although it does not seem to be able to support a military force as effective as those of other peoples).

In fact, their tools and technical skills, together with the effective ways in which they organized themselves to acquire food and other resources available in their environments, appear to have served foragers well until they were forced to compete militarily with other systems of adaptation. Ethnographic work carried out since the 1960s among the few remaining hunter-gatherers indicates that their lives are easier than industrial peoples might expect.

We in industrialized countries believe ourselves to be relatively affluent. We eat and drink well (sometimes *too* well!). We think of ourselves as healthy and long-lived. Almost all of us believe that modern technology has reduced the amount of time we must work to "make our living," and thus has provided us with more "leisure time." We all know about the many pockets of poverty that exist in all modern nations. But we think that even the poor of today have it better than Average Joe of the "stone age." Indeed, we think that human history reveals fairly steady progress because our medical and technological ingenuity has largely freed us from nature's constraints.

Anthropologists have no simple answer as to whether our notions of progress and development are entirely cultural or represent a genuine improvement in the objective quality of our lives. (It is likely that many of our ideas about "progress" are created to justify the way we live and the way our political and economic systems work.) Certainly, terms like *progress* and *development* imply "better," and the relativistic minds of most anthropologists want to know "better with respect to what?" If we mean "with respect to the quantity and variety of goods consumed per individual," then progress is real, but then are we not making a cultural judgment that high levels of material consumption are inherently valuable? If we mean "with respect to the satisfaction of human biological, psychological, and cultural needs," we have perhaps a more objective criterion. But in this respect it is not clear that we have progressed over some of our preindustrial ancestors. For what we learn from foragers—especially from the quantitative data on their working hours and diet collected by ethnographers since the 1960s—is that "development" is a mixed blessing.

You might think (as practically all experts thought until the 1960s) that hunting and gathering is a hard life. After all, foragers are at the mercy of natural forces over which they exercise no control, as we have seen with the Cheyenne, Netsilik, Shoshone, and !Kung. With no human control over the distribution and abundance of life-sustaining resources, most foragers are unable to stay in one place, live in large settlements, accumulate many possessions, or produce much of a surplus over their immediate needs. But when some imaginary prehistoric genius finally figured out that plants grow from seeds, which could be planted to produce a crop in a few months, all these natural constraints on humanity were reduced. Once some ancient Einstein realized that wild animals—as well as plants—could be domesticated, people no longer were at the mercy of uncontrolled movements of their meat supply or of the natural fluctuations in numbers of game. For the first time (this story goes) the supply of both plant and animal foods became controllable and, hence, greater, more reliable, and less labor intensive to harvest. After this agricultural revolution, populations could settle down in large permanent villages, begin to accumulate wealth, produce a surplus that allowed the development of specialists, and at last have the free time

*Because they acquire their nutritional needs with comparatively little effort, hunting-gathering peoples such as the !Kung have been called the original affluent society.*

needed to develop their culture. Almost certainly, if you have learned or thought about this subject of agricultural origins at all, something like the preceding story is what you learned or figured out on your own.

Our best evidence is that this story is a fairy tale. Ethnographic studies of foragers who survived into modern times—generally in marginal, unproductive biomes—indicate that in many respects, the overall quality of their lives is at least equal to that of farming peoples. It is unfortunate that the studies are so few. By the time ethnographers began questioning the preceding tale, peoples still practicing foraging were rare. Even they were affected by Western technology, such as steel tools. So the conclusions will forever remain tentative. What we present here is some of the evidence that foragers have much better lives than most people think.

By far the best evidence comes from multidisciplinary studies conducted of the !Kung. Thanks to the work of Nancy Howell, Richard Lee, Marjorie Shostak, John Yellen, Melvin Konner, and others, we have a fairly detailed knowledge of !Kung working hours, nutrition, reproduction, health, and longevity.

Taking working hours first, in 1964 Richard Lee kept records for four weeks during the dry season for the !Kung who lived around the permanent water hole called Dobe. From his data he estimated that each !Kung adult spent an average of only 2.4 days (or about seventeen hours) per week in foraging activities. Women, it turned out, spent less time gathering wild plants than men did hunting (actually, men did much plant collecting as well). Women spent around thirteen hours weekly in gathering, men about twenty-two hours per week in foraging. Further, the elderly (over sixty) and young people, who constituted 40 percent of the population, did practically no subsistence work. This means that the 60 percent of the Dobe people who foraged supported themselves and their dependents with an average subsistence effort of only seventeen hours per week. The !Kung were not out grubbing for food all the time.

Still, there is more to work and survival than food-getting activities. The products have to be prepared, huts built, tools and clothing made and repaired, and so forth. Lee studied the time devoted to these activities as well. Dividing "work" into the categories of "subsistence work" (time actually spent foraging), "tool making and fixing," and "housework," he found that the "total work week" of an average !Kung was forty-two hours, or about six hours a day. Men worked slightly longer than women. The !Kung spend the rest of their ("spare") time visiting other camps, entertaining guests, or organizing dances—that is, socializing.

These figures compare favorably with most people who live in industrialized societies. According to recent studies of labor time in twelve European countries and in the contemporary United States, employed women spend between 10.5 and 12.6 hours daily in their jobs and housework combined, and nonemployed women average between 5.9 and 9.5 hours per day in work inside their homes. Men spend about 7 or 8 hours daily at their jobs and working around the house. All these figures, incidentally, include "weekends off"; that is, they are averaged over a seven-day period, so the figures can legitimately be compared with those of the !Kung. The worries of some people about how people in modern societies will spend the "new leisure" made possible by industrialization are somewhat misplaced.

But how productive is the subsistence labor of the !Kung? Perhaps they are living at the edge of survival and do not spend more time foraging because wild foods are so scarce that it would be a waste of energy that they could ill afford. Lee's figures do not support this view. For the same four-week period Lee weighed everything foragers brought back into camp. The major foods—mongongo nuts, assorted fruits, berries, roots, and melons—were analyzed in the laboratory for their nutritive composition. In the end, Lee estimated that the !Kung consumed an average of 2,355 calories per person per day and an average of 96 grams of protein per person per day and received an adequate supply of vitamins and minerals from their diet. These figures were well above the estimated requirements established by nutritionists for people of the !Kung weight and activity level.

The !Kung are not the only foraging population for whom these conditions are reported. Comparable low working hours have been estimated for some hunter-gatherers in Australia, for the Hadza of Tanzania, and for the BaMbuti pygmies of Zaire. Studies such as these have led some anthropologists to conclude that foragers are "the original affluent society" because they seem to acquire their food with minimal expenditure of time and energy. As always, we need to be careful with such sweeping generalizations about some segment of humanity: The Inuit of the Arctic, the Western Shoshone, and some other foragers living in harsher biomes undoubtedly had a much harder time acquiring food than the tribes of California and the Northwest Coast. Nonetheless, we have many reasons to believe that in general the hunting and gathering way of life followed by humanity for most of its existence was efficient and satisfying.

If this is true, we might well wonder why people ever abandoned foraging for the cultivation of domesticated plants. The answer is probably that cultivation does offer certain advantages over hunting and gathering. In the next chapter we consider adaptations based on domestication of plants and animals and some of the implications of domestication for human cultures.

## SUMMARY

Adaptation is the process by which organisms acquire characteristics that allow them to survive and reproduce in their habitats. Humans adapt to changes in their environments primarily by cultural changes, not by biological changes. This chapter discusses various components of adaptation, and one major variety of human adaptation—foraging.

Part of a population's adaptation is production—activities by which people exploit the raw materials and energy available in their environments. By expending their labor and applying technology to the raw materials they culturally define as resources, people transform resources into goods that satisfy their wants and needs. Because production is nearly everywhere a social activity, production must be organized: Labor must be divided up, patterns of cooperation must be decided on and regulated, and rights of access to natural resources must be assigned. Production thus requires organization as well as labor, technology, and resources.

Foragers, or hunter-gatherers, adapt to their habitats not by controlling the distribution and abundance of resources but by exploiting resources when and where they are naturally available. Until about 10,000 years ago all humans were foragers, but cultivators, pastoralists, and industrial peoples have spread into the biomes suitable for their mode of adaptation, and today only a handful of foragers survive.

There is great diversity in the foraging adaptation; yet certain patterns predominate, and a foraging existence has certain widespread effects on the cultures of those people who live(d) by it. The most common elements of the foraging way of life include high rates of mobility;

regular and usually seasonally based congregation and dispersal of groups; and small, flexible units called *bands* as the major enduring territorial-based association. Not all foragers exhibited these characteristics. Where resources were abundant and reliable, as on the North American Northwest Coast, people settled in fairly permanent villages and differences in rank developed.

Life among foragers was not as nasty, brutish, and short as sometimes it is made out to be. The few quantitative ethnographic studies made of those foragers who survived into the mid-twentieth century suggest that they did not have to work long and hard in the food quest, nor in other kinds of work, and that their diets were adequate. If anything, most foragers studied worked fewer hours than many cultivators. They appear to have had more leisure than most citizens of modern industrialized nations.

## KEY TERMS

adaptation
biome
production
factors of production
division of labor

patterns of cooperation
rights of access
foragers (hunter-gatherers)
bands

## SUGGESTED READINGS

Bicchieri, M. G., ed. *Hunters and Gatherers Today*. New York: Holt, Rinehart and Winston, 1972.

*A collection of original short ethnographies covering eleven twentieth-century foraging societies scattered throughout the world.*

Campbell, Bernard. *Human Ecology*. New York: Aldine, 1985.

*Describes how humans have adapted to various biomes, both prehistorically and today.*

Cohen, Yehudi. *Man in Adaptation: The Cultural Present*. Chicago: Aldine, 1974.

*A collection of important essays on human adaptation, many of which examine foraging societies.*

Jochim, Michael A. *Strategies for Survival*. New York: Academic Press, 1981.

*An advanced, theoretically oriented textbook with a novel approach.*

Lee, Richard B., and Irven DeVore, eds. *Man the Hunter*. Chicago: Aldine, 1968.

*Contains thirty-six articles on foragers from around the world.*

Schrire, Carmel, ed. *Past and Present in Hunter-Gatherer Studies*. Orlando, Fla.: Academic Press, 1984.

*A collection of essays that attack many of the more popular ideas about foraging societies.*

**The following ethnographies are excellent descriptions of particular foraging groups.**

Balikci, Asen. *The Netsilik Eskimo*. Prospect Heights, Ill.: Waveland Press, 1989.

*A study of Netsilik adaption, technology, kinship, marriage, and religion.*

Hoebel, E. Adamson. *The Cheyenne*. New York: Holt, Rinehart and Winston, 1978.

*A reconstruction of Cheyenne life during the mid-nineteenth century.*

Holmberg, Allan R. *Nomads of the Long Bow*. Garden City, N.Y.: American Museum of Natural History, 1969.

*A very readable and interesting account of Siriono, a foraging society living in the tropical forest of eastern Bolivia.*

Jenness, Diamond. *The People of the Twilight*. Chicago: University of Chicago Press, 1959.

*A highly readable, classic account of Inuit life in the Canadian Arctic based on field research conducted between 1913 and 1918.*

Lee, Richard. *The Dobe !Kung: Foragers in a Changing World*. Fort Worth, Texas: Harcourt Brace Jovanovich, 1984.

*A study of the !Kung of the Kalahari desert of southern Africa.*

Steward, Julian. *Basin-Plateau Aboriginal Sociopolitical Groups*. Smithsonian Institution, Bureau of American Ethnography, Bulletin no. 120. Washington, D.C.: U.S. Government Printing Office, 1938.

*A classic study of the economy and culture of the Native American groups who lived in the Great Basin and Plateau region of the western United States.*

Thomas, Elizabeth Marshall. *The Harmless People*. Revised edition. New York: Vintage, 1989.

*A readable account of the !Kung written from a personal perspective.*

Turnbull, Colin. *The Forest People*. New York: Simon and Schuster, 1962.

*An ethnography of the BaMbuti (pygmies) of Zaire. Good description of their hunting and organization.*

Van Stone, James. *Athapaskan Adaptations: Hunters and Fishermen of the Subarctic Forest*. Chicago: Aldine, 1974.

*A study examining the Native American groups of interior Alaska and northwestern Canada.*

## CHAPTER 8

# ADAPTATION: DOMESTICATION

*Adaptations based on the domestication of plants and animals dramatically affected human cultures. These rice terraces in mountainous Nepal require coordination to supply irrigation water.*

## CONTENTS

Domestication—or the intentional planting of food crops and the taming of certain species of animals—was probably the major adaptive transformation in the history of humanity. Once plant foods began to be intentionally planted and cared for, enormous changes in human cultures followed. Because they could produce more food in a given area of land, people began to remain in one place for long periods, and they settled in more permanent and much larger villages. Whole new ways of organizing groups and societies eventually developed, giving rise to cultures much different from the bands of hunters and gatherers. In this chapter we discuss adaptations based on domesticated plants and animals. We also consider some of the major changes in cultural systems that resulted from farming and herding.

## ADVANTAGES OF DOMESTICATION

For tens of thousands of years, foraging nourished humanity well enough to allow hunting and gathering bands to spread over most of the land surface of the earth. As we saw in chapter 7, most evidence suggests that hunters and gatherers usually were well nourished and healthy and did not have to work long and hard to acquire their food. However, hunting and gathering suffers from one major disadvantage compared with other adaptations: the number of people that can be supported per unit of land by foraging is relatively small. Only rarely does the population density of foragers rise above one or two per square mile; in many regions several square miles of foraging area are needed to support a single individual.

The reason that foraging can support only low population densities seems clear: Uncontrolled nature is indifferent to human desires, so the plants and animals that foragers use do not always occur in the abundance

they would like and are not always found when and where people would like them to be. Until people began to exert some control (which is never total) over the distribution and abundance of their food supply, the number of people that an area could support could not rise above a fixed limit. If an area's population rose above its long-term **carrying capacity**, either the environment degraded because natural food resources were harvested at a rate greater than their rate of recovery or part of the population left the region. In fact, this budding off and subsequent dispersal of people due to local population pressure may be the principal reason for humanity's geographical expansion across the globe in prehistoric times.

Planting (cultivating) crops and keeping domesticated animals offers one major advantage over foraging: a great many more people can be fed from a given area of land. In effect, cultivation (and, to a lesser degree, herding animals) raises the carrying capacity of the available territory, supporting greater population densities.

Cultivation supports higher population densities for several reasons. The main one is that virtually all the plants growing in a cultivated area (a garden plot or field) are edible by humans. In essence, cultivators

*As this just harvested Japanese rice field illustrates, plant cultivation makes it possible to produce far more food on an area of land than hunting and gathering. The population density of cultivators is correspondingly far higher than that of foragers.*

The domestication of plants and animals occurred independently in the Old World (Europe, Asia, Africa) and the New World (North and South America). Before the age of European colonization the crops grown in the two hemispheres were completely different. A description of where some of the most familiar food crops were first grown follows.

## OLD WORLD CROPS

Apparently, the first domestication occurred in southwest Asia (including parts of modern Iran, Iraq, and Turkey). Wheat, barley, lentils, peas, carrots, figs, almonds, pistachios, dates, and grapes were first grown in this region. Oats, cabbages, lettuce, beets, and asparagus were first domesticated in the Mediterranean. In West Africa, sorghum, finger millet, watermelons, and African rice were domesticated; sorghum and millet still feed millions of people on the African continent. Oriental rice, eggplants, cucumbers, bananas, taro, and coconuts originated in southern Asia and South-

## BOX 8.1

# DOMESTICATES IN THE OLD AND NEW WORLDS

east Asia. Soybeans, citrus fruits, and tea were domesticated in China. We get our morning caffeine from coffee, first domesticated in Ethiopia.

## NEW WORLD CROPS

Maize, red pepper, avocado, cacao, and the squash family (squash, pumpkins, and gourds) originated in Central America and Mexico. From Peru came numerous crops that are still important to the region and indeed to the world, including potatoes, sweet potatoes, and lima beans. From elsewhere in South America came manioc, peanuts, pineapple, Brazil nuts, and cashews.

Some plants were domesticated not just once but several times in various parts of the world. Separate species of rice were domesticated in Africa and Asia, apparently independently. Cotton was domesticated independently in three places: South America, Central America, and either in India or Africa. Three yam species were grown in West Africa, Southeast Asia, and tropical South America.

In the two or three centuries after Spain, Portugal, France, Britain, and the Netherlands established colonies in most of the preindustrial world, many of these crops were taken to other continents. As a result, most people in the modern world are not aware of the origins of the plant foods they consume every day. North American meals include roots, greens, grains, seeds, and fruits that were originally domesticated in various parts of the earth. We all owe much of our diet to the prehistoric peoples of the Middle East, Asia, Africa, Mexico, Peru, and elsewhere. ✦

*SOURCE:* Fagan (1986).

select areas of their habitat and attempt to control the kinds and numbers of plants that grow there. So the domesticated plants (or *cultigens*) grow more densely in plots or fields than do the wild plants gathered by foragers. Most modern scholars believe that this benefit—supporting larger numbers of people on a given area of land—is the chief (and perhaps the only) advantage of cultivation over hunting and gathering. (As we shall see, this benefit is far from cost-free.)

In the Old World, plant domestication was accompanied by the taming of several species of herd animals, including sheep, goats, horses, and cattle. These animals were kept for their hides, wool, meat, and milk as well as for their ability to carry heavy loads. Animal domestication reduced, and eventually nearly eliminated in some areas, the time men devoted to hunting. When

harnessed to the plow, cattle, horses, and water buffalo also supplemented human labor in farming.

The prehistoric origins of plant domestication are outside the scope of this text. Suffice it to say that in the Old World, domestication had occurred by about 10,000 years ago in the Middle East and by about 9,000 years ago in southeast Asia. In the next few thousand years it spread to encompass most of the environments in southern Asia, Africa, and Europe that were well suited to it. In the New World a different set of plant species were domesticated in Mexico by 5,000 years ago and in northern Peru by 4,000 years ago (see Box 8.1). Unlike the Old World, the Americas contained few herd animals suitable for domestication; only llamas, alpacas, guinea pigs, dogs, and turkeys were kept by people until after European colonization of the two continents.

(What about the horse, on which some Native American peoples were so intimately dependent in historic times? It was domesticated about 5,000 years ago on the grasslands of Asia—possibly in Ukraine—and brought to the New World by the Spanish. It did not reach North America until the 1600s. It was not until then that the Indians mounted horses to fight off white settlers and hunt bison.)

So the domestication of plants and animals occurred not just once, but several times in prehistory and in different parts of the world. The main advantage of adaptations based on domestication is that they can support many more people per unit of available territory. The remainder of this chapter describes the various forms of domestication found among humanity today and analyzes the profound impacts of domestication on human ways of life. To organize our discussion, we divide this chapter into (1) adaptations based mainly on domesticated plants, or **cultivation**, and (2) adaptations based on domesticated animals, or **pastoralism**.

## CULTIVATION

Cultivators acquire their vegetable foods by creating and maintaining an artificial community of plants that have been intentionally selected for their usefulness to humans. These cultigens are the product of generations of human selection for their edibility, resistance to disease and drought, suitability for local soil and climate, and so forth. In the process of domesticating a plant species, people select (sometimes unintentionally) those individual plants with the characteristics they like. They cultivate (plant, care for, and harvest) those individual plants with the greatest usefulness and allow the less desirable varieties to go unpropagated. Modern cultivators thus enjoy the benefits of the efforts of hundreds of past generations, from whom they have inherited a store of cultigens with useful genetic qualities.

As mentioned, the chief advantage of cultivation over foraging is its ability to support more people per unit of land. To get this benefit, people must pay some costs. Cultivators create and maintain an artificial community of plants on their plots. Such creation and maintenance require labor, time, and energy. First the plot must be prepared for planting. The plants that occur naturally on the plot must be removed—they become defined as unwanted "weeds." In some kinds of cultivation the landscape itself must be modified by constructing furrows, dikes, ditches, terraces, or other artificial landforms. Second, the crops must be planted, requiring

more labor. Third, natural processes destroy the artificial plant community and landscape that people have created: weeds invade and compete for light and soil nutrients, animal pests are attracted to the densely growing cultigens, and rainfall and floods may wash away physical improvements. Cultivators, therefore, must "beat back nature" by periodically removing weeds, protecting against pests, rebuilding earthworks, and so forth. Fourth, the act of cultivation itself reduces the suitability of a site for future harvests by reducing soil fertility if nothing else. In future years the cultivators must somehow restore their plots to a usable condition or their yields will fall. All these necessities require labor and other kinds of energy expenditures.

Numerous types of cultivation exist, depending on environmental conditions (such as soil, temperature, and rainfall), the types of crops grown, and the technology used in working the land. Two of the most important differences between cultivation systems are (1) the frequency with which particular plots are cropped and (2) the tools and kinds of energy used to keep the system running.

*Cropping frequency* refers to how often a particular plot of land is planted and harvested (how frequently a plot is used for cultivation). In *extensive* land use systems, plots are planted, worked, and harvested for only a year or two. They then are left alone for several years or, in some cases, for two or three decades. During this resting (or *fallow*) period, as the natural vegetation regrows it restores fertility, shades out weed species, and reduces insect infestations. In *intensive* land use the same plot is cultivated almost every year. In tropical areas where temperature, sunlight, and available water allow, the same plot may be planted and harvested two or even three times each year. Extensive and intensive are relative terms. We can compare cultivation systems to each other based on their degree of intensity: the more intensive a system, the more frequently plots are planted and harvested. The intensity of a system is directly related to the number of people who must be supported from the cultivation system: The more intense the land use, the more people can be supported per acre of available land.

The *technology and energy sources* used are also major factors in distinguishing types of cultivation. Some tools—such as hoes, shovels, rakes, and digging sticks—require only the energy of human muscles to operate. Here human labor provides most of the energy needed to clear, plant, maintain, and harvest plots. Other systems add animal muscle energy to human labor. Animal power is used to pull plows, power irrigation works, and fertilize fields. Still other (modern, twentieth-century) systems largely dispense with both human and animal energy and rely on inanimate power sources such as electricity and fossil fuels. As with land use, no sharp boundary exists between these technological and energetic systems.

We can use these two sets of differences to identify three basic types of cultivation:

✦ **Horticulture.** Technology and energy sources include mainly hand tools powered by the cultivators' own muscles. Land use tends to be extensive, meaning that plots are cultivated for a year or two and then abandoned to fallow for several years to allow their renewal.

✦ **Intensive agriculture.** People plant and harvest their crops semiannually, annually, or biannually, so land use is intensive. Old World intensive agriculturalists used the animal-powered plow to turn the soil over before planting. In regions of inadequate or seasonally variable rainfall, irrigation works were constructed to provide water. In the Americas there were no domesticated animals suitable for harnessing to plows, and hence no plows until the settlement of the New World by Europeans. Other methods were adopted by New World intensive agriculturalists to keep plots under cultivation for many years.

✦ **Mechanized agriculture.** Farmers also use land intensively. This type of cultivation is made possible by

*Over the centuries, various peoples have developed a variety of specific technologies used in cultivating the soil. Some tools are powered by human muscles, as in highland Guatemala (upper left). Other cultivators harness the muscle energy of oxen or other domesticated animals (upper right). Where natural rainfall is inadequate or ill-timed, irrigation is used to increase yields, as in this Thailand rice paddy (lower left). Recently, farm machinery powered by fossil fuels has replaced both human labor and animal power as a source of energy inputs into agriculture (lower right).*

the energy and materials supplied by complex machinery, irrigation facilities, artificial fertilizers and pesticides, and other products of the modern agricultural supply industry. This high-tech agriculture allows a high degree of control over ecological conditions in agricultural fields, and hence is enormously productive in yields. But it, too, has its costs, as we shall see in part 4.

Human muscle power is used in all three kinds of cultivation, although in mechanized agriculture it is quite unimportant compared with other sources of energy.

In the remainder of this chapter we concentrate on horticulture and intensive agriculture, the two preindustrial systems that anthropologists have studied most. Mechanized agriculture did not even exist until the twentieth century because it is a product of industrialization. The mechanized farmers of the developed, industrialized nations of North America, Europe, and Japan rely on the market for their livelihood. They purchase their machinery, agricultural chemicals, fuel and electricity, and other inputs from the market, and they sell their product to canneries, food processors, middlemen, and consumers. All these inputs require large amounts of energy, metals and minerals, water, and other resources, on which modern farmers are dependent and that are quite expensive.

In these and other ways modern *commercial* farmers differ from the *subsistence* farmers of much of the preindustrial world. The latter grow much or even all their own food and have no national government or social welfare system to bail them out when harvests are insufficient for their food needs. Not surprisingly, then, people who rely on horticulture or intensive agriculture to support themselves usually know very well how to farm their land. Furthermore, their traditional methods rely mainly on resources that are locally available and inexpensive, and the technology does not require huge amounts of energy to be effective. These are good points to keep in mind the next time you hear that "traditional" agricultural methods need to be replaced with "modern" ones. We return to this issue when we discuss world hunger in chapter 19.

## ◼◼ HORTICULTURE

Horticultural peoples break up the soil using only hand tools, such as hoes, spades, and sharpened sticks. They clear the land for planting with simple tools such as knives, adzes, and axes, although fire is also frequently used for removing unwanted trees and grasses. Usually they do not fertilize the earth or increase the supply of water to their fields by irrigating. Although horticulture usually is regarded as the simplest form of raising crops, it is nonetheless true cultivation. That is, the crops are fully domesticated—and have been for millennia—and the people expend much time and energy creating and maintaining the artificial community of plants they raise.

Horticulturalists vary in the way they obtain meat. Some—such as those who live in the Amazon basin of South America—continue to rely largely on wild game and, therefore, are hunters and fishers as well as horticulturalists. Others keep a stock of domesticated animals, such as cattle, pigs, chickens, dogs, or goats, which supplement their primary reliance on cultivated foods. By definition, horticultural peoples do not keep domesticated animals for purposes of powering the plow.

Horticulture is a subsistence method that works in a variety of environments. Of the major biomes, only in the tundra and northern coniferous forests is it absent. It is most common in temperate and tropical forests and in temperate and tropical grasslands and savannas (compare Figure 7.1 with Figure 8.1). Some people practice horticulture even in deserts and mountains, although in these biomes it usually is accompanied by herding (for reasons discussed later). Two abiotic factors seem to limit its overall distribution. One is low average temperature in high latitudes or altitudes, which reduces the length of the growing season. The other is insufficient water availability, which makes cultivation without irrigation impossible or too risky to be viable.

The cultures of horticultural peoples differ from those of foragers in several respects. First, with a dense community of edible plants growing under partly controlled conditions in a small area, the size of horticultural settlements increases. Rather than living in bands or camps of around twenty to fifty, horticulturalists aggregate into villages, sometimes numbering in the hundreds.

Second, these settlements are more permanent than those of foraging bands; villages remain in the same location for a longer time, usually years, decades, or centuries rather than the weeks or months typical of foragers. This relative permanence is not simply because cultivation allows people to settle down, as is often thought. Although cultivation does in fact allow a more sedentary existence, of equal importance is the fact that it provides a positive incentive for increased sedentariness. The members of a horticultural village have in-

FIGURE 8.1
Principal Regions of Horticulture at Contact Period

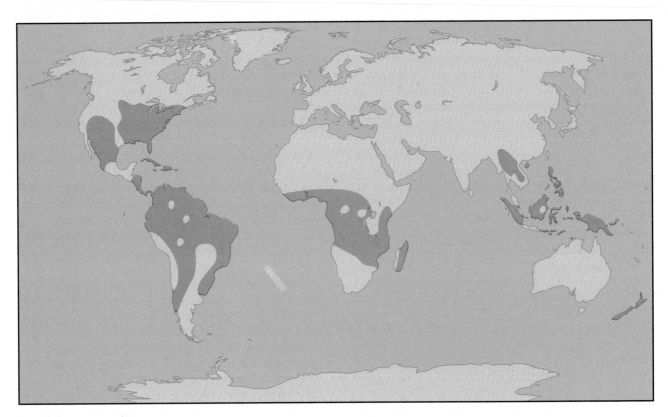

vested considerable labor in creating their gardens; some of this labor would be wasted if they moved away before the gardens were fully harvested or before the plot was used to its full potential over many growing seasons. This labor input makes horticulturalists—and in fact all cultivators—reluctant to abandon an area that has been successfully cultivated. Thus the labor investment encourages sedentariness by raising the costs of premature mobility.

In chapter 7 we noted that adaptation involves more than just applying technology and labor to raw materials to transform them into goods. It requires also that people develop an organization that allows them to produce food and other necessities efficiently, given their technology, local environmental conditions, and the resources they exploit in their habitat. These organizational features of a population include division of labor, patterns of cooperation in production, and assignment of rights of access to resources. We already have seen some of the ways hunter-gatherers organize themselves to exploit their environments. Do horticultural peoples exhibit a similar set of widespread organiza-

tional patterns? To broaden the question, do they share many common cultural features?

Unfortunately for our desire for simplicity and consistency, the answer is no. Horticultural peoples are diverse in the ways they organize production activities and in their cultural systems generally. In some the drudgery of day-in, day-out subsistence labor is allocated largely to women, and men spend much of their time politicking, hunting, guarding the settlement, or making wealth objects. In others garden work is split up among the sexes in various ways: The men may take on the heavy work of clearing new land with axes or knives, whereas the women may do the planting, weeding, and harvesting.

Cooperative patterns and decision-making authority also vary. Among some peoples a whole village will clear and plant a common parcel of land as a single unit, with village elders or leaders deciding when and where the work will occur. Sometimes the members of a large kin group work together. In other populations individual families work alone in their gardens and the family heads make most of the important cultivation decisions.

A similar degree of variation exists in how rights of access to land are assigned to individuals and groups. Sometimes any land not under cultivation at the moment is virtually free to all—whoever clears and plants an unused parcel first has full rights to cultivate it so long as he or she works that land; but once they have completed their last harvest, the plot again becomes freely available. Among other horticulturalists all land (in use or not) is held collectively by one or another kin group; the head of each group is responsible for granting use rights over specific plots of land to individual members. In other systems individuals or nuclear families have ownership rights to specific tracts of land, which they may pass along to their offspring or dispose of in any way they choose.

Thus generalizing about horticulturalists can be even more misleading than doing so about foragers. We can, however, make one generalization that applies to most of these populations: In horticulture, families or other kinds of kinship groups invest their labor in improving a specific and relatively well defined territory. Each kin group lays a claim to a specific area of land by clearing, planting, and applying their labor to it. Their claim (that is, their rights over a specific area, minimally including the right to deny other people access to it) arises from their having worked on the land, improving its usefulness to humans. Everyone with a claim to a specific parcel passes his or her rights along to his or her children. In any generation any given individual or family group thus has ownership rights (recall here that these vary cross-culturally) over a specific territory. This territory includes the gardens they are cultivating. It also frequently includes abandoned plots that they or their ancestors cultivated in the past and to which they or their children may return in future years.

In studying how horticultural peoples allocate rights of access to resources, anthropologists usually find ownership rights by kin groups over specific parcels of land with relatively well defined boundaries. With foragers it is more common to find use rights over large territories that have vague boundaries. Further, kin groups in horticultural populations usually claim ownership over the land itself because the earth may be made productive by planting crops on it. For foragers it usually is the wild resources of the territory over which any use rights are exercised because the territory itself is valuable only because of the wild plants and animals that naturally occur on it.

Numerous subtypes of horticulture are practiced in the preindustrial world. Here we discuss only two of the most widespread: *dry land gardening* and *shifting cultivation*.

## Dry Land Gardening

**Dry land gardening** is defined by the main ecological and climatic factor with which cultivators have to cope: low, erratic, and unpredictable rainfall. Like all horticulture, it uses no plow, and simple hand tools—hoes,

*Dry land gardeners cope with the problem of growing crops in arid or semiarid regions.*

spades, and so forth—powered by human muscles are the characteristic technology. Dry land gardening occurs in the American southwest, in parts of Mexico and Central America, in some of the Middle East, and in much of sub-Saharan Africa. In the more arid regions of Africa sometimes it is supplemented by cattle raising, because rainfall is too erratic and unpredictable for people to depend entirely on their crops. Preindustrial dry land gardening is distributed in temperate grasslands, chaparral, and tropical savannas and grasslands.

In this type of horticulture, low and highly variable precipitation impedes the growth of crops. Cultivation in arid lands is risky: even if in most years rainfall and harvests are adequate, there is a good chance that in any given year not enough rain will fall. Therefore, people who cultivate in dry regions have developed various gardening strategies to cope with the possibility of drought, which occurs unpredictably. One method is to combine gardening with the keeping of domesticated animals, which offers several advantages that we describe later. Another is to plant only along rivers and streams, where the roots can tap into the high water table.

The Pueblo peoples of the North American Southwest exemplify another way to cope with aridity. In this desert region annual rainfall averages only ten inches, concentrated in the spring. Further, in this high country the growing season for corn—the major source of food—is only about four months long. The people are faced with extreme uncertainty: If they plant too early, a late spring frost may kill their crops; if they wait too long, they will lose some of the critical moisture from the spring rains. The people, then, must concentrate their efforts into a short spring–early summer period, and they must take measures to cope with potential frost and insufficient rainfall.

One way the Pueblo peoples make the most of available water is to plant corn in those areas that are most likely to flood because there soil moisture usually lasts until harvest time. Yet in some years—they do not know in advance which years—the rains are so torrential that floods wash away the crops. The people, therefore, diversify both the place and the time of their planting. They sow the seeds of corn, squash, beans, and other crops in several locations, so that no matter what weather occurs, some gardens produce a harvest. For example, gardens on the flood plains may be lost during an unusually wet year, but upland gardens still yield a crop. Staggering the time of planting likewise lowers the risk of cultivation; by planting crops weeks apart the risk of losing all of a planting because of an untimely

frost is reduced. Thus by mixing up where and when they plant, the Pueblo peoples reduce the risk of cultivation in an arid, highly seasonal environment.

## Shifting Cultivation

**Shifting cultivation** involves cutting and burning an area of land to clear it of natural vegetation; planting crops on it for one to three years (seldom longer); then cutting, burning, and planting a new area for a new garden. The old garden is left alone (fallowed) for several years (often ten or more) to allow the natural vegetation to reestablish itself. A harvested garden is not abandoned all at once, but little by little, for often long-lived fruit trees are planted and people return for several years to pluck the fruits. After a fallowed plot has regrown, its soil fertility is partially or wholly restored, most weeds have been shaded out by regrown trees, and insect pests that invaded the garden when it was full of crops have gone elsewhere. The same parcel of land again may be cleared and burned for a new garden. Shifting cultivation is an extensive method of land use.

Also known as **slash-and-burn** and **swidden**, this method is practiced largely in heavily forested areas. Early cultivators in the temperate forests of Europe used it, and some white settlers of eastern North America were taught the method by the Native Americans. Today shifting cultivation is largely confined to the tropical forests of South and Central America, Africa, and Southeast Asia.

The tools of most shifting cultivators are quite simple, yet remarkably efficient in labor requirements. When a new garden plot is to be cleared from the forest, the largest trees are felled with the adz or axe. The smaller trees and undergrowth are slashed down using a knife with a long blade. These tasks are done in the dry season (if there is one) because the woody material that has been cut down is not hauled off but is left to dry out for several weeks. When it is dry enough and when the winds are right, the whole plot is set on fire. Thus the clearing of land for new gardens usually requires only an adz or axe, a knife, and fire, which does much of the work.

Burning is more than a labor-saving method of clearing the land of vegetation; it also rids the plot of insects and provides nutrients for the crops. The usefulness of the burn arises partly from the ecological characteristics of tropical forests. Ecologists have clearly established that most of the nutrients in a tropical forest are found in the biomass (that is, in the living material, mainly the trees), not in the soil. The high heat and humidity of the tropics result in remarkably high rates of decay of dead organic matter. The decay process releases the nutrients into the soil, where they are quickly taken up by the shallow, splayed roots of the trees. The nutrients recycle as leaf litter, fallen branches, and dead animals (who have consumed the plants) accumulate on the ground, decay, and are reused.

Tropical soils, then, are not the repository of nutrients familiar to most temperate folk. Despite the luxuriant vegetation of the tropics, the soil is usually nutrient poor. In many areas it cannot support the permanent cultivation of crops—at least not without a heavy investment of fertilizers and other materials. Rather, the heavy precipitation washes nutrients too deeply down into the soil for plant roots to penetrate (a process called *leaching*) or simply carries them away with eroding topsoil into streams and rivers.

Thus swiddeners have to overcome two problems of cultivating a tropical forest. First, most of the nutrients are locked up in the living vegetation and must be released before they can be used by the crops the swiddener hopes to grow. Burning is a labor-saving way to accomplish this release (it is not, however, very efficient at conserving some nutrients because most of the nitrogen and sulfur in the dried vegetation goes up in smoke). After the burn the crops must be planted soon; otherwise, tropical downpours will wash the ash away, and the intense tropical sun will bake the soil.

Second, shifting cultivators frequently face the problem of nutrient loss by leaching or erosion. Underneath the natural forest the soil is protected by the treetop canopy of leaves that shields the ground from the worst force of rainstorms. Many swiddeners shield the soil of the garden plots they plant in the forest in a similar way. They leave some of the tallest trees standing when they originally clear the plot. They often are careful to spread the chopped and slashed plant matter evenly over the plot to protect the soil while the material is drying. Another way to cope with leaching and erosion in the tropics is to plant an enormous variety of crops in a single plot; some crops are taller than others and have leaves that spread horizontally, thus protecting the soil in much the same way that the canopy does in the natural forest.

A few examples will indicate the enormous variety of crops that many shifting cultivators plant in a single garden. The Hanunoó of the Philippines plant up to forty distinct crops in a plot, including rice, corn, sweet potatoes, yams, manioc, banana, and cacao. The gardens

of the Maring, who live in the highlands of interior Papua, New Guinea (north of Australia), regularly contain more than thirty species of cultigens. The Yukpa, slash-and-burn cultivators of tropical Colombia and Venezuela, cultivate about fifty species, most of which are found in a single garden.

On the other hand, other swiddeners have less diverse crop inventories. The Iban of Sarawak (Malaysia) rely mainly on dry rice grown under slash-and-burn conditions, supplemented by a few other crops. And many shifting cultivators of Central America are heavily dependent on corn and beans, which grow symbiotically: The cornstalk provides the support needed by the beans, whereas the beans fix atmospheric nitrogen—a nutrient that corn requires in abundance—in their roots, where it becomes water-soluble and available to the corn.

It was once common to condemn the slash-and-burn method as an extremely wasteful use of land. This judgment was based on the simple observation that many more acres of land are required to support a population than would be needed using intensive agriculture with shorter or no fallow periods. This observation is indeed correct: If a plot is cropped for two years and fallowed for twenty, then ten times the amount of

*As this garden on the island of Tanna in Melanesia illustrates, shifting cultivators use fire to clear the land of natural vegetation.*

land is needed per person than if there were no fallow, for example. For human populations the main implication of this extensive land use is that high densities of people cannot be supported by shifting cultivation. Densities of less than one hundred per square mile characterize most shifting cultivators. By contrast, intensive agriculture supports densities of several hundreds per square mile in many parts of the world. In some intensive agriculture areas—notably the island of Java (Indonesia) and parts of China under wet rice—densities per square mile reach into the thousands.

But it does not follow that shifting cultivation is a more wasteful method than its *viable alternatives*. Agricultural experts from temperate regions frequently have attempted to apply "advanced modern methods" to the tropics: clear-cutting wide swaths of the forest, planting a single crop in a plot (called *monoculture*), applying commercial fertilizers, tilling with plows, and so forth. They found that once enormous tracts of forest were clear-cut, there was nothing to protect the soil from the rains, so leaching and erosion occurred. They often discovered that monoculture is too susceptible to viruses, fungi, and insects to work without an enormous input of chemical agents, which were washed off by the rains. Because it is not the major storehouse of nutrients, the soil was too infertile to support more than a crop or two; attempts to improve its productivity with artificial fertilizers often were unsuccessful because of the leaching and erosion of the unprotected soil. Plowing turned the earth over, greatly disturbing its structure and making it more susceptible to erosion and leaching. Prevention of the natural recolonization of the plot from the surrounding forest for several seasons led to the invasion of hardy tropical grasses, which became so well established on the impoverished earth that trees could not regain a foothold. As a result of such experiences, many of those who used to claim that swidden was primitive and wasteful now admit that the methods that work in the temperate latitudes often fail in the tropics.

## From Extensive to Intensive Land Use

As we have seen, the chief limitation of shifting cultivation and other extensive land use systems is that they can support only relatively low population densities. If we look broadly at the history of cultivation—if we take a bird's-eye view of the long-term evolution of farming methods on our entire planet—we find that methods have grown more intensive: Plots have been planted more frequently and fallow periods have grown shorter

or even disappeared. The reasons for this broad shift in land use and methods are complex and controversial, but there is little doubt that population growth was an important factor. As densities grew and regions became filled up with people, plots had to be kept under cultivation longer. In some parts of the world with high densities, fallow periods eventually almost disappeared.

As cultivation periods grew longer and fallow lengths shorter, farming tasks changed. For example, less labor time was spent in reclearing fallowed plots, but more labor had to be devoted to maintaining plots already under cultivation because natural fallow no longer was sufficient to restore soil conditions, reduce pest infestations, and shade out weeds. If not removed, weeds greatly reduce yields by competing with crops for water, nutrients, and light, so human labor had to be used to remove them. Turning over the soil between plantings became necessary, both to remove unwanted vegetation and to bring nutrients to the surface. For this task a new tool, the plow, and a new source of energy, draft animals, proved useful, and harnessing domesticated animals to plows developed in several regions of the Old World. Oxen, horses, or water buffalo commonly serve as the power (energy) source for the plow. In some regions, animals were harnessed to mechanical pumps to bring water to fields or harnessed to heavy stone wheels used to grind grain. Besides supplementing human muscle energy in these and other ways, the animals' manure was used to fertilize fields, a step made necessary by the practice of keeping fields under cultivation year after year.

Before the coming of Europeans, New World peoples had no domesticated animals suitable for pulling plows. In the valley of Mexico and in the Andes, as populations grew and land use intensified, human labor continued to be the main source of energy. In the valley of Mexico, for example, natural swamps were reclaimed by filling in earth and constructing raised fields that were planted with crops like tomatoes, squash, and corn. By continually adding new materials to these so-called floating gardens, the people could keep them under almost continuous cultivation. In the Andes, stepped terraces were constructed to reduce erosion and an incredible variety of sweet potatoes and other crops were grown during the summer.

These kinds of changes occurred over many centuries, the details varying with crop variety, climate, soil, local technology, and the like. But the end result was that in many regions extensive systems evolved into more intensive ones, culminating in the modern type of cultivation known as intensive agriculture.

## INTENSIVE AGRICULTURE

Intensive agriculture differs from horticulture in several ways. Most important, the land is used more fully: Over a period of years intensive agriculturalists plant and harvest plots more frequently. Many use the same field for many years with only a year or two of fallow. This more intensive use of the land is made possible mainly by fertilization and relatively thorough removal of weeds. Intensive agriculturalists usually apply some form of organic fertilizer to maintain the productivity of their soil. Domestic animals often are turned loose after harvest or in fallowing fields to replace soil nutrients with their dung. Manure is gathered and spread over fields. In some areas, including modern China, human excrement ("night soil") is collected and used to recycle nutrients back into the soil. Frequent removal of invading weeds is practiced so that growing crops have less competition.

Most intensive agriculturalists establish some form of artificial irrigation works because rainfall occurs only seasonally where they live or because yields would be limited by low or unreliable rainfall but can be increased by artificial watering. Therefore, to farm during the dry season, they store water in reservoirs or tanks. Various irrigation methods are used around the world. Sometimes streams are dammed to conserve runoff, and ditches are dug to transport water to the fields. In

Mexico's arid Oaxaca valley farmers of the valley floor plant maize and other crops around shallow wells and water the crops with pots. In some Asian river valleys channels are dug to transport water (and fertile silt!) to fields during the annual monsoons, when the rivers overrun their banks. In many mountainous regions of Southeast Asia the level of water in hillside rice fields is controlled with an elaborate system of diked terraces.

Intensive agriculture can support much greater numbers of people on a given area of land—five, ten, and even twenty times the densities of horticultural methods. In essence, intensive agriculture further raises the carrying capacity of the habitat. Some scholars believe that this advantage is the main or even the only benefit intensive methods offer over horticulture.

Higher densities are possible mainly because plots yield their harvests more frequently, there being little fallow, but this is not the only reason an area of land supports more people. Preparing land more thoroughly, tilling the soil more completely, controlling the supply of water, removing weeds, artificially adding nutrients— these activities give intensive agriculturalists greater control over the conditions under which their crops grow. This control also contributes to greater outputs per unit of land.

Of all forms of modern intensive agriculture, wet rice cultivation is the most widespread and feeds the greatest number of people. It serves as our example of intensive methods.

*Intensive agriculturalists use the animal-powered plow to prepare the soil for planting. In the Phillipines, water buffalo are commonly used.*

## Wet Rice in Asia

The wet rice fields of Asia are the most productive of all preindustrial intensive agricultural systems. This method provides food for most of the rural population of the Far East, including China, South Korea, Taiwan, Vietnam, the lowlands of Thailand, the river valleys and coastal plains of South Asia, and Indonesia (Figure 8.2)

As the term *wet rice* suggests, the method involves flooding the fields for most of the growing season. In some areas the water comes entirely from the natural rainfall of the monsoons, but the water level often is controlled by artificial irrigation. Most wet rice is, therefore, grown on the flood plains of rivers. In parts of Southeast Asia, southern China, and the Himalayan fringes wet rice is grown on terraced hillsides originally constructed centuries ago.

Perhaps the most remarkable feature of wet rice cultivation is the capability of a plot to yield a harvest year in and year out, with little or no fallow. Indeed, where the seasonal availability of water is adequate, the same plot may yield two or even three harvests in a single year, being under almost continuous cultivation. According to agricultural economist D. B. Grigg, this capability is attributable to four factors: (1) the protection from erosion the water gives the soil, (2) the high water table of the rivers' flood plain that reduces leaching, (3) the replacement of soil nutrients by the silt carried in the rivers' flooding, and (4) nitrogen fixation from the blue-green algae that live in the floodwater. The chief benefit of wet rice—its ability to grow in the same field year after year—is then related to the practice of flooding the fields and allowing the water to remain throughout most of the maturation period.

Like horticultural peoples, wet rice growers have developed a diversity of patterns to organize agricultural tasks and access to land. Besides the difficulties faced by all cultivators, wet rice growers must solve other problems relating to the management of water because the proper supply of water at the proper time is important for a good yield. It is more efficient if storage ponds or tanks, canals or ditches, and other improvements are

**FIGURE 8.2**
**Principal Regions of Intensive Agriculture at Contact Period**

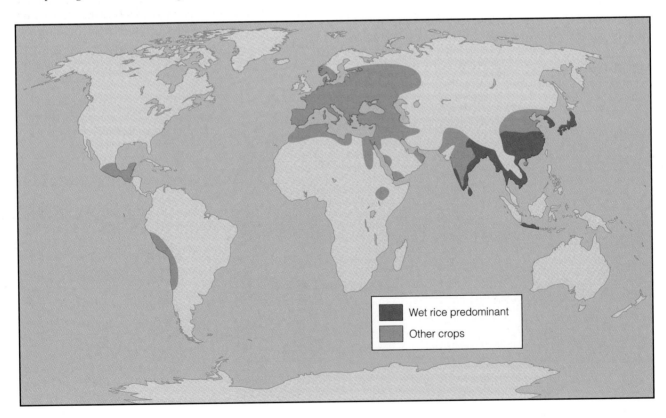

Wet rice predominant
Other crops

held and managed communally, because less labor is required to construct and maintain them than if each family owned their own. Water may be stored in small lakes or ponds, or captured and held in tanks until it is used to flood the fields. It is important that the water level be controlled fairly precisely while the rice is growing: If it rises too high, the plants will be unable to photosynthesize; and if it falls too low, the benefits of having standing water in the fields will be reduced. Unless the land is naturally flat, the plots, therefore, must be leveled to keep the height of the water constant in different areas of the field. The water level must be controlled by low dikes, usually constructed of earth, which can be easily breached to drain the plot for the harvest.

Managing the supply of the water that is so critical in growing wet rice requires sophisticated organization, especially with respect to cooperative labor patterns and rights of access to both land and water. Each family may work its lands on its own, but who will construct and maintain public irrigation works? Who will decide when dikes, dams, ditches, and tanks need to be repaired, and how will the labor to repair them be coordinated? The water used on the fields of one family is not available to other families. How shall the consumption of water be coordinated? Who will get how much water and when? How, in short, will use rights to water be determined? These are all, essentially, problems of organizing production in wet rice areas.

Here is how one population, the Sinhalese of the dry zone of Sri Lanka, traditionally solved the problem of organizing the allocation of water to fields. Each village subsists from wet rice cultivation, the water for which is drawn from a collectively owned rain-fed reservoir constructed from earth. Most villages have their own separate reservoirs filled with water that their residents alone may use. The people of the village are responsible for maintaining the earthworks of the reservoir and for managing the allocation of water to each family plot. The capacity of the tank determines the maximum number of acres of land that the village may have in cultivation. This is because the supply of water is so critical to wet rice cultivation that land cannot be farmed without it (especially in this part of Sri Lanka, in which all the rain falls in one season, and water must be stored the rest of the year).

All the cultivated land of a village is in a single area, below the reservoir. The entire field is laid out into bounded, diked plots of equal size. Each plot receives a fixed amount of water from the communal reservoir. The number of owners of a single plot varies: Poor

*In East and South Asia, wet rice continues to be the major source of food for hundreds of millions of people.*

families must share rights of access to one plot with other families, whereas other (richer) families have access to several plots with their accompanying ration of water. Thus the ownership of plots within the entire village field carries with it rights to a certain proportion of the communal water supply. By allocating each plot (rather than each family) a fixed proportion of irrigation water, the chance that a given plot will receive insufficient moisture is reduced.

## Cultural Consequences of Intensive Agriculture

The development of intensive agricultural methods had profound cultural consequences. Some of these arose from the need to manage the supply of irrigation water, which gave rise to a variety of new social organizations. (The Sinhalese are only one of many variants.) Other consequences result from a potential that is greater in intensive agriculture than in either foraging or horticulture: the production of a food **surplus**. That is, a single worker using intensive agricultural methods can feed many more people than just himself or herself and his or her family.

As we have seen, intensive agriculture produces significantly more food per unit of available land than horticulture. As Box 8.2 shows, intensive agriculture

How do the food production systems we have discussed so far compare in how hard people work to produce their food and how much each worker produces per unit of labor? Available data on this subject are scanty, so only rough comparisons can be given.

For a few populations we know about how much time producers actually spend in subsistence labor. We therefore can state the *labor input into subsistence*; but we must keep in mind that time spent in making tools, processing food, cooking food, and so forth usually is not recorded by fieldworkers. We also know how much food is produced per unit (e.g., hour) of labor input, measured in weight. If we can determine how much food value is locked up in the foods produced, we can state roughly how *productive* a system is in the amount produced per unit of subsistence labor. To do this, we need a common measure that will apply to all kinds of foods and that, therefore, can be used to compare them. (To see why, ask, How do we

## BOX 8.2

## LABOR AND ENERGY INPUTS AND OUTPUTS

compare the food value of a pound of mongongo nuts eaten by the !Kung with that of a pound of rice consumed by the Sinhalese?) The only common measure available is kilocalories (commonly called *calories*), which are a unit of energy. By determining in a laboratory the number of kilocalories contained in a gram of mongongo nuts and a gram of rice, we can compare the productivity of mongongo nut gatherers with that of rice growers.

Table B.1 compares working hours and productivity of sample foragers, horticulturalists, and intensive agriculturalists. The figures in the column "Subsistence Working Hours" refer to the approximate number of hours a

subsistence worker spends per week in food production. The figures under "Output/Input Ratio" show the approximate number of calories of food energy obtained per calorie of human labor input. This column also might be headed "labor efficiency," since it shows how much food energy an average worker produces from each unit of muscle energy he or she expends in subsistence labor.

On the basis of these limited data it seems that foraging and horticulture are roughly comparable in the hours actually spent in producing food and in the amount of food a worker produces. Only intensive agriculture is notably more productive: Agricultural workers produce about five times the amount of calories with their labor as do horticultural workers. We can see that an intensive agricultural village can potentially produce enough food to support many people who are not themselves engaged in food production.

In chapter nineteen we compare the output/input ratio—or labor efficiency—of these preindustrial food production systems with that of mechanized agriculture. As we discuss further, the latter is far more efficient in its output/input ratio; a single mechanized agricultural worker in the United States or Great Britain produces enough food to feed sixty or seventy persons. But this labor efficiency is achieved only with an enormous input of energy in the form of fossil fuels and electricity. The "energetic efficiency"—the number of calories of energy needed to produce one calorie of food energy—of mechanized agriculture is far lower than that of any of the preindustrial systems discussed in this chapter. ✦

SOURCES: Lee (1979), Harris (1985), Waddell (1972), Leach (1976), Little and Morren (1976).

TABLE B.1 Working Hours/Productivity Comparisons

| PRODUCTION SYSTEM | POPULATION | SUBSISTENCE WORKING HOURS | OUTPUT/INPUT RATIO |
|---|---|---|---|
| Foraging | !Kung | 17 | 10 |
| Horticulture | | | |
| Hoe cultivation | Genieri (Gambia) | 16 | 11 |
| Grassland gardening | Enga (Papua New Guinea) | 19 | 9 |
| Swidden plus pigs | Maring (Papua New Guinea) | ? | 10 |
| Intensive agriculture | | | |
| Wet rice | Luts'un village (China) | 22 | 54 |

also is more productive per unit of *labor*—and for many reasons. In the Old World, animal muscle supplemented human labor in preparing the land for planting. Milk and meat from cattle, sheep, horses, pigs, and other domesticated animals reduce the need to hunt, conserving male labor that can be put into cultivation. In both hemispheres the labor needed to clear land and establish irrigation was put in long ago, so fields and irrigation works need only be maintained and extended occasionally. Even more so than horticulturalists, intensive agriculturalists live partly off the labor of past generations. For these and other reasons it is clear that—at least after intensive agriculture is fully established in a region—a single worker or farm family can produce a significant surplus over their own immediate needs.

What happens to this surplus? To answer this question, we must realize that most intensive agricultural peoples are not politically independent and economically self-sufficient societies. Instead, they are incorporated into larger political units. By this we mean that the villages in which most of them live are part of an inclusive political system that dominates or rules them in some way. The surplus is used to support people who do not themselves perform agricultural labor, such as rulers and aristocracies, priests, armies, traders, and craft specialists.

The association of intensive agriculture with large-scale political organization is an ancient one. In prehistoric times intensive agricultural peoples were incorporated into the four major civilizations of the ancient Old World: the valley formed by the Tigris and Euphrates rivers of Mesopotamia, the Nile valley of Egypt, the Indus River valley of Pakistan, and the Shang cities of China. The food supply of these civilizations was produced by intensive agriculturalists, who paid tribute or taxes to support the rulers, priests, armies, and officials who ran the government apparatus. In the New World, too, agricultural peoples were part of large-scale political units, such as the Mayans of the Yucatan peninsula, the Toltecs and Aztecs of Mexico, and the Incas of highland Peru (Figure 8.3).

In these parts of the world, within a few centuries or millennia after the development of intensive agriculture, the socially and politically complex organization we call

**FIGURE 8.3**
**Ancient Civilizations**

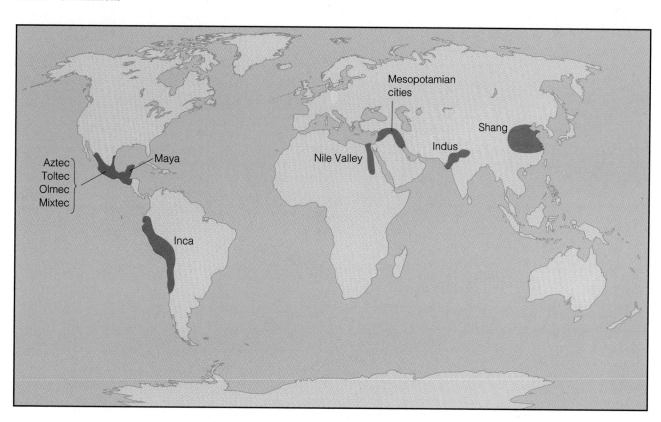

civilization (or "living in cities") emerged. All these ancient civilizations were supported by intensive agriculture, and all involved large-scale irrigation works and water control. In fact, some prehistorians have argued that civilization—and the despotic control of rulers and priests that everywhere accompanied it—developed out of control over the supply of irrigation water. (This theory is controversial, and numerous alternatives have been proposed.) Certainly, it appears from current evidence that intensive agriculture is virtually a prerequisite for civilization. No known civilization ever developed out of a horticultural cultivation system. (The Mayan civilization was once thought to have been an exception, but recent evidence shows that the Mayans, too, used intensive methods.)

In the modern world most people are incorporated into large-scale political units, namely, into nations.

Even in some developed regions—notably in Europe, South Korea, and Taiwan—intensive agriculturalists survive. In most industrial nations, however, intensive agriculture has been largely replaced by mechanized agriculture based on energy derived from electricity and fossil fuels rather than from humans and animals. Today most intensive agriculture occurs in the less developed countries of southern Asia and Southeast Asia, Latin America, and Africa. Intensive agriculturalists typically fit into these nations economically as peasants.

**Peasants** are rural people who are integrated into a larger society politically (i.e., they are subject to laws and governments imposed from outside their communities) and economically (i.e., they exchange products of their own labor for products produced elsewhere). In many Third World countries they make up the bulk of the population and produce much of the food consumed

*Peasants in the ancient civilizations of both hemispheres were required to contribute their labor to the construction of roads, buildings, irrigation works, and other public projects. This mural depicts the building of a Tula temple in the Maya civilization.*

*Peasants make up the majority population of many modern Third World nations, including India.*

by town and city dwellers. Peasants typically subsist mainly from foods they grow themselves, although many also produce nonagricultural products for market sale. Peasant households produce goods that are sold for money, traded or bartered for goods produced by other people, paid to a landlord as rent, or rendered to a central government as taxes.

But subjection to external political authorities and exchange with a wider economy are not enough to define the term *peasant.* (Otherwise, Midwestern farmers would be classified as peasants.) Peasantries nearly always fit into their larger societies at or near the bottom of the social and economic pyramid. They have little prestige in the view of other categories of people in their nations. Although the foods they produce often feed almost everyone else, their labor is not valued and their life-style is not envied. Also, they are among the poorest people in the country because in one way or another they are dominated or exploited.

The peasantry first arose in the ancient civilizations just discussed. The agricultural labor of prehistoric peasants fed the craft workers, the merchants, the state-sponsored priesthoods, the political elite, the warriors, and the builders of transportation facilities, buildings, and cities themselves. The tribute (usually paid in food, labor, or both) rendered by peasants was extracted from them by armed force or threat of force. This rendering of goods and labor by peasants to members of a more powerful social category continued into historic and modern times. The peasantry of medieval Europe, for example, eked out a meager living, paying a substantial portion of their annual harvest to their lords or working many days a year on their lord's estate.

Given this information, we might well wonder whether the development of intensive agriculture was a curse or a blessing for most of humanity. There is little doubt that it is a blessing to those who throughout history have received the surplus made possible by intensive methods. And most scholars agree that the productivity of intensive agriculture allowed the specialized division of labor that led to writing, metallurgy, monumental architecture, cities, and the great religious and artistic traditions we associate with civilization.

But how about the peasants, who produced the food that made such "progress" possible? For them, writing meant that more accurate accounts could be kept of their tribute payments or of the number of days they worked for overlords. Iron and other metals meant that peasants had better agricultural tools; yet for the most part they were not allowed to use them to ease their own labor, but only to produce more surplus for others to consume. Metal also meant that weapons became more effective, so that the citizens of one state could slaughter the citizens of another state more effectively. Most peasant families continued to live in hovels, even while great palaces, religious structures, and walled cities and towns were constructed and the workers were fed by the peasants' agricultural labor. Both prehistorically and historically, peasants around the world have been denied many of the benefits offered by technological progress, although their agricultural labor has made much of this progress possible.

*Because of the seasonal mobility needed to supply livestock with food and water, the dwellings of pastoralists are portable. This a camp of herders in Afghanistan.*

Peasants occasionally have organized themselves to resist these conditions. In the twentieth century, peasant revolts have occurred in many areas. Peasants in Mexico, Russia, China, and Vietnam played an important role in the revolutions of these countries. Guerrilla movements have been backed by many peasants in Guatemala, El Salvador, Nicaragua, Peru, and the Philippines. Denied most of the benefits of whatever progress their nations have managed to achieve, modern peasants often join these movements in the hope of obtaining a greater share of the land and other resources that have been denied them.

## PASTORALISM

Except for some New World peoples in precolonial times, cultivators usually keep domesticated animals. For example, Southeast Asian and Pacific horticulturalists raise many pigs and chickens. Intensive agriculturalists raise horses, oxen, water buffalo, and cattle, which they use to pull their plows, fertilize their fields, and provide dairy products and meat. These domesticated animals are not merely supplementary to the horticul-

tural or agricultural adaptation: Because of the meat, eggs, milk, hides, wool, transportation, fertilizer, and horsepower they provide, they usually are critical to the survival and nutrition of assorted cultivators.

Cultivators do not depend on their domesticated animals to the same extent as do peoples known as *pastoralists,* or herders. Herders acquire much of their food by raising, caring for, and subsisting on the products of domesticated animals. With a few exceptions, the livestock are gregarious (herd) animals, with cattle, camels, sheep, goats, reindeer, horses, llamas, alpacas, and yaks being the common animals kept in various parts of the world.

But the simple degree of dependence on domesticated animals is not all that distinguishes pastoralists from cultivators because a great many pastoralists also cultivate; indeed, many acquire the bulk of their food calories from their crops rather than from their animals. More important, when we characterize a people as "pastoral," we mean that the needs of their animals for naturally occurring food and water profoundly influence the seasonal rhythms of their lives. The key phrase here is "naturally occurring." Most cultivators raise crops that they feed to their livestock or maintain fields in which their animals graze. In general, pastoralists do neither of these. Their herds subsist on natural forage and therefore must be moved to where the forage naturally occurs. Some or all of the people must take their livestock to wherever the grasses or other forage is available in a given season. This high degree of mobility, known as **nomadism**, characterizes most pastoralists. Most commonly, pastoralists are seasonally nomadic—they do not wander aimlessly. Their migrations often are "vertical," meaning that animals are taken to highland areas to graze during the hottest season of the year.

Few pastoralists subsist entirely from the products of their livestock; animal products nearly always are supplemented by cultivated foods. Herders acquire these in one of four major ways.

✦ They practice some horticulture or agriculture themselves (often men and boys watch the herds and women cultivate).
✦ They trade animal products for vegetable foods and other goods with neighboring cultivators.

✦ They sell livestock, meat, hides, wool, milk, cheese, or other products of their animals for money, which they use to buy food and other supplies.
✦ They use their livestock partly as beasts of burden, which allows them to undertake long-distance trade from which they profit.

We briefly discuss some examples of these methods in upcoming sections. First, we need to discuss the distribution of the pastoral adaptation and the characteristics that make it advantageous in some kinds of environments.

## Distribution of Pastoralism

Herders are scattered across the globe, but not in a random distribution. By comparing Figure 7.1 with Figure 8.4, you can see that the pastoral adaptation occurs largely in deserts, grasslands, savannas, and mountains. (A few peoples, such as the Sami of north-

**FIGURE 8.4**
**Principal Regions of Pastoralism at Contact Period**

*Pastoral people live primarily off their herds, eating their flesh and drinking their milk, trading animal products with their neighbors, or—like this Egyptian—selling the animals themselves.*

ern Scandinavia and the Tungus and Chukchee of Siberia, were reindeer herders in the tundra biome.) These areas do have something in common: Cultivation is impossible, extremely difficult, or highly risky because of low average annual precipitation, great fluctuations in rainfall from year to year, or short growing seasons. As always, there are exceptions to our generalizations, but pastoralists usually are found in regions that are not well suited to cultivation using preindustrial technologies.

Some of these regions are too cold or have a short growing season, such as the northern Scandinavian and Siberian tundra or the high mountains of the South American Andes and parts of Tibet. In the northern Scandinavian and Siberian tundras the high latitude makes cultivation impossible. The meat and milk of reindeer and the trade in reindeer products allow the Lapps, Chukchee, and Tungus to exploit these areas. In the high mountains of the Andes, Tibet, and parts of Afghanistan the high altitude greatly shortens the length of the growing season. In parts of the Andes people move their llamas and alpacas to highland pastures for the summer, making much of their living from selling wool and using the animals for transport. In Tibet the yak not only serves as a beast of burden for long-distance trade but also is harvested for its flesh, milk, and hide. In central Asia, north and west of the Hima-

layas, the horse herders known as the Kazakh roam the grassy plains. They subsist partly from mare's milk and periodically shear the wool from their herds of sheep to trade with neighboring peoples.

In other areas cultivation is possible and does occur, but precipitation is so low or unreliable from year to year that droughts frequently cause crop failure. This is the case in eastern and southern Africa, parts of Turkey and the eastern Mediterranean, and certain arid regions of modern Iran and Iraq. In the savannas of eastern and southern Africa peoples such as the Karimojong, Dinka, Nuer, Swazi, and Tswana combine cattle raising with the cultivation of African grains such as millet. In the chaparral and grasslands of the eastern Mediterranean herding is the dominant activity among several ethnic populations, including the Yörük and some local Bedouin groups. Adaptive patterns vary, but most of these peoples subsist only partly off the meat and milk—made into butter, cheese, and yogurt—of their sheep, camels, and goats. More important, they sell or trade the meat, dairy products, and wool to their cultivator neighbors and receive vegetable foods and other necessities in return. Sometimes the wool is dyed locally, woven on hand looms into beautiful rugs, and exported to neighboring townsmen—or nowadays to the international market.

Still other regions in which the pastoral adaptation occurs are outright deserts, in which aridity makes cultivation difficult or impossible, such as the African Sahara and much of the Arabian peninsula. Here the dominant livestock is the camel. Both its milk and its flesh are consumed, but the animal is equally significant as a resource because of its well-known ability to survive long periods with little water. The camel is used as a beast of burden on the long-distance caravans for which these regions are famous. Many traditional peoples of the Sahara (such as the Tuareg) and the Middle East make their living primarily through the trade made possible by their camels.

## The Benefits and Costs of Herding

In such arid or cold environments the breeding and exploitation of domestic animals offer several advantages over the planting and harvesting of domesticated plants. First, most of the vegetation of grasslands and arid savannas (grasses and shrubs) and of tundras (lichens, willows, and sedges) is indigestible by humans. Livestock such as cattle, sheep, and reindeer are able to eat this vegetation and transform it into milk, blood, fat,

Parts of the arid Middle East are still inhabited by nomadic peoples who herd camels, sheep, and goats. Here Bedouin women of the Egyptian desert are preparing tea.

and muscle, all of which are drunk or eaten by various pastoral peoples. Thus in some areas livestock allow people to exploit indirectly certain wild resources not directly available to them.

Another advantage of herding may be called *subsistence risk reduction*. Under preindustrial conditions in areas of low and unreliable rainfall, crops often fail because of drought. Livestock provide an insurance against these periodic, unpredictable droughts and accompanying low yields. Not only do they store meat "on the hoof," but they also can be traded to neighboring peoples for cultivated foods.

Finally, a big advantage of keeping livestock is their mobility: Herds can be moved to the areas of freshest or lushest pasture, to sources of water, away from neighbors who have grown too aggressive, or even out of easy range of tax-seeking governments who often want the nomads to settle down.

With advantages like these you may well wonder why pastoralism was not more widespread in the preindustrial world. Why did the herding adaptation not spread to areas where cultivators lived? Part of the reason is that environmental conditions are not always conducive. For example, until recently pastoralism seldom was found in tropical forests, largely because of lack of

forage. (Today enormous tracts of tropical forest in Central America and Brazil are cleared and replanted in grasses suitable for cattle grazing, with all this implies for the destruction of the tropical forests.) Livestock diseases also limit the distribution of pastoralists. For example, much of eastern and southern Africa is occupied by cattle herders (most of whom also farm, however). Herders would presumably be even more widespread on the continent were it not for the limitations imposed by the presence of the tsetse fly, which transmits the debilitating disease sleeping sickness to cattle.

Perhaps the main factor limiting the distribution of pastoralism is that herding is not the most productive way of using the land of areas in which cultivation can be carried out reliably. The best way to understand why is to apply the ecologists' "10 percent rule." The food energy produced by photosynthetic plants lies at the base of any ecosystem except the deep oceans. In the presence of sufficient water, carbon dioxide, and minerals, plants convert the energy of sunlight into simple sugars, from which they derive the energy to grow and reproduce. Herbivores (plant-eating animals) consume the vegetation and use it to maintain their own bodies and produce offspring. Carnivores (animal-eating animals) in turn feed on herbivores. At each of these levels

One advantage of herding is that animals can be moved when the local environment is unfavorable, carrying people and possessions on their backs. These Chadians are relocating in face of a drought.

of the food chain most of the energy is lost as it is carried to the next level. Thus herbivores transform only about 10 percent of the plant energy they consume into their own flesh and blood (and hoofs and horns); and only around 10 percent of the energy carnivores acquire by eating herbivores is available to make more carnivore flesh (and teeth and claws). At each level 90 percent of the energy consumed is lost to respiration, waste production, and other processes. The 10 percent rule says that only 10 percent of the energy locked up in living matter at one level is available to the next level.

Now we can see why herding is not as efficient a way of exploiting an environment as cultivation: Overall, pastoralists eat higher on the food chain. Local abiotic and biotic conditions permitting, more total energy can be obtained from an environment by cultivation because much more energy can be gained from (cultivated) plants than from (herded) animals. People are not directly concerned with how much total energy they can extract from an environment; populations did not figure out that they could most productively exploit an environment by growing crops rather than raising animals and then opt for cultivation. More likely, cultivation won out over herding—in areas that are suitable for both—because of its greater labor productivity. If several times the food energy can be gained from an area of land by cultivating it rather than by grazing livestock on it, then 100 herders would have to range over a much larger area to support themselves than would 100 culti-

vators, and these movements would consume time and energy. Further, the 10 percent rule also would translate into higher potential (and actual) population densities for cultivators, who in the past may have outcompeted pastoralists for those territories that both could exploit.

For reasons such as these, cultivation rather than pastoralism occurs in areas well suited for growing crops, although people frequently also could live in these areas by herding. The pastoral adaptation occurs in regions where cultivation alone is unreliable, usually because of short growing seasons or inadequate precipitation.

Aridity, temperature, short growing seasons, and other ecological and climatic factors do not totally explain the distribution of the pastoral adaptation, however. Some pastoralists live in areas where crops could be grown, and they certainly know how to cultivate, but they consciously choose not to grow crops. The cattle-herding Masai of Kenya and Tanzania are an example. In some parts of the Masai territory cultivation is possible, and in fact most neighboring tribes combine cattle herding with cultivation of sorghum and other crops. The proud Masai, however, look down on cultivation because their herds represent wealth and are the main symbol of their cultural identity relative to their neighbors. Masai, therefore, live largely off the products of their cattle—blood, milk, meat, curds—and trade with their neighbors for the cultivated foods they do eat. The reasons they continue their pastoral adaptation are, therefore, as much "cultural" as "ecological."

## Herding and Social Organization

When people acquire much of their foods and other necessities from livestock, this adaptation inevitably affects other aspects of their way of life. As we define *pastoralism* in this text, the herds subsist largely or entirely from natural forage. Because the location of water and the best forage for livestock typically varies from season to season, the herds—and at least some of the herders—must also be seasonally mobile. Herds must also be managed, which requires some minimum number of people of the appropriate sex and age in a settlement at any given time. Finally, herders must have some ways of deciding whose animals have access to which areas of forage—the rights of access of people's livestock to land.

All these necessities of the pastoral adaptation—mobility, herd management, and regulating access to pasture land—affect how herders organize themselves to survive, persist, and even thrive in their often harsh environments. To illustrate how the herding adaptation affects social organization, we now consider two specific pastoral cultures, one from Iran and one from Uganda.

**BASSERI**    The Basseri are one of several nomadic pastoralists of the desert and arid grasslands of southern Iran. When studied by Norwegian anthropologist Fredrik Barth in the late 1950s, the 16,000 Basseri made their living by herding. Sheep and goats provided much of their food in the form of milk, cheese, and meat. Donkeys, camels, and horses provided transportation for people and possessions. The Basseri traded products made from the fur and hides of sheep, goats, and camels with their cultivator neighbors. In return they received cereals and other foods produced by irrigated agriculture. Although much of their diet thus came from exchange with surrounding peoples, the Basseri culturally looked down on agriculture and did little of it themselves. Basseri and their agricultural neighbors also benefited from each other's activities in another way: In their seasonal migrations the Basseri flocks grazed on the stubble in the harvested fields of the cultivators. For their part, the farmers were glad to have the Basseri livestock fertilize their just-harvested and fallow fields with their manure.

The Basseri had traditional rights to exploit pasture lands on which their livestock relied. The grazing rights were complex, but in essence Basseri could pasture their animals on a strip of land (their "tribal road") that ran from the mountains in the north through some central grasslands to the hot, arid desert of the south. On this strip, about 300 miles long and 20 to 50 miles wide, different areas contained good pasture at different times of the year. In the winter snow covered the northern mountains, but pasture was available in the south. In the spring people and livestock began moving northward, arriving in the highlands in time to take advantage of the summer pasture. In autumn they made their way south again, the livestock grazing largely on the cereal stubble of the harvested fields of the cultivators who lived along the central portion of the tribal road.

Because of their frequent moves, the Basseri lived in portable tents woven by women from goat hair. Each tent ordinarily was occupied by a single family. Each family owned its tents, textiles, and other household equipment and, on average, about 100 sheep and goats. If a family was to manage its flocks and run its other activities independently, it would need at least three members: a man, a woman, and a shepherd (usually a boy). But many young couples were childless, so they either had to acquire a shepherd through a contract (of which there were several kinds) or make an arrangement with another family to intermingle their flocks. In fact, because a single shepherd could look after a flock of around 400, it was common for several tents to use a single shepherd, for this required less labor. So two to five tents typically formed a "herding unit," the members of which cooperated by using a single young shepherd. Ownership of the livestock always remained separate, however, and tent families frequently pulled their livestock from one herding unit and associated with another.

The number of tents that camped together and jointly used an area of pasture varied seasonally. In the winter, when most Basseri lived in the arid southern lowlands, grass for the flocks was so sparse that the animals had to range widely to acquire sufficient food. Accordingly, the typical winter settlement group was the herding units of two to five families, which lived scattered throughout the territory, separated by a mile or more from other herding units. At other times of the year grass was more abundant, and the number of tents that associated together in a single area increased to as many as forty. These larger "camps" migrated as a single group under the limited authority of a headman, who consulted with the heads of the various tents in deciding when to move, where to move to, what route to take, and where to pitch the tents.

Tents, herding units, and camps were not the only groups formed by the Basseri. Camps were in turn associated into an overarching group called the *oulad* (a term that has no suitable English translation). The *oulad* was an important group because the camps that comprised it had joint rights to exploit certain areas of pasture along the tribal road. These grazing rights to specific areas were use rights, not ownership rights. No *oulad*—much less any lower-level group—could permanently claim an area of pasture as its own because the various *oulad* were subgroups of yet a higher level of organization.

The entire Basseri "tribe" of 16,000 was subject to the authority of a single chief, who inherited his office from his father. The chief exacted small, irregular taxes from the general population. He represented the tribe as a whole to surrounding sedentary cultivators and often settled disputes between tribal members. The tribal chief also periodically reallocated use rights to pasture lands between the *oulad,* so the various camps that made up a single *oulad* shared grazing rights to pastures allocated to them by the tribal chief. As the size of an *oulad* increased or decreased, the chief allocated it more pasture or reduced the area of pasture to which it had grazing rights. Through this organizational mechanism the members of each *oulad* knew to which areas they enjoyed grazing rights at any given time. Presumably, this reduced disputes over pasture between members of different *oulad*.

We see that the Basseri developed a fairly complex organization. Livestock were owned by families; families formed herding units to save labor; herding units aggregated into camps most of the year, which migrated as a single group; several camps composed an *oulad*, whose constituent camps had joint grazing rights over specific pasture lands; in turn, *oulad* formed a tribe, which was subject to the authority of a single chief, who periodically reallocated use rights to pasture among the *oulad*. Through the complexity you can see how the various levels of organization helped to relate the Basseri and their livestock to their habitat, organized their migrations, and regulated access to pasture lands without much internal dispute and conflict.

**KARIMOJONG.**     The Karimojong are an East African people of Uganda. Living on an arid savanna with marked seasonal differences in rainfall, they subsist by a combination of horticulture and cattle pastoralism. The 60,000 Karimojong are a fairly representative example of a cultural area known to anthropologists as the "East African cattle complex." In this complex, found throughout the East African savannas, cattle are more than an ordinary source of food. The East African man loves his cattle like some North Americans love their cars. Cattle represent wealth and manliness. They are the source of prestige, influence in tribal affairs, and wives (for an East African man must transfer cattle to his wife's relatives to marry her, a practice we discuss in chapter 10). When sacrificed ritually, cattle are religious symbols and are the source of benefits from the supernatural. Underlying these other cultural elements of the cattle complex, according to Rada and Neville Dyson-Hudson, who studied the Karimojong, is the important role of cattle in subsistence: "First, last and always the role of cattle in Karimojong life is to transform the energy stored in the grasses, herbs and shrubs of the tribal area into a form easily available to the people" (Dyson-Hudson and Dyson-Hudson 1969, 4).

This transformation is not mainly achieved by eating the animals' flesh, as we Westerners might expect. Rather, the Karimojong—and most other East Africans—consume the products of living cattle: milk and blood. Lactating cows are milked twice daily. Every three to five

*East African pastoralists live mainly from the products of living cattle. This ox is about to yield blood.*

months several pints of blood are taken from the jugular of some animals and drunk, usually immediately. Cattle meat is consumed mainly on religious occasions; the meat is shared among all participants.

There is a marked sexual division of labor in Karimojong subsistence activities. The central portion of the tribal territory is crossed by several rivers, and hence is relatively well watered during the rainy season. Here the women live in permanent settlements, where they cultivate sorghum (an African grain) and a few other crops. The central area, however, produces good grasses only during the rainy season, so for most of the year the cattle must be taken to greener pastures, often miles away from the settlements. The Karimojong thus also have another kind of settlement, the mobile "cattle camps" that are manned by males, especially by young men. Rainfall is quite unpredictable, especially during the driest half of the year. But localized storms do occur, and for many days afterward grass grows well in restricted areas. The men of the cattle camps—accompanied by the cattle—therefore move frequently in search of pasture. While living in the cattle camps, men live largely from the milk and blood of their animals, supplemented by the beer made from sorghum that the women sometimes bring when they visit.

Both cultivated crops and livestock are necessary foods for the Karimojong. Even a short three-week drought during the sorghum-growing season will seriously reduce the harvest, but the mobility of the livestock allows them to be taken to places where there is sufficient forage. Cattle thus provide an insurance against climatic and other forces that make cultivation too risky to rely on. They also allow the Karimojong to make use of those parts of their territory that are too dry to support cultivation. The cattle transform vegetation indigestible to humans into milk, blood, and meat, which eventually are eaten by the people.

## Summary

Adaptations based on domestication control plants and animals so as to increase their use value to humans. Domestication's major advantage is that it increases the carrying capacity of a habitat over adaptations based on foraging.

Cultivation refers to adaptations based mainly on domesticated plants. The three basic varieties of cultivation—horticulture, intensive agriculture, and mechanized agriculture—differ mainly in their intensity and in the amount of nonhuman energy they use in the production of foods. They also have certain generalized impacts on other elements of the way of life of people who live by them.

Whether they practice dry land gardening or shifting cultivation, horticulturalists live in larger and more permanent settlements than foragers, partly to recover and protect their labor investments in their plots. Horticultural people are quite diverse in the way they organize production and establish access rights to resources. Commonly, a group of relatives establish a claim to an area of land by first clearing and investing their labor in it and then passing their ownership rights along to future generations.

Over long spans of time cultivation methods became more intensive—plots were kept under cultivation for longer periods. Increasing intensity led to changes in production methods—more labor was devoted to maintaining the plots by weeding, adding animal dung, turning over the soil, and so forth. For such tasks new tools (plows) and a new source of energy (draft animals) became useful, and intensive agriculture developed. Intensive agriculture greatly increases an area's carrying capacity, which is its major advantage over horticulture. It can also raise the amount of food an average farmer is able to produce and thus allow the production of a large surplus.

The surplus potential of intensive agriculture made possible the development of civilization in several regions of both the Old and the New Worlds. Peasants produced the food supply for the government officials, priests, artisans, miners, warriors, and other specialists of the ancient civilizations. The peasantry is a consequence of the emergence of civilization; and peasants continue to exist in Asia, Latin America, Africa, and Europe.

Pastoralists acquire many of their material needs and wants from their herds of domesticated animals, either directly or indirectly. Because by definition the herds of pastoral people depend on naturally occurring water and forage, most pastoralists lead a seasonally nomadic life. Herders acquire food and other products they do not take from their livestock by engaging in cultivation, trading with neighboring cultivators, selling the products of their herds, or using their livestock as beasts of burden on long-distance trade.

Pastoralists are found in regions that are not well suited to reliable cultivation, typically because of rainfall or temperature. In these arid or cold environments herding allows people to transform plant matter that is indigestible to humans into edible animal products. It also reduces the risk of living in certain environments both because livestock are a way of storing food and because the herds can be taken to a more favorable location in times of drought. Despite these advantages, herders acquire less food from an area of land than cultivators because most of the energy locked up in the plant matter eaten by livestock is lost to the animals' waste and respiration. The pastoral adaptation affects social organization in many ways, two of which are exemplified by the Basseri of southern Iran and the Karimojong of East Africa.

# KEY TERMS

domestication
carrying capacity
cultivation
pastoralism
horticulture
intensive agriculture
mechanized agriculture
dry land gardening

shifting cultivation
  (slash-and-burn, swidden)
surplus
civilization
peasants
nomadism

# SUGGESTED READINGS

Cohen, Mark Nathan. *Health and the Rise of Civilization.* New Haven: Yale University Press, 1989.
  *Argues that health and nutrition deteriorated after civilization evolved.*

Johnson, Allen W., and Timothy Earle. *The Evolution of Human Societies.* Stanford: Stanford University Press, 1987.
  *Text discussing the cultural consequences of changes in human adaptation.*

Potter, Jack M., May N. Dias, and George M. Foster, eds. *Peasant Society, A Reader.* Boston: Little, Brown, 1967.
  *An edited volume that reprints many classic articles on peasants.*

Wolf, Eric. *Peasants.* Englewood Cliffs, N.J.: Prentice-Hall, 1966.
  *A relatively brief theoretical treatment of peasants, which serves as a good introduction to the subject.*

**The following ethnographies provide excellent descriptions of particular pastoral and farming peoples around the world.**

Barth, Fredrik. *Nomads of South Persia.* Prospect Heights, Ill.: Waveland Press, 1986.
  *A study examining the culture of the Basseri, a pastoral, sheep- and goat-herding society of southern Iran.*

Evans-Prichard, E.E. *The Nuer.* Oxford: Clarendon Press, 1940.
  *A beautifully written ethnography of the Nuer, a cattle-herding people of the Sudan.*

Geertz, Clifford. *Agricultural Involution.* Berkeley: University of California Press, 1963.
  *A case study of agricultural intensification of wet rice in Indonesia caused by population growth and Dutch colonial policy.*

Hanks, Lucien M. *Rice and Man: Agricultural Ecology in Southeast Asia.* Chicago: Aldine, 1972.
  *A discussion of historical changes in methods of rice cultivation in Southeast Asia and the effects of various modes of production on the culture of the people.*

Harner, Michael J. *The Jívaro: People of the Sacred Waterfall.* New York: Natural History Press, 1972.
  *A very readable and interesting ethnography about a horticultural society of the Ecuadorian Amazon.*

Reader, John. *Man on Earth.* New York: Perennial Library, 1990.
  *A photographic and textual survey of a variety of cultures and their adaptations.*

Wagley, Charles. *Welcome of Tears: The Tapirapé Indians of Central Brazil.* New York: Oxford, 1977.
  *A well-researched study of a horticultural society of the Brazilian Amazon.*

**CHAPTER 9**

# EXCHANGE AND CONTROL IN ECONOMIC SYSTEMS

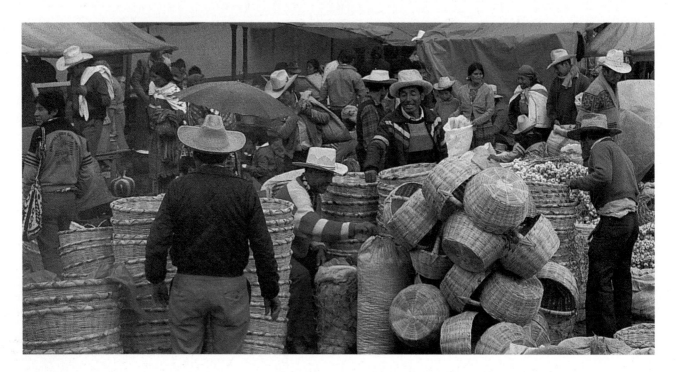

*Exchange is part of the economic system. This Guatemalan scene illustrates one form of exchange known as market exchange.*

## CONTENTS

In the previous two chapters we introduced the basic types of human adaptation and looked at some of the ways these adaptations affect cultures. As we saw, the ways in which a people organize themselves to produce the food and other products they need affects many aspects of their way of life. Productive activities and how they are organized are part of a culture's **economic system**, defined as the patterned activities by means of which people procure and distribute the material goods they consume. This chapter considers two other dimensions of economic systems: (1) some of the ways in which goods are exchanged between individuals and groups and (2) some of the ways in which control over resources, labor, and the distribution of wealth is organized.

## EXCHANGE

Production may be only the first step toward the final use (consumption) of goods. Once they are produced, many goods change hands before they are consumed; that is, those who produce the products transfer them to someone else, who may in turn transfer them to yet another person, until they finally are consumed. The transfer of goods between individuals or groups is **exchange**. Different human populations organize the exchange of products in different ways, some of which we consider in this section.

Anthropologists usually classify exchanges into three modes or types:

✦ **Reciprocity,** in which two individuals or groups pass goods back and forth, with the aim of (1) helping someone in need by sharing goods with him or her; (2) creating, maintaining, or strengthening social relationships; or (3) obtaining goods for oneself.
✦ **Redistribution,** in which the members of an organized group contribute goods or money into a common pool or fund; a central authority usually has the privilege and responsibility to make decisions about how the goods or money later will be reallocated among the group as a whole.
✦ **Market,** in which goods are sold for money, which in turn is used to purchase other goods, with the ultimate goal of acquiring more money and accumulating more goods.

Although most goods change hands through the market mode in capitalist, industrial economies, enormous quantities of goods also are transacted through reciprocity and redistribution. Examples of reciprocity are various gifts we give and receive on holidays, birthdays, weddings, baby showers, and other culturally special occasions. If you are employed, every pay period you participate in redistribution, for the federal and state governments collect a portion of your wage or salary as taxes, which they expend on public purposes or transfer to other members of society.

Although all these exchange forms exist in modern societies, not all preindustrial cultures have all three. Some kind of reciprocity occurs in all human populations. But redistribution implies the existence of a central authority to organize the collection of goods from the group and to make decisions about how the goods will be reallocated. Redistribution, therefore, is an

*Before being consumed most products are exchanged. Here a bullock is being carved into 75 pieces for distribution to Chinese villagers.*

insignificant exchange mode in societies that lack strong leaders who make decisions on behalf of the group. The market mode of exchange requires money, private property, and certain other features that are absent in many preindustrial populations.

## Reciprocity

Reciprocity refers to the giving and taking of objects without the use of money or other media of exchange. It can take the form of sharing, hospitality, gift giving, or barter. To cover these varieties, anthropologists identify three forms of reciprocity.

**GENERALIZED RECIPROCITY.** The defining feature of **generalized reciprocity** is that those who give goods do not expect the recipient to make a return of goods at any definite time in the future. Generalized reciprocity occurs between individuals who are (or are culturally expected to be) emotionally attached to one another and, therefore, have an obligation to help one another on the basis of relative need. In North America parents who provide their children with shelter, food, vehicles, college educations, and interest-free loans are practicing generalized reciprocity. Giving without expectation of quick return also should occur between parties to certain other kinds of social relations, such as wives and husbands, siblings, and sometimes close friends.

This exchange mode occurs in all human populations. Among some peoples it is the dominant form of exchange, meaning that more goods are passed around using this form than any other. For example, most foragers expect band mates to share food and be generous with their possessions. (This fits with the fact that most members of a small hunting and gathering band are relatives of some kind.) Among the !Kung (see chapter 7), only some band members search for food on any given day. But the products of men's hunting and women's gathering are passed around within the band, so that even those families who did not participate in foraging that day receive an equitable share. The band or camp itself is a social group within which food sharing is culturally expected, and those who are stingy with possessions or who fail to share food with band mates are subjected to ridicule (or worse). Broadly speaking, generalized reciprocity is the dominant mode of exchange in very small human groups in which most members are relatives.

**BALANCED RECIPROCITY.** In **balanced reciprocity** goods are transferred to someone and the donor expects a return in goods of roughly equal value (i.e., the exchanges ideally should "balance"). The return may be expected immediately, or whenever the donor de-

Among !Kung and most other hunting and gathering peoples food is shared with other members of the camp, on the principle anthropologists call generalized reciprocity.

In many preindustrial societies balanced reciprocity helps to establish and maintain political alliances. This pig about to be slaughtered on Tanna, Vanuata, will be given as a gift to someone, who is obliged to return a pig to the donor. The goal is sustaining political relations between the island's communities.

mands it, or by some specified time in the future. With generalized reciprocity the giver continues to provide material assistance even though the receiver is unable to return anything for a long time. With balanced reciprocity the giver refuses to continue to transfer goods to the receiver if the latter does not reciprocate within the appropriate time period. Donors may merely be angry if the receivers fail to reciprocate, may complain or gossip to others, may try to force reciprocation, or may end all further relations until goods of equal value are returned.

Although the value of the goods transacted is supposed to be equal (at least roughly), balanced reciprocity is characterized by the absence of bargaining between the parties. In some preindustrial economies the exchange of goods without having to negotiate for each transaction (How much of A will you give me for my B?) frequently is organized by a special relationship between two individuals known as a *trade partnership*. Individuals of one tribe or village pair off with specific individuals (their "partners") from other regions with whom they establish long-lasting trade relationships.

For instance, in the Trobriand Islands off the eastern tip of the island of New Guinea there was a form of balanced reciprocity called *wasi*. Residents of coastal villages traded fish for yams and other garden crops produced in the mountainous interior. The *wasi* exchange was formalized: A coastal village paired off with an interior village, and within each village individuals formed trade partnerships. The rates at which garden produce exchanged for fish were established by custom, so there was no haggling at any particular transaction.

In *wasi* each trade partner received foods not readily available locally, so parties to the transaction gained a material benefit. In many other cases balanced reciprocity takes the form of mutual exchanges of gifts or invitations for social and political purposes. That is, the exchange is not motivated primarily by the desire of the parties for the objects (unlike *wasi*) but by their desire to establish and maintain good relations with one another. (On your friend's birthday, instead of giving her a gift in exchange for a gift of about equal value on your own birthday, you both could save the cost of wrapping paper and cards by buying the objects for yourselves. But then the social goal of the gift—expressing and strengthening your friendly relationship—would not be attained.)

We all are familiar with the anger or disappointment of not having our gifts or dinner invitations reciprocated. Many of us also know the embarrassment of being unable to return a gift of equal value to one we have received. We also are familiar with the use of gift giving for social and political goals. We know that friends make gifts to one another because giving a gift to someone re-creates and strengthens feelings of goodwill. Gifts are a material symbol of good relations. They sustain relations of solidarity and mutual aid between individuals and groups. This is why, cross-culturally, gift-giving ceremonies frequently are part of peacemaking between formerly hostile groups; the gifts symbolize the beginning of a new period of peaceful coexistence.

In our personal lives, too, the back-and-forth flow of tangible objects often symbolizes warm personal feelings about a relationship as well as words—or perhaps better than words, since "talk is cheap." The failure to present objects of appropriate value on certain occasions also symbolizes one's personal feelings, although in a less "warm" way.

But gifts not only express existing social relations with material symbols; they can also be used to create social bonds that are useful to the giver and to obligate people from whom the giver wants something. Gift giving makes someone indebted to you, and therefore can be used to create an obligation to return a favor. Lobbyists and sales representatives know this use of balanced reciprocity.

For a preindustrial example of how balanced reciprocity helps to create and sustain political alliances, we turn to the Maring of highland Papua New Guinea. These people live by a combination of shifting cultivation, pig keeping, and hunting. The Maring live in settlements composed of clusters of kin groups. Each settlement is engaged in periodic warfare with some of its neighbors. Unless a settlement is unusually large, its members form a political alliance with one or more nearby settlements. When warfare occurs the warriors of each settlement rely on their allies for military support and, should defeat occur, for refuge. Most Maring settlements must establish and sustain military alliances if they are not to be defeated in warfare.

An important expression of continued goodwill between allied groups is periodic invitations to feasts and exchanges of wealth objects and other goods between the friendly settlements. Every few years, whenever they accumulate sufficient pigs, the members of a settlement invite their allies to an enormous feast, appropriately called a *pig feast*. At the pig feast, which is attended by hundreds of people, allies bring large quantities of wealth objects to exchange and pay off debts; they consume enormous quantities of pork provided by their hosts; they are on the lookout for potential spouses and

sexual partners; and they aid the host settlement in the ceremonial dancing that the Maring believe is ritually necessary for success in the fighting that will soon occur. The host group uses the occasion of their pig feast to gauge the amount of military support they can expect from their allies: The more people who attend the feast, the more warriors the host settlement will be able to put on the battleground. Later the guests will have accumulated enough pigs to sponsor their own pig feast. They will reciprocate by hosting a pig feast for their allies, who come with wealth objects and pledge their military support by helping the host group in their ceremonial dancing.

The Maring pig feast, and the reciprocal exchanges between the hosts and guests from various allied groups that occur during it, is an important event in maintaining good relations between allies. A group sponsors a pig feast to compensate their allies for their previous military aid as well as to reciprocate previous pig feasts they have attended. The failure to organize a pig feast large enough to compensate one's allies can result in the weakening and sometimes even termination of an alliance. Thus mutual invitations to feasts are critical to the military success and continued survival of a Maring settlement.

**NEGATIVE RECIPROCITY.** The distinguishing characteristics of the third kind of reciprocity—known as **negative reciprocity**— is that both parties attempt to gain all they can from the exchange while giving up as little as possible. It usually is motivated largely by the desire to obtain material goods at minimal cost.

Insofar as it is motivated by the desire for material goods, negative reciprocity is like market exchange; it is different mainly because no money changes hands between the participants. In economies that use money to purchase goods and services, market exchange partly or largely replaces negative reciprocity.

But in economies with no money negative reciprocity is an important way for individuals and groups to acquire goods that they do not produce themselves. Few populations are entirely self-sufficient: Some foods they like to eat do not occur in their habitats; some materials they need to make tools are not found locally; or they lack the skill to produce some of the objects they use. To acquire these goods, people produce other goods to exchange for "imports."

Negative reciprocity in the preindustrial world often takes the form of barter. In the interior highlands of

Papua New Guinea many indigenous peoples manufactured money or wealth objects by stringing shells together into long chains or belts. Because these shells did not occur naturally in the interior, they were traded from people to people until they reached their final destination. Salt also was a trade object because it occurred in only a few areas.

In western North America the obsidian (volcanic glass) used to make stone tools occurred in only a few areas; other peoples acquired it through trade. In some cases these trade routes stretched for hundreds of miles, with the obsidian passing through the hands of numerous middlemen before finally being made into a tool.

## Reciprocity and Social Distance

Can we do anything more with this typology of reciprocity other than merely noting its existence and providing an example or two of each type? Indeed, we can. As Marshall Sahlins, who first distinguished the three varieties, noted, the kind of reciprocity that occurs between two individuals or groups depends on the **social distance** between them. By *social distance* is meant the degree to which cultural norms specify they should be intimate with or emotionally attached to one another. In other words, a given mode of reciprocal exchange is culturally appropriate with only certain kinds of social relationships.

This is seen clearly in North American cultural norms. We expect an individual to practice generalized reciprocity with his or her children and perhaps with siblings and elderly parents; in fact, we are likely to judge them as uncaring or selfish if they do not. But if a middle-income person repeatedly lends money to a cousin or puts a niece through college, we are likely to regard him or her as either unusually generous or a bit foolish. He or she has extended generalized reciprocity beyond the range of relatives to whom we culturally consider it appropriate.

A cultural association of exchange form with kinds of relationships applies to market transactions, which, as we have seen, have largely replaced negative reciprocity in modern societies. In market exchange, individuals are supposed to be "looking out for their own private interests," "trying to get the most for their money," and so forth. We regard this as fine—in fact, as smart shopping—with transactions between strangers in a department store or car lot. But when the seller and buyer are friends or relatives, it is difficult for them to disentangle their economic transaction from their personal feelings for each other. Most of us believe that kinship and friendship bonds cannot easily be mixed with market exchange, because kinship and friendship are supposed to have an element of selflessness, whereas buying and selling are assumed to have selfish motives. Therefore, although I may buy my friend's used car, I feel uneasy about the transaction: What will I do if the car is a lemon?

Further, as our social relations with other people change, so does the kind of reciprocity we practice with them. Most adults have experienced one way in which this occurs: As we grow up, our increasing independence from our parents is manifested by a change in the way we exchange goods with them. We go from being the recipients of generalized reciprocity to more of a balanced reciprocity as we become more independent and finally—at least until the advent of social security—to being the provider of generalized reciprocity.

Finally, changing one form of reciprocity into another can be used as a way of changing the nature of a social relationship. Because the form of reciprocity practiced between two individuals is related to the degree of social distance between them, the social distance can be decreased or increased by one party beginning to initiate a new form of exchange. Or someone can signal his or her wish to draw another person closer (reduce the social distance between them) by tentatively initiating a relationship of balanced reciprocity. In other words, reciprocity has social uses in our culture, just as it has among preindustrial peoples. It also probably has significant consequences for our market economy (see Box 9.1).

Thus I can let you know of my desire to become your friend by giving you an unexpected gift or invitation to dinner. In turn, you tell me whether you share my feelings by whether you return my gift on an appropriate occasion, or repeatedly find reasons to refuse my dinner invitation, or come to dinner several times at my place without reciprocating. If we both use this "strategy of reciprocity," neither of us needs to be put in an embarrassing position of verbalizing our feelings. I signal my wish by my initial gift or invitation, and you decline or accept my offer of friendship by your response.

In sum, forms of reciprocity are culturally associated with types of social relations, so the reciprocity practiced between people changes as their relationship changes. And we can use reciprocity to achieve social

BOX 9.1

RECIPROCITY AND THE
AMERICAN ECONOMY

In many preindustrial economies most exchanges are organized by the principles of reciprocity and redistribution rather than by the market principle. As we have seen, reciprocal and redistributive exchanges are by no means absent in modern market economies. In fact, many economists spend most of their time analyzing the impacts of different redistributive policies (taxation rates, transfer payments, and so forth) on the market. What is less well studied is the impact of reciprocity on the American economy.

The basic difference between reciprocity and market exchange is the essentially social nature of the former. When you give a compact disk as a gift, you have in mind social goals: creating a new relationship, maintaining an old one, reciprocating something that was given to you, and so forth. Further, when you give a gift to a friend or to many relatives, something usually comes back to you in the future because most gift giving is based on balanced reciprocity. This means that gift giving reproduces itself: One gift breeds

another on some future occasion in a cycle that need never end as long as the relationship continues.

So we, too, have a gift economy. Certain kinds of relationships practically require gifts on certain culturally defined occasions, such as Christmas or Hannukah, birthdays, parents' days, valentine's days, and so forth. Gift giving is necessary to maintain and improve relationships that individuals value in their own right. One gift usually is paid back with another, so the gift economy is self-perpetuating, although it does respond to changes in relationships.

This gift economy probably has important effects on the "real" economy.

Because we feel socially obliged to give gifts, we buy goods on the market that we would not otherwise need or want. For example, we buy perfumes and flowers for our wives and girlfriends, tools and belt buckles for our husbands and boyfriends, toys and games for our children, and clothing and recreation equipment for everybody. Whole industries are supported almost entirely by the gift economy, such as floral, greeting card, and gift shop businesses. Other industries—such as businesses involving tools, toys and games, clothing, jewelry, music, cosmetics, publishing, and many other products—enjoy a dramatic increase in the sales of their products because of the gift economy.

To our knowledge, no quantitative studies exist of the magnitude of the gift economy, its impact on consumer-spending habits, or its aggregate effects on the economy as a whole. If you want to gain some idea of how important gift giving might be, try keeping a record over several months of how you spend

*continued on next page*

goals: Reciprocating or refusing to reciprocate gifts or invitations sends messages that are too embarrassing to say outright. Finally, reciprocity can serve as a way to shorten or lengthen social distance.

## Redistribution

The major difference between reciprocity and redistribution—the second major mode of exchange—is the way the transfer of goods is organized. With reciprocity, goods pass back and forth between two participants, with no third party to act as intermediary. With redistribution, goods or money collected from many individuals or groups is taken to a central place or put into a common pool or fund. Some overarching author-

ity (who is empowered to make decisions on behalf of those who contributed) later draws from this pool or fund in returning public goods and services that allegedly benefit the group as a whole.

In modern nations redistribution takes the form of taxes on wages, profits, retail sales, property, and other income and assets. To understand redistribution it is instructive to review how our tax system is supposed to operate. Federal tax revenues, for example, are used for two main purposes. First, they are expended in such a way as to benefit the whole country. The citizens receive police protection, law enforcement, national defense, infrastructure (e.g., dams, roads, airports), regulation of polluting industries, and so forth. Resources collected from the citizenry are expended on public goods and services. Second, taxes are used to provide assistance for individuals in need. These are "transfer payments" in the

*The demand for many goods is increased because American cultural norms require gifts on certain occasions.*

got each item and roughly estimating its dollar value. We think you might be surprised at how much you've received as gifts over the years.

From a strictly utilitarian perspective, all this gift giving is quite unnecessary. Much of it is even wasteful because much of what we receive as gifts we never would have bought for ourselves. (If you make an inventory, ask yourself whether you would have bought all those shirts or blouses or sweaters for yourself. Better yet, ask yourself if you ever wear them!) But the purpose of gifts usually is not to supply the receiver with some object he or she needs or wants; it is rather to supply the giver with the continued goodwill of the receiver by offering an object that symbolically expresses the character of their relationship. Florists, jewelry dealers, and cologne manufacturers depend on these symbolic expressions for most of their living. In the gift economy we glimpse the impact of cultural norms and symbolic expressions of social relationships on material life. ✦

your discretionary income (the money you have left after essential bills are paid). How much of it is spent on some form of gift—including taking someone out to dinner? Or make an inventory of your possessions, recalling where you

form of Aid to Families with Dependent Children, social security, Medicaid, disaster relief, and so forth. Such public expenditures are based on moral norms and cultural values about social justice, equal opportunity, and helping those in need. Redistribution systems around the world are used for similar purposes: to provide public goods and services and to provide assistance to individuals and groups in need.

But there is another side to most systems of redistribution, a side with which we also are familiar. First, there often is conflict over who should provide the public resources, how the resources should be expended, and how much of a share of them should be given to those who collect and distribute them. One common social and political problem with redistribution is disagreement: When many individuals have contributed to the public pool or fund, not everyone is

likely to agree on how the "public resources" should be spent for the "public good."

Second, those who control the redistribution frequently apply the public resources toward their own pleasure or ambitions rather than to benefit the entire population. In modern nations officeholders frequently use redistribution for political purposes. For instance, taxpayers finance dams, allegedly for flood control, hydroelectric power, irrigation, or recreation. Actually, the purpose is to get "federal money" (i.e., tax dollars from elsewhere in the country) into some elected official's district to provide jobs or serve special-interest groups. (Americans even have a term that describes this political use of redistribution: *pork barrel*.) So, like reciprocity, redistribution can be manipulated.

A common form of redistribution in the preindustrial world is known as **tribute**. The subjects of a chief or other officeholder contribute goods (usually including food) into a common pool. Some of the accumulated products are consumed by public officials and other specialists and some are redistributed to the whole population.

Good examples of redistribution systems using tribute payments exist on many of the islands of Micronesia and Polynesia. The entire population was divided into at least two classes. Members of the noble class did little agricultural work but instead ran the political system and sponsored religious ceremonies. The commoner class produced the food and other material goods that supported the nobility. Each commoner household or settlement periodically was obliged to render tribute to the chief who had authority over them. The chiefs used part of these payments to support—and sometimes to enrich—themselves and their families as well as their servants, attendants, and officials. The rest of the tribute was redistributed among the population in various ways. It fed the commoners who worked on public buildings or trails; sometimes it was used for famine relief; and it was consumed on various enormous public feasts and celebrations.

## Market Exchange

To say that goods are exchanged "on the market" means that they are bought and sold at a price measured in money. Person A possesses goods that person B wants to acquire; B acquires the goods by giving A some quantity of money that both A and B agree on; A then uses the money to acquire goods from other people. Market exchange thus requires (1) some object used as a medium of exchange, that is, money; (2) a rate at which goods exchange for money, that is, prices; and (3) parties to exchanges who have alternative buyers or sellers and are free to make the best deal they can, that is, prices determined by supply and demand. On the third point, markets imply the absence of physical coercion: If prices are set by supply and demand, neither party to a transaction can be forced to buy or sell from the other party. This is what we mean by a "free" market—no third party (a government, for example) sets prices or forces anyone to buy or sell from anyone else, and no single supplier of a good controls enough of the market to force people to buy from him, her, or it (in the case of firms).

Because markets (as we define them in this text) require the presence of money, we begin by discussing some of the diversity in money objects and money uses.

**MONEY.** Money consists of objects that serve as media of exchange in a wide range of transactions of goods, services, or both. This facilitation of exchange is the main function of money, in most cases. If an economy uses money, individual A can acquire something from individual B without having to return an object desired by B; money can be given instead, and B can then use the money to buy an object or a service of her or his choice.

Some other characteristics of money are derived from its function as a medium of exchange. For example, money serves as a standard of value: The value of the goods and services that can be exchanged for money can be compared with one another because money serves as a common measure of "how much things are worth." Money also is a store of value: Because it can be used to purchase various goods, it represents wealth in a portable form.

These characteristics mean that not just any object is suitable to be used as money. Money objects must be durable or the value they store deteriorates over time. The supply of the money object must be controllable because if people can get all they want of it, its value inflates and it becomes worthless as an exchange medium. The monetary supply can be controlled by a government, which manufactures the only "legal tender" in the society; or the supply can be controlled by using only imported or rare objects as money. Imported shells are especially common, partly because of their durability. The supply also can be controlled by having the money stuff require a lot of labor to manufacture: Money remains scarce because it takes much time to make it.

An enormous variety of objects serve as money in one or another region of the world. We already are familiar with currencies of modern nations, issued by governments that control the money supply. In preindustrial economies the kinds of objects that take on the characteristics of money are surprisingly diverse. In Africa, for example, the following objects served as money in one or another part of the continent: iron, salt, beads, cowry shells, cloth, slaves, gin, gold dust, metal rods, brass bracelets, and livestock. In Melanesia the list of money objects is also diverse: assorted shells (often modified in some way and sewn into fibers to form long belts), salt, the red feathers of a certain bird (also woven into belts), and pigs.

There are nonmonetary economies in which all exchanges are based on one of the three forms of reciprocity. But even in economies that do have an exchange medium, the range of goods that can be acquired with money varies greatly. In some the range is broad: many kinds of resources and goods can be bought and sold, including labor, land, tools, and sometimes even people (slaves). In these systems money serves as a *generalized medium of exchange*; that is, it can be used to acquire many kinds of goods and services, including land and labor. Anthropologists call this **multipurpose money.**

Money is multipurpose in modern North America. In principle, privately owned natural resources, labor, goods, and money itself can be sold for money. Some preindustrial peoples also have multipurpose money. For example, the Kapauku people of Irian Jaya, which is now part of Indonesia, used imported cowrie shells and two types of necklaces as currency. Kapauku money could be used to purchase almost anything, including land, labor, crops, pigs, tools, and medical services. In fact, Kapauku money can be said to be even more multipurpose than our own. Leopold Pospisil (1963), the ethnographer, writes:

Among the Kapauku an overwhelming amount of goods is exchanged through sales. . . . In their selling and buying most of the Kapauku are strictly profit motivated. Often they invest money in pigs, chickens, large *woti* (bailer shell), inner bark, or animal teeth, for the purpose of breeding the animals for profit, speculating on sales of the bailer shell, or for making artifacts for sale. . . . Besides the necessity of having to buy with money such commodities as land, manufactured products, labor, and services such as surgery, curing, and midwifery, the Kapauku have to pay for favors and acts for which even in our capitalistic society there is no charge. For example, one pays a bride price for a wife, the services of a foster father have to be paid for by the grown boy, a grief expressed by strangers or distantly related people over the death of a close relative has to be recompensed in money, and almost all crimes can be settled through a proper transfer of shell currency. (21–22)

Kapauku sales occurred on a daily basis, much as we make purchases of one or another item regularly. Periodically, however, Kapauku political leaders (called *big men*) organized enormous ceremonies often attended by hundreds of people who came to sell and buy and to make and pay off loans.

The Kapauku represent an extreme in the range of uses to which money could be put as well as in their intense desire to accumulate wealth. More often we find the range of money uses in preindustrial economies to be narrow: Only a few categories of goods are purchased with money. For example, it may be possible to buy food, clothing, and a few other goods, but land is not available for sale at any price and labor is almost never sold. Here money is called **limited-purpose money.**

A famous example of limited-purpose money comes from among the Tiv of Nigeria, studied by Paul Bohannan. Tiv money consisted of metal rods, but the rods could not be used as an exchange medium for all other goods. For one thing, land could not be sold, and labor was exchanged among relatives on the principle of generalized reciprocity. For another, among these people goods circulated in different *exchange spheres*. Certain kinds of goods could only be transacted for certain other kinds of goods. Goods were culturally classified into categories, within which they were freely exchangeable but between which exchange was difficult.

The "subsistence sphere" category included cultivated crops, chickens and goats, and some tools and household goods. Goods within this sphere were exchangeable for one another by means of barter. The "prestige sphere" included slaves, cattle, a special kind of white cloth, and metal rods. Within the prestige sphere metal rods functioned as an exchange medium: One could sell cattle for metal rods and then use the rods to acquire white cloth or slaves, for example, but the monetary function of metal rods normally was limited to the prestige sphere.

However, it was *possible* to acquire subsistence goods in exchange for metal rods; but these transactions were rare, for two reasons. First, few people were willing to trade their metal rods for subsistence goods. This is because goods that circulated in the prestige sphere had much greater cultural value to Tiv than subsistence goods. Second, metal rods were worth an enormous amount of subsistence goods. Yet the metal rods had no denominations; that is, unlike our dollars and cents, they were not divisible into fractions. So for a Tiv to try to exchange one metal rod for subsistence goods would be like an American taking a thousand-dollar bill into a grocery store to buy food, with the clerk unable to make change. As a result of these two factors, Tiv metal rods were largely limited-purpose money.

The Tiv example serves to remind us that just because we find it convenient to call some object "money" does not mean that it has all the characteristics of our own currency. Indeed, some anthropologists believe that money objects are lacking in preindustrial economies and that money is a Western concept that we should not attempt to apply to other cultures. This problem is mainly semantic, however: If we define money simply as a medium of exchange, it is found in many other economies. To avoid confusion and false impressions, we do need always to specify its uses and its cultural meaning to the local people.

As we discuss next, we also need to be careful with the use of the term *market*, because many non-Western markets do not work the same way as ours.

MARKET ECONOMIES AND MARKETPLACES. Two uses of the term *market* can be distinguished. The first refers to the **market principle**. The market principle exists when goods and services are mutually exchangeable at a price determined by supply and demand. In some economies—such as those of the capitalist nations of today—a wide range of goods and services are exchanged according to the market principle. In this case we speak of a market economy, which has four characteristics.

✦ Practically all goods and services have a monetary price: The value of one good (e.g., a piece of land) can be compared with the value of something else (e.g., an auto or so many hours of someone's labor) using a common measure (money).

✦ Most people make their living by selling something— goods, services, or their own labor—on the market. For most people this means selling their labor to someone else, either to another individual or, more often, to a group (firm or public agency) in return for a wage. Workers sell their labor because they themselves do not own the natural resources and capital with which to produce goods.

✦ The factors of production are allocated by the market: Natural resources, capital, and labor are bought and sold on the market, which implies that the supply of and demand for these factors of production determine the uses to which they will be put. The market allocates them in such a way that they flow into those uses in which they receive the highest return (profit).

✦ The economy is self-regulating. This means that the interaction of impersonal forces such as supply and demand—rather than a government or particular individuals—regulates the kinds of economic activities that occur. For example, if the worldwide supply of oil dwindles, people get upset about an "energy crisis." But the market for energy is self-regulating: Energy prices rise, which encourages new exploration, increased production, and a switch to alternative sources of power. In the end the "energy crisis" becomes an "oil glut," during which prices fall because of the market's "invisible hand." (This last point is a somewhat idealized view of market systems: It represents the way the market is supposed to work.)

These four features characterize market economies. But it is possible for the market *principle* to operate

without having a market *economy*. For example, only a few goods may sell for money; only a few individuals make their living by selling something on the market; land, technology, and labor are seldom or never sold; and the economy is regulated by the quite "visible hand" of centralized leadership. In these cases the market principle still exists; but it operates only for certain categories of goods because only some kinds of things are bought and sold. This leads us to the second meaning of *market*.

In its second meaning *market* refers to the location— the **marketplace**—where buyers and sellers meet for purposes of acquiring goods and making money. For example, peasant marketplaces are common in West Africa, southern and Southeast Asia, the Caribbean, and Central and South America. Peasant vendors sell food, cloth and clothing, leather products, livestock, and other goods produced by their families. Traveling merchants (middlemen) bring commodities imported from the developed world or from elsewhere in the region to sell to local people at the marketplace.

Although much buying and selling occurs, peasant marketplaces are not the same as modern shopping malls or department stores. Several notable differences exist between peasant markets and the markets with which people of highly urbanized, industrialized societies are familiar. First, the categories of goods sold at the marketplace are limited, and in fact, most people produce most of their own subsistence using family labor. Most people do not acquire their livelihood from selling their labor for a wage. Rather, they rely on the marketplace for only certain categories of goods that they cannot produce for themselves efficiently. The existence of marketplaces thus does not imply a market economy because most people are not making their living by selling something (goods, labor) on the market.

Second, producing and marketing goods for monetary profit are part-time activities for many vendors. Many marketplaces are staffed mainly by peasants, who market small quantities of food, pottery, furniture, fibers, crafts, or other goods they have produced with family labor. Indeed, marketplaces frequently are periodic, meaning that they do not open every day, but only for a day or two a week. Peasant vendors sell their products on whatever days the market is open in their region. Traveling merchants typically visit several markets in different regions in a single week, often buying products for sale at one market and reselling them at a distant market a day or two later.

Third, peasant vendors usually sell products that they or their family members, rather than hired laborers,

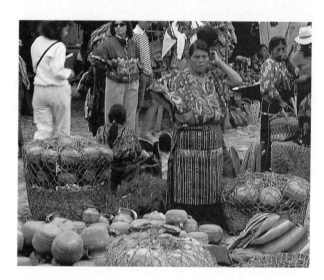

*In peasant marketplaces such as these in Guatemala, a variety of foods and crafts goods are available. Most wares are produced by the vendors and their families. Marketplaces in highland Guatemala existed in pre-Columbian times.*

produce. This means that the kinds and quantities of goods offered for sale by any single vendor usually are small. Most marketplaces also feature goods sold by people who specialize in buying goods wholesale and selling them retail. Such people are dependent on the market—with all its insecurities and risks—for their livelihood. They therefore have developed various marketing strategies to reduce the risks they face. We conclude this section by considering some of these strategies.

When we who live in a market economy visit a marketplace—a store or car lot, for instance—we normally buy goods from strangers. We do not expect any special treatment. We pay the same price as everyone else. If we need credit, we expect to pay the market rate of interest. We expect sellers to be looking out for themselves, just as sellers expect us to be trying to get the most for our money. This characteristic of our market exchanges is referred to as the "impersonality of the marketplace." This impersonality is expressed nicely by the saying that "one person's money is as green as anyone else's."

Marketplace vendors in much of the preindustrial world frequently develop more intimate and personal relations with their customers. In the Caribbean nation of Haiti, for example, the parties to a market exchange commonly establish long-lasting special relationships with one another. The market intermediary (whom we know as a middleman, although most of them are women in Haiti) purchases food and other goods wholesale from several farmers for transport and retail sale at a marketplace. She establishes a special relation, known as *pratik,* with many of her suppliers and customers. *Pratik* involves certain concessions an intermediary makes to many of her suppliers and customers. For instance, when she buys produce from a farmer, she may pay a little more than the market rate or give the producer a loan against a future crop. Market vendors give special treatment to some of their best customers as well. When a *pratik* partner approaches her stall, she quotes the going price for the good on that particular day; but when the transaction is consummated the seller throws in a few extra items of produce.

According to Sidney Mintz, who studied Haitian marketplace relations, *pratik* are not "economically irrational." Because they themselves usually are poor and because competition between them is severe, Haitian market intermediaries seek long-term security in their relations. They therefore are willing to grant concessions by giving better deals to their *pratik* than the market rate

because this increases the chances of maintaining their suppliers and customers.

The same personalistic relations are reported for a marketplace in a Philippine town studied by William Davis. Here, also, sellers attempt to reduce their risks by gradually building up a steady, large clientele of customers rather than by squeezing all the money they can from a single transaction. Each vendor maintains "special customer" relationships (called *suki*) with numerous people who regularly buy his wares. The customers receive credit, favorable prices, extra quantities of goods at a given price, the best quality goods his *suki* partner has to offer on a particular day, and certain services. The vendors benefit as well: Their *suki* customers are expected not to patronize any other suppliers of goods they carry. This is a great advantage in calculating the minimum quantities of goods they will be able to sell and, hence, helps to keep them from unintentionally stocking more of some categories of goods than they can sell.

In both Haiti and the Philippines the impersonality of the marketplace is modified by the formation of personal ties between sellers and buyers. Both *pratik* and *suki* increase the security of marketplace trade for vendors, their suppliers, and their customers.

As we have noted, in market economies the kinds of economic activities that occur are regulated by impersonal forces. Supply and demand are impersonal because—assuming a free market—no small number of individuals or groups controls them, prices, or the overall allocation of the factors of production. The market regulates what and how much is produced, the activities to which labor is allocated, the uses made of capital, how wealth is distributed, and so on.

In nonmarket economies, in contrast, the complex of activities we call an economic system is more under the control of particular people who hold certain statuses and belong to certain groups. We now consider these mechanisms of control.

## CONTROL IN ECONOMIC SYSTEMS

As discussed in chapters 7 and 8, in the process of production people expend their labor and apply their technology to natural resources with the goal of producing the goods they need or want. In all cultures someone controls this process of production. By *control* we mean who decides how the factors of production are allocated to produce goods: who works and how hard, which natural resources are used and how, what is produced and when, and so forth. This control over production is yet another component of the organization of production, along with the division of labor, patterns of cooperation, and assignment of rights of access to resources (see chapter 7). In some systems control is diffuse; that is, those who carry out the production make most of the decisions. In others control is centralized; that is, decision making is hierarchically organized and producers do not control the allocation of much of their own labor.

But production is not the only activity that is subject to control in economic systems. As seen in the previous section, exchange also is universal, although the form it takes varies from people to people. Exchange moves goods or money around between individuals and groups. Because of exchange, those who consume goods may not be the same people who produced them. Potentially, by controlling exchange activities, a few people can transfer the products of other peoples' labor to themselves.

Here it is useful to distinguish exchange from *distribution*. *Exchange* refers simply to a transfer of any kind of good between parties, using one of the three forms already discussed. Economic activity goes on continually, but imagine that we could freeze all acts of production and exchange in an economy for a short period. During that period we would find that individuals and groups have a certain quantity of goods in their possession that they expect to consume or to continue to own. We also would find that individuals and groups have rights to exploit certain areas of land or other natural resources and rights to use certain technologies for future production. The way the use or possession of goods, resources, and technology is spread out among the members of a population is known as **distribution**. Distribution is the relative share of these valuable things (we shall now call them *wealth*) that different individuals and groups consume or possess.

The distribution of wealth can be relatively equal: All families consume about the same quantities and kinds of goods, and they all enjoy about the same access to resources and tools. Or the distribution of wealth may be unequal: Only a few people possess and consume a large share of the goods (including money) produced, and only a few people control the natural resources and technology used in production.

What major kinds of control over production and distribution do we find in preindustrial economic systems? If we want to make fine distinctions, we could certainly identify dozens of types of control. For purposes of this text, we collapse this variety into only four forms: band, kin group, chiefly, and state control. In each form some individual or the members of some group decide how production will occur and how products will be distributed.

## Band Control

In chapter 7 we emphasized the small size, mobility, and flexibility of hunting and gathering bands. These are the major organizational features associated with the foraging adaptation. Here we discuss the organization of control over resources and distribution of products among most foragers.

The members of a band harvest the plants and animals of the region in which they live, but they do not deny access to other bands. Indeed, the composition of bands fluctuates greatly from season to season as individual families of one band receive rights to harvest resources in the territories of other bands for long periods. Why doesn't a stronger association of a specific band with a well-defined area of land develop among most foragers?

Rada Dyson-Hudson and Eric A. Smith suggest that the reason bands do not maintain exclusive access to a territory is that wild resources usually are not "economically defendable." This hypothesis begins with a simple observation: The time and energy required to defend a territory against intruders increase as the area of territory increases (all else equal). Further, the more sparsely resources occur in the territory, the less the reward (in food) of defending any territory of a given size. Finally, the rewards from maintaining exclusive access to a territory are less if the resources found in the territory are unreliable in their abundance, that is, if resources are abundant in one year or season but scarce at other times. The economic defendability hypothesis states that exclusive access to territories will not be maintained if resources are sparsely distributed and unreliable in their abundance. Under these conditions it is "uneconomic" (i.e., the costs outweigh the benefits) to "defend" (i.e., maintain exclusive access to) a given territory.

This hypothesis seems to apply to numerous foraging populations, including the !Kung, the Hadza, and the Western Shoshone. Among these peoples, low, erratic, seasonal, and unpredictable variations in rainfall—and hence in the distribution and abundance of resources—made it uneconomic for the members of a band to defend a specific area.

*Among foragers such as the !Kung of southern Africa, control over access to resources in decentralized and there is minimal inequality in consumption and wealth.*

How is the production process controlled in foraging bands? The individual families or adult members of the band usually decide by consensus what individuals of the family or whole band are to do on a given day: who hunts or gathers and where. Many bands do have headmen, who are respected for their intimate knowledge of the environment or for their hunting prowess. But headmen do not "control" labor in the usual sense of the word; rather, they give advice and make suggestions, and most people heed their advice because their opinion often is correct. Control over production is, therefore, decentralized and individualized among foragers.

Finally, what about control over the distribution of food and wealth objects in hunting and gathering cultures? There is little inequality in food consumption or in possession of tools, jewelry, or other forms of wealth in band societies. There are many reasons for the social and economic equality typically found among foragers. First, the need to pack up and move every few weeks inhibits the accumulation of large quantities of possessions. Second, the value placed on sharing of goods helps to prevent any individual or family from becoming wealthier than their band mates. Third, as a rule, control over distribution is acquired and maintained by restricting other peoples' access to resources, and the ability of any individual to limit access to resources typically is low or absent among most hunter-gatherers. This inability to maintain control over resources is, in large part, because of the seasonal and annual fluctuations in wild resources: Sometimes would-be controllers of rights of access to territory need to hunt and gather in other territories, so they need to allow other individuals access to their own. For such reasons there is little inequality in the distribution of food and wealth in most hunting and gathering populations.

## Kin Group Control

*Domestic group* or *household* refers to a group that shares a common dwelling or domicile. In North America many domestic groups are made up of nuclear families. Further, our households or nuclear families are relatively independent units economically: Wage earners spend most of their income on themselves and their families, and bills are paid largely from the income earned by family members. (As usual, we are here speaking generally, and we mean "relative to other societies we are about to mention.")

In contrast, among most preindustrial peoples, related families are united into much larger associations of kinfolk known as *kin groups,* which often number in the dozens or even hundreds. We consider some of the kinds and functions of these kin groups in later chapters. Here we concentrate on how kin groups control access to resources and how they make decisions about production and distribution.

In many horticultural societies land is not owned by individuals or even by the members of a single nuclear family; rather, it is owned jointly by a kin group. Within each kin group the individual families are allocated temporary use rights to specific plots of land for their subsistence needs. This allocation may be done by consensus of the family heads of the kin group, by decree of the head of the entire kin group, or by simply being the first family to plant crops on a specific plot. But the rights allocated to a family do not include the authority to transfer the land they are using to members of other kin groups. Domestic groups thus exploit land to which they have use rights but not disposal rights. If we look at overall control of land and resources in the whole society, we find that each kin group believes that its members have the right to cultivate particular areas of land. Their rights, however, frequently are disputed, and each kin group may have to be prepared to defend them militarily. Warfare is widespread in kin group control systems, and changes in access to land occur mainly whenever larger and expanding kin groups defeat smaller and declining groups and take over a portion of their territory.

What about control over technology and labor? In general, all families have access to the same tools and knowledge. Each household (or its head) decides which crops it will produce, which of its members will work the plot, how hard they will work, and so forth. Further, by and large, the head or members of the household control what happens to the products of their labor. They themselves consume most of the food and other goods they produce.

But nowhere do households consume everything they produce. For one thing, they share food with other relatives, often on the principle of generalized reciprocity. For another, the kin group as a whole participates in exchanges with other kin groups, usually based on balanced reciprocity. The households contribute vegetable foods, domestic animals, wealth objects, or other goods to the exchanges organized by their common kin group. From time to time each household thus contributes a portion of its products to the activities of a higher-level kin group.

There are several reasons for engaging in these exchanges. They may customarily be required between kin groups whose members have intermarried (see chapter 10). Or exchanges may be made between groups that need to maintain political alliances with one another for purposes of cooperative offense and defense, as we discussed for the Maring in the previous section. So people produce goods for social or even military purposes, not merely to satisfy the needs of their families for food, shelter, and other necessities.

To summarize economic systems using kin group control: The population is divided into numerous large kin groups. Each group has rights of access to a given territory, and it allocates use rights to specific parcels among its constituent individual families. Within a single group there is not much inequality in the distribution of life-sustaining resources because kinship obligations lead to much generalized reciprocity. Kin groups may compete for or fight over land with other like groups, with larger groups often displacing smaller ones and appropriating all or part of the latter's territory. Everywhere kin groups engage in exchanges—usually of the type called *balanced reciprocity*—with other kin

groups for purposes of cementing social, political, and military alliances.

Kin group control is found mainly among horticultural and pastoral peoples. Among horticulturalists, producing and sometimes fallowing lands are allocated among the many kin groups that make up the population. Among pastoralists, sometimes rights to pasture lands are split up on the basis of kinship. Among other herders, such as the Karimojong, grazing lands are allocated on a first come–first served basis, and only the livestock themselves are owned by families or kin groups.

Many horticulturalists and herders have political leaders whose authority extends beyond the members of their own kin group. Control over production and distribution among these peoples may be called *chiefly*.

## Chiefly Control

A *chief* is not just any kind of leader in a "primitive society," although this is the way the term is used in everyday conversation. Rather, chiefs occupy formal offices or hold titles. Most chiefs are formally installed into their office in a public ceremony. The right to occupy the office or hold the title is limited to only some people in the society, usually to the members of a special kin group or to a special family within a kin group. Societies whose political leaders have these characteristics are called *chiefdoms* (discussed further in chapter 13).

Chiefly systems of control incorporate some elements of the kin group system. Each individual's use rights to resources are acquired from the kin group to which he or she belongs. But with kin group control, the rights of the kin group to territory cannot legitimately be taken away from the group by any overarching, higher-level authority. Indeed, such higher-level leaders often are absent altogether in kin group control; even if they are present, they have no rights to strip kin groups of their land or to reallocate lands among kin groups. In chiefdoms, however, a group's use rights to resources can be taken away and reallocated to another group by the chief, who is an overarching political leader with the authority to reallocate rights to resources within his political domain. (In some chiefdoms the chief's power to do this may only be nominal; that is, serious resentment and perhaps bloodshed result if a chief tries to seize the land used by a kin group.)

Further, some labor and a portion of its products are under the control of chiefs, rather than being largely controlled by households and kin groups. Sometimes the chief has the right to call out people to work on public projects, such as making trails, clearing land, building canoes or storehouses, or going on cooperative trading expeditions. Here people are obliged to contribute their work for some public purpose, under the direction of the chief. In other systems the population's labor obligations to their chiefs are only partly for public purposes. A chief periodically demands that his subjects contribute labor for his personal benefit: to cook food for himself and his family, build his dwelling, paddle his canoe, make his clothing, and so forth.

Many chiefs collect tribute as well. Members of various kin groups under the control of a single chief render a portion of their harvest or present some of their animals to the chief. This is another way in which chiefly systems differ from kin group systems of control: Domestic groups still produce most of their own subsistence, but they also must produce an excess that is rendered to a holder of a political office who has traditional rights to receive some share of the products. The amount of tribute taken by chiefs varies. In some systems only a token is offered—an animal or two a year, or the first fruit harvested from a family's garden. In others the demands of chiefs for tribute are quite onerous; people may spend as much or more time laboring to fulfill their tribute obligations as they do working to produce food for themselves and their families.

Through their collection of tribute sometimes chiefs control a sizable proportion of the products of the labor of ordinary people. This means that they also have a great deal of control over the overall distribution of wealth in the society. Again, how chiefs use this control varies. In some chiefdoms most of the food and other goods collected by chiefs are redistributed to the population at large. In such systems chiefs are obliged to give away most of the tribute they receive in large public feasts, provide hospitality, or feed those who contributed their labor for public projects. The rewards of chiefly office in these cases are largely nonmaterial. Some chiefs are allowed to have more wives than other men, but in many cases they merely receive the respect and love of their people in rough proportion to their generosity.

On the other hand, chiefs can potentially use the products they collect for political and selfish purposes. A chief expands or consolidates his political control by means of his control over the resources he collects from his subjects. In one way or another he rewards other, lesser chiefs or those of his subjects who support him.

They receive additional land, food, wealth objects, titles, spouses, or whatever rewards are locally valuable. A chief and his relatives (who sometimes make up a "nobility") also appropriate part of the tribute rendered by their subjects for their own private use, thus enriching themselves and their families. By these processes we see in many chiefdoms the beginnings of marked inequalities in the distribution of wealth, discussed further in chapter 14.

Chiefly control may be summarized as follows. To varying degrees, rights to land and resources are subject to chiefly consent or reallocation. Chiefs have traditional rights (which sometimes need to be backed up by armed force) to receive tribute from their subjects and to call out labor for public purposes. The degree to which chiefs use this control over tribute and labor to enrich themselves varies: Sometimes most of the tribute they receive is redistributed; sometimes most of it is consumed by chiefs and their families or converted into wealth for the chief's noble relatives. Ordinary people, then, work both to support themselves and to support or enrich the chief who has control over the resources they exploit and much of their labor.

### State Control

No sharp line separates chiefly from state systems of control. In both, natural resources are allocated by a formal authority. But in state control the central authority is stronger, and the government is run by a bureaucracy staffed by officials who specialize in administration.

The geographical area and population subject to overarching control also are larger in state systems. The residents of a large region (hundreds or thousands of square miles) are subject to governmental commands for their labor and its products. In a chiefdom hundreds or, occasionally, thousands of people are subject to the tribute and labor demands of a chief. In states tens or hundreds of thousands (and sometimes millions) of people are united under a single ruler and government. Taxes paid to the government pass through several levels of bureaucracy, and each level intercepts some share of the total.

State systems also have more levels than do chiefdoms. For example, households may be grouped into villages, villages into districts, districts into provinces, and provinces into the whole state. At each level control is hierarchically organized: Kings or other rulers pass commands to provincial governors, who give orders to district officials, who pass them along to village headmen, who organize the households of the village to carry them out.

States also have a greater number and variety of occupational specialists—including priests, merchants, artisans, and often standing armies—than do chiefdoms. These specialists must be fed if they are to devote full time to their crafts. Many states include large central places that serve as governmental, religious, and commercial centers.

The ancient civilizations mentioned in chapter 8 are examples of state systems of control over production and distribution. In these civilizations peasants produced the food that fed the elite classes of rulers and priests as well as artisans, warriors, merchants, and other specialists. Peasants often were ordered to participate in large-scale public works projects under a forced-labor arrangement. We can best see how state control works with an example.

In the civilization of prehistoric Peru the ruling dynasty, known as the *Inca,* had great power to allocate natural resources and control the distribution of wealth within the empire. The empire was divided into provinces, each governed by a member of the aristocratic class. In turn the provinces were divided into many village communities, each administered by an official we call an *overseer.* Under this hierarchical power structure the Inca ruler was able to exert control over several million people who lived scattered over thousands of square miles in one of the most mountainous regions of the planet.

At the community level village males held and worked some land in common, subject to the orders of the overseer. Use rights to other land were allocated to the kin groups that made up the village. Peasant men of a single village apparently maintained at least four sets of fields: one they farmed for the subsistence of their families, one for the subsistence of their overseer, one for the Inca, and one for the Sun (the Inca god). The community's men were obliged to work the fields of the overseer, the Inca, and the Sun as a tax. They also kept the llamas and alpacas of the Inca because the village's women wove fine textiles from the wool of these animals to pay their tax.

How were these products distributed? Part of the food grown as tax labor for the Inca maintained the courts of the provincial governors, the ruler himself, and other members of the Inca aristocracy. Part fed the many servants and crafts specialists (miners, goldsmiths and

*The emperor of the Inca state, shown here, ruled over a vast and complex empire.*

silversmiths, weavers, potters, stoneworkers, and so forth) who produced the wealth of the empire that so attracted the Spanish conqueror Pizarro. Part was used to provide subsistence to the peasants, who periodically were called on to construct and maintain public works. Finally, the food that peasants grew on the lands of the Sun supported the large religious bureaucracy and financed temples and sacrifices.

Growing food under the labor-tax laws was not the only obligation of the peasants. Peasants cleared and terraced new lands for intensive agriculture under the labor-tax laws. But because the Inca considered this land to be state property, the peasants received few rewards for extending the area under cultivation. When the central government needed labor for some construction project, villagers were recruited and their labor was directed by engineers. The workers constructed huge ceremonial centers, fortresses, irrigation canals, bridges, and an extensive network of roads (complete with resthouses) that linked the empire together for purposes of communication and trade.

Knowing all this, it is not surprising that the Inca aristocracy controlled the overall distribution of productive resources and wealth objects in the empire. Censuses were made periodically and the land was reallocated among the communities to adjust their landholdings to their population size. Aside from these lands held and worked communally by peasants, sometimes the Inca ruler made a private "land grant" to individuals who gave him unusual service as warriors or engineers.

The empire had *sumptuary laws,* that is, laws regulating the possession of wealth objects, such as certain kinds of cloth and jewelry. Overseers and provincial governors taxed the peasantry for food, which was used partly to feed the artisans who produced fine cloth and objects made from precious metals. Yet under the sumptuary laws, overseers themselves could not possess this kind of wealth unless it had been given to them by the Inca, so they presented such items to the Inca as gifts and relied on Inca generosity toward them for their wealth objects.

The Inca example reveals the main elements of state control. A centralized government allocates most or much of the productive resources among the population. The organization of this control is hierarchical: There are administrative levels between the ordinary person and the top echelons of the state. Commands and some services and public goods flow "down" the hierarchy under the principle of redistribution, but the flow of goods is mostly "up": Peasant families produce food and other products for their tribute or tax obligations as well as for their own subsistence. Part of the products of their labor support artisans, warriors, priests, and other specialists. Another part supports others of their class who work on public projects under the direction of the state. But much of their tax or tribute supports an aristocracy in grand style. By controlling the distribution of wealth in the empire, rulers and other officials reward their supporters and punish their detractors. They thus use their control over the tax and tribute system to reinforce their political power.

## An Evolutionary View

We conclude by stepping back and taking a bird's-eye view of these four systems of economic control over production and distribution. First, the order in which we discussed these systems is the evolutionary order in which they developed among humanity. There was a time in the prehistoric past when all humans lived in foraging bands; all adult members of a band had a say in decisions about work, access to resources was relatively equitable, and little inequality existed between families in possessions or wealth. Some time after the evolution of domestication, kin group control developed among most cultivators and pastoralists as a way of assigning rights of access to particular areas of land to definite kin groups—although a group's rights often had to be defended militarily. Still, economic and political inequality remained relatively undeveloped, because within a kin group generalized reciprocity equalized access to life-sustaining food and other resources. In some parts of the earth kin group control persists even today, but in other areas chiefly control developed out of the kin group system. (How and why this happened are subjects of considerable controversy.) In some chiefdoms the chiefs' control is only nominal and their rewards are mainly honorific because custom obliges them to redistribute most of the tribute they collect from their subjects. But in others chiefs use their authority to exact onerous tribute and command labor, which they use to increase their own wealth and power. Finally, in a few parts of the earth, state control developed out of the chiefly system. Again, the hows and whys of this transformation are controversial, but it is likely that one chiefdom conquered surrounding peoples by means of superior military power and established a ruling dynasty. It forced subject peoples to pay tribute or tax and to contribute labor. Over time a complex social machinery evolved to administer the region, and out of this developed the complex administrative hierarchy, specialization, economic and political inequality, intricate tax and tribute systems, and other features by which we define the state system of control.

Second, notice that a major difference between the four systems is their *scale:* Control of natural resources, of labor, and of the distribution of food and wealth is exerted over ever-larger territories and over ever-increasing numbers of people. Foraging bands typically number around twenty to fifty members; kin groups, a hundred to several hundred; chiefdoms, several hundred to several thousand; and states, tens of thousands, or even millions. Accompanying this increased scale of control is ever-increasing concentration of wealth and power. Such things are difficult to measure, but it is likely that the peasants of the ancient civilizations (as well as many of those of modern nations) lived no better than prehistoric foragers. Almost certainly they had to work harder and longer because they were no longer working mainly for themselves and their families. Rather, they worked partly to feed specialists whose crafts they seldom were able to own and partly to support an aristocracy whose wealth they could enjoy only vicariously.

## SUMMARY

Economic activities encompass the patterned ways people acquire and distribute material goods. This chapter covers two aspects of economic systems: exchange, or the ways goods are acquired by means of transfer from one individual or group to another, and control, or the diverse ways in which ownership or use rights to resources, power to allocate labor, and ability to acquire wealth are organized.

One form of exchange is reciprocity, or the giving and receiving of objects without the transfer of money. Generalized reciprocity usually occurs between parties who are culturally obliged to assist one another in times of need, as among relatives and sometimes close friends. With balanced reciprocity a return of an object of equivalent value is expected. The goal of balanced reciprocity may be the acquisition of goods for their utility, as in the Trobriand *wasi*. More often it is motivated by the desire to create or sustain good relations between individuals (as in gift giving) or political alliances between groups (as with the Maring pig feast). Negative reciprocity is characterized by the desire of both parties to acquire as many goods as possible while giving up as few as possible, as in barter.

The variety of reciprocity that is likely to characterize transactions between individuals and groups depends on the normative degree of social distance between them, so exchange relations alter if social relationships change. Conversely, one party can initiate an attempt to alter a relationship by an offer of a good, and the other party can signal acceptance or rejection by his or her response. Therefore, varying the type of reciprocity can be used to draw people closer together or to push them further apart.

Another form of exchange is redistribution, in which the members of a group contribute goods or money into a pool or fund and a central authority reallocates or uses them for public purposes. Taxes in modern nations and tribute in chiefdoms are examples. Normatively, redistribution is supposed to provide resources to increase public welfare, either to provide public goods or to support those in need. In fact, there is much conflict over the collection and allocation, and those officials who do the collecting and allocating frequently use their authority for private rather than public interest.

Market exchange involves the buying and selling of goods; it therefore requires money and prices determined by supply and demand. Money functions as a medium of exchange, a standard of value, and a store of value. These functions mean that money objects must be durable, and their supply must be limited or controlled in some way. The range of goods and services that can be bought with money varies between economies. Money types can be characterized as multipurpose (like modern currencies) or limited-purpose (like Tiv metal rods).

It is important to distinguish between the market principle, or the principle by which modern market economies operate, and the marketplace, or the physical location at which buyers and sellers exchange money for goods. In many peasant and other preindustrial economies the market principle exists, but it allocates only a limited range of resources because most people do not make their living by selling goods or their labor on the market. Market vendors in peasant economies frequently seek to reduce their risks by developing special relationships with some of their customers, as illustrated by the Haitian *pratik* and the Philippine *suki*.

Systems of control over production and the distribution of wealth may be classified into four overall forms. In the bands that characterize most foragers ownership over productive resources is rather loose and flexible, partly because wild resources usually are not economically defendable. There is little inequality in access to resources within a band because families make production decisions for themselves or by consensus, and it is difficult for any individual or family to maintain exclusive control over territory or technology.

In kin group control, characteristic of many horticulturalists and pastoralists, kin groups control access to land, allocating use rights to specific parcels to particular families. Entire kin groups participate in balanced reciprocal exchanges with other groups into which their members have married to strengthen military alliances or to acquire political influence. Each kin group must be prepared to defend its access to territorial resources from other groups.

Chiefly control exists when there are formal offices or titles that only members of certain kin groups or families are eligible to acquire. Chiefs have the formal authority to reallocate land or resources among the kin groups subject to their control. Some labor or tribute is rendered to chiefs, who use it for public projects and sometimes to support themselves and their family and retainers. In some systems chiefs have extensive control over the distribution of wealth, which leads to marked inequalities. But in others chiefly control is only nominal and the rewards of office are mainly honorific because chiefs are obliged to give away most of what they receive.

Compared with chiefly systems, in state control extralocal political authority is stronger, the geographical area and population subject to state control are much larger, more administrative levels exist, and a greater number and variety of occupational specialists exist. The central government, usually in the person of a single ruler, has the authority to allocate productive resources among the citizenry. Control is hierarchically organized, with commands flowing "down" to peasants and workers. Food and other goods move "up" administrative levels, with each level intercepting some portion of the total for their own consumption and riches. Enormous inequalities in wealth, power, and honor exist because states always include a rich aristocracy and a poor peasantry. The Inca empire of ancient Peru illustrates all these features.

These systems of control emerged in the history of humanity in the order discussed. Taking a bird's-eye view, the scale of control has increased in economic evolution: Control has been achieved over ever-larger territories and over increasing numbers of people. The trend has been toward increased concentration of control and more unequal distribution of wealth.

## KEY TERMS

| | |
|---|---|
| economic system | social distance |
| exchange | tribute |
| reciprocity | multipurpose money |
| redistribution | limited-purpose money |
| market | market principle |
| generalized reciprocity | marketplace |
| balanced reciprocity | distribution |
| negative reciprocity | |

## SUGGESTED READINGS

Belshaw, Cyril S. *Traditional Exchange and Modern Markets.* Englewood Cliffs, N.J.: Prentice-Hall, 1965.
    *A good, short introduction to exchange systems.*

Davis, William G. *Social Relations in a Philippine Market.* Berkeley: University of California Press, 1973.
    *An empirical study of a marketplace in a Philippine town, emphasizing market relationships.*

Douglas, Mary, and Baron Isherwood. *The World of Goods: Toward an Anthropology of Consumption.* New York: W. W. Norton, 1979.
    *An examination of cultural theories of consumption.*

Leclair, Edward E., Jr., and Harold Schneider. *Economic Anthropology: Readings in Theory and Analysis.* New York: Holt, Rinehart and Winston, 1968.
    *A collection of important articles in economic anthropology that includes both theoretical and descriptive case studies.*

Neale, Walter C. *Monies in Societies.* San Francisco: Chandler and Sharp, 1976.
    *A good, brief book about the uses, forms, and functions of money in a variety of economies.*

Plattner, Stuart, ed. *Economic Anthropology.* Stanford: Stanford University Press, 1989.
    *A collection of recent articles on economic systems.*

Rubel, Paula G., and Abraham Rosman. *Your Own Pigs You May Not Eat.* Chicago: University of Chicago Press, 1978.
    *Based on existing ethnographic accounts of numerous societies in Papua New Guinea, this comparative study analyzes the symbolic nature of exchange relations.*

Rutz, Henry J., and Benjamin S. Orlove, eds. *The Social Economy of Consumption.* New York: University Press of America, 1989.
    *A collection of articles focussing on consumption in various regions of the world.*

Sahlins, Marshall. *Stone Age Economics.* New York: Aldine, 1972.
    *Deals with the organization of production and modes of exchange in preindustrial economies.*

Schneider, Harold. *Economic Man.* New York: The Free Press, 1974.
    *A theoretical study of social exchange and economic life.*

Service, Elman R. *Origins of the State and Civilization.* New York: W. W. Norton, 1975.
    *A description and functionalist analysis of the evolution of states and civilizations and the control over production and distribution that accompanied their emergence.*

## CHAPTER 10

# DOMESTIC LIFE: MARRIAGE, FAMILY, AND RESIDENCE

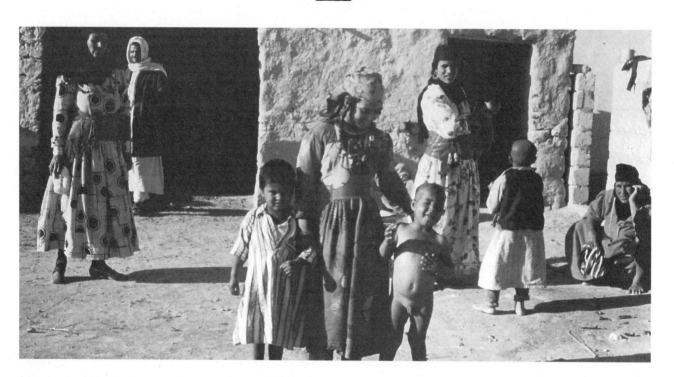

*Human societies vary in their marriage patterns, family forms, and domestic organizations. This Bedouin man is polygamous, which is permitted in his society.*

**CONTENTS**

No matter what their adaptation or economic organization, almost all peoples recognize culturally variable relationships between men and women that we call marriage. Marriages create new nuclear families, which in most cultures are largely responsible for the nurturing and enculturation of children. Newly married couples may establish their own independent households, as is common in North America, or they may reside with the parents of either the husband or the wife, as often happens in other cultures. How and why do cultures vary in their marriage customs? What major types of families exist among humanity, and how are they formed? Why do American newlyweds move into their own place, whereas couples in many other cultures live with one of their parents? We address such questions in this chapter.

*All cultures have nuclear families, including the Maasai of Africa.*

## DEFINITIONS

We must first define some terms. **Kin group** refers to a group of related people who share common interests and a sense of common identity and who cooperate in certain kinds of activities. **Domestic group** refers to those individuals who live together in a single household, or domicile. Because the residents of a household usually are also relatives, a domestic group is one type (but only one type) of kin group. Other kinds of kin groups (much larger than domestic groups) also exist, as we shall see in chapter 11.

Anthropologists use the term **consanguines** to refer to "blood" relatives—people related by birth. We use the term **affines** to refer to "in-laws"—people related by marriage. So a *consanguine* is any blood relative, and a person's *consanguineal relatives* are all of her or his blood relatives. An *affine* is any relative by marriage, and one's *affinal relatives* are all of one's relatives by marriage. Your parents, siblings, grandparents, parents' siblings, and all

cousins are examples of your consanguines. Your sister's husband, wife's mother, and father's sister's husband are some of your affines. Note that affinal relationships are always created by marriage; for instance, a woman is an affine to you because one of your consanguines married her or one of her blood relatives.

Societies everywhere have domestic groups and kin groups, and all peoples distinguish between consanguineal and affinal relatives. But the nature of these groups and relations between kin are highly variable cross-culturally. In North America and most other highly industrialized, urbanized societies, the most important domestic unit is made up of a married couple and any unmarried children they may have. We call this the **nuclear family**, and this kind of group is what Americans ordinarily mean when they say "my family." In many other societies nuclear families are embedded in and merged into much larger kin groups. Some of these are enormously large, consisting of hundreds of members. We discuss these larger kin groups in the next chapter; here we deal only with domestic groups, showing some of the ways they are formed and the major types of groups that exist in the world's cultures. The best place to start is marriage, for this relation is the basis of all kinds of kinship groupings and relationships.

## MARRIAGE: DEFINITIONS AND FUNCTIONS

If someone were to ask you for a definition of marriage, you might well offer something like the following:

Marriage is a personal relationship between a woman and a man involving love, exclusive sex, cohabitation, reproduction and childrearing, and sharing the joys and burdens of life.

People trained in law might also note that marriage has legal aspects, such as joint property rights. Those who are familiar with the writings of some economists might add that the marriage tie creates new households, which are important consumption units in industrial society. Religious people will want to include their beliefs that marriage is a relationship sanctioned by God, a relationship that should last until the parties are separated by death.

This definition is fairly serviceable in North America, but it is not broad enough to include all the diversity in the marital relationship that anthropologists have uncovered in the past 100 years. For example, we think of marriage as a private matter between a man and a woman, although we usually seek the "blessing" of our parents and other relatives before the wedding. In many cultures marriage is much more likely to be a public matter that concerns a broad range of kinfolk of the bride and groom, who must consent to—and often even arrange—the marriage of a couple. Also, cohabitation in the same house is by no means universal: in many villages in Melanesia, Southeast Asia, and Africa the men sleep and spend much of their time in a communal house (called, appropriately, the *men's house*), whereas their wives and young children live and sleep in a separate dwelling.

Similarly, more often than not romantic love between a man and woman is not considered necessary for marriage, and sometimes it is not very relevant to the relationship. Couples do not marry because they "fall in love." For example, in traditional China and Japan a man and woman had no chance to fall in love before they married because they usually hardly knew each other and often had not even met. Sometimes boys and girls were betrothed at birth or as children. In both Japan and China, even when couples were married as adults, the marriage was arranged by their parents with the aid of a matchmaker, usually a female relative of the groom's family or a woman hired by them. She tried to find a woman of suitable age, wealth, status, and disposition who would become a wife for the young man. The matchmaker would "match" not only the couple to each other, but also the woman to the husband's parents. Once she married, the wife would be fully incorporated into her husband's family; her labor would be very much under the control of her husband's parents, especially her mother-in-law; she would worship the ancestors of her husband's family, not those of her own parents; her behavior would be closely watched lest she disgrace her in-laws; and her children would become members of her husband's kin group, not her own.

The same ideas apply to most other Western cultural notions of and customs about marriage: Things we consider normal to the marital relation are not practiced among other peoples. Sex is not always confined to the marriage bed (or mat). The marital tie may be fragile or

In traditional China, marriages were arranged by the parents of the couple and the wife and children became part of the husband's family.

temporary, with individuals expecting to have several spouses during the course of their lives. Or the tie may be so strong that even death does not end it. In much of traditional India there are strict rules against the remarriage of a high-caste widow, and such a widow often follows her husband to the grave by throwing herself onto his cremation fire. There are even a few cases—notably the Nayar of southern India—in which marriage is not the normal relationship that conceives children, and husband-fathers and wife-mothers are not the primary statuses responsible for enculturation. There are culturally legitimate marital relationships that are not between a man and a woman: Among the Nuer of the southern Sudan, sometimes an old, well-off woman pays the bridewealth needed to marry a girl; the girl takes male lovers and bears children, who are incorporated into the kin group of the old woman.

Formulating a definition of marriage that encompasses all the cross-cultural variations in the relationship is, then, a difficult task, for somewhere there will be a human society that does not fit the definition. As you can imagine, numerous definitions have been offered, but still there is no agreement on the "best" or "most encompassing" one. Most anthropologists agree, however, that marriage ordinarily involves

✦ a culturally defined special relationship between a man and woman from different families, which regulates sexual intercourse and provides for reproduction;
✦ a set of rights the couple and their families obtain over each other, including rights over the couple's children;
✦ an assignment of responsibility for enculturation to the spouses or to one or both sets of their relatives; and
✦ a division of labor in the domestic group.

This conception of marriage has the virtue of defining the term by its most common and distinctive features, although doubtless it is possible to roust out human populations whose "marriage" does not share all these features.

In most cultures (an exception will be presented shortly) marriage is the relationship that normatively gives rise to new nuclear families. Sociologists distinguish between an individual's family of orientation and his or her family of procreation. The *family of orientation* is the one a person is born into (i.e., the family formed by the marriage of one's parents). The *family of procreation* is the new one a person forms on his or her marriage (i.e., the family one forms with her or his spouse and children). Marriage usually is the relation-

*Marriage creates new families of procreation and new relations between individuals and groups. The relatives of the couple have gathered for this French wedding.*

ship through which new families of procreation are formed in a population.

This way of defining marriage also is useful because it points to the major, nearly universal functions and social benefits of marriage:

✦ a reduction (but not elimination) of conflict over sexual access;
✦ a formation of social bonds that provide for the material needs, social support, and enculturation of children;
✦ an establishment of relations between intermarrying families or other kinds of kin groups;
✦ a provision for the exchange of domestic services between the sexes; and
✦ the formation of new families of procreation in a population.

Some kinds of relationships—usually a marital relationship—must perform these functions in a human society because of several universal characteristics of humanity. These characteristics include (1) the human female's ability to receive sexual partners continuously, regardless of her ovulatory cycle; (2) the prolonged infancy and childhood dependency of human children; (3) the sexual division of labor found to varying degrees in all cultures; and (4) the definition of sexual intercourse within the nuclear family as incestuous. We now look at how each of these characteristics gives rise to needs that usually are satisfied by the marital bond and the families it creates.

Unlike females of other primates, human females are continuously receptive sexually, and most human males are able and willing to have intercourse with a female regardless of the chances of impregnating her. Marriage establishes special relationships that constrain people's sexual behavior by defining and limiting most people's sexual access to certain individuals. (It does not, however, always limit everyone's sexual partners to their spouses alone, the way our own cultural norms prescribe.) This undoubtedly reduces the amount of conflict over sexual access. Do not conclude, however, that it eliminates the conflict because people still quarrel over who will marry whom and over who has the right to have intercourse with whom.

Human children also have special requirements. Until they reach ten or more years of age, they are totally or largely dependent on adults for food, shelter, protection, and other bodily needs. Equally important, they require the presence of adults for the social learning crucial to complete psychological and cultural development. It is theoretically possible that only one adult, the mother, is required; but almost everywhere marriage helps to create and expand the relationships through which children receive the material support and enculturation necessary for their immediate survival, future maturity, and eventual reproduction.

Humanity also differs from other mammals in the degree to which economic tasks are assigned to sexes. As discussed in chapter 12, a sexual division of labor exists worldwide: men do some kinds of activities, women other kinds. The tasks ordinarily overlap, but there is enough differentiation that the goods and services produced by women somehow must be made available to men, and vice versa. Marriage usually establishes domestic relationships between men and women in which these goods and services pass back and forth. It also defines the duties each partner is normatively obliged to render to the other and to their offspring.

Finally, in some societies nuclear families are able to survive independently, but in very few societies are people allowed to mate and marry within their own family. Almost everywhere sexual relations between parents and children or between sisters and brothers are defined as incestuous and prohibited. Violation of this prohibition—known as the **incest taboo**—usually is severely punished, often by death. Except for a few cultures, the incest taboo applies to members of one's own nuclear family, but it usually is extended to some

*One reason that marriage is found in nearly all cultures is the prolonged dependency of children on adults, especially the mother in infancy. This is a Sherpa woman with her child.*

cousins, to uncles and nieces, to aunts and nephews, and to other kin that a culture defines as close relatives. The incest taboo means that people take their sexual partners and spouses from other nuclear families. Individuals must leave their families of orientation if they are to form families of procreation. Because of the incest taboo, families intermarry with one another, and in many cultures the affinal ties created by intermarriage form the basis for establishing important trade relations or political alliances. Such marriage alliances are covered later in this chapter.

These universal characteristics of humankind—continuous sexuality, prolonged infant dependency, sexual division of labor, and the incest taboo—make a relationship like marriage and a group like the family nearly universal. They do not, however, make any particular *form* of marriage or the family universal. Sexual access must be defined, children must be cared for, the products of the sexes must be exchanged, and people must leave their families of orientation to seek their mates—these universal needs do not impose any specific form of marriage or family on a culture. Indeed, human societies have evolved diverse solutions to these problems. Some of these solutions are considered in the remainder of this chapter. For now, to show how very different from our own marriage and family system other peoples can be, we consider one of the most unusual systems recorded by anthropologists, the Nayar of southern India.

## Nayar "Marriage"

Before Great Britain assumed colonial control over part of India in 1792, the Nayar were a caste (see chapter 14) whose men specialized in warfare. A great many Nayar men were away from their villages much of the time because as a warrior caste, they served as soldiers for several surrounding kingdoms and in other parts of India. Nayar women were required to confine their sexual activity to men of their own or a higher subcaste. They suffered severe penalties—death or ostracism—if they transgressed this norm. The fascinating thing about the Nayar is that they almost certainly lacked nuclear families and—by the conception of marriage just described—lacked marriage as well. What alternative system did they use?

Nayar villages were composed of a number of kin groups. Each child joined the kin group of his or her mother. Each kin group was linked for certain ceremonial purposes to several other kin groups: some from its own village, others from neighboring villages. Any Nayar caught having sexual relations with anyone in his or her own kin group was put to death because intragroup intercourse was regarded as incestuous. Every few years all the girls of a kin group who had not yet attained puberty gathered for a large ceremony. This ceremony was attended also by people from the linked kin groups, for the purpose of the event was to ceremonially "marry" these young girls to selected men from the linked kin groups (whether these really deserve to be called "marriages" depends, as you will see, on how we define the term). At the ceremony each "groom" tied a gold ornament around the neck of his "bride," and each couple retired to a secluded place for three days, where they may have had sexual relations if the girl was nearing puberty. After this period the "grooms" left the village, and each had no further responsibilities to his "bride"; indeed, he might never even see her again. For her part, the "bride" and the children she would later bear had only to perform a certain ritual for her "husband" when he died. The ritual tying of the ornament by a man of a linked kin group did, however, establish a girl as an adult, able to have sexual liaisons with other men when she reached sexual maturity.

After her "marriage" each girl continued to live with her own kin group. When she reached sexual maturity she began to receive nocturnal male visitors from other kin groups. She established long-lasting sexual relations with some of her partners, who were expected to give her small luxury gifts periodically. Her other, more casual partners had no obligations toward her, and any of her sexual relationships were easily terminated. None of her partners supported her or her children in any way other than these occasional gifts; indeed, they also visited other women and sired other children. The food and clothing of a woman and her children were supplied by her brothers and other members of her kin group, who were also responsible for disciplining and providing an inheritance for her children. A woman's early "marriage," then, did not establish a nuclear family, nor did her later sexual partners ever live with her or support her children. There was only one other thing a Nayar woman required from her partners: when she became pregnant one of them had to admit that he could have been the father of her child by paying the fees for the midwife who helped to deliver the baby. If none of her partners did so, it was assumed that she had had sexual intercourse with someone of a lower caste, and she, and sometimes her child, would be expelled from her kin group or killed.

We see that a Nayar girl's early, prepuberty "marriage" ceremonially marked her entry into adulthood; only after she had been "married" to someone of a linked kin group should she begin (legitimately) to receive male visitors. Later, when she bore a child, the infant was believed to be the product of a legitimate union if one of its mother's partners paid the birth fees. Her child then became a member of the kin group of herself, her sisters, and her brothers, who gave the child material and social support. No nuclear families—or any other kind of family of procreation—existed, and the Nayar had no marriage as the term is used in this book.

## MARRIAGE: A CROSS-CULTURAL PERSPECTIVE

The taboo on sexual activity within the nuclear family means that people ordinarily leave their families of orientation to establish new families of procreation. When they do so they enter into a relationship—known as *marriage*—with one or more people of the opposite sex, but the nature of this relationship varies enormously cross-culturally. For one thing, most preindustrial peoples allow multiple spouses. For another, the nature of the marital relationship—living arrangements, what wives and husbands expect from each other, who decides who marries whom, authority patterns, how the kinfolk of the couple relate to one another, and so forth—differs from people to people. We can only provide a glimpse of this diversity.

## Marriage Rules

Everywhere the choice of a spouse is governed by cultural norms that identify members of some social groups or categories as potential spouses and specify members of other groups or categories as not eligible for marriage. One set of rules is called **exogamous rules.** Exogamy ("outmarriage") means that an individual is prohibited from marrying within her or his own family or other kin group or, less often, village or settlement. Because the incest taboo applies to those people whom the local culture defines as close relatives, members of one's own nuclear family and other close kin are almost everywhere prohibited as spouses. Exogamous restrictions often extend to large kin groups with hundreds of members—no one in the kin group may marry any other member, although many of these individuals are not closely related biologically.

Other kinds of marriage rules are known as **endogamous rules.** Endogamy ("inmarriage") means that an individual must marry someone in his or her own social group. The classic example of endogamous groups is the castes in traditional Hindu India (see chapter 14). Other kinds of endogamous categories are orthodox Jews, races in the American South during the slave days and, more recently, in South Africa, and noble classes in many ancient civilizations and states.

The purpose of endogamous rules most often is to maintain social barriers between groups of people of different social rank. Rules of endogamy maintain the exclusiveness of the endogamous group in two ways. First, they reduce the social contacts and interactions between individuals of different ranks. Intermarriage creates new relationships between the families of the wife and husband and potentially is a means of raising the rank of oneself or one's offspring. Endogamy has the effect of keeping affinal relationships within the caste, class, ethnic group, race, or whatever; this reinforces ties within the endogamous groups and weakens those between the groups. Second, endogamy symbolically expresses and strengthens the exclusiveness of the endogamous group by preventing its contamination by outsiders. This is most apparent with Indian castes because the cultural rationale for caste endogamy is to avoid ritual pollution: The Hindu religion holds that physical contact with members of lower castes places high-caste individuals in a state of spiritual danger, precluding the possibility of marriage between them.

Technically, the term *endogamy* applies only to cultural rules or laws about confining marriage to those within one's own group. But it is important to note the existence of *de facto* endogamy, meaning that although no formal rules or laws prohibit outmarriage, most people marry those they consider to be like themselves. De facto racial and class (here in the sense of "social status" or "rank") endogamy exist in most modern nations, including North America. This is partly because opportunities for members of different classes to get to know one another often are limited. For instance, members of different classes often go to different kinds of schools and hang out with different sets of friends. Such practices decrease social interactions and, hence, the possibilities for people of different classes to meet and fall in love. De facto endogamy also exists because of powerful norms against marrying outside one's own "kind." Members of elite classes (and parents and other relatives of young people) may worry that would-be spouses of lower-class standing would not fit in with their social circle (to put their objection politely). Likewise, interracial couples are warned about the social stigma attached to their relationship and about the "problems" they and their children will encounter.

(Incidentally, notice how the norm against interracial marriage and even dating is self-reinforcing. The norm exists partly because of racial prejudice and partly because of the cultural fact that so many people think interracial couples and their children will face special difficulties. So interracial marriages are uncommon, mainly because of the norm. In turn the rarity of interracial marriage reinforces the widespread opinion that society is not yet "ready" for them; if it were, there would surely be more interracial couples!)

## How Many Spouses?

One way in which cultures vary in marriage practices is in the number of spouses an individual is normatively allowed at a time. There are four logical possibilities:

✦ **Monogamy,** in which every individual is allowed only one spouse
✦ **Polygyny,** in which one man is allowed multiple wives
✦ **Polyandry,** in which one woman is allowed multiple husbands

✦ **Group marriage**, in which several women and men are allowed to be married simultaneously to one another

The last three possibilities are all varieties of **polygamy**—meaning "plural spouses." Notice that the three types of polygamy refer to the number of spouses allowed to a person, not necessarily to how many spouses most people have. For example, in cultures that we characterize as polygynous, men are permitted more than one wife, but only a minority of men actually have more than one.

It may surprise members of monogamous societies to learn that most of the world's cultures allow polygamy. The most common form of plural marriage is polygyny, which is allowed in about 75 percent of the societies of the world. Polyandry, on the other hand, is rare. There are less than a dozen societies in which it is well documented—less than 1 percent of the world's cultures. Group marriage, so far as we know, has never been a characteristic form of marriage of a whole human society. Indeed, most anthropologists believe that group marriage, where it has occurred, has been a short-lived phenomena brought about by highly unusual circumstances, such as in utopian or communitarian groups (see Box 10.1).

Comparisons of frequencies such as those just mentioned face difficulties in assigning a particular people unambiguously to one of these four categories. (To appreciate this problem, answer the following question: Did the Nayar have polyandry, group marriage, or no marriage at all?) But they do give an accurate impression of how common or rare each form of marriage is in the human species.

Most monogamous peoples misunderstand the nature of polygamous marriages, seeing them mainly as attempts, usually by men, to get access to more sexual partners. We fail to recognize the social and economic conditions that make these forms of marriage advantageous. We now look at these conditions for polygynous and polyandrous societies.

**POLYGYNY.** Even though most peoples allow polygynous marriage, only a minority of men in these societies actually have more than one wife. Thus polygyny exists as an alternative form of marriage in these societies, rather than as the predominant (most common) form. In those societies that allow it, polygyny ordinarily is the preferred form of marriage for men and often for women. Men, in particular, desire to have multiple spouses, although most men are unable to achieve their goal.

*Polygyny is permitted in most of the world's cultures. This Iraqi man is shown with two wives, their children, and his mother.*

Even with only a minority of men married polygynously, an obvious problem exists for some other men: if some men have plural wives, this reduces the number of marriageable females so that some men cannot marry. This is in fact often the case. But in other cases this problem is not as acute as one might think because in many populations there are more marriageable women than men at any one time, for several reasons.

The main reason there are more females than males eligible for marriage is that in many cultures, teenaged females are considered to be prepared sexually and socially for marriage. Most males, however, wait until they are in their twenties or even thirties to marry because they have other important duties (such as serving as warriors) to perform, because they are regarded as irresponsible, or because they have insufficient resources to acquire or support a wife. Thus many women are ready for marriage at a young age (often soon after puberty), and in many cultures girls are betrothed even earlier (often at birth). The fact that women are ready for marriage at a younger age than men has the effect of raising the ratio of marriageable women to men and thus increases the number of men who can marry.

Also, in some cultures more males than females die prematurely because they engage in more hazardous

Most Americans know about the communes popular with many young people in the 1960s and 1970s, which practiced free love and renounced personal property. Whether these communes represent cases of group marriage is debatable, because there are questions about whether "love" was quite as "free" in them as usually depicted. At any rate, most lasted only a few years. No doubt many of their former members are now monogamous stock brokers and attorneys.

So "hippie" communes may or may not represent group marriage, depending on how strictly we define the term. But there is at least one well-documented case of group marriage in the United States. It occurred in an unexpected time—the nineteenth century—and among an unexpected subculture—conservative Christians.

Mainstream Christians of this time stressed premarital chastity and marital fidelity. Ever since the Reformation, however, Christian sects that draw important elements of their doctrine from small passages of scripture have sprung up. One such passage is from Acts 4:

[2] The host of believers were one in heart and soul; no one claimed his belongings just for himself, but everything was theirs in common. . . .[4] Not one among them suffered need; for those who owned fields or houses sold them, brought the proceeds of the sale[5] and deposited the money at the feet of the apostles. Then it was distributed to each according to his need.

This passage served as the basis of a radical utopian experiment in Oneida, New York, initiated in 1847 by a theologian named John Humphrey Noyes. Noyes believed—not unreasonably—that the preceding scripture exhorted

BOX 10.1

# GROUP MARRIAGE IN THE UNITED STATES

believers to hold property in common. He attracted some converts and founded a community based on his beliefs.

But he took the exhortation one step further. Not only were Noyes's followers required to sign over their worldly goods to the community, to eat together, to live in a single enormous house (still standing), and to work together like a giant family; "private property" in marriage and sexual matters was also forbidden. All men and women were to consider themselves husbands and wives and were allowed sexual access to one another. The tricky part was that during the first twenty years of the community, the men were not supposed to ejaculate because no children were allowed to be born, and Noyes believed that the spilling of semen was debilitating to male strength. But Noyes did make one concession to human frailty: He required young men to sleep only with postmenopausal women until they learned to control themselves. Astoundingly, in a community of around 500, only two children were born between 1848 and 1868!

The sexual aspects of group marriage in the Oneida community apparently worked as follows. A committee (no doubt under the control of Noyes, who was something of an autocrat) had the final word over who spent the night with whom. A man who wanted to

sleep with a particular woman submitted a written request to the committee, who sought the consent of the woman. The woman could refuse permission, or the committee itself could deny the request on the grounds that this man and woman were showing too much "special love" for one another rather than loving all community members equally. This rather unusual arrangement was a bit titillating to outsiders, and the community supplemented the income that it got mainly through the manufacture of steel traps by selling lunches to thrill-seekers who came up from New York City to see the community.

After 1868 children were allowed, but not just anyone could have them. Noyes thought that only the worthiest and most mentally and physically fit members should be allowed to reproduce. He set up another committee to which members could apply for a child-bearing permit. Thirty-eight men and fifty-three women were selected as parents, and they had about sixty children. Children knew their parents and had some special contact with them, but they were raised in a communal nursery; and all adults were supposed to love and nurture the children as if they were their own.

The Oneida community disbanded as such in 1879, largely because of internal discord and resentment caused by the elderly Noyes's attempt to monopolize the young women. But many former members continued to live nearby and formed a successful company, also known as Oneida. Perhaps you have some of their silverware. ✦

SOURCES: Van den Berghe (1979), Whitworth (1975).

activities, such as warfare and hunting. Higher male death rates also increase the number of men who are able to find wives even though some men are polygynous.

So polygyny does not necessarily mean that most men cannot marry because some men are monopolizing the women. Indeed, looked at from the female perspective, polygyny may have the beneficial effect of assuring that virtually all women find husbands. This is important for a woman because marriage legitimizes children, and in many preindustrial cultures children are her main or only source of social security—they are the people she depends on to support her in old age. There is another reason why it is important for a woman to marry in polygynous societies: to ensure that her children are well provided for. In the vast majority of polygynous societies, inheritance of land, livestock, and other wealth and productive property passes from fathers to sons. A woman need not marry to bear children, but she does want a husband to assure her sons of having rights to an adequate inheritance; her married daughters usually acquire their rights of access to resources from their husbands. Thus, in societies in which for some reason there are more adult women than men, polygyny provides a means for almost all women to gain the benefits of a husband for both herself and her children.

As mentioned, in societies that permit it, polygyny is the preferred form of marriage. Men, in particular, want multiple wives. A man has both social and economic incentives for marrying several women. Socially, in many of these societies a man's status is directly related to the size (number of wives and children) of his family. Economically, there are short-term and long-term benefits, especially when a woman's labor is important in providing food and wealth to her family. The more wives and children a man has, the larger the work force available. In pastoral societies in Africa and elsewhere, polygyny enables a man to increase the size of his herds, since he has more herders (wives and children) to tend livestock. Similarly, in those farming societies in which female labor is important, a polygynous man has more workers to tend fields and harvest crops. As he grows older he will have more children and grandchildren to look after his herds or work his fields and care for him. Thus as long as he has the resources to support them, a man usually tries to acquire additional wives.

What determines whether a particular man is *able* to acquire more than one wife? The answer usually is wealth: Only well-to-do men are able to afford more than one wife. "Afford," however, does not mean what North Americans might think; it more often is a matter of being able to acquire additional wives than of being able to support them. Most polygynous peoples have the custom of bridewealth (discussed later), which requires a prospective groom and his relatives to give livestock, money, or other wealth objects to the kin of the bride. Although fathers and other relatives typically are obliged to help a young man raise bridewealth for one wife, only a minority of men can get together sufficient resources to provide bridewealth for additional wives.

Thus far we have emphasized the benefits to the husbands of polygynous marriages. There are also social and economic advantages for the wives. Many North Americans think a woman would not want to be part of a "harem." But the most prestigious marriages for a woman are to husbands of wealth and status—the very men who are most likely to have married other women. Not only are these women economically better provided for by their husbands, but polygynous marriages frequently lighten their workloads. Co-wives usually work together and cooperate on chores such as producing, processing, and preparing food; tending livestock; and caring for children. Thus it is not unusual for a wife to encourage her husband to take additional wives to assist her in her chores.

Although they have advantages for both men and women, polygynous marriages also have inherent problems. A frequent problem is rivalry between co-wives and favoritism by husbands. Several strategies are used in polygynous societies to minimize friction within these families. One strategy is for a man to marry women who are sisters, a practice called *sororal polygyny*. Among groups who practice sororal polygyny, sometimes the husband of the oldest daughter of a family will have a marriage claim on her sisters as they come of age. The reasoning is that sisters are raised together, have sentimental ties, enjoy working together, are less jealous of one another, and are thus more compatible. In cases where a man marries a number of unrelated women, each wife usually has her own separate dwelling to minimize potential conflict with other wives. In these cases the husband lives or spends time with each of his wives alternatingly. Regardless of whether the wives live in one dwelling or several, or whether they are sisters or unrelated, these societies emphasize that the husband should show no overt signs of favoritism.

POLYANDRY.    Polyandry, the marriage of one woman to two or more men, is documented in less than a dozen societies. Although much has been written about the practice, anthropologists disagree on the factors that lead men to share a common wife and a woman to take more than one husband. Here we can discuss only two such factors: (1) female infanticide, which results in fewer marriageable females than males, and (2) resource scarcity, in which polyandry has the effect of limiting family size.

The Inuit foragers of Canada occasionally practiced polyandry up to the nineteenth century. Life in the Canadian arctic was seasonally difficult and starvation was always a possibility. Recognizing such potential problems, the Inuits tried to limit family size. One common form of population control was infanticide; unwanted babies were taken at birth and killed. Both boys and girls were killed, but male children were considered more desirable than females, and thus a disproportionately higher number of female babies fell victim to infanticide. The higher accident rate among Inuit males while hunting partly compensated for the difference in the infanticide rates, so the sex ratio usually was fairly balanced in a region. The Inuits were so widely scattered, however, that social contact frequently was limited to only a few hundred people from among whom potential spouses would be obtained. Not surprisingly, shortages of marriageable females occasionally occurred within some Inuit groups.

Among the Inuits, a husband and wife working as a team was more necessary to ensure survival than among most other peoples. For example, during winter months game frequently was scarce, and the Inuits lived in small family units, moving regularly in search of game. Because an individual cannot survive long in the open during the winter, every move in search of food required the building of an igloo—a dome-shaped structure made of snow blocks. Only about one hour was spent in igloo construction, but the task required the labor of two persons. Neither a man nor a woman alone could travel or secure food. For these and other reasons, a man whose wife died or left him had to quickly find another wife, so sometimes he joined the family of and became a co-husband with a brother or close friend. This arrangement usually was considered neither desirable nor necessarily permanent. The "second" husband usually moved out and married the first eligible woman who became available. Conversely, an Inuit woman whose husband was killed or died had also to find a new husband immediately. As a result, polyandry, polygyny, and monogamy were practiced by the Canadian Inuits, according to circumstances.

Resource scarcity has also led some people to practice polyandry. The problem of a family having too many heirs for available resources has confronted many farming peoples. Often the family farm would support only a single couple, yet some families had three or four sons. Many European groups faced this problem during the Middle Ages and even up to the nineteenth century. In Ireland and some other parts of Europe the problem was solved by the rule of primogeniture, under which the oldest son inherited the land and the younger sons had to make their own ways in the world. Some sons served in the army. Others might join the church as a priest or a monk or in some other capacity. Daughters who could not find husbands usually either remained at home or joined a nunnery.

Some peoples of the Himalayas found another solution—polyandry. The rugged topography and high altitude of Tibet and Nepal sharply limit farmland. Traditionally, all sons, regardless of age, have an equal claim on Tibetan family property. A farm may be adequate to support only a single family, but a couple may have three or more sons. If the sons divide their inheritance, the land would become so fragmented that

*Although it is allowed in only a few cultures, polyandry is a fairly common form of marriage in parts of Tibet.*

the brothers' families would be impoverished. To solve this problem, sometimes all the sons marry one woman. This form of polyandry, called *fraternal polyandry,* helps to keep the farm and family intact and limits the number of children in the family. Although the oldest son assumes primary responsibility for the wife and children, he is not supposed to be shown sexual favoritism by the wife, who has sexual relations with all her husbands. When children are born each brother treats them as if they were his own, even if he knows that a particular child was fathered by one of his brothers. To the brothers, the advantage is that polyandry preserves the family property, keeping the land, the livestock, the house, and other wealth together. Also, one brother can stay behind and work the family land during the summer, while another brother takes the livestock to high mountain pastures and a third brother (if present) visits the lowland for purposes of market trade. This system also has advantages for the wife, who has multiple husbands to work for and help support her and her children. Her life usually is less physically strenuous and she usually has a higher standard of living than a woman married to only one man.

Although polyandry has its economic advantages, sometimes problems arise. A younger brother can at any time decide to end the arrangement, claim his portion of the family property, marry another woman, and establish his own family. The oldest brother does not have this option because as head of the family he bears primary responsibility for supporting their wife and children.

## Marriage Alliances

In a few cultures getting married and being married are treated rather casually. In fact, considering our own marriage practices—as opposed to our marriage norms—from a comparative perspective, many North Americans treat their marital duties rather lightly. In two studies conducted in the 1940s, Alfred Kinsey found that one half of American husbands and one quarter of American wives had had extramarital affairs. (The nation was shocked, but apparently much of the surprise was faked!) Marriages also are quite liable to be terminated in the contemporary United States: The chances that a 1990s marriage will ultimately end in divorce approach 50 percent. We call ourselves monogamous—which we are—but divorce is sufficiently common that some sociologists have suggested that the phrase *serial monogamy* (meaning "only one legal spouse at a time") is

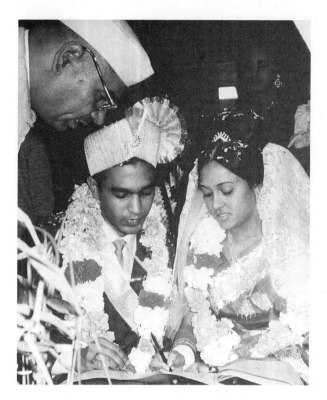

*In many cultures a new marriage creates bonds between the families of the couple. This is an Indian wedding.*

more appropriate. There is a large gap between our actual behavior and our norms of marital fidelity and lifelong commitment.

Most peoples treat marriages as a far more serious business—so serious in fact that it cannot be left entirely to the free choice of the partners. Marriage frequently establishes a bond not just between the couple itself but also between their relatives. The affinal ties between kin groups created by the fact that one or more of their members are married to one another frequently are important not just socially but also economically, politically, and, often, ritually. Marriage establishes an *alliance* between the members of two kin groups, and sometimes **marriage alliances** are critical for the well-being and even survival of the intermarried groups. This appears to have been the case, for example, among the ancient Israelites because Moses wrote in Genesis (34:16): "Then we will give our daughters unto you, and we will take your daughters to us, and we will dwell with you, and we will become one people."

A good example of how intermarriage creates and maintains ties between kin groups comes from among the Yąnomamö, a horticultural and hunting tribe of the

Amazon rain forest of South America. Every Yạnomamö village had numerous enemies with whom it was engaged in warfare. Each village constantly was under threat of attack, so each had to be prepared to defend itself; likewise, the men of each village periodically went on raids intended to capture the women and other resources of its enemies. It was, therefore, advantageous for a village to establish and maintain alliances for mutual defense and offense with other villages, for the more men a village could mobilize as warriors, the more likely it was to be successful in conflicts. The smaller villages were in fact obliged to enter into military alliances or they soon would be victimized by their more numerous enemies. Another advantage of alliance formation was realized in the case of military defeat: A defeated group could take refuge with an allied village, whose members would feed and protect the refugees until they could establish producing gardens in a new location.

Marriage was a key strategy in creating and maintaining these alliances. When the men of a Yạnomamö village wanted to make an alliance with another village, they began by trading. For instance, one village might tell the other it needed clay pots and would be willing to trade its bows for them; or it might say that it needed hallucinogenic drugs used in shamanistic curing and would trade its hammocks for them. The people of each village were capable of making all these products for themselves, but no matter: Trade provided the excuse that villages used to visit one another to begin alliance formation. If no trouble broke out during the trading—for a Yạnomamö village did not even trust its long-time allies, much less its prospective allies—the relation might extend to mutual invitations to feasts. If the feasts did not turn violent, the men of the two villages would agree to give some of their "sisters" (female consanguines) to one another. This was considered the final stage of alliance formation; once the villages had exchanged women, the alliance was—by Yạnomamö standards—secure.

The Yạnomamö illustrate how intermarriage creates bonds and establishes important political relations between villages. In many cultures these bonds and relations are important to families or settlements. If marriages are one means of establishing ties that are critical to a group's material well-being or survival, then the choice of which group to marry into may be too important to be left entirely up to the woman and man whose marriage creates the relationship. Older, wiser, and more responsible people should be making such critical decisions. This helps to explain one widespread custom—arranged marriages—that many Westerners believe is an infringement on people's freedom.

The importance of the ties between kin groups created by intermarriage is also revealed by two more widespread customs. In one, called the **levirate**, if a woman's husband dies, she marries one of his close kinsmen (usually a brother). The relations between the intermarried kin groups are too valuable for a woman to be returned to her own family of orientation because then she might marry into another kin group. Therefore, a male relative of her deceased husband takes his place, and because both her dead and her new husband belong to the same kin group, the affinal relationship remains intact. The converse custom, the **sororate**, also preserves the affinal ties between kin groups even beyond the death of a spouse. With the sororate, if a woman dies, her kin group is obliged to replace her with another woman, for which no additional bridewealth need be transferred. The Zulu of southern Africa, as well as many other African peoples, practiced both the levirate and the sororate. In societies with these customs, marriages—and the affinal ties they create—endure even beyond death.

## Marital Exchanges

In most cultures the marriage of a man and a woman is accompanied by some kind of a transfer of goods or services. These transfers—called *marital exchanges*—take numerous forms. The North American custom of wedding showers and wedding gifts is only one variety. In these, the presents given by the kin and friends supposedly help the newlyweds to establish an independent household. Part of our cultural knowledge is knowing the kinds of gifts that are appropriate for someone's wedding. We give things that are useful to the couple jointly, with food-preparation and eating utensils easily the most common type of gift. From a cross-cultural perspective, the most unusual feature of North American marital exchanges is that nothing is transferred between the relatives of the groom and bride: the couple treats the gifts as their private property. Like most of our other customs, this seems natural to us. Of course the goods go to the couple—what else could happen to them?

Plenty else, as we shall see in a moment. For now, notice that the fact that the goods go to the couple fits with several other features of Euro-American marriage. First, it usually is the bond through which new independent households are started, so the husband and wife

*In most cultures, some kind of an exchange of goods accompanies the marriage ceremony. Here are gifts being brought by a wedding party in the Trobriand Islands.*

"need their own stuff." If, in contrast, the newlyweds moved in with one of their relatives, they would not have as great a need for their own stuff. Second, our marriage-gift customs fit with the importance our culture gives to the privacy of the marital relationship: It is a personal matter between the husband and wife, and their relatives should keep their noses out. If the in-laws like each other and socialize together, well and good, but our marriages generally do not create strong bonds between the families of the bride and groom. (In fact, the two families often compete for the visits and attention of the couple and their offspring.) As we saw in chapter 9, gifts make friends and vice versa; the fact that the affines do not exchange goods with each other is a manifestation of the absence of a necessary relation between them after the wedding. If, in contrast, the marriage created an alliance between the two sets of relatives, some kind of an exchange would probably occur between them to symbolize and cement their new relations. Third, the gifts are presented to the couple, not to the husband or wife as individuals, and are considered to belong equally and jointly to both partners. But there are marriage systems in which the property of the wife is separate from that of her husband; if divorce should occur, there is no squabbling over who gets what.

With this background in mind, what kinds of marital exchanges occur in other cultures?

**BRIDEWEALTH.** **Bridewealth** (also known as *bride-price*) is the widespread custom that requires a man and his relatives to transfer goods to the relatives of his bride. It is easily the most common of all marital exchanges, found in more than one-half the world's cultures. The term *bridewealth* is well chosen because the goods transferred usually are among the most valuable symbols of wealth in the local culture. In sub-Saharan Africa cattle and sometimes other livestock are the most common goods used for bridewealth. Peoples of the Pacific Islands and Southeast Asia usually pay their bridewealth in pigs or shell money and ornaments. Many Native Americans of the Great Plains used horses after the Spanish reintroduced them into the continent, although not all Great Plains tribes had the custom of bridewealth.

Much anthropological ink has been devoted to answering the question of whether men who pay bridewealth are "buying" their wives. Is bridewealth to be equated with *bride-price*? Bridewealth does indeed often have some elements of a commercial transaction: The "price" of the bride often is negotiated; the rights over the woman are not given to her husband until the "deal" is sealed by the handing over of the appropriate quantity of goods; the goods often must be "refunded" to the husband's relatives if the woman proves barren or troublesome; and the goods used in the transfer commonly serve as media of exchange in other contexts.

Despite these similarities to our own commercial transactions, most anthropologists do not think it useful to consider the bridewealth transaction as equivalent to our own "buying and selling." For one thing, the object of the transaction—the woman herself—usually has at least some voice in who her husband will be. For another, unlike commodities, she has rights of her own in her marital relationship, and she and her kinfolk

usually can end the marriage if she [is]
mistreated or if her husband does not m[eet his obliga-]
tions to her and her children. And fina[lly,] [the buying]
and selling of most commodities are o[ne-time affairs.]
We pay our money and get our goods, a[nd our relation-]
ship with the seller usually terminates a[nd has no other]
aspects to it. In contrast, bridewealth [creates or]
establishes an enduring bundle of recipr[ocal rights and]
obligations between the relatives of the [bride and groom,]
and obligations that will last at least [as long as the]
marriage itself (and sometimes longer).

One of the most common rights a [husband and his]
relatives acquire when they transfer brid[ewealth to a]
wife's family is rights over the woman's c[hildren. Recip-]
rocally, one of a wife's most important ob[ligations is to]
bear children for her husband. This is we[ll illustrated]
by the Swazi, a traditional kingdom of so[uthern Africa.]
A Swazi marriage is a union between two families as
well as between the bride and groom. The payment of
bridewealth—in cattle and other valuables—to a woman's relatives establishes the husband's rights over his
wife. A woman's main duty to her husband is to provide
him with children. If she is unable to do so, her relatives
must either return the bridewealth they received for her
or provide a second wife to the husband, for which he
need pay no extra bridewealth. Reciprocally, a man must
pay bridewealth to gain rights of fatherhood over the
child of a woman, even though everyone knows he is

marital exchange; it is the usual compensation given to
the family of a bride in roughly one-eighth of the world's
cultures. However, sometimes it occurs alongside other
forms of marital exchange and occasionally can be used
to reduce the amount of bridewealth owed.

**DOWRY.**     A culture is said to have a **dowry** when
the families of a woman transfer a portion of their own
wealth or other property to their daughter and her

*Dowry is usually the inheritance that parents give to a woman to take into her marriage. As with this Tunisian bride, jewelry is often a major part of dowry.*

husband. The main thing to understand about dowry is that it is *not* simply the opposite of bridewealth; that is, it is not "groomwealth." It is, rather, the share of a woman's inheritance that she is allowed to take into her marriage for the use of her new family, although her parents are still alive. The woman and her family do not acquire marital rights over her husband when they provide a dowry, as they would if dowry were the opposite of bridewealth; rather, the bride and her husband receive property when they marry rather than when the bride's parents die. By doing so parents give their female children extra years of use of the property and also publicly demonstrate their wealth.

Dowry transfers largely are confined to Europe, southern Asia, and the Middle East. Most peoples that have it are intensive agriculturalists and have significant inequalities in wealth. It is a relatively rare form of marital exchange, occurring in only about 5 percent of the peoples recorded by anthropology.

Dowry is well documented for parts of India, where it includes jewelry, household utensils, women's clothing, and money. Much of the dowry is presented to the bride on her wedding day, but her parents and maternal uncle often provide gifts periodically throughout her marriage. Dowry, then, is not always a one-time expense for a family but may represent a continual drain on their resources.

## KINSHIP DIAGRAMS

At this point we need to introduce a set of notational symbols that will be useful in the remainder of this chapter and the next. This notation allows us to express diagrammatically how any two persons are (or believe themselves to be) related by bonds of kinship. The symbols appear in Figure 10.1, along with an example of how they would be used to show a married couple with five children. By stringing a number of symbols together, it is possible to make a complete chart—called a *genealogy*—that shows all the relatives of a given individual and how they are related to that individual. In these charts, or kinship diagrams, it is useful to have a reference individual, or a person to whom everyone on the chart is related. It is customary to call this reference individual "ego." In Figure 10.1 ego is symbolized by a square to show that his or her gender is irrelevant for the purposes of the genealogy. (If ego's gender mattered, we would symbolize him or her with either a triangle or a circle.)

FIGURE 10.1
Symbols Used on Kinship Diagrams

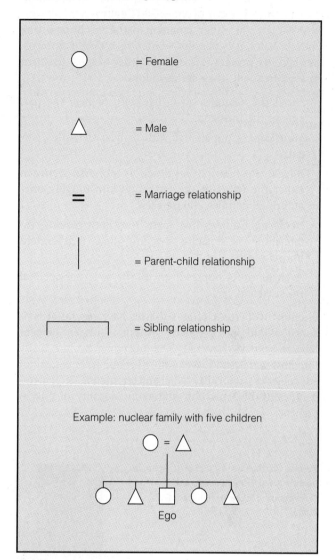

## POSTMARITAL RESIDENCE PATTERNS

A newly married woman and man establish a new family of procreation. In modern Euro-American societies they also establish a new domestic group (household)—most newlyweds get their own apartment, condo, or house. Couples do not always set up a new household in human populations. They often move into an existing household, either that of the husband or that of the wife. Where most new couples in a society establish their residence is known as the **postmarital residence pattern.** Cross-cultural research shows that our own pattern, in which couples form new households separate from their parents, is uncommon; in fact, it occurs in only about 5 percent of the world's cultures.

What are the other common patterns? By splitting enough hairs, it is possible to identify a dozen patterns, but here we present only five. In order of most frequent to least frequent, they are as follows:

*Patrilocal:* Couples go to live with or near the parents of the husband.

*Matrilocal:* Couples live with or near the wife's parents.

*Bilocal:* Postmarital residence is optional between either the wife's or the husband's kin; roughly one-half of all couples choose each.

*Neolocal:* Couples live apart from both parents, establishing a separate dwelling and independent household.

*Avunculocal:* Couples live with the maternal uncle of the husband.

Roughly 70 percent of all societies have patrilocal residence as the predominant pattern. Thirteen percent have matrilocal residence. The preceding two are easily the most widespread, accounting for about 83 percent of all societies. Bilocality is characteristic of 8 percent, neolocality of 5 percent, and avunculocality of only 4 percent.

What kinds of factors affect postmarital residence patterns? What determines whether newly married couples live separately or move in with some kind of relative? There is no simple answer, but property rights and inheritance forms are important influences on postmarital residence patterns. In societies in which the most important productive property is held by men, and in which inheritance passes from fathers to sons, brothers will have good reasons to join their fathers (and each other) in a common household to cooperate and protect their interest in land, livestock, or other wealth. And when the sons of most families in a society bring their wives and children into their father's existing household, this results in the residence pattern anthropologists call patrilocal. (The people themselves do not know they are practicing "patrilocal residence," of course—this is a term anthropologists use to describe and compare systems to one another.) Where important resources are controlled or owned by women, and especially if female labor is also important in supplying food for their families, then sisters tend to live and work together, and matrilocal residence is most likely to develop.

Neolocal or bilocal patterns are most often found in societies in which inheritance of life-sustaining resources passes through both sexes, or in which rights of access to resources are ill defined, or in which most people rely on wage labor for their livelihood. This may be why both foragers and modern industrialized coun-

*Patrilocal residence is the most common form. Here a Tunisian wife is ceremonially taken to her husband's home.*

tries are usually neolocal or bilocal. Among foragers, people need to maintain access to several territories, so rights to critical resources are loose and flexible (as explained in chapters 7 and 9). Nuclear families may live off and on with the husband's and wife's bands, according to sentimental ties, short- or long-term availability of resources, or idiosyncratic considerations.

Modern industrialized peoples usually are neolocal, for two major reasons. First, job availability forces many couples to move away from their home town. This is especially true for "upwardly mobile" couples seeking increased income, better opportunities, and the more materially rewarding life-style valued by many in the late twentieth century. Second, in industrial countries most workers do not rely on their family connections for access to their livelihood but sell their labor on an impersonal market for labor to an employer they have never met. In other words, most ordinary citizens do not inherit productive property (capital) from their parents and do not rely on their parents for their livelihood, so they establish independent domiciles free from parental control and interference. The result is neolocal residence and an emphasis on nuclear family ties.

No single factor "determines" postmarital residence. Patterns of control over resources and inheritance form are important overall influences. For instance, if most couples rely on the wife's family for access to the resources they need to survive and raise children, then most couples will live with the wife's family and matrilocal residence will be predominant in the society. But a multitude of other factors also affect residence choices. Consequently, in some societies women have much control over land, yet residence is not matrilocal because these other factors are locally more important than keeping sisters together in a common household. The same complexities apply to the other residence patterns.

## FAMILY AND HOUSEHOLD FORMS

At first thought, the subject of postmarital residence seems trivial (almost like a topic anthropology professors thought up to befuddle their students!). What differences does it make where newly married couples go to live? In fact there is a good reason why residence patterns are worth studying. A moment's thought shows that the prevalent pattern of postmarital residence spatially locates a new family of procreation with one set of relatives and isolates it from other sets. In turn this influences which sets of relatives a newly married

couple cooperates with. If the postmarital residence pattern is patrilocal, for instance, the husband lives and works with his own consanguines (father and brothers) and the wife cooperates in household chores or gardening with her affines, not with her own consanguines. Postmarital residence affects the relatives with whom children are most likely to develop strong sentimental attachments. If the residence pattern is matrilocal, for example, the children of sisters live together in a single household, much like brothers and sisters, and are likely to conceive of their relation as being like "real" siblings. The residence pattern also influences who has main authority over the couple and their offspring. If it is avunculocal, for instance, the mother's brother of the husband is the head of the household and manages its activities. So residence patterns affect all kinds of family relationships in a society.

Perhaps most important, the prevailing form of residence affects the kinds of household and family units that exist among a people. Consider neolocal residence, for example. If all or most newlyweds set up their own households, separate from and independent of that of either of their parents, then a new household and family unit is established with each new marriage. This emphasizes the social and economic importance and independence of nuclear families because mothers and fathers—and not more distant relatives—are most likely to be the main teachers of children and "breadwinners" for the household. The couple maintains relations with their parents, siblings, and other relatives, of course, but neolocal residence tends to lead to an emphasis on nuclear families as the most culturally important and stable family unit.

(You can see this phenomenon in modern North America: When sociologists, psychologists, and politicians worry about the decline or breakup of the American family, they are talking about the nuclear family, which they think is threatened by high divorce rates, unmarried couples living together, absent or deadbeat fathers, high illegitimacy rates, homosexuality, and so forth. In recent years so many "families" have "split up" that family stability has become a major "social problem." But no one worries much about the "decline" or "breakup" of relations between married children and their parents, or about how many married siblings do not speak to one another or have not seen one another for years. We consider it normal—which is to say, we do not consider it to be a "social problem"—when married children move out on their parents and away from their siblings. Indeed, it is regarded as unfortunate if newlyweds live with either set of parents, because we think that only economic necessity could force them to do so. Many of us believe that young marrieds who visit or seek advice from their parents too often are a little strange for not making their own choices and establishing their own friendships.)

Other kinds of households and family groupings exist among the world's peoples. These units—known as **extended families**—are made up of related nuclear families. Because the related nuclear families usually live in a single household, here we use *extended family* and *extended household* as synonyms. Extended households typically include three and often four generations of family members.

Many anthropologists think that the form of family (household) that is prevalent in a society depends on its postmarital residence pattern. For example, with patrilocal residence the married sons of an older couple remain in the household of their parents (or often each son builds his own house on his parents' land, near their dwelling). As they grow up and marry, the daughters go to live with their husbands' parents. If all the sons and daughters of a couple do this, the resulting household is of a type called *patrilocally extended*—brothers live in a single household with their own nuclear families and parents (see Figure 10.2a). If all families in the village, town, or other settlement follow this pattern, then the settlement consists of patrilocally extended households. Notice that the residents of each household are related to one another through males. The married women of the community live scattered in the households of their husbands, or perhaps many of them have married out of the community altogether.

The converse occurs with matrilocal residence. The mature sons leave as they marry, and the daughters bring their husbands to live with them in or near their parents' households. The household type formed by the co-residence of daughters and sisters with their parents is called the *matrilocally extended household* (see Figure 10.2b). The sons of an elderly couple are scattered in the households of the women they have married, either in their own home community or in another community into which they have married. If most people follow this residence pattern, then the community consists of numerous households, each of which is lived in by women related through females plus their husbands and children.

The same relationship between residence and prevalent household form applies to the other residence patterns. With bilocal residence there is no consistency in whether households are made up of people related through males or females: Some couples live with the husband's family, others with that of the wife. The household type is *bilocally* (or *bilaterally*) *extended* (see Figure 10.2c). The community's households are a mixture of people related through both sexes, in roughly equal frequency. With neolocal residence the settlement—be it village or modern suburb—consists of relatively small domestic units made up of nuclear families.

The avunculocal residence pattern associates nuclear families with the husband's mother's brother; if everyone

*Extended families like that of these Muslims from North India are common cross-culturally.*

FIGURE 10.2
Household Forms

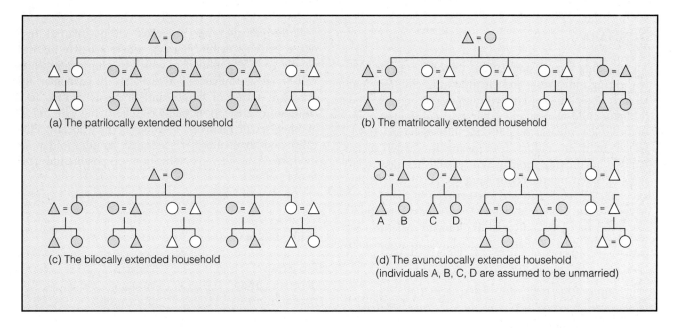

(a) The patrilocally extended household

(b) The matrilocally extended household

(c) The bilocally extended household

(d) The avunculocally extended household
(individuals A, B, C, D are assumed to be unmarried)

in the community adopted this practice (which they usually do not), then the community would consist of households composed of older men (the household heads) and the families of their sister's sons. This is called the *avunculocally extended household* (see Figure 10.2d). It includes men (and their wives and children) who are related to one another through women (their mothers)! (Confused by this one? We shall see in the next chapter that avunculocal residence makes good sense in many societies that trace their main kinship relationships through women.)

We can now see one reason why postmarital residence patterns are important: They give rise to various household and family forms. The kinds of family and domestic groups found among a people result from where newly formed families of procreation go to live. Stated differently, the prevalent household type in a human community represents the crystallization of the pattern of postmarital residence. And who lives with whom— the household type—is important, since households so often hold property in common, cooperate in production and other economic activities, enculturate children together, and sometimes even worship the same ancestral spirits.

Because the prevalent household form varies with postmarital residence, the same things that influence residence also affect household form—notably ecological and economic factors like the sexual division of labor, property rights, and inheritance patterns. For instance, in most pastoral societies men are most responsible for maintaining the herds, men own the animals (either as individuals or as groups of brothers), and men inherit their livestock from their fathers. Patrilocally extended families are, therefore, characteristic of most pastoral people. Again, though, we need to be careful with such generalizations. Adaptation to environment and economics are important, but their effects may be overridden by social and political factors.

In this chapter we have given an overview of some variations in domestic life. If we were writing a book about industrial societies, we might stop our discussion of groupings formed on the basis of kinship relations at this point. This is because, among the industrialized portion of humanity, other kinds of relations and groupings—economic, educational, political, religious, and so on—are organized by relationships other than kinship—by specialized firms, schools, parties, governments, churches, and so on. But, as we discuss in the next chapter, in preindustrial cultures kinship principles are used to form much larger kin groups that organize and perform a range of other activities.

## SUMMARY

All surviving human populations reproduce themselves by bearing, nurturing, and enculturating children, and all have some kind of family groupings to organize and facilitate child-rearing and other essential domestic activities. New nuclear families are formed by marriage, which reduces conflict over sexuality, forms social bonds that provide for children, establishes new relations between intermarrying families, and involves the exchange of goods and services between husbands and wives. Human biological characteristics make a relationship like marriage universal in human societies, although the form of marriage, the kinds of rights and duties it establishes, and many other aspects of the marital relationship vary. The Nayar illustrate an unusual form of marriage, if it is marriage at all.

Marriage is everywhere governed by rules. Marriage systems commonly are classified by the number of spouses an individual is allowed: polygyny, monogamy, polyandry, and group marriage, in order of relative frequency in human societies. In preindustrial societies marriage often is the cornerstone of alliance relations between families or larger kin groups. The Yąnomamö illustrate the use of strategic marriages to create and sustain military alliances, a practice quite common in the preindustrial world. The levirate and sororate are customs that preserve affinal relationships even after the death of a spouse.

New marriages ordinarily are accompanied by the exchange of goods or services between the spouses and the families of the bride and groom. The most common forms of marital exchange are bridewealth, brideservice, and dowry. These exchanges are used to create affinal relationships, compensate a family or larger kin group for the loss of one of its members, provide for the new couple's support, or provide a daughter with an inheritance that attracts a husband.

*Postmarital residence patterns* refers to where newly married couples establish their residence. In order of most common to least common, the patterns are patrilocal, matrilocal, bilocal, neolocal, and avunculocal. There are many influences on which of these forms will be most prevalent in a given community, including economic forces and inheritance patterns. No single factor is adequate to explain the cross-cultural variation in residence patterns.

Anthropologists are interested in postmarital residence patterns mainly because where a newly married couple go to live influences which kinship relationships will be most emphasized in a society. In particular, the prevalent forms of family and domestic groups in a community arise out of many couples living with one or another set of relatives. Patrilocally, matrilocally, bilocally, and avunculocally extended families often are interpreted as the crystallization of postmarital residence patterns.

## KEY TERMS

kin group
domestic group
consanguines
affines
nuclear family
incest taboo
exogamous rules
endogamous rules
monogamy
polygyny
polyandry
group marriage
polygamy
marriage alliances

levirate
sororate
bridewealth
brideservice
dowry
postmarital residence
    pattern
patrilocal residence
matrilocal residence
bilocal residence
neolocal residence
avunculocal residence
extended family (household)

## SUGGESTED READINGS

Bohannon, Paul, and John Middleton, eds. *Marriage, Family, and Residence.* New York: Natural History Press, 1968.
> *A collection of studies with descriptions of marriage, family, and residence from societies around the world.*

Goody, Jack, and S. J. Tambiah, eds. *Bridewealth and Dowry.* Cambridge: Cambridge University Press, 1973.
> *A collection of papers examining the causes and consequences of bridewealth and dowry.*

Suggs, David N., and Andrew W. Miracle, eds. *Culture and Human Sexuality: A Reader.* Pacific Grove, Calif.: Brooks/Cole, 1993.
> *An outstanding collection of articles dealing with sexuality and related topics from a cross-cultural perspective. Includes both case studies and theoretical articles.*

Most ethnographies contain a description of the domestic life of the people studied. The following are a few ethnographies specifically focused on domestic life.

Blesdoe, Caroline. *Women and Marriage in Kpelle Society*. Stanford: Stanford University Press, 1980.

*A description of an African society.*

Hart, C. W. M., and Arnold R. Pilling. *The Tiwi of North Australia*. New York: Holt, Rinehart and Winston, 1979.

*A brief ethnographic study of an Australian culture with a most unusual marriage system.*

Malinowski, Bronislaw. *The Sexual Life of Savages*. New York: Harcourt, Brace, Jovanovich, 1929.

*Not what you may think from its title. An ethnography that describes courtship, sexual norms, marriage, domestic relations, and love magic in the Trobriand Islands.*

Stack, Carol B. *All Our Kin: Strategies for Survival in a Black Community*. New York: Harper and Row, 1974.

*An outstanding ethnography that shows how blacks in a midwestern city use family ties to cope with poverty.*

Turnbull, Colin M. *The Mountain People*. New York: Simon and Schuster, 1972.

*A very well written and readable account of the Ik of east Africa. The study is disturbing because it shows the deterioration of the family under extreme economic pressures.*

Wolf, Margery. *The House of Lim*. Englewood Cliffs, N.J.: Prentice-Hall, 1968.

*A very readable study of family life in a Taiwanese Chinese farm family.*

## CHAPTER 11

# KINSHIP: FORMING RELATIONSHIPS AND GROUPS

*Kinship ties often organize a variety of cooperative activities in human cultures. These Gorotire hunters in Brazil are bringing racks of turtles back to their village.*

**CONTENTS**

Humans are among the most social of animals. Young children rely on parents or other adults to satisfy their needs. Most humans rely on cooperation with others for survival and material well-being. In many cultures the social roles and groupings established and maintained on the basis of kinship relationships organize many kinds of economic and political activities. Emotional well-being is also a powerful force in human life, and people seek companionship and affection for their own sake. In most societies people rely heavily on their relatives for emotional support and turn to their kinfolk in times of crisis and need.

For these and other reasons, kinship is among the most important features of any human culture. In this chapter we show how principles of kinship are used by various human societies to create social groupings of all sizes and to organize cooperative relationships. We also cover some of the ways different cultures classify relatives into labeled categories.

## KINSHIP

In every culture people have ideas about how they are biologically related to one another. These ideas are in part cultural because they vary from people to people. Nonetheless, how any given people trace their ties to their many relatives seems quite natural to them. In the United States, for example, the children of one's parents' siblings all are considered to be the same kind of relative: first cousin. *Cousin* seems like a natural (i.e., biologically given) category of kinship. In actuality the people you call *first cousins* are related to you differently. Some are your mother's sisters' children, some your mother's brothers' children, some your father's brothers' children, and the rest are your father's sisters' children. If

you reply, "Yes, but they all are the children of my aunts and uncles," then someone with another kinship system might ask, "But what makes you think that both your father's sister and your mother's sister are the same kind of relative (aunt)? After all, you call your mother and your father by different terms because of their gender; why then do you ignore the gender of your parent when you call the sisters of both your parents *aunt?*" You might ask in disgust, "How else would you do it?"

In fact, there are several other ways to do it. There are human kinship systems in which the brothers of your father are not culturally categorized as the same kind of male relative as the brothers of your mother. In some of these, the brothers of your father are called *father* (like your biological father), whereas the brothers of your mother are called by a kinship term that translates roughly as *male mother.* There are kinship systems in which your relatives through your mother are considered to be different kinds of kin to you than your relatives through your father. In its kinship systems humanity is surprisingly diverse: Various populations view the biological connections between relatives differently and make use of them differently in forming groups, allocating roles to people, culturally classifying kin, and establishing norms of proper behavior between relatives.

Before proceeding further, we should note why anthropologists have devoted so much attention to kinship.

### Significance of Kinship

In industrialized nations there are thousands of kinds of groups that organize different aspects of our lives—some groups are economic, others social, political, and religious. Each individual participates in the common activities of a number of formal and informal groups. For example, we might belong to formal groups such as a labor union, the Audubon Society, the Republican party, and the United Methodist Church. At the same time, we are active in many informal gatherings made up of our co-workers, neighbors, and friends, with whom we socialize or share common interests.

Notice two important characteristics of these groups. First, they are *voluntary:* If individuals' interests change, or if they find some other group of people who better meet their goals, they are free to change jobs, churches, neighborhoods, friends, and so forth. Second, for the most part, they have *nonoverlapping membership:* Each group typically consists of a different collection of

*Kinship relationships and groups are multifunctional in most preindustrial communities. This is a Quechua family in Peru. Quechua are cultural descendants of the ancient Inca empire.*

people; we cooperate and interact with different individuals in the various groups to which we belong. Members of each of these groups have varying and sometimes contradictory expectations about how we should behave because we perform different roles in each of the groups. In many ways our behavior differs according to the context of the particular group of people we are associating with at the moment—we act one way at home, another at church, and yet another at work. Our fellow church members might be surprised if they could see how we act on the job, but—probably fortunately—they ordinarily don't.

In contrast, among most preindustrial peoples, one lives with, works with, socializes with, and often worships with the same people, most of whom are relatives. Kin groups and kin relationships are *multifunctional*, meaning that they organize many kinds of activities. It is as if most of the activities organized by the firms, schools, governments, churches, and other specialized groups in our own society were organized by one or another kind of kin group. Thus kinship relations are far more important to the organization of these preindustrial societies than they are to our own. In fact, when we study their organization we often find that it is based on the bonds created by kinship. We can no more understand these societies without studying their kinship systems than we could understand the modern world without knowing about nations.

## How Cultures Vary in Kinship

Before describing some of the cross-cultural diversity in kinship, we present an overview of the major ways that different cultures vary in kinship.

**KINDS OF KIN GROUPS.** Much of human activity is cooperative, meaning that people work together with one another in social groups to get tasks accomplished and to solve common problems. Families of various types are one kind of human group (see Chapter 10), as are churches, schools, companies, and sororities. Any group that endures longer than a human lifetime has some means of replacing its members as they die, graduate, retire, drop out, or otherwise leave. For example, a university recruits new students (freshmen) to replace graduating seniors, whereas companies hire new employees to expand their work force or replace retired workers.

A **kin group** is a kind of social group that a person joins because she or he is a relative of other members. One usually becomes a member of (joins) a kin group by virtue of the fact that his or her mother and/or father is a member. In the American kinship system people become members of the family groups of both their mothers and their fathers. There is no systematic societywide pattern of cooperating with relatives through one's mother or father, although particular individuals may develop closer ties with one or another side of their family.

In contrast to the American kinship pattern, many other cultures place primary importance on one side of the family—either the paternal or the maternal side—in preference to the other. For example, in many cultures most individuals become members of their father's kin group. They might live with their father's relatives, cooperate with their paternal relatives, inherit property from their fathers but not their mothers, and worship their paternal but not their maternal ancestors. In such systems relatives through one's mother usually are recognized as kin, but kin of a fundamentally different and less important kind than paternal relatives. There are also systems in which kin groups are organized around maternal relationships, and paternal kin are culturally de-emphasized.

**NORMATIVE EXPECTATIONS OF KIN RELATIONSHIPS.** The kinds of social relations a people believe they should have with individuals related to them in a certain way are part of the norms of a kinship system. Cross-culturally, these norms are surprisingly variable. There are systems in which husbands and wives do not sleep and eat in the same dwelling; in which brothers must rigidly avoid their sisters after puberty; in which sons-in-law are not supposed to speak directly to their mothers-in-law; in which a boy is allowed to appropriate the property of his maternal uncle but must show utmost restraint and respect toward his paternal uncle; and in which people are expected to marry one kind of cousin but are absolutely forbidden to marry another kind of cousin. In sum, many of the patterns of behavior toward relatives that members of one culture regard as normal are absent from other ways of life.

**CULTURAL CLASSIFICATIONS OF RELATIVES.** Kinship relationships are created through biological reproduction. When a woman gives birth the relatives of herself and her mate become the biological relatives of the child. In this sense, who your relatives are is determined for you by who your parents are. Thus the kinship relationship between any two people depends on how these individuals are related biologically. Despite this, anthropologists claim that kinship is a cultural, rather than a biologically determined, phenomenon. We make this claim mainly because societies differ in the way they use the biological facts of kinship to create groups, allocate roles, and classify the domain of relatives into various kinds of relatives. They vary in how they perceive and categorize their biological relationships. In our own kinship system, for example, whether a woman is our maternal or paternal aunt makes no difference: We still call her *aunt* and think of both our maternal and paternal aunt as the same kind of relative. But side of the family makes a difference in some other kinship systems: Father's sisters and mother's sisters are completely different kinds of relatives and are called by different terms.

Keeping this overview of kinship diversity in mind, let's look at kinship in more detail.

 **UNILINEAL DESCENT**

Consider how people know who their relatives are and how individual relatives are related to them. As mentioned previously, people are your biological relatives because you and they share a common ancestor in some

*Many cultures, including that of this Pakistani family, place primary emphasis on kinship relationships traced through males.*

previous generation. Thus your sister is the female child of your parents; your aunts and uncles are children of your grandparents; your first cousins are the grandchildren of your grandparents; and you and your second cousins share a common set of great-grandparents. Stated differently, someone is your biological relative if you and they are descended from a common ancestor who was alive some number of generations ago. The greater the number of generations back this ancestor lived, the more distantly related a particular person is to you. Figure 11.1 shows how different kinds of cousins are related to you. (The central person of the diagram, labeled "ego," is the reference point, or the person to whom everyone else on the diagram is related.)

Realizing this fact, you can see that you have an enormous number of living biological relatives. You have or had two parents, four grandparents, eight great-grandparents, and sixteen great-great-grandparents. All the people descended from your sixteen great-great-grandparents are your relatives (third cousins). Going back in time, the number of your ancestors doubles every generation. Assuming twenty-five years between generations, twenty generations ago (in the year 1500)

you had more than one million ancestors, and all the descendants of these ancestors are biologically related to you, however remotely.

Just being biological relatives does not mean much, since we all have so many of such relatives. From the total range of potential biological kin, all cultures consider some kinds of relatives as more important than others. The reduction in the number of relatives is accomplished in two main ways: (1) forgetting or ignoring the remoter kinship relationships and (2) emphasizing some kinds of kinship relationships and de-emphasizing others. In North America we use mainly the first method: Most people forget who their kin are beyond the range of second cousin because they have little reason to keep track of their more distant relatives.

Many cultures—especially preindustrial ones—use the second method: They consider that some kinds of relatives are more important than others. The most common means of making some relatives more important than others is to use the gender of connecting relatives as the basis for defining which kin are close. For example, if people consider that kin relationships traced through males are most important, then individu-

**FIGURE 11.1**
**Types of Cousins and Other Relatives**

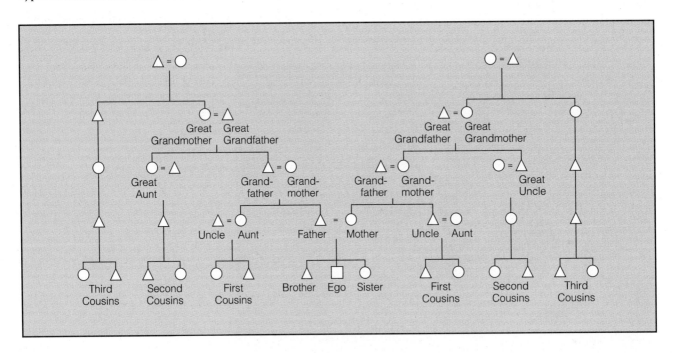

## FIGURE 11.2
### Patrilineal Descent

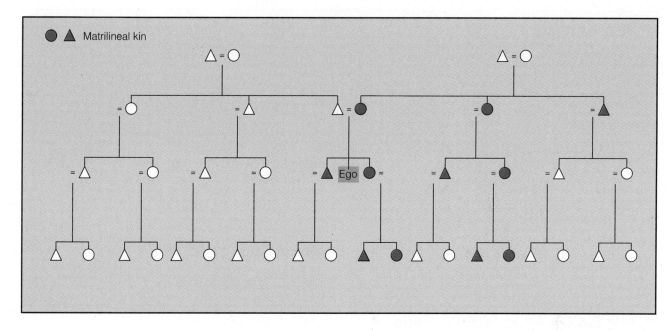

als will think that their father's relatives are more important than their mother's relatives—for some purposes at least. Relationships through females will be de-emphasized and perhaps forgotten in two or three generations. If you lived in such a culture, some of your second cousins on your father's side of your family would be quite important relatives, but you might not consider your second cousins through your mother as relatives at all.

Kinship relationships, then, are defined by how people trace their descent from previous generations. How people in a given culture trace their descent is called their **form of descent**. Descent can be traced through males, females, or both genders. This section considers cultures that trace descent through only one gender.

In many cultures relationships traced through only one gender are considered most important. Anthropologists say that such cultures have **unilineal descent**, a term that refers to the fact that people place importance on either their mothers' ancestral line or their fathers' ancestral line, but not both. Depending on which gender is the most important for tracing kinship relationships, two categories of unilineal descent are most common:

✦ **Patrilineal descent**. People trace their primary kinship connections to the ancestors and living relatives of their fathers (see Figure 11.2). In cultures with patrilin-

eal descent a person's father's relatives are likely to be most important in his or her life. Individuals are likely to live among their fathers' kin, and most property is inherited from fathers to sons.

✦ **Matrilineal descent**. People trace their most important kinship relationships to the ancestors and living relatives of their mothers (see Figure 11.3). In matrilineal descent it is the mother's relatives who are most important in a person's life. People are most likely to live with or near their mothers' relatives and usually inherit property from their mothers or mothers' brothers.

Of these two forms of unilineal descent, patrilineal is the most common. There are about three times as many patrilineal as matrilineal cultures.

Let's look at each of these forms of unilineal descent more closely, to see which relatives are considered most important for an individual. In Figure 11.2 the patrilineal relatives of the person labeled *ego* are shaded in. The kinship diagram shows that ego's patrilineal kin include only those relatives related to ego through males. For instance, ego's father's brother's children are related to ego through two males, whereas ego's other first cousins are not.

Looking at patrilineal descent another way, ego's patrilineal kin include all the people descended through males from the man labeled *founder* on Figure 11.2. In fact, any two individuals shaded in the diagram are

FIGURE 11.3
Matrilineal Descent

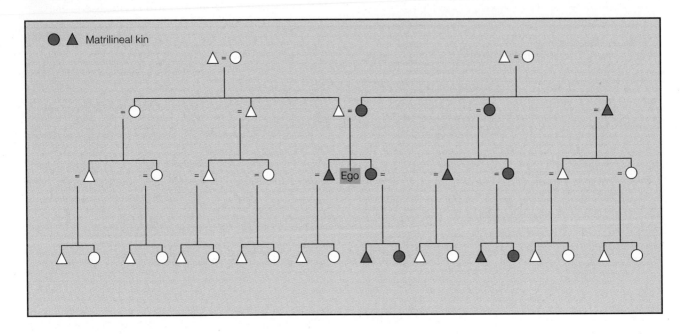

related to one another through males. This includes women as well as men, but the children of these women are not related through males and, therefore, are not patrilineal kin. The children of the women have their own set of patrilineal relatives, which they take from their fathers.

How does patrilineal descent affect behavior toward different relatives? Probably the most widespread and noticeable effect is in the inheritance of property. In patrilineal societies property is passed down through the male line or, in other words, from fathers to sons. We can see the significance of this effect on inheritance by contrasting it with inheritance in North American society, where the dominant ethnic group traces their kinship relationships through both genders. You probably do not distinguish between your two grandfathers but think of yourself as related in the same way to both. You may potentially inherit from both. But if your culture was patrilineal, your father's father would play a far more significant role in your life and it would be from him that you would expect to inherit wealth or receive land rights. Your mother's father would pass his property on to his sons and sons' sons—not to you because you are related to him through your mother, not your father. A similar distinction exists between paternal and maternal uncles: Paternal uncles are far more important.

Finally, some of your four sets of cousins are more important than others—those related to you through males, or your father's brothers' children. It is these people who would be primarily responsible for your economic and social welfare, and it is with them and your own siblings that you would probably cooperate and associate.

We can use the same logic to examine matrilineal descent. Your matrilineal kin are related to you through female links. They include, as core members, your mother, mother's mother, mother's mother's mother (if she is alive), plus the daughters of all these women and their children. The sons and brothers of these women are your matrilineal kin, but their children are not. In Figure 11.3, we have shaded the people who are ego's matrilineal relatives. Note that only one set of cousins— ego's mother's sisters' children—are shaded in the diagram. They are the individuals who are related to ego through female links, and therefore, ego is likely to have closer relationships with them than with other cousins. Property is most likely to be inherited from one's mother and maternal grandmother and from the brothers of these women. In matrilineal societies men usually leave most of their property not to their own children but to their sister's children. As a result, maternal uncles (mother's brothers) are important figures in one's life, and in some respects they assume the role we usually associate with fathers.

As we have seen, in unilineal descent systems relations such as aunt, uncle, and cousin differ from those we are accustomed to. Some cousins, in particular, will be more important relatives than other cousins: father's brothers' children in patrilineal systems, mother's sisters' children in matrilineal systems. The recognition of the fact that not all cousins are "alike" in unilineal societies has led anthropologists to distinguish between *parallel cousins* and *cross cousins*. Two sets of cousins are parallel cousins if their parents are of the same sex: so your parallel cousins are your mother's sisters' children and your father's brothers' children. People are cross cousins if their parents are siblings of the opposite sex: so your cross cousins are your father's sisters' children and your mother's brothers' children. The significance of this distinction is that in unilineal descent systems, one set of parallel cousins is always in the same kin group as ego, as you can see by contrasting the cousins shaded in Figures 11.2 and 11.3. On the other hand, no cross cousin is ever in ego's kin group in a society with a unilineal descent form.

## Unilineal Descent Groups

Culturally defined relationships between individuals serve as the basis for forming kin groups. In chapter 10 we saw how extended families and household groups are formed when nuclear families associate together in patterned ways. Much larger kin groups of people—also known as **descent groups**—can be established on the basis of kinship ties.

Take matrilineal descent, for example. A matrilineal descent group exists when people descended from the same woman through females recognize their group identity and cooperate for some purposes. When a matrilineal rule of descent establishes a group of people all related to one another through females, we say that the group is created using the *matrilineal principle*. We can state the matrilineal principle as "everyone joins the descent group of his or her mother." Alternatively, we can say "only the children of the female members of a group become members," or "only the group's women transmit membership rights and duties in the group to their offspring." Looking back to Figure 11.3, all the individuals on the diagram are members of a single descent group. Check for yourself that only the female members pass their membership in the group along to their offspring. (What happens to the children of the group's men? They join the descent groups of their mothers, which usually are a different group because incest and exogamy rules typically prohibit sex and marriage between any of the group's members.)

Groups also can develop by repeated application of the *patrilineal principle*. In any given generation only males transmit their membership in the group to their offspring. The result of applying this principle for several generations is a group of people related to one another through males. Check this on Figure 11.2: All the shaded individuals are in the same descent group, and everyone joined the groups of their fathers. Assuming the patrilineal kin group is exogamous, the children of the group's women become members of their father's patrilineal group.

A **unilineal descent group** is a grouping of relatives all of whom are related through only one sex. A *matrilineal descent group* is a group whose members are (or consider themselves to be) related through females or who trace their descent through female links from a common ancestress. A *patrilineal descent group* comprises people who trace their descent through males from a common male ancestor.

Using either of the unilineal descent principles, groups of various sizes can be formed in such a way that smaller groups are nested inside larger groups. A nuclear family can be made part—or a "segment"—of a unilineally extended family. The unilineally extended family is a segment of a somewhat larger group, which in turn is a segment of a still larger unilineal group. This segmentation of unilineal groups can continue until groups with thousands of members are formed. It is not even necessary that two members of the larger and more inclusive groups know exactly how they are related. If the descent principle is patrilineal, for example, everyone only need remember to which group their fathers belong. So long as only the males of the group transmit this membership to their offspring, everyone whose fathers were members will know that they, too, are members of the same patrilineal descent group and, therefore, are somehow related through males.

Unilineal descent groups can be small or enormous, depending on the fertility of members of previous generations and on the genealogical depth of the group—that is, on how far back in time any two members of the group must go to trace their relationship to each other. Genealogical depth provides a convenient way to classify the kinds of unilineal descent groups that are most common cross-culturally. From "shallowest" to "deepest,"

*Among the Maasai, a cattle herding people of Kenya and Tanzania, patrilineal descent groups organize many economic and ritual activities.*

they are unilineally extended families (chapter 10), lineages, clans, phratries, and moieties (see Figure 11.4).

**LINEAGES.** A **lineage** is a unilineal group composed of several unilineally extended families whose members are able to trace their descent through males or females from a common ancestor or ancestress. By the conventional definition, the extended families that make up the group must be able to state how they are related to one another for anthropologists to call the group a lineage. Lineages may be either patrilineal (patrilineages) or matrilineal (matrilineages), depending on the form of descent prevalent among a people.

In many societies small lineages are in turn aggregated into larger ones. This happens because the size of

**FIGURE 11.4**
**Typology of Unilineal Kinship Groups**

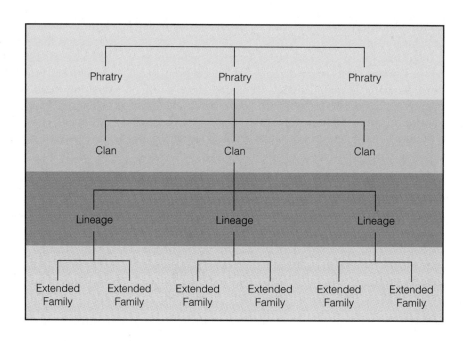

lineages grows through several generations. Consider a small patrilineage, for example. The lineage will increase its numbers as long as its male members, on the average, have more than one son who lives to reproduce. After several generations each member can trace his or her relations to some other members by counting back three generations (for example) to their common great-grandfather. But for other members ego must go back five generations, to their common great-great-great-grandfather. So the largest patrilineage is segmented into smaller patrilineages; or stated conversely, small lineages are "nested inside" larger ones.

CLANS.    Clans are unilineal descent groups whose members are descended from either a common ancestor through the male line (patriclans) or a common ancestress through the female line (matriclans). The major difference between a clan and a lineage is generational depth. With clans the common ancestor or ancestress lived so far in the past that not all the members of the clan are able to state precisely how they are related to one another. Like lineages, clans usually are exogamous. Members of the clan think of themselves as relatives and frequently refer to one another as "clan brother" or "clan sister." In many societies clans own or control land and other forms of property. Most clans are *totemic,* meaning that their members are symbolically identified with certain supernatural powers associated with particular

animals, plants, and other natural forces such as lightning, the sun, and the moon. Clans commonly take the name of their primary totemic symbol, and thus have names such as the bear clan, the sun clan, and the eagle clan. The association with particular supernatural powers gives specific clans control over particular religious rituals. Although the function of clans varies from one society to another, they usually are among the most significant economic, social, and political units in the society.

Whereas lineages may exist without being aggregated into clans, clans are almost always subdivided into lineages. Clans themselves are also frequently aggregated into larger groupings called *phratries* and *moieties.*

PHRATRIES AND MOIETIES.    Phratries and moieties are not technically descent groups because their members are not thought of as being descended from a common ancestor or ancestress. *Phratries* and *moieties* are simply loose associations of clans, based on historical or religious factors. Some societies have only phratries, others have only moieties, and still others have both.

A society has phratries if its clans are grouped into three or more, usually named associations. A myth may exist telling why a particular association of clans forms a phratry. Sometimes the myth tells of the clans living

*Two Micronesian women weaving. In most of the small islands of Micronesia, matriclans owned land and determined a person's social rank.*

together in the distant past and later joining with the other clans to form the existing society. The functions of phratries vary greatly. In some societies phratries are exogamous. In other societies the clans of a phratry may collectively have the responsibility for a particular religious ceremony. In still other societies phratries are only of symbolic or historical significance.

A moiety (from the French word for "half") is any grouping of clans or phratries into two associations. Moieties are named, formally organized groups. Membership in a moiety is based on membership in a particular clan. There usually is a myth telling why particular clans or phratries belong to a particular moiety. The reasons given in the myth may be either historical or religious in emphasis. Moieties play a variety of roles in the societies in which they occur. They usually are exogamous: The members of the two moieties intermarry. Many villages are divided into two halves, one for the dwellings of each moiety. Moieties may also be political units, with each moiety having its own political head. Moieties also frequently play a significant role in religious rituals. The moieties may be symbolized by contrasting elements in the universe: earth-sky, war-peace, night-day, summer-winter, or land-water. The name of the moiety usually is taken from this symbolic association, such as earth people, land people, and summer people.

## Descent Groups in Action

Thus far we have described the two major forms of unilineal descent and outlined some of the major kinds of groups formed by the application of the matrilineal and patrilineal principles over several generations. All this has been abstract and somewhat technical, and you may well wonder why ethnologists bother so much with kinship.

We bother because descent groups are made up of living people who work in gardens, quarrel, conduct rituals, go to war, teach their children, construct their dwellings, and carry out innumerable other activities together. If people are to work together for common purposes, they must have ways of creating groups and ensuring their continuity over time; they must have ways of assigning group members to roles and allocating tasks to them; they must have ways of making decisions that affect the members. In short, they must be organized. More often than not, descent groups and kinship relations provide the organizational basis on which various cooperative activities are carried out.

Two examples illustrate how unilineal descent principles organize cooperative activities. One is a patrilineal people of a Pacific island who call themselves the *Tikopia*. The second is the *Hopi*, a matrilineal Native American people of the Southwest.

**TIKOPIA: A PATRILINEAL SOCIETY.** Tikopia is a western Pacific island covering about six square miles. In the late 1920s, when it was studied by Raymond Firth, Tikopia had a population of about 1,200. Tikopians traced their descent patrilineally and used this principle to establish groupings of people related through males. They viewed their society as composed of four patriclans, each with a name that passed from fathers to sons. Each patriclan was subdivided into several patrilineages, averaging about thirty to forty members. The members of each patrilineage traced their descent in the male line back to a common ancestor—the founder of the patrilineage—who lived four to six generations ago. Each patrilineage ordinarily considered the oldest male descendant of this founder to be its head. The women of a lineage married men of other lineages, so the children of the lineage's women did not become members of it.

What were the functions of Tikopian lineages and clans? To consider the lineage first, it controlled rights over land and certain other kinds of property. Each lineage owned several parcels of land that were planted in crops, including yams, taro, coconut, and breadfruit. The families that made up the lineage had the right to plant and harvest crops on lineage land; once they had planted a parcel they had the right to continue to use it. They could not, however, sell, trade, or give it away to members of other lineages. The same rights applied to the parcels of land on which a family established their dwellings: They could live on one of the lineage's house sites but could not dispose of it to outsiders. The patrilineage then owned land and allocated use rights to parcels among its members, and each family acquired most of its subsistence through its members' access to the land of their lineage.

Ordinarily, each nuclear family cultivated primarily the lineage land of its husband-father. In Tikopia, unlike in most other patrilineal societies, the female members of a patrilineage retained their use rights to lineage land even after they married. When a woman married a parcel of the land of her lineage was divided off for her own and her husband's and children's use. A woman could not, however, pass any of her rights to this land along to her children; when she died the use of the parcel reverted to the patrilineage she was born into, and her children had no more use rights to it. Thus each patrilineage allowed its female members who had married out of it to use plots of land for subsistence during their lifetimes but not to transmit rights in the land to their offspring. (The children of the women of the patrilineage received use rights to land from their own father's lineage.)

Land was not the only property controlled by Tikopian patrilineages. Much of the food supply came from the surrounding ocean. Effective harvesting of the sea required various kinds of fishing equipment and canoes. Many canoes were owned jointly by the members of a patrilineage, whose male members used them on cooperative fishing expeditions. A lineage thus counted ownership of another factor of production—the canoe—among its functions and organized some kinds of labor—fishing expeditions.

The social rank of individuals also was determined largely by which kin group they belonged to and their status within it. As we have discussed, the various lineages were aggregated into four patriclans. One lineage of each clan was considered the senior lineage. Because its living members were believed to be directly descended (through males) from the founder of the clan, it was the highest ranking lineage of that clan. They received certain kinds of respect from their clanmates. The senior lineage of each clan also had the right to select one of its male members to serve as the clan chief. Just as the lineages were ranked relative to one another on the basis of genealogical closeness to the senior lineage, so families within a single lineage were ranked by their closeness to the head of the lineage. Tikopian kinship thus had a political aspect, since authority over others was granted or refused to an individual or group largely through their descent group membership and rank.

Tikopians did not live by breadfruit alone. The Tikopian world view included a belief in certain supernatural powers. These beliefs also were tied into the descent system because each descent group was allocated ritual duties to perform. Each of the four clan chiefs served as the religious leader and organizer of certain religious ceremonies. Each clan had its own ancestral spirits, which were the deceased former chiefs of the clan. Each clan also had its own gods, with whom its chief acted as intermediary.

One religious function of a clan was to carry out rituals that ensured the availability of food. Each of the four major subsistence crops was spiritually associated with one of the clans. The gods of this clan were

believed to control the crop. The chief of the clan performed important rituals that ensured the continued supply and fertility of whichever crop "listened to" (as the Tikopia phrased it) the gods of his clan. Thus each clan—in the person of its chief—had ritual responsibilities toward the other three clans.

Like clans, Tikopian patrilineages cooperated in religious contexts. Patrilineages were not residence units; rather, the members of a single patrilineage usually lived scattered among several settlements. Each patrilineage did, however, have a house that its scattered members regarded as sacred because it was believed to be the ancestral home of the entire lineage. The members of a lineage periodically held religious ceremonies at this place to honor the deceased ancestors of their kin group.

The Tikopian example shows the diverse kinds of functions that often are assigned to kin groups in preindustrial populations. Patrilineages controlled use rights to land and some other kinds of property, influenced an individual's social rank, and performed joint rituals. Patriclans also had political functions, and their chiefs carried out rituals that Tikopians believed were essential for the well-being of all islanders.

**HOPI: A MATRILINEAL SOCIETY.** In northeastern Arizona live a matrilineal people known as the Hopi. The Hopi divide themselves into about fifty exogamous matriclans (some of which are now extinct). Clans are not residential groups, for most have members who live in more than one of the Hopi's nine *pueblos*. A Hopi pueblo, or village, often is a single large apartment-like building divided into many rooms in which families reside. Each clan is subdivided into several matrilineages. The female members of a Hopi matrilineage usually live in adjoining rooms within a single pueblo.

The Hopi postmarital residence pattern is matrilocal, so after marriage a man joins his wife, her sisters, and her other matrilineal relatives to form a matrilocally extended household. Most Hopi extended families consist of one or more older women, their daughters together with their husbands, and sometimes even their granddaughters and their husbands. Because of lineage and clan exogamy and matrilocal residence, husbands are outsiders and—as the Hopi say—their real home is with their mothers' extended family. The residential core of a matrilineage thus consists of its women, who live close to one another throughout most of their lives. The married men of the lineage are scattered among the households of their wives, although they frequently return to their matrilineal home for rituals and other responsibilities or in case of divorce.

Most property, both secular and ceremonial, is inherited matrilineally. Living space, for instance, is passed from mother to daughter. Farmland, on which the Hopi formerly depended for most of their subsistence, is owned by a clan, with each lineage having use rights over particular parcels at any one time. The husbands of the lineage's women do most of the farming to support their families, although they themselves do not own the land.

Membership in a matriclan not only defines one's primary social relationships but also establishes one's relationships with the supernatural world. Each clan is mystically associated with a number of supernatural powers called *wuya*. Clans usually take their name after their principal wuya, such as bear, rabbit, corn, snake, cloud, sun, and reed. The members of a matriclan pray to their wuya, asking them for protection and for bountiful harvests.

Hopi religion features a ritual calendar that includes a large number of annually required ceremonies. In most cases each ceremony is "owned" by the members of a certain clan, meaning in Hopi culture that this clan has primary responsibility to see that the ceremony is performed on time and in the proper manner. Every clan represented in a village has a clanhouse in which the masks, fetishes, and other sacred items used in the ceremonies it owns are kept when not in use. The clanhouse usually consists of a room adjoining the dwelling of the senior female member of the clan. This woman, known as the *clan mother*, is in charge of storing ritual paraphernalia and of seeing to it that they are treated with the proper respect. The position of clan mother is passed down from a woman to either her younger sister or her daughter, depending on age and personal qualities. There is also a male head of each clan whose duties likewise are partly religious because he is in charge of the performance of ceremonies owned by his clan. A male clan head passes his position, together with the ritual knowledge required to hold it, down to either his younger brother or his sister's son. In this way culturally important ritual knowledge is kept within the clan.

Among the Hopi, as with most other matrilineal systems, the roles of father and husband differ from those in patrilineal systems. As we have seen, husbands move in with their wives and her relatives after marriage. A man brings little property into the marriage other than his clothing and a few personal items. Nor

does he accumulate much property as a result of his marriage because the house, its furnishings, the food stored there, and other goods remain the property of his wife's family. Although a man provides food for himself and his family by working in the fields of his wife, the products of his garden labor belong to his wife. The children similarly are viewed primarily as members of their mother's lineage and clan, and indeed they have no rights to use land or any claim to ritual knowledge or property of their father's kin group.

All these factors mean that a Hopi husband has a rather anomalous position in his wife's household because each spouse owes his or her main loyalty to his or her own matrilineal relatives, and there is little common property in which they share an interest. This feature of the kinship system seems to put stress and strain on marriages because divorce rates are comparatively high. After separation or divorce a man retires to the residence of his own mother and sisters until he remarries.

The combination of matrilineal descent and matrilocal residence profoundly affects relationships between fathers and their children. A child's relationship with his or her father usually is close and tolerant. A man seldom punishes his own children. Culturally this is not considered his appropriate role, for—after all—children and fathers belong to different descent groups. The father's sisters and brothers likewise exhibit warm feelings for their nieces and nephews, often spoiling them with gifts and affection. The main disciplinarians of children are their mother's brother and other members of their mother's kin group. This is partly because a child's behavior reflects well or poorly on the kin group of the mother, so members of this group have the primary duty of monitoring and correcting children.

The Hopi illustrate how the matrilineal principle recruits individuals into kin groups, in which they perform various economic, religious, and social roles. They also show how the form of descent found among a people influences interpersonal relationships between relatives, such as between husbands and wives and between fathers and children.

Neither the Tikopia nor the Hopi "typifies" patrilineal and matrilineal kinship. A wide range of diversity occurs in patrilineal and matrilineal systems: Sometimes men and women have important ritual responsibilities toward their maternal relatives even in patrilineal systems; even in matrilineal systems men often have rights over land in their fathers' kin group or are able to extract favors from their fathers and their fathers' brothers; and so on. The Tikopia and Hopi do illustrate some of the

How often have you heard it said that "the family is the backbone of our nation"? From a comparative perspective, our nuclear family is a rather weak and insignificant kind of group for society as a whole. You can see this in several ways now that you have some feeling for the cross-cultural diversity in marriage, family, and kinship.

First, what do we typically want to know about people as individuals? When we meet someone for the first time, do we ask "Who is your father?" or "Who is your mother?" No, we ordinarily do not. Who a stranger's kinfolk are is of no special interest to us. We are much more likely to ask "Where do you work?" or "What do you do?"—the latter being a question that could mean lots of things but (significantly) usually is a question about occupation. College-age students may instead ask "What's your major?" This last question usually means "What occupation will you perform when you've finished school?" (You can see this by answering "anthropology" and waiting for the question that often follows: "And what are you going to do with *that?*") Culturally, we identify an individual by his or her occupation; the occupational status

of a person is his or her *master status,* as the sociologists call it.

Second, how do you think about and culturally categorize the organization of your society? Certainly, you do not think of it as a kinship group. You do not think of small domestic groups fitting into larger kin groups, which in turn fit into still larger kin groups, and so on. More likely, you think of it as one political and territorial unit fitting into others: cities into states, and states into the nation as a whole.

Third, what are the functions of the nuclear family—our most important kin group—in North American society, and how do they compare with the functions of kin groups in other human populations? The kinds of activities organized by the family are fewer in number than in most preindustrial societies. Even these functions are increasingly

becoming alienated from the family in our society. For example, enculturation and child care, which are among the most important "traditional functions" of a husband-father and wife-mother, increasingly are being handled by babysitters and professionals in day-care centers. Domestic chores are being farmed out to housekeepers, gardeners, and others, and not just among the elite. Restaurants cook much of our food and wash the dishes afterward. Elderly people typically live by themselves or in retirement communities and rest homes rather than with their adult children. Television shows and commercials entertain and—whether we know and like it or not—enculturate our children.

You may think that all this is for the better. But the next time you hear a politician using the cultural theme of "traditional family values" to win your vote, you might pause to consider what he or she means by the phrase. In particular, if you are a woman, you might wonder how this politician plans to arrange things so that you can enjoy these "family values" by staying at home with chores and children and still achieve the standard of living you would like. ◆

differences between patrilineal and matrilineal peoples with respect to recruitment into groups, the allocation of roles, the nature of sentimental attachment, and the organization of common activities. They also exemplify a fundamental organizational feature of many preindustrial societies: Kin groups carry out most of the cooperative activities that more specialized groups perform in industrialized nations. If we compare ourselves with many preindustrial peoples for whom kinship ties are the organizational basis for most activities, we see that family relations are not the backbone of our nation,

contrary to the statements of some politicians (see Box 11.1).

## Avunculocality Revisited

Comparatively speaking, Hopi women have a great deal of influence on domestic life and control over property—land in particular. (As we discuss in chapter 12, Hopi women owe their relatively high status partly to their control over land and partly to matrilineality and matrilocality.) Because they are a matrilocal people, sisters live together and their husbands live apart from their matrilineal relatives for as long as the marriage lasts.

But not all matrilineal people are matrilocal. The most common pattern of postmarital residence among matrilineal peoples is avunculocality, in which married couples live with or near the husband's mother's brother (chapter 10). More than one-third of all matrilineal societies have avunculocal residence as the predominant pattern. Most of the others are matrilocal or patrilocal. Now that we are aware of matrilineal descent groups and know that they often control property, we can understand this seemingly bizarre residence pattern.

First, the fact that a people are matrilineal does not mean that women control property and politics. That is, *matrilineality*—descent through females—should not be confused with *matriarchy*—rule by women. Even in matrilineal societies men control and make decisions about the use and allocation of land and other forms of wealth and have more of a say than women do in public affairs. The oldest competent man of a lineage usually has the greatest control over life-sustaining or culturally valuable property in a matrilineal society. Unlike patrilineal peoples, in a matrilineal society a lineage elder has authority over his sister's children rather than his own children because the latter are not members of his own descent group and supposedly have their property and loyalties with the group of their mothers.

How can a lineage elder have his sisters' sons living with or near him, where he can keep an eye on them, and where they can look after their own interest in land and common property? The answer is avunculocal residence. If a man's sisters' sons bring their wives to live with them in a common residence, then the elder and young male members of a single matrilineage are localized in a single place. The married women of the matrilineage are scattered among the households of their husbands' mothers' brothers. The children of the matrilineage's women are likewise scattered among the households of their fathers, so long as they are unmarried. But as they marry they return to their own mothers' brother's households—the place of their own lineage. In short, avunculocal residence has the effect of localizing male matrilineal relatives who have a common interest in land, wealth, or other property. It therefore is explicable once we understand how the matrilineal principle forms kin groups that hold common property, and once we realize that men usually have most control over wealth and public affairs even among matrilineal peoples.

 ## COGNATIC DESCENT

In cultures that trace descent patrilineally most people become members of the kin groups of their fathers. If enough people do this over several generations, patrilineages and perhaps patriclans develop, the members of which are related through males. Conversely, in matrilineal cultures most people join the groups of their mothers, and over time matrilineal descent groups develop, the members of which are related through females.

In real societies that practice either of these unilineal systems the membership of lineages and clans are not as well defined as the descent principles make them appear. For instance, in matrilineal systems adoptions, childless women, inability to get along with one's matrikin, insufficiency of land owned by the matrigroup, and other factors make it likely that some individuals will affiliate with a group other than that of their mothers. As a result, many matrilineages will include members who are not matrilineally related. To state the point differently, even in unilineal descent systems there often is some degree of choice about which group to join, depending on personal preferences and circumstances. Most people, however, follow the norms by joining the culturally proper or preferred group.

Cultures with **cognatic descent** have no formal principle or rule about whether individuals join the groups of their mothers or fathers. Some people join with their fathers, others with their mothers, entirely or largely according to preferences and circumstances. A **cognatic descent group**, then, consists of all the individuals who can trace their descent back to the common ancestor (or founder) of the group, through both female and male links.

Much more so than in unilineal systems, in cognatic descent people make choices about the groups they want to join. The choice commonly is based on factors such as ego's chances of inheriting rights to land use or other forms of property or wealth; on the desire to associate with a relative of high status or rank; on childhood residence; and on emotional ties. For example, in a cognatic system you might decide to reside and cooperate with your mother's relatives if her kin group has a lot more land available for you to cultivate than does your father's group. Or if a coveted political office or honorific title is about to become vacant in your father's group, you might decide to try to acquire it by moving in and working with his relatives.

## Cognatic Descent in Polynesia

Cognatic descent is found in all continents, but it is especially prevalent among Polynesians, including the Samoans, Hawaiians, Tahitians, and New Zealand Maori. The residents of these and most other Polynesian islands were divided into numerous cognatic kinship groups, the membership of which sometimes numbered in the thousands. Details varied from island to island, but generally speaking, a person could join any cognatic group or groups to which he or she could trace ancestry. Membership in the descent group bestowed rights to agricultural land, house sites, and some other kinds of property.

As we have seen, in cultures with patrilineal and matrilineal descent a person ordinarily becomes a member of only one group—that of her or his father or mother, respectively. With cognatic descent it might seem that everyone becomes a member of either their mothers' or their fathers' group, or of both. In fact, everyone potentially belongs to several groups because everyone has the opportunity to join all the groups to which their parents belong, and each parent probably is a member of at least two groups. If the kin groups intermarry, everyone potentially will belong to a great many groups—perhaps even to most of the groups that exist in their society.

Unlike unilineal systems, then, cognatic descent groups have overlapping membership. This potentially poses a problem for access to land and other culturally valued things. For example, if all members of a group have rights to the land collectively owned by the group, and if one-half or more of the entire population potentially has such rights, then the "right" does not mean much.

The problem of overlapping membership may be solved in several ways. Effective membership commonly is restricted only or largely to those individuals who reside on or use the group's land. Among the Maori—the original inhabitants of New Zealand—the *hapu* (kin group) *potentially* consisted of everyone who could trace their ancestry back to its founder. However, only people who lived on the land and participated in the daily life of the *hapu* were *effective* members. More often than not, a couple would live with the *hapu* of the husband's parents. The husband's and wife's connections and membership in other *hapu* would be remembered, but the claim of their children and grandchildren to membership in these *hapu* might be forgotten.

In some Polynesian cultures people keep up their membership in several groups simultaneously by con-tributing labor and foods to feasts sponsored by the group and generally showing their interest in and commitment to the group. The islands of Samoa provide an example. Each Samoan village has a council that plans public activities, levies fines, and performs other functions for the whole community. Each village is composed of several cognatic kin groups known as *'aiga*. Although each *'aiga* has branches represented in several villages, every *'aiga* has an ancestral homeland village. In its homeland village each *'aiga* has the right to select one or more of its men to hold titles, or *matai,* and it is these titleholders who serve as the *'aiga's* representative to the village council. Acquisition of a *matai* carries great honor as well as authority to regulate use of the *'aiga's* land, resolve disputes among the *'aiga's* members, organize feasts and ceremonial gifts, and assess the members for contributions to marriages, funerals, and other events.

When a title becomes vacant because of death or some other reason, all members of the entire *'aiga* have a voice in choosing the new *matai,* whether they live in the homeland village or not. Because people belong to several (often six or more) *'aiga* simultaneously, they have a voice in choosing the new *matai* for several groups, although they may not exercise their rights in all the *'aiga* to which they belong. Because men belong to several groups, they have the right to compete for and gain a title in these groups. A young man might anticipate a future title vacancy in one of his *'aiga* and decide to move to the village where that *'aiga* is represented on the council to concentrate his energies on acquiring that particular *matai.* This general kinship and village-level political organization persist in rural Samoa to this day.

The Maori *hapu* and the Samoan *'aiga* illustrate some of the common functions of cognatic kin groups: They can hold property and regulate access to land, organize cooperative activities, and serve as the structural basis for acquiring honored and authoritative political roles. In these respects they are similar to the lineages and clans of unilineal systems. But in cognatic systems the range of individual choice about group membership is much wider than in unilineal descent.

## ▰▰ BILATERAL KINSHIP

**Bilateral** (two-sided) kinship systems differ from unilineal descent in that kinship relationships are traced through both genders. An individual regards his or her relatives through both parents as equal in importance; cousins are seen as the same kind of relative, for

In bilateral kinship, there are no large descent groups that commonly own property or act cooperatively. Marriages, such as this one in Hungary, and other important events in an individual's life provide occasions at which a person's kindred gather.

instance, regardless of whether they are related to ego through the mother or the father.

Bilateral kinship, as you may recognize, exists in most contemporary Western countries, but it is also common in other parts of the world. Bilateral kinship differs from both unilineal and cognatic descent in that no large, well-defined, property-holding groups exist in bilateral systems. Rather than lineages and clans, the tracing of kinship relationships bilaterally produces associations of relatives known as the **kindred**. A kindred consists of all the people that a specific person recognizes as bilaterally related to himself or herself.

To understand bilateral kinship and the kindred, imagine a Canadian or an American woman named Liz. Liz recognizes her relatives through her father and mother as equivalent and interacts with them in much the same way (unless she has established strong bonds with someone because they live close by or for some other reason). The more distant the relationship, the less likely Liz is to interact with or even know who her relatives are. The only times she is likely to see many of her kindred in the same place are at events such as weddings, funerals, and, perhaps, family reunions. Many of Liz's relatives do not know one another (her cousins on her mother's side are unlikely to know her cousins through her father, for example). All the members of her kindred do not consider themselves relatives, and they certainly do not own any common property. The only thing that ever brings them together is the fact that they are all related to Liz.

As this hypothetical example shows, a kindred is *ego-focused,* meaning that each individual is the center of his or her own set of relatives. Only you and your siblings share the same kindred; your mother has a different kindred, as do your father and all your cousins. Unilineal and cognatic descent groups, in contrast, are *ancestor-focused,* meaning that people are members of a descent group by virtue of the fact that they recognize descent from a common ancestor.

The Iban, a people of the tropical island of Borneo in Malaysia, provide a non-Western example of bilateral kinship. The Iban are shifting cultivators who traditionally lived in longhouses that were subdivided into numerous apartments. Each apartment was occupied by a single bilocally extended family called a *bilek.* Most bilek included three generations: an elderly couple, one of their married children and his or her spouse, and their grandchildren. The *bilek* owned the section of the longhouse in which its members resided. It also formed an economically independent unit: Its members cooperated in the growing of dry rice, and it owned its own land.

The *bilek* is the main residential and property-owning group among the Iban. Compared with the unilineal and cognatic descent groups, the *bilek* is relatively small, averaging only six or seven members. When an individual Iban needs more people for some purpose, he can ask for help from his kindred, people who are related to him through bilateral ties. In organizing hunting or periodic long-distance trading or warfare expeditions, for example, a man would call out dozens of his first and second cousins to get enough people together to help him for this specific purpose. In other words, a man mobilized his kindred to help him accomplish some particular task or achieve some goal. The bilateral relatives he mobilized, however, came together and cooperated only occasionally. They did not constitute a permanent kin group and did not hold any common property because the *bilek* was the property-holding unit.

## ▦ INFLUENCES ON KINSHIP SYSTEMS

As we have seen, kinship relationships establish groups of relatives that perform various functions and cooperate in many activities. Why does a given culture develop one form of kinship rather than another? Are there any general explanations for patrilineal, matrilineal, and cognatic descent and for bilateral kinship? Ethnologists have worked on this question for decades, but so far none has identified a single factor or even a small number of factors that account for why different cultures develop different kinship systems. There are, however, a number of factors that seem to *influence* (as opposed to *cause*) which form of kinship a people will have.

One of the most important influences is the primary mode of adaptation (see chapters 7 and 8) of a people. For example, about 60 percent of all cultures that exploit their environments by foraging are bilateral or cognatic, according to a cross-cultural study by David Aberle. Bilateral kinship and cognatic descent allow individuals a great deal of choice about which of many possible groups to affiliate with. In foraging cultures this choice allows individuals and families to maintain relationships with many bands. They can move to and harvest the resources of any band to which they trace a kinship relationship. Given that hunters and gatherers usually are subject to seasonal, annual, and spatial fluctuations in wild food availability, keeping one's territorial options open is advantageous (for more discussion of band flexibility, see chapters 7 and 9).

The nomadic pastoral adaptation (chapter 8) likewise influences the way most herding cultures trace their descent. About three-fourths of pastoral peoples are patrilineal. According to one hypothesis, the association between nomadic herding and patrilineal descent exists because livestock most often are owned and managed by men. To conserve labor devoted to protecting and moving animals to seasonally available pastures, a group of brothers often combine their animals into a single herd. Also, inheritance of animals typically passes from fathers to sons. Brothers tend to stay together to cooperate in herd management and look after their inheritance; therefore, they will reside patrilocally. Patrilocal residence associates male relatives together in a single location, whereas it disperses the females. Descent through males develops as a consequence.

Patrilineal descent also has been interpreted as a way to improve success in intergroup warfare. It keeps a group of related males together and thereby increases

*The way people adapt to their environments is an important influence of the kind of kinship system their culture will develop. These are aboriginal peoples of Australia.*

Bedouin herders taking their sheep to market. Most pastoralists are patrilineal, partly because men usually own and manage the livestock.

their willingness to cooperate in battles as well as decreases the chances of male relatives becoming antagonists. Several cross-cultural studies have found a strong association between patrilineal descent and frequent intergroup warfare. But exactly why this correlation exists is a subject of much dispute.

What are some hypotheses about the causes of matrilineal descent? It was once thought that the tracing of kinship ties through the maternal line was a primeval characteristic of early human cultures. That is, in the early stages of cultural evolution descent must have been matrilineal. The logic was that in "primitive hordes"—as these imaginary early populations often were called—people would have been ignorant that the sexual act is responsible for children, so they could have had no concept of paternity. But such a concept seems to be required to develop descent through males. At any rate, it was argued that mating in these primal hordes was so promiscuous that people could not have known which of their mothers' many sexual partners were their fathers. If these "savages" were ignorant of the biological basis of reproduction, and promiscuous besides, then descent had to have been reckoned through one's mother. The matrilineal cultures of today were explained as holdovers from this primitive condition, which once characterized all of humankind.

Thanks to the ethnographic research of the twentieth century, we now know that few, if any, "savages" fail to realize the connection between sexual relations and children. We also know that mating and marriage are everywhere governed by cultural norms of incest and exogamy and are nowhere promiscuous. Matrilineality must have an alternative explanation.

Anthropologists do not agree on the nature of this alternative. Some think that matrilineal descent is somehow connected to the way matrilineal peoples acquire their food. Matrilineal descent is more likely to be found among horticultural peoples (see chapter 8) than it is with any other adaptation; nearly 60 percent of matrilineal cultures are horticultural. This association is probably related to the fact women perform so much of the daily subsistence work in most horticultural populations.

A study by Melvin Ember and Carol Ember suggests that horticulture plus long-distance warfare or trade is likely to lead to the development of matrilineal descent. The reasoning is that if the men are far away fighting or trading much of the time, they cannot at the same time be gardening to feed their relatives; so women will have to take over most of the subsistence labor. They are unlikely to do this effectively if postmarital residence is patrilocal because then they would be working for their husbands' relatives rather than for their own. At any rate, a middle-aged or elderly couple will want to keep their daughters around after they marry, to work their land and help support them in their old age. So postmarital residence typically is matrilocal in horticultural cultures in which men often are absent. Matrilocality has the effect of localizing a group of sisters and other female matrikin in a single household or village. Their brothers move away after their marriage, and the children of these brothers develop closer relationships with their mothers' families than with their fathers' relatives. This ultimately leads to the tracing of descent through females (i.e., to matrilineal descent). This hypothesis is not accepted by all anthropologists, many of whom believe that there is no universal explanation. It does seem to work reasonably well for some matrilineal cultures, such as the Iroquois and the Huron of North America and the Nayar of south India. Almost certainly, no single determinant can explain all cases of matrilineality, or for that matter the other forms of kinship. It may be that the cross-cultural variations in kinship are influenced by so many kinds of complex factors that no generalized explanation is possible.

## CLASSIFYING RELATIVES: KINSHIP TERMINOLOGIES

In chapter 2 we noted that one of the major components of cultural knowledge is the way a people classify natural and social reality. As is by now apparent, kinship relationships and kinship groups are a major part of social reality in human cultures. Just as cultures differ in the ways they trace their descent and form social groupings of relatives, so do they differ in the way they classify types of relatives. That is, cultures differ in how they place relatives into types or labled categories. The labeled categories are called **kin terms**, and the way in which a people classify their relatives into these categories is called their **kinship terminology**. For instance, *aunt* is an English kin term, and the fact that most native English speakers consider all the sisters of both their parents as the same type of relative is part of the English kinship terminological system.

We think of kin terms as reflections of biological (genetic) relationships between individuals: We think that the people we call *cousin* are related to us through certain biological connections, for instance. This is true for some English kin terms: The terms *mother, father, son, daughter, sister,* and *brother* define individuals related to us in distinct genetic ways. However, this is not true for all our kin terms. Consider the term *uncle.* It classifies together into a single term men who are related to you in four ways: your father's brother, mother's brother, father's sister's husband, and mother's sister's husband. Note that both consanguineal and affinal kin are included in the term *uncle.* The same idea applies to some other English terms; a particular term groups together several individuals related to you in different ways. Thus *grandfather* includes both mother's father and father's father; *grandmother* is used for both mother's mother and father's mother; and *aunt* is applied to all female siblings of parents as well as to the wives of all male siblings of one's parents. The term *cousin* likewise applies to a wide range of relationships.

A peoples' kinship terminology only partly reflects the biological relationships between individuals. More fundamentally, it reflects the various norms, rights and duties, and behavioral patterns that characterize social relationships between kinfolk. Collapsing relatives of different kinds into a single term reflects the cultural fact that people think of them as the same kind of relative; in turn, people conceive of them as the same kind of relative because they have similar kinds of relations with them. Thus the men we call *uncle* have the same general kinds of social relationship with us regardless of whether they are our mother's or our father's brothers. Under most conditions people in American society would not expect to inherit much from their uncles (unless the uncles were childless or very rich), but if a parent or grandparent left you out of the will, you probably would be hurt.

Before we can discuss particular kinship terminologies, we need to understand the logic by which they are constructed. No matter how strange some systems may appear to us (and some seem strange indeed), all are logically constructed. For one thing, every term has a reciprocal term. For example, the reciprocal of *grandfather* is either *granddaughter* or *grandson.* If you call a woman *mother,* she will call you *son* or *daughter.*

Kinship terminologies are constructed using several criteria. Three of the most important criteria are (1) gender of referent, (2) generation, and (3) side of the family. In the following discussion *ego* refers to the person using the given kin term.

The gender of the individual to whom the term refers (the referent) usually is a relevant criterion for the kin term used. In English, gender matters for terms like *brother* and *sister, uncle* and *aunt,* and *grandfather* and *grandmother.* Indeed, gender is the only criterion that distinguishes the relatives just mentioned from one another. Gender is irrelevant, however, for another of our kin terms, *cousin.*

Kinship terms usually reflect whether the individual referred to is of the same or a different generation than ego's. In English, specific terms are used for relatives in ego's own generation (*cousin*), in ego's parents' generation (*aunt*), and in ego's childrens' generation (*niece*). In describing kinship terminologies we call ego's parents' generation the *first ascending generation* and ego's children's generation the *first descending generation.* Although the terms used in most kinship terminologies reflect generational differences, two systems of terminology use terms that transcend generations.

Side of ego's family is the third criterion by which kin terminologies are constructed. In English, side of the family is irrelevant: Relatives through the mother receive the same terms as relatives through the father. As we know, many other cultures place special emphasis on relationships through females (mothers) or males (fathers), and this emphasis is reflected in their terminological systems.

## Varieties of Kinship Terminology

We shall discuss only the five most common types of kinship terminology: Eskimo, Hawaiian, Iroquois, Omaha, and Crow. Do not be misled by the names of these systems. Lewis Henry Morgan, the American anthropologist we mentioned in chapter 4, developed the basic classification system for kinship terminology in 1871. He named each system after the first people among whom he discovered it. Although four terminologies are named after Native American groups, all are found scattered around the world. To simplify our discussion, we consider only terms used for consanguineal relatives in ego's generation and in ego's first ascending (parental) generation. To make these systems easier to understand, we translate the terms into what would be their closest English equivalents. Keep in mind that these translations are only rough approximations, and that some terms have no exact English equivalents.

**ESKIMO.**    Eskimo terminology is the easiest for English speakers to understand because this is the system we use (see Figure 11.5). In this system ego's biological mother is called *mother* and ego's biological father is called *father.* These are the only two persons to whom

these terms apply. The term *aunt* is used for both ego's father's sister and ego's mother's sister, and the term *uncle* is used for father's brother and mother's brother. The terms *brother* and *sister* are used only for the children of ego's mother and father. The term *cousin* is used for all children of ego's uncles and aunts.

**HAWAIIAN.**    Hawaiian kinship terminology is the simplest because it uses the fewest terms (see Figure 11.6). All relatives in ego's first ascending generation are called either *mother* or *father.* The term *mother* is extended to include ego's mother's sister and ego's father's sister, and *father* is extended to include father's brother and mother's brother. In ego's own generation everyone is called either *brother* or *sister.* Thus Hawaiian terminology includes no terms equivalent to the English terms *uncle, aunt,* or *cousin.* Although the Hawaiian system extends the terms *mother* and *father,* this does not mean that individuals do not know or are unable to distinguish their biological parents from their other relatives of the parental generation.

Hawaiian often is called a generational system because only the generation of the term's referent is relevant; if Figure 11.6 showed the first descending generation, people whom English speakers call *niece* and *nephew* would be shown as ego's *daughter* and *son.*

**IROQUOIS.**    Iroquois terminology categorizes relatives very differently than do either the Hawaiian or the Eskimo system (Figure 11.7). The term *father* includes father's brother but not mother's brother. *Mother* includes mother's sister but not father's sister. The term *uncle* is used only for mother's brother; *aunt* is used only

FIGURE 11.5
Eskimo Kinship Terminolgy

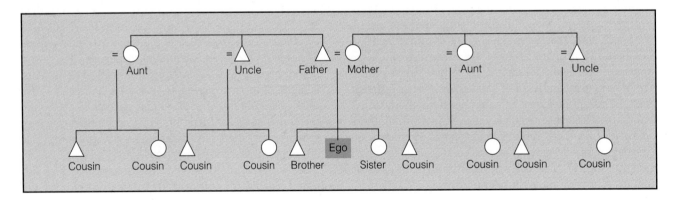

FIGURE 11.6
Hawaiian Kinship Terminology

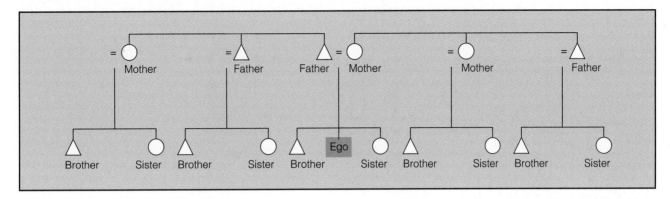

for father's sister. If we look at ego's generation, we also see a difference. The children of father's brother and mother's sister are called *brother* and *sister.* The term *cousin* is used only for the children of mother's brother and father's sister. Thus in the Iroquois system ego differentiates cousins. Although this distinction may seem unusual to us, it also exists in the Omaha and Crow systems, so we need to understand the reasoning behind it.

The Iroquois system distinguishes between parallel and cross cousins. Parallel cousins are terminologically classified with ego's own brothers and sisters. Cross cousins are distinguished from parallel cousins and called by a term that we would probably translate as *cousin.* To understand the logic behind calling parallel cousins *brother* and *sister* and cross cousins *cousin,* we have to go back to the terms used for ego's parents' siblings. Ego's father's brother and mother's sister are

called *father* and *mother,* respectively. Thus it is logical to call their children *brother* and *sister* (what do you call the children of the people you call *mother* and *father?*). Ego calls his father's sister *aunt* and his mother's brother *uncle,* so it is logical to call their children (ego's cross cousins) by a term we would translate as *cousin.*

OMAHA.    Omaha is a difficult kinship terminology for English speakers to understand (see Figure 11.8). The terms used in the first ascending generation are identical to the Iroquois system. Also, as with the Iroquois system, parallel cousins are called *brother* and *sister.* The only difference between Iroquois and Omaha is how cross cousins are treated. Omaha terminology has no equivalent to the English term *cousin.* In addition, in Omaha terminology a distinction is made between cross cousins on the mother's side (the children of

FIGURE 11.7
Iroquois Kinship Terminology

FIGURE 11.8
Omaha Kinship Terminology

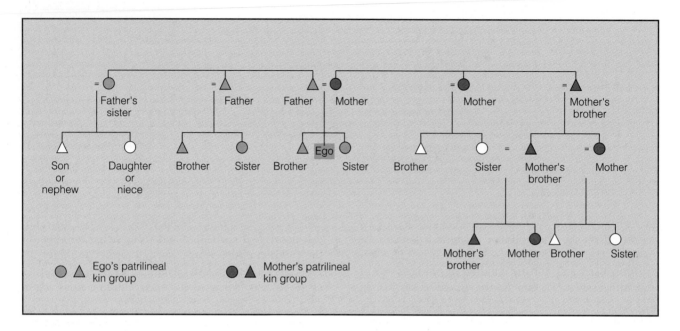

mother's brother) and cross cousins on the father's side (the children of father's sister). Mother's brothers' daughters are called *mother,* and mother's brothers' sons are called *mother's brother* (or *uncle*). Thus ego's maternal cross cousins are grouped with individuals in ego's parents' generation. The situation appears even more confused for ego's paternal cross cousins, since the terms used depend on ego's sex. If ego is a male, he calls his father's sisters' children *niece* and *nephew.* If ego is a female, she calls her father's sisters' children *son* and *daughter.*

Why are there two separate terms for father's sisters' children, depending on the sex of ego? This distinction is perfectly logical. Remember that kinship terms are reciprocal and that we have only indicated the terms used by ego. To understand why the sex of ego is important in this relationship, we must ask: What would father's sisters' children call ego? In Figure 11.8 you can see that ego is their mother's brothers' child. Thus if ego is female, they would call her *mother,* and she would reciprocate by calling them *son* or *daughter.* If ego is male, they would call him *uncle* and therefore he would call them *niece* or *nephew.*

CROW.    Crow terminology is said to be the mirror image or reverse of Omaha (see Figure 11.9). First ascending generation terms are the same as in the Omaha and Iroquois systems. As in the Omaha and Iroquois systems, parallel cousins are called *brother* and *sister.* Once again the difference is in the terms used for cross cousins. In the Crow system father's sisters' children are called *father* and *father's sister* or *aunt.* Using the same logic discussed for the Omaha system, in the Crow system mother's brothers' children are called *son* or *daughter* if ego is male and *niece* or *nephew* if ego is female.

There are a few other systems, but these five are the most widespread. This diversity is surprising, and some of the ways of classifying relatives are puzzling. Can we account for them?

### Determinants of Kinship Terminology

In previous chapters we have emphasized that cultures are integrated: One aspect "fits" with others and sometimes makes sense only when understood in context. In kin terminology systems we have a prime example of this integration, so it is worthwhile to see how we can make sense of them.

A good way to begin is by noting that the five terminologies described can be separated into two types. In the Eskimo and Hawaiian, the side of the family does not matter in classifying relatives; in the Iroquois, Omaha, and Crow it does. Stated another way, among the diverse peoples who use the Eskimo or Hawaiian system, the logical principle of distinguishing relatives according to side of ego's family is irrelevant; they *could* recognize the distinction between mother's and father's kin, but (like ourselves) they do not. Among the many cultures who use the Iroquois, Crow, or Omaha system, the logical principle of distinguishing relatives according to family side is relevant. Why should the side of the family matter in some terminological systems but not in others?

You might already have guessed the answer. The side of the family matters in some terminologies because some people trace their descent through only one of their parents. The side of the family makes no difference in other systems because these populations trace their kin connections equally through both parents. The prevalent rule of descent and the relationships between kin are the most important "other aspects" of a peoples' cultural system that influence the way they culturally classify their relatives. *In general,* the way a people trace their descent affects the relationships between kin, which affects how relatives are placed into cultural categories, which affects the terms used to refer to various kin.

Why say "in general"? Because the correlations between types of kinship terminologies and forms of descent are far from perfect. In a moment, for example, we shall show that the logical principles underlying the

Omaha classification make sense for systems in which patrilineal descent is predominant; but not all patrilineal systems also have Omaha terminologies and not all Omaha terminologies occur in patrilineal systems. Here again, humankind's complexity defies our attempts to explain something totally, and we must be satisfied with general correlations that have many exceptions.

Because the Eskimo classification is most familiar, we begin with it. If we compare it with the other terminologies, it differs in two main ways: (1) it makes no distinctions between ego's father's and mother's relatives and (2) no other relatives of any kind are lumped together with nuclear family relatives. Assume that these two features reflect peoples' ideas about how various kin are related. We might conclude that people think (1) that both sides of the family are of equal importance to an individual (or, rather, there is no systematic *pattern* of importance through one side over the other) and (2) that nuclear family relatives are somehow special and thought of differently than are other kinds of relatives. In the case of the contemporary United States we happen to be right. Our surnames are inherited mainly through males, but other than this, we are no more likely to have special relationships with our kin through our fathers than through our mothers. And, generally, the members of our nuclear families *are* special: We do not expect to inherit much, if anything, from other relatives; we usually do not live in extended

**FIGURE 11.9**
**Crow Kinship Terminology**

households; we do not have any ancestors to worship as a large kin group; kin groups larger than the nuclear family usually do not own property in common; and so on. The hypothesis that the prevalent forms of descent, groupings, and relationships are reflected in kin terminology seems to account nicely for why the Eskimo system developed among ourselves.

More generally, we ought to expect the Eskimo classification of relatives to be associated with cognatic or bilateral kinship. And usually it is: About 80 percent of all societies that use the Eskimo terminological system have either bilateral or cognatic kinship. This is because neither side of any given ego's family is consistently emphasized, nor does any ego consistently join the kin group of her or his mother or father. Ego, therefore, does not think of his or her mother's or father's relatives as being any different. The absence of a special relation with kin through either parent is reflected in the terminological system.

What about the Hawaiian system? Like the Eskimo, family side is irrelevant. Logically, it ought, then, to be associated consistently with cognatic or bilateral kinship. The fact that it lumps other relatives with nuclear family members seems to indicate that the nuclear family is submerged or embedded in larger extended households. Ego should have important relations with the siblings of his or her parents and with their children. Despite this logic, the Hawaiian terminology is not as consistently associated with cognatic or bilateral kinship as is the Eskimo terminology: In fact, about 40 percent of societies that use the Hawaiian classification are unilineal. The Hawaiian system apparently is also compatible with unilineal descent.

And the Iroquois? Ego's father and father's brother are assigned a single term, which is different from mother's brother. Mother and mother's sister are given the same term, which is not the same term as ego uses for father's sister. Thus ego distinguishes between maternal and paternal aunts and uncles in the first ascending generation. The fact that the side of the family matters in this generation seems to imply unilineal descent. And in fact the Iroquois system usually is found among peoples who trace their descent unilineally: Around 80 percent of all Iroquois terminologies occur in unilineal descent forms. If you look back to Figure 11.7, you will see that ego classes with his own brother and sister the children of relatives he classes with mother and father. This certainly makes logical sense—if you call someone *mother*, it is sensible to call her son *brother*. The cross cousins have a separate term because their parents are

not classed with ego's own biological parents, which again is logically consistent.

The Omaha system also distinguishes between sides of the family, like the Iroquois. In fact, it carries the distinctions between the mother's and father's side "down" into ego's own generation. If you look back to Figure 11.8, you will see that the Omaha differs from the Iroquois by its splitting of cross cousins according to whether they are related to ego through ego's mother or father. Mother, mother's sister, and mother's brother's daughter are lumped, although they are members of different generations. Mother's brother and mother's brother's son likewise are lumped together under a single term.

What can explain this way of classifying relatives, which you probably find confusing? The fact that these relatives are all related to ego through ego's mother must mean something; and the fact that they are classified ("lumped") together and distinguished only by their gender must be significant. Indeed, both these features are clues to the logic behind the Omaha terminology. It is found among peoples who use the patrilineal principle to form kin groups.

How does patrilineal descent make sense of the Omaha system? In Figure 11.8 we have drawn a line around all those relatives in the diagram who belong to ego's own patrilineal group. Notice that the cousins in ego's group are called *brother* and *sister*, to reflect the fact that they are in ego's own lineage. We have drawn another line around those relatives who are members of ego's mother's patrilineal group. Notice that all the members of this latter group are assigned only two terms—one for the male members of the group and one for the female members of the group. We might translate the two kin terms that apply to them as "female member of my mother's group" and "male member of my mother's group." Their common social characteristic as members of ego's mother's kin group overrides the biological fact that they are members of three generations. If you have followed the argument, you will agree that the Omaha system makes perfect sense, provided it is associated with patrilineal descent forms. And, indeed, more than 90 percent of all cultures who use the Omaha terminological system are patrilineal.

Because the Crow system is the mirror image of the Omaha, we can make sense of it by showing how it reflects kinship relationships among matrilineal peoples. Go back to Figure 11.9 and look at the lines drawn around ego's own matrilineal descent group and around the matrilineal group of ego's father. You will see that all the male members of ego's father's group are called by the same term, as are all the female members of the same group. The underlying logic of the Crow terms is apparent, given matrilineal descent: Ego lumps together relatives who belong to the same descent group as his or her father. More than 70 percent of all people who use the Crow terms are also matrilineal.

The preceding discussion shows how the strange-looking Hawaiian, Iroquois, Omaha, and Crow terminological systems make sense once we understand that they reflect the prevalent relationships and groupings of kin produced by various ways of tracing kinship connections. The ways in which various people classify and label their relatives looks mysterious until we put these classifications and labels in the context of the kinship systems that give rise to them. The Eskimo terminology used by ourselves would probably look rather exotic to people who use, say, the Crow or Omaha terminology. Our failure to distinguish between relatives through one's mother and father would be strange because to them these relatives would be clearly differentiated, given the way their kinship systems place people into different kin groups.

Along these same lines, the various peoples who use one or another of these kinship classification systems cannot state the logic of their classifications in the same way as we just did. For instance, people who use the Omaha terminology cannot tell you why they label their relatives as they do because they lack a comparative perspective on their own kinship system. To them, their mother, mother's sister, and mother's brother's daughter are called by the same term because all these women are the same kind of relative, just as aunts are all the same kind of relative to us. They do not realize that in Eskimo systems these females all have separate terms; nor are they aware that their terminology reflects the groupings and relationships of their kinship system. But then again, people who use the Eskimo system cannot account for their own classification system either unless they are aware of the diversity in human kinship systems discovered in the past century by anthropologists. The way a people classify their kinfolk seems quite natural or obvious to them until they become aware that other people do it differently.

▼▼▼▼▼▼▼▼▼▼▼▼▼▼▼▼▼▼▼▼▼▼▼▼▼▼▼▼▼▼▼▼▼▼▼▼▼▼▼▼▼▼▼▼▼▼▼▼

## SUMMARY

Relationships and groups based on kinship are an especially important component of the social organization of preindustrial peoples. Although kinship is everywhere based on biological relatedness, societies vary in their kinship systems. There is diversity in the kinds and sizes of groups formed using kinship principles, in the norms attached to kin roles, and in the way people culturally categorize their relatives.

One way cultures vary is in how people trace their relationships back to previous generations—in how they trace their descent. Cross-culturally, the most common forms of descent are patrilineal, matrilineal, and cognatic. All three kinds of descent principles place people into kinship groups and assign roles to them. In preindustrial cultures, the multifunctional groupings established on the basis of kinship usually are more important than in industrialized nations. The latter societies have groups that specialize in the performance of only a

few kinds of tasks or functions and for the most part the membership of these groups is not based on kinship.

Matrilineal and patrilineal descent are both unilineal forms of descent, meaning that a person traces his or her descent through either females or males, but not through both sexes. Unilineal descent groups may be formed using the matrilineal or patrilineal principle, yielding kin groups composed of people related through females and males, respectively. In order of increasing inclusiveness and genealogical depth, the main kinds of descent groups are extended families, lineages, clans, phratries, and moieties. All may be based on either the matrilineal or patrilineal principle. The multifunctional nature of descent groups and the diverse kinds of activities organized by such groups are illustrated by the patrilineal Tikopia and the matrilineal Hopi.

The avunculocal residence pattern is understandable once we realize that it is consistently found in matrilineal cultures. Avunculocal residence has the effect of forming households composed of men (and their families) with a common interest in the property of the matrilineal kin group.

In cognatic descent people trace their ancestry through both males and females, depending on choice and circumstance. Kin groups whose members have use rights to common property or resources and who cooperate socially, economically, politically, and ritually are found in many parts of the world. The Maori *hapu* and the Samoan *'aiga* illustrate the functions of cognatic descent groups.

Peoples who trace their kinship relationships bilaterally have no true kin groups larger than extended families, because the kindreds of different people overlap so much. In most industrialized nations, kinship is bilateral, and large numbers of an individual's relatives are likely to congregate only on certain occasions such as weddings, funerals, and family reunions. Individuals in preindustrial bilateral societies such as the Iban mobilize their kindreds to help them in various tasks, such as hunting, trading, and construction.

One important influence on the kinship systems of a culture is its mode of adaptation. Cognatic descent and bilateral kinship are common among foragers, who find it beneficial to maximize social contacts and access to diverse territories.

Nomadic pastoralists usually are patrilineal, which is probably related to the tendency for males to own and manage herds. Patrilineal descent also is likely to be found among peoples who are heavily engaged in warfare with close neighbors. Matrilineality is most likely to occur among populations who are horticultural and whose men are absent for prolonged periods when engaged in long-distance trade, warfare, or both. These general associations have been supported by cross-cultural studies, but so many forces influence descent forms that no single explanation suffices to account for their occurrence.

People culturally classify their relatives into labeled categories by recognizing some differences between relatives and ignoring others. This classification gives rise to systems of kin terminology. Five systems are most widespread: Eskimo, Hawaiian, Iroquois, Omaha, and Crow. With the exception of the Iroquois, each terminological system is associated with one form of descent. This is because the ideas people have about how they are related to one another are strongly influenced by how the descent form of their society sorts people into groups and establishes relations of one or another kind between kinfolk.

# KEY TERMS

| | |
|---|---|
| kin group | cognatic descent group |
| form of descent | bilateral |
| unilineal descent | kindred |
| patrilineal descent | kin terms |
| matrilineal descent | kinship terminology |
| descent groups | Eskimo |
| unilineal descent group | Hawaiian |
| lineage | Iroquois |
| clan | Omaha |
| cognatic descent | Crow |

# SUGGESTED READINGS

There are a number of excellent texts and collections of readings on kinship, descent groups, and the classification of relatives. The following is a list of such books.

Collier, Jane F. and J. Yanagisako, eds. *Gender and Kinship: Essays Toward a Unified Analysis.* Stanford, Calif.: Stanford University Press, 1987.

> Collection of recent articles focussing on relationships between the sexes and kinship.

Fox, Robin. *Kinship and Marriage: An Anthropological Perspective.* Baltimore: Penguin, 1968.

> An excellent introduction to the topics covered in this chapter.

Graburn, Nelson, ed. *Readings in Kinship and Social Structure.* New York: Harper and Row, 1971.

> Collection of about 60 essays, many of which were influential in the anthropological study of marriage, family, and kinship.

Keesing, Roger M. *Kin Groups and Social Structure.* New York: Holt, Rinehart and Winston, 1971.

> An introduction to the theory of kinship but can be difficult reading for undergraduate students.

Pasternak, Burton. *Introduction to Kinship and Social Organization.* Englewood Cliffs, N.J.: Prentice-Hall, 1976.

> A short introductory text with a cross-cultural orientation.

Radcliffe-Brown, A. R., and Daryll Forde, eds. *African Systems of Kinship and Marriage.* London: Oxford University Press, 1950.

> A collection of still-valuable essays by British anthropologists on kinship among nine African peoples. Radcliffe-Brown's introduction is regarded as a seminal paper.

Schneider, David M. *American Kinship: A Cultural Account.* 2nd ed. Chicago: University of Chicago Press, 1980.

> A symbolic account of American kinship written by a leading idealist.

Schneider, David M., and Kathleen Gough, eds. *Matrilineal Kinship*. Berkeley: University of California Press, 1961.
> *Contains a description of nine matrilineal systems and an analysis of some dimensions of variation in matrilineal societies. Introductory essay by Schneider is a good overview.*

Schusky, Ernest L. *Manual for Kinship Analysis*. 2d ed. New York: Holt, Rinehart and Winston, 1972.
> *A short text designed to teach students how to diagram kinship ties and analyze kinship systems.*

**The following ethnographies include excellent descriptions of specific kinship systems.**

Chagnon, Napoleon A. *Yanomamo*. 4th ed. Fort Worth: Harcourt Brace Jovanovich, 1992.
> *Description and interpretation of a patrilineal horticultural and hunting people of the Brazilian and Venezuelan rainforest. Shows how conflict and cooperation are based on kinship ties between individuals and lineages.*

Colson, Elizabeth. *The Plateau Tonga of Northern Rhodesia*. Manchester: University of Manchester, 1962.
> *An ethnographic account of a southern African people.*

Eggan, Fred. *Social Organization of the Western Pueblos*. Chicago: University of Chicago Press, 1950.
> *A study in which the author describes and compares the social organization of the Hopi, Hano, Zuni, Acoma, and Laguna pueblos.*

Evans-Pritchard, E. E. *The Nuer*. Oxford: Clarendon, 1940.
> *An ethnography of an African society, long considered one of the classic studies in social organization.*

Firth, Raymond. *We, the Tikopia*. Boston: Beacon Press, 1936.
> *An ethnographic study of domestic life, kin relationships, descent groups, and marriage on a tiny Polynesian island.*

## CHAPTER 12

# GENDER IN COMPARATIVE PERSPECTIVE

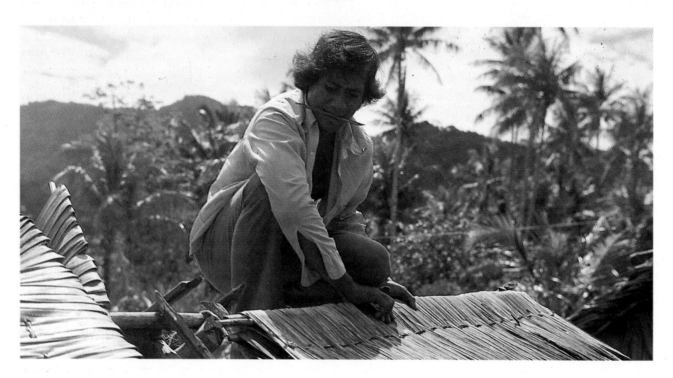

*Gender is everywhere relevant for self-identity and the kinds of roles people perform, but cultures vary in the significance they attach to maleness and femaleness. A Micronesian man ties the thatch on a cookhouse roof.*

**CONTENTS**

Scholars do not work in a cultural vacuum. The teaching and research of anthropologists and other scholars are influenced by events and concerns in the societies in which they themselves live. So it is not surprising that the feminist movement—one of the most important social and political events of the late twentieth century—has led to increased interest in and research about gender relationships. Before about 1970 only a handful of anthropologists conducted research on gender; today many hundreds do so.

In this chapter we make no effort to cover all aspects of the anthropological study of gender. Instead, we concentrate on three areas in which much work has been conducted: (1) the cultural construction of gender, (2) variations in the sexual division of labor, and (3) influences on the status of women in human societies. In all three topics we deal with fieldwork and cross-cultural studies that focus on the human diversity in gender relationships. When relevant we also note the implications of some particular fact or conclusion for gender issues and problems in industrialized societies.

In all cultures gender matters for an individual's self-identity, roles, social relationships, access to culturally valued resources, overall status in the group or society, and so forth. But gender matters to different degrees and in different ways in various cultures. Even within a single culture the importance of one's gender identity varies according to specific social contexts and circumstances. In North America, for example, consider how the consciousness and relevance of gender loom large as one applies for a job subject to affirmative action guidelines and become smaller in the context of a group setting such as a classroom or meeting.

A good topic to begin our discussion of cultural variations in gender patterns is by making the point that gender is a culturally determined construct and not entirely a biologically given characteristic.

## CULTURAL CONSTRUCTION OF GENDER

Anthropologists often say that gender is culturally constructed, not biologically determined. The **cultural construction of gender** is best introduced by making a technical distinction between *sex* and *gender*. A person's sex is determined biologically, by chromosomes—your genitalia, predominant hormones, and secondary sexual characteristics (breasts, hair, body size and musculature, and the like) are fixed by your chromosomes. (Although not considered here, note that a person's sex is not always unambiguously female or male. Gender, in contrast, is culturally defined. A person's sex is a physical reality, but how males and females view themselves and each other, what it means to be a woman or a man, how women and men relate to each other, what roles are appropriate for men and women—all these and most other elements of maleness and femaleness are socially learned during enculturation, not biologically fixed at birth. They are culturally variable, not constant or universal.

To say that gender is culturally constructed is to say that being biologically male or female has different implications in various cultures. Maleness among the Yanomamö is one thing, maleness among the Maasai another thing, and maleness among the Tahitians yet something else. Likewise, womanhood among the Yanomanö, Maasai, and Tahitians has different implications and meanings.

To exemplify the cultural construction of gender, we turn to Anna Meigs's study of the Hua, a New Guinea people. The Hua—who number about 3,500—are horticulturalists who live in villages of around 100 to 300. Each Hua village contains one or more huge men's houses, occupied by initiated people of the patrilineages of the village. Initiated people include men who have completed the complex "male" initiation ceremonies and women with more than two children who have passed through menopause and been initiated themselves. Other women and girls as well as boys who have not yet been initiated live in separate houses, away from people who have been initiated.

To describe Hua conceptions of femaleness and maleness, we focus our discussion on solving a puzzle. Cross-culturally, there is nothing uncommon about male initiation ceremonies (discussed further in chapter 16) or about husbands and wives spending most of their time apart in separate houses. Many cultures in New Guinea and in other regions traditionally have initiation ceremonies, after which males move into houses reserved for men. However, the Hua practice of initiating postmenopausal women with more than two children and having them live with initiated men is unusual and, possibly, unique. The puzzle is, Why were postmenopausal women with more than two children initiated and allowed to live in the men's house? The answer takes us into how Hua culture constructs categories of gender and attributes certain characteristics to these genders.

Hua believe that bodies contain a life-giving substance (like a vital essence) that they call *nu*. *Nu* is thought of as a real, physical substance—not a mystical or magical thing—that can be transferred from one person to another and gained and lost in various ways. Female bodies contain an excess of *nu*, which in Hua thought makes women grow faster and age more slowly than men but also makes them unattractively moist. On the other hand, men naturally contain a smaller amount of *nu*, so they have difficulty with growth and maintenance of vitality later in life but they are attractively dry and hard. Hua explain many of the differences between men and women by the amount of *nu*: Men are stronger and fiercer because they are dry, for example.

*Nu* takes several forms. It is both gaseous (breath) and liquid (blood, sweat, semen, female sexual secretions). A transfer of *nu* between individuals may be either harmful or helpful, depending on the nature of the relationship between the giver and the recipient. Transfer of *nu* may occur during eating, sexual intercourse, and other kinds of direct and indirect contact. For example, a woman transfers her *nu* to people when she serves food to them. *Nu* from her bodily secretions adheres to the food and gets ingested by her children or her husband. A woman also transfers *nu* to her husband when she has intercourse with him. But the giving of feminine *nu* to a man in the act of intercourse is harmful to the man because it pollutes and debilitates him. Intercourse is also damaging to a man because he contributes his scarce *nu* (in the form of breath and semen) to a woman during sex, so she gains strength and vitality at his expense.

The amount of *nu* one has can be regulated by one's activities and by the kinds of food one eats. Various events in the lives of people require regulation of the amount of *nu* they should have. Women need extra *nu* during pregnancy, so they eat lots of foods that are considered rich in *nu*. (Broadly speaking, these are fast-growing foods with high moisture content.) During menstruation women have too much *nu*, so they avoid the same kinds of food. For their part, men naturally lack enough *nu* for full growth and maturation, so during certain periods of boyhood they are encouraged to eat foods with lots of *nu*. At other times, when they are undergoing the initiation ceremonies that make them into strong men able to fight to defend the village, they are supposed to rigorously avoid *nu*-rich foods because such foods will weaken and pollute them. In fact, during initiation ceremonies there are strict taboos not only on the eating of these foods but also on eating foods from gardens tended by women or foods prepared by women. These taboos exist to keep the boys free of the pollution caused by contact with women.

*Nu* is what makes women polluting to males, and the greater the difference in *nu* between a woman and a man, the more dangerous that woman is to the man. But both men and women can and do lose or gain *nu*, depending on their activities, their diet, and how old they are. After decades of engaging in sexual intercourse with and eating foods touched by their wives and other women, middle-aged and elderly men have picked up lots of *nu*. They become invulnerable to further contamination by contact with females and therefore may eat *nu*-rich foods and participate in sexual intercourse with less anxiety than younger men. Gaining *nu* over the years makes them become "like women."

Women lose *nu* whenever they menstruate, handle and prepare food, and have babies. Their *nu* is transferred to others by these activities and events. Over their life course women thus are drained of *nu*, and this draining means that they become less and less dangerous to males as they grow older. Women who have given birth to more than two children are considered to have lost enough *nu* that they are no longer polluting. They therefore have become "like men."

In these ways Hua culture constructs gender categories on the basis of quantity of *nu* as influenced by a person's stage in the life cycle. If gender categories are culturally constructed using these criteria, there is no necessary reason why there are only two highly discrete (either/or) genders. Indeed, Hua culture recognizes gender distinctions based on a person's genitals (in which case one is either male or female) and distinctions based on the quantity of *nu*. The latter criterion gives rise to two additional nondiscrete (more/less) gender categories that the Hua call *figapa* and *kakora*. Although the *figapa/kakora* distinction is relevant only in certain ritual contexts, it is significant that people who are genitally male or female can be classified with the opposite gender for certain purposes.

*Figapa,* which ethnographer Meigs translates as "uninitiated person," are people whose bodies contain lots of substances associated with feminity (e.g., menstrual blood, vaginal secretions, fluids associated with childbirth). *Figapa* include the following kinds of people:

✦ children of both sexes because they have recently been in intimate contact with a woman, their mother;
✦ women in their child-bearing years because they are the essence of femininity and their bodies contain maximum amounts of feminine substances;
✦ postmenopausal women who have not had at least three children because their bodies are not sufficiently drained of feminine substances; and
✦ elderly men because female *nu* has been transmitted to them by their lifetime of activities that exposed them to contact with women.

These people—whether or not their genitals are female—are all "like women" because their bodies contain lots of substances symbolically considered feminine.

*Kakora,* translated by Meigs as "initiated person," consists of

✦ males in their early teens through the prime years who have been initiated (except elderly men) because during the initiation procedures they have rigorously avoided female foods and contact with women and so have minimal quantities of *nu;* and
✦ postmenopausal women with more than two children because three or more childbirths have drained them of most feminine substances, so they are no longer a source of danger to males.

These people are eligible to live in the men's house and to obtain the secret "male" knowledge gained during initiation ceremonies. To return to our original puzzle: Postmenopausal women are eligible to join the men's house because Hua culture constructs gender categories in such a way that they can be initiated and become *kakora,* and *kakora* live in the men's house. As Meigs (1990, 109) puts it, the feminine substances in their bodies have been "massively cleaned out three or more times," and without these substances culturally associated with femininity they are "like men."

This example is presented in such detail because the Hua so clearly illustrate our point about the cultural construction of gender. The objective physical distinctions between the sexes—genitals, beards, breasts, and so on—are differences that are recognized and relevant for behavior in all known cultures. But, as the Hua show, cultures use the raw material (to speak metaphorically) of these differences to construct varying beliefs about the ways in which females and males differ. (Thus Hua believe that men and women differ not only in the obvious physical ways but also in the quantity of *nu* each has.) These beliefs in turn affect the attitudes each sex holds about the other and the behavior each sex adopts toward the other. (Thus Hua men in some contexts and at some ages are fearful about the possibility of feminine pollution and therefore try to minimize their contact with women, their intake of food prepared by women, and their sexual relations with women.)

The more different some culture's beliefs are from one's own, the more obvious it is that those beliefs are a cultural construct rather than a biological imperative. Therefore, because their beliefs pertaining to male-female relationships seem exotic to most Westerners, the fact that gender is culturally constructed among a people such as the Hua is readily apparent. However, all people's ideas about gender are culturally constructed. To stimulate thought, we very briefly present some ideas on the construction of gender in Euro-American culture.

Fairy tales, stories, movies, and numerous modern computer games reflect Western ideas about male dominance and self-reliance over against female passivity and dependence. Princesses, maidens, and other kinds of young, attractive, and usually helpless women are rescued by brave, dashing men who use their physical prowess to overcome unbeatable odds and win the fair damsel's heart and body. There are many exceptions, but they often illustrate the rule: One reason the recent movie Thelma and Louise was so controversial is because its plot featured two women who fought back against male harassers, *and won.*

Speaking more generally, many Americans see females as caring of others, emotional, socially skilled, physically fragile, family oriented, and patient. Males are taken to be more selfish, rational, tolerant of physical discomfort ("tough"), coordinated, and individualistic.

Now consider the possible effects of these cultural conceptions on the uneven distribution of occupational roles between women and men in the modern American economy. The predominant pattern is for members of each sex to move into jobs for which they are held to be best suited, given American cultural conceptions of

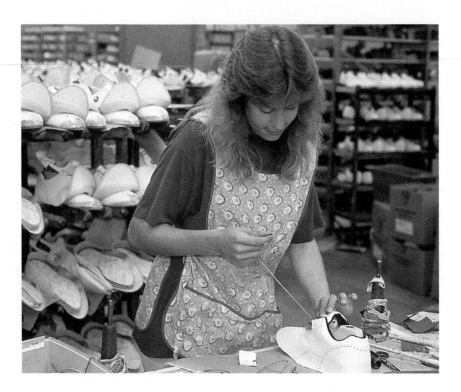

*Gender in the United States is culturally constructed, just as it is among people such as the Hua. This Pennsylvania woman puts her "fine motor skills" to work in a shoe factory.*

gender. This happens for at least two reasons: (1) Individual men and women more often seek those jobs that they find appropriate for their sex or believe they have the best chance of getting or succeeding in; people apply for certain kinds of jobs according to their preferences based in part on their beliefs about "sex roles." (2) Employers tend to hire people according to their own cultural conceptions of which sex is likely to do well in a particular job; the employment market itself allocates men and women into certain kinds of jobs.

This is changing rapidly today, but many jobs remain disproportionately female or male. Thus, women predominate in jobs that involve nurturing (e.g., nursing, day care, teaching of elementary students, pediatric medicine), routine interactions with the public (e.g., receptionists, store clerks, restaurant waiters), repetitive and patient use of fine motor skills (word processing, sewing and stitching), and cleaning and housekeeping. A few of the jobs in which men predominate are those involving outdoor activity (equipment operation, driving, carpentry and construction), high level decision making (management, administration), and knowledge of mathematical principles (science, engineering, computer programming). How much of the occupational difference between the sexes results from the American cultural construction of gender, which defines females

as having certain inherent characteristics, males as having a contrasting set?

To say that gender is culturally constructed is not equivalent to saying that physical differences between males and females are irrelevant. In fact, such differences are everywhere relevant in many ways, including the allocation of work activities. But, as discussed in the next section, biological differences between the sexes are relevant in diverse ways and to varying degrees in the world's cultures.

## ▰▰ THE SEXUAL DIVISION OF LABOR

The **sexual division of labor** refers to the patterned ways in which productive and other economic activities are allocated to men and women. The sexual division of labor is a cultural universal. It implies, necessarily, that males and females share or pool some of the products of their labor. Each sex has access to the goods produced by the other, so that the tasks of males and females are, to some extent, complementary.

In modern North America the sexual division of labor, and indeed the overall social roles of males and females in general, is rapidly changing: Males are carrying out activities and performing roles that twenty or thirty years ago were associated with females, and vice versa. In many other societies, however, the social roles of females and males are sharply divided and the sexual division of labor is clearly defined. Among the Plains Indians, for instance, men and women ordinarily were engaged in different but complementary economic activities. Yet sex role "options" existed for individuals: There were culturally allowable and even socially rewarded ways in which males could assume the normal roles of females, and vice versa (see Box 12.1).

The past 100 years of ethnographic fieldwork provide all the information needed to demolish one common idea on this topic: that it is only natural for men to be the breadwinners for and women the caretakers of the family. Breadwinning—that is, producing the supply of food and other material needs and wants of domestic groups—is definitely not an activity of men exclusively, or even largely. As we shall discuss, in many socieites men produce most of the food, but in many others women's contribution to daily subsistence equals or exceeds that of men; it is the rule rather than the exception for women to produce a significant propor-

tion of the food supply for the camp, household, or domestic group.

This finding of ethnographic research contradicts the opinion of those who think that the domination of men over women is rooted in the "fact" that men's labor is more important to physical survival and material well-being than women's labor. Those who hold this view argue that women are everywhere dependent on men, which in turn makes women everywhere subordinate to men. But where females are subordinate to males, it is not because the things men do are somehow more important to family and group survival than the things women do. (What could be more important to group survival than bearing children?) This ethnocentric idea probably comes from the way most modern industrial economies worked until the mid-twentieth century: By and large, men earned the money that allowed their families to purchase the goods they needed to survive. It is falsely concluded that the same economic dependence of wives on husbands characterized other peoples.

This is our usual warning about confusing the practices and ideas of one's own culture with those of

*In many cultures, women produce much or most of the everyday food supply for their families. These Papua New Guinea women are fishing.*

The Plains Indians of the nineteenth century made a sharp distinction between male and female social roles and behavior. As hunters and warriors, men were aggressive and independent in their social behavior. In contrast, women were mainly involved in the domestic sphere—with activities such as cooking, working hides, making clothing, and decorating items with quill and beadwork. Women were supposed to be passive and reserved in their public behavior.

Even among Plains tribes not all individuals adhered to the normatively appropriate role and behavior of their gender. There was *gender mixing* (sometimes called *gender crossing*), here meaning that some men or women adopted some of the attributes usually accorded the other gender. Particular types of gender mixing were culturally defined alternatives to normatively prescribed gender roles and behaviors. Among the Plains Indians gender crossing took three main forms: (1) berdaches, in which men took on some aspects of feminine roles; (2) manly hearted women, in which a female acted like a male normally acted; and (3) women chiefs, in which a woman assumed a role usually occupied by only men.

## BERDACHES

A berdache was a man who dressed in women's clothes, performed women's work, and, in general, assumed the social behavior normatively appropriate for women. Among the tribes of the plains, the Arapaho, Arikara, Assiniboine, Blackfoot, Cheyenne, Crow, Gros Ventre, Hidatsa, Iowa, Kansa, Mandan, Omaha, Osage, Oto, Pawnee, Plains Cree, Ponca, and Sioux are

## BOX 12.1

# ALTERNATIVE SEX ROLES AMONG THE PLAINS INDIANS

known to have recognized berdaches as alternatives to the normal male role. There is little specific information about the frequency of berdaches among these tribes, but early traders and explorers commonly remarked that they were "numerous" among some tribes.

Variation did exist in the particular characteristics of berdaches from one plains society to the next. Sioux berdaches are the best reported in the literature. The Sioux called berdache *winkte*. Winkte dressed like women and lived in their own separate tepees at the edge of camp. They performed women's tasks such as tanning hides and working with quills and beads. In these activities winkte were said to excell. Ceremonial and ritual items made by a winkte were especially sought after because of their fine quality. To say that a woman had "fine possessions like a winkte's" was the highest compliment to her skill.

It is not clear when a man began to exhibit the characteristics of a winkte. Some began dressing as girls while quite young; others not until after they reached puberty. It was not thought that a man chose to become a winkte but became one by dreaming about female supernatural forces. Through their visions winkte had supernatural powers, such as the ability to cure the

sick. They appear to have had the right or supernatural authority to grant children special secret names, which protected the children from illness and prolonged their lives.

Although most of their activities were those normally associated with women, winkte did take part in male activities. Many were outstanding hunters. This, together with their great skills as craftspeople, made many of them wealthy. Some winkte also participated in war parties and thus engaged in the male role of warrior.

Many questions remain unanswered concerning the winkte in traditional Sioux society, such as whether they were homosexuals. The degree to which they were accepted by other members of the community is also uncertain. Some say that they were well accepted and respected in the community for their skill, hard work, and supernatural powers and that they were intelligent and compassionate individuals who frequently cared for the aged and infirm. Others say that the winkte were disliked and discriminated against. Probably, different Sioux individuals had different opinions about the winkte.

## MANLY HEARTED WOMEN

In the northern Plains tribes certain women adopted elements of male social behavior, acting aggressive and domineering. The Blackfoot called them *ninauposkitzipxe,* which means literally "the manly hearted women." Women ordinarily were passive and docile, but manly hearted women were aggressive and outspoken in public affairs. At the same time they were wives and mothers and were involved in female tasks.

*continued on next page*

Manly hearted women were invariably wealthy women. In large part, their greater wealth came from their own industry. They worked harder and longer at their tasks. They could tan more buffalo robes and produce better quality and greater amounts of quill and beadwork than other women. Many were also medicine women, which not only enhanced their status but also brought them additional wealth. Their wealth was a key factor in their relations with men, because among the Blackfoot wealth and generosity were more highly regarded than bravery and war deeds in determining social status.

Because of their wealth and industry, manly hearted women were major economic assets to their husbands, and thus desirable wives. These same characteristics also made them independent. Within the family a manly hearted woman had an equal say, if not the dominant voice. As a Blackfoot once commented to Oscar Lewis (1941:181), "it's easy to spot a manly-hearted woman; the husband simply has nothing to say." Not only did they retain control of their own wealth, but they frequently controlled the property of their husbands as well. Because they were economically more self-sufficient than other women, many manly hearted women chose to divorce their husbands and support their children by their own industry.

Their public behavior also distinguished them from other women. Their wealth made it possible for them always to dress in the finest clothes. Whereas other women modestly covered themselves with shawls and blankets, manly hearted women usually did not. Whereas most women were retiring and quiet in public discussions, manly hearted women joined in and even argued with others, "just as though they were men." Whereas other women were shy at dances, manly hearted women aggressively chose their own partners. They were known for their sharp and cutting remarks, and it was said that a manly hearted woman would "take no lip" from either a man or another woman. Not surprisingly, they were believed to be sexually aggressive and passionate.

## WOMEN CHIEFS

Among many Plains tribes, sometimes women assumed the role of chiefs. Detailed information is lacking, but an early trader (Edwin Denig) wrote a biographical account of a Crow woman, called "Woman Chief," who lived in the early nineteenth century.

Woman Chief was born into the Gros Ventre tribe. At age ten she was captured by the Crows and adopted by a Crow family. As a girl she showed a fondness for such typically male activities as riding horses, hunting, using bows and arrows, and shooting guns. She was indulged by her foster father, who made her guard of the family's horses—a responsibility usually assumed by a son. She became an excellent rider and markswoman and spent most of her time hunting deer and bighorn sheep as she grew older. She was said to be able to kill four or five bison in a single chase, to butcher the animals, and to pack the meat and hides back to camp with no assistance. When her foster father died she assumed the role of family head, hunting to feed her mother and siblings.

While Woman Chief was still a young woman her camp was attacked by the Blackfoot. Several Crow men were killed, and the survivors took refuge in a fortified trading post nearby. After surrounding the post the Blackfoot asked for a parley, but fearing a trap, the Crow men refused. Finally, Woman Chief ventured out alone and was attacked by the Blackfoot. She killed one and wounded two before running back to the post. Accorded the honors of a warrior for her acts of bravery, the next year Woman Chief led a raid on the Blackfoot. Her party captured seventy horses, and she herself killed one Blackfoot and took the gun of another. In the following years she organized numerous raiding parties against the enemies of the Crow.

Accepted as a family head and warrior, Woman Chief was admitted to full participation in the council deliberations of the men. She eventually came to be ranked third out of the 160 family heads in her band. Because of her role as a frequent leader of raiding parties, she became wealthy in horses. Disdaining traditional women's tasks such as tanning, sewing, quilling, and beading, she paid the brideprice for and married four women to do these jobs for her.

Although Woman Chief was unusual, she was not unique. Women chiefs and women warriors were reported among other Plains tribes. The cases of the berdache, manly hearted women, and Woman Chief show us how individuals are not forced to conform rigidly to the normal social roles and activities of their gender in many cultures. Alternatives frequently are available to both sexes, even in those preindustrial societies in which sex role "deviance" is—according to our stereotypes—supposedly not allowed. ◆

SOURCES: Benedict (1934), Callender and Kochems (1983), Demallie (1983), Denig (1961), Hassrick (1964), Lewis (1941), Medicine (1983).

humanity in general: Our own cultural ideas about what is and is not natural for people to do and think often are wrong. They are wrong because those who espouse them have little knowledge of the cultural diversity of humanity, so they regularly—and mistakenly—conclude that the ideas and practices of their own society are only natural and universal.

We now look at some of the patterns anthropologists have discovered in the sexual division of labor and at some of the hypotheses they have offered to explain these patterns.

## Patterns and Hypotheses

Table 12.1 summarizes the cross-cultural similarities and differences in some specific tasks. Those activities toward the left of the table are more likely to be male; those to the right, more likely to be female. The nearer an activity is to the right, the more likely it is to be done by females, and vice versa for males. Notice both the patterning of differences and the range of overlap. A few tasks, such as hunting and smelting, are almost exclusively male activities in those societies in which they are carried out; some, such as clearing land and tending large animals, are predominantly the work of men almost everywhere; others, such as planting crops, are done by both sexes with about equal frequency; still others are done by women in most societies.

Note that Table 12.1 includes *only* those activities in which some kind of material good is produced. Other activities that are predominantly or exclusively male, such as holding political offices and fighting wars, are discussed later. Also not included is one activity— nursing infants—that is universally allocated to women. There is another—caring for young children—that is predominantly women's work. Of course, there is a sense in which all activities are "productive" (of social order or offspring, for example), but for convenience our discussion is restricted to activities popularly known as "economic tasks."

We want to account for two things revealed by Table 12.1. First, we would like to know why there are widespread similarities between cultures in how productive labor is divided up. For instance, hunting, land clearing, working with hard materials (bone, etc.), and cutting wood are entirely or predominantly men's work everywhere. Gathering wild plants and processing plant foods are mainly female work everywhere. Table 12.1 also reveals that many tasks are not sex-specific—that is, they are allocated to either males or females, depending on the society. In Table 12.1 the tasks in the column labeled "Either or Both Sexes" are performed by women in some cultures and by men in others. The second thing we would like to account for is the cross-cultural variations in the sexual division of labor.

This section focuses on hypotheses that deal with the first issue: the fact that some tasks (such as hunting and land clearing) are regularly assigned to men and others (such as gathering and preparing plant foods) are assigned to women in all or most cultures. In the next section we discuss hypotheses about the differences or cross-cultural variations in the sexual division of labor.

First, what can explain the similarities? The physical differences between males and females provide one possible explanation. Perhaps men are biologically well equipped to handle certain kinds of tasks and women to perform other tasks. These activities are allocated in such a way that each sex does what it is biologically or physically able to do best. Because men and women differ in the same biological ways everywhere, these differences are reflected in widespread similarities in the sexual division of labor.

This idea is not simple and potentially sexist biological determinism. Most of those who believe that physical differences between the sexes play a part in explaining the sexual division of labor say only that these differences are *relevant* in accounting for why societies allocate different tasks to the two sexes. They do not claim that biological differences alone explain the sexual division of labor. This would be an absurd claim because only hunting, lumbering, smelting, and metal working are exclusively male tasks in nearly all cultures.

What, then, are the claims of those who believe that the biology and physiology of males and females are important influences on the sexual division of labor? Because of biological factors, they contend, men are better equipped to handle some tasks than women and vice versa, and these physical differences are reflected in how labor is divided in human populations.

For example, anthropologists used to say that there was at least one task that was everywhere done by men: hunting. Hunting seems to require certain biological capabilities—such as speed, strength, and endurance— that men have more of than women. It also was thought to be incompatible with certain responsibilities universally borne by women for biological reasons: pregnancy, lactation (breastfeeding), and child care. Pregnant women would have a hard time chasing game; lactating mothers would have to quit the hunt several times a day to nurse their infants; and the risk of injury to both mother and child would be high. Because men could

TABLE 12–1   Patterns in the Sexual Division of Labor

|  | TASKS PERFORMED BY GENDER | | | |
|  | Exclusively Males | Predominantly Males | Either or Both Sexes | Predominantly Females |
|---|---|---|---|---|
| **Extracting food and other products** | Hunting<br>Trapping<br><br>Woodworking<br>Mining<br>Lumbering | Fishing<br><br>Clearing land<br>Preparing soil<br>Tending large animals | Gathering small land animals<br>Planting crops<br>Tending crops<br>Harvesting crops<br>Milking animals | Gathering wild plant foods<br>Gathering shellfish, mollusks<br>Tending small animals<br>Gathering fuel<br>Fetching water |
| **Manufacturing, processing, and preparing goods for consumption** | Butchering<br><br>Boat building<br>Working with stone, horn, bone, shell<br>Smelting ore<br>Metalworking | House building<br>Making rope, cordage, nets | Preparing skins<br>Making leather products | Making clothing<br>Matmaking<br>Loom weaving<br>Making pottery<br>Processing, preparing plant foods<br>Cooking |

SOURCE: Adapted from Murdock and Provost (1973).

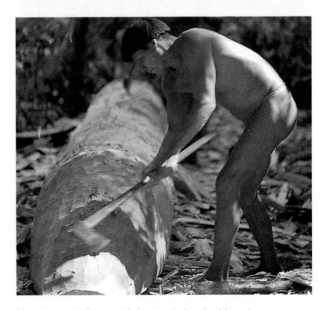

*Six tasks that are assigned to males in all or most cultures (clockwise from upper left): carpentry (Kashmir, India); housebuilding (Indonesian village); hunting (here with a blowgun on Palawan, Philippines); boatbuilding (carving a dougout, Brazil); wood carving (Irian Jaya, Indonesia); metalworking (copper forging, Philippines).*

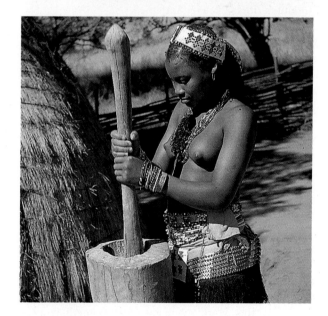

*Six tasks usually assigned to females (clockwise from upper left): making clothing (spinning yarn, Ladakh, India); gathering wild foods (!Kung); cooking (Tarascan woman, Mexico); processing food (grinding corn, Zulu); gathering firewood (Yanomamö, Amazon); weaving (Guatemala).*

hunt more effectively than women, foraging populations allocated hunting to men. Gathering, in contrast, required less strength and ability to run fast and long, so gathering is allocated largely to women.

These arguments are probably correct, but female and male biological differences do not make it mandatory that males are the hunters and females are the gatherers in foraging populations. For one thing, not all kinds of hunting and not all tasks connected to hunting require strength, speed, and endurance. For another, there are questions about whether males have more endurance than females. Finally, there is no necessary *biological* reason why a woman could not give up hunting only during her pregnancy and lactation and leave her older children in camp under the care of someone else.

In fact, it is just not true that hunting is *universally* an exclusively male activity. When the BaMbuti pygmies of the Zaire rain forest hunt animals with nets, the women help by driving game into the nets manned by men. In another part of the world Agnes Estioko-Griffin has reported on hunting by women among the Agta, a mountain tribe of the Philippines who live on the island of Luzon. Agta men do most of the hunting, but women often accompany them in teamwork efforts, and women frequently hunt together without the company of men. Interestingly, sometimes women take their infants with them on the hunt, carrying the children on their backs. There are some differences between the methods used and types of game hunted by women versus men. Still, cases such as the Agta and BaMbuti show that the "man the hunter" image is oversimplified.

It is not, however, wrong. The great majority of cultures in which hunting is a significant means of acquiring food are foragers or horticulturalists. There is no question that in most of these cultures women do most of the gathering of wild plants or the planting, weeding, and harvesting of cultivated plants, whereas men hunt to provide meat. The male hunting/female gathering pattern is not universal, as we have just seen, but it is clearly the predominant pattern. The images of "woman the gatherer" (or gardener) and "man the hunter" do not apply to all people everywhere, but they are common enough that many anthropologists believe that there must be some physical differences between men and women that contribute to this particular division of labor.

What kinds of differences between the sexes seem to matter most? The simplest idea—which we call the **strength hypothesis**—is that men are stronger than women, so that work requiring great strength is allocated to males. Relative strength does play a role in

The strength hypothesis holds that women cannot perform tasks that require great strength. Superior male strength does affect the sexual division of labor, but women are not always assigned "light work," as this Nigerian woman can testify.

explaining why some tasks are nearly universally allocated to males, such as working with hard materials, cutting wood, mining, and perhaps hunting. It also might explain why males predominate in two important cultivation tasks—clearing land and preparing soil for planting. But male strength has no obvious relation to other predominantly male tasks, such as trapping, butchering, and working with fibers. Also, women often do tasks that require significant strength, such as gathering fuel and fetching water.

Women have another physical characteristic that might explain why some activities are allocated to males. Modern female athletes—especially long-distance runners—often do not menstruate and ovulate monthly. Apparently, this is because of a low ratio of body fat and complex hormonal changes in women who engage in prolonged physical exercise. It has been suggested that productive activities that require comparable exertion—notably hunting—would depress a woman's fertility, and thus help to explain why most hunting is done by men. We might call this the **fertility maintenance hypothesis**. It suggests that female reproduction would be so decreased by the strenuous exercise involved in activities such as hunting that the population might not be able to maintain its numbers over the course of many generations. It is difficult to know whether this hypothesis adequately accounts for why women so rarely hunt or cut down trees. For instance, we do not know how much (or even if) the exertion involved in hunting would lower women's ability to bear children. This is because we must locate and study several cases of women hunting in the same way as men before we can measure hunting's effects on female fertility. How much would the exercise of hunting depress a woman's fertility? We do not know.

A third idea is the **child-care-compatibility hypothesis.** First proposed in 1970 by Judith Brown, this hypothesis holds that women tend to perform those tasks that they are able to combine effectively with nursing and other child-care duties that they have almost everywhere. Brown argued that such tasks have several characteristics:

✦ They are fairly routine and repetitive, so they do not require much concentration.
✦ They can be interrupted and resumed without harming their efficient performance.
✦ They do not place the children who accompany their mothers to the site of the task in potential danger.
✦ They do not require women to travel very far away from home.

The gathering of various products and the domestic work listed in Table 12.1 are highly compatible with

*The child-care compatibility hypothesis of the sexual division of labor holds that females are assigned work that can be combined with caring for young children. This African woman can process grain with her child on her back, for example.*

child care. In addition, among horticultural peoples, garden tasks such as planting, weeding and tending crops, and harvesting usually are done by women; these activities, too, seem to be highly compatible with caring for children.

None of the three hypotheses can explain the variability in the allocation of tasks. In fact, no biological difference between the sexes can explain the cross-cultural *diversity* in the sexual division of labor. The biological differences between males and females are about the same everywhere. A condition that is constant across all cultures cannot, by itself, account for conditions that vary across these cultures. We need another explanation for the variations shown in Table 12.1. Such an explanation would take the physical differences between the sexes into account but would see these differences as manifesting themselves in various ways because of variations in local conditions.

## Intensive Agriculture and Women's Labor

Anthropologists have given considerable attention to one cross-cultural variation in the sexual division of labor: that between women's relative importance to subsistence in horticultural versus intensive agricultural populations. (See chapter 8 for a discussion of the distinction between these two systems of cultivation.)

It is fairly well established that women usually do much or most of the garden work in horticultural populations. Of the major tasks involved in growing food using horticultural methods, only two—clearing land for cultivation and, to a lesser extent, preparing the plot for planting by removing natural vegetation and turning over the soil—seem to be almost always done by men. Other tasks, including planting, weeding, guarding, and harvesting, are most often activities of women.

Why do women contribute a relatively large amount of garden labor in horticultural adaptations? Whether a people practice shifting cultivation, dry land gardening, or some other variety of horticulture, most female gardening tasks do not require great strength and are compatible with child-care demands. But this statement merely says that women (or, rather, mothers) *can* contribute effectively to subsistence; it does not say why they *will*.

No satisfactory answer has been offered. One suggestion is that in horticultural populations, men frequently are absent in trading expeditions or hunting, so women do most gardening by default. For instance, in the Americas before contact with the West, most of the meat supply came from men's hunting because no large animals had been domesticated outside the Andes. Because men were so occupied with hunting, one of the nearly exclusively male tasks, women were left to garden. Yet we do not know how much of male time hunting usually required, so this suggestion is difficult to evaluate.

Along the same lines, others suggest that men in horticultural societies were so heavily involved in warfare and guarding the settlement against attack that they had little time for cultivation. But warfare was *not* more frequent in horticultural than in intensive agricultural populations, so why should it interfere more with men's ability to grow food in the former? The reason is that so many of the world's intensive agriculturalists were part of large-scale, state-organized societies (chapter 9), which had specialized, standing armies. Among horticulturalists, in contrast, most able-bodied men were expected to be active in defensive and offensive warfare, which detracted from their subsistence activities.

Both of these hypotheses state that because women are able to do most garden tasks in horticultural adaptations, and because men are so busy with other things that women cannot do as well, most garden work falls to women. Another possibility is simply that gardening is not much fun—remember the "routine, repetitive" nature of so many women's tasks noted previously. Stronger men/husbands may force weaker women/wives to do

such work whenever they can. Essentially, males exploit females by making them do the "drudge work," according to this argument.

Whatever the reason why females contribute so much to the everyday vegetable food supply among horticulturalists, the importance of women's labor relative to men's declines as cultivation systems become more intensive. ("Intensity" increases as cultivators increase the amount of food they harvest from a given amount of land by putting in more hours of work per acre, by plowing with animal power, by digging irrigation wells and ditches, by gathering dung and spreading it over the fields as fertilizer, and so on—see chapter 8.) Women usually contribute much less agricultural labor than men in intensive agricultural systems. Why should this be?

One possibility is that the work involved in intensive systems demands more strength and stamina than the work required by horticulture. For instance, tilling the soil with a plow might be too heavy a type of work for women. Yet this hypothesis has never been demonstrated to be true (animals provide most of the strength, at any rate). Besides, because plowing usually is done only once or twice a year, there is no reason why men should not handle the plowing while women continue to perform other agricultural tasks.

The relative strength and stamina of the sexes alone are insufficient to account for why women contribute relatively less labor in intensive systems. A number of anthropologists have proposed a more complicated hypothesis. Their ideas are based on studies suggesting that, as cultivation becomes more intensive, two changes occur in women's domestic work loads. First, domestic tasks that women generally perform require more of women's time in intensive systems. Second, in intensive systems, new kinds of tasks emerge that are generally done by women. Both sets of changes—the increased time required for old domestic tasks and the addition of new kinds of work—divert women's time from cultivation, so they work relatively less than men in supplying food.

One such hypothesis was proposed in 1983 by Carol Ember. Using studies comparing how much time men and women spend in food production versus domestic work in horticultural and intensive agricultural societies, she suggested that women typically have significantly more domestic work to perform in intensive agricultural societies. There are several reasons that women's domestic work load generally increases with increasing intensity. For one thing, about one-half of all horticulturalists concentrate on root crops (such as

*Women contribute less labor to direct food production in intensive agricultural societies. One hypothesis for this is that women lack the strength needed to work with the plow. As this photo shows, this hypothesis is questionable.*

yams, potatoes, manioc, taro, and sweet potatoes) rather than cereal crops. In contrast, about 90 percent of all intensive agriculturalists subsist mainly from cereals (such as wheat, rice, corn, oats, barley, and millet).

How could this general difference in the kinds of crops grown affect the kinds of tasks women perform in the two systems? In 1975, Kay Martin and Barbara Voorhies suggested an important implication of this seemingly insignificant difference—showing us how subtle differences can have major effects on cultural patterns of behavior. The root crops grown more often by horticultural peoples tend to be harvested continuously rather than seasonally. Edible roots can be stored in the ground for relatively long periods, allowing cultivators to harvest them more or less at will (within limits, of course). Cereals (grains), however, are the seeds of cultivated plants, so they mature at about the same time every year. The seeds will fall off and rot (or sprout) unless harvested at the proper time. Therefore, cereals typically are harvested seasonally, dried, and stored for processing and eating the rest of the year. This increases both cooking and processing time—picture the Mexican peasant woman grinding corn to make tortillas, or the Greek woman winnowing, grinding, making flour, and baking bread from wheat. Because, overall, cereals require more labor to process and prepare for eating than roots, and because in almost all societies such domestic tasks are done by females, women tend to devote more hours to domestic work in intensive agricultural societies. They therefore have relatively less time to spend in the fields.

Douglas White, Michael Burton, and Malcomb Dow pursue this line of reasoning. In a 1981 cross-cultural study they noticed a fairly consistent relation between crop type and the average length of dry season: The longer the dry season, the more likely cereals rather than roots are to be the main crops of a people. They also found a relation between crop type and the importance of animal husbandry: Domesticated animals are more important to people who grow cereals, since cereal-growers tend to be intensive agriculturalists who use animals to pull plows.

In summary, and in general, most intensive agriculturalists live in regions with a long dry season, grow cereals as an important part of their diet, and keep domesticated animals for both traction and food. How might the association between these factors explain the lower involvement of women in intensive agriculture than in horticulture?

First, consider the possible effects of a long dry season. Because of the lack of rain for many months of the year, the timing of crop planting needs to be adjusted so that the growing plants will have adequate water. Therefore, planting tends to be concentrated during a few weeks of the year; harvesting is later concentrated into a small time period as a result. So the seasonality of agricultural tasks is greater than that of horticultural tasks. There is an increased need for agricultural laborers who can do a lot of hot, heavy work in a short period that cannot be interrupted by other tasks, that is, for men's rather than women's labor (see previous section).

In contrast, root-growing horticultural peoples living in regions with a short or no dry season, or in which the time of planting is relatively unaffected by climate, spread cultivation tasks out more evenly over the entire year. Gardening is a day-in, day-out activity but also requires less muscle power and is relatively interruptible. So women are able to do it effectively.

Now consider the possible effects on women's time of the keeping of large numbers of domesticated animals used to pull plows, supply meat and dairy products, and fertilize fields in intensive systems. Burton and White cite some evidence that many of the labor burdens involved in keeping domesticated animals are borne by women (as well as children). Women do most of the work of collecting fodder for the animals to eat, of gathering dung, of watering livestock, and of milking cows as well as several other animal husbandry tasks. This also tends to divert their labor from direct involvement in agricultural chores, Burton and White believe. (Their evidence that women do most of the care of domesticated animals is weak, however.)

In summary, some cross-cultural researchers suggest that a combination of the following factors explains why women contribute less labor to cultivation in intensive agricultural than in horticultural adaptations:

✦ The cereals grown using intensive cultivation methods require more processing time than the root crops of horticultural peoples.
✦ Cereal-growing intensive agriculturalists tend to live in parts of the world with a long dry season, which increases the efficiency of using men's rather than women's labor in the fields.
✦ Intensive agriculturalists tend to keep more domesticated animals, which directly or indirectly increases the nonagricultural work load of women.

We note here something you may already have noticed: These associations are generalized. Intensive agriculturalists "tend to" live in regions with a long dry season; domesticated animals are "generally" cared for more by women than by men; and so on. These hypotheses are not very precise, and there are serious questions about whether the cross-cultural tests support what those who conduct them claim they support. And, as always, there are numerous exceptions—some specific culture may have intensive agriculture without any of the things it is "supposed to" be associated with. Despite these and other problems, these hypotheses are plausible; they do not merely restate in fancy language what everyone already knows; and they do have some empirical support in the form of cross-cultural tests. So long as we do not accept them as the final word, as *the truth,* they are useful guides for further research.

Right or wrong, the preceding ideas are a good example of the materialist theoretical orientation, introduced in chapter 4. The preceding argument assumes that the way a population exploits its habitat (by horticulture or more intensive methods) greatly affects the kinds of tasks women and men do (given the physical differences between the sexes and the biological fact that women give birth to and nurse children). So the material conditions of life in a certain kind of adaptation interact with biological differences between women and men to produce an overall pattern of the division of labor along gender lines. (Or so those scholars who proposed these hypotheses believe.)

Does this have any relevance for the relation between gender and occupational roles in a modern, industrialized society? If it is true that the essential differences between men and women that account for the sexual division of labor in preindustrial populations are (1) male strength (and perhaps the ability to run fast or long) and (2) the fact that only women bear and nurse children, then this matters for modern employment patterns. It matters, first, because advanced technology and machinery have greatly reduced the need for strength and stamina to perform tasks; so there is less of a biological basis for allocating some tasks ("jobs," they have become) exclusively to males. It matters, second, because the economies of Japan, Western Europe, and North America are increasingly service- and high tech–oriented; so the biological differences that once mattered need not matter so much (if at all) today. It matters, third, because the birthrate of industrialized nations is lower than that of most preindustrial peoples; so child-care burdens may be lessened for modern women. It matters, fourth, because one reason some tasks were allocated to women in preindustrial societies was their compatibility with women's child-care duties; but today these duties are delegated during work hours to child-care specialists, with no harm to children.

A more general implication arises from the fact that the sexual division of labor shows great, but not unlimited, variability in human populations. In the materialist hypotheses we have discussed, this variability is seen as resulting from the interaction between female-male biological differences and the overall economic conditions of a people. If these hypotheses have merit, then, the sexual division of labor responds to other changes in a peoples' way of life—particularly to changes in their adaptive, productive, and economic systems. That the sexual division of labor in industrialized nations is responding and will continue to respond to similar changes is not surprising. That the long-term development will be toward a decreasing emphasis on gender as a basis for allocating tasks and roles is consistent with many anthropological hypotheses about the sexual division of labor. As technological, economic, and demographic changes reduce the importance of male-female differences in the ability to perform most jobs, the gender of the job holder will come to matter less and less.

## THE STATUS OF WOMEN

Another issue in the anthropological study of gender relations is how and why the status of women varies cross-culturally. By **status of women** we mean how women and men relate to each other on the basis of the gender difference between them. The overall status of women in a society includes numerous components: the kinds of social positions men and women hold and the roles they perform; the economic importance of and cultural value attached to women's contributions to their families and to society at large; whether or how much women defer to men with whom they have important bonds, such as their husbands and male relatives; female access to positions of power and influence; the degree to which women have the right to control their own bodies and to make marital, sexual, child-bearing, and other important decisions for themselves; and so on.

Comparative data on variations in the status of women is relevant for the present and future of gender relations in modern society for two reasons. First, if ethnographic information shows that women's status is low to the same degree and in the same ways in most societies, then it may be more difficult to improve women's status in modern nations. Conversely, if there are preindustrial cultures in which women have status

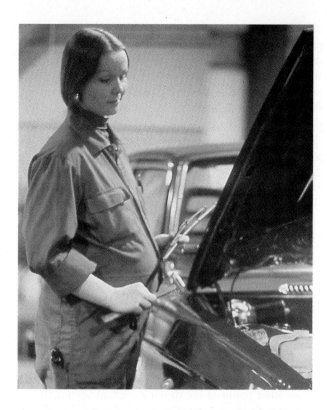

*In industrialized economies, technological changes reduce the importance of physical strength in efficient task performance. Physical differences between the sexes therefore matter less for employment.*

higher than or equal to men, then our confidence that modern societies can reach the same state is increased.

Second, assuming that we find that women's status varies significantly cross-culturally, we may be able to discover why it does so. We might be able to find a key economic, political, domestic, sexual, or religious factor that determines how women are treated and regarded everywhere. If so, then modern feminists will need to work to alter this key factor, and in the long term our societies will develop greater equality between the sexes.

Before proceeding we need to recognize how difficult it is to determine "the" status of women in any given society. This difficulty exists because relations between the sexes are complex and have many dimensions or aspects. For example, many anthropologists who study family life (see chapter 10) report that women have a great deal of independence and control over child-rearing and domestic activities in most societies. Even in male-dominated societies like traditional Japan and China the eldest female in a household usually had the right to manage household affairs with a fair degree of

autonomy. Yet in China, Japan, and many other societies women were not allowed to participate in public affairs, had hardly any property of their own, had little say over whom they married, and were clearly subordinate to their fathers and husbands socially and even legally.

Further complicating the concept of women's status is the fact that in most cultures, a woman's status changes over the course of her life. As Judith Brown (1988, 74) states, "overwhelmingly, the cross-cultural evidence indicates positive changes" in women's status as they become middle-aged. This improvement is revealed in many ways. For example, fewer restrictions usually are placed on an older woman's behavior because, in many cultures, her sexual reputation is now secure. Also, middle-aged women frequently exercise authority over younger relatives, including the spouses of their married children. In the patrilocally extended families typical of traditional China, Japan, India, and other places the senior woman exerted authority over inmarried daughters-in-law, whose day would come when they themselves took over the management of the household. Brown suggests that an important reason for this widespread pattern of improvement in status with age is that older mothers in most cultures receive respect and deference from their grown children, who support their mothers' decisions.

So it is misleading to think of women's status as a unitary phenomenon: The way men regard and treat

*In most cultures, a woman's status improves as her children grow into adulthood.*

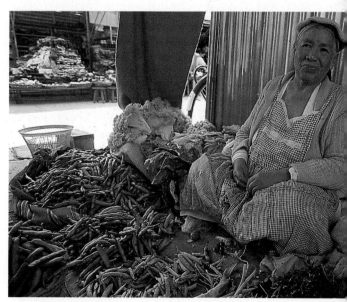

women and the rights of women have many dimensions, and the factors that constitute women's status are not always consistent with one another. Like other kinds of relations, gender relations are complex. This is not surprising: People of other cultures do not arrange their relations between males and females in such a way that modern social scientists can understand and label them with the simple phrase "women's status."

Nonetheless, we shall continue to use this phrase. It serves as a useful shorthand for the overall way women are regarded, the kinds of property and political rights they lack or enjoy, how highly their material and nonmaterial contributions are valued, and so forth. Most important, the phrase is a meaningful one for discussing the degree to which women are subordinate to men, a subject to which we now turn.

## Universal Subordination?

A main question asked by anthropologists interested in gender is whether females are everywhere subordinate to males. Are there societies in which women and men are equal? Are there societies in which women dominate men?

The answer to the second question is no. Despite the stories we sometimes read or the occasional old adventure movie in which the hero is captured by "amazons," not a single instance of clear female domination over men has ever been found by ethnographers. Matriarchy—rule by women over men—does not exist, nor has it ever existed, to the best of our knowledge. Certainly there have been and are individual women who hold great power, control great wealth, and are held in high esteem. Certainly there are queens, female chiefs, and individual *matriarchs* of families and kin groups. But no instance of *matriarchy*—women as a social category holding power over men as a social category—has been documented.

The first question, of whether cultures exist in which men and women are equal, has a more uncertain and complex answer. Even anthropologists who have devoted their careers to studying gender relations do not agree on the answer. On the one hand, some scholars believe that women are never considered to be fully equal to men. They interpret the ethnographic record as showing that an asymmetry always exists between the sexes in one or more areas of life—in sexual freedom, familial relations, participation in religious rituals, political influence, or other realms. Even in domestic life, where women often have relative equality and autonomy, there is almost everywhere a cultural expecta-

tion that it is right and proper for husbands to dominate their wives and to make most of the important decisions. In social relations generally women everywhere are likely to defer to men in a multitude of subtle and not so subtle ways—assuming that other dimensions of their relationship (such as age or class) do not overpower the gender dimension.

Those who believe that male dominance/female subordination is universal point to two fairly well established ethnographic generalizations. One applies to political institutions. In political life sexual asymmetry almost always exists: In no society on record are the primary political leadership and authority roles regularly performed by females; but in many socities any woman is denied the right to succeed to political offices. In the majority of cases even kin-group leadership roles are dominated by men. Male elders of the lineage or clan decide how the group's land and other resources are to be used and allocated, how the group's wealth objects are to be disposed of, whether the group is to engage in a battle to avenge a wrong, and so on. (But as we shall soon see, women often do have significant influence over these matters, especially in matrilineal societies.)

The other realm of life in which sexual asymmetry is found is religion. In many societies women are excluded from performing major religious leadership roles and are forbidden to participate in the most important rituals. For example, sometimes the death of a man is blamed on the witchcraft of his wife, and she is cruelly punished for her alleged "homicide." In many New Guinea societies—the Hua, for instance—men believe that their health or masculinity is jeopardized if they come into contact with women's menstrual discharges, so women must seclude themselves during their periods to avoid harming the men. (Chapter 16 discusses menstrual pollution in more detail.)

Widespread patterns of intersexual relations such as these led Michelle Zimbalist Rosaldo (1974) to generalize about the universal status superiority of men in these words:

What is perhaps most striking and surprising is the fact that male, as opposed to female, activities are always recognized as predominantly important, and cultural systems give authority and value to the roles and activities of men. Contrary to some popular assumptions, there is little reason to believe that there are, or once were, societies of primitive matriarchs, societies in which women predominated in the same way that men predominate in the societies we actually know. . . . An asymmetry in the cultural evaluations of male and female, in the importance assigned to women and men, appears to be universal. (19)

According to Rosaldo and some other scholars, then, the activities of males are everywhere regarded as more important than those of females. Women as a social category are everywhere culturally devalued relative to men as a social category. Women are everywhere subordinate to men.

But the ethnographic record can be interpreted differently. Many scholars note that most fieldworkers—and hence most of the ethnographic data available to shed light on the issue of universal female subordination—have been biased in two ways. The first is the *androcentric* (male) bias. Most of the fieldwork until the 1970s was done by males, who usually were uninterested in the females of the cultures they studied. At any rate, simply because they were themselves males, fieldworkers had little access to women's points of view, so they often unwittingly took the men's values, attitudes, and opinions as "the" values, attitudes, and opinions of the culture.

The second source of fieldwork bias in the study of gender is *Eurocentric* bias. Because of the inequalities in wealth, power, and status in Western (European-derived) societies, Western anthropologists might perceive relations of inequality, hierarchy, and domination/subordination even among cultures where they are less developed. For instance, when a wife greets her husband by bowing her head or stays behind him while walking, Western fieldworkers may interpret such behaviors as indications of female subordination, when in fact they are merely public demonstrations of politeness.

In short, some scholars think that many fieldworkers have been sexually and culturally biased. Because of this bias, the ethnographic record is not objective; it "records" a universal female subordination not justified by the real world. Note, however, that even those who accuse others of bias may be biased themselves, albeit in another direction!

Those who argue in favor of the existence of societies with female-male equality also cite specific ethnographic cases that they think document their point. The Iroquois, a matrilineal people of northeastern North America, are the most famous ethnographic example of women achieving equality (or is it only relative equality?) with men. Iroquois women produced the corn and other cultivated foods, put them in storage, and largely controlled how they were distributed from the storehouses. Iroquois men were away from their apartments in the longhouse much of the time, engaged in warfare or cooperative hunting expeditions. After the introduction of the fur trade into northeastern North America in the seventeenth century, men were away searching for beaver pelts or raiding their neighbors for pelts. The matrilineally related women of a longhouse influenced their inmarried husbands' behavior by withholding provisions from their hunting trips and war parties. Only men had the right to hold the most powerful political leadership offices because only males could be elected to the great council of chiefs. But representatives to the council were selected by the older women of the various matrilineages, and these women also had the right to

*Iroquois women's control over cultivated foods and their distribution gave them relatively high status.*

remove and replace men who did not adequately represent the group's interests. Also, women had a voice in the deliberations of the council itself: They could veto declarations of war and introduce peace-making resolutions.

So who is right? Are women subordinate to men in all societies or not? Certainly, some male ethnographers have been biased—but does this bias explain their reports of female subordination? Certainly, the Iroquois and other peoples demonstrate that women in some cultures have achieved considerable control over their own lives and over public decision making—but do such cases represent full equality of males and females? Indeed, would we know "total gender equality" if we saw it in a society? What would it look like? Would men and women have to carry out the same kinds of economic tasks before we could say they are equal? Is monogamy necessary, or can a society be polygynous and still qualify? Shall we require that women occupy 50 percent of all leadership roles before we say they have equal rights? How should family life be organized before we can say that husbands in general do not dominate their wives?

As you can see, many questions must be answered before we can say whether women are everywhere subordinate—not the least of which is how we would know complete gender equality if we were to encounter it!

But perhaps too much weight is given to the issue of universal male dominance. Many anthropologists (especially feminist ones) are prone to think that their discipline must ferret out human cultures in which women and men are equal for ethnographic data to lend support for the feminist cause. Feminist psychologists, sociologists, historians, biologists, and other scholars likewise have turned to the ethnographic record to support their positions. Their reasoning is that if numerous ethnographic cases can be found in which women have achieved equality, then women will be more likely to be able to achieve equality in the future. Their hope is that there are many such cases. Conversely, their fear is that the ethnographic record shows few or no such cases.

But how much does it matter for the cause of gender equality if women are universally or nearly universally subordinate? Perhaps it does not matter as much as some think it does. Perhaps what matters most is that women and men are a good deal more equal in some societies than they are in others, which allows us to study the conditions under which future equality is likely to be possible. To argue that because women have always been subordinate they are forever doomed to be subordinate is analogous to many pre-twentieth-century arguments that humans will never be able to fly. Just because no human society has achieved some state in the past does not mean that none will achieve it in the future. It does not mean that we should give up trying to achieve it today. And it certainly does not mean that late-twentieth-century Euro-American women have achieved about all the equality they are likely to be able to achieve, and therefore ought to shut up and be happy.

## Influences on Women's Status

What influences the status of women in a human society? No one can generalize about this subject with confidence. Women's status is affected by such a multitude of factors that thus far no one has shown that any small number of forces are the primary determinants of women's status in all times and places. Here we discuss only a few hypotheses that point to influences that are most widespread and important.

**WOMEN'S CONTRIBUTIONS TO MATERIAL WELFARE.** Many materialists argue that women's role in production strongly influences their property rights, their role in public affairs, men's attitudes toward them, their degree of personal freedom, and so on. One hypothesis is that where women produce a sizable proportion of the food, shelter, clothing, and other necessities of existence, their contributions will be recognized and rewarded with influence, property, prestige, dignity, and other benefits. In other words, the sexual division of labor, together with the proportion of valued goods women produce, are strong influences on women's overall status.

Such ideas might apply to some foraging and horticultural people, among whom women's gathering or gardening contributes a sizable amount of resources to their domestic groups. Women's productive labor might give them a status that is closer to equality with men than they have in other forms of adaptation in which their subsistence contributions are not as great.

But everyone's status is "closer to equality" in most hunter-gatherer and many horticultural populations (see chapters 7, 8, 9, and 14). So perhaps the relative equality of women in these two systems of adaptation results not from their importance in subsistence but from something else that "levels out" social inequalities of all kinds.

**WOMEN'S CONTROL OVER KEY RESOURCES.**    A more complex proposal is that women's contribution to production, by itself, is not enough to "earn" them relative equality. It is necessary for women to contribute heavily to material welfare to gain resources, rights, and respect, but this alone is not sufficient. (After all, slaves contributed a lot to production in the Americas and the Caribbean in the eighteenth and nineteenth centuries, but they were not rewarded with social equality!) One specific hypothesis is that women must also own productive resources (land, tools), or have considerable control over the distribution of the products of their labor, or both. If women own productive resources and have a great deal of say over what happens to the goods they produce, then they can have some influence on the activities of men. Overall, this gives them more equality. Peggy Sanday found some support for this hypothesis in a cross-cultural study (1973).

This hypothesis seems to account reasonably well for some specific cases. For instance, Iroquois women controlled the production and distribution of important resources. They used this control to nominate their kinsmen to chiefly positions and to influence the public decision making from which they were formally excluded. Likewise, Hopi (see chapter 11) women owned land and had considerable control over the distribution of its products. Women had relatively high status in both these societies.

Along the same lines, in many West African and Caribbean societies, women are more active than men in market trade in foodstuffs, handicrafts, textiles, and other goods produced by themselves. Sometimes market-trading women are able to transform their independent control over exchangeable resources into more equitable relations with men. Wives commonly maintain separate income from their husbands, which they are free to expend on themselves and their children. One such culture is the Yoruba, who make up most of the population of many towns in Nigeria. Yoruba women are active in market trade and in craft production, which gives them access to income and economic security independent of their husbands and other men. Many women purchase houses in urban areas and use the rent to improve their and their children's economic well-being and social autonomy. According to ethnographer Sandra Barnes (1990, 275):

Property frees the owner from subordinating herself to the authority of another person in domestic matters. It places her in a position of authority over others and in a position to form social relationships in the wider community that are politically significant. Property owning legitimates her entry into the public domain.

*Where women commonly earn income for themselves by marketing products, as in Jamaica, their overall status in society tends to be relatively high.*

The economic independence that some Yoruba women are able to acquire translates into increased participation in neighborhood associations and other public affairs and allows them much freedom from male authority.

Thus many ethnographic and comparative studies suggest that controlling resources is one way for women to get respect and independence from their husbands, brothers, and other men. This ability to acquire some measure of control over family resources helps to account for why many late-twentieth-century wives are demanding and receiving more help from their husbands in housework and child care. Since the 1950s many married women have left hearth and home for wage employment. Increased female employment stems from many factors, including inflation, widespread cultural desires for an ever-increasing living standard, increasing worries about divorce, and structural changes to a more service-oriented economy. (Some ideas about how these forces led to increases in women's employment and to the women's movement are presented in Box 12.2.) Not only do working wives now have psychological ammunition against their husbands' domestic indolence ("I work forty hours a week just like you do!"), but they also have the wherewithal to back up their demands. With most women now out in the world of work, and with the families of married women now virtually dependent on their income to pay the bills, more women are demanding equal pay for equal work, equal treatment and opportunity in the workplace, equal legal rights, and equal respect.

**DESCENT AND POSTMARITAL RESIDENCE.** The form of descent and postmarital residence also influences women's overall status. Some scholars have noted that women in matrilineal and matrilocal societies have greater equality in many areas of life. What is it, specifically, about matrilineality and matrilocality that gives relatively high status to females? It is *not* that "females rule" in these societies. Men hold positions of both political and domestic authority in matrilineal societies (see chapter 11). The main difference is whom among their relatives men have authority *over*: their sisters and sister's children in matrilineal systems versus their sons, unmarried daughters, and son's children in patrilineal systems.

But other elements of matrilineality and matrilocality benefit females. In a cross-cultural study Martin Whyte found that women enjoy more authority in domestic matters, have more sexual freedom, and have more worth placed on their lives in these societies. Two

factors contribute to their equality. First, because it is husbands who go to live with the families of their wives; sisters remain with or close to one another throughout their lives. Inmarrying husbands face a relatively cohesive and enduring group of related women. A typical wife thus has her mother, sisters, and perhaps other female relatives around to support her in domestic quarrels. Second, in many matrilineal and matrilocal societies domestic authority over a married woman is divided between her husband and her brother. Alice Schlegel suggests that this arrangement increases her freedom because each man acts as a check on the other's attempts to dominate her.

Contrast this situation to patrilineal and patrilocal China before the mid-twentieth century. When a Chinese woman married she was incorporated as a member of her husband's household. This was symbolized by the fact that she began to pay homage to his deceased patrilineal ancestors rather than to her own. A woman's relationships with her own parents and siblings were sharply curtailed when she married. Her main duties were to work for her husband and his parents, to obey them in all things, and to bear them male heirs. In many respects a new wife was treated as a domestic servant to her father- and mother-in-law: She was given arduous household tasks to perform for most of her waking hours, and she could be berated and even beaten with impunity. Only when she herself bore sons and heirs to her husband's family did her status improve, and only when she herself became a mother-in-law to her sons' wives could she relax a bit. The Confucian social and moral philosophy, which held that women must always be submissive to men, affected the way wives and daughters-in-law were treated. But also important were the social facts that wives were fully incorporated into the households of their husbands' parents and the lines of authority over them were clearly and legally redrawn on their marriage. A Chinese wife had few viable alternatives to submission to her husband's family and few sources of social support when she was treated poorly. In contrast, in most matrilocal and matrilineal cultures women do have alternatives to suffering the dominance of their husbands, and they likewise receive support from their own relatives.

**OVERALL SOCIETAL COMPLEXITY.** So far, we have discussed ideas that try to account for the variations in women's status synchronically. That is, we have treated societies as if they are frozen in time, and we have looked at what kinds of cultural factors might be associated with variations in women's status. Another approach considers women's status in general evolutionary terms (chapter 4). That approach largely ignores specific societies with their specific variations and asks instead what has happened to women's overall status in the very long term.

Rather than present an overview of existing evolutionary hypotheses, here we concentrate on one. This hypothesis claims that women's overall status has decreased as social complexity has increased (at least until the development of industrialized technology and the profound cultural changes that accompanied it). This idea comes mainly from the work of Jack Goody, Ester Boserup, and Martin Whyte, whose ideas we shall sketch and integrate. The following argument is complex, but it is worth the effort to understand it. Not only is it a fascinating attempt to show how women's place in societies has changed throughout history, but it is yet another example of how alterations in one subsystem affect other subsystems in subtle and unexpected ways.

Recall the strong relation between cultivation systems and the relative degree of importance of women's labor to subsistence. As the intensity of cultivation increases, women participate less and less in agricultural tasks for reasons suggested earlier in this chapter. Recall also (from chapter 9) that intensive agriculture is associated with societies that are highly stratified, with economies featuring much centralized control, with well-developed craft and other specializations, with marked distinctions between rulers and ruled, and so on. Such large-scale hierarchically organized societies are called *complex* by anthropologists. How does increasing agricultural intensity, together with these other features of complexity, affect the status of women?

Jack Goody provides a hypothesis that makes connections between increasing complexity and the (seemingly unrelated) overall status of women. In a cross-cultural study he compared the predominantly horticultural societies of sub-Saharan Africa with the mainly intensive agricultural societies of Eurasia (Europe, the Middle East, and Asia). In Eurasia, land is relatively scarcer because of higher population densities. It is also more intensively exploited, with plows, irrigation, and fertilization with animal droppings used to increase yields. Because land is scarcer and more productive in Eurasia, there is more competition for it, family wealth and prestige depend more on access to it, and a family has a greater chance of losing it to someone else. Finally, because Eurasian societies are more stratified than African societies, in the former there is a real danger of downward mobility for one's children and grandchildren

unless access to resources is maintained through the generations. Therefore, in Eurasia, parents are concerned about maintaining their male and female children's access to land, since so much else depends on it.

Goody argues that these differences between Africa and Eurasia have important cultural consequences. In Africa, land and other property is transmitted through males. An African man passes land rights down to his sons; his daughters receive little or no inheritance but rely largely on their husbands to supply them with access to land, cattle, and other productive resources. In Eurasia it is relatively more important that parents make a "good match" for their daughters, meaning that their daughters marry someone of at least equal wealth. So in most Eurasian societies, parents divide property among their daughters as well as their sons to maintain their daughters' and daughters' children's access to adequate resources. By giving property to their daughter, parents improve her chances of attracting "the right kind of husband," one with sufficient resources to maintain the social and economic standing of her and her children. Bilateral inheritance thus is typical of Eurasia.

*Much evidence suggests that the overall status of women declines as cultural complexity increases, at least until the industrial era. In the Islamic Middle East, males exercise great control over their daughters, sisters, and wives. These Bedouin women are required to wear veils because unrelated males are present.*

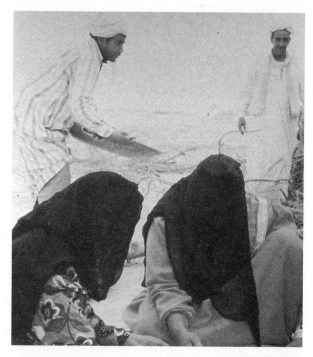

BOX 12.2

## ON WOMEN'S LIBERATION

In the late 1960s a social movement organized by and for women got under way in the United States. In the 1970s many thousands of women joined the National Organization for Women, and millions more joined it in spirit by supporting economic and legal equality and an end to all forms of discrimination based on gender. Why did the women's movement occur when it did? Why were so many American women attracted to its goals of equality of opportunity in hiring and promotion, in salaries and wages, in divorce settlements, in domestic chores, and so forth?

One possible answer is women's rising "gender consciousness." The civil rights struggle and the antiwar movement in the 1960s made some women aware of their oppression. These movements also showed women that they could do something about it by organizing other Americans to pressure legislatures and companies, and even amend the Constitution to gain and guarantee equal rights.

No doubt the activism of the 1960s changed the political climate of the country, making women aware of their low status. And no doubt the experience gained by activist women in the political movements of the 1960s provided them with organizational knowhow, which they put to good use in attracting other women to their cause. But political movements are grounded in social and economic problems. People are not attracted to movements in large numbers unless they are dissatisfied.

The major source of discontent in a country such as the United States, in which money and wealth are so highly valued, is economic conditions. We can understand the women's movement, which represented a change in women's consciousness (ideas) about their proper roles, by considering economic circumstances, which changed in a certain way in the 1950s through the 1970s.

Anthropologist Marvin Harris analyzes these economic shifts. They can be reduced to two interrelated overall changes in the past three decades: (1) increased employment of women and (2) alterations in the structure of the American economy.

Roughly 50 percent of single American women have had jobs since the 1940s. But except during the Great Depression and World War II, relatively few married women worked for a wage. In 1947 only 21 percent of married women worked outside the household. Over the next four decades this percentage rose steadily to 32 percent in 1960, 42 percent in 1970, 51 percent in 1980, and nearly 60 percent today. Surprisingly, but significantly, the increase in the employment rate for women with preschool-aged children has been even greater than the overall rate since 1970: In 1948 only 11 percent of women with children under six were employed, but this number rose to 19 percent in 1960, to 30 percent in 1970, to 45 percent in 1980, and to 60 percent in 1991. Why did so many women, especially married women with young children, have the desire to find jobs during the past two to three decades? Why were their husbands agreeable to their employment?

Part of the answer is rising consumer expectations, spurred on by advertising that created new desires in the mass market. More important, high rates of inflation in the mid-1960s through the 1970s seriously eroded the purchasing power of a family's income. Prices of housing (both for sale and rent), autos, medical care, education, energy, food, and other necessities skyrocketed. The purchasing power of Average Joe's single paycheck could not keep up with inflation. In fact, the average American family with only the husband employed actually lost real income in some years—between 1969 and 1970, single-earner families lost 6.9 percent in real earnings. To keep up with inflation and achieve the American Dream became impossible for millions of families with a single income.

*continued on next page*

Eurasian daughters often receive their inheritance when they marry—that is, as a dowry (chapter 10). Dowries usually include money, jewelry, and household goods rather than land itself. The purpose of a dowry is not to provide a daughter and her children with land but to attract a man with a sizable inheritance of land and other property as her husband. Therefore, dowry is part of the marital transaction in European and Asian societies. In contrast, dowry is practically nonexistent in sub-Saharan Africa, where bridewealth is the predominant form of marital exchange.

All these factors influence patterns of marriage. In horticultural Africa, where female labor is so important to subsistence, men who can pay bridewealth for several

But getting a job requires that jobs be available and that the job seeker have the skills to qualify for them. As is well known, the American economy has undergone important structural changes in the past few decades. Automation, overseas competition, and other factors have resulted in the rise of the so-called *service economy* and have led to what is sometimes called the *postindustrial economy*. Jobs in services became available in vast numbers. Most women who filled jobs beginning in the 1950s became typists, secretaries, receptionists, cashiers, waitresses, file clerks, nurses, retail clerks, teachers, and other people-processing and information-processing jobs (as Harris calls them).

Because these were traditionally women's jobs, male employees were not threatened by female hirees. Because so many women were looking for work and because married women were not considered the primary source of income for their families, employers could get away with paying them low wages. (In this, the opinions of bosses were reinforced by many husbands, who salvaged their male egos by saying they let their wife work because she wanted to "get out of the house more.") Women were passed over for most promotions because many of their bosses thought women unsuitable for managerial positions, considered female employees liable to resign, and didn't want flak from those male employees who got beat out by women and who would have to take orders from them. So on

the job most women were second-class employees—they earned only 50 to 60 percent of what men made for comparable work, were usually the first laid off, and had little chance of moving up.

This situation might have been more tolerable if so many husbands had not insisted on having the best of both worlds: the wife's paycheck as well as her continued household duties and subordination. As we mentioned in chapter 7, job-holding women in the United States and Europe spend between ten and thirteen hours daily on their jobs and housework combined, as compared with only seven to eight hours daily for men. Large numbers of women were caught in a double bind: Underrewarded at work and overworked at home, they were willing to pay attention when the leaders of the feminist movement told them that they were exploited by bosses, husbands, and the male sex in general.

This analysis helps to correct a popular misconception about the women's movement—that a small clique of radical feminists succeeded in making large numbers of American women dissatisfied with their so-called traditional roles as homemakers, wives, and mothers. Feminists have been blamed for making housewives feel guilty about their lack of independence, for making women not want to have babies, for making women into hedonists, for making women want to be just like men, for the high divorce rate, for abortions, and for many other "problems."

But feminists are not to blame. Like all social movements, feminism does indeed promote and channel the direction of change, but it also is a response to other kinds of changes. Feminist leaders did not stir up women who were otherwise happy, nor did they plant ideas into heads that were otherwise empty. Rather, millions of Americans supported the women's movement because changing economic conditions provided women with the opportunity to work, even as the maintenance of their family's living standards required them to leave home. Yet neither their bosses nor their husbands—the one benefiting from their cheap wages, the other from their domestic services—were willing to grant them rewards proportionate to their efforts. ◆

SOURCES: Berch (1982), Harris (1981), United States Bureau of the Census (1992:387–88).

wives acquire a critical resource: their wives' labor. But more wives mean more children, which in turn means the need to find spouses for all these children. In a bridewealth society a man acquires wives for his sons partly out of the bridewealth he receives for his daughters. So, unlike dowry, bridewealth "circulates" in a single generation rather than "passes down" to the next.

If, in contrast, an African man had to provide all his daughters with dowries, the daughters would become more of an economic liability than an asset to him. So we see how the importance of female labor to subsistence, polygyny, and bridewealth all go together in most African populations; they form a system, each reinforcing the other.

In contrast, Eurasian societies with bilateral inheritance tend to be monogamous. This is because (1) women's labor has less value in accumulating wealth in intensive agricultural systems and (2) it would be difficult for all but the very rich to provide an adequate dowry for the daughters of more than one wife. It is relatively more important for parents to control who their daughters marry because a bad match could impoverish her and her offspring and lower the wealth and honor of the whole family. A woman therefore has little say about whom she marries. As part of their effort to control whom their daughters marry, parents place restrictions on their unmarried daughter's relations with males. In the Islamic Middle East and northern India a woman's virtue strongly reflected on the honor of her whole family, so extreme steps (to Western eyes) were taken to ensure that no question could arise about her virtue: Daughters lived secluded lives in the houses of their fathers and had to veil their faces and cover their heads when out in public.

## What About the Status of Modern Women?

We conclude by pulling together some of the ideas covered in this chapter and suggesting their relevance for male/female relations today. Some scholars try to show what has happened to the overall status of women throughout the course of cultural evolution. Generally, they believe that women in foraging and many horticultural populations had relative equality with men, especially in matrilineal and matrilocal societies. As agricultural systems grew more intense, the sexual division of labor was affected, and women's labor was pulled out of agriculture and into domestic tasks. A whole set of cultural changes accompanied intensification. Goody argues that as stratification increased, there was a greater chance for downward social mobility unless control over productive resources was passed along to the next generation. This led to changes in inheritance and marriage patterns. Together, these "developments" led to the deterioration of women's overall status in more complex societies: Women lost the ability to choose their marital partners, a double standard of sexual morality became pronounced, and women had less of a say in domestic matters and less independent property of their own.

This evolutionary trend has been reversed in some countries in the twentieth century, although complexity certainly has continued to increase. Perhaps this reversal is because industrial technology increasingly substitutes for labor and muscle power, reducing the relevance of biological differences for recruitment into economic tasks ("jobs"). Perhaps, as materialists would argue, it is because so many modern married women feel obliged to seek employment to maintain the living standards to

*Many anthropologists who follow the materialist theoretical orientation believe that the provision of equal economic opportunities will lead to an improvement in women's overall status in society.*

which they and their spouses have (or would like to) become accustomed. Or perhaps, as idealists might argue, it is all attributable simply to an autonomous change in values and beliefs—the development of women's "gender consciousness" of their low status and common interests.

Whatever the reason, anthropological ideas about gender relations provide modern women with a hope and a warning. The hope derives from the fact that the roles, rights, and restrictions placed on women vary throughout humanity, from place to place and time to time. As we have seen, we cannot say whether there has ever been a human culture in which women had an overall status equal to men. We can certainly say that women enjoy more equality in some societies than in others. So there is reason to think that equality of opportunity and achievement (if not the elimination of all distinctions based on sex, an idea to which some feminists subscribe) is a possible future for womankind.

The materialist hypotheses we have described suggest that the provision of equal economic/employment opportunities for women will be a key factor. It will bring with it improvements for women in other realms of life, such as sexuality, legal equality, participation in political life, and husbands' sharing of child care and housework.

Or will it? This is our warning: Anthropological studies have not yet uncovered the magic key that unlocks the door leading to equality between the sexes. No one thing that feminists can do will inevitably lead to equal treatment for women in the workplace, in the household, in the bedroom, and in the voting booth. No one male-dominated institution, chauvinistic attitude, or discriminatory practice that modern societies could change will suddenly and radically improve the position of women in various realms of life. For example, if lawmakers should outlaw sexual discrimination in the workplace or make comparable pay for comparable work legally mandatory, it might take decades for the effects to "work through" the cultural system and be realized in greater female-male equality. It is possible that passing laws—including amending the "supreme law of the land"—against discrimination on the basis of gender will have little effect on male-female social relations or on male attitudes toward women. So anthropological ideas suggest that modern feminists must continue to work on a broad front to achieve their goals.

## SUMMARY

Physical differences between females and males are recognized and relevant in all known cultures. Although whether one is male or female matters to all peoples, it matters in different ways and to different degrees.

A person's *sex* is determined biologically by chromosomes, but *gender* is a cultural construct. The cultural construction of gender means that cultures vary in how they perceive the physical differences between the sexes, in the significance they attribute to those differences, and in the ways those differences are made relevant for self-identity, task and role allocation, access to property and power, and so forth. The Hua of New Guinea illustrate how one culture constructs gender categories and interprets the meaning of those categories.

Much attention has been given to how and why the sexual division of labor varies cross-culturally. One firm conclusion of this research is that our sexual stereotypes that men are breadwinners and women are caretakers are not based on natural differences between the sexes. Male domination is not rooted in men's supplying the necessities of existence because women's labor frequently produces much or most of the food supply.

There are certain widespread patterns in the sexual division of labor, as shown in Table 12.1. Three major hypotheses have been offered to explain the broad cross-cultural similarities in the allocation of economic tasks: superior male strength, the depression of fertility that seems to occur when a woman engages in heavy exercise, and the compatibility of a task with care of infants and young children, which is everywhere primarily a female responsibility.

No biological difference can account for the cross-cultural variations in the sexual division of labor. A difference to which much attention has been given is the higher importance of female labor in horticultural populations relative to intensive agriculturalists. Credible hypotheses explain why women's contributions to subsistence decline as intensity increases. The seasonally maturing cereal grains grown by most intensive agriculturalists require seasonally heavy work (done by males), more processing of food before it is eaten (done by females), and more time spent in caring for domesticated animals (done by females). As a result, males spend more time in cultivation, and females experience a greater domestic workload. As technology reduces the importance of biological differences in task performance and as the birthrate declines, gender will matter less for occupational recruitment in industrialized nations.

Another issue in gender studies is the nature and causes of diversity in the status of women. Even specialists in this subject cannot agree whether ethnographic studies reveal that females are universally subordinate to males. This is mainly because no explicit criteria can be used to judge whether there are populations in which males and females are fully equal. It does seem to be true that females as a social category are never dominant over males as a social category.

A multitude of forces influence women's overall status in a culture, including their relative contributions to subsistence, their control over key resources, the prevalent pattern of descent and postmarital residence, and overall societal complexity. Studies that document the variability in women's status suggest that greater sexual equality is an achievable goal for modern women, but there may be no single attitude or institution that feminists can alter that will give women equality in all realms of life.

## KEY TERMS

cultural construction of gender
sexual division of labor
strength hypothesis
fertility maintenance hypothesis
child-care-compatibility hypothesis
status of women

## SUGGESTED READINGS

Books that are excellent brief introductions to the anthropological study of gender include:

Friedl, Ernestine. *Women and Men: An Anthropologist's View.* New York: Holt, Rinehart and Winston, 1975.

Tiffany, Sharon W. *Women, Work, and Motherhood.* Madison, Wisc.: Four Seasons Press, 1982.

The following books investigate some particular dimension of gender from a comparative perspective:

Buckley, Thomas, and Alma Gottlieb, eds., *Blood Magic: The Anthropology of Menstruation.* Berkeley: University of California Press, 1988.

Collier, Jane. *Marriage and Inequality in Classless Societies.* Stanford, Calif.: Stanford University Press, 1987.

Dahlberg, F., ed. *Woman the Gatherer.* New Haven, Conn.: Yale University Press, 1981.

Gilmore, David D. *Manhood in the Making: Cultural Concepts of Masculinity.* New Haven, Conn.: Yale University Press, 1990.

Margolis, M. *Mothers and Such: American Views of Women and How They Changed.* Berkeley: University of California Press, 1984.

Martin, M. K., and B. Voorhies. *Female of the Species.* New York: Columbia University Press, 1975.

Sanday, Peggy R. *Female Power and Male Dominance.* Cambridge: Cambridge University Press, 1981.

Schlegel, A., ed. *Sexual Stratification: A Cross-Cultural View.* New York: Columbia University Press, 1977.

A number of edited volumes are useful. On the list below the best single resource for both students and professionals is the 1989 volume edited by Morgen. In addition to an excellent introductory essay, it covers gender studies in all four anthropological subfields. It also contains chapters on gender relations in the major world regions: Africa, Middle East, Latin America, and so forth.

Collier, Jane, and Sylvia Yanagisako, eds. *Gender and Kinship: Essays toward a Unified Analysis.* Stanford, Calif.: Stanford University Press, 1984.

di Leonardo, Micaela, ed. *Gender at the Crossroads of Knowledge: Feminist Anthropology in the Postmodern Era.* Berkeley: University of California Press, 1991.

MacCormack, Carol, and Marilyn Strathern, eds. *Nature, Culture, and Gender.* Cambridge: Cambridge University Press, 1980.

Morgen, Sandra, ed. *Gender and Anthropology: Critical Reviews for Research and Teaching.* Washington, D. C.: American Anthropological Association, 1989.

Ortner, Sherry B., and Harriet Whitehead, eds. *Sexual Meanings: The Cultural Construction of Gender and Sexuality.* Cambridge: Cambridge University Press, 1981.

Reiter, Rayna R., ed. *Toward an Anthropology of Women.* New York: Monthly Review Press, 1975.

Rosaldo, M. Z., and Louise Lamphere, eds. *Women, Culture, and Society.* Stanford, Calif.: Stanford University Press, 1974.

Sanday, Peggy Reeves, and Ruth Gallagher Goodenough, eds.

*Beyond the Second Sex: New Directions in the Anthropology of Gender.* Philadelphia: University of Pennsylvania Press, 1990.

**Readable case studies of gender relations in particular cultures include:**

Abu-Lughod, Lila. *Writing Women's Worlds: Bedouin Stories.* Berkeley: University of California Press, 1992.

Goodale, Jane. *Tiwi Wives.* Seattle: University of Washington Press, 1971.

Mead, Margaret. *Sex and Temperament in Three Primitive Societies.* New York: William Morrow, 1963.

Mitter, Sara S. *Dharma's Daughters: Contemporary Indian Women and Hindu Culture.* New Brunswick, N. J.: Rutgers University Press, 1991.

Nanda, Serena. *Neither Man nor Woman: The Hijras of India.* Belmont, Calif.: Wadsworth Publishing Co., 1990.

Roscoe, Will. *The Zuni Man-Woman.* Albuquerque: University of New Mexico Press, 1991.

Saitoti, Tepilit Ole. *The Worlds of a Maasai Warrior: An Autobiography.* Berkeley: University of California Press, 1988.

Shostak, Marjorie. *Nisa: The Life and Words of a !Kung Woman.* Cambridge, Mass.: Harvard University Press, 1981.

Wolf, Margery. *Women in China.* Stanford, Calif.: Stanford University Press, 1975.

# CHAPTER 13

# THE ORGANIZATION OF POLITICAL LIFE

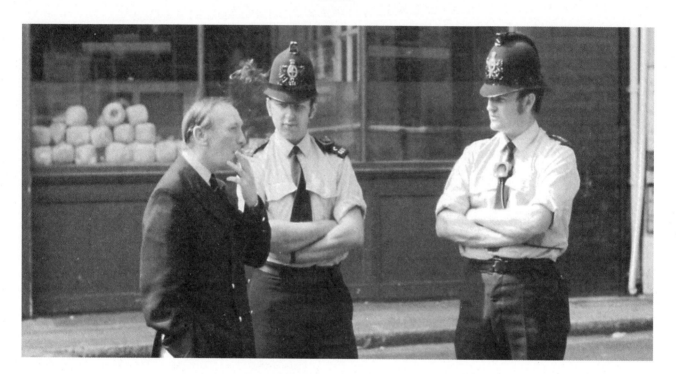

*When we think of law and social control, we usually think of the police.*

**CONTENTS**

Every society has some form of political system, meaning those institutions that organize and direct the collective actions of the population. In small societies political leadership and organization may be informal and even ad hoc. Only when a specific need for leadership arises does some individual assume an overt leadership role. In general, the larger the population, the more formalized the leadership and the more complex the political organization.

Likewise, as mentioned in chapter 2, all societies demand some minimal degree of conformity from their members. All, therefore, develop mechanisms of social control by which the behaviors of individuals are constrained and directed into acceptable channels. There are always behavioral patterns that are approved or acceptable and patterns that are disapproved or unacceptable. By means of social control a society encourages normatively proper behavior and discourages unacceptable actions, the objective being the maintenance of harmony and cooperation. The most serious deviations from acceptable behavior, which threaten the cohesiveness of the group, fall under that aspect of social control known as *law,* also discussed in this chapter. In the least organized societies law and political organization exist independently of each other. As political organization becomes increasingly formalized and structured, governmental institutions take over legal institutions, until legal institutions become part of the formal political structure.

## FORMS OF POLITICAL ORGANIZATION

When we speak of the political organization of a particular cultural system, we frequently are left with the impression that political boundaries and cultural boundaries are the same. But the boundaries of a *polity,* or politically organized unit, may or may not correspond with the boundaries of a particular way of life. For example, the Comanche of the Great Plains shared a common language, customs, and ethnic identity, yet politically, they were never organized above the local group. Thus the term *Comanche* refers to a people with a common language and culture who never united to carry out common political activities.

At the other extreme we find highly centralized polities that incorporate several culturally distinct peoples. In these instances the political boundary is suprasocietal and multicultural. The United States is unusual in this regard only in the degree of cultural heterogeneity that exists in the population. France, although predominantly "French," also includes Bretons and Basques. India has several hundred different ethnic groups. Russia, China, Indonesia, and the Philippines also integrate highly diversified populations into a single polity. In fact, every large and most small countries in the world today politically integrate several ethnic groups (see chapter 18).

Political organization falls into four basic forms. From the least to the most complex, these forms are **bands** (**simple** and **composite**), **tribes, chiefdoms,** and **states.** Today few societies exist that are not integrated into state-level political systems. Thus, to understand societies organized at less complex levels, we have to reconstruct the structure of such societies at an earlier period.

### Bands

As the least complex form, bands were probably the earliest form of human political structure (see chapter 7). As more complex political systems developed, band-level societies were unable to compete for resources. Thus bands survived until the modern period only in regions of the world with limited natural resources. Most known band-level societies were found in the dry deserts and grasslands of Australia, Africa, and the Americas. A few others lived in the tropical forests of Africa, Asia, and South America and in the boreal forest and tundra regions of North America and Asia.

Bands consist of a number of families living together and cooperating in economic activities throughout the year. Band-level organization most frequently was found among peoples with foraging economies, which usually dictated low population densities and high seasonal mobility. As a result, only a relatively small number of people could stay together throughout the year. Bands ranged in size from only a dozen to several hundred individuals. The adaptive significance of the band's size and seasonal mobility is described in chapter 7. In this chapter we are concerned with leadership statuses and political organization of bands.

The smallest bands, called *simple bands,* usually were no larger than an extended family and were structured as such. Leadership was informal, with the oldest or one of the older male members of the family serving as leader. Decision making was reached through consensus and involved both adult males and adult females; simple bands operated as families. Because all members of the band were related either through descent or by marriage, they were exogamous units, and members of the band had to seek spouses from other bands. Thus, although an autonomous economic and political unit, every band was, by social necessity, allied through intermarriage with other bands, usually territorially adjacent ones. Simple bands usually had names, although names may have been informal and may have simply referred to some prominent geographical feature associated with the band's usual territory.

Resource availability influenced the formation of such small groups. Simple bands often were associated with the hunting of nonmigratory game animals, such as deer, guanaco, moose, or small mammals, which occupy a limited territory on a year-round basis and are found either singly or in small herds. The foraging activities of simple bands usually did not generate any significant surpluses of food, which necessitated the year-round hunting of game animals. Effective hunting of these animals required only a few male hunters who had intimate knowledge of the seasonal shifts in range of these animals within their territory. The game resources of such areas could be exploited most effectively by a small and highly mobile population. In addition, such bands depended on the seasonal collection of wild roots, berries, nuts, and other edible plants as well as on limited fishing and shellfish collection.

*Composite bands* consisted of a larger aggregation of families, sometimes numbering in the hundreds. In contrast to simple bands, composite bands encompassed a number of unrelated extended families. Although leadership in composite bands was informal, it was more defined. Such leaders frequently have been called **big men**. Big men did not hold formal offices, and leadership was based on influence rather than authority over band members. **Influence** is merely the ability to convince people that they should act as you suggest. **Authority** is the recognized right of an individual to command another person to act in a particular way. Thus a big-man leader could not, by virtue of his position, make demands or impose rules on the members of the band; and his decisions were not binding on others. Because big-man status did not involve a formal office, no prescribed process for attaining leadership status existed. A man might emerge as the leader through a variety of personal accomplishments or qualities, such as his proven ability in hunting or warfare, the supernatural powers he possessed, or merely his charisma. There was no set tenure in the position, which was filled by a man until he was informally replaced by some other leader.

Like simple bands, many composite bands are nomadic groups that move within a relatively well defined range. Because of their greater size, composite bands are not as cohesive as simple bands and are politically more volatile. Disputes between families may result in some members joining another band or even the band splitting into two or more bands.

The formation of composite bands resulted from economic pressures that facilitated or necessitated the cooperation of a larger number of individuals than found in a single extended family. As in the case of simple bands, the behavior of the principal game animals was an important influence. Composite bands were associated with the seasonal hunting of migratory animals that form large herds, such as bison and caribou. Migratory herd animals usually appeared only seasonally in the range of a particular composite band as the herd moved between its summer and winter ranges. Because bison and caribou migrate in herds that sometimes number in the tens of thousands, there was no difficulty in locating the herds on the open grasslands and tundra. Unlike the nonmigratory-animal hunters, who secure game steadily throughout the year, hunters of migratory animals take most of their game only twice a year, as the herds pass through their territories during migrations.

Hunting large herds of animals effectively required directing the movements of the herd into situations where large numbers could be slaughtered. Herds might be run over a cliff, into a holding pen, or into a lake, where hunters in boats could kill them. Regardless of the method used, all these strategies required the presence of a larger group of hunters than was available in a simple band. Thus composite bands were formed to bring together a sufficiently large number of hunters to control the movements of large herds of animals.

The Comanche of the southern Great Plains of the United States illustrate the nature of composite bands. These horse-raising, bison-hunting people were politically autonomous until the Red River War of 1875. During the early and middle years of the nineteenth century the Comanche numbered about 6,000 to 7,000, divided between five and thirteen main bands. Comanche bands had only vaguely defined territories, and two or more bands frequently occupied the same general area or had overlapping ranges. Membership in Comanche bands was fluid: Both individuals and families could and did shift from one band to another, or a number of families might join together to establish a new band. Some anthropologists have theorized that there were only five major bands, with a varying number of secondary bands appearing and disappearing from time to time.

*Among the Comanche, "peace chiefs" lead the band villages. Quanah Parker, pictured here, was one of the most famous Comanche peace chiefs.*

A band consisted of a number of families, each headed by an older male member who was "peace chief" or "headman." One of these family heads also served as the peace chief for the entire band. There was no formalized method of selecting either the family heads or the head of the band. As the Comanche say, "No one made him such; he just got that way." A Comanche peace chief usually was a man known for his kindness, wisdom, and ability to lead by influencing other men. Although a war record was important, peace chiefs were not chosen from among the most aggressive or ambitious men. Such men usually remained war chiefs—great warriors who periodically recruited men to raid neighbors—but frequently had little influence outside war and raiding.

A band peace chief was responsible for the well-being of the band. Through a consensus of the family heads, he directed the seasonal movement of the band and the bison hunts. He did have men who voluntarily assisted him. In the morning the peace chief usually sent out two men to scout the area around the camp for the presence of enemy raiding parties. He also sent a crier through the camp periodically to announce plans for the movement of the camp, an upcoming hunt, or some other cooperative activities. During the bison hunts the peace chief called on a number of men from the camp to police the hunt and restrain overly eager hunters from scattering the herd and thus spoiling the hunt for others.

In an extraordinarily individualistic and egalitarian society Comanche band leaders had to strive for and maintain consensus. If a dispute arose and a consensus could not be reached, individuals and families were free either to shift residence to another band or even to form a new band under another leader.

Comanche bands were economically and politically autonomous units. Only seldom did two or more bands come together for any unified action, and never did leaders of the bands come together to discuss issues. At the same time, there was a strong consciousness of common identity, of being Comanche. Comanches freely traveled between bands to visit, marry, and even shift residence. There was an informally reached general consensus on whether relations with a particular neighboring group were friendly or hostile. Comanche bands also usually refrained from attacking other Comanche bands, although on occasion some Comanche bands did ally themselves with foreign groups.

Thus, on the band level of political organization, populations are fragmented into numerous independent political units that operate only at the local-group level. These various communities share a common cultural identity and usually attempt to maintain harmonious relations with one another, but they lack any political structure capable of organizing all the various communities into a single unit for collective actions.

## Tribes

Tribes differ from bands in that they have formally organized institutions that unite the scattered residential communities, give the society greater cohesiveness, and make possible a more united response to external threats. These institutions are called **sodalities**. Sodalities take various forms: They may be based on large kin groups, such as clans and lineages; on nonkinship units, such as age sets (see chapter 16); or on voluntary associations, such as warrior societies. Regardless of their exact nature, sodalities unify geographically dispersed communities into political units. Although tribal-level societies usually are egalitarian, with leadership dependent in part on the persuasive abilities of individuals, formalized political offices with institutionalized authority exist. Although tribes vary greatly in structure, here we can examine only one tribal-level society.

The Cheyenne of the Great Plains, whose adaptation we discussed in chapter 7, numbered between 3,000 and 3,500 during the early 1800s. The Cheyenne, like the neighboring Comanche, were horse-mounted bison hunters. They were divided into ten main nomadic villages, which averaged between 300 and 350 persons. Village membership was not based on kinship, although the members of a particular village usually were related either by blood or by marriage. Village membership was relatively stable, and marriages between villagers were common. Despite this stability, myths concerning village origins were not well developed, and band names were only nicknames (e.g., Grayhairs, Hair-rope Men, Ridge Men, or some other trivial characteristic). Although a particular village usually frequented a certain range, there was no sense of village territoriality. Periodically and seasonally, family camps and subvillage camps broke off from the main village.

The only time the entire tribe came together was in early summer, when all the widely scattered villages gathered into a single camp at a predetermined location. This crescent-shaped encampment stretched for several miles from end to end, with the open portion facing east. Within the tribal encampment every village had a designated location; and while camped together, they performed the great tribal ceremonies (e.g., the Arrow Renewal, the Sun Dance, or the Animal Dance). At least one and possibly two of these rituals were performed, depending on the particular ritual needs of the tribe at that time. After the performance of the ritual the tribe as a unit staged the great summer bison hunt. After the hunt the tribe again scattered into smaller village camps.

Politically, the tribe was controlled by the Council of Forty-four and the warrior societies. The Council of Forty-four, which had both political and religious duties, was headed by the Sweet Medicine chief, who was responsible for keeping the Sweet Medicine bundle, a sacred package of sweet grass. Second to him in importance were four other sacred chiefs, each representative of specific supernatural beings. Under these five sacred chiefs were thirty-nine ordinary chiefs.

Chiefs served in their positions for ten years and could not be removed for any reason. Serving as a chief placed a burden on the individuals. Chiefs usually were selected from among the older men, all of whom had war records. When an individual was chosen as a chief, he was to act like a chief, not an aggressive warrior. If the man was an officer in one of the warrior societies, he had to resign his position, although he remained a member of the society. A chief was to be generous, kindly, even tempered, and aloof from everyday disputes. In short, he was expected to display ideal human behavior at all times: He was to take care of the poor, settle disputes between individuals, and be responsible for the ritual performances that protected the tribe.

There were five original warrior societies, but this number was not fixed. These were formal voluntary associations of men, each with its own style of dress, dances, songs, and set of four leaders. As young warriors, men were recruited by the different societies until all had joined one or another of the societies. Theoretically, there were no status differences between the societies; in actuality, they did vary somewhat in prestige.

The term *warrior societies* is slightly misleading. Each warrior society had four leaders, one of whom served as its head. The heads of the various societies constituted what some call the *tribal war chiefs*. Although this group planned and led attacks on their enemies, the different societies did not fight or operate as military units in battles. In battles men fought as individuals, and members of several societies may have been present in a particular raiding party.

Subordinate to the council of chiefs, the warrior societies cooperated as a group only in the policing of the camps. During the summer tribal encampment the Council of Forty-four appointed one of the societies as camp police. Later, when the villages scattered into separate camps, the members of the council resident in the village appointed one of the warrior societies to police the camp. After being appointed the warrior society usually carried out its function with little direction from the chiefs. Its members scouted the area around the camp to check for the presence of any enemy raiding parties, corrected young boys involved in any mischief, and intervened in any serious disputes between village members.

But it was during bison hunts that the policing role of the warrior societies became most evident. Successful bison hunts required a strategy that caused the herd to stay together and not scatter; only in this way could the maximum number of animals be killed. Before the hunt, as the village moved into a position near the herd, hunting by individuals was prohibited; and the warrior society in charge of the camp enforced this order. If any man flagrantly violated the order, the society might beat him with whips, shoot his horses, and destroy his tipi. As the hunters gathered on their horses to begin the hunt, the society in charge restrained any overly eager hunters and made certain that every man had an equal opportunity to secure game for his family.

There are two points to be emphasized about the political organization of tribal societies. First, although there were some formalized political and religious offices that bequeathed some limited authority and prerogatives, on the whole, tribal societies were basically egalitarian (see chapter 14). Few positions were hereditary, and most leaders were selected on the basis of personal qualities and individual merit.

Second, there was little economic specialization, either individual or regional, among tribes. Except for cooperation in communal hunts, families produced their own food and manufactured their own clothes and other material goods. From an economic perspective, each band or village was virtually a self-contained unit, capable of sustaining itself without support from other communities; therefore, it was not economic necessity, convenience, or efficiency that led to the supracommunity political organization of tribes. Although sodalities unite tribes at a higher level of cohesiveness than bands, the mere existence of sodalities is not sufficient to generate or maintain the cohesiveness of a tribe. It is likely that external threats, either real or perceived, necessitated the cooperation in warfare of a large group of people and was the major factor that united geo-graphically dispersed communities. Thus warfare—the existence and activities of hostile human neighbors— was an important force in creating the political integration of separate communities.

## Chiefdoms

Like tribes, chiefdoms were multicommunity political units. Unlike tribes, chiefdoms had a formalized and centralized political system. A chiefdom (see chapter 9) was governed by a single chief, who usually served as both political and religious head of the polity. The chief had authority over members of the chiefdom, and the position often was hereditary within a single kin group, which based its chiefly rights on supernatural powers. Thus a chiefdom was not an egalitarian society but a ranked or stratified society (see chapter 14) with access to resources based on inherited status. With authority and power conferred by supernatural beings, governing was not by consensus but by decree.

Most chiefdoms were associated with horticultural societies in which craft or regional specialization in production had emerged. There was a need for regularized exchanges of goods either between geographically dispersed communities or, at times, within a single community. This economic exchange was managed through redistribution, with the chief occupying the central position in the flow of goods (see chapter 9).

In earlier historic periods chiefdoms probably were found throughout much of the Old World. During more recent periods such political systems were primarily concentrated in Oceania (Polynesia, Micronesia, and Melanesia) and in the Americas (the circum-Caribbean and coastal portions of South America and the northwestern coast of North America).

The Polynesian-speaking people of Tahiti, an island in the southeastern Pacific, illustrate many characteristics typical of a chiefdom. This relatively large, mountainous, volcanic island had a population of about 100,000 at the time of European discovery. Tahiti was divided among about twenty rival chiefs. Although most of these chiefdoms were about the size of the average tribe and significantly smaller than the largest tribes, their political organization differed significantly.

The economy of Tahiti was based largely on farming: Taro, breadfruit, coconuts, and yams were the main crops; pigs and chickens were also raised, and fish and other seafoods supplemented the food supply. Food production was sufficient not only to meet the needs of the population but also to produce surpluses for export to other islands. Although sufficient food was produced in all regions, there were significant regional differences in types of food produced because Tahiti varied ecologically.

Tahitian society had at least three, and possibly four, distinct classes, depending on how finely one wants to divide the units. *Arii*, or chiefs, and their close relatives formed the ruling elite. The arii were divided into two groups: the *arii rahi*, or sacred chiefs, and the *arii rii*, or small chiefs. Under these chiefs were the *raatira*, or subchiefs, and the *manahune*, or commoners. The sacred chiefs were viewed as descended from the gods, whereas the commoners were merely created by the gods for their use. The subchiefs were the offspring of intermarriage between the sacred chiefs and commoners, whereas the small chiefs were the products of still later intermarriages between sacred chiefs and subchiefs. Once these four classes were established, class endogamy became the rule.

The sacred chiefs, viewed as gods on earth, evoked both reverence and fear. Whatever the highest-ranking sacred chiefs touched became *tabu*, or sacred, and could not be used for fear of supernatural punishment. Such chiefs had to be carried on the back of a servant, lest the ground touched by his feet become tabu. They could not enter the house of another individual, for the same reason. The life-style of the chief's family differed from that of other individuals: They had larger and more elaborate houses, the largest canoes, insignia of their rank, and particular clothing.

Unlike in band and tribal-level societies, resources in chiefdoms were individually owned. Land was owned mainly by the chiefs and subchiefs, but ultimate authority rested with the sacred chiefs within the polity. Although sacred chiefs could not withhold the title to lands from the families of subchiefs, they could banish an individual subchief. Crafts were specialized, and craftspeople were attached to particular sacred chiefs and produced goods for them. Communal fishing equipment was made by these craftspeople, and the chiefs regulated their use. Thus the sacred chiefs directly controlled craft production and communal fishing. The chiefs could make any demands on the property of the subchiefs and commoners. If someone refused, the chief could have the recalcitrant banished or make him or her a sacrificial victim. Theoretically, the sacred chief was the head judicial figure in the polity, but some believe that the chief seldom intervened in disputes between individuals; the chief usually used these powers only against people who challenged his authority.

The sacred chief in each polity was the focal point for redistributive exchanges. The chief periodically demanded surplus production from all his subjects for a public redistribution. Such events were associated with a number of occasions: a rite of passage for a member of the chief's family, the organizing of a military attack, religious ceremonies, or the start of the breadfruit harvest. During such ceremonies the chief distributed the goods collected to all his subjects.

## States

Although they had a centralized political system, chiefdoms were still kinship-based structures. Even in Tahiti the sacred chief's authority rested in large part on his control over families of subchiefs, each of whom had his own inalienable rights to lands—and thus families—of commoners. As a result, the number of people who could be effectively integrated into a chiefdom was limited. In Polynesia most chiefdoms ranged from only a few thousand to 30,000 persons. Polities with larger populations require a political structure based on institutions other than kinship.

States, like chiefdoms, have a centralized political structure, but what distinguishes them from chiefdoms is the presence of a bureaucracy. A chiefdom is basically a two-level system: (1) the chiefs (which in Tahiti included the subchiefs), who have varying levels of authority and power, and (2) the commoners, or great mass of the populace. A state has three levels: (1) the ruling elite, (2) a bureaucracy, and (3) the populace.

In states, as in chiefdoms, highest authority and power reside in the ruling elite, the formal political head or heads of the polity. States vary greatly in the types of political leaders present and in the basis for the leaders' authority and power. Leaders in the earliest states frequently were considered to be the descendants of gods, and thus themselves gods on earth. The Inca of Peru (discussed in chapter 9) and the pharaohs of Egypt were leaders who ruled as gods. Other political leaders, although not claiming to be gods, have legitimated their positions with claims of having been chosen by god. Early European kings legitimated their claims to leadership on such a basis; and as English coins still proclaim, the queen rules *Dei gratia*—by the "grace of God." Other states have evolved political leadership that uses strictly secular ideas to justify its power. In countries where leaders are elected by a vote of the populace, rule is legitimated by the internalized acceptance of such ascendance to office. Even strictly secular kingdoms, dictatorships, and oligarchies can, if in power for a sufficient time, have their rule accepted by the populace as "legitimate." We have more to say about legitimation in chapter 14.

Although they differ greatly in political leadership, states all share one characteristic: the presence of a bureaucracy that carries out the day-to-day governing of the polity. In simple terms, a bureaucrat is a person to whom a political leader delegates certain authority and powers. The bureaucrat thus acts on behalf of the political leader. Lacking any inherent authority or powers personally, bureaucrats depend on the continued support of political leaders. The emergence of bureaucracies allowed for both qualitative and quantitative changes in political systems. Using bureaucrats as intermediaries, political leaders could expand the size of their polities both geographically and demographically, while strengthening their political control over the population. Bureaucrats could engineer such expansion without threat of revolution and political fragmentation because they lacked any personal claims to independent political legitimacy.

The emergence of states increased the complexity of political units, and bureaucracies not only allowed for specialization in governmental functions but also made possible the effective integration of large land areas and population into political units. For example, chiefdoms seldom exceeded 30,000 persons, whereas modern states such as China may have populations of one billion people. In addition, political units could incorporate multiple ethnic populations.

## ▚ SOCIAL CONTROL AND LAW

In all societies there are clearly defined rules that govern the relationships between members. Not all individuals in any society will conform to these rules. There will always be some individuals who behave in a socially unacceptable manner. Thus among all peoples there exist formal and informal ways to correct the behavior of individuals. In general, we call these mechanisms social control. One form of social control is called law.

### Social Control

**Social control** refers to the diverse ways in which the behaviors of the members of a society are constrained into socially approved channels. All cultures have certain behavioral norms that most people learn and begin to conform to during enculturation. But all societies have individuals who, to one degree or another, deviate from those norms. Violations of norms usually result in sanctions or punishments for the offender, which serve both to correct the behavior of particular people and to show others the penalties for such deviance. The severity of sanctions and the process by which sanctions are imposed differ greatly, depending on the seriousness culturally attached to the violated norm, the perceived severity of the violation, and the overall political and legal system of the people.

Children who get into mischief usually are corrected by their parents. In our own society parents may impose sanctions ranging from physically spanking children to verbally scolding to withdrawing privileges such as television viewing or activities with friends. The correcting of children trains individuals in proper behavior at an early age.

The community also applies informal sanctions against individuals—both children and adults—who are not behaving properly. Gossip, or fear of gossip, serves as an important method of social control in most societies. Most people fear the contempt or ridicule of their peers, so most individuals try to conform to acceptable behavioral norms. People attempt to hide behavior that would be the subject of gossip, scandal, and ridicule. Individuals whose known behavior consistently violates social norms may even find themselves ostracized by friends and relatives (the severest of informal punishments). Informal economic penalties also may be imposed. A family may withdraw economic support in attempts to modify errant behavior of a member.

A wide variety of supernatural sanctions may assist in controlling individual behavior, and in some cases these supernatural sanctions are automatically imposed on particular types of behavior. Whether the commission of these acts becomes public knowledge or not, and thus regardless of whether other punishments are inflicted on the individual, the commission still endangers one's immortal soul. Supernatural sanctions can be more specifically directed. In many societies, including some Christian ones, an individual may place a curse on another person by calling on a supernatural being to punish that individual. Fear of sorcery or witchcraft (see chapter 15) frequently serves as another important form of social control. Most victims are people who in some way offended a witch or sorcerer, often through a breach of social norms.

## Law

Law is the highest level of social control, and legal punishments usually are reserved for the most serious breaches of norms. The question of how law can be distinguished from other forms of social control is not easy to answer. In societies with court systems the distinction is formalized, but in societies without such formalized legal systems the division is not as clear.

E. Adamson Hoebel (1954, 28) defined law in the following way: "A social norm is legal if its neglect or infraction is regularly met, in threat or in fact, by the application of physical force by an individual or group possessing the socially recognized privilege of so acting." Law so defined was and is present in virtually every society. Leopold Pospisil, building in part on Hoebel's work, defined law as having four attributes: *authority, intention of universal application, obligatio,* and *sanction.*

In a legal action some individual or group must have publicly recognized authority to settle a case or punish a violation. In societies with courts who has the authority is obvious, but in societies that lack courts the authority becomes less clear. What emerges frequently is an ad hoc authority; that is, because of the peculiarities of the case, a particular individual or group becomes recognized by the community as the authority responsible for its resolution. In some cases the victim himself or herself may be the recognized authority. In the victim's absence (as in the case of murder) the victim's family or clan or kin group may be placed in the role of authority. Such ad hoc authority is discussed later in some of the examples.

Implicit in all legal actions is the intention of universal application, which means that in identical cases the sanction imposed is the same. Although one might argue that no two legal cases have been or will ever be identical, the notion of universal application requires that the law be consistent and thus predictable; the arbitrary imposition of sanctions is not law.

Obligatio refers to the legal relation between two or more living individuals. All individuals are immersed in a complex web of rights and duties, and every individual has both certain rights and certain duties to others. In some cases an individual's rights and the correlative duties of others are well defined; in other cases some ambiguity exists. Most civil legal cases and arguments in our own court system focus on questions about rights and duties. For example, when two drivers argue after a traffic accident, they argue about who was properly exercising rights and who was negligent regarding duties. An act breaches the law only if the abridgment of one's individual rights resulted from another person's failure to perform a legitimate duty.

Whereas Hoebel limited legal sanctions to physical sanctions, Pospisil argued that this definition is too narrow. A legal sanction does not have to be some form of corporal punishment, nor does it have to involve the loss of property. Based on his work with the Kapauku of New Guinea, Pospisil contended that the impact of psychological sanctions can be severer than that of actual physical punishment. For this reason he stated, "We can define a legal sanction as either the negative behavior of withdrawing some rewards or favors that otherwise (if the law had not been violated) would have been granted, or the positive behavior of inflicting some painful experience, be it physical or psychological" (Pospisil 1958, 268).

The legal institutions of a society consist of two distinct components: (1) **procedural law** and (2) **substantive law.** Procedural law refers to the manner in which a breach of the law is adjudicated or resolved, and it focuses on questions such as the following: Who assumes the role of authority? How is it determined that a breach of the law has taken place? How is the proper sanction determined? Who imposes the sanction on the offending party? Substantive law, on the other hand, is concerned with defining the types of behavior that are categorized as illegal—in other words, violations of the rights and duties of individuals and the appropriate sanctions to be imposed. Substantive laws—or at least the relative significance of such laws—differ greatly, and thus they are extraordinarily difficult to categorize. For example, some societies have laws against witchcraft. Witchcraft, however, is not illegal under American law because we deny the existence of true witchcraft. In many societies adultery is considered a serious crime punishable by death, whereas in other societies adultery is of little consequence and is either ignored or subject to only a small fine.

Although substantive laws vary widely in particulars, they do fall into two main categories: (1) criminal laws and (2) civil laws or torts. Criminal law is concerned with breaches of social norms that are considered to be crimes against the state or against society as a whole. They are handled by the society acting in a collective manner through its legal institutions, such as courts, prosecutors, judges, and police. In contrast, civil laws or torts are breaches of social norms that are considered to affect only an individual or groups of individuals. The society may or may not have formal organized institutions to adjudicate such cases. As we discuss later, not all societies make a distinction between criminal and civil law. In some societies there are only civil laws or torts, even for the more serious breaches of norms, such as murder.

# LEGAL SYSTEMS

On the basis of procedural characteristics two main levels of complexity and formality can be defined: (1) **self-help legal systems** and (2) **court legal systems**.

## Self-Help Systems

Self-help systems, also called *ad hoc systems,* are informal and exist in the absence of any centralized or formalized legal institutions capable of settling disputes. Such systems are associated with band-level societies and most tribal-level societies. In such systems there is only civil law. All legal actions concern only the principal parties and/or their families. The reason for terming the legal procedure in these societies *self-help* will become clear.

Self-help legal systems fall into two main forms: (1) *familial* and (2) *mediator.* In familial systems all actions and decisions are initiated and executed by the families or larger kin groups involved. In mediator systems there is the formal presence of a neutral third party—the mediator—who attempts to negotiate and resolve the dispute peacefully.

In familial systems legal actions are handled by the families involved. A legal offense only indirectly concerns the community as a whole. When an individual and/or family determines that its rights have been violated, the imposition of the proper sanction falls to the plaintiffs; in other words, the offended party assumes the role of authority. Such a system in which the redress of a legal grievance falls to the victim, or in the case of murder to the victim's family, has some problems in implementation but not as many as one might anticipate. This is not a system of "might makes right." Certainly cases arise in such societies in which the physically (or militarily) weak are victimized by the strong. However, in cases of legal redress there is a collective consensus of the community in support of the victim and usually a recognized means by which even the weakest members of the community can gather support adequate to impose appropriate sanctions on the strongest.

The Comanche exemplify how a familial legal system operated and how victims weaker than their opponents could nonetheless obtain redress. One of the most frequent Comanche offenses was "wife stealing." Most older Comanche men were polygynous, and some of their wives were significantly younger than their husbands. Among young Comanche men it was considered prestigious, although illegal, to steal the wife of another man. Under Comanche law the injured husband could demand either his wife back or some property, usually horses, in compensation. The husband had the responsibility of imposing these sanctions. In such actions the community played no direct role, but a husband could not ignore the loss of a wife. If he did ignore it, the community would ridicule him, and his prestige would decline. Thus not only did the community support the husband in pressing his claim, but they informally pressured him to act.

In imposing these sanctions the husband was allowed to use whatever physical force was needed, short of killing the individual. In cases in which the men involved were physically about equal, the two men met to negotiate and discuss the husband's demands. Behind these negotiations was the potential threat that the husband might physically assault the defendant.

In cases where the husband presented little or no personal threat to the defendant, institutionalized means existed whereby the husband could gain the physical backing needed. Although it lowered his prestige in the community, he could call on his relatives for support; the husband, with his male relatives present and prepared to support his demands physically, could then negotiate with the defendant. The defendant always had to stand alone. He would not even consider asking his relatives for support because he would lose prestige, and wife stealing was motivated in large part by prestige. Even if he had asked his kinsmen for support, they would not have responded for fear of community ridicule.

In cases where the husband was an orphan or lacked kinsmen to negotiate successfully, another cultural avenue was open: The aggrieved man could call on any other man he wanted to prosecute his case. He usually called on the assistance of one of the powerful war leaders in the band. Such a request was so prestigious that a war leader could not refuse. At the same time, such a request was demeaning to the man asking for help and greatly lowered his prestige. As a result, it usually required a great deal of social pressure to force a man to ask for assistance; once the request was made, the issue was between the defendant and the war leader alone. On approaching the defendant the war leader would call out, "You have stolen my wife," and then proceed to exact whatever demands the husband had requested. For his action the war leader received nothing in payment other than the admiration of the community; the husband received the settlement. Although this process most commonly was used in wife-stealing cases, it could be used for other issues as well. Thus Comanche legal institutions gave any individual the means to marshal overwhelming physical force in the protection of his rights.

As the Comanche example shows, familial systems often work relatively well in protecting individual rights. There are exceptions, and in some situations this system can fail. The Caribou Inuit illustrates one of the inherent problems. In cases of murder the authority and responsibility for imposing the sanction—execution— fell to the family of the victim. Execution of the murderer was not always immediate. The family might wait years until the opportunity presented itself to kill the murderer with impunity; shooting the man in the back while he was working was considered an ideal situation. For the system to work, a relative of the victim had to be left alive to impose the sanction. To prevent being killed himself, a murderer might not stop with the killing of his intended victim but proceed to kill the entire family as well. For example, a Caribou Inuit man was rebuffed by the family of a girl he wanted to marry. He killed the girl's father, mother, brothers, and sister—a total of seven or eight persons—and then took the girl as his wife. Such massacres were thought by many Inuit to be prudent behavior and sometimes enhanced the prestige of the individual.

The Caribou Inuit case illustrates the problems with familial systems of law; yet we must remember that all legal systems have defects, and manipulative individuals frequently escape sanctions in all societies. Sometimes murderers escape punishment because of legal technicalities under the American legal system. Also, the fact that an individual may enhance his prestige by committing a particular illegal act does not necessarily reflect on the law—after all, American folk heroes include Jesse James and Pretty Boy Floyd.

A more formalized type of legal procedure is found in the mediator system. Under this system disputes are still between individuals and families. The offended party and/or his or her family fills the position of authority. However, a third party is called on, usually by the offending individual or his or her family, to attempt to negotiate a mutually agreeable solution. The mediator has no authority to impose a settlement. The aggrieved party and/or his or her family must agree to accept the compensation negotiated.

The Nuer, a pastoral tribal society of the Sudan, provide an example of how mediator systems operate. The Nuer live in small villages of related families. Although villages are tied together through lineages and clans, there is no effective leadership above the village level. The only formalized leaders who transcend the local units are individuals called *leopard-skin chiefs,* whose position is indicated by the wearing of a leopard-skin cloak. These men have no secular authority to enforce their judgments but only limited ritual powers to bless and curse.

The most important function of leopard-skin chiefs is mediating feuds between local groups. The Nuer are an egalitarian, warrior-oriented people. Disputes between individuals frequently result in physical violence, and men occasionally are killed. The killing of a Nuer requires that his kinsmen exact retribution. Any close patrilineal kinsman of the murderer may be killed in retaliation, but at least initially the kinsmen of the victim attempt to kill the murderer himself. Immediately after committing a murder the killer flees to the house of a leopard-skin chief. This dwelling is a sanctuary, and as long as the man stays in the chief's house he is safe. The

*The cloak of this Nuer man indicates that he is a leopard-skin chief. As such, he is in charge of mediating disputes.*

victim's kinsmen usually keep the house under surveillance to try to kill the murderer if he ventures out.

The leopard-skin chief keeps the murderer in his house until a settlement is arranged. The chief will wait until tempers have cooled, which usually requires several weeks, before he begins to negotiate the case. First, he goes to the family of the murderer to see if they are willing to pay cattle to the victim's family in compensation. Seldom do they refuse because one of them might be killed in retaliation. After the murderer's family has agreed to pay, the chief proceeds to the family of the victim, offering so many cattle in compensation. Initially the victim's family invariably refuses, saying that they want blood, that cattle cannot compensate them for the death of their beloved kinsman. The leopard-skin chief persists, usually gaining support of more distant relatives of the victim who also pressure the family to settle. The leopard-skin chief may even threaten to place a curse on the family if they continue to refuse to settle for a payment rather than blood. The family finally agrees and accepts cattle, usually about forty head, as compensation. Even though the matter is formally settled, the killer and his close patrilineal kinsmen will avoid the family of the victim for some years so as not to provoke spontaneous retaliation.

Up to this point we have examined legal systems that operate without a formalized or centralized political structure capable of resolving disputes. In many of these societies law, not subordination to a common set of formal political institutions, defines the boundaries of the society. To see what we mean, consider the Nuer. The Nuer distinguish between a *ter,* or a feud within a Nuer tribe that is a legal action subject to arbitration; a *kur,* or a fight between members of two Nuer tribes that cannot be arbitrated; and a *pec,* or a war with non-Nuer people. Nuer believe that disputes within a tribe should be resolved by legal means (that is, peacefully), whereas disputes between individuals who are not members of the same tribe should be resolved by extralegal means, including organized warfare. Legal processes serve to repair and maintain social relations between families; thus law serves both to maintain the cohesiveness and to define the boundaries of the society.

The Jívaro, a horticultural and foraging people of eastern Ecuador, illustrate how law defines social boundaries. The Jívaro are best known for their former practice of severing the heads of their enemies and shrinking them to the size of a fist. By the 1950s the Jívaro had been reduced to slightly more than 2,000 persons settled in more than 200 scattered family households. Such households usually consist of a man, his wife or wives, their children, and, possibly, a son-in-law or other relatives. These households are grouped into "neighborhoods," which consist of a number of households living within a few miles of one another; the membership of such a neighborhood is poorly defined and fluid. Poor hunting, a dispute with other households, or some other factors might result in a family's moving away. Neither corporate kin groups nor formalized leadership positions exist. Except for household heads, only a few men are called *unta,* or "big," but their informal leadership role is limited and transitory. Politically, the Jívaro are organized at a band level. Although they have only limited political institutions, the Jívaro have a strong sense of common cultural identity and territorial boundaries. Living in adjacent or nearby territories are four other "Jívaroan" groups, who speak mutually intelligible dialects, share the same basic customs, and at times trade with Jívaro households. Despite their minimal political integration, there is little question about which households are Jívaro and which belong to the other four groups.

With this political organization the methods in settlement of disputes define the effective boundaries of the society. Disputes between Jívaros are resolved by legal means, whereas disputes with members of other societies are resolved through extralegal means. Like the Nuer, the Jívaro make a sharp distinction between a **feud** and a war. A feud is the legal means by which a sanction is imposed on another family for the murder of a kinsman. As a legal procedure, a feud proceeds in a manner quite different from a war.

As in most societies, murder is the most serious offense. According to Jívaro beliefs, few deaths are attributable to natural causes; most deaths are the result of physical violence, sorcery, or avenging spirits. Deaths caused by physical violence and witchcraft are considered murders, which have to be avenged by the kinsmen of the deceased. In most cases of physical violence the murderer is readily identifiable. In cases of poisoning and witchcraft, divination is used to determine the guilty party.

Determination of the guilty party and whether they are Jívaro or non-Jívaro affect how the victim's kinfolk avenge the death. If the guilty party is Jívaro, the kinsmen of the victim attack the household of the murderer with the goal of killing the man himself. If they are not successful in finding him, they may kill a male relative of his, even if it is only a young boy. They normally will not harm women or children, except in cases in which the victim was a woman or a child. Even if they have the opportunity to kill more, only one individual will be killed. This is a legal action, and Jívaro law allows only a life for a life. The head of the victim cannot be taken.

If, on the other hand, the guilty party is determined to be a non-Jívaro, different actions are taken. The relatives of the murdered person attack the household of the guilty party, trying to kill as many people as possible. They attempt to massacre the entire family, with no regard for either sex or age. In some cases they attack nearby households as well, attempting to kill even more members of the group. This is a war, not a legal action, and the heads of all victims are taken.

The Jívaro, the Nuer, and other peoples who lack centralized and formal political structure nonetheless have definite means of maintaining social control. To those of us who have formal governmental institutions that are supposed to handle our grievances and right the wrongs done to us, self-help systems such as those of the Comanche, Caribou Eskimo, Nuer, and Jívaro look rather anarchic. However, rules govern such systems. Some anthropologists believe in fact that the best definition of *society* in self-help systems is those individuals whose vengeance-taking activities are constrained by procedural rules.

## Court Systems

A number of factors distinguish a *court legal system* from a self-help legal system. First, authority resides not with the victim and/or his or her family but with a formalized institution, the court. The court has the authority and the power to hear disputes and to unilaterally decide cases and impose sanctions if they are deemed warranted. Authority in legal matters is a component of political authority; thus fully developed court systems can exist only in societies that have centralized formal political leadership, that is, chiefdoms or states. Second, most court systems operate with formal public hearings, presided over by a judge or judges, with formally defined defendants and plaintiffs. Grievances are stated, evidence is collected and analyzed, and, in cases of conflicting evidence, oaths or ordeals may be used to determine truthfulness. Finally, only in court systems does one find substantive law clearly divided into criminal law and civil law.

Court systems in turn may be divided into three categories; (1) **incipient courts**, (2) **courts of mediation**, and (3) **courts of regulation**. All court systems mediate disputes as well as regulate behavior; however, as societies become increasingly complex, the primary focus of the courts shifts from mediating disputes to regulating behavior. This shift results in a qualitative difference not only in courts but in the nature of the law itself. Associated with this shift is an increasing codification of the laws. Laws and their associated sanctions become standardized and rigid, and civil laws are steadily transformed into criminal laws. Court systems begin to emerge with the concept of "crime against society"—the need to control individual acts that might endanger the society as a whole, as opposed to acts that threaten only individuals. Herein lies the distinction between criminal law and civil law.

**INCIPIENT COURT SYSTEMS.**     True court systems can only be found in societies with centralized political systems—chiefdoms or states. However, in some tribal societies are what might best be termed *incipient courts*. Although a tribal-level society, the Cheyenne, as described earlier in this chapter, demonstrate the development of an incipient court system. At times both the Council of Forty-four and the warrior societies assumed the role of de facto judges and courts. The Cheyenne recognized that certain individual actions threatened the well-being of the group and thus had to be controlled. Some of these actions were purely secular, whereas others were religious. Designated warrior societies were formally empowered by the council to enforce secular laws and regulations on the camp members. For example, in preparation for a communal bison hunt camp members would be told to refrain from independent hunting for some days before the hunt. If the policing warrior society discovered someone hunting illegally, the men present became the de facto judges and court and immediately imposed sanctions on the offender. Such an offender often was beaten with whips, his horses were shot, and his tepee was slashed with knives. Other secular criminal violations were handled just as swiftly. The Council of Forty-four was responsible for the religious or sacred well-being of the tribe; thus any action that endangered the supernatural well-being of the Cheyenne was their concern. The murder of a Cheyenne by another Cheyenne was the most heinous of crimes. Such a crime was said to bloody the sacred arrows, the most sacred of Cheyenne tribal medicine bundles. The arrows were symbolic of Cheyenne success in hunting (their main economic activity) and warfare. Murder within the tribe polluted the arrows and thus made the Cheyenne vulnerable to their enemies and less successful in their hunting. When a Cheyenne died at the hands of another Cheyenne the Council of Forty-four became a de facto court. Although there was no formal hearing, the council met and discussed the case: Was it a murder? If so, then the sacred arrows had to be "renewed," or ritually purified. They also decided on the sanction to be imposed—usually exile for a period of years. With the Cheyenne there could be no capital punishment without again polluting the sacred arrows. (See Box 13.1 for further discussion of the Cheyenne system.)

**COURTS OF MEDIATION.** The key difference between court systems is not how the legal hearings are conducted, but the manner in which breaches of the law are determined and suitable sanctions imposed. In courts of mediation few laws are codified, and the judges follow few formalized guidelines as to what constitutes a legal violation or the sanction that should be imposed. This is not to say that judges act arbitrarily in these matters, but that they have tremendous latitude in their actions. What they apply is a **reasonable-man model**. Using prevalent norms and values, they ask the question, How should a reasonable individual have acted under these circumstances? To determine this an individual's actions have to be examined within the social context in which the dispute occurred: What was the past and present relationship between the parties involved? What were the circumstances leading up to the event? Thus they attempt to examine each case as a unique occurrence. Although some sanctions are imposed as punishments, other sanctions are designed to restore as fully as possible a working, if not harmonious, relationship between the parties involved.

One difficulty in attempting to describe courts of mediation is our limited knowledge of such systems. Polities having courts of this nature were some time ago brought under European colonial rule. Their courts were soon modified by and subordinated to European colonial courts, which were more regulatory in nature. The example we use is that of the Barotse judicial system, as described by Max Gluckman. The Barotse made up a multiethnic state in southern Africa that at the time of Gluckman's study in the 1940s had been under British rule for forty years. More serious offenses had been removed by the British from the jurisdiction of this court. Despite these factors, the basic Barotse legal concepts aptly illustrate this type of court system.

The Barotse state had two capitals—a northern capital, where the king resided, and a subordinate southern capital, ruled by a princess. All villages in the state were attached to one or the other of these capitals. The

*The British integrated existing native court systems of Africa into their colonial administrations. Here a policeman and a local headman preside over a meeting in Botswana.*

capitals were identical in structure; each had a palace and a council house. Courts of law were held in the council house.

The titular head of the court was the ruler; in practice the ruler seldom was present at trials. In the center at the back of the house was the dais, or raised platform, for the ruler to be seated on if present. There were three ranked groupings of judges. The highest-ranking group of judges were the *indunas,* or "councilors," who sat to the right of the dais. The second highest ranking group was the *likombwa,* or "stewards," who sat to the left. These two groups were divided into senior members, who sat in the front, and junior members, who sat behind. The third group consisted of princes and the husbands of the princesses, who represented their wives. This group sat at a right angle to the likombwa.

A case was introduced by a plaintiff, who was allowed to state his or her grievance at length with no interruption; the defendant was then allowed the same privilege. The statements of witnesses for both sides followed. There were no attorneys for either side; the judges questioned and cross-examined the witnesses. After all the testimony had been heard the judges began to give their opinions, starting with the most junior indunas, followed by the others in order of increasing seniority. The last judge to speak was the senior induna, who passed judgment on the case, subject to the ruler's approval.

## BOX 13.1

## MURDER AMONG THE CHEYENNE

The killing of one Cheyenne by another Cheyenne was not only a "sin" that "polluted" the murderer and endangered the well-being of the tribe but also a crime against the society. This pollution of the sacred arrows caused the game animals that Cheyenne depended on for their subsistence to shun their hunting territory. A killing of one Cheyenne by another required the ritual purification of the sacred arrows. However, not every killing was considered a criminal act. On hearing of a killing within the band, the members of the Council of Forty-four assembled. Exactly how and what they discussed in such cases we shall never know; but the council members had to decide when a killing was to be treated as a murder: Was suicide murder? Was abortion murder? Was a killing ever justifiable? Was drunkenness a mitigating circumstance? If the council determined that a murder had taken place, the chiefs ordered the immediate banishment of the murderer. Such banishment usually included not only the murderer but his or her family, and sometimes friends who went along vol-

untarily. This banishment usually lasted between five and ten years. During the period of exile the banished individual usually lived with a friendly group of Arapahos or Dakotas.

The act of a Cheyenne taking his or her own life was not typically considered murder. Several cases are known of Cheyenne women committing suicide for what were considered trivial reasons. Such cases were not considered murder, and as far as can be determined, the sacred arrows were not renewed. In other instances, however, suicide was treated as murder. For example, one mother became infuriated when her daughter eloped with a young man of whom she did not approve. The mother found the girl and beat her with a whip while dragging her home. Inside the tepee the girl

seized a gun and shot herself. In another case a young girl divorced her husband and returned to her parents' home. At some later time her mother found the girl participating in a young persons' dance and beat her; the girl subsequently hung herself. In both cases the chiefs ruled that the girls were driven to suicide by their mothers, who were thus considered the murderesses. In both cases the sacred arrows were renewed, and the mothers were banished.

Was a killing ever justifiable? In one case a man attempted to rape his daughter, who resisted and used a knife to kill her father. The sacred arrows were renewed, but the chiefs did not order the girl banished, nor did the people treat her as a murderess. In another case a man named Winnebago took the wife of another man, who retaliated by taking one of Winnebago's wives. Winnebago was enraged and killed the second man; the murderer was then banished. After his return from banishment Winnebago argued with and killed a second man, so he

*continued on next page*

In judging a case a reasonable-man model was used. With the Barotse the reasonableness of behavior was related to the social and kinship relationships of the individuals involved. Also, a breach of the law usually did not happen in isolation, and many individuals were at fault; so one case frequently led to a number of related cases. In passing judgment and imposing sanctions the judges considered numerous factors. One of the most important factors was the kinship relationship between parties. The judges attempted to restore the relationship and reconcile the parties—but not without blaming those who had committed wrongs and not without imposing sanctions. The judges' opinions frequently

took the form of sermons on proper behavior. As Gluckman (1973, 22) notes:

Implicit in the reasonable man is the upright man, and moral issues in these relationships are barely differentiated from legal issues. This is so even though . . . [they] distinguish "legal" rules, which the . . . [court] has power to enforce or protect, from "moral" rules which it has not power to enforce or protect. But the judges are reluctant to support the person who is right in law, but wrong in justice, and may seek to achieve justice by indirect . . . action.

Courts of mediation have great potential for meeting the basic social purpose of the law, which is the maintewas banished again. While living among the Arapaho, Winnebago became involved in a dispute with a Cheyenne named Rising Fire, who knew of Winnebago's murders and therefore shot Winnebago out of fear. Although the facts are unclear, it appears that Rising Fire was not exiled for this killing. Thus, under some circumstances, such as incestuous rape and the fear of a known murderer, the chiefs thought that killing was justifiable. In such instances the sacred arrows had to be renewed, but the killer was not exiled.

Was drunkenness a mitigating circumstance? During a drunken brawl Cries-Yia-Eya killed Chief Eagle. In another case, during a drunken party, Porcupine Bear stabbed Little Creek and then called on his relatives to stab Little Creek as well. They did so and killed Little Creek. Cries-Yia-Eya and Porcupine Bear and his guilty relatives were banished by the chiefs; drunkenness was not a defense for murder.

The chiefs were faced with a second issue regarding Little Creek's killers. After their banishment Porcupine Bear and his relatives had continued to stay close to the band camp. When the tribe organized a revenge attack on the Kiowas, Porcupine Bear and his relatives kept their distance but followed along with the other Cheyenne. In the attack on the Kiowas, Porcupine Bear and his six relatives distinguished themselves by bravely attacking first and killing about thirty Kiowas. What about war honors for acts of bravery accomplished during banishment? The council ruled that exiles could not receive recognition for their military acts, no matter how courageous they might be. In a sense, during their period of banishment they were not Cheyenne.

Was abortion murder? In one case a fetus was found near a Cheyenne camp. An investigation by a warrior society discovered that a young girl had concealed her pregnancy. The young girl was banished, but only until after the sacred arrows had been renewed. Thus the chiefs considered abortion to be a less serious type of murder that required a shorter period of banishment.

The chiefs had to answer many other types of questions concerning murder and banishment. About 1855 one of the chiefs, a member of the Council of Forty-four, killed another Cheyenne. The sacred arrows were renewed, and the chief was banished; but what was to be done about his position on the council? The council ruled that the man could not be removed from office and that he remained a chief even though he could not participate in the council.

From the discussion of these cases emerges some of the reasoning behind Cheyenne legal decisions. The chiefs considered a range of factors in reaching their final determinations. Murder included not merely the cold-blooded killing of one Cheyenne by another; it also included abortion and acts that compelled one to commit suicide. At the same time, the chiefs thought that in particular instances killing was justifiable, but that intoxication at the time was not a mitigating factor. ◆

*SOURCE:* Llewellyn and Hoebel (1941).

nance of group cohesiveness. There is one serious drawback: Such a system is workable only in a culturally homogeneous political unit; that is, it works only if the judges and the parties involved share the same basic norms and values.

COURTS OF REGULATION.    In the second millennium B.C. the Code of Hammurabi, the earliest known set of written laws, was created in Babylon. The code covered a variety of laws. One section dealt with physicians. It set the prices to be charged for various types of operations, based on the ability of individuals to pay. It also decreed, among other things, that if a surgeon operated on an individual using a bronze knife and the patient died or lost his eyesight, the surgeon's hand was to be cut off. The laws defined in the Code of Hammurabi reflect the emergence of regulatory laws. The role of the court was no longer to merely arbitrate disputes and strive for reconciliation but to define the rights and duties of members of an increasingly heterogeneous community.

Courts of regulation were a natural outgrowth of state-level polities, which evolved socially and economically distinct classes and encompassed numerous culturally distinct peoples. As relationships between individuals in the population became depersonalized, the law, too, became increasingly depersonalized. This change in the nature of law was compounded by the political incorporation of diverse peoples who frequently had conflicting cultural norms and values. The use of a reasonable-man model is workable only as long as there is a general consensus on what is "reasonable." In increasingly complex and stratified societies the possibility of such consensus declined. Mediation of disputes works well in small kinship-based societies, where all parties recognize the need for reconciliation through compromise. In sharply divided societies the need for mediation is not as great because reconciliation in itself is not seen as a gain. Compromise is viewed only in terms of what is lost. Laws were thus created to bring order and stability to the interactions between individuals, particularly between individuals who were not social equals. With law divorced from social norms and values, justice was no longer simply a moral or ethical issue but came to be viewed in terms of consistency, or precedent.

The separation of law from social norms and values also allowed for the "politicization" of the laws. Laws were created to serve political ends, as various groups vied with one another for the creation of laws that would protect, express, or further their own goals, interests, and values. This situation is particularly evident in multiethnic and religious and economically diverse state-level systems such as that of the United States. Given the cultural pluralism, religious diversity, and economic inequality of the United States, it would be impossible to create a code of laws that could equally protect the interests of all classes and that would be consistent with the norms and values of all groups. As a result, many people find themselves subject to laws and sanctions, many of which they judge either immoral or unethical; at times people find that laws violate their own cultural values. We see this with the right-to-life advocates who think that abortion is murder and thus should be made illegal. We see this with groups who oppose capital punishment on the grounds that the state does not have the right to kill individuals. During the Vietnam war we saw it with the draft resisters who argued that the state did not have the right to order men to fight in a war that they considered immoral. Less obvious is the manner in which numerous ethnic minorities, notably Native Americans, subordinate their cultural norms and values to comply with the legal system. With the emergence of states and courts of regulation, law ceased to be an expression of social norms and values and became their molder.

---

## SUMMARY

In this chapter we discussed two distinct but overlapping cultural institutions: political organization and social control. Humans live in cooperative groups. Group action—in both economic and social activities—is a prerequisite for the survival of the population. To be effective, group activities must have leadership and organization, which are the basis for political structure. At the same time, individual differences, conflict, and competition within the group must be controlled and channeled in such a manner that the internal cohesiveness and cooperation of the individual members of the group are maintained—thus the need for social control.

Four major categories of political organization are found: bands, tribes, chiefdoms, and states. Found among foraging societies, the band is the simplest and least formal level of political organization. Two forms of band organization exist: simple bands and composite bands. In simple bands the highest level of political organization is the extended family, with the highest level of political leadership being the heads of the various families. These simple bands are economically self-sufficient and politically autonomous. Because a simple band has as its core a group of related individuals, band members are forced to seek spouses from outside the band; they are exogamous units. Thus kinship ties through marriage serve as the primary link between bands. Simple bands most commonly are found among foragers who depend on the hunting of game animals that are present in small numbers year-round.

Composite bands are larger than simple bands and include a number of distinct families. Leadership in composite bands is vested in "big men," or informal leaders, who have influence but not authority. Composite bands most often are found among foragers who depend on the hunting of migratory herd animals.

At the tribal level formal institutions transcend local residence groups and bind the geographically scattered members of the society into a cohesive unit. The key element in tribal societies is sodalities, which may be either kinship-based, as in the case of clans, or nonkinship-based, as in the case of warrior societies or age grades. Leadership in such groups is more structured, with formal political offices.

Chiefdoms have formal, hereditary leadership with centralized political control and authority. The associated redistributive economic exchange system focused on the chief serves to integrate economically the various communities within the political unit.

The state is the most complex level of political organization. States have centralized power and control, but the key characteristic of a state is the presence of a bureaucracy—individuals acting on behalf of the political elite, thus enabling the centralized power figures to maintain control of a greater number of individuals.

Social control consists of the various methods used to control and channel the behavior of individual members of a society into approved behavior. Law and legal systems are merely the highest level of social control. Law is defined as having four attributes: (1) authority, (2) obligatio, (3) intention of universal application, and (4) sanction. By this definition all societies have law. All legal systems consist of two elements: substantive law is concerned with the types of unacceptable behavior and their associated sanctions, and procedural law is concerned with handling breaches of substantive law and imposing sanctions.

In societies without centralized political systems legal systems are self-help. In self-help systems the responsibility and authority for determining a breach of the law and imposition of the proper sanction fall to the victim or his or her family (or both). As we discussed, this system is not as arbitrary as we might think. In the case of murder or killing the result may be a feud between families; but a feud—sharply distinguished from a war—is part of the legal process.

Law in societies with centralized political systems is handled by courts. Court systems in turn usually can be categorized as either courts of mediation or courts of regulation. In relatively homogeneous societies most court systems take as their primary objective the mediation of disputes between individuals and the restoration of harmonious social relationships. In more heterogeneous groups courts usually become more regulatory in nature, with formally defined laws and sanctions.

# KEY TERMS

| | |
|---|---|
| simple bands | law |
| composite bands | procedural law |
| tribes | substantive law |
| chiefdoms | self-help legal systems |
| states | court legal systems |
| big men | feud |
| influence | incipient court systems |
| authority | courts of mediation |
| sodalities | courts of regulation |
| social control | reasonable-man model |

# SUGGESTED READINGS

Cohen, R., and Elman Service, eds. *Origins of the State: The Anthropology of Political Evolution.* Philadelphia: Institute for the Study of Human Issues, 1978.

> *A collection of essays from various perspectives examining the development of state-level political systems.*

Fried, Morton. *The Evolution of Political Society.* New York: Random House, 1967.

> *A theoretical study that traces the development of political systems from egalitarian societies through ranked to stratified and state-level societies.*

Hoebel, E. Adamson. *The Law of Primitive Man.* Cambridge, Mass.: Harvard University Press, 1964.

> *The first major comparative study of non-Western legal systems. Although somewhat dated, it remains a classic study.*

Mair, Lucy. *Primitive Government.* Baltimore: Penguin, 1966.
> *Concerned exclusively with African peoples, this is an excellent introduction to preindustrial political systems.*

Newman, Katherine S. *Law and Economic Organization: A Comparative Study of Pre-Industrial Societies.* Cambridge: Cambridge University Press, 1983.

> *A cross-cultural analysis of sixty societies to show that legal institutions systematically vary with economic organization.*

Service, Elman. *Primitive Social Organization: An Evolutionary Perspective.* New York: Random House, 1966.
> *Traces the evolution of political systems from bands to chiefdoms.*

**The following ethnographies are excellent descriptions of political and/or legal systems within particular societies.**

Barth, Fredrik. *Political Leadership among Swat Pathans.* London: Athlone, 1959.
> *A description and theoretical analysis of political life of a people on the Pakistan and Afghanistan border.*

Fortes, M., and E. E. Evans-Pritchard, eds. *African Political Systems*. London: Oxford University Press, 1940.

    *A collection of short descriptions of the political organization of eight African societies.*

Gluckman, Max. *The Ideas in Barotse Jurisprudence*. Manchester: Manchester University Press, 1965.

    ————. *The Judicial Process among the Barotse*. Manchester: Manchester University Press, 1973.

    *These two studies of the Barotse of Zambia not only describe a system in a non-Western state but also—and more important—illustrate the legal reasoning used in their court systems.*

Hoebel, E. Adamson. *The Political Organization and Law–Ways of the Comanche Indians*. American Anthropological Association, Memoir 54, 1940.

    *Good description of the political structure and legal system of a band-level society.*

Kuper, Hilda. *The Swazi: A South African Kingdom*. 2d ed. New York: Holt, Rinehart and Winston, 1986.

    *An excellent short ethnography of Swaziland, now an independent nation. Has a good discussion of recent changes.*

Leach, Edmund. *Political Systems of Highland Burma*. Boston: Beacon Press, 1965.

    *Describes the cyclical political changes of the Kachin.*

Llewellyn, Karl, and E. Adamson Hoebel. *The Cheyenne Way*. Norman: University of Oklahoma Press, 1941.

    *One of the best descriptions of the legal system of a tribal society.*

Meggitt, Mervyn J. *Blood Is Their Argument: Warfare among the Mae Enga Tribesmen of the New Guinea Highlands*. Palo Alto, Calif.: Mayfield, 1977.

    *Perhaps the best ethnography ever written about warfare and war-related practices among a preindustrial people.*

## CHAPTER 14

# Social Inequality and Stratification

*Inequality in access to culturally valued rewards characterizes some but not all human societies. This is a New Delhi street shoemaker.*

## CONTENTS

We hold these truths to be self-evident, that all men are created equal, that they are endowed by their creator with certain unalienable Rights . . .

As you can guess by now, whether in fact all "men" are believed to have been created equal depends on which society you happened to have been born into. Whether you have certain "unalienable rights," and the nature of these rights, also varies from people to people. In this chapter we consider another dimension of cultural systems—the differential allocation of rewards.

## SYSTEMS OF EQUALITY AND INEQUALITY

Societies differ in the degree to which there is **inequality** between individuals and groups. *Inequality* refers to the extent to which culturally valued material and social rewards are allocated disproportionately to individuals, families, and other groups.

Before discussing these variations in inequality, it will be helpful to consider the different kinds of rewards that exist. They are broken down into three categories. The most visible reward is *wealth,* or access to or ownership of valued material goods. Another kind of reward is called *power,* or the ability to make others do what you want based on coercion or legitimate authority. A final type of reward is *prestige,* or the respect, esteem, and overt approval granted by others to individuals they consider meritorious. Prestige (or honor) is a social reward, based on judgments about an individual's personal worthiness or the contributions the individual makes to others in the group.

Each of these kinds of rewards varies from people to people. For instance, how individuals and groups acquire power, how the exercise of power is organized, the uses to which power is put, and so forth vary between societies. Similarly, many Americans admire so-called self-made men who have supposedly gained wealth and power through their own drive, talent, and effort, whereas such men would be looked down on as self-centered and ungenerous in many other cultures. Despite the diversity, this typology of rewards is useful because in all cultures the desire for wealth, power, or prestige motivates at least some individuals to "get ahead" of others. But, as we shall see, some cultures inculcate these motivations more than others. And some groups make it possible for ambitious individuals to acquire wealth, power, and prestige, whereas others make it difficult for anyone to accumulate resources and possessions, achieve control over others, and put themselves above their peers socially.

We can classify societies by "how much" inequality they exhibit with respect to wealth, power, and prestige. Imagine a continuum. At one end can be placed societies that feature only slight differences between individuals and groups in access to these rewards. At the other end appear those societies with marked contrasts in access to rewards. In the middle are a myriad of societies that are intermediate between the two extremes: Some have contrasts in prestige but lack significant differences in wealth, for example.

A large body of information has accumulated about inequality in various societies. In 1967, Morton Fried formulated a threefold classification of the kinds and degree of inequality found in diverse human cultures. He labeled the three basic types of inequality **egalitarian, ranked,** and **stratified.** A description and examples of each type appear later in this section. Three points need to be noted about Fried's classification.

First, Fried's three categories have nothing to do with access to rewards based on gender or age. When we call a society *egalitarian,* for example, we do not mean that females and males receive equal or nearly equal rewards, or that elderly people and young people are economically or socially equal. Even in egalitarian societies there are social distinctions based on gender and age (see chapters 12 and 16). Essentially, *egalitarian* means that there are few differences in access to rewards between families or other kinds of kin groups within a society. At the other end of the continuum, in societies we call *stratified,* there are major differences in access to rewards between families and/or kin groups, in addition to any distinctions based on gender or age. For example, as we shall see, the United States is a stratified society, but the class structure of American society crosscuts distinctions based on gender or age. It therefore is possible for the United States to remain a stratified society, even if greater equality based on gender should be achieved in the future.

It also is important to understand that these categories are merely points along a continuous spectrum of systems of inequality. It is impossible to pigeonhole all human societies into one of these types because most fit somewhere in between the three categories. The terms *egalitarian, ranked,* and *stratified* are useful mainly as short descriptions of the kinds and range of variation in inequality found cross-culturally.

Finally, it should be noted that egalitarian-ranked-stratified is the temporal order in which the three forms developed. Until about 10,000 years ago practically everyone on earth lived in egalitarian societies. Ranked societies developed in a few areas about then, and a few thousand years later stratification developed in the great civilizations (see chapters 8, 9, and 13 on the economic and political dimensions of chiefdoms and states). Stratified societies in the next 4,000 to 5,000 years spread throughout most of the world, as some peoples and nations conquered and ruled over others.

## Egalitarian Societies

Egalitarian societies are at the low end of the inequality continuum. There is little noticeable difference in wealth and power between individuals, aside from distinctions based on gender and age. There are always differences in personality, skill at certain tasks, willingness to work, and other personal qualities. Individuals with attractive personalities, unusual talents, and high diligence may receive the esteem of other members of the group; but in egalitarian societies they are unable to transform their admirable personal qualities into power and possessions, for reasons to be discussed.

Mobile foragers such as the Inuit, the western Shoshone, the Hadza, and the !Kung (see chapter 7) are highly egalitarian. James Woodburn identified several reasons why such peoples maintain relatively equal access to social rewards. First, and most obviously, effective adaptation demands frequent seasonal movements of the band or camp, and this high rate of mobility inhibits one's ability to accumulate possessions.

Second, among mobile foragers, individuals are not tied to specific territories but have the right to live in and exploit the resources of a variety of areas to which they have rights of access because of bilateral kin relations (see chapters 9 and 11). They therefore are free simply to leave and live elsewhere if any other individual should attempt to exercise control over their behavior. In fact, interpersonal disputes are among the most commonly reported reasons for the frequent move-

ments of individuals between camps in groups such as the !Kung and Hadza.

Third, the hunting-and-gathering adaptation places a great advantage on sharing of food products. This seems to produce a generalized cultural value on generosity and deprecation of one's own abilities and contributions. Sharing on the principle of generalized reciprocity is *expected* behavior—the recipients of what nonegalitarian peoples might consider largesse seem to feel less compelled to make a return. Indeed, there is strong social pressure not to make oneself stand out as worthy of greater rewards. Among the !Kung, BaMbuti, and Hadza foragers, men who boast about their hunting skill are ridiculed or subject to other kinds of informal sanctions.

Fourth, sharp contrasts in wealth usually develop out of differential control of productive resources, but it is difficult in a nomadic foraging adaptation for any individual or group to maintain exclusive access to the natural resources of a territory or over the labor of other people for a prolonged period, for reasons discussed in chapter 9.

In sum, if individuals have a range of alternatives about where to acquire what they need to survive, if sharing of products is expected and failure to share is socially punished, and if no one can exercise long-term control over necessary resources, then inequality in access to valued rewards does not have much chance of developing. And if it should develop, it does not have much chance of persisting for very long.

Not all foragers are egalitarian. The Indians of the North American Northwest Coast, for instance, developed a ranked society because in this area the abundance of anadromous fish and the relative reliability of their occurrence allowed greater sedentariness and territoriality (see chapter 7). Further, not all mobile foragers were as egalitarian as those just discussed.

Egalitarian people do have leaders. Some individuals serve as leaders of certain kinds of activities because others recognize their special skill at some valuable task or because of special religious or practical knowledge they are believed to possess. Their leadership role is quite informal and limited to the activities in which they have special abilities. And leaders have only influence, not authority (chapter 13). Their influence is derived from their ability to persuade others. Leaders cannot coerce adherence to their decisions, and others may or may not defer to their opinions on some matter. If they do, it is usually because they believe that the leaders' knowledge or skill is superior to their own.

In egalitarian societies leadership does not take the form of political offices for which people compete or to

*Most foraging peoples are egalitarian, partly because their adaptation makes it difficult for any local group to maintain long-term control over culturally valuable resources.*

which certain people automatically succeed. In this respect, egalitarian societies contrast with ranked societies.

## Ranked Societies

In ranked societies there are a fixed number of social positions, usually titles or some kind of formal office, that certain individuals occupy by virtue of birth into families that are culturally considered to have high social status. Certain families, lineages, or clans have the traditional right to have their members hold these titles or offices. High social rank is thus restricted to certain kin groups and is largely or entirely hereditary within those kin groups.

The significance of the fact that rank is mainly hereditary is realized when we contrast ranked with egalitarian societies. In the former, individuals who are born into kin groups culturally defined as lower ranking usually cannot acquire the most valued rewards offered by their societies, regardless of their skill, diligence, ambition, or other personal qualities considered admirable. In the latter, leadership, prestige, and other valued rewards can be attained by almost anyone (often restricted to males, however), regardless of their birth.

In one of the most common types of ranked societies all kin groups are ranked relative to one another: Each group has its own unique rank relative to each and every other kin group. Further, within each kin group each and every member is ranked relative to all others, usually on the principle of genealogical seniority (elders being superior in rank to younger people). The most valued positions that bring the highest rewards in prestige, wealth, and power are held by the highest-ranking individuals of the highest-ranking kin group. This way of ranking individuals and kin groups is most well documented for several ancient Polynesian chiefdoms.

An excellent example of a ranked society is Tikopia, a tiny Pacific island whose kinship system is described in chapter 11. In the 1920s, Tikopia's 1,200 persons were divided into four patrilineal clans, each with its own chief who exercised authority over his clanmates. Each clan in turn was divided into several patrilineages. Every Tikopian patrilineage had a head, who was believed to be the oldest living male descendant of the man who founded the lineage about four to six generations ago. Alongside this ranking of individuals within a single lineage, the various lineages of a single clan were ranked relative to one another. One lineage of each clan, supposedly the original, "senior" lineage from which the "junior" lineages had budded off, was considered the noble lineage. Members of other lineages of the clan had to defer socially to members of the noble lineage, according to Tikopian standards of etiquette. In addition, the noble lineage of each clan selected one of its members to be the chief of the whole clan.

Chiefs and other members of the noble Tikopia lineages had little more wealth than anyone else. The nobility did receive tribute from other lineages of their clan, but they gave away most of it in the many public activities that they organized and financed through redistribution (see chapter 9). The chief and nobility of each clan had no way to deny access to land and ocean resources to members of other lineages, for each lineage was considered to have inalienable rights to certain pieces of land. The Tikopia nobility, then, received much prestige and token tribute from other islanders, but they did not use this tribute to enrich themselves, and their sphere of power was limited. They were honored, but their wealth and power were not great. It is mainly in this respect that ranked societies contrast with stratified societies.

## Stratified Societies

Stratified societies are at the high end of the inequality continuum. A society is said to be stratified if

◆ there are marked inequalities in access to all three kinds of rewards: wealth, power, and prestige;
◆ this inequality is based primarily on unequal access to productive resources such as the land and tools people need to make their living; that is, a few people control access to the resources others need to survive at culturally acceptable levels;
◆ unequal access to rewards has a strong tendency to be heritable throughout the generations, regardless of the personal qualities or aptitudes of individuals.

The last point means that most individuals (and families) do not move very far up or down the social ladder during their lifetimes. Although upward social mobility for individuals and families may be theoretically possible in stratified societies, it is uncommon. This is because peoples' **life chances**—their chances to receive rewards in proportion to their talents, efforts, and so on—are largely determined by the social stratum into which individuals happen to have been born. As in ranked societies, hereditary factors are the main determinant of where one fits into the social hierarchy.

Stratified societies vary in the cultural ideas they have about the possibilities of social mobility. In some, such as North American and other contemporary Western and Western-derived democracies, upward or downward mobility is considered possible, although numerous studies have shown it to be uncommon. In others, especially in preindustrial societies, one's class membership is culturally considered fixed, often because of beliefs that existing inequalities are hereditary or ordained by supernatural beings.

In stratified societies individuals, families, and other groups are differentiated on the basis of their relative access to rewards. A social group whose members share about the same degree of access to rewards is called a *social stratum*. The two major kinds of strata are **classes** and **castes**.

*Appalachian children have poorer life chances than do children of middle- or upper-class Americans.*

Two general differences between class and caste systems stand out. First, by definition, castes are endogamous groups: They have cultural norms or laws that require individuals to marry within their caste. As discussed in chapter 10, rules that mandate marriage within one's own group have the effect of maintaining the distinctiveness of the group relative to other groups. This is because there is no possibility of upward mobility through intercaste marriage, and because there are no children who have potentially anomalous group membership. Class societies allow an individual to marry someone of a different class; in fact, intermarriage between classes commonly is an avenue of social mobility. It follows from the endogamous nature of caste that one's caste membership is theoretically hereditary: One is born into the caste of one's parents, one marries someone in the same caste, and one's children are likewise born into and remain members of one's own caste. (We say "theoretically" because sometimes social reality differs from cultural norms, in caste societies as in all others.)

Second, caste systems have some kind of prohibition against contact between members of different castes. High-caste members, for example, sometimes believe that they will be spiritually polluted if they should come into contact with members of other castes. Indeed, they often must perform rituals to cleanse themselves after accidental contacts.

Both of these general differences mean that castes have more permanent membership and more rigid social boundaries than classes. This does not mean that it is easy to tell whether some particular stratified society "has" castes or classes. Some societies have elements of both. For instance, some scholars have suggested that black-white relations in the American South were more caste-like than class-like until the mid-twentieth century. There was no possibility of upward mobility into the white "caste" for blacks because no one could overcome the cultural stigma of black skin color. Interracial marriage was legally prohibited or culturally taboo, so that the two races were endogamous. Explicit laws against certain kinds of "intercaste" contacts and interactions—known as *segregation laws*—forced blacks to live apart from whites, forbade them to enter certain white business establishments and public restrooms, made them send their children to all-black schools, and so forth.

## CASTES IN TRADITIONAL INDIA

The most well known caste system is that of India. India's caste system is complex and varies from region to region, so we can present only a generalized picture. There are four main caste categories, or *varnas*. (A varna is not itself a caste.) Each varna is ranked relative to the others in honor and degree of ritual purity, and each is broadly associated with certain kinds of occupations.

The highest varna is the Brahmins, or priests and scholars; next is the varna of nobles and warriors, the Kshatriyas; third are the Vaishas, or merchants and artisans; and ranked lowest are the farmers, craftspeople, and certain other laborers, the Shudras. A fifth category—outside and ranked below the varna—are the untouchables, to whom falls work considered polluting to the varna.

The varnas (which, incidentally, first arose in the second millennium B.C. when the Aryans invaded and conquered what is now northern India) are the largest, most inclusive categories into which India traditionally

is divided. The villages in which most people live are divided into much smaller and specific occupational groupings called *jati* (castes, as the term usually is used). For example, in a particular village the Shudra varna might be represented by several jati with names such as weaver, potter, and tailor. There are thousands of these castes in India, distributed among the many thousands of villages, with each village containing a variable number of castes.

To better understand Indian castes, it is necessary to understand the basic tenets of Hinduism, the traditional religion of India. (Hinduism is incredibly diverse and complex, so here we can present only a simplified depiction of it.) Hindu religion holds that spiritual souls are reborn into different physical bodies at various stages of their existence—this is the doctrine of *reincarnation*. Souls ultimately desire an end to the cycle of earthly birth, death, and rebirth, but to achieve this end each soul must be reborn many times into many bodies, both animal and human. Souls attempt to move up the "ladder" of reincarnation, from lower forms of life to higher ones: from animals to humans (of various ranked castes) to gods.

The particular body (be it human or animal) that a soul is born into depends on how closely that soul adhered to proper standards of behavior in previous lifetimes. For souls that had made it up to human forms in their previous incarnation, these standards include avoidance of activities that Hindus believe are polluting. Among the most polluting activities are handling and working with animal carcasses or the bodies of deceased humans, touching excrement and other waste materials, dealing with childbirth, and eating meat. People who regularly perform these activities are not only polluted themselves, but anyone of a higher caste who comes into physical contact with them likewise becomes polluted and must bathe ritually to cleanse himself or herself. One's present place in society—one's "station in life"—varies with the degree to which one is associated with pure and impure activities. In turn, because of reincarnation, whether one is associated with pure or impure activities depends on one's behavior in previous lives—such as the degree to which one has allowed oneself to become polluted or failed to cleanse oneself.

India's traditional caste hierarchy is so intimately tied up with Hindu doctrines that the two are almost inseparable. First, the caste into which one is born depends on the behavior of one's soul in previous incarnations. People are low caste either because their soul has not yet been through enough lifetimes to have reached a higher form, or because their sins in a previous lifetime merit

*The Hindu religion regards certain things and activities as spiritually defiling or polluting. Ritual bathing removes the pollution, as here in the Ganges River.*

reincarnation into a low caste. In the present life people have what they deserve. Thus all "men" were not created equal, in the Hindu world view; it is legitimate that some castes have more power and privilege and more status and wealth than others.

Second, caste categories are associated with certain occupations. Each village contains a number of castes, most of which are named according to the occupation traditionally performed by their members. Thus a village might include castes of priests, merchants, blacksmiths, potters, tailors, farmers, weavers, carpenters, washers, barbers, leather workers, and "sweepers" (the last refers to those who remove human waste matter from peoples' houses). Just as activities are ranked in Hindu beliefs according to their degree of purity and impurity, so occupations and those who perform them are ranked. Working with animal carcasses is defiling, so leather working is a defiling occupation and leather workers are so polluting as to be untouchable. The same applies to sweeping: People who remove human wastes from houses or spread excrement over village fields are polluted, and their touch pollutes those of higher castes. Therefore, members of the leather working, sweeping, and other castes associated with defiling occupations were traditionally untouchable. (Discrimination against people of untouchable ancestry is illegal in modern India, although it still occurs.) Untouchables usually live in their own special section of the village, separate from members of higher castes. Because they contaminate temples by their entry, they cannot go inside a temple. Their touch contaminates water, so they have to use separate wells. These and other restrictions on their behavior sometimes are extreme.

However, members of high-ranking castes, such as priests, landowners, warriors, and merchants, need the services of low-ranking castes. Again, this is because Hinduism defines some activities essential for life as polluting, so castes who would be defiled by these activities need lower castes to perform these services for them. The bullocks essential for farming die, so someone has to remove dead cattle from the village; Brahmin women give birth just as other women, so the women of some low-ranking caste have to serve as midwives, since other Brahmin women would become polluted by so serving; everyone passes bodily wastes, so someone must remove these wastes from the houses of high-caste members lest they pollute their occupants. Accordingly, each caste has its proper role and function in the economic, social, and religious life of the village.

Likewise, each caste has its religiously ordained duties to the other castes. In Hindu beliefs one's soul is reincarnated into a higher or lower form partly according to how well one fulfills the obligations of his or her caste in the present life. Leather workers, for instance, cannot do much to improve their lot in this life; but by faithfully fulfilling their obligations to members of higher castes their souls will receive higher reincarnations in future bodies.

In much of India (especially in the north) caste membership provides the organizational basis for some kinds of economic cooperation. Individual members of the various castes represented in a region are involved in hereditary patron-client relationships with one another known as *jajmani*. A village farmer, for example, might require the services of a blacksmith, carpenter, leather worker, potter, tailor, barber, or other specialized craftspeople or workers. The farmer does not have to search for someone to perform these jobs for him, nor do those who perform these services have to make special deals with other farmers to obtain their livelihood; rather, the farmer and the individual members of the castes who specialize in the appropriate occupation inherit these "contracts" from their parents. So during the course of the year, the blacksmith fixes the farmer's plow, the leather worker makes the shoes for the farmer's family, the barber cuts their hair, the washers do their laundry, and so on.

These specialists are not paid each time they perform their tasks. At the end of the agricultural season, when the farmer's grain is harvested, each specialist receives a portion of the total harvest. The amount of grain each specialist receives is supposedly fixed by tradition: so much is sent to the temple priests, so much given to the blacksmith, so much to the leather worker, and so on. Each specialist has a jajmani relationship with many other people and acquires food or other goods or services from each of them according to the traditional allotment of the occupation. Many members of a caste inherit the jajmani relations of their parents, which provides them with patrons whom they serve and with clients who serve them. Individuals of various castes in a village or region thus are involved in economic relationships with one another, exchanging their specialized services or goods for those of other castes.

One should not conclude that intercaste relations are harmonious, or that the complementary tasks associated

*A member of the barber caste in Rajasthan trims the moustache of another villager. Among traditional village Hindus, caste and occupation are closely related.*

with each caste are entirely mutually beneficial. A great deal of friction and outright conflict exist between individual members of different castes. In fact, local castes as a whole group sometimes organize themselves with a council to pursue their common interests. It is even possible for a caste to improve its rank in the local caste hierarchy, despite the normatively unchanging relative position of castes. This is done in several ways, including adopting the customs and prohibitions of a higher caste and "reinventing" the history of one's caste to make it seem that it originally came from a higher varna.

 ## CLASSES

Class societies are subdivided into strata—the classes—that have different degrees of access to material goods or control over land, tools, and other kinds of productive resources; have different degrees of control over or access to the public decision-making apparatus of government; and are ranked by esteem or respect from the society at large. We first discuss an unusual example of a preindustrial class system and then consider classes in industrial societies.

### Preindustrial Class Systems: The Natchez

We already have mentioned some examples of class-stratified preindustrial societies, such as the Inca (chapter 9) and other representatives of the state level of political structure (chapter 13). Here we shall discuss only one additional example.

In the lower Mississippi valley of North America lived the Natchez, a society of about 5,000 persons known to us only through ethnohistorical reconstruction. Until their society was destroyed in a war with the French in 1731, the Natchez had one of the most unusual and interesting class systems of the preindustrial world. Among these horticultural, matrilineal people were two major classes: rulers and commoners. The rulers in turn were divided into three ranked social categories: Suns, Nobles, and Honored People.

The highest-ranking member of the Sun rank was the Great Sun. He and his matrilineage were believed to be at the apex of the society because the Natchez believed that God (the real Sun) had sent the Great Sun and his wife to rule them, giving them their laws and the sacred fire. Because of his divine origin, the Great Sun assumed the attributes of a living god and had great authority over the lives of the people. As the link between humans and God, the Great Sun had ritual duties. Each morning he went to the temple of the sacred fire and blew tobacco smoke toward the rising sun and in the four cardinal directions, to bless the people.

The Great Sun also had wealth and many privileges denied to others. His large house, complete with a wooden throne, sat atop an earthen mound located across the plaza from the temple of the sacred fire. When traveling he sat on a litter carried by eight servants. A large number of other servants, who were given to him at his birth by their parents, served his household, hunted for him, and planted his fields. Only he could wear a beautiful headdress made from black and white feathers. He received and redistributed game killed on communal hunts. The first corn harvested from the fields was presented to him. He had substantial political control, because he could order the execution of anyone whose actions offended him.

The Great Sun was a member of the small Sun matrilineage (with between eleven and seventeen members). At the death of a Great Sun a new Great Sun was chosen from among the male members of this lineage who were "without physical blemish." Other Suns lived in houses near the residence of the Great Sun. Like him, they had many privileges, including servants whose work freed them from most physical labor and the right to wear fine headdresses that marked their rank. The senior female member of the Sun matrilineage, called White Woman, also was carried around on a litter.

Other members of the ruler class—the Nobles and the Honored People—also had certain privileges. Noble and Honored People males could wear black breechclouts, whereas commoners were allowed to wear only white. Children of the ruling class wore two or three sacred pearls from the temple around their necks, whereas commoner children went naked. Although all Natchez were tatooed on their faces, rulers were elaborately tatooed on their bodies and limbs as well.

Suns, Nobles, and Honored People filled virtually all positions conferring authority and leadership, including the status of Great War Chief, temple priests, village chiefs, and councilors to the Great Sun. The commoner class was thus excluded from positions that carried privileges and authority.

But—and this next feature was what made this system so unusual—Natchez marriage rules required all rulers to take their spouses from among the commoners. (Because there were many more commoners than nobles, most commoners married one another, how-

ever.) If a Sun woman married a commoner man, their offspring became Suns (because of matrilineal descent). But if a Sun man married a commoner woman, their children received the status of Noble. So Nobles were the children of marriages between Sun men and commoner women. When in turn a Noble woman married—as she was required to do—a commoner man, their children remained Nobles. But the children of Noble men and commoner women dropped to the status of Honored People, the lowest rank in the ruler class. When an Honored People man married a commoner, their children dropped to the class of commoners, whereas the children of Honored People women remained Honored People. As you can see, in essence children took the rank of their mother if she was in the ruler class; if their father was a ruler and their mother a commoner, their rank was one notch below that of their father. No satisfactory explanation for this unusual (and possibly unique) class system has been offered.

The Natchez class system allowed for the possibility of mobility: The offspring of any commoner who married one of the rulers would rise in class. In addition to interclass mobility by means of marriage, commoner men who distinguished themselves in war could be advanced into the rank of Honored Person, as could their wives and children. Finally, at the death of a Great Sun a commoner family could become Honored People by offering one of their children as a sacrifice.

## Industrial Class Systems: The United States

In industrial societies upward mobility between classes is possible through interclass marriage, personal talent and effort, or good luck. In actuality, few individuals rise much higher in the class system than their parents. Members of different classes have differential access to the material resources (income, wealth), social contacts, and cultural knowledge (education, "social graces") that are valued and rewarded in the culture.

The kind of work one does often is assumed to be the best single overall indication of class membership. (Is this perhaps the reason one of the first questions adults ask new acquaintances is, "What kind of work do you do?") Occupation is popularly assumed to be the main determinant of income, and one's income influences so much else: overall life-style, the access of one's children to education, the kinds of individuals with whom one associates, the kind of church or club to which one belongs, and so on.

Sociological studies reveal how highly Americans regard certain occupational categories. Below is a sample of twenty-five occupations, listed from highest to lowest prestige ranking:

- ✦ physician
- ✦ college professor
- ✦ attorney
- ✦ stockbroker
- ✦ registered nurse
- ✦ high school teacher
- ✦ social worker
- ✦ electrician
- ✦ plumber
- ✦ police officer
- ✦ dental assistant
- ✦ carpenter
- ✦ welder
- ✦ mechanic
- ✦ truck driver
- ✦ hairdresser
- ✦ cashier
- ✦ assembly-line worker
- ✦ housekeeper
- ✦ coal miner
- ✦ waitress/waiter
- ✦ babysitter
- ✦ garbage collector

## BOX 14.1

# OCCUPATIONAL PRESTIGE IN THE UNITED STATES

- ✦ janitor
- ✦ hotel chambermaid

Apparently, the main influence on how people rank occupational categories is how much formal education is required to assume the occupational role: Generally, "brain work" is ranked above "manual work."

The interesting thing about these prestige ranks is that a great many of them do not reflect income levels typical of the occupation. College professors, nurses, teachers, and dental assistants receive significantly higher prestige than plumbers, carpenters, welders, and assembly-line workers. Yet, largely because of unionization of the latter occupations, many of them earn more yearly income than those who do "brain work." This is not a contradiction—because being in a high-prestige professional career offers other, nonmaterial rewards—but it does make it difficult to decide exactly to which "class" some individuals and families belong. ✦

*SOURCE:* Tischler 1990.

---

Unfortunately for our desire to make things neat and orderly, there are problems with defining a class on the basis of occupation or any other single criterion. For one thing, different criteria used to define class membership do not always agree. For instance, people do not agree on the prestige of many occupations—attorneys are despised by some but granted high prestige by others. The same applies to politicians, physicians, academicians, police, and numerous other professionals. Further, the degree to which some occupation is respected by the population at large does not always reflect the relative wealth and/or access to power of those who practice it (see Box 14.1).

So it often is difficult to decide to which class some individual belongs. One way around this ambiguity, favored by some sociologists, is to separate the three kinds of rewards from one another and define a separate class ranking for each reward. We can distinguish classes defined on the basis of prestige (*status groups,* as some call them) and on the basis of income or wealth (*economic classes*), for instance. The definitions and methods used for ranking the classes depend, to some extent, on the interest of the social scientist as well as on the nature of the society under study.

In the United States probably the most widely accepted approach to stratification uses the concept of economic class. Individuals and families are placed into classes based on their wealth. Using wealth as the primary basis of class ranking has four major advantages. First, it is more measurable than other indications of class membership (although cash income alone does not measure it adequately).

Second, wealth is the best single indication of the overall benefits individuals and families are receiving from their citizenship in the nation. Money cannot buy you love, happiness, or many other things, but it can buy you much of what Americans value.

Third, wealth generally (but not completely) matches up with an individual's or a family's access to what Marxians call the *means of production* (see chapter 4). That is, high wealth is correlated with ownership of productive resources such as factories, financial institutions, and income-producing real estate. By and large, the very wealthy people in the country own the nation's large businesses. They either built their companies themselves or their ancestors made fortunes through business activity and passed their ownership along to the current generation.

Fourth, wealth levels broadly determine people's access to political power. Through campaign contributions the wealthy have a greater say in who gets nominated and elected to important offices. Through lobbying efforts the rich enjoy greater influence on the laws and policies of the nation than their numbers warrant. By providing much of the funding for think tanks and other public advisory groups, the wealthy subsidize the expertise of many economists, political scientists, sociologists, and other social scientists who advise government. Many appointed officials in the executive branch of the federal government are members of the elite. Some appointees move back and forth between business and government service regularly. (These generalizations are documented convincingly in William Domhoff's [1983] book *Who Rules America Now?*)

For these and other reasons, we can learn most about inequality in the United States by focusing our discussion on the distribution of wealth. Most Americans know something about economic inequality in their country. If we consider annual cash income, for example, the poorest fifth of Americans received only 4.6 percent of the nation's total income in 1990, whereas the richest fifth received 44.3 percent (see Table 14.1). This distribution of annual income has been quite consistent over the past thirty to forty years. Year after year the poorest 20 percent of Americans earn around 5 percent of all the money earned in the country, whereas the richest 20 percent earn more than 40 percent. The wealthiest 5 percent of Americans received more than 17 percent of all income earned in 1990, and this percentage also has altered little over the past thirty years.

That great wealth and poverty coexist in the United States is well known. What is less well known—or at any rate less talked about—is how much of the nation's wealth is owned by a small minority of its citizens.

TABLE 14.1 Distribution of Family Annual Income in the United States, 1990

| PERCENTAGE OF INCOME EARNED BY | | AMOUNT EARNED, 1990 |
| --- | --- | --- |
| Poorest fifth | 4.6 | Less than $16,846 |
| Second fifth | 10.8 | Between $16,847 and $29,044 |
| Third fifth | 16.6 | Between $29,045 and $42,040 |
| Fourth fifth | 23.8 | Between $42,041 and $61,490 |
| Richest fifth | 44.3 | Over $61,491 |
| Richest 5% | 17.4 | Over $102,358 |

SOURCE: U.S. Bureau of the Census (1992, 450).

Middle-income people, and in fact people who are considered fairly affluent, own little in comparison with the truly wealthy.

Figures on annual income such as those given in Table 14.1 greatly underestimate the degree of economic inequality in the United States. People's material standards of living are not determined in any simple way by their income, nor is their influence over local, state, and national political decision making. Living standards and political influence are more greatly determined by a person's or family's net worth, that is, by all assets (property) minus all indebtedness. Ther are two kinds of assets: *financial* and *tangible*. Financial assets include property such as savings and checking accounts, stocks, bonds, money-market funds, and trusts. Tangible assets include material property such as real estate, houses, automobiles, and other personal property. Like financial assets, tangible assets can be assigned a dollar value equal to what they would be worth if they were sold on the market. The assets a particular family owns are a better measure of its wealth than its annual income. Tangible assets directly affect material standards of living, and both tangible and financial assets represent stored-up purchasing power, since by selling them families can acquire additional money.

In 1983 the Federal Reserve Board conducted a study of the assets and liabilities of a random sample of more than 4,000 American households. The findings of the 1983 study revealed the remarkable inequality in net worth between the wealthiest families and everyone else. The Economic Policy Institute, a private think tank, updated this study in its 1993 report titled *The State of Working America: 1992-3*, written by Lawrence Mishel and Jared Bernstein. The following data are taken from this 1993 report, which summarizes the latest available figures on the distribution of wealth (net worth) for the year 1989.

The report divides American families into the following four economic categories:

✦ Super rich: the 0.5 percent of families with the most wealth
✦ Very rich: the next 0.5 percent of richest families
✦ Rich: the next 9 percent of richest families
✦ Everyone else: the rest of the American families, or 90 percent of all the nation's families

How much of the nation's privately owned wealth is owned by families of these four categories?

✦ The super rich and very rich families (the wealthiest 1 percent) together own 38 percent of all assets.
✦ The rich families own 33 percent of all assets.
✦ Everyone else owns 29 percent of all assets.

The richest 1 percent of American families thus hold 38 percent of the nation's wealth, and the richest 10 percent of families own 71 percent of the nation's wealth. The net worth of the bottom 90 percent of the population is only 29 percent of the wealth under private ownership. The distribution of wealth is thus highly concentrated in the United States.

By comparing the 1983 data with the 1989 data we see that wealth became more concentrated in the 1980s. In 1983 the super rich and very rich families owned 31 percent of all wealth, whereas the bottom 90 percent owned 34 percent of all wealth. So between 1983 and 1989 the richest 1 percent of American families gained an additional 7 percent of the nation's wealth, whereas the 90 percent majority lost 5 percent over the same period. Almost all the wealth gains in the 1980s in fact went to the wealthiest 1 percent of Americans.

Just as important as the fact that wealth is unequally distributed is the nature of the assets owned by the very wealthy and by everyone else. Financial assets represent wealth that produces future income for their owners in the form of interest, dividends, and other returns on savings and investments. How much of American financial assets are owned by the four categories of families?

✦ Super rich families own 37 percent of stock, 64 percent of bonds, 33 percent of trusts, and 34 percent of all real estate not used as the owner's residence.
✦ Very rich families own 9 percent of stock, 9 percent of bonds, 19 percent of trusts, and 10 percent of nonowner-occupied real estate.
✦ Rich families own 37 percent of stock, 21 percent of bonds, 38 percent of trusts, and 37 percent of real estate not occupied by the owner.
✦ Everyone else owns only 16 percent of stocks, 6 percent of bonds, 10 percent of trusts, and 19 percent of real estate not used as their residence.

Putting this information together a little differently, the wealthiest 1 percent of American families own 46 percent of all stocks, 73 percent of all bonds, 52 percent of all trusts, and 44 percent of all real estate not used as the owner's residence. The wealthiest 10 percent of families

*Wealth is unequally distributed in the United States. This is the terrace of a mansion that used to be owned by an Oklahoma oil family.*

*As this homeless man reminds us, in the United States great wealth co-exists with brutal poverty.*

own 84 percent of stocks, 94 percent of bonds, 90 percent of trusts, and 81 percent of nonowner-occupied real property. Again, all these kinds of wealth produce income continuously for their owners. Further, possession of stocks, bonds, trusts, and real estate enormously increases a family's economic security.

## ◫ MAINTAINING INEQUALITY

The persistence of inequality in stratified societies demands an explanation. As the United States illustrates, a small percentage of the population typically controls most of the wealth and wields a great deal of influence over public affairs. Why does the relatively underprivileged majority allow them this power and privilege?

One answer is that this question is ethnocentric: Even to ask it assumes that the cultural value North Americans supposedly place on human equality is universal, which, of course, it is not. One might argue that we find high degrees of inequality puzzling, especially if wealth and power are largely inherited, because we believe that all people are created equal. But people brought up in other cultural traditions accept inherited inequalities as a normal part of human life.

This response will not suffice. First, it is no response: It says merely that not everyone in the world has the same hangups about inequality that we do, but it explains neither our hangups nor why others lack them. Second, there is evidence of widespread conflict between strata in a wide range of stratified societies. Resentment, rebellion, and occasional attempts at revolution occur in stratified societies from all parts of the world (which is not to say that they are universally present). A great many powerless and poor people do not simply accept their place in the social hierarchy, so we need some understanding of why so many others do. Finally, although our knowledge of the history of preindustrial stratification systems is scanty, we know that in a great many societies a conquering militaristic group imposed their rule over the indigenous population of a region. This was true in African states such as Bunyoro and Zulu, in the ancient civilizations of the Americas such as the Aztec and Inca, in China and India, and in many other regions. In many and probably most stratified societies the lower strata did not consent to their low standing but had it forced on them.

Another possible explanation of how inequality persists is that members of the highest stratum (hereafter called the *elite*) use their wealth and power to organize an armed force stronger than that of their opposition. If the elite somehow manage to monopolize control over weapons or to organize a loyal army, then they can use coercion and threat to maintain their access to rewards and resources. Sometimes armed force is used by the elite to put down rebellions, and no doubt the ever-present threat of coercive sanctions does deter resistance to the elite's wealth, prestige, and power.

Yet in most systems of stratification, including even modern military dictatorships, only occasionally do the elite find it necessary to actually use force. Besides, use of actual force and the threat of force have disadvantages to the elite itself. Suppose the elite wait for rebellions to occur and then use superior military force to put them down. Even though none succeed, each time a rebellion is suppressed, more hatred and resentment and more awareness of the relative wealth and power of the elite are produced. Increased hatred and awareness caused by suppression can backfire and lead to a greater probability of future rebellion. Notice also that the elite's reliance on oppression to maintain wealth and power reduces or eliminates their honor and esteem, one of the three major rewards offered by stratification, and one that they presumably covet. Further, those who supply the military might—the army, henchmen, thugs, or police—must be paid or otherwise provided for by the elite; this requires resources. The elite can either take these resources from their own wealth, thus reducing it, or they can increase their exploitation of the majority population, thus breeding more hatred and resentment toward themselves. Finally, relying entirely on the loyalty of an army is risky because their allegiance may change. In sum, reliance on threat and armed force alone is costly and risky.

This is not to deny that military might is an important reason why high degrees of inequality are maintained for many generations. Probably few elites have maintained themselves for many generations without occasionally using the deterrent value of force and periodically suppressing rebellions and dissent. Nonetheless, stratification systems that rely entirely or largely on force seem to be short-lived and unstable and have been replaced by those that use other mechanisms. What other mechanisms are available?

### Ideologies

We can begin to answer this question by noting yet another reason that inequality seldom persists because of force alone. A single rebellion can have many causes, but a persistent *pattern* of rebellion is caused mainly by the lower strata's perception that they are exploited or not receiving their fair share of rewards. Putting down rebellions does nothing to change the reasons why people rebel. The instigators may be sanctioned or eliminated, but the underlying discontent that causes persistent conflict remains. Sooner or later there will be new instigators who organize new rebellions. Armed force cannot eliminate the perceptions of unfair distribution of rewards that cause rebellions.

One mechanism available to an elite to reduce dissent without coercion is to change the perceptions of the underprivileged about why they are underprivileged. For example, if poor people think it is God's will that they are poor, they are less likely to rebel than if they believe that they are poor because of exploitation. Or if they think that the elite use their property and power to benefit everyone in the society, then they are less likely to begrudge the elite their rewards. Or if they think that a concentration of property and power is inevitable because that's just the way life is, they will be less likely to resist. Or if they think that they, too, can acquire property and power through their own achievements, they are likely to put their effort into improving their own position rather than into causing trouble.

If, to state the general point, members of the lower strata adopt a set of cultural ideas that justifies and legitimates the rewards received by the higher strata, then they are more likely to try and join the system rather than to beat it. In such beliefs the elite have a powerful and relatively cheap tool with which to reduce the amount of opposition to their power and privileges. Further, these ideas increase the prestige of the elite. If people believe that inequality is God's will, or that the activities of the elite benefit all, or that the elite became elite through intelligence and hard work, then the elite deserve the honor and respect of everyone else.

We shall call those ideas and beliefs that explain inequality as desirable or legitimate **ideologies**. The term ideology also has a broader meaning, referring to any set of ideas held by a group—as in the phrases *leftist political ideology* and *feminist ideology*. Here we use it in the narrow sense, to refer only to ideas that justify the status quo of inequality.

In many stratified societies ideologies are based on religion. We are familiar with the notion of the "divine right of kings" from feudal Europe—certainly a handy supernatural mandate for kings and aristocracies! Similar notions are common in non-Western stratified societies. For instance, in Bunyoro, a kingdom in East Africa, the health and welfare of the ruler were mystically associated with the fertility and prosperity of the

whole kingdom. Anything that threatened his life was believed a threat to everyone. In many ancient civilizations, such as the Aztec, the Inca, the Japanese, and the Egyptian, the ruler himself was believed to be a divine or semidivine being. In pre-twentieth century China the emperor was believed to rule because he had the "Mandate of Heaven," meaning that Heaven itself had granted him secular authority over the vast Chinese empire for so long as he ruled it wisely and humanely. In traditional India, as we have seen, Hindu beliefs about reincarnation and pollution were so intertwined with the caste system that they rendered its inequities both explicable and legitimate.

In the ancient chiefdoms of Hawaii there was a marked social distinction between the noble and the commoner class. The nobility was believed to be endowed with a supernatural power called *mana. Mana* was partly hereditary, and within a single family the eldest child inherited the most *mana* from his or her parents. The highest-ranking noble, the paramount chief, was believed to be descended from one of the gods of the islands through a line of eldest sons. This descent gave him the right to rule because he had more *mana* than anyone in the chiefdom. Other nobles (lesser chiefs and their families) were relatives of the paramount and thus also were endowed with *mana. Mana* gave chiefs the power to curse those who were disloyal or disobedient or who violated some taboo, which further reinforced their authority. Hawaiians believed that the prosperity of a chiefdom and everyone in it depended on the performance of certain religious rituals held in grand temples. Because commoners did not have enough *mana* to enter a temple, only priests and the nobles could perform the rituals needed to ensure prosperity. Everyone in the chiefdom thus relied on the social (and religious) elite for their well-being.

The preceding examples illustrate some of the ways religion serves ideological functions in some societies. In stratified societies religion commonly gives the elite a supernatural mandate, provides them with the supernatural means to punish people, and gives them ritual functions to perform that are believed to benefit the whole population.

## American Secular Ideologies

What about ideologies in modern industrial societies, most of which are as highly stratified as any in the preindustrial world? Take the contemporary United States, for instance. Certainly the beliefs of the dominant religion in the United States, Christianity, often are said to provide support for the American way of life. Sometimes the Bible is claimed to teach that it is okay to be rich—many television evangelists even preach that wealth is a sign of God's blessing to the faithful. In many parts of the country few politicians win elections without periodic references to God in their speeches.

Still, many American citizens regard themselves as too sophisticated to believe ideologies based on supernatural mandates. Politicians may find it politically expedient to invoke God's name periodically, but few contemporary politicians go far by claiming that they are chosen by God. Likewise, the super rich and very rich do not justify their wealth and access to power by invoking supernatural authority. In other words, there is religious reinforcement for American institutions and "basic values," but religious ideologies justifying the wealth and power of particular *individuals* and families are not as widely accepted (and hence not as powerful) as they are in other societies and in Western civilization a few centuries ago.

This does not imply that industrial societies such as the United States no longer have ideologies because ideologies do not have to be based on religious beliefs; a **secular ideology** may exist. The three necessary characteristics of an ideology are that

✦ it must reinforce inequality by reducing activities that would redistribute wealth and power more equally;
✦ it must perform this function by affecting the popular consciousness (cultural beliefs, attitudes, values, world views, and so forth), not by threatening physical coercion;
✦ it must be believable, based on existing standards of cultural knowledge.

In the first requirement *activities* refers not just to rebellions against the elite but also to legitimate political activities such as demonstrations, to economic activities such as strikes and work stoppages, to attempts to redistribute wealth through influencing government social welfare policies, and so forth. On the third point, an effective ideology must match up with other ideas people have about the world, especially their ideas about how their political and economic systems work. It must make sense and be plausible, or it will be ineffective and (presumably) will not survive.

In other words, there must be a consistency between workable ideologies and other aspects of a people's culture. It would not "fit" with most Americans' ideas about how their society works if wealthy individuals

claimed a supernatural mandate for their privileged and powerful position, or if a congressional candidate claimed that "God wants me to win this election." They must justify their access to power and wealth in ways that the rest of us find acceptable, or the ideas they put forward will be ineffective. What are these "other beliefs" with which American ideologies must fit?

Like the citizens of most nations with market economies, most Americans believe that people will not scramble to get an education, work hard on the job, and so forth—that is, will not give their best efforts—unless they have an incentive to do so. To bring out the best in individuals, it is necessary that they be rewarded for their efforts, or at least that they think they have the possibility of being rewarded in the future. Many of us think that this is only part of a universal "human nature." Also, Americans accept it as morally fair and just that, given equal opportunity, people who work the hardest, have the most talent, and are the most ambitious should receive the highest rewards. If the rich and powerful in the United States are to promote an ideology that justifies their position, it must be compatible with these other cultural opinions and values of most Americans.

In the context of this cultural knowledge many scholars suggest that two major kinds of ideas justify the high degree of inequality in the modern United States. First is the idea that our whole nation benefits from inequality—because a few are wealthy, everyone else is better off than they would be if wealth were distributed more equally. This is because the possibility of gaining wealth motivates individuals to do their best, and we all win when our fellow citizens perform up to their potentials. Besides, the concentration of wealth is believed necessary to create jobs, from which everyone benefits. Second is the belief that the elite have earned their rewards through their own meritorious qualities and efforts—skill, intelligence, hard work, ambition, willingness to take risks, and other qualities that we consider laudable in an individual.

Some Americans believe these ideas; others do not. But to the extent that they are believed, these two ideas fit together with Americans' other ideas about how their nation works to legitimate inequality. The first says that inequality is socially necessary and even beneficial. The second says that the present way rewards are distributed is, in general, just. Wealthy and powerful people justify their rewards with these ideas without any recourse to the will of supernatural beings. They do so with ideas that many of us find acceptable according to our cultural premises because we share the belief in the neces-

*According to secular ideologies, members of the elite class deserve their wealth and influence because they have earned it through ambition, talent, and hard work.*

sity of incentive and because we agree in the fairness of greater rewards for greater efforts and talents.

## THEORIES OF INEQUALITY

You may or may not personally believe the ideas just summarized. (If you do not believe them, then they are not effective ideologies to you.) Or you may believe that these ideas are a fairly accurate representation of how American society allocates rewards (in which case, you will think that they are objectively true, not ideologies). Your personal opinion depends on your class, your upbringing, your political philosophy, your other ideas about human nature, and so forth.

Are these ideas accurate representations of reality, as some conservatives believe? Or are they ideologies, as many liberals hold? The answer boils down to two questions: (1) Who benefits from inequality? and (2) Do the elite themselves perform any functions for which they deserve to be rewarded with the amount of power and privilege that they have?

There is—as usual—disagreement on the answers to these questions. Two distinct political and philosophical views exist. One view is that a high degree of inequality in the final distribution of rewards is necessary, just, and beneficial to all the members of society. Stratification is the only way to provide unequal rewards for unequal talents and efforts. Without such unequal rewards, this view holds, collective mediocrity will result. This is called the **functional theory of inequality.**

Another opinion holds that a high degree of inequality is not only unjust but robs the whole society of the benefits of much of its talent, which lies undeveloped in those at the bottom of the social ladder. Stratification and its accompanying ideologies are ways that the privileged and powerful have devised over the generations to ensure the maintenance of their access to resources and the machinery of government. Called the **conflict theory of inequality,** this view holds that stratification preserves the social, economic, and political position of the well-off but offers no benefit to society at large and indeed is the major source of conflict in class and caste societies.

We now consider each of these theories in more detail.

### Functionalist Theory

Scholars who follow the functionalist theory believe that inequality is necessary if a society is to motivate its ablest members to perform its most important roles. Any valuable social role must have some means to motivate qualified individuals to perform it. Some jobs or roles require more skill and training than do others. Ordinarily, the more skill and training required to perform a role, the fewer the number of members in the group who are qualified to "do the job" and, all else equal, the more valuable their talent is to the whole group. Functionalists argue that unequal rewards—and the system of stratification that results from them—are an effective way to recruit the most trained individuals with the scarcest talents into the most socially valuable roles. Unless there are rewards for those with the personal qualities that most of us lack, they will have no incentive to put those qualities to work in activities that benefit all of us. Further, inequality is not only advantageous, it also is socially just in the functionalist view. If society as a whole is to enjoy the fruits of the labor of its small number of well-trained, talented, and hard-working individuals, it is only fair that it reward these individuals with material goods, respect, and control over public decision making.

How can we evaluate this argument? Two objections are possible within the framework of the theory itself. First, there is little reason to believe that the high degree of inequality in most stratified societies is needed to ensure that scarce talent is put to its most valuable uses. This is true even in industrialized societies. As an example, how many dollars does it take to motivate a qualified individual to run a major oil or auto company? If the income levels of top oil and auto executives were reduced to, say, $100,000 annually, would we have inferior executives and less well managed and profitable companies? Or would oil and auto workers simply receive a greater slice of the company pie, and the rest of us enjoy lower gasoline and car prices? To broaden the question: Is the *high degree* of inequality empirically found in stratified societies needed to realize the benefits of *some degree* of inequality? Or could some of the wealth now controlled by the rich be redistributed without reducing anyone's incentives to perform critical roles? One objection to the functionalist theory, then, is as follows: Granted that unequal rewards are needed to motivate people, no one knows how unequal the rewards must be. Certainly, no one knows whether the rewards must be as unequal as they are in some particular stratified society.

Second, functionalists assume that the system of stratification *effectively* places qualified individuals into important roles. But it is a large assumption, and perhaps only an ideology, that those who are best able to perform the most important roles are those who usually are recruited into them. In all systems of stratification there is a powerful element of inheritance of wealth, prestige, and power. Assume it is true (and it is not) that all those individuals who acquired their rewards in previous generations did so by performing roles that the rest of the population was willing to reward them for performing. There still is no guarantee that their children and children's children have the same enviable and scarce personal qualities, yet their descendants have a head start. If we think of much of economic, social, and political life as analogous to a race—like a 100-meter dash—then to ensure that the fastest runners finish first,

we need to start them all off from the same place. But the tendency for rewards to be inherited is analogous to starting some runners at the starting line, others at the 40-meter mark, and a few at the 80-meter mark; who finishes first and last is not determined mainly by who is the fastest.

Only if a society were able to devise some way of beginning each generation on an equal footing, with truly equal opportunities to compete, would the functionalist theory of inequality be adequate. No stratified society has ever achieved this condition, partly because the wealthy and powerful would have to consent to such a change, and they have no incentive to do so. In sum, the second objection to functionalism is that stratification is an inefficient way to recruit talented individuals into the most valuable roles because it virtually ensures unequal life chances or opportunities.

## Conflict Theory

The conflict theory takes off from objections to functionalism, such as the two just given; but it argues that such objections do not get to the heart of the issue. We could argue endlessly about how much inequality is needed for a society to function effectively, and about whether society A or B currently has more than the required amount. We also could try mightily to institute a system in which wealth is redistributed each generation (say, by high and progressive inheritance taxes); but the well-to-do would find a way around such laws, even if they should allow them to pass, and even if the laws were not impossibly unwieldy. According to the conflict theorists, what the functionalists do not realize—or are trying to cover up with a "theory" of inequality that in fact is only an ideology!—is that stratification is based on the exploitation of the many by the few. They also ignore the fact that stratification creates many problems for a human population.

Conflict theorists claim that stratification is based ultimately on control over the means of production (see chapter 4), that is, over productive resources such as land, technology, and, indirectly, labor. Once some people gain control over these resources—by whatever means—they use their economic power to coerce other people into working for them. The way this coercion operates varies between different kinds of economic systems. In ancient preindustrial states and some chiefdoms the noble class controlled the land and the commoners had to provide tribute and labor to the nobility

*Conflict theorists hold that inequality originates from control over the means of production. These Mississippi sharecroppers have only their labor to sell on the market.*

in return for the privilege of using it. In parts of feudal Europe the serfs were tied to their estate and ordinarily could not be denied access to the land they worked, but they still had to contribute a certain number of days of work or a certain proportion of their harvest to their lord per year.

As for the capitalist economic system, Karl Marx—the "father" of conflict theory—argued that capitalist societies include only two fundamental classes. Members of the capitalist class (or *bourgeoisie*) own the factories and other means of production. Members of the working class (or *proletariat*) have only one thing to sell on the market: their labor. To earn their living, workers must sell their labor to some capitalist. This seems like an equitable arrangement: The capitalists buy the labor they need to operate their capital to sell goods and make profit; the workers get the jobs they need to support their families by selling their time and skills for a wage.

But, Marx noted, the goods the workers produce must be worth more on the market than the workers themselves receive in wages or there would be no profit for the capitalists. The difference between the amount the capitalists receive for the goods they sell and their costs (including the amount they pay their workers) is *profit*. Thus, although the workers are not fully aware of it, a portion of every one of their workdays is spent in labor for the owners of the equipment they operate to make their living. Because workers do not receive the full market value of what they produce, part of their labor benefits not themselves but the capitalist who employs

them. For this reason, workers are exploited, Marx believed. The notion that the exchange of workers' labor for wages is mutually beneficial is merely an ideology. Sooner or later the workers will see through the ideologies and realize what the exploiters have been doing to them, and they will rise up and overthrow the ruling (capitalist) class. They will establish a new economic system in which the means of production are owned collectively, by workers themselves, and hence exploitation will disappear.

In one way or another, then, the owners of productive resources exploit the labor of nonowners, according to conflict theorists. Members of the elite class maintain their control over the means of production despite their smaller numbers by their control over ideas (i.e., by ideologies), over armed force, and/or over the kinds of laws that are passed and enforced by governmental authority.

Conflict theorists have been criticized for being ideologues themselves, although of a different political persuasion than functionalists. If one wants to find exploitation in a relationship, one can always do so. Critics of conflict theory claim that the value-laden term *exploitation* does not adequately characterize relations between chiefs or kings and commoners, between lords and serfs, or between capitalists and workers. Conflict theorists ignore the valuable services and/or resources that elite classes perform, such as maintaining social control, organizing the society for the provision of public goods, and accumulating productive resources (capital) put aside to increase future production.

Many conflict theorists assume that it is possible to create a complex social system without unequal rewards. This is a rather unrealistic view of human nature, according to some critics of the approach. Complex social systems are always hierarchically organized, with centralized leadership of the system's parts (if not of the whole). It is naively idealistic to think that leaders who have power over the activities of so many other people will not use this power to benefit themselves, their families, and their friends. Indeed, many critics believe that the functions of leaders, controllers, and organizers are so valuable to society at large that they deserve the rewards they receive.

## Who Benefits?

Contrasting the two theories, we see that functionalism emphasizes the positive aspects of stratification, whereas conflict theory emphasizes the negative side. Conflict theory points to the costs of stratification not just to those on the bottom of the social ladder but also to society at large. Society loses the undeveloped potential of its less fortunate members and must suffer the periodic violent conflicts (rebellions, revolutions) and/or ongoing disorder (crimes, political dissent) caused by a high degree of unjust inequality and inherited privilege.

The functionalist and conflict theories imply different philosophical and moral views of inequality, views that have contemporary relevance for industrial societies. The first implies that inequality should be maintained; the second that it should be reduced or even eliminated. The first argues that the best and the brightest naturally gravitate to the top; the second that much goodness and brightness never have a chance to reveal themselves. The first suggests that government get out of the business of redistributing wealth; the second proposes an active government policy to redistribute wealth to maximize the chances that hidden genius in the ghettoes will have a chance to manifest itself. Profound issues of social policy are involved.

Does the comparative perspective of anthropology have anything to offer to a solution of this issue? Who does benefit from inequality? If we review some of the information given in this chapter, and in chapters 9 and 13, we find that preindustrial elites did indeed perform some vital roles for the whole population, just as functionalists claim. For example, elites often organized labor for the construction and maintenance of public works projects, provided relief to regions struck by famine, and raised a military force to provide for the defense of the political unit. Some kind of central authority may indeed be necessary for such tasks to be coordinated effectively. Cooperative activities require organization; organization requires leaders and controllers; leaders and controllers deserve to be rewarded.

On the other hand, preindustrial elites performed some roles that probably were created mainly to maintain their positions as rulers. Thus their religious functions often were viewed as indispensable to the general welfare by ordinary people, but in fact the rituals they sponsored did not ensure rain or the fertility of land or women. Their regulation of access to land and other resources might have been necessary, but it was partly because they themselves controlled so many resources that other peoples' access to them had to be "regulated." The social order they helped to maintain benefited everyone, but the elite's power, wealth, and internal political rivalries produced conflicts that otherwise would not have existed.

We see, then, that some of the functions of nobles, lords, and other elite classes in the preindustrial world are useful for the whole population. But other "functions" are imaginary and exist only because of prevailing (usually religious) ideology. Still other "benefits" that the population receives from the elite are beneficial only because of the control of the elite itself over society. The existence of inequality itself produces some societal "needs" that the elite help to meet, and then they claim to deserve rewards for fulfilling the so-called needs.

With the insight gained from this comparative perspective, we can be fairly certain that some of the "functions" carried out by the elite in industrialized nations likewise are imaginary. We also can imagine that some of the "benefits" the rest of the people receive from the roles performed by the elite exist only because the past and present elite class itself has set up society's institutions in such a way that their roles are popularly perceived as necessary or beneficial. (To take a provocative and only half-serious example, if there were no such occupation as lawyer, how often do you think you would need one?) It is difficult for insiders to pick out which functions of an elite are and are not needed— most people are enculturated to see these functions as necessary for the general welfare. But with a comparative view of humanity we can see that much of what is needed for the general welfare is relative to time, place, and cultural conditions. In turn, such conditions are influenced by those with wealth and power.

Along these same lines, note that many of the institutions we regard as beneficial to all in fact do not benefit everyone to the same degree. A good example of this is our laws regarding the government's protection of private property. Most Americans are enculturated to believe that private property is a basic human right and that the general welfare requires laws to protect everyone's property. But, as shown previously, the bulk of the private property is owned by a small percentage of the population in the United States, as in most industrialized nations. It may be true that we all benefit somewhat from the legal safeguarding of our private property, but we do not all benefit equally. For one thing, we differ vastly in the amount of property that needs to be protected. For another, because big thefts are investigated more thoroughly and prosecuted more vigorously than small thefts, the poor receive less protection than the rich.

So who does benefit from the inequality found in stratified societies? The functionalists probably are correct in their assumption that some degree of inequality is needed for motivation. We might also agree that unequal rewards for unequal efforts is a fair and just standard. But we do not know how much inequality is necessary to provide incentives, much less whether some particular stratified society has just the right amount. We do know that power and privilege are partly—and usually largely—inherited in stratified societies and that therefore the current members of the elite class are not automatically more talented and diligent than everyone else. By comparing stratified societies, we see that elites do provide some useful services for the population at large. But we also see that many popular ideas about their functions are ideologies, and that many of their roles are useful only under circumstances that they themselves had a hand in creating.

Probably most of us would benefit from some degree of inequality, if only there were some way to find out what the optimum amount of inequality is for some given society, if only there were some way to achieve this optimum initially, and if only there were some way to reset opportunities at equal in future generations. But no known human society has ever achieved this utopia.

## SUMMARY

Inequality refers to the degree to which individuals and groups enjoy differential access to socially valuable rewards of wealth, power, and prestige. Fried's typology of egalitarian, ranked, and stratified societies provides a useful description of the range of cross-cultural diversity in inequality.

Most foragers are egalitarian. This is largely because their adaptation makes it difficult for anyone to exercise control over productive resources and the behavior of others. Such adaptive features include high rates of mobility, ability of individuals to choose their band affiliation, a cultural value placed on sharing and the social pressure against making oneself stand out, and the difficulties of maintaining exclusive access to a territory. Leadership is largely situational and informal.

In ranked societies there are a set number of honored positions (chiefs, titles, offices) to which only a small number of people are eligible to succeed. Succession may be determined by genealogical ascription, or membership in a particular kin group may establish a pool of candidates from which one will emerge or be selected. Tikopia illustrates one form of ranking.

Stratified societies are defined by three characteristics: they have marked inequalities in access to all three kinds of rewards, this inequality is based largely on unequal access to productive resources, and the inequality is strongly heritable. One system of stratification is the caste system. Castes are best known from India, where they were intimately associated with the Hindu doctrines of reincarnation and pollution.

Class systems are more common in the preindustrial world and are characteristic of all modern nations. In modern nations the class into which one was born is a strong determinant of one's life chances, although in theory interclass mobility is possible. Assigning a particular family to a particular class is not always easy, but in the United States the best criterion of class membership is wealth. Studies conducted by scholars and by the federal government reveal an enormous disparity in the distribution of wealth, especially if net worth rather than annual cash income is used to measure a family's wealth.

How such highly unequal distribution of rewards persists in stratified societies is puzzling. The mobilization of armed force by the elite is an insufficient explanation. Cultural beliefs that inequality is inevitable, divinely ordained, legitimate, and/or beneficial to society as a whole provide ideologies that justify and reinforce the power and privilege of elite classes. Among preindustrial peoples, religious beliefs were the main form of ideology, as exemplified by ancient Hawaii. In modern countries ideologies are more secular in orientation, because effective ideologies must be compatible with a peoples' overall cultural ideas about how their society works. In the United States, Americans' ideas about the social and economic usefulness of inequality, about the fairness of unequal rewards for unequal talents and efforts, and about how the well-to-do achieved their wealth may be interpreted as secular ideologies.

The two major theories about inequality are the functional and the conflict theories. Functionalists hold that societies offer unequal rewards to those individuals who have the scarcest talents and who use them to perform the most socially valuable roles. Conflict theorists claim that inequality is based ultimately on control over the means of production, which allows those who own productive resources to exploit those who do not. The two theories imply contrasting views of the nature of inequality. Anthropology's comparative perspective suggests that although elites often do perform valuable services for society at large, many of their "functions" are illusory. Others exist only because past elites have set up the structure of society so that their "services" are necessary. Although functionalists are correct that some degree of inequality is necessary for incentive, we have no way of knowing whether any society has the amount it "needs," nor has any society ever succeeded in establishing the equal opportunity required for the functionalist theory to be correct.

## KEY TERMS

| | |
|---|---|
| inequality | ideology |
| egalitarian society | secular ideology |
| ranked society | functional theory of in- |
| stratified society | equality |
| life chances | conflict theory of in- |
| class | equality |
| caste | |

## SUGGESTED READINGS

Bendix, Reinhard, and Seymour M. Lipset, eds. *Class, Status, and Power: Social Stratification in Comparative Perspective*. 2d ed. New York: The Free Press, 1966.
> *A reader intended primarily for sociologists. Contains many seminal articles, although now dated.*

Berreman, Gerald D., and Kathleen M. Zaretsky. *Social Inequality: Comparative and Development Approaches*. New York: Academic Press, 1981.
> *A collection of papers discussing social inequality in a number of societies.*

Fried, Morton. *The Evolution of Political Society*. New York: Random House, 1967.
> *A well-known book with an extensive discussion of ranking and stratification and how they relate to political organization.*

Goldman, Irving. *Ancient Polynesian Society*. Chicago: University of Chicago Press, 1970.
> *A comparative study of social stratification in a variety of Polynesian islands.*

Lenski, G. *Power and Privilege*. New York: McGraw-Hill, 1966.
> *A treatment of stratification comparing the range of inequality in preindustrial and industrial societies. Best known as an attempt to reconcile the functionalist and the conflict perspectives.*

Shepher-Hughes, Nancy. *Death Without Weeping*. Berkeley: University of California Press, 1992.
> *How poor northeast Brazilian families cope psychologically with high rates of infant and child mortality.*

**Several studies treat the concentration of power and wealth in the United States in great detail.**

Domhoff, G. William. *Who Rules America Now?* Englewood Cliffs, N.J.: Prentice-Hall, 1983.

Dye, Thomas R. *Who's Running America? The Conservative Years*. 4th ed. Englewood Cliffs, N.J.: Prentice-Hall, 1986.

Hurst, Charles E. *Social Inequality: Forms, Causes and Consequences*. Boston: Allyn and Bacon, 1992.
> *A textbook on inequality in the modern United States. Includes chapters on inequality based on race and gender as well as summaries of various explanations of inequality and stratification.*

Levy, Frank. *Dollars and Dreams: The Changing American Income Distribution*. New York: Norton, 1988.
> *Analysis of increasing economic inequality in the United States in the 1980s.*

Newman, Katherine. *Falling from Grace: The Experience of Downward Mobility in the American Middle Class*. New York: Vintage, 1988.

*Written by an anthropologist, the interview and observational data in this book show the impacts of job loss or declining income on former members of the American middle class and how they cope with downward mobility.*

Mishel, Lawrence, and Jared Bernstein. *The State of Working America, 1992-93.* Economic Policy Institute Series. Armonk: M. E. Sharpe, 1993.

*Excellent source of quantitative data on the distribution of income and wealth in the contemporary United States. Also includes chapters on taxation, wages, unemployment, poverty, costs of living, and how inequality in United States compares with that in other industrialized nations.*

## CHAPTER 15

# RELATIONS WITH THE SUPERNATURAL

*Guatemalan Catholics in a ritual procession. Rituals are part of all religions.*

**CONTENTS**

All cultures believe in the existence of supernatural powers and attempt to maintain positive relations with them through the performance of rituals. Beliefs and rituals pertaining to the supernatural make up the religion of a culture. Religion is in one respect different from the other aspects of cultures covered in previous chapters. It is easy to understand why any people need to exploit their environment, have domestic and kinship groups, organize political decision making, maintain social control, and the like. But what kinds of individual and group needs or wants are met by religion? This question is one topic of the present chapter.

Anthropologists as well as other scholars have long been fascinated by the varieties of religion that exist in human cultures. Field-workers have studied and written detailed ethnographies about the diverse religions of humanity. Most ethnologists believe that a people's religious beliefs and rituals are related to other aspects of their way of life, especially the main features of their economic and political organizations. This chapter introduces the diversity of religions and outlines how religion is related to economic and political organization.

## DEFINING RELIGION

What is religion? How can we best define it so as to encompass all the diversity of religion found in the human species? It is ethnocentric to define religion simply as "belief in God," for the same reason it is ethnocentric to define politics as "the activities and organization of a government." Just as some societies have no formal government, so are there societies that lack a belief in any kind of deity, much less in the Judeo-Christian God. We need a definition that can be applied cross-culturally.

The oldest anthropological definition of religion is E. B. Tylor's **animism**, or "belief in spiritual beings" (see chapter 4). Most modern conceptions follow Tylor's lead: They specify that, at the least, all religions include beliefs that some kind of spiritual or supernatural powers exist. But Tylor's definition leaves out much about religion. By expanding on it we can present an overview of religion in cross-cultural perspective.

### Supernatural Powers: Beings and Forces

"Beings" are not the only kind of spiritual powers that people believe in. Many religions posit the existence of other kinds of powers that are more like "forces" than "beings." For example, in aboriginal times the peoples of Polynesia believed in *mana*, a diffuse, impersonal, incorporeal force. Mana lent supernatural potency to things, which explained unusual qualities; or to people, which explained unusual success. People and objects could be infused with greater or lesser amounts of mana. Having a lot of mana explained why some chiefs always won battles, why some fishing equipment seemed to work so well, why certain gardens produced such fine crops, and so forth. But mana could be withdrawn by the gods: A chief defeated by a rival in battle had lost his mana, which had been given instead to the victor.

The widespread belief in powers such as mana make it useful to divide supernatural powers into beings and forces. Spiritual *beings* usually are believed to have qualities such as a bodily form, some way of appearing before people, a personality, and a fairly predictable way of responding to human actions. The characteristics people attribute to supernatural beings vary enormously: They can be capricious or consistent, stubborn or reasonable, vengeful or forgiving, amoral or just. Some beings have human origins, such as souls or ancestral ghosts, which reside or resided in a specific individual. Other kinds of beings have nonhuman origins, such as many gods or demons.

Supernatural *forces* likewise are believed to have definite properties, which vary from people to people. Because forces usually have no will of their own—no power to refuse humans who know how to command or manipulate them in the proper manner—they often can be used for either good or evil purposes. In most cases people believe that supernatural forces can be manipu-

*Gods are honored and worshipped through prayer. Devout Muslims pray five times daily.*

lated by humans who know the proper rites and spells. The manipulation of forces by means of rites and spells, known as *magic,* is discussed later in this chapter.

## Myths

Belief in the existence of supernatural powers (beings and forces) is only part of religion. Religion also includes **myths**—oral or written stories about the actions and deeds of supernatural powers in the past. Myths commonly tell of the actions of cultural heroes and supernatural powers of long ago. Sometimes they explain how the entire universe was created. They may recount how and why people, animals, plants, and natural features originated. Myths explain how a people acquired their tools and customs and how they came to live where they do. They often tell why people should or should not act in certain ways and what happened to

someone in the past who did something people are forbidden to do.

North Americans mostly learn their mythology in formal settings: Myths are taught at church and, to a lesser extent, at home. (Here we need to emphasize that calling Bible stories "myths" does *not* mean that we regard them as false.) In many societies people learn the mythology of their religion as an ordinary part of enculturation. Elders recount myths in moments of leisure. Myths are repeated regularly on days set aside for religious performances. They are sung or chanted while one is doing daily tasks. The fact that myths sometimes are recounted rather casually does not mean that their importance in a people's way of life is negligible. A people's world view is greatly affected by their mythology.

It has been argued, for example, that the Judeo-Christian mythology makes it easy for North Americans to view nature as something to be conquered and used for their own profit. When God made humans he gave us "dominion" over nature and told us to "subdue" the earth and its living creatures (see Genesis 1:26–30). When it suits our purposes and interests we thus have no supernatural commandments to keep us from fouling the water and air, from destroying the habitats of other creatures with dams and other developments, from destroying hills with strip mines, and so forth. According to this argument, if individual Americans have any opinions about the way God wants them to relate to nature, they are more likely to believe that he gave it to humans to conquer and exploit than to believe that he wants them to restrict their consumption so that they can preserve it for its own sake or for future generations.

In contrast, we might show more respect for other living things if (like some cultures) we had a religious heritage with sacred myths telling that some of us came from bears, some from rabbits, some from whales, and so forth. We might be more reluctant to tear up a mountain for its minerals if we thought that some of us came from a hole in its side. We might hesitate to destroy a forest if the Bible told us explicitly that trees are just as precious to God as humans.

A people's myths—and this is the general point we are trying to make—are more than stories they tell after dark or recite on appropriate occasions. They do more than satisfy idle curiosity and help pass the time. Myths are part and parcel of a peoples' world view: their fundamental conceptions of nature and society and how people ought to relate to the world and to one another. They therefore affect how people behave in their everyday lives.

## Rituals

Religions include behaviors as well as beliefs and myths. People everywhere believe that gods, ghosts, demons, devils, and other supernatural beings take an active interest in worldly affairs, particularly in the lives of human beings. Such beings can be asked for blessings or aid, or sometimes they can be commanded to do things for or to people. Similarly, people can use supernatural forces to cause helpful or harmful effects. Because people believe that supernatural beings and forces can make natural events occur and can intervene in human affairs, all cultures prescribe certain behaviors that are used to interact with and influence various powers.

The organized performance of behaviors intended to influence spiritual powers is known as **ritual**. Rituals are always stereotyped: There are definite patterns of speech

or movement, or definite sequences of events, that occur in much the same way in performance after performance. In general, people performing rituals want supernatural powers to do things on their behalf: to make someone (or everyone) healthy or fertile, to bring rain, to make the crops grow, to save their souls, to bring back the game, to provide blessings, and so forth. People may pray, worship, make sacrifices, and follow ritual procedures scrupulously to ensure that their gods, their personal spirits, or the ghosts of their dead ancestors intervene favorably in their lives.

The performers of ritual often want supernatural powers to harm their enemies in some way: to make them sick or barren, to bring floods or pestilence to their land, to drive the animals out of their territory, to make their spears fly crooked in the upcoming battle, and so forth. If we can ask supernatural powers to harm our enemies, our enemies may have the same ability; they can cause supernatural harm to us, making us sick or prone to misfortune. So ethnographers commonly report that members of some society believe that many or all illnesses, deaths, and accidents are caused by the supernatural powers of evil or enemy humans. And many kinds of rituals exist whose explicit purpose is to counteract the harm caused by other rituals performed by enemies.

Rituals the world over have symbolic aspects. They often occur in *places* that have symbolic significance to the performers. For example, they may be held where some mythological event occurred, or where the women who founded a matrilineage were born. Rituals often involve the display and manipulation of *objects* that symbolize an event (e.g., the cross), a holy person (statues of Jesus and Mary), a relationship (wedding rings, the symbol of holy matrimony), and a variety of other things. Symbolic significance usually is attached to the *language* and *behavior* of ritual, as in the Christian rituals of worship, hymn singing, prayer, baptism, communion, and confession. (The symbolic places, objects, language, and behaviors used in rituals are sometimes said to be sacred, but our cultural distinction between sacred and profane must be applied with great care in describing non-Western religions.)

Anthropologists classify rituals on two bases. The first basis is their conscious purposes—the reasons people themselves give for performing them. For example, there are divination rituals, which are performed to acquire information from a supernatural power about the future or about some past event that people have no other way of finding out about. There are also curing, sorcery, sacrificial, and exorcism rituals. There are ritu-

*All religions have rituals. This Tibetan priest is officiating at a cremation.*

als to renew the world, to make a man out of a boy and a woman out of a girl, and to free the soul from a dead person's body. There are rituals held for single individuals, for kin groups, for people of similar age, for whole societies, and so forth. A few examples of these are discussed in this chapter.

The second basis of classification is when rituals occur—whether they are held on a regular schedule (like Sunday church services) or simply whenever some individual or group wants or needs them (like funerals or prayers for a sick person). If rituals are held regularly (seasonally, annually, daily, monthly, etc.) they are called *calendrical rituals*. *Crisis rituals* are organized and performed whenever some individual or group needs, wants, or asks for them—for purposes of curing, ensuring good hunting or fishing, or other events that happen sporadically or unpredictably.

The three components of all religions, then, are (1) beliefs about the nature of supernatural powers, (2) mythologies about the historical deeds of these powers, and (3) rituals intended to influence these powers to intervene favorably on behalf of the performers. With this conception of religion we can glimpse the ways in which cultures vary in their religious dimen-

sion. There is diversity in beliefs about the nature of supernatural beings and forces, in what spheres or realms of life their powers extend to, in how they can be requested or commanded to intervene in human affairs, and in who can organize the rituals that make such requests or demands. We consider some of these variations in this chapter.

With this brief and broad overview of religion in mind, we now look at a few aspects of the anthropological study of religion. A good place to start is with some of the major theoretical orientations offered to understand or explain religion.

## THEORIES OF RELIGION

So far as we know, every culture has religion. The fact that religion is universal is a bit surprising, for two reasons. First—with regard to beliefs and myths—it can never be proved that supernatural powers such as ghosts, gods, devils, demons, angels, souls, mana, and so forth exist, much less that myths about them are true. Indeed, from an outsider's ("nonbeliever's") perspective, other peoples' religious beliefs and myths often seem irrational. Yet in every culture we know about, many, most, or all people believe in supernatural powers and recite myths about their actions. Why?

Second—with regard to rituals—religious behavior may not be effective at achieving the goals the performers have in mind. From an outsider's perspective, many rituals seem to be a huge waste of time and resources. For example, when a Trobriand Islander plants a yam garden, he does some things that "work" in the way he thinks they do: He clears the land, removes weeds, and so forth, just as anyone should for success. But a Trobriander believes that acts that many outsiders consider superfluous are also necessary for success in gardening. He hires a magician to perform rites and spells that will keep his yams from leaving his garden at night and roaming around, because he knows that other people are performing magic to steal his yams by luring them into their own gardens. We—meaning those outside the culture's belief system—easily understand what the Trobriand gardener gets out of the first kind of activity: a yam harvest, if nature cooperates. But what does he get out of the magical rites and spells? How did Trobrianders come to believe that magic is needed?

We can state this second problem another way to see the major puzzling thing about rituals. When the Trobriander clears land, plants a crop, and weeds his garden, his actions are effective in attaining the goal he has in mind—they work in more or less the way he thinks that they do. But when the garden magician performs rites and spells to keep his client's yams from being stolen by a neighbor during their nightly wanderings, his actions do not achieve the result he has in mind. Yams do not really roam around; the magic does not really work. (Again, remember that these statements are made from an outsider's perspective.) How, then, did the Trobrianders get the idea that they do?

Speaking generally, rituals do not work the way the performers imagine they do—the rain does not fall because of the rain dance; the crazy woman is not made sane by exorcizing the devil within her; no spirits enter the body of the medicine man; there were no witches in Salem, Massachusetts, in 1692. Why, then, do so many people believe in the power of ritual?

You may already have thought of possible answers. If rituals do not work in the way the performers believe that they do, perhaps they work in some other way. If they do not have the effects people believe that they have, they may have other effects that people find useful or satisfying. As for myths, if they are not accurate historical accounts, perhaps they are symbolic statements that help people make sense of reality and give meaning to real-world things and events.

We all have heard people who consider themselves sophisticated and educated say that religious beliefs rest on simple ignorance and superstition—"they believe because they don't know any better." This nonanswer to the question "Why religion?" is (or should be) rejected by all anthropologists. Its ethnocentrism is apparent: Superstition is something that someone else believes in but you do not; but many of your own beliefs seem superstitious to others, and probably many of the accepted truths of the twentieth century will be considered superstitious in the year 2050. Besides, even if we admit that such beliefs and practices are superstitious, we have not explained them. Why does one form of superstition develop in one place and another form in another place?

Few, if any, modern anthropologists believe that religious beliefs and rituals can be explained as simple delusions. That is, few of us claim that religion results from ignorant folk making mistakes in logic that lead them to perform ritual activities that are a total waste of energy and resources. Practically all of us believe that religion has some kind of positive value to individuals, to society, or both. It is difficult to explain its universality in any other way: How could something that is totally worthless be found among all humanity?

We do not, however, agree on what this positive value is. This leads us to the functions of religion—its useful effects to individuals, to society as a whole, or to some social group within a society. Broadly, social scientists have proposed three types of functions of religion: the **intellectual** (or **cognitive**), the **psychological**, and the **social**.

## Intellectual/Cognitive Functions

Many scholars think that humans actively seek explanations for things and events, for the human mind does not tolerate uncertainty and unanswered questions (or so some believe). According to the cognitive approach, religions perform the function of explaining things and events that would otherwise remain inexplicable. Religion provides people with myths and beliefs that account for the origin of the sun, moon, stars, world, animals, people, and so forth. It allows people to interpret natural and social phenomena and events. As we have seen, this was E. B. Tylor's theory of the origins of animism—people sought explanations for things they saw in dreams and imaginations and mistakenly came to believe in spiritual beings (see chapter 4).

Around the turn of the twentieth century, Sir James Frazer proposed a similar theory. He noticed that "savages"—as he called peoples whom he imagined were living representatives of the earliest cultures—usually believe in some kind of magical power that can be manipulated by people who perform the proper rites and spells. He saw this belief as a prescientific one: People wanted to influence natural occurrences and other people, but they did not understand true scientific cause-and-effect relations. Believers in magic thought, for example, that a magician could cause harm to people by performing rites and spells on things that were once in contact with their victims, such as hair, nails, feces, or even footprints. Such beliefs had a kind of logic—by doing something to things once in contact with a man, you can do something to him—but the logic was based on false premises. Frazer thought that people gradually realized their logical errors and eventually gained knowledge of true scientific cause and effect. Frazer thus believed that magic and science are alternative world views: Each provides people with an intellectual model of the way the world works and a means to manipulate events and people. But whereas magical beliefs are false, scientific theories are objectively correct—in Frazer's view. Because Frazer thought that science is a superior system of knowledge, it is in the process of replacing magical and religious beliefs.

The idea of Frazer and others that religious beliefs provide people with explanations for things and events is correct, as far as it goes, but it is an incomplete explanation for religion. Religion does satisfy curiosity about the world, but this is not its only function. "Savages" possess and use practical knowledge just as we do—a Trobriander knows that he must care for his yams as well as perform garden magic. Conversely, many "civilized" and "scientific" folk believe in and practice religion—even many of those who make their living practicing the science for which religion supposedly substitutes. Religious beliefs do not take the place of practical or scientific knowledge; in some way that we do not fully understand, they supplement it.

Few scholars today believe that religion exists because some peoples are the victims of erroneous thought processes. But the intellectual approach is by no means passé. Clifford Geertz, a leading modern cultural theorist, holds that religion provides its believers with the assurance that the world is meaningful—that events have a place in the grand scheme of things, natural phenomena have causes, suffering and evil happen to specific individuals for a good reason, and injustices are corrected. Cultural beings (i.e., humans) cannot tolerate events that contradict the basic premises, categories, and world view of their cultural tradition. Yet such events do occur periodically. Because of religion, people are able to maintain their world view in spite of events that seem to contradict it. Religion, Geertz believes, reassures its believers that the world is orderly rather than chaotic, all within the framework of their existing cultural knowledge.

## Psychological Functions

The notion that religion helps people cope psychologically (here meaning emotionally) with times of trouble, stress, and anxiety is a common one. Sicknesses, accidents, misfortunes, injustices, deaths, and other trials and tribulations of life can be handled emotionally if one believes that there is a reason and meaning to them or that one's troubles can be controlled or alleviated by means of ritual.

One psychological theory holds that humans are unique among animals in that we are aware of our own mortality. The knowledge that we will eventually die produces anxiety and a denial of the finality of death. We invent afterlifes and imagine them to be pleasant to calm our fears. This notion is tainted by ethnocentrism—although belief in life after death is common, a great many peoples believe that the soul's existence in the other world is greatly inferior to its life in the earthly body. Hardly a "comforting" belief!

In anthropology a well-known psychological theory of religion is that of Bronislaw Malinowski, whom we introduced in chapter 4. Malinowski thought that religion (including magic) serves the valuable function of giving people confidence when they are likely to be unsuccessful despite their best efforts. There are always natural phenomena that people cannot control and that constantly threaten to ruin their plans and efforts. Belief in the power of ritual to control these (otherwise uncontrollable) elements instills confidence and removes some of the anxiety that results from the uncertainties of life.

There is little doubt that religion is psychologically useful: It relieves our anxieties, reduces our fears, and helps us to cope with life. That religion serves such functions (at least for some people some of the time) is not subject to dispute. On the other hand, there is little doubt that sometimes religious beliefs increase our anxieties and fears. Consider the Kwaio, a people of the Solomon Islands. Kwaio believe that women are spiritually dangerous to men, so Kwaio wives are expected to take elaborate precautions to avoid polluting their husbands when preparing their food or performing other services for them. If a man dies of an illness, his wife is likely to be blamed, and perhaps killed, for her "offense." Just whose "anxieties and fears" are "relieved" by this belief?

## Social Functions

"Societies need religion to keep people in line," you may have heard people say. The idea here is that religion maintains common values, leads to increased conformity to cultural norms, promotes cohesion and cooperation, promises eternal reward for good deeds and eternal damnation for evil acts, and so forth. Those who champion the social function (also called the sociological) theory hold that religion exists because of the useful effects it has on human societies: It maintains social order by discouraging individuals from violating the culturally legitimate rights of others and by urging them to perform their proper duties.

Consider the Ten Commandments, for example, which serve as a moral code for Christians and Jews. Two prescribe how people ought to feel and act toward God and other people and eight proscribe actions, including the five "thou shalt nots" (see Exodous 20:3–

*The French sociologist Emile Durkheim proposed that rituals enhance social solidarity by imparting feelings of harmony within a group. These people are gathered for a sago ceremony in Irian Jaya, Indonesia.*

17). Note that five of the divinely ordered prohibitions are against the commission of acts that could result in harm to others, such as killing and stealing. God gave us commandments that will, if obeyed, lead to good relations with others and therefore promote earthly social order. More general Christian moral guidelines are the Golden Rule ("do unto others as you would have them do unto you") and love of one's neighbor (Matthew 19:19), both of which are useful prescriptions for harmonious social life.

Another social function of religion is to enhance the cohesion of society by making people feel their interdependence on one another and on their traditions. Emile Durkheim, a French sociologist of the early twentieth century, was influential in formulating this perspective. Durkheim's view was that the main function of religion in human society is to promote *social solidarity,* meaning that religion has the effect of bringing people together and enhancing their sense of unity, cohesion, and reliance on their society's customs. Groups of people who share the same beliefs and who gather periodically to perform common rituals experience a feeling of oneness and harmony. Religion exists, Durkheim believed, because it is socially useful or—stated differently—functional for society as a whole.

Numerous social scientists have championed the sociological interpretation of religion. (In fact, if any interpretation can be said to be *the* most popular, this is it.) Because we present several examples of sociological approaches to specific religious phenomena in this chapter, for now we merely discuss why one popular sociological interpretation is unlikely to apply to all religions. This is the idea that religion promotes order and conformity by promising supernatural retribution for immoral or antisocial behavior and by holding out worldly or otherworldly rewards for culturally defined clean living.

Because of their Judeo-Christian heritage—in which eternal reward or damnation is a key belief—Westerners might easily assume that supernatural powers are everywhere believed to be concerned with whether people behave well or poorly in this life. Deities might, for example, reward virtue with earthly wealth and power or with eternal heavenly bliss. Or supernatural powers might punish troublemakers with illness, misfortune, and even death or with an unpleasant afterlife. Indeed, such beliefs are common.

They are not, however, characteristic of all religions. Many cultures have no belief that supernatural powers punish wrongdoers or sinners—in fact, many cultures have no concept of sin, in the sense of violations of edits issued by the supernatural. All peoples have conceptions of morality, of course, but not all believe that supernatural powers apply sanctions against violators of moral standards.

What determines whether a religion does or does not include the belief that deities, ancestors, or other spiritual powers punish and reward people according to the moral worthiness of their actions? According to Guy Swanson's cross-cultural study, the presence or absence of such a belief is related to the degree of inequality in a society: The greater the inequality found in a society, the more likely that society's religion is to include the belief that supernatural powers reward and punish individuals according to how well they behave. There is an especially striking relation between social classes and supernatural sanctions for morality, as shown by the following cross-cultural tabulation:

|  | SUPERNATURAL SANCTIONS FOR MORALITY | |
| --- | --- | --- |
| SOCIAL CLASSES | Absent | Present |
| Present | 2 | 25 |
| Absent | 12 | 8 |

The religions of class societies are likely to include beliefs that supernatural powers reward and punish, whereas the religions of classless societies are much less likely to include such beliefs. This association of a high degree of inequality with the presence of supernatural sanctions may be related to a topic discussed in chapter 14. The power, wealth, and prestige of the haves may be reinforced and legitimated if have-nots believe that spiritual powers punish wrongdoing.

## ▆▆ SPHERE OF SUPERNATURAL INTERVENTION

One cross-cultural variation in religions is the sphere—or the range of human activities and natural occurrences—in which spiritual powers are believed to have an influence. A modern North American Christian is likely to have a relatively narrow conception of the realms of personal and public life in which God intervenes. (This varies with denomination and personal belief.) Most of us do not use divine action to explain the failure of a company, car wrecks, illnesses, great wealth, poverty, or the outcome of elections. We are more likely to blame poor business practices, carelessness, coincidence, poor eating or drinking or exercise habits, and personal skill or laziness for misfortune or

success. The same is true for natural occurrences: Most of us do not blame God for earthquakes, floods, hurricanes, volcanoes, and other natural disasters, which we attribute to natural forces.

In contrast, in most religions of the preindustrial world, people believe that spiritual powers actively intervene in a wide range of human activities and natural events. Rituals are performed to request or command that their future intervention be favorable or that they remove the effects of their previous malevolent interference. A few examples will illustrate.

✦ The matrilineal Ndembu of Zambia attribute various female health problems to the actions of ancestral spirits. Infertility, frequent miscarriages, stillbirths, and other reproductive disorders are explained by the actions of one of the victim's ancestresses, who is punishing the woman for "forgetting her ancestress" or for doing something of which her ancestress disapproves. The cure for the affliction consists of a lengthy ritual that makes the victim "remember" her dead relative.

✦ Some central Canadian Inuit believe that prolonged inability to find game may be caused by a goddess who is angry over the misconduct of members of the camp. They persuade the goddess to release the game by performing a ritual in which camp members publicly confess their violations.

✦ To help them locate caribou, the Naskapi foragers of eastern Canada used divination. They heated a caribou shoulder blade over a fire until it cracked. The pattern of cracks in the scapula told them the direction in which to look for game.

✦ The Trobriand Islanders periodically go on long overseas voyages to acquire the shell valuables that are symbols of status and wealth in their culture. They perform magic to induce their trading partner to give a certain valuable to them rather than to someone else. The ocean trip is hazardous because of the possibility of sudden storms, so before they depart the voyagers also perform magic to ensure favorable weather.

✦ The Hopi of the American Southwest believe that rainfall is brought by supernatural beings. These beings, called *kachinas,* live in the peaks of mountains to the southwest of Hopi villages. In the spring and summer Hopi believe that kachinas dwell in the villages. During this period men wearing masks of the kachinas perform ritual dances. The spirit enters the body of the dancer, who thus becomes the kachina. Rain is brought to the Hopi's cornfields by the dances.

These examples illustrate three areas of human life in which the supernatural commonly is believed to intervene. First, various peoples believe that supernatural powers are responsible for success or failure of many group activities, such as hunting and trading. Second, spiritual beings or forces frequently must be asked to bring about some desired natural event, such as good weather and the return of game. Finally, supernatural powers are believed to interfere in the lives of individuals, making them ill or poor, or healthy and wealthy. This last kind of intervention is universal, or nearly so. We now consider how religion helps people account for and deal with misfortunes.

## SUPERNATURAL EXPLANATIONS OF MISFORTUNE

One occurrence that many peoples attribute to the action of spiritual powers is personal misfortune, including death, illness, and events that many Westerners consider accidents. Many beliefs and rituals of various societies are concerned with explaining, preventing, and curing illness and disease. Cross-culturally, two major complexes of beliefs about illness are most common.

First, many peoples believe that sickness is caused by the direct action of some spiritual power. Sickness often is thought to be brought on by a taboo violation, which some supernatural being or force is punishing. Other societies believe that the ancestral spirits of kin groups cause their members to become ill because of conflict or bad feelings within the group. (We consider ancestral cults later in this chapter.) The same kinds of beliefs may apply to accidents that many Westerners attribute to bad luck or carelessness. Drownings, falls, snakebites, prolonged failure to succeed at some activity—such events are likely to be seen as evidence of unfavorable supernatural intervention. The victim has offended a god or spirit, who brings an "accident" as punishment.

Second, many peoples think that all or most illnesses or other misfortunes are caused by the action of some evil human who is using special supernatural powers against the afflicted person. Belief that certain people, called *sorcerers* and *witches,* have powers to harm others by mystical means is enormously widespread among humanity. Sometimes witches and sorcerers are thought to strike randomly and maliciously against people who are innocent of any wrongdoing. More commonly they direct their evil magic or thoughts toward those against whom they have a grudge. Sorcery and witchcraft are among the most fascinating of all religious phenomena— well worth considering in more detail.

*A Brazilian Indian shaman cures a woman by sucking the illness out of her body. Sickness is often thought to have supernatural causes and, hence, the rituals are used to cure patients.*

### Sorcery

**Sorcery** is the performance of rites and spells intended to cause supernatural forces to harm others. In some cultures sorcery may be carried out by almost anyone because everyone learns to harm their enemies by sorcery as an ordinary part of enculturation. Among other peoples sorcery is a more specialized practice: Only certain people inherit or acquire the knowledge of how to recite the spells and perform the rites correctly.

In 1890, Sir James Frazer proposed that magic (including sorcery) is based on two kinds of logical premises or assumptions. Both kinds of logical principles involve a symbolic identification of something (e.g., an object or action) with something else (e.g., an event or a person).

One kind of logical principle on which magic is based is called the *imitative principle,* which is based on the premise that like produces like. That is, if an object resembles (is like) a person and the sorcerer mutilates the object, then the same effect will occur to the person. The so-called voodoo doll is a familiar example of the imitative principle: An image or effigy is made of the enemy; some act is performed on the effigy; and the enemy supposedly experiences the same fate. The effigy symbolically represents the person, so to mutilate the effigy is believed to harm the person. In another kind of imitative magic the magician or sorcerer mimics the effects she or he wants to produce. For example, sorcerers among the Dobu of Melanesia cast spells by imitating the symptoms of the disease they want to afflict on their victims.

The second kind of logical premise underlying magic and sorcery is called the *contagious principle of magic,* which is based on the assumption that power comes from contact. That is, things that were once in contact with someone can be used in rites and spells to make things happen to that person. By performing the correct rites and spells on such objects as hair clippings, bodily excretions, nail parings, infant umbilical cords, or jewelry and clothing, harm can be done to one's enemies. In societies in which sorcery rests on the contagious principle, people must be careful to dispose of objects they have been in contact with, lest one of their enemies use them for sorcery. As with the imitative principle, a symbolic identification is made between the objects and the victim. But in the case of the contagious principle the symbolic equation comes from previous contact rather than from resemblance: By acquiring possession of something once belonging to a person, supernatural power is acquired over that person.

Because sorcery relies on beliefs about the manipulation of supernatural forces, anthropologists consider it part of a culture's religion. Sorcery affects and is affected by other dimensions of culture. We next consider two of many possible examples of these effects.

**PATTERN OF ACCUSATIONS.** In most societies bad feelings are most likely to occur between individuals and groups who stand in certain relationships to one another—co-wives of a polygynous man, people who have married into a lineage or village and hence are seen as outsiders, brothers who are rivals for a political office, members of other kin groups with whom one group is in conflict, and so forth. In all societies certain kinds of relationships are especially subject to conflict. Which relationships are most likely to be strained vary with the way the society is organized: In one society brothers-in-law usually are friends and allies, but their interests conflict in another society, for instance.

Sorcerers are believed not to strike randomly but to direct their evil magic against people toward whom they feel hatred, anger, or envy. So when I or my relative becomes ill or suffers a misfortune, neither of us suspects just anyone of sorcery. We ask ourselves who has a motive to perform evil magic against one of us: Whose interests have we harmed? Who envies our success? Who will profit from our illness or death? It is these people whom we suspect and these people whom we are most likely to accuse. Because all societies have built-in conflicts and stresses, we are most likely to suspect and accuse people with whom we have certain kinds of

relationships. So ethnographers frequently report that accusations of sorcery (and witchcraft, to be discussed shortly) are patterned in a society: They reflect the patterned conflicts of interest, disagreements, and so forth that develop because of the relationships in particular forms of social organization.

**SORCERY AS A POLITICAL WEAPON.** You might imagine that sorcerers everywhere would be despised and punished or killed whenever their practices become public knowledge. This is not always the case. In many societies there are ambivalent feelings about people widely suspected of practicing sorcery: They may be despised, but they are also feared and respected for their powers. A common strategy on the part of a person suspected of using sorcery against his enemies is to deny the charge but to leave enough room for doubt that no one is sure that he is not indeed guilty. By this strategy, people will fear his powers enough to give him an advantage in political or other kinds of rivalries. Sorcery (more precisely, fear that one may practice sorcery or be allied with sorcerers) can be used as a political weapon.

A fine example of the use of sorcery as a weapon in political competition is provided by the Abelam, a Papua New Guinea people studied by Anthony Forge. Like most other Melanesians, the Abelam have no hereditary chiefs or other formalized political officials. Rather, leadership is vested in a "big man" (see chapter 13), who achieves prominence through his ability to persuade others to follow his directives. Rivalries between the aspiring big men of a single village are the major focus of political life, and big men use other people's fear of sorcery in their competitions for followers.

The Abelam believe that all deaths not obviously caused by violence result from sorcery carried out by members of an enemy village. Their beliefs are based on the contagious principle; so to perform his deed, an enemy sorcerer must have access to objects (which we shall call here *leavings,* including feces, hair, etc.) that have been in direct contact with his victim. Yet everyone is careful not to leave their leavings lying about in other villages, so that sorcerers cannot acquire the things necessary to work their powers from the victims themselves. But the Abelam believe that sorcerers are operating against someone in their village almost constantly (why else would people be sick or have other kinds of troubles?). This means that someone in the village must be supplying outside enemies with the bodily secretions or other leavings of his co-villagers.

It is the big man in the village, and his rivals, who are thought to be the suppliers. They have secret caches of almost everyone's leavings. Although a big man does not work contagious magic against his own villagemates, he is believed to employ a foreign sorcerer to make his rivals and nonsupporters sick. If a big man is accused of complicity with an outside sorcerer, he makes a half-denial; that is, he denies the charge but leaves the possibility open. The fear that his cache of leavings will be turned over to an enemy is a major source of power over his rivals and co-villagers. In fact, a man who is not suspected of magical complicity with outside enemies has little hope of becoming a powerful big man, because he lacks one of the political weapons essential for success.

## Witchcraft

Witchcraft is the second explanation that people in many societies give for misfortune. There is no universally applicable distinction between sorcery and witchcraft. Whereas sorcery usually involves the use of rites and spells to commit a foul deed, here we define **witchcraft** as the use of psychic power alone to cause harm to others. Sorcerers manipulate objects; witches need only think malevolent thoughts to turn their anger, envy, or hatred into evil deeds. (Our own language's distinction between the two—witches are female, sorcerers usually male—is not useful cross-culturally.) Many cultures believe in the existence of both kinds of malevolent powers, so sorcery and witchcraft often are found among the same people.

Cultures vary in the characteristics they attribute to witches and in how witches cause harm. A few examples illustrate some of the diversity.

✦ The Navajo associate witches with the worst imaginable sins—witches commit incest, bestiality (sex with animals), and necrophilia (sex with corpses); they change themselves into animals; they cannibalize helpless infants; and so on.

✦ The Nyakyusa of Tanzania hold that witches are motivated mainly by their lust for food; accordingly, they suck dry the udders of peoples' cattle and devour the internal organs of their human neighbors while they sleep.

✦ The Zande of the southern Sudan believe that witches possess an inherited substance that leaves their bodies at night and gradually eats away at the flesh and internal organs of their victims. Witches, as well as their victims, are considered to be unfortunate, because the

Zande believe that a person can be a witch without even knowing it. Witches can do nothing to rid themselves permanently of their power, although they can be forced to stop bewitching some particular individual by ridding themselves of bad feelings against their victim.

✦ The Ibibio of Nigeria believe that witches operate by removing the spiritual essence (soul) of their enemies and placing it into an animal; this makes the victim sick, and he dies when the witches slaughter and consume the animal. Sometimes Ibibio witches decide to torture, rather than kill, a person. In that case they remove the victim's soul and put it in water or hang it over a fireplace or flog it in the evenings; the afflicted person will remain sick until the witches get what they want out of him or her.

✦ The Lugbara, a people of Uganda, claim that witches—who are always men—walk around at night disguised as rats or other nocturnal animals. Sometimes they defecate blood around the household of their victims, who wake up sick the next morning.

Such beliefs, it might appear to someone who does not share them, are logically outrageous; no one's soul leaves his or her body at night to cavort with other witches, for example. It might seem that these beliefs are socially harmful as well; beliefs in witchcraft, fear of witchcraft, and accusations of witchcraft engender unnecessary conflict and aggression among a people. Finally, the treatment many suspected and "proven" witches receive offends our notions of social justice. As we know from the witch hunts of European and American history, the truly innocent victims of witchcraft often are the accused witches, who sometimes are cruelly executed for crimes they could not have committed.

## Interpretations of Sorcery and Witchcraft

Anthropologists wonder about why beliefs in witches and sorcery are so widespread, given their seemingly harmful effects and the injustices that frequently result from them. Why should so many cultures independently have developed such beliefs? Why should most of the world's peoples think that some or all of their misfortunes are caused by the supernatural powers of their enemies? What use or value could a human society possibly derive from accusations of witchcraft or sorcery?

Many answers have been offered to these questions. In line with the overall theoretical approaches discussed earlier, the answers fall into two categories: cognitive and sociological. (In the following discussion for simplicity we use the term *witchcraft* to refer to both witchcraft and sorcery because the ideas presented have been applied to both kinds of beliefs.)

## COGNITIVE INTERPRETATIONS.

The most influential of the various cognitive approaches is that witchcraft explains unfortunate events. The argument is that most people find the idea of coincidence or accident intellectually unsatisfying when some misfortune happens to them or their loved ones, so they search for other causes. Their logic is something like this: I have enemies who wish me harm, and harm just came to me, so my enemies are responsible.

The best example of how people account for misfortune by reference to the actions of witches comes from among the Azande, whose beliefs we just described. The Azande attribute prolonged serious illnesses and many other personal misfortunes to witchcraft. Ethnographer E. E. Evans-Pritchard (1976) describes their beliefs:

Witchcraft is ubiquitous. . . . There is no niche or corner of Zande culture into which it does not twist itself. If blight seizes the groundnut crop it is witchcraft; if the bush is vainly scoured for game it is witchcraft; if women laboriously bail water out of a pool and are rewarded by but a few small fish it is witchcraft; . . . if a wife is sulky and unresponsive to her husband it is witchcraft; if a prince is cold and distant with his subject it is witchcraft; if a magical rite fails to achieve its purpose it is witchcraft; if, in fact, any failure or misfortune falls upon any one at any time and in relation to any of the manifold activities of his life it may be due to witchcraft.(18)

All this does not mean that the Azande are ignorant of cause and effect and therefore attribute every misfortune to some witch who is out to get them. When a Zande man seeks shelter in a granary and its roof falls and injures him, he blames witchcraft. But Zande know very well that granary roofs collapse because termites eat the wood that supports them. They do not attribute the collapse of granaries in general to witchcraft; it is the collapse of this particular granary at this particular time with this particular person inside that is caused by witchcraft. Do not granaries sometimes fall with no one sitting inside them? And do not people often relax in granaries without the roof falling? It is the coincidence between the collapse and the presence of a particular person—a coincidence that many other peoples consider bad luck—that witchcraft explains.

Another benefit people gain is that witches serve as scapegoats. When things are going poorly, people do not always know why. Witchcraft provides an explanation. It also provides people with a means to do something about the situation: identify, accuse, and punish the witch responsible. If, as often is the case, things still do not improve, there are always other yet-to-be-identified witches! People can blame many of their troubles on witches—evil enemies conspiring against them—rather than on their personal inadequacies or on the failures of their own societies. Although most of us do not attribute them supernatural powers, evil enemies still are blamed by modern folk for many problems of our nations (see Box 15.1).

## SOCIOLOGICAL INTERPRETATIONS.

One sociological hypothesis is that witchcraft reinforces the cultural norms and values that help individuals live harmoniously with one another. Every culture has notions of how individuals ideally ought to act toward others (chapter 2). Witches typically are the antithesis of these cultural ideals. They act like animals, or actually change themselves into animals. They mate with relatives. They often put on a false front, pretending to be your friend by day while they eat your liver by night. They have no respect for age or authority. They are in league with the forces of evil (in the Judeo-Christian tradition witches made compacts with the Devil, agreeing to be his servant in return for worldly pleasures.) All the most despicable personal characteristics of people are wrapped up in the personality of witches, whom everyone is supposed to hate. So witches symbolize all that is undesirable, wicked, and hateful. Just as one should despise witches, so should one abhor all that they stand for. In short, this argument is that by providing a hated symbol of the abnormal and the antisocial, the witch strengthens cultural conceptions of normatively approved social behavior.

Another argument is that witches provide an outlet for repressed aggression, and thus beliefs about witches lower the overall amount of conflict in a society. Writing about the Navajo in 1944, Clyde Kluckhohn argued that Navajo culture emphasizes cooperation and maintenance of good relationships between members of the same extended household. Bad feelings do develop within the household, yet Navajo culture leads people not to express them. But pent-up hostilities have an outlet in the form of witches, whom people are allowed to hate and gossip about. Because most people whom the Navajo believe to be witches are members of distant groups, little action usually is taken against them. Solidarity between relatives of the in-group is preserved by displacing hostility to people of the out-group.

Many North Americans find great tragedy in the scapegoat function of witches in earlier times and foreign places; innocent people were punished or cruelly put to death as witches. But we should always examine comparable beliefs among ourselves before we feel morally or intellectually superior to others.

Modern societies are too complex for people to comprehend the interaction of all the forces that cause social, political, and economic problems. The most knowledgeable experts and scholars admit that they know only a part of the story, and they cannot even agree among themselves on what causes poverty, crime, the so-called decline of the family, voter apathy, and other social problems. Many of us fall into the trap of personifying the reasons for the troubles of our society; rather than recognizing the complexities of our problems, we simply lay the blame on specific individuals and groups. Is our economy in trouble? Outside powers— for example, the Japanese—are to blame. Is the nation beset by laziness, crime, incompetence, and moral decay? Social workers, unions, permissive lib-

## BOX 15.1

## MODERN WITCHES

erals, and the secular humanists are the reason. Johnny and Suzie can't read? Blame their teachers and the colleges that trained them.

It is nearly always incorrect to blame specific individuals and groups for complex social problems. Such problems result from little understood cultural forces, over which particular individuals and groups exert only partial control. Rather than attempting to understand these forces, or at least to appreciate their complexity, it is easier intellectually to personify them, to scapegoat, to witchhunt. We have seen that the Azande and other peoples blame witches for accidents and sickness, two kinds of personal misfortunes for which they have no scientific explanation. Similarly, we find scapegoats for misfortunes on the societal level for which we likewise have no explanation.

Politicians are eager to feed our desire for the simple answer scapegoats provide. By identifying scapegoats, politicians divert responsibility from themselves— foreigners and the other party are to blame. This also increases their reelection chances—what voter wants to hear that the modern world is so complex that candidate Smith does not know how to make our cities safe and all Americans prosperous? And scapegoating makes us feel good about ourselves—the American people and the American system are not at fault after all.

Scapegoating is not harmless, no matter how good it makes us feel. Most Americans know the tragedy of the McCarthy era, when anti-Communist sentiment in the country was manipulated by a U.S. senator to further his own career. We know that Jews were the witches of Hitler's Germany, burnt at the stake by the millions. Jews, blacks, Catholics, Communists, and gays serve as witches for certain rightwing organizations in the modern United States. When will our next witchhunt occur and who will its victims be? ◆

Another hypothesis is that witchcraft beliefs serve as a mechanism of social control. This might work in two ways. First, it commonly is the case that a people believe in the existence of witchcraft but do not know which specific members of their community are witches. This leads individuals to be careful not to make anyone angry, since the offended party may be a witch. Second, it often is the case that individuals who fail to conform to local cultural norms of behavior are most likely to be suspected and accused as witches. People who are always mad at somebody; who carry grudges for prolonged periods; who are known to be envious and resentful of the success of others; who have achieved wealth but selfishly refuse to share it in the culturally accepted manner—such violators of these and other standards for behavior frequently are believed to be the

likely perpetrators of witchcraft. Fear of being accused and punished presumably increases adherence to norms and ideals of behavior.

These are the major ideas that anthropologists have proposed about the benefits people derive from beliefs that witches and sorcerers cause many of their misfortunes. But notice that none of them explain the origin of such beliefs. They all state: "Assuming a people believe in witches or sorcerers (or both), individuals or groups derive positive benefits from these beliefs." Like other functionalist approaches (chapter 4), they state what kinds of rewards individuals or society gains as a *consequence* of beliefs in witches and sorcerers. They do not answer the *causal* question: "Why do some cultures develop a belief that misfortune is caused by the supernatural powers of their enemies?" For not all cultures have such beliefs: Some hold that illness is attributable to punishment by ancestors, or violations of a taboo, or divine retribution, or invasion of their bodies by invisible microorganisms that they themselves have never seen but that experts assure them exist.

# ▥ VARIETIES OF RELIGIOUS ORGANIZATION

There is no way to present an overview of the diversity of human religions without great distortion. Just as we oversimplify a given culture when we classify it as (for example) horticultural, polygynous, patrilineal, tribal, and egalitarian, so do we simplify when we pigeonhole its religion as (for example) shamanistic or monotheistic. Nonetheless, a typology of religion is useful, because it gives a general picture of religious diversity among humanity.

In his 1966 book *Religion: An Anthropological View* Anthony Wallace proposed a fourfold classification that we use for convenience. His typology is based on the concept of **cult**. A cult is an organized system of cultural beliefs and practices pertaining to the control over specific supernatural powers. A cult is not the same as the religion of a people. Rather, religion is a more inclusive concept: A society's religion may include several cults, some of which are devoted to curing, some to controlling weather, some to praying to their ancestors, some to foretelling the future, and so on.

Wallace's classification distinguishes four kinds of cults.

✦ **Individualistic cults.** Each individual has a personal relationship with one or more supernatural powers, who serve as his or her guardians and protectors. The aid of the powers is solicited when needed for personal goals.

✦ **Shamanistic cults.** Some individuals—shamans—are believed to have relationships with the supernatural that ordinary people lack. They use these powers primarily for socially valuable purposes, to help (especially cure) others in need. They may also act on behalf of their band or village to cause supernatural harm to the group's enemies.

✦ **Communal cults.** The members of some kind of group gather periodically for the performance of rituals that are believed to benefit the group as a whole, or some individual in it. There are no full-time religious specialists, as is also true of individualistic and shamanistic cults.

✦ **Ecclesiastical cults.** The hallmark of ecclesiastical cults is the presence of full-time religious practitioners who form a religious bureaucracy. The practice of religion is carried out by formal, specialized officials—priests—who perform rituals that are believed to benefit the society as a whole. The priesthood usually is materially supported by institutionalized governmental authorities through taxation or redistributive tribute (chapter 9).

Although any given culture usually has more than one of these kinds of cults, the cults are not randomly distributed among the peoples of the world. Rather, there is a rough evolutionary sequence to their occurrence. Many foraging bands and horticultural tribes, such as the Netsilik, !Kung, and Yanomamö, have only shamanistic cults, and ecclesiastical cults occur mainly in stratified chiefdoms and states, for example. If we consider the religion of a people to be composed of some number of cults, more kinds of cults are found in states than in tribes.

But the evolutionary matching of kinds of cults with kinds of economic and political organizations is only very rough and general. For instance, the aboriginal peoples of Australia had communal cults, although they were foragers and lived in bands. Many tribes of the North American Great Plains had individualistic, shamanistic, and communal cults, although they were primarily foragers.

We now look at some of these varieties of religious organization in more detail.

## Individualistic Cults

The defining characteristic of individualistic cults is that individuals intentionally seek out particular spirits or other supernatural powers to protect and help them in their endeavors. Individualistic cults thus emphasize direct, personal interactions between people and the supernatural.

The most well-known example of individualistic cults is the **vision quest.** It is widespread among Native American peoples but is especially important for the Great Plains tribes. To the Plains Indians the world is charged with spiritual energy and supernatural power. Power exists in inanimate objects such as rocks or mountains and in living animals and plants. Human beings require the aid of the supernatural in many activities—in hunting, warfare, and times of sickness or other troubles.

Spiritual power comes to individuals in visions. These visions play an important role in the religious life of the people because it is through them that people achieve the personal contact with the supernatural that is essential in various endeavors. Spiritual powers occasionally make contact with individuals for no apparent reason, coming to them as they sleep or even as they are walking or riding alone.

More often humans—especially young men—have to seek out these powers through an active search, or a quest whose purpose is to acquire a vision. There are places that supernatural powers are believed to frequent: certain hills, mountains, or bluffs. A young man goes to such a location alone. There he smokes and fasts, appealing to a power to take pity on him. Among one tribe, the Crow, sometimes a man will even amputate part of a finger or cut his body to arouse pity. The vision commonly appears on the fourth day, since four is a sacred number to the Crow. Many young men fail at their quest but others do achieve visions.

The supernatural power that contacts a man and the manner in which it manifests itself varies. Sometimes he only hears the spirit speak to him. Sometimes it comes in the form of a dream-like story. In other instances it simply materializes before his eyes, taking the form of a bear, a bison, an eagle, or some other large animal. Sometimes small animals like rabbits, field mice, and dogs also appear.

The power tells the man how it will help him. It might give him the ability to predict the future, locate enemies, find game, become a powerful warrior, or cure illness. It tells him the things he will have to do to keep his power—what songs to sing, how to paint his war shield, how to wear his hair, and so forth. It also tells the man some things he cannot do; for example, if the power comes from the eagle, the man might be prohibited from killing "his brother," the eagle. As long as he continues to behave in the prescribed manner, the power will be his supernatural protector, or guardian spirit. It aids him in his endeavors and gives him special powers other men do not have.

There is no known culture in which individualistic cults constitute the entire religion. Even among Plains Indians, in which this kind of cult is unusually well developed, shamanistic and communal cults also exist.

## Shamanism

A **shaman**, or **medicine man**, is a person with a culturally defined special relationship to supernatural powers, which he frequently uses to cure sickness. In many societies (especially among many foraging peoples) the shaman is the only kind of religious practitioner; that is, he practices the only kind of ritual and possesses the only kind of abilities not available to ordinary people. Shamans seldom are specialized practitioners. They carry out their tasks whenever their services are needed, usually in return for a gift or fee; but otherwise they live much as everyone else.

Shamans are believed to possess several qualities. They have access to the power of spiritual beings, called *spirit helpers*. The effectiveness of a shaman in curing (or causing harm) is believed to derive from the potency of his spirit helpers and from his ability to contact them and get them to do his bidding. Contact with one's spirit helpers commonly is made by achieving an altered state of consciousness. This altered state (referred to as a *trance*) is reached in various ways: through intake of drugs, ritual chanting, or participation in rhythmic music. People quite often believe that one of a shaman's spirit helpers has physically entered (possessed) the

*A !Kung shaman in a trance state. Trance makes shamans spiritually powerful and able to cure people.*

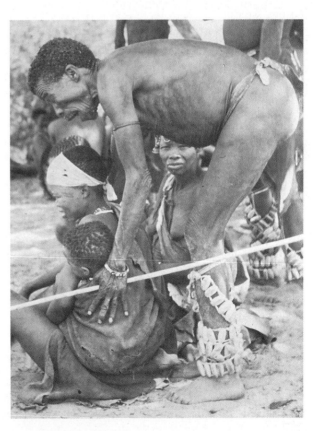

shaman's body. The spirit takes over his body and speaks to the assembled audience through his mouth. When possessed the shaman becomes a *medium,* or mouthpiece for the spirits—he may lose control over his actions and his voice changes quality because a spirit is speaking through him.

The way in which a person becomes a shaman varies from people to people. Shamans usually are considered to have knowledge and powers lacking among ordinary folk. They acquire these in three major ways. In some societies they undergo a period of special training as an apprentice to a practicing shaman, who teaches the novice chants and songs and how to achieve the trance state. Many shamans must have endured difficult deprivations, such as prolonged fasting, the consumption of foods culturally considered disgusting, or years of sexual abstinence. Finally, in many societies shamans are people who have experienced some unusual event. For example, they have miraculously recovered from a serious illness or injury, or they claim to have had an unusual dream or vision in which some spirit called them to be its mouthpiece.

In most cultures the shaman's major role is curing. Again, how the shaman performs this role varies. By considering an ethnographic example of sickness and curing, we can see shamans in action. We also can use the case to suggest an answer to one of the questions frequently asked about shamanism: How does the belief that shamans have the power to make people well persist, even though many of their clients die?

The Jívaro are a rain forest people of Ecuador. Jívaro believe that most sickness is caused by the actions of their human enemies (rather than by natural causes). Jívaro shamans acquire their power from their control over their personal spirit helpers, which live in their bellies in the form of tiny magical darts. A man becomes a shaman by presenting a gift to an existing shaman, who regurgitates some of his spirit helpers, which the novice swallows. If the novice drinks a hallucinogenic drug nightly for ten days and abstains from sexual intercourse for at least three months—the longer the better—he will acquire the power to transform any small objects (insects, worms, plants, etc.) he ingests into magical darts.

The Jívaro recognize two kinds of shamans: bewitching shamans, who have the ability to make people sick, and curing shamans, who try to make people well by counteracting the evil deeds of bewitching shamans. By ingesting and storing many magical darts in his body, a bewitching shaman can later harm his enemies. He causes illness by propelling one or more magical darts

into the body of his victim; unless the darts are removed by a curing shaman, the victim will die. To effect the cure a curing shaman first drinks tobacco juice and other drugs, which gives him the power to see into the body of the victim. Once he locates them, the curer sucks out and captures the magical darts; if the cure is successful, the darts return to their owner and the patient recovers.

Many patients die, which means that curing shamans often are ineffective. How, then, does the belief that curing shamans really cure persist? The answer is that the Jívaro believe that a kind of supernatural battle is waged between the bewitching and the curing shamans. Bewitching shamans have two special spirit helpers. One, called a *pasuk,* looks like an ordinary tarantula to people who are not shamans; the other takes the form of a bird. A bewitching shaman can order his pasuk or spirit bird to remain near the house of the victim, shooting additional magical darts into him as the curing shaman sucks them out. If the victim dies, it may be because the darts shot by the pasuk and spirit bird were too many for the curing shaman to remove. Or, because the supernatural power of shamans varies, it may be because the bewitching shaman has more power than the curing shaman.

Aside from serving as an example of shamanism, the Jívaro show how beliefs about supernatural causes and shamanistic cures for illness form a logically coherent system. If the patient recovers, as usually happens, the ability of the shaman to cure is confirmed. If the victim dies, this event, too, is explained (rationalized, an outsider might say) in terms that are consistent with existing beliefs. Events in the real world—getting better or getting worse, living or dying—do not disprove the beliefs because the belief system itself covers such events and contingencies.

Faith healers, those shamans of modern times, use similar premises. God's power to heal is unquestionable, and faith healers seldom publicly doubt their own calling. If the cancer is not cured, if the blind do not see, if the disabled do not walk away, if the heart patient does not recover, the fault often is with themselves: They had too little faith.

## Communal Cults

Like shamanism, communal cults have no full-time religious specialists. Rituals organized communally frequently have leaders—often an elderly person or someone with a special interest in the outcome of some ritual—who manipulate the symbolic objects or who address the supernatural. But the cult leaders are unspecialized—they do not make their living as religious practitioners.

Communal rituals are held to intercede with the supernatural on behalf of some group of people, such as a descent group, an age group, a village, or a caste. To illustrate, we consider two widespread kinds of communal rituals organized by descent groups: **ancestral cults** and **totemism**.

ANCESTRAL CULTS.    Practically all religions hold that people have a spiritual dimension—what we call a *soul*—that lives on after the physical body has perished. Beliefs about the fate of the soul after death vary widely. Some religions—such as Hinduism—believe that it is reincarnated into another person or animal. Others hold that the soul passes into a spiritual plane, where it exists eternally with a community of other souls and has no further effects on the living. Still others believe that souls become malevolent after death, turning into ghosts that cause accidents or sickness or terrifying anyone and everyone.

One of the most common beliefs about the fate of souls after death is that they interact with and affect their living descendants. A great many peoples hold such beliefs. They usually practice rituals to induce the spirits of their deceased ancestors to do favors for them or simply to leave them alone. Beliefs and rituals surrounding the interactions between the living and their departed relatives are called *ancestral cults*. (They are also known as *ancestor worship*, but *worship* is not an accurate term to describe what goes on in many of these rituals!)

The Lugbara, a people of Uganda, illustrate ancestral cults. The patrilineage is an important social group to Lugbara. Its members are subject to the authority of lineage elders. As the most important members of the lineage, elders are expected to oversee the interests and harmony of the entire group. They serve as the guardians of the lineage's morality, although they have no power to punish violations physically.

Lugbara believe that the spirit of a deceased person may become an ancestral ghost of her or his lineage. The ghost punishes living descendants who violate Lugbara ideals of behavior toward lineage mates. People who fight with their kinsmen (especially a relative older than oneself), who deceive or steal from their lineage mates, or who fail to carry out their duties toward others are liable to be punished by an ancestral ghost. Sometimes this happens because a ghost sees an offense committed

and causes illness to the offender. More commonly the ghosts do not act on their own initiative to make someone sick. Rather, the ghosts act on the thoughts of an elder who is indignant because of the actions of some member of the lineage. John Middleton (1965) describes Lugbara beliefs about the power of lineage elders to cause illness by invoking ghosts.

[The elder] sits near his shrines in his compound and thinks about the sinner's behavior. His thoughts are known by the ghosts and they then send sickness to the offender. He "thinks these words in his heart"; he does not threaten or curse the offender. For a senior man to do this is part of his expected role. It is part of his "work," to "cleanse the lineage home." Indeed, an elder who does not do so when justified would be lacking in sense of duty toward his lineage.(76)

In the Lugbara example we see how elders maintain harmony and cooperation in the lineage. This is a common feature of ancestral cults.

Why do some societies have ancestral cults in which ghosts are believed to punish their descendants who violate cultural prescriptions of right behavior? Like most "why" questions, this one is controversial. But many anthropologists agree that such beliefs are related to the degree of importance of large kin groups in a society. The greater the importance of kin groups such as lineages and clans in making public decisions, regulating access to resources, allocating roles, controlling behavior, and so on, the more likely a society is to develop an ancestral cult.

TOTEMISM.    Totemism, another widespread form of communal cult, is the cultural belief that human groups have a special mystical relationship with natural objects such as animals, plants, and, sometimes, nonliving things. The object (or objects) with which a group is associated is known as its *totem*. The group most often is a unilineal kin group, such as a clan. The totem frequently serves as a name of the group, for example, the Bear clan, the Eagle clan.

The nature of the relationship between the members of the group and its totem varies widely. Sometimes the totem is used simply for identification of the group and its members, much like our surnames. Often there is a mystical association between the group and its totem object: People believe that they are like their totem in some respects. Members of other groups also resemble their totems. In many populations—most notably among some of the aboriginal peoples of Australia—the members of a clan treat their totem like a clanmate, believing that the totem gave birth to their ancestors in

*At this funeral in Tanna, Vanuatu, the relatives of the deceased demonstrate their sorrow. The ghost may cause trouble for relatives who do not show their grief by mourning.*

a mythical period. The welfare of the clan is mystically associated with the welfare of the totem, so periodically the clan gathers for rituals that ensure the reproduction of its totem.

Despite its many variations, everywhere totemism exists the totem is a symbol of the group, to a greater or lesser degree. Why are some living things "chosen" as totems rather than others? There are several answers to this question. Perhaps the most influential is that offered by the French structural anthropologist Claude Lévi-Strauss (see chapter 4). He noted that totemic beliefs classify a peoples' social world into kinds of groups. The natural world likewise is divided into kinds of plants, animals, and other things. In essence, totemic logic posits an association between natural categories (kinds of things) and social categories (kinds of people, or groups). According to his argument, particular natural objects are chosen because they are a convenient way to represent (symbolize) kinds of groups and their relationships to one another. As Lévi-Strauss puts it, certain animals are used as totems because they are "good to think"—they have (concrete, constant) properties that provide useful metaphors for conceptualizing and thinking about (abstract, variable) groups and social relationships.

## Ecclesiastical Cults

In chapter 9 we saw that a high degree of specialization accompanied the development of civilization. Among New World peoples such as the ancient Incas, Aztecs, Mayans, and Toltecs and in the Old World cities of ancient Mesopotamia, Egypt, China, Japan, and India, this specialization extended into the religious dimension of cultural systems. Rather than organizing rituals on a communal basis—in which a wide range of people controlled and participated in the performance—a formal bureaucracy of religious specialists controlled most public rituals. The religious bureaucracy probably also had a large voice in formulation of the religious laws, which ordered certain kinds of punishments for those who violated them.

These religious specialists are known as **priests**. It is instructive to compare priests with shamans. In addition to their more specialized status, priests differ from shamans in several respects. First, most shamans perform their ritual functions without aid from other shamans; indeed, as we have seen, many peoples believe that enemy shamans engage in supernatural battles with one another. In contrast, priests are organized into a hierarchical priesthood under the sponsorship of a formal government, the state. Second, priests undergo a lengthy period of special training because they must master the complex rituals needed to perform their role. Third, the priesthood was at or near the top of the social ladder in the ancient civilizations, so individual priests lived much better than the population at large. Fourth, shamans typically perform mainly crisis rituals, whenever some person requires their services. The rituals at which priests officiate tend to be calendrical—they occur at regular intervals because the gods that the rituals are intended to appease demand regular praise or sacrifice.

A final difference is especially revealing. With the development of a *priesthood* there comes to be a strong distinction between priest and layperson. The layperson has little control over the timing and content of religious performances or the content of myths. The population at large relies on the priesthood to keep it in proper relation to supernatural powers. This creates a sense of spiritual dependence on the priesthood and on the state apparatus that sponsors it, a dependence that reinforces the high degree of stratification found in states.

These state-sponsored cults are called *ecclesiastical* (meaning "of or pertaining to the church") because their priesthood was highly organized and their rituals usually were held in grandiose buildings that served as temples. The entire ecclesiastical cult was under the control of the government. Officials exacted tribute or taxes to finance the construction of temples, the livelihood of the priesthood, the sacrifices that often accompanied state rituals, and other expenses needed to

*Ecclesiastical cults include an organized priesthood, which officiates at rituals usually held in temples. Most religions familiar to Westerners include ecclesiastical cults, as this photo of a Protestant church illustrates.*

support and organize religious activities on a fantastically large scale.

There is little question that ecclesiastical cults provided a body of myth and belief that supported the domination of the ruling dynasty. (This is not to say that this function totally explains these cults or that it constitutes their entire significance.) This is seen by the content of the cults' beliefs, myths, and rituals, which almost invariably express the dependence of the entire population on the ruler's well-being and on the periodic performance of rituals. A common belief of official state religions is that the ruler is a god-king: He not only rules by divine mandate but is himself a god or somehow partakes of divine qualities. This was true of most of the ancient civilizations and of the states that developed in sub-Saharan Africa.

Many official rituals of ecclesiastical cults are held to keep the entire polity in beneficial relationship with supernatural beings. For example, the state religion of the ancient Aztec taught that the gods had to be periodically appeased or they would cause the world to end in a cataclysm. To keep the gods' goodwill the priesthood periodically performed human sacrifice at temples, offering the heart of the victim (usually a war captive) to the deities. The ancient Egyptians believed that their pharaoh would rule in the afterlife—just as in the present world—so when he died, he took much of his wealth, his wives, and his servants into the next world with him.

Ecclesiastical cults everywhere consumed enormous resources in the civilizations, but they did not wipe out other kinds of cults. Common people usually continued to rely on local shamans for curing, to practice magic, to believe in witches and sorcerers, and to worship their ancestors. In China, for example, each household and lineage continued to revere its ancestors while participating in the state religion.

Most Christian denominations—Catholic and the diverse Protestant sects—have an ecclesiastical character. In medieval Europe the authority of the Catholic Church was tightly interwoven with the exercise of secular power, although there often was conflict between pope and king. Only in the past few centuries has the formal alliance between the power of government and the power of God been broken for any length of time. (Informally and unofficially, religion continues to prop up political systems—God seems always to be on "our side," according to many religious people in our own and other modern nations.) We should not assume that even this official separation between church and state will necessarily be permanent. As the recent history of Iran suggests, the intermingling of political and ecclesiastical authorities can be reborn even in the modern world.

## ▣ REVITALIZATION MOVEMENTS

So far we have discussed religions in cultures that are changing only slowly. Under conditions of rapid change many peoples have turned to supernatural beings for aid and protection when their way of life or their lives themselves are threatened by contact with powerful outsiders. To preserve their way of life or to cope with changing conditions, large numbers of people join organized movements, usually called **revitalization movements**.

Revitalization movements are most likely to occur in a society when three conditions coalesce: (1) rapid change, often caused by exposure to unfamiliar people, customs, and objects; (2) foreign domination, which leads to a sense of cultural inferiority, especially common in colonial situations; and (3) the perception of relative deprivation, meaning that people see themselves as lacking wealth, power, and esteem relative to those who dominate them. The movements are especially common in situations of colonialism, but colonialism does not always produce them.

### Prophets and Revelations

Revitalization movements usually originate with an individual—a **prophet**—who claims to have had a dream or vision. Sometimes the prophet says that he or she is a messiah, or savior, sent by a spiritual being to save the world from destruction. In the dream or vision the prophet received a message—a **revelation**—from a god, an ancestor, or another spiritual power.

Revelations typically include two kinds of information given by the spirit. The first is a statement about what has gone wrong with the world, about why peoples' lives have changed for the worse. The introduction of corrupting foreign objects and habits—such as tobacco, alcohol, money, religions, or formal schooling—commonly are blamed for the troubles of today.

Second, prophets' revelations usually include a vision of a new world and a prescription for how to bring it about. In some cases the message is vague and secular, the prophet claiming that earthly lives will improve if people do (or stop doing) certain things. The message often is *apocalyptic:* The prophet says that the present world will end at a certain time, and only those who heed his message will be saved. The expulsion or death of foreigners is a frequent theme of apocalyptic visions: Foreigners will be drowned in a flood, burned in a fire, swallowed up by an earthquake, or killed by dieties or ancestors. Another common theme is the reversal of existing political and economic dominance relations: Foreigners will work for us, we will have the wealth instead of them, we will tax them and make laws that they must obey, or some other inversion of the existing structure. Nearly always the prophets' revelations are *syncretic;* that is, they combine elements of traditional myths, beliefs, and rituals with introduced elements.

Examples from two regions illustrate prophets, revelations, and the syncretism of revitalization movements.

### Melanesian Cargo Cults

The area called *Melanesia* in the southwest Pacific has experienced numerous revitalization movements in the twentieth century. Melanesians placed great cultural emphasis on wealth—and the manipulation of the flow of wealth—as the route to becoming a big man or powerful leader. It is therefore not surprising that they were most interested in the material possessions of German, English, French, and Australian colonial powers. Because European wealth was brought to the islands by ship or plane, it became known as *cargo,* and the various movements that sprang up with the aim of acquiring it through ritual means became known as **cargo cults**.

To Melanesians, all Europeans were fantastically wealthy; yet the Melanesians seldom saw them do any work to earn their possessions. The whites who lived in the islands certainly did not know how to make tanks, cars, canned food, radios, stoves, and so forth. In many traditional religions technology was believed to have been made by deities or spirits, so it followed that European objects likewise were made by their God. Further, when the whites living in Melanesia wanted some new object, they simply made marks on papers and placed them in an envelope or asked for the object by speaking into metal things. Some weeks later the object was delivered in ships or airplanes. It seemed to appear from nowhere. Surely the goods were made by spirits, and the meaningless acts the whites did to get their spirits to send cargo were rituals. Melanesians therefore believed that they, too, could acquire this wealth through the correct ritual procedure, which they

*Some members of the John Frum cargo cult in Tanna, Vanuata, perform a ritual march. They await the day that John Frum, their messiah, will return, bringing freedom and wealth. This movement has been in existence for more than forty years.*

frequently believed the whites were selfishly withholding from them.

Numerous prophets sprang up among diverse Melanesian peoples, each with his own vision or dream, each with his own story for why the Europeans had cargo and the Melanesians had none, and each claiming to know the secret ritual that would deliver the goods. The prophet often claimed to have received a visit from one of his ancestors or a native deity, who told him that the whites had been lying to people about how to get cargo.

The Garia, of the north coast of Papua New Guinea, illustrate some common themes of cargo cults. Like most other indigenous peoples, the Garia were visited by missionaries. Also, like many other peoples, the Garia initially adopted Christianity for reasons other than those the missionaries had in mind. They assumed that the whites knew the ritual that was the "road to cargo." The missionaries would give it to the Garia if only they practiced what the missionaries preached: church attendance, monogamy, worship of the true God, cessation of pagan practices such as sorcery and dancing, and so forth. Based on their belief that the missionary life-style and Christian rituals held the secret of cargo, many Garia converted to Christianity early in the twentieth century.

But the cargo did not arrive. The Garia grew angry with the missions because they concluded that the missionaries were withholding the true ritual secret of how to get cargo to deceive the Garia and keep all the wealth for themselves. In the 1930s and 1940s two Garia prophets arose. They told the people that the missionaries had been telling them to worship the wrong gods! God and Jesus both were really deities of the Garia, not of whites. The Europeans knew the secret names of God and Jesus and asked them for the cargo with secret prayers. All along Jesus had been trying to deliver the goods to the Garia, but the Jews were holding him captive in heaven. To free him the Garia had to perform sacrificial rituals. To show him how poor they were and to make him feel sorry for them, they had to destroy all their native wealth objects. If they did these things, Jesus would give the cargo to the ancestral spirits of the Garia, who would in turn deliver it to the living.

## Native American Movements

Revitalization movements occurred among American Indians, whose tragic sufferings at the hands of white traders, settlers, armies, and administrators are known to all twentieth-century Americans. Two movements were especially important, both of which were precipitated by a deterioration of tribal economic, social, and religious life.

**HANDSOME LAKE.** By 1800 the Seneca of New York had lost most of their land to the state, settlers, and land speculators. Whites committed many atrocities against the Seneca in the 1780s and 1790s, partly because many Seneca supported the British during the American Revolutionary War. There were also the usual diseases—such as smallpox and measles, which wiped out hundreds of thousands of Native Americans all over the continent—that reduced the tribe to a fraction of its former numbers. Seneca men had been proud warriors, hunters, and fur traders, but all these activities became more difficult because of the loss of land and the presence of whites. The American government waged psychological warfare against them, intentionally corrupting their leaders with bribes and liquor and generally attempting to dehumanize and demoralize them.

Seneca men became victims of alcoholism and drank up most of what little money they could still earn from the fur trade. Neighboring peoples, once subject to the authority of the Seneca and other members of the League of the Iroquois, ridiculed them. A growth in witchcraft accusations increased the internal conflict and divisions of their communities. Many women lost their desire for children and took medicines that caused them to abort or become sterile altogether. A way of life—and indeed a people themselves—was dying.

In 1799 a Seneca man named Handsome Lake lay sick. He was cured by three angels, who gave him a message from the Creator. Handsome Lake reported that the Creator was saddened by the life of the people and angry because of their drunkenness, witchcraft, and taking of abortion medicines. The Seneca must repent of such deeds. Handsome Lake had two more visions within the next year. There would be an apocalypse in which the world would be destroyed by great drops of fire, which would consume those who did not heed Handsome Lake's teachings. People could save themselves and delay the apocalypse by publicly confessing their wrongs, giving up sins such as witchcraft and drinking, and returning to the performance of certain traditional rituals.

The apocalypse did not occur, but Handsome Lake was able to give his teachings a new, more this worldly twist between 1803 and his death in 1815. He continued to preach temperance because the Creator had never intended whiskey to be used by Indians. He taught peace with both whites and other Indians. He urged that the scattered reservations of the Seneca be consolidated, so that the people could live together as one community. Domestic morality must be impeccable: Sons were to obey their fathers; divorce (commonplace among the Seneca in aboriginal times) was no longer to be allowed; adultery and domestic quarreling were to cease. Most

important, Handsome Lake succeeded in changing the traditional division of labor, in which cultivation of crops was done by women and garden work by men was considered effeminate. Seneca men took up farming and animal husbandry and even fenced their fields and added new crops to their inventory.

**PEYOTE RELIGION.** Peyote is a small cactus that grows in the Rio Grande valley of Texas and northern Mexico. It produces a mild narcotic effect when eaten. The ritual use of peyote among Mexican Indians predated European conquest. However, its consumption as the central element in a revitalization movement dates only from the last two decades of the nineteenth century.

In 1875 the Southern Plains tribes, the Kiowa and Comanche, lost their land after they were defeated militarily. During their confinement to reservations in southwestern Oklahoma the Lipan-Apache introduced them to peyote. By the 1880s the two tribes had made the cactus the center of a revitalization movement. Like many movements, peyotism subsequently spread, reaching about nineteen Indian groups in Oklahoma by 1899. It ultimately was incorporated as an official church in 1914, with the name Koshiway's First Born Church of Christ. During the early twentieth century the church spread rapidly to other Indian communities throughout the western United States and Canada. It exists today as the Native American Church.

The peyote movement had no single prophet or leader. Local churches developed their own versions of services and rituals. One early leader was John Wilson, a Caddo/Delaware from western Oklahoma who had learned to use peyote from the Comanche. While eating dinner in the early 1890s, Wilson collapsed. Thinking him dead, his family began preparations for the burial. But Enoch Parker, a Caddo, told the family that he had learned in a vision that Wilson was not dead. Indeed, Wilson revived three days later. He reported that a great Water Bird had sucked the breath and sin out of his body, causing his collapse. Jesus brought him back to life three days later, telling him that his sins had been removed and that he was to teach the Indian people to believe in God and to use peyote to communicate with him.

Until his death in 1901 Wilson proselytized the peyote religion among the Osage, Delaware, Quapaw, and other groups. He preached that they needed to believe in God and Jesus, work hard, act morally, and abstain from alcohol consumption. They were to abandon their traditional religious practices because the spirits that formerly had aided them could be used for evil as well as good purposes. Wilson attracted the greatest number of adherents among the Osage, who combined the use of peyote in worship services with the Christian teachings they had learned in mission schools.

Peyote was not integrated into Christian teachings among all Native Americans who adopted it for ritual use. It did, however, provide meaning and moral direction to Indian life during a period of rapid and harmful change. Thousands of Native Americans continue to use it in religious services.

What is the fate of revitalization movements? Many with apocalyptic messages simply disappear when the end of the world does not occur. Other movements were remarkably tenacious. In Melanesia certain areas saw the rise and fall of numerous prophets, each claiming to have the cargo secret. People followed again and again because they had no other acceptable explanation for the existence of cargo, for why whites had it and they lacked it, or for how they could acquire it. Certainly their own worldly efforts—working for Europeans in mines and plantations, growing and selling coffee, copra, cocoa, and so forth—showed no signs of rewarding them with the fantastic wealth that whites enjoyed with virtually no effort. Cargo cults did not exactly disappear in some regions; instead, they transformed into a political movement or party. This was the fate of cargo cults among the Garia, Manus, Tannese, and some Malaitans.

Other movements do not wither away or transform into a more secular, political movement. They retain their religious character, frequently teaching that contentment is to be found within oneself rather than in worldly material things. After his death in 1815, Hand-

*Members of the three Southern Plains tribes are shown here with objects used in peyote rituals. Thousands of Native Americans continue to practice the peyote religion.*

some Lake's exhortations on how to live became codified and still persist as a Native American church—the Old Way of Handsome Lake, also known as the Longhouse religion.

Peyotism also became formally organized. Like many other revitalization movements that give birth to new religions, the adherents of peyotism are thus far largely confined to a single ethnic category: Native Americans. Other movements, however, grow in scale over the centuries. From humble beginnings they eventually attract millions of believers. They develop a formal organization complete with priests rather than prophets. Revelations become sacred writings. Beliefs become formal doctrines. Followers and disciples become organized into a church. Most of the major religions of the modern world began as revitalization movements, including Islam, Judaism, and Christianity.

## SUMMARY

In comparing religions, it is useful to identify three components that all share: beliefs about the nature of supernatural powers (beings and forces), myths about the past deeds of these powers, and rituals intended to influence them. All known human societies have such beliefs and myths and practice such rituals, so all have religion.

Religion is universal despite the facts that beliefs and myths can never be proved true or false and that

rituals are not effective in achieving the goals people have in mind when they perform them. One puzzling thing about religion is what it does for people as individuals or for society as a whole. Various social scientists have proposed that religion performs intellectual/cognitive, psychological, and social functions. No consensus exists about which of these functions are most important. Religion probably fulfills all these kinds of "needs," but none of these functions seems able to explain religion itself or the great diversity of human religions.

Religions vary in the range of human activities and natural occurrences in which spiritual powers are believed to intervene. Most religions include a belief that supernatural beings or forces cause or influence group or personal misfortune, such as deaths, illnesses, and "accidents." The malevolent powers of sorcerers and witches are blamed for misfortune in a great many societies. Accusations of sorcery and witchcraft tend to be patterned and to reflect prevalent conflicts and tensions in the organization of society. Those known or suspected of having malevolent powers can use other peoples' belief that they have such powers as a political weapon because witches and sorcerers are feared as well as despised. Although beliefs in sorcery and witchcraft might seem to be harmful, a number of anthropologists have argued that they have psychological and social functions.

Religions may be classified according to the types of cults they include, although any such classification is inadequate to depict the diversity of the world's religions. Cults may be characterized as individualistic, shamanistic, communal, and ecclesiastical. In a generalized way there is an evolutionary sequence to cults in that they tend to be associated with different degrees of cultural complexity.

Revitalization refers to religious movements that aim to create a new way of life to replace current conditions that are intolerable. Most revitalization movements originate with prophets who claim to have received a revelation, which usually is syncretic and often apocalyptic. Twentieth-century Melanesian cargo cults are among the best studied movements. The Handsome Lake religion among the Seneca of New York and the peyote religion are two of many North American revitalization movements.

# KEY TERMS

animism
myths
ritual
intellectual/cognitive
    functions of religion
psychological functions
    of religion
social functions of
    religion
sorcery
witchcraft
cult
individualistic cults

shamanistic cults
communal cults
ecclesiastical cults
vision quest
shaman (medicine man)
ancestral cults
totemism
priests
revitalization movement
prophet
revelation
cargo cults

# SUGGESTED READINGS

**Numerous books are available that provide basic introductions to the anthropological study of religion, including the following.**

Howells, William. *The Heathens: Primitive Man and His Religions*. Salem, Wisc.: Sheffield, 1986.
> *This book was originally written in 1948. Interpreted with the date of its first publication in mind, it is a good place to start for an overview of human religious diversity.*

Lehman, Arthur C., and James E. Myers, eds. *Magic, Witchcraft, and Religion*. 3d ed. Palo Alto, Calif.: Mayfield, 1993.
> *An excellent reader prepared mainly for undergraduates.*

Lessa, William, and Evon Vogt, eds. *Reader in Comparative Religion*. 4th ed. New York: Harper and Row, 1979.
> *A collection of essays that examine religion from various perspectives and introduce students to the range of anthropological ideas concerning the subject.*

Levack, Brian P., ed. *Anthropological Studies of Witchcraft, Magic and Religion*. New York: Garland, 1992.
> *Reprints of twenty-one influential articles published at various times in the twentieth century. Especially good on witchcraft and religion.*

Mair, Lucy. *Witchcraft*. New York: McGraw-Hill, 1969.
> *Excellent introduction to witchcraft and its analysis.*

**The following ethnographies examine religion and religious movements.**

Boyer, Dave, and Stephen Nissenbaum. *Salem Possessed*. Cambridge, Mass.: Harvard University Press, 1974.
> *Historical study of the witchcraft outbreak in 1692 in Salem, Massachusetts. Shows that the accusations closely reflected long-standing lines of conflict in the community.*

Brown, Michael Fobes. *Tsewa's Gift: Magic and Meaning in an Amazonian Society*. Washington, D.C.: Smithsonian, 1986.
> *Detailed study of shamanism among the Aguaruna of Peru.*

Evans-Pritchard, E. E. *Witchcraft, Oracles, and Magic among the Azande*. Abridged ed. Oxford: Clarendon, 1976.
> *An abridgement of the 1937 edition that loses little of the information found in the original. One of the best descriptions of witchcraft among an African people ever written.*

Geertz, Clifford. *The Religion of Java*. Glencoe, Ill.: The Free Press, 1960.
> *One of the great case studies of non-Western religions.*

Grim, John A. *The Shaman: Patterns of Religious Healing among the Ojibway Indians*. Norman: University of Oklahoma, 1983.
> *Empirical study of Ojibway shamans that also compares Ojibway with shamanism in other parts of the world.*

Jorgensen, Joseph. *The Sun Dance: Power for the Powerless.* Chicago: University of Chicago Press, 1972.
> *An analysis of the historic adoption of the sun dance by the Ute Indians of Utah.*

Keesing, Roger. *Kwaio Religion*. New York: Columbia University Press, 1982.

*Study of the religion of a Solomon Island society.*

Kehoe, Alice Beck. *The Ghost Dance: Ethnohistory and Revitalization*. Fort Worth: Holt, Rinehart and Winston, 1989.

*Descriptive account of the 1890 Ghost Dance that began among the Nevada Paiute and spread to the Lakota and other peoples of the plains. Shows the impact of the religious movement on Native American cultures today.*

Kluckhohn, Clyde. *Navaho Witchcraft*. Boston: Beacon, 1967.

*Well-written study of witchcraft among the Navajo of the Southwest, originally published in 1944.*

Luhrman, T. M. *Persuasions of the Witch's Craft: Ritual Magic in Contemporary England*. Cambridge, Mass.: Harvard University Press, 1989.

*Detailed and lengthy ethnographic study of witchcraft and the use of magic in England. One focus is how people maintain beliefs in the powers of magical rituals.*

Malinowski, Bronislaw. *Coral Gardens and Their Magic*. New York: American Book Company, 1935.

*A detailed description of garden magic and horticultural practices in the Trobriand Islands.*

Myerhoff, Barbara. *Peyote Hunt: The Sacred Journey of the Huichol Indians*. Ithaca, N.Y.: Cornell University Press, 1976.

*An ethnography describing how the Huichol Indians of northern Mexico locate and acquire peyote, which they use in their rituals.*

Neihardt, John G. *Black Elk Speaks*. 2d ed. Lincoln: University of Nebraska Press, 1961.

*A very popular and readable account of an Ogalala Sioux holy man and an excellent introduction to the religious beliefs and practices of this American Indian people.*

Stewart, Omer. *Peyote Religion*. Norman: University of Oklahoma Press, 1987.

*Detailed study of the peyote religion.*

Stoller, Paul, and Cheryl Olkes. *In Sorcery's Shadow: A Memoir of Apprenticeship among the Songhay of Niger*. Chicago: University of Chicago Press, 1987.

*Personal and adventurous account of Stoller's efforts to learn sorcery techniques from a famous Songhay sorcerer.*

Turner, Victor. *The Forest of Symbols*. Ithaca, N.Y.: Cornell University Press, 1967.

*Collection of papers on the religion of the Ndembu of Zambia. Turner's descriptions are rich in detail, and his analysis of the meaning of symbols used in rituals has been influential.*

Wallace, Anthony F. C. *The Death and Rebirth of the Seneca*. New York: Vintage, 1969.

*A highly readable and interesting account of the Longhouse religion, a revitalization movement that first appeared among the Seneca of New York State in the early 1800s.*

Worsley, Peter. *The Trumpet Shall Sound: A Study of "Cargo" Cults in Melanesia*. New York: Schocken, 1968.

*A comparative study of the origins and development of cargo cults.*

**Of the numerous studies of religion in contemporary America, these are especially useful.**

Chalfant, H. Paul, Robert E. Beckley, and C. Eddie Palmer. *Religion in Contemporary Society*. Palo Alto, Calif.: Mayfield, 1984.

*A textbook on the sociology of American religion. Twelve articles analyzing the mobilization of evangelical Christians for the conservative cause.*

Rochford, E. Burke, Jr. *Hare Krishna in America*. New Brunswick, N.J.: Rutgers University Press, 1985.

*Participant observation study of Hare Krishna by a noted sociologist.*

Stark, Rodney, and William Sims Bainbridge. *The Future of Religion*. Berkeley: University of California Press, 1985.

*A theoretical analysis of religious change and diversification, focusing on Protestant denominations in the United States.*

## CHAPTER 16

# PERSONALITY FORMATION AND THE LIFE CYCLE

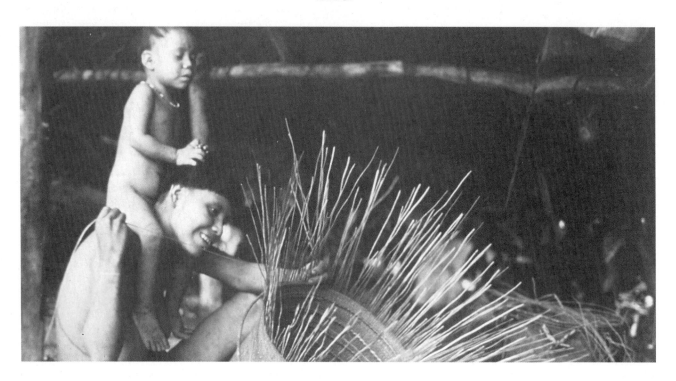

*Cultural categories of age, with corresponding roles and responsibilities based on age, vary from people to people.*

**CONTENTS**

Like most other dimensions of human existence, the way infants and children are treated by and interact with their parents and other adults varies from culture to culture. Cultural anthropologists are interested in how the process of nurturing and enculturating children affects the development of an individual's motivations, emotional states, behavioral predispositions, and the like. They are, in other words, interested in the relation between the culture of a group and the personalities of its members. How personality and culture mutually affect each other is one topic of this chapter.

People experience a series of life cycle changes, meaning the stages they pass through as they reach puberty, marry, become parents, reach middle age, and grow old. The movement of people through the various stages of life is also discussed in this chapter.

## PERSONALITY AND CULTURE

A child learns how to think, feel, speak, and behave by growing up and participating in a social environment made up of other people and the cultural traditions they live by. No two children experience the same social and cultural environments during their childhood, but people brought up in similar environments do develop similarities in their emotions and reactions to people and events. The specialization within ethnology known as *psychological anthropology* studies the relation between individuals and their cultural systems. One major interest of psychological anthropology is the relation between personality and culture.

What do we mean by the word **personality**? A concise definition appears in the 1991 *Dictionary of Concepts in Cultural Anthropology:* "The characteristic modes of thought, motivation, and feeling, conscious and unconscious, which guide the behavior of an individual"

(Winthrop 1991, 213). This definition implies that to the extent that two individuals share a similar personality, their behavioral reactions to similar events and situations will be similar.

The type of personality an individual develops is a product of the complex interaction between that individual's unique biological constitution and total life experiences. A discussion of how these two forces interact to fashion a unique human individual is outside the scope of this book. Psychological anthropologists have focused much more on life experiences than on biological influences on personality. They are especially concerned with the effects of how children are cared for and enculturated on the type of personality they are likely to develop. If nurturing and enculturation practices differ from culture to culture, then these differences might be reflected in the personalities of the members of these cultures.

## Child-Rearing Practices and the Formation of Personality

The phrase **child-rearing practices** refers to a culture's consistent and widespread behavioral patterns involved in caring for and enculturating children. These include practices such as how children are nursed, weaned, and toilet trained; how adults and people their own age interact with children; the kinds of behaviors that are punished and rewarded and how they are punished and rewarded; how much time children spend with various caretakers; how much attention and love they receive from adults and other family members; and the like.

It is largely during their childhood years that people learn the norms, values, world views, attitudes, and other elements of cultural knowledge (see chapter 2) that will guide their behavior throughout their lives. Child-rearing practices also are important influences on the type of personality people acquire. All else equal (and all else never is equal) children exposed to similar child-rearing practices tend to develop common elements of personality.

Although scholars find it convenient to speak of "the" way the members of a culture raise children, it is important to note that there is always variability in how families interact with their young, even within a single cultural tradition. Nonetheless, people share much in common by virtue of the fact that they were raised in the same culture, and the cultural knowledge they share has at least some impacts on how they rear their children.

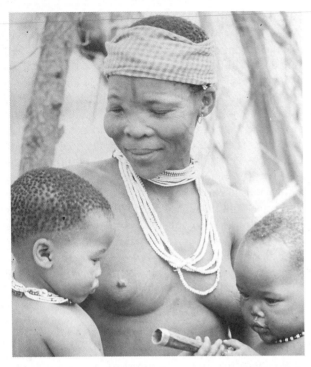

*!Kung woman with her children. How parents and other adults interact with children is one of many influences on personality formation.*

mothers coat their nipples with bitter substances to discourage nursing after a certain age.

Norms about disciplining children likewise vary from people to people. In some societies people believe that physical punishment is an integral and necessary part of childhood discipline (as in the saying "spare the rod and spoil the child"). In other societies correcting children's behavior by slapping or beating them is rare. Parents and siblings may cruelly ridicule (by our standards) a child for misbehaving. Or children may be quite indulged until they reach a certain age, after which they are punished severely for their misdeeds. In many Micronesian and Polynesian islands an infant of either gender is caressed, fondled, played with, and generally the center of interest of the whole family. Such indulgence and attention continue until a younger sibling is born. Then attention shifts to the newborn, and the child finds herself or himself just another member of a (usually large) family. Prolonged tantrums often result.

In some cultures children are threatened by animals, ghosts, spirit beings, and the like (the equivalent of "the boogey man will get if you act like that"). Among the Hopi children are threatened by *kachinas,* or masked dancers impersonating spiritual beings whom Hopi believe live in the mountains near their villages (see chapter 15). When a Hopi child seriously misbehaves, parents often get someone to put on a costume (including a frightening mask) of an "ogre" kachina believed to eat children. When the kachina tries to steal the child for misbehaving the parents come to his or her rescue. Children are so grateful to their parents for saving them that they accede to their wishes—for a while, anyway. Kachinas also reward "deserving" children by passing out gifts during their dances. Boys often are given a small bow and arrow, whereas girls receive carved wooden figures shaped and painted like the spirits.

Numerous other differences in child-rearing norms and practices exist between societies. Age and methods of toilet training are diverse. The kind of social interaction with adults varies widely—children are constantly fussed over among one people, left alone more to amuse themselves among others. Youngsters are punished for playing with their genitals in one society but are fondled playfully by adults in another. Pubescent boys and girls are allowed to associate freely with one another in some societies but are discouraged or forbidden from doing so in others. Fathers often are hardly involved with their children and in fact are absent much of time, but sometimes men are more or less equal partners in child care. Caretaking roles vary: in some cases virtually all the care is the responsibility of the mother, but other

They may broadly agree, for instance, on the proper age and methods for nursing and weaning infants, on physical punishment, and on other practices that they regard as appropriate or inappropriate. Likewise, in culturally homogeneous societies families may be subject to similar kinds of economic or social pressures that lead to similar child-rearing practices. For example, if males frequently are away on hunts or wars, then fathers and other male relatives may not be as active in child care as women, and this may have impacts on their children's personality formation.

Conversely, significant differences exist *between* cultures in behavioral patterns related to child-rearing. To illustrate this diversity we use two examples: weaning and discipline methods.

Cultures differ in their ideas about whether infants should be allowed to nurse whenever they desire or only at certain times. There are culturally variable norms about the proper age of weaning and how it should be accomplished. Reportedly, some Inuit allowed children to nurse as long as they desired; even ten-year-olds might occasionally be given the breast. Weaning methods likewise vary: Some people believe that infants should be allowed to wean themselves, whereas other relatives of the child (e.g., grandparents, uncles, aunts, older siblings) frequently share the duties.

These are only a few of the many ways cultures vary in child-rearing norms and practices. Not surprisingly, as a result of these variations members of different cultures develop some differences in adult personality. A major question of psychological anthropology is, How are differences in adult personality related to different child-rearing practices? More broadly phrased, How do cultural systems affect the personalities of their members?

The answer is not simple. Early studies often assumed a one-to-one relationship between personality and culture. That is, largely through its child-rearing practices, each culture was seen as molding the personalities of its members into a certain basic type. It commonly was believed that "a" culture fashioned the individual personalities of its members into the kinds of persons "it" needed to persist.

The most famous exponent of this approach was Ruth Benedict, whose 1934 book *Patterns of Culture* was

*There are many ways parents induce children to behave appropriately and acceptably. This carving represents a Hopi ogre kachina that parents sometimes use to frighten misbehaving children.*

enormously influential. Benedict argued that from the vast array of humanly possible cultures, each develops only a limited number of "themes," "patterns," or "configurations" that come to dominate the thinking and responses of its members. These patterns are essentially emotional: Each people develop a unique set of feelings and motivations that govern their behavior. Each culture has a conception of an ideal personality type, and these ideals vary from culture to culture. People's personality reflects and is consistent with the basic pattern of their culture. The essence of both the culture and the personality of a people could be described in simple terms—sometimes even by a single word. Behavior that one people considered crazy or otherwise abnormal would be acceptable, normal, and even ideal among another people.

For instance, Benedict wrote that the Kwakiutl of the Northwest Coast of North America are individualistic, competitive, intemperate, and egoistic to the point of megalomania. This culture (or is it a personality?) affects Kwakiutl customary behaviors. They stage ceremonies known as *potlatches* in which one kin group gives away enormous quantities of goods to another. The aim is to shame the rival group because if the rival is unable to return the presentations on certain occasions, it suffers a loss of prestige. In fact, to avoid losing prestige the recipient group is obliged to return gifts of even greater value. Over time the presentations often snowball until the members of one group, in their ceaseless quest for prestige, are left destitute (or so Benedict imagined). The whole complex of behavior connected to the potlatch reflects the cultural configuration of the Kwakiutl—so caught up is Kwakiutl culture by the prestige motivation that groups impoverish themselves to achieve this goal. Benedict used the term "Dionysian" to describe the Kwakiutl, after the Greek god known for his excesses.

Benedict contrasted this configuration to the Zuni villagers of the North American Southwest. Zuni control their emotions; they are moderate, modest, stoical, orderly, and restrained in their behavior; they do not boast or attempt to rise above their fellows but are social and cooperative. This "Apollonian" cultural theme, as Benedict called it, penetrates all of Zuni life. Unlike a Kwakiutl leader, a Zuni man does not seek status; indeed, a leadership role practically has to be forced on him.

So, according to Benedict, each culture has its unique patterns and themes, which produce images of the ideal personality that vary from culture to culture. One culture's crazed megalomaniac is another culture's ideal person. And culture programs personality more or less completely.

Benedict's approach is not highly regarded today by most psychological anthropologists. Her notion that whole cultures can be described, compared, and contrasted with fairly simple labels that depict their basic emotional patterns is regarded as simplistic. It is invalid to apply single labels to *the* personality type of the members of a culture, such as that Kwakiutl are Dionysian (given to excesses), whereas the Zuni are Apollonian (moderate in all things). Yet labels comparable to those used by Benedict are common even today. They often take the form of stereotypes that one people have about the "personality" of another. For example, the Japanese are popularly said to have "authoritarian" personalities because they seem to submit to instituted authority more than some other people. Italians are "excitable" to North American perceptions because they seem to be so enthusiastic about love, food, and family and so quick to take offense at slight indiscretions. Similarly, according to common American stereotypical labels, French are passionate, Irish have bad tempers, Swiss are humorless, Germans are scatological, and Swedes sensual.

In fact, wherever researchers have tried to measure the personality "type" of a people, they have found considerable variability in personality between individuals. Individuals do not share the same personality just because they belong to the same culture and have experienced similar child-rearing practices and other influences. There is always variability, due to hormonal and other biological differences between individuals, to idiosyncratic caring practices of parents, and to other factors. The best we can do is to identify and describe the **modal personality** of a people, meaning those elements of personality that many or most members of a culture share, or the type of personality that is most common.

Keeping in mind this variability, there do seem to be some interrelationships between child-rearing practices and modal personality. Here we illustrate these studies by describing one finding, and it is suggestive rather than definitive, like other analyses you have encountered in this book.

On the island of Timor in eastern Indonesia live a people known as the Alor. The Alorese were studied in the 1930s by Cora DuBois, who gave them psychological tests and had the tests interpreted by several psychologists when she returned from the field. The Alorese get most of their food by gardening. Women are responsible for most food production. When a woman gives birth she devotes most of her attention for several weeks to her newborn, nursing the baby whenever he or she cries and generally nurturing the infant. After only two or three weeks the mother returns to work almost daily in the family gardens. From early morning until late afternoon the child is left with grandparents, siblings, or other relatives. An Alorese father often is absent, engaged in the borrowing and lending of pigs and other wealth objects that are so important to these people.

During the long hours his or her mother is away the infant is not suckled, although attempts are made by caretakers to give it premasticated foods to quiet its crying. As the child matures his or her emotional demands are met only irregularly and by various individuals. Children are not often caressed or praised, and they frequently are teased and lied to. Their demands for attention often are ignored by their caretakers. Weaning is accomplished by pushing the child away from the breast; sometimes a recently weaned child is deliberately provoked by nursing another child because adults find the child's reaction humorous. All in all, the Alorese child lives in an uncertain, insecure, and, to some degree, hostile social environment.

As a result of these childhood experiences, many Alorese develop a personality described (by DuBois) as suspicious, antagonistic, uncooperative, prone to violent outbursts of jealousy, and lacking in self-confidence and social responsibility. These features of Alorese modal personality affect adult interpersonal relationships. Relations between husbands and wives, for instance, usually lack intimacy and often are downright hostile.

The Alorese case study suggests that the modal personality of a people is significantly affected by the degree to which parents and other caretakers reject or nurture children. How can we know whether this same relationship between a relatively low degree of nurturing and modal personality type applies elsewhere? And how do we know whether it is the relative neglect of children, rather than some other child-rearing practice, that produces a personality type like that of many Alorese?

One way to investigate such questions is with cross-cultural methods. For a variety of societies we can study their child-rearing practices with respect to the degree of parental and caretaker nurturing they receive and see whether rejection/nurturing has similar effects on modal personality among them. Ronald Rohner has conducted such a study. He found that parental lack of affection does produce certain similarities in modal personality: People who experience rejection and neglect in childhood develop personality traits such as hostility, low self-esteem, and emotional instability.

Child-rearing practices seem to be the major link between culture and the personalities people are most likely to develop. The cultural system influences how adults raise their children, and child-rearing practices in turn influence modal personality. The Alorese case illustrates how these influences might operate in one society, and many comparative studies like those of Rohner suggest that the same influences might produce the same kind of modal personalities generally.

## Cultural Consequences of Modal Personality

So far we have considered only one-half of the relation between personality and culture: how culture (particularly, child-rearing practices) affects modal personality. The other half of the relation is the impact of personality "type" on culture, that is, how the common elements of peoples' personalities affect culture. We would like to have a way to analyze how personalities and cultures interact and *mutually* affect each other.

Such a way is available. Clearly certain parts (subsystems) of a peoples' overall culture have greater impact on child-rearing practices than other subsystems; that is, some aspects of a culture affect the kinds of personalities individuals develop more than other aspects. In turn, because many individuals share certain elements of their personality, they relate in certain patterned ways to other individuals, and they find certain kinds of behaviors and ideas more attractive than others. Modal personality, therefore, influences other subsystems of the cultural system.

According to this approach, then, for purposes of relating cultural elements to personality, we divide a cultural system into two parts: (1) those subsystems that importantly affect child rearing and hence influence the kind of personality many or most individuals develop and (2) those subsystems that are partly determined by this modal personality.

What, specifically, about a peoples' overall way of life is most likely to have important effects on how they raise their children? The norms, values, attitudes, world views, and other kinds of shared cultural ideas are important. For instance, parents who view the world as a hostile place with many dangers to be avoided may impart feelings of insecurity to their children. Or adults who mistrust other people may have children who grow up suspicious of others.

But some psychological anthropologists believe that they can make conclusions more important than to simply say that "it all depends on a culture's ideas and beliefs." They can conclude more than this because child-rearing *practices* are affected by more than people's *ideas*. People's norms, values, world views, attitudes, and beliefs about the proper way to raise children affect how they actually raise children, but they do not entirely determine how they do so. For example, in the case of the Alor we saw how the sexual division of labor leads mothers to leave their children for many hours a day, forcing other relatives to assume the role of caretaker. In modern North America mothers with jobs make child-care arrangements for their children, leaving them with relatives, baby-sitters, or day-care centers. Alorese or North American mothers (and fathers, too, for that matter) may believe that they ought to spend more time with their children. But their actual child-rearing practices are affected by more than just their beliefs. Economic and social conditions impact what parents do. And parents themselves have other values and goals that may conflict with their desire to bring up their children the way they or others think that they should.

A more sophisticated and realistic model recognizes that child-rearing practices are affected by more than just people's ideas about the proper way to care for and rear children. The relation between modal personality and the cultural system is explained by the social systems model, developed by John Whiting and Irvin Child. The model is diagrammed in Figure 16.1.

In the figure, the *maintenance system* essentially is those specific aspects of cultures we have discussed in chapters 7 through 14. It includes how people acquire energy and materials from their environment; the organization of production, exchange, and control over resources; the prevalent forms of family and domestic groups; the kinds and sizes of kin groups and the strength and breadth of kinship relations; prevalent inequalities in access to resources and to social rewards; and the organization of political life, legal systems, and warfare. A maintenance system, in short, consists of a people's basic adaptation to nature and how their society is organized to persist, cooperate, allocate rewards, defend itself, and maintain internal order. It is influenced by technology, natural environment, and historical forces.

The maintenance system affects child-rearing practices and the overall learning environment of children: how soon they are made to take on household chores, how and how much they are punished or rewarded, how children interact with their caretakers, and so on. The kinds of personality children develop in turn depends on the total learning environment to which they are exposed, as the Alorese example shows. To the extent

**FIGURE 16.1**
**The Social Systems Model**

*SOURCE:* Adapted from "A Model for Psychocultural Research," by John Whiting in *Culture and Infancy,* P. Herbert Leiderman, Steven R. Tulkin, and Anne Rosenfeld, eds. Orlando, Fla.: Academic Press, 1977. Reprinted by permission.

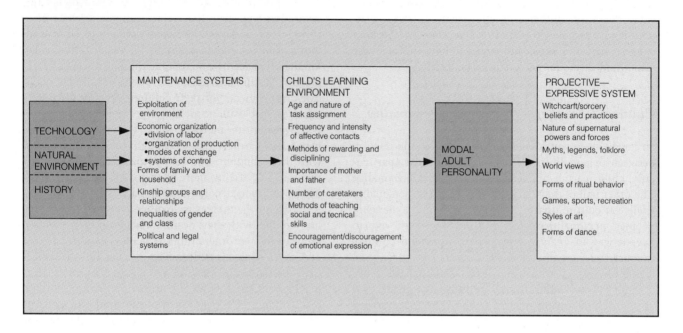

that most or many children experience the same learning environment, they will develop similarities in personality as adults, which we have called the *modal personality*. Thus similar modal personalities result from economic pressures, familial and kinship relationships and groupings, inequalities based on class and gender, and political forces.

The social systems model suggests how modal personality influences culture as well as being influenced by it. Because so many people develop similar personalities, they find certain kinds of activities and ideas about the world more attractive (or congenial) than others. For example, they are likely to attribute certain qualities to supernatural beings and forces; to find some kinds of games, art styles, and stories more enjoyable to play, view, and hear than others; and to find some kinds of rituals and ceremonies more meaningful than others. Cultural elements that are strongly influenced by modal personality are called the *projective-expressive system*.

One important suggestion of the social systems model is that economic, social, and political factors outside the control of parents and other caretakers are *universally* important influences on how parents rear their children. Working parents in modern industrial nations often think that there is something unique about their failure

*According to the Social Systems Model, modal personality is affected by a people's adaptation, including whether work requires parents to leave their children with other caretakers. This Burkina-Faso woman cares for her child while she works.*

to spend as much time with their children as they would like, or as much as they believe is necessary for their children's emotional well-being or intellectual development. To make up for the hours spent on the job instead of at home with the kids, the idea of devoting quality time to one's children has developed. The implication is that in the past no one had to worry about such things. But parents everywhere face conditions such as those identified by the social systems model that affect how they rear children. Societies have adjusted to these conditions, and they have readjusted as these conditions have changed. Thus far in the United States working parents themselves have had to make most of the familial rearrangements needed to find child care. Perhaps it is time for more employers to find ways of accommodating their employees' familial needs. Given the alleged concern for family values in the United States, perhaps it is time to change "an occupational system that operates 'as if' the family did not exist." (Cohen 1987, 72).

## ▄▄ AGE CATEGORIES AND AGE SETS

In all societies an individual's chronological age makes a difference in the kinds of roles he or she adopts and in the activities he or she performs. Everywhere individuals are culturally classified on the basis of their age: infant, child, adult, elderly person, and so forth. People of similar age often are allocated the same kinds of roles. Although all peoples have such age categories, societies vary in the number of categories, the sharpness with which they are defined, their importance relative to other distinctions such as gender and class, and the roles members of the category are expected to adopt.

Like other people, Westerners classify people on the basis of their age. In the United States we make subdivisions of age categories as needed by the context (e.g., the age category "child" may be divided into infant, toddler, preschooler, first-grader, and so on). Many other cultures establish more formal and highly organized groups of individuals of similar age, and these age groupings assume definite and important rights in and duties to the society as a whole. One such grouping common in the preindustrial world is the *age set association*.

An **age set association** is a permanent, formally organized named group of males or females, the members of which are recruited on the basis of similar age. It is more common for males to be organized into age sets, although some societies have such organizations for both males and females. Because age sets include all members of a society of a particular sex and age cohort, they cut across kinship lines and often serve as pantribal sodalities (chapter 13). In many societies age sets take over many functions usually assigned to kin groups and frequently surpass the kin group in relative importance for the individual. If a society has age sets, people usually enter them about or a little after the time they reach sexual maturity. Although age sets are found among peoples in North and South America, Melanesia, and Asia, they are especially common in Africa. There are two distinct types of age sets: *cyclical age sets* and *lineal age sets*.

Societies with *cyclical age sets* have a limited number of named associations based on age. Although the same individuals continue to associate with one another throughout their lives, the members move as a group from one association to another in rank or age order. The Hidatsa of the Great Plains are an example of this type of system. Periodically, about every four to six years, all adolescent Hidatsa boys banded together. With the help of their parents they purchased the lowest ranking of the ten age set associations from the members of that association. This lowest-ranking association was called the *Kit-Foxes*. The purchase of the age set gave the new members the sole rights to wear the insignias of this group as well as to perform its dances and songs. In addition, many rights and duties of the individual members were defined by the association of which they were members. After they themselves sold the lowest-ranking age set, the former members of the Kit-Foxes association purchased the rights and privileges of the next highest association, and within a short period all the groups had moved up a step to the next age set. The few surviving old men in the highest-ranking association withdrew from the system after selling their age set because there was no higher place for them to go within the system. Among the Hidatsa age sets were primarily men's social clubs with limited economic and political significance. Among the Cheyenne and other Great Plains peoples these organizations frequently filled the role of camp police.

*Lineal age sets* offer a contrast. In a lineal age-set system an individual remains a member of the same association throughout his or her life. The Swazi of southern Africa provide an example of lineal age sets. Every five to seven years the king of the Swazi announced that a new age set would be created to include all the adolescent boys in the kingdom. This announcement coincided with the proclamation that the members of what had up to then been the youngest set were now free to marry. The role of the youngest set was to serve as active warriors and thus its members could not be married. Many of them moved to barracks near the royal family, and even those who remained in their home communities were organized into military units. Every association had its own leaders and insignias, and a man belonged to the same age set for his entire life. All sets participated in wars, each as a separate and distinct military unit. Indeed, after English contact age sets commonly were called regiments.

Loyalty was fostered between the members of a given Swazi age set. Whether they were living in a royal barracks or at home, the members of a particular set were expected to work together. All members were equals who ate, worked, and smoked together. They used the term *brother* or *age mate* in referring to one another. Some anthropologists have argued that age set ties were stronger than kinship ties, and that a man's identity became more closely linked with his age set than with his family. Rivalries between age sets were intense, and fighting occasionally broke out between members of different sets, which pitted close relatives against one another.

Age sets illustrate how different societies use the principle of age differently to allocate statuses and roles to individuals and even to place them into groups. In a sense, age sets represent one extreme in the use of age as a principle—age differences are sharply (although partly culturally) defined, and they become the organizational basis of many cooperative activities. One African people, the Nyakyusa, even used age together with

sex to establish residence. Male members of the same age set lived in the same age-based village, bringing their wives to live with them.

Why do some societies have age sets, whereas most do not? Age sets most commonly are found among peoples who lack a centralized political system yet frequently are engaged in warfare. This correlation has led some anthropologists to suggest that age sets are a means of organizing males for warfare among people who lack formal political leadership and specialized armies.

## LIFE CYCLE

A person's **life cycle** consists of the culturally defined age categories through which he or she passes between birth and death. It includes stages such as birth, childhood, sexual maturation (puberty), marriage, adulthood, old age, and death. Each stage in the life cycle carries certain cultural expectations; as individuals move through these stages their overall role in society changes. All societies recognize at least three major distinctions in the life cycle: childhood, adulthood, and old age. These stages serve as a convenient way to organize our discussion of the life cycle, but it is important to recognize that peoples vary in how they conceive of these stages and in how transitions from one to the other are recognized and marked.

Transitions between stages may take place gradually and not be the object of any particular notice, or they

*Life cycle changes are significant in all cultures, but in varying ways and degrees. South Asian children with grandparents.*

may be sharply and formally defined by a rite of passage. A **rite of passage** is a public ceremony or ritual that marks a change in status, usually brought about or related to increasing age. Examples of rites of passage in North America include baptisms, conferrals, bar mitzvahs, graduation ceremonies, weddings, and funerals.

## Childhood

One might think that childhood begins at birth. Actually the issue is more complex. Like all phases of the life cycle, "child" is a culturally defined category of person as well as a physical state. Childhood may be said to commence only when an individual is accorded "human" status within some society, and the time when this happens varies from people to people. Does one become a person at the time of conception, at some period during the mother's pregnancy, at birth, or sometime after birth? As we discussed in chapter 13, all societies have legal systems, which are partly concerned with protecting the individual rights of the members of the society. Societies differ in how and when such rights are conferred on an individual, so the time when childhood begins may be said to vary.

In our own society this question has not been resolved. Members of right-to-life (antiabortion) groups believe that human life, and thus legal protection, begins at the time of conception. From their perspective, abortions constitute murder of a human being. Data from other societies concerning this question reveals a similar lack of consensus. As discussed in Box 13.1, the Cheyenne considered the murder of one Cheyenne by another as the most serious of crimes, and they categorized a woman who had an abortion as a murderer. In contrast, in many cultures even birth itself does not automatically convey human status. Infanticide (the killing of infants) has been a widespread practice. Among the Canadian Eskimo a child, particularly a female child born during the winter, could be placed outside immediately after birth to die of exposure. No stigma was attached to such an act. In ancient Greece, even in Athens itself, parents of sickly or unwanted newborn babies could abandon them along the road to die. Any passerby was free to adopt such an infant or to raise it as a slave to be sold, as in the famous story of Oedipus, the Greek king who unknowingly married his mother. In preindustrial societies with a high infant mortality rate the conferring of full human status sometimes is delayed until infancy has passed; thus the responsibility for providing formal burials for the large

numbers of children who die in infancy is avoided. Even where infanticide is not practiced the bestowal of full human status sometimes is delayed for some period after the birth of a child.

The formal naming of a child frequently is associated with the conferring of human status and often is the first rite of passage. For the Osage, a Native American people, the naming rite was the most important rite of passage: It bestowed human status on the individual. Osage parents often waited several months—in the case of a sickly child, possibly more than a year—before naming a child. If the child died before acquiring a name, he or she was quietly buried and the family did not have to observe a year of mourning. After they were convinced that the infant was going to survive, parents began to prepare for a naming ritual. A ritual specialist called a *non-hon-zhinga* (or "little-old-man") from the child's father's clan was chosen leader to organize and direct the ceremony. Little-old-men representing all twenty-four Osage patrilineal clans gathered in the "lodge of mystery," a ritual structure in the village, to hold the ceremony. One at a time the leader gave a trade blanket to all the little-old-men, each of whom recited a long and complex ritual prayer asking *Wa-kon-tah's* (god's) blessing for the child and outlining the supernatural powers associated with his particular clan. After all twenty-four clan prayers had been recited, the child was handed to each of the little-old-men, who in turn blessed the child. Some anointed the baby with water, others rubbed the child with cedar or touched the child with ground corn. Then the baby was seated on a specially prepared robe in the center of the lodge and given a name belonging to his or her clan by the leader. The giving of this name symbolized the acceptance of the child as a member of a particular clan. The ritual participation of members of the other twenty-three clans indicated the acceptance of the child as an Osage. The ritual ended with the father of the child giving horses and blankets to the main little-old-men and lesser gifts to the other little-old-men. Only after the naming ritual might one say that Osage childhood truly began.

Childhood is the stage in which the essentials of cultural knowledge are acquired, including the linguistic and social skills that people use later in life. It is also the period when people begin to acquire the technical and mechanical skills required in their culture for full adult status. In most societies the learning of technical skills begins early by Western standards, by about age five or six. Simple tasks not demanding great strength are done even earlier—three-year-olds may sweep the house, feed the animals, wash the baby, pick up the

*Games help children learn the technical, physical, and social skills of their society.*

yard, run errands, deliver messages, and so forth. In industrial societies much technical learning takes the form of formal education in schools, where children are instructed by trained specialists. Elsewhere children learn most skills informally by watching and imitating adults and following their instructions. Boys begin spending more time with their fathers and other male relatives, who instruct them in skills and knowledge they will need as men. Among cultivators, children begin going to the fields with their parents and performing minor tasks that are suited to their physical abilities. In herding societies children begin caring for the herds at a young age. For example, among the Navajo, six- and seven-year-old boys and girls begin helping with the herds of sheep and goats. While Navajo boys learn the technical skills needed by men, girls learn the skills of women by imitating their mothers and playing with toy animals. As they become older they help their mothers by preparing wool for weaving, preparing foods, making clothing, and caring for their younger brothers and sisters.

## Becoming an Adult

A person usually reaches puberty (sexual maturation) between ages twelve and fifteen. Female sexual maturation is indicated by the menarche, or first menstruation.

With boys the physical indicators develop more gradually: increase in body hair, change in voice, development of musculature, and so forth. In most societies sexual maturation alone does not convey full adult status, with all its rights and responsibilities. Biologically determined sexual maturation usually precedes culturally defined social maturation, especially for males. This intermediate stage of transition from childhood to adulthood is what we call *adolescence.*

In American society adolescence often is a trouble period of life, filled with conflict, experimentation, rebellion against parental authority, moodiness, and the like. Some researchers attribute the problems that arise during this period primarily to physiological changes, but others consider cultural factors to be the major causes. In the 1920s Margaret Mead examined adolescence in a Pacific culture in her classic study *Coming of Age in Samoa.* Mead found that adolescence was not a particularly traumatic time in the life of Samoan girls, and she argued that the problems associated with adolescence were the result of cultural factors, not physiological changes. In 1983 Derek Freeman challenged Mead's Samoa findings in his book *Margaret Mead in Samoa,* arguing that Samoan adolescents have about as much trouble and conflict as do American teenagers. He went on to suggest that the physiological changes that occur during adolescence have similar effects among all peoples, so this stage of the life cycle is always stressful despite the cultural context. Most modern anthropologists would probably contend that the universal physiological changes do create problems for adolescents everywhere, but that these problems are manifested in various ways, depending on the cultural context.

Not only are there physical changes and the associated intensification of sexual urges, but changes in culturally expected behavior also occur during adolescence. Although adolescents begin to take on many of the social and legal responsibilities of adulthood, they usually are not accorded the full prerogatives of adults. For example, in the United States adolescents frequently can be tried and sentenced in an adult court for a criminal offense yet cannot vote in local, state, or national elections; purchase liquor; marry without parental consent; or get a bank loan without a co-signer. Until the voting age was lowered to eighteen in 1971, a male could be drafted into the army before he could vote. Thus in the United States an adolescent has some of the legal obligations of an adult but lacks full adult privileges. There are similar disparities in many other societies. Among the Cheyenne older adolescent boys were expected to join war parties and to be daring and aggressive warriors and raiders. Along with adult males they were expected to take part in hunts and help supply food for their family. At the same time they could not hold an official position within the tribe and had to remain silent in the presence of the elders of the tribe.

## Initiation Rites

The manner in which individuals are incorporated into adulthood and into adult rights and responsibilities varies from people to people. In the United States the transition to the adult stage of life is marked by rites of passage we call graduation ceremonies (from high school or college): One leaves the status of "student" and (we hope!) becomes an independent, wage-earning adult. In preindustrial societies the transition from childhood to adulthood frequently is marked by an elaborate set of ceremonies known as **initiation rites.**

Initiation rites often occur around puberty, so sometimes they are called *puberty rites,* although they do far more than simply mark off a person's sexual maturation. During many rituals the initiates are educated in the intricate responsibilities of adulthood, being told of the changes that will from then on be expected in their behavior and often being let in on ritual secrets.

Some societies have initiation rituals for males only, others for females only, and still others for both sexes.

But even those societies that hold initiation rites for both males and females almost always have separate ceremonies for each sex. This generalization suggests that an important function of initiation rituals is to incorporate children not just into adulthood but also into the adult roles and responsibilities culturally appropriate for their gender (see chapter 12). In fact, the most common theme of initiation rituals is to make girls into women and boys into men.

Some of the most interesting male initiation rituals occur in the highlands of New Guinea. Before describing an example we must point out that in many of these societies (and there are many hundreds of them) people believe that females can pollute males. Above all else, men fear contact with women's menstrual discharges, which they believe can cause them to sicken and die. Ethnographer Mervyn Meggitt (1970) describes the beliefs of one New Guinea people, called the *Enga,* about women's pollution:

Men regard menstrual blood as truly dangerous. They believe that contact with it or a menstruating woman will, in the absence of counter-magic, sicken a man and cause persistent vomiting, turn his blood black, corrupt his vital juices so that his skin darkens and wrinkles as his flesh wastes, permanently dull his wits, and eventually lead to a slow decline and death. Menstrual blood introduced into a man's food, they say, quickly kills him, and young women crossed in love sometimes seek their revenge in this way. Menstrual blood dropped on the bog-iris plants . . . that men use in wealth-, pig-, and war-magic destroys them; and a man would divorce, and perhaps kill, the wife concerned. (p. 129)

Because of such beliefs that their menstrual discharges are dangerous to their husbands and to other men, among many New Guinea peoples women must remain in seclusion during their periods, either in a menstrual hut away from the main settlement or in a special place in their houses, which men never enter. An Enga woman may do garden work during her period but only in gardens that contain "female crops"; if she should enter any garden that contains "male crops", such as taro and sugar cane, the crops would die.

These beliefs about feminine contamination have many implications for women's lives. Women must take precautions to avoid accidentally causing injury to their husbands by polluting the food they serve to their husbands. In some New Guinea societies women must travel on separate paths from men, lest a man unknowingly step on a female secretion and become polluted. Sometimes a wife is believed to "murder" her husband by introducing her bodily fluids into his food; a woman occasionally is killed in retaliation if her husband dies suspiciously. Women have to suffer through having their young sons taken away from them by force because according to beliefs the sons are endangered by continued association with their mothers once they reach a certain age.

Finally, it is common in these societies for husbands and wives to live in separate dwellings. A man's wife or wives have their own house, where they live with their children. Their husband lives in a separate men's house, together with all the older boys and men of the hamlet or village. By the time they are around ten years old boys usually are taken away from their mothers—because even contact with one's own mother is dangerous for a boy—and brought to live in the men's house. Male initiation rituals usually begin when a boy is dissociated from the company of his mother and other women and inducted into the men's house.

The details of male initiation vary from people to people in New Guinea. One common cultural rationale of the rituals is to transform a boy into a man: Boys do not grow up naturally but must go through a lengthy series of rituals to give them masculine qualities. Masculine courage, strength, aggressiveness, and independence are desirable not only for the boys themselves but are needed by the group as a whole because most New Guinea peoples traditionally were heavily involved in warfare with their neighbors and so needed warriors to survive. Another goal of the rituals is to protect boys from feminine contamination: Initiates learn ritual procedures that will allow them to have sexual relations in relative safety.

The Awa, a New Guinea people numbering about 1,500 who were studied by Philip Newman and David Boyd, illustrate both themes: "maturation" and "protection." Like many of their neighbors, Awa men believe that if female substances penetrate male bodies, the men will become sick or old before their time—or even pregnant! Beginning in their early teens boys go through a series of rituals that have five stages and last well into their twenties. When several boys in a region have reached the appropriate age of twelve to fourteen they are taken from their mothers' houses. They are inducted as a group into the men's house during an intimidating ritual involving food and water restrictions, beating with stinging nettles to toughen them, and rubbing the inside of their thighs with a coarse vine. This is the first stage of their initiation.

In the second stage, about one year later, the boys experience the first cleansing of their bodies from female pollution. At a secluded site in the forest they are forceably bled and made to vomit. The purpose of these acts is to protect their general well-being and promote their physiological maturity by removing female substances from the boys' bodies. Small bundles of sharp-edged swordgrass are jabbed into their nostrils and two small cuts are made in the glans of their penises to bleed out contamination. A vine is looped and thrust down their throats, inducing the vomiting that also cleanses and helps dry out their bodies—for the Awa believe that dessication is necessary for boys to achieve maturity.

The third ritual stage occurs when the males are between eighteen and twenty. They again are purged of female contamination by nose bleeding, penis cutting, and induced vomiting. They also are let in on certain ritual knowledge, known to all adult men but kept secret from women and boys. After they have been through the third stage the young men are taught why too much contact with women is so dangerous. They learn how menstrual pollution can overstimulate their growth and age them prematurely, and how it is possible for a man to become pregnant. Because they have not yet learned to protect themselves from female substances, they are warned to avoid sexual intercourse altogether until they are married.

About five years later, when the men are in their midtwenties, they go through the "sweat ceremony," which is the fourth stage of initiation. They sit together next to the fire in the men's house and sweat profusely for a week or more. The older men lecture to them about their upcoming responsibilities as husbands and fathers. They are told about how to protect themselves from the dangers of sexual intercourse and are emphatically warned about the evils of adultery. When the men emerge from the men's house after the sweat ceremony they receive new clothes and body ornaments, including a pair of boar's tusks that they wear in their pierced noses as a symbol of their adult status. After this stage young women chosen as brides are brought to the hamlet of their future husbands.

The fifth stage—appropriately called the "severe penis cutting"—occurs only a few days later. The young men are again subjected to food and water taboos, to nose-bleeding and vomiting, and to penis cutting. This time, however, canes are driven deep into their noses to cause severe bleeding. Small wedges of flesh are cut from either side of their penises, producing deep gashes in the glans. In fact, at the final stage of initiation all the adult men present line up and expose their penises to puncture wounds made by tiny stone-tipped arrows. This treatment is held to be necessary periodically to remove harmful female substances that have entered the body through the penis during sexual intercourse. In Awa

*Beginning in their early teens Awa boys participate in a lengthy series of rituals intended to strenthen, protect, and instruct them. This second-stage initiate is having his nose bled to remove harmful female substances from his body.*

beliefs a married man may become pregnant if he has sex too often, has intercourse with a menstruating woman, or penetrates the vagina too deeply, causing his penis to contact the blood and water contained in the womb. Womb blood moves up into the man's body and can make him pregnant. He therefore must have the female blood removed by being shot with miniature arrows, which will halt the pregnancy. Once a man has been through the fifth stage, Awa believe that he has been sufficiently strengthened by the hardships of initiation that he is capable of withstanding feminine pollution, although he must continue to undergo ritual bloodletting to maintain his strength and to fight the dangers of male pregnancy.

The Awa illustrate several themes common in male initiation rituals: inducing physical maturation, strengthening and protecting, imparting secret knowledge, and learning the importance of masculine responsibilities. Awa initiation also exemplifies another practice, common not just in New Guinea but around the world: The rituals are almost always painful and traumatic to the boys. They frequently involve scarification, beatings, genital mutilation, tattooing, intimidation by threats and frightful stories, social seclusion, fasting, going without water, and so forth. These pains and traumas usually are considered to be necessary to strengthen the boys and prepare them for the rigors of adulthood (see Box 16.1 for one mildly comparable ritual in the United States). Certainly such ordeals indelibly mark the transition from boy to man in the minds and usually the bodies of the males.

Initiation rites for females are not as common as those for males, but similar themes are apparent where they occur: an emphasis on maturation, instruction in sexuality, reminders of a woman's duties as a wife and mother, and so forth. There is a parallel to circumcision among males, known as *cliterectomy,* in which a woman's clitoris is removed. The female also commonly is harassed and frightened during her initiation.

When a girl among the Tucuna Indians of the Amazon has her first menstruation she is immediately placed in the loft of the large communal dwelling where she lives. She remains there until a special seclusion room next to the dwelling is constructed for her. She stays isolated in this room while preparations for her puberty rite are made. During this period the older women tell her about the danger from various spirits to which she as a woman is now subject, and they also inform her of what will be expected from her as a wife and mother. The ritual itself involves the presence of forty to fifty masked dancers who imitate spirits that both terrify and instruct her. Toward the end of the ceremony the girl is placed on a tapir hide in the middle of the house, and a group of elderly women slowly pull all the hair out of her head to the sound of a drum and rattle. The girl has to endure this pain without crying out. Although the Tucuna have an elaborate puberty rite for females, they have no such rite for males.

*These two Apache girls are being initiated.*

The late anthropologist Victor Turner pioneered the modern study of rites of passage. In his study of initiation rites among the Ndembu of Zambia, Turner noted that the rites have three phases: separation, liminality, and incorporation. These phases correspond to the basic nature of rites of passage: individuals who go through them are separated from their former statuses in society, go through a transition ("liminal") period during which they are "betwixt and between" normal statuses and social categories, and finally are reincorporated into society as a new person with new rights and obligations.

These phases are seen clearly in common cultural themes and behaviors involved in male initiation rituals among numerous peoples. The boys often are forcibly removed from their homes, a frequent practice being to separate them from the company of women (especially their mothers, who sometimes are expected to mourn as if their sons had died) so they can become real men. The boys often are secluded during the rituals and subjected to tests of their ability to endure pain without crying out. They may have to fast or go without drink for days. Nearly always some painful operations are performed on their genitals; they may be circumcised or have their penises mutilated in other ways. Scarification of face and body is common because it is a visible symbol that a male has gone through the proceedings and is entitled to the privileges of manhood. Although sometimes the proceedings last for years, the initiates may have to refrain from eating certain foods or from coming into contact with females or female things because the period of transition into manhood is regarded as a dangerous time. A simple social structure characterizes the liminal period: The initiates are equal in status and utterly subordinate to the control of the men who are in charge of the proceedings. The boys

## BOX 16.1

## LIMINALITY AND BECOMING A SOLDIER

typically are stripped of all possessions, their faces or bodies are painted in an identical way, they are dressed alike, and their heads are shaved, all to make them look alike and to emphasize their common identity.

Modern folk have rites of passage that serve similar functions: Births, graduations, marriages, and deaths are marked by some kind of public ceremony signifying the social transitions involved. Baptisms, betrothals, promotions, installations of new public officials, birthdays, and many other ceremonial gatherings also are rites of passage.

But one of our most interesting rites of passage—because of its similarity to the initiation rituals just discussed—is entering military service. Many of the behaviors involved in entering the military are reminiscent of puberty rites. Basic training is a liminal period—recruits have been separated from civilian life but have not acquired the secret knowledge and skills needed to become a soldier. Recruits are stripped of possessions, their hair is cut, they are issued identical uniforms, they are secluded from most contact with the outside, they all have identical (low) rank that requires complete subordination to sergeants and superior officers, they must undergo arduous trials and perform daring physical feats (such as getting up before sunrise), and they live in a common barracks where they have identical sleeping and eating facilities. In the military, too, the aim is to grind down a boy so that he can be rebuilt into a man (as the Marines used to say). Masculine qualities of courage, toughness, dedication, discipline, and determination are supposed to be instilled. When the recruit has successfully completed his training he is incorporated into a new group, the military, and acquires a new status (rank and job).

We should not carry the analogy too far—recruits are not operated on (but note that voluntary tattooing used to be fairly common), nor is it necessary for a boy to enter the military to be a real man (although many men who were not in the military are looked down on by many of those who were). Still, the similarities are striking enough for us once again to see our common humanity with preindustrial peoples. Their behaviors and beliefs may seem strange to us, but we often engage in similar activities that only seem perfectly natural because we are used to them. ✦

*Pain and physical mutilation are frequent aspects of male puberty rites. Not only was this Nuer man circumcised, but the six scars across his forehead are the result of deep cuts made during his initiation.*

contact with their families, moving to retirement communities or to other areas of the country such as California, Arizona, and Florida. Thus many individuals culturally classified as elderly are segregated and isolated (sometimes by their own wishes) from younger adults and children, living in their own relatively closed communities. In industrialized societies in general and in the United States in particular old age often is associated with the inability to maintain a meaningful economic or social role in the community. This in turn frequently results in a loss in self-esteem.

There is no easy explanation for the variations in the treatment of elderly people. One argument is that the elderly receive the greatest respect and authority in those societies in which they control the land, livestock, and other resources of their kin group. Younger members rely on them for use rights to land, and their children (or sister's children in matrilineal societies) may maximize their chance of a large inheritance by acceding to their wishes and deferring to their judgments. In such kin group systems of control (see chapter 9), almost everyone who lives long enough will gain the status of elder and the esteem and authority it brings.

Some anthropologists argue that the explanation lies not in economic control per se but in the contrast between literate and nonliterate people. In societies without writing elderly people become the major repositories of historical, religious, and technical knowledge. They function as the de facto libraries of these societies. Their control of knowledge makes them indispensable to the community and gives them power over its members, thus enhancing their social value and the respect they receive. This might be termed the "knowledge is power" explanation.

Another contributing factor is the rate of change a people are experiencing. In slowly changing societies with relatively stable technologies knowledge is seen as cumulative and wisdom as the product of experience. Thus wisdom is thought to increase with age. The older individuals within the group are viewed as the valued

*Among many peoples elderly people play an important role in the everyday life of the family. Here two elderly Indonesian women care for their grandchildren in Jakarta.*

repositories of community wisdom and cultural knowledge, so they are the individuals most capable of making important political and economic decisions. In contrast, industrialization has unleashed rapid and profound changes in the technologies of modern societies, and existing technologies quickly become obsolete. Therefore, we view knowledge not as cumulative but as ever changing and transitory; and in our view experience alone does not generate the wisdom necessary for effective decision making. Like yesterday's technology, elderly people often are viewed as obsolete, old-fashioned, and out of step with today's realities. Their ideas and knowledge are thought by many to be antiquated and thus of limited value in decision making. From this perspective, it is not surprising that older individuals are frequently forced out of positions of authority and replaced by younger individuals thought more capable of making the critical leadership decisions.

## Summary

Personality refers to those mental processes that guide a person's behavioral reactions to events and situations. The kind of personality an individual develops is greatly influenced by the way he or she is reared, as the Alorese case illustrates. Cultures differ in their child-rearing practices—in nursing and weaning norms, the degree and methods of discipline, toilet-training practices, nurturing, sexual permissiveness, caretaking roles, and so forth. Therefore, differences in the modal (i.e., typical, or most common) personality found among different peoples are expected. But in any society a wide range of personality types exist, so we cannot accurately characterize "the" personality of a people in any simple way.

The relation between modal personality and culture is complex, but several attempts have been made to order this complexity. One such attempt is the social systems model. In this model the maintenance systems of a people affect the overall learning environment of children, which results in a tendency for children to develop some important similarities in personality. In turn individuals with similar personalities develop or find attractive other cultural elements, known as the *projective-expressive system*.

The changes that occur in peoples' lives as they mature and age are referred to as *life cycle changes*. In some populations relative age serves as the recruitment principle for formal groups known as *age sets*, two forms of which are illustrated by the Hidatsa and the Swazi. Most societies lack age sets, but age is everywhere a relevant social characteristic used to allocate roles. This is shown by the fact that transitions from one age category to another so often are marked by formal public ceremonies called *rites of passage*.

Exactly when childhood begins and ends is culturally, not biologically, determined. Often, as among the Osage, a naming ritual confers human status to an infant. Childhood is universally a period of intense social learning and of personality formation. Among preindustrial peoples it is typical for children to begin contributing to the support of their families at a much younger age than among ourselves.

The passage from childhood to adolescence often is accomplished and marked by an initiation ritual, which often involves severe physical and psychological trauma, as illustrated by the Awa. In preindustrial societies marriage frequently is necessary to attain full adulthood because marriage creates critical rights and obligations between individuals and groups.

Human societies vary enormously in their regard for and treatment of their elderly members. The chronological age at which an individual is considered elderly likewise varies, and our own cultural notion that sixty-five is the age of retirement is largely a historical accident. The degree to which elderly people exercise control over important property and its inheritance seems to be important in how they are regarded. Other influences include the degree of literacy—for among preliterate peoples elderly people serve as a repository of knowledge—and the rate of technological change a people are experiencing.

## KEY TERMS

| | |
|---|---|
| personality | life cycle |
| child-rearing practices | rite of passage |
| modal personality | initiation rite |
| age set association | |

## SUGGESTED READINGS

Barnouw, Victor. *Culture and Personality*. 4th ed. Homewood, Ill.: Dorsey, 1985.

>A work that has long been a standard text in psychological anthropology. A well-written introduction to the subject for students.

Bernardi, Bernardo. *Age Class Systems, Social Institutions and Policies Based on Age*. New York: Cambridge University Press, 1985.

>A comparative study of the significance of age in social institutions.

Freeman, Derek. *Margaret Mead and Samoa: The Making and Unmaking of an Anthropological Myth*. Cambridge, Mass.: Harvard University Press, 1983.

>A critique of Margaret Mead's description and analysis of Samoan adolescence. Freeman argues that Mead's findings were erroneous and that Samoan girls experience the same kinds of psychological processes as Western girls during their adolescence.

Hammond, Dorothy. *Associations*. Reading, Mass.: Addison-Wesley Modular Publications, 14, 1972.

>A dated and short study that nevertheless contains a good review of the anthropological literature on age.

Leiderman, P. Herbert, Steven R. Tulkin, and Anne Rosenfeld, eds. *Culture and Infancy: Variations in the Human Experience*. New York: Academic, 1977.

>A volume of twenty-three articles, mostly dealing with infancy in various cultural settings.

LeVine, Robert. *Culture, Behavior and Personality*. Chicago: Aldine, 1973.

>A provocative text in psychological anthropology.

LeVine, Robert, ed. *Culture and Personality*. Chicago: Aldine, 1974.

>A book containing twenty-three readings covering most aspects of psychological anthropology.

Maretzki, Thomas and Hatsumi. *Taira: An Okinawan Village.* Six Cultures Series, vol. 7. New York: Wiley, 1966.

    *An in-depth case study of one of the six societies analyzed in Whiting and Whiting (1974).*

Marsella, Anthony J., George DeVos, and Francis L. K. Hsu, eds. *Culture and Self: Asian and Western Perspectives.* New York: Tavistock, 1985.

    *Nine articles on cultural conceptions of selfhood in the West, Japan, and China, and in Hinduism and Confucianism. First two chapters are quite good.*

Mead, Margaret. *Coming of Age in Samoa.* New York: Morrow, 1928.

    *A highly readable account of adolescent girls in Samoa and one of anthropology's great classics. Few anthropological studies have been more widely read by the general public.*

Minturn, Leigh, and William W. Lambert. *The Rajputs of Khalapur, India.* Six Cultures Series, vol. 3. New York: Wiley, 1966.

    *An in-depth case study of one of the six societies analyzed in Whiting and Whiting (1974).*

Turnbull, Colin. *The Human Cycle.* New York: Simon and Schuster, 1983.

    *A readable summary of life cycle changes in various populations from all parts of the world.*

Whiting, Beatrice B., and John W. Whiting. *Children of Six Cultures: A Psycho-Cultural Analysis.* Cambridge, Mass.: Harvard University Press, 1974.

    *A comparative psychocultural analysis of children from six societies around the world, discussing the influence of culture on personality and vice versa.*

Wilson, M. *Good Company: A Study of Nyakyusa Age-Villages.* Boston: Beacon, 1963.

    *An interesting and readable account of the unusual age set village organization of the Nyakyusa of East Africa.*

# PART IV

# ANTHROPOLOGY IN THE MODERN WORLD

In the first three parts of this text, you might have gained the impression that anthropologists are concerned largely with people of long ago and far away. To some extent this is an accurate impression—more than any other discipline that deals with humans, anthropology is concerned with the description and analysis of non-Western peoples. But part of the reason for this is our assumption that our comparative, relativistic, and holistic perspectives allow us to better understand what is happening to our own sociocultural system and, indeed, in the world as a whole. We have from time to time suggested some insights on Euro-American societies derived from anthropological theory or ethnographic data. And we have suggested that the economic and political system of the modern world make an understanding of and tolerance for members of other sociocultural traditions increasingly useful. In part 4, our focus shifts explicitly to anthropology's contributions to understanding life in the modern world.

# CHAPTER 17

# THE CHANGING HUMAN WORLD

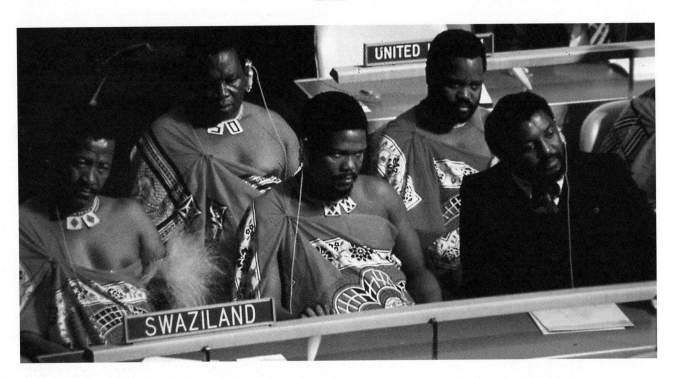

The world has changed greatly during the post-World War II era. Former colonial possessions are now playing an increasingly important role in international politics. Here we see the delegation from Swaziland at a meeting of the United Nations.

**CONTENTS**

The world you live in is not the world of your grandparents' youth. Some of these changes are readily apparent. Technological advances have "made the world smaller." We can watch Operation Desert Storm on our televisions live from Baghdad and Dhahran. On our telephones we can call or fax messages to our friends or colleagues in any major city in the world in a matter of seconds. Airline travel has caused us to think of travel time in terms of hours, not days, weeks, or months. In this chapter we look at the major political, economic, and demographic changes that have occurred over the past fifty years and the consequences of these changes. You might find that the world is much different and even smaller than you thought.

## THE WORLD SINCE 1945

World War II was a major watershed in world history. As we discuss in chapter 6, the period from 1492 to the start of World War II was a time of ever-increasing European control over the peoples of the world. By 1900, European nations controlled virtually every major region on the globe. Most of Africa, Asia, and Oceania had been carved up into colonial empires for the benefit of the English, French, Germans, Dutch, Belgians, Russians, Spanish, Portuguese, and Italians. At the same time, in the Americas the resident European (Euro-American) population had virtually completed their conquest of the Native Americans. Politically dominant European peoples economically restructured the world to serve their own economic needs while imposing their own cultural norms, values, ideas, and institutions on the world's peoples.

Political dominance also served to enhance European feelings of racial and cultural superiority. Non-Western peoples and their cultures were looked on as inherently inferior. Non-Western cultures, if studied at all, were looked at only out of curiosity for the strange and the exotic. For the most part, the attitude was that there was nothing of significance that non-Western peoples could teach Europeans. The unilineal evolutionary ideas of Lewis Henry Morgan and Edward Tylor, discussed in chapter 4, were, in part, a response to this thinking. There were more advanced and less advanced cultures, and the Europeans were at the top. Thus they were the only people whose ideas and cultural systems mattered, and colonialism was morally justified on the basis of European superiority.

So complete was European dominance that many non-Western peoples began to question the worth of their own cultural institutions and to adopt and emulate the European life-style. There was, however, one major non-Western people who successfully resisted European domination—the Japanese. Having adopted European military technology beginning in the 1870s, the Japanese defeated the imperial Russian forces in Manchuria during the Russo-Japanese War of 1904–1905. This defeat marked the first time a major European power had been decisively beaten by a non-Western people, and the inherent superiority of Europeans was brought into question. At the time, other Europeans dismissed the war as being of little consequence, which in fact was true. It did, however, set the stage for later events. More than any other event, the Russo-Japanese War encouraged the development of nationalist independence movements in the colonial world. Between World War I and World War II nationalist movements had taken root in many colonial possessions. The best known of these movements was the one led by Gandhi in India.

World War II created the conditions necessary for the success of these movements and the collapse of the colonial world. In Asia the Japanese army quickly overran a number of important European colonies: the Dutch East Indies, Hong Kong, Indo-China, Malaya, North Borneo, Sarawak, Burma, and the Philippines. In the wake of their eventual defeat the Japanese left behind not only a destroyed colonial infrastructure, but numerous well-organized and well-armed nationalist groups as well. Meanwhile in Europe the war with Germany had destroyed the home economies and the industrial bases of the major colonial powers. Their own cities and factories damaged or destroyed, they could not resist the rising forces of nationalism. One by one their former colonies gained independence; by the late-1960s the colonial world had almost vanished.

The past half-century has been a time of far-reaching and profound changes in the lives of the world's peoples. The collapse of the colonial world signaled the beginning of a decline in the power and influence of Euro-

*Modern technology has penetrated even the remotest regions of the globe. These Australian aborigines in Arnhemland call relatives to a ceremony using a solar battery–powered shortwave radio.*

pean peoples. No longer can European leaders alone dictate the course of world events. The centers of political, economic, and cultural power and influence are increasingly dispersed and ethnically diverse. At the same time, technological changes have increased industrial and agricultural production and greatly intensified the social contacts between and economic interdependence of the various countries and peoples of the world. A highly integrated global economy has evolved. Concurrent with these changes, a population explosion has more than doubled the earth's population. Virtually every country in the world has, since 1945, experienced major internal economic and demographic shifts as well as significant changes in external relations with other countries. As a result, there have been fundamental changes in the economic, demographic, and political structure of the world.

## The Global Economy

For better or worse, the market principle increasingly integrates the economies of the world into a global economy in which manufactured goods, foodstuffs, and raw materials are marketed worldwide. Thus the price we pay for a sack of flour in Kansas or a gallon of gasoline in Texas is determined in large part by the world price for wheat and oil. In turn oil prices are

greatly influenced by whether the leaders of OPEC (Organization of Petroleum Exporting Countries) can control the production of its member nations, and thus the world price. The price we pay for a Ford in Detroit is no longer solely influenced by competition from General Motors and Chrysler but also by auto manufacturers in Japan, Scandinavia, and Germany. Foreign imports not only place American auto companies and dealers in competition with foreign companies but also put American auto workers in direct competition with their foreign counterparts. American farmers, oil producers, businesspeople, and workers are now finding that they have to compete on a global level for the prices they can charge for their goods and labor.

Three main factors have been instrumental in the development of this global economic system. First, to varying degrees, the colonial powers economically monopolized their colonies, using them as sources of raw materials as well as markets for their manufactured goods. With the end of colonialism the export products of these regions could be sold on the world market and imported goods could be purchased in the same competitive world marketplace. Second, technological improvements in transportation have resulted in a drastic lowering of the cost of transporting ores, metals, manufactured goods, and foodstuffs. Supertankers have been developed for the shipping of oil. The use of containers in transporting and loading has greatly reduced the cost of shipping manufactured goods. Larger and faster cargo planes have revolutionized the international transportation of lightweight, high-value goods. Geography no longer protects markets or limits the products produced by a region. Third, international banking and financial institutions have evolved and loaned money to capital-poor Third World nations for economic development, ultimately increasing both the exports and the imports of these countries. (see Figure 17.1)

These and other changes have stimulated and expanded the volume of world trade. World trade stagnated between World War I and World War II. After World War II the volume of world trade began once again to expand, until by 1990 it was more than nine times the level it had been just before and after the war (see Figure 17.2).

Until the 1950s the industrialized regions of the world were concentrated in Europe and North America, with Japan being the only non-Western country that had industrialized to any significant degree. The rest of the world served basically as a source of raw materials and a market for the manufactured goods of these regions. Since 1960 several "second-wave" industrialized regions

FIGURE 17.1
**Map of Commodities and Manufacturing Flow**

The modern world is linked together by the flow materials and manufactured goods creating a global economy.

Manufactured goods

Fuels and minerals

Tropical crops

have emerged, particularly in Asia: Hong Kong, Taiwan, South Korea, and Singapore. With sophisticated technology and low labor costs, these regions have been able to undercut the prices and invade the markets of the established "first-wave" industrial countries. Initially involved in the production of textiles, clothing, and footwear, these countries have steadily moved into the production of electronics and, in the case of South Korea, into heavy industry—steel, automobiles, and shipbuilding. As a result, the global competition for both raw materials and markets for manufactured goods has intensified.

The changing economic relation between the United States and the rest of the world over the past forty years illustrates the increasing degree of global interdependence. Just before World War II the United States was what geographer L. Dudley Stamp characterized as a "young nation," meaning that more than 50 percent of the U.S. exports consisted of foodstuffs and raw materials such as oil, raw cotton, wheat and other grains, and

*Today modern and traditional cultures often exist side by side. Here in Punjab, India, Sikh farmers in bullock carts travel on a paved road past a modern gasoline station.*

**FIGURE 17.2**
Growth of World Trade: 1905–1990

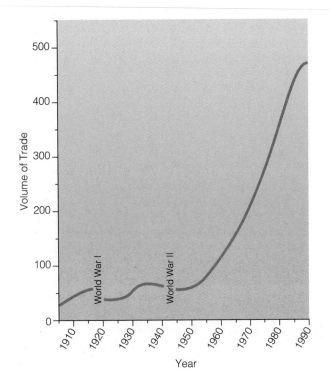

deed, the United States was an exporter of these items. In turn, American industrial output was more than sufficient to meet domestic needs for most categories of manufactured goods.

The postwar era has seen major shifts in both the kinds and the quantities of goods that the United States imports and exports. As the volume of trade has increased, the nature of American imports and exports has changed. From a strategic perspective, the most significant change is that the United States now has to rely on other countries for many of the critical raw materials for industries and fuels that it once produced (see Table 17.1). The increasing dependence of Americans on the importation of metals, petroleum, and other raw materials is the result of several factors. The expanding economy of the United States has resulted in an increased consumption of energy fuels and raw materials. At the same time, either domestic energy and raw-material reserves have declined in production or production cannot be increased to meet demands.

While the United States has become increasingly dependent on foreign sources for basic energy needs and raw materials, the nature of American industry itself has been changing. The American shoe industry is almost gone, replaced by factories in Brazil, Italy, Taiwan, and South Korea. Segments of the American electronics industry have lost out to foreign competition; most television sets, radios, and videocassette recorders are now produced in Japan, Hong Kong, or Singapore. The American garment industry is rapidly losing its domestic market to clothing imported from South Korea, Hong Kong, and Taiwan. The American automobile industry, traditionally the bulwark of the manufacturing econ-

tobacco. Imports were dominated by products that did not occur naturally or grow well domestically, notably tropical foodstuffs and raw materials such as rubber, sugar, coffee, and silk. The United States was self-sufficient in most minerals critical for industry, including iron, copper, potassium, coal, and petroleum. In-

---

**TABLE 17.1  Percentage Imported of Selected Minerals and Metals, United States, 1960–1986**

| MINERALS & METALS | 1960 | 1970 | 1980 | 1990 | MAJOR SOURCES 1982–1985 |
|---|---|---|---|---|---|
| Manganese | 89 | 95 | 98 | 100 | South Africa, Gabon |
| Bauxite | 74 | 88 | 94 | 98 | Jamaica, Guinea |
| Cobalt | 66 | 98 | 93 | 84 | Zaire, Zambia |
| Tin | 82 | 81 | 79 | 71 | Malaysia, Thailand |
| Potassium | Exp. | 42 | 65 | 68 | Canada, Israel |
| Titanium | 22 | 24 | 32 | Wh. | Australia, Canada |
| Petroleum | 16 | 22 | 37 | 42 | Mexico, Canada |
| Iron ore | 16 | 30 | 25 | 21 | Canada, Venezuela |
| Iron and steel | Exp. | 4 | 15 | 13 | Europe, Japan |
| Vanadium | Exp. | 21 | 35 | Wh. | South Africa, Canada |

Note: *Exp.* indicates export of surplus production; *Wh.* indicates that this figure is officially "withheld to avoid disclosure."
SOURCE: U.S. Bureau of the Census (1980 and 1989).

omy, has lost a significant portion of both its domestic and its world markets to Europe, Japan, and South Korea. In 1950 American factories produced 75 percent of all motor vehicles manufactured in the world, dominating not just their own domestic market but most of the world market as well. By 1991 American production had dropped to only 18 percent of the world's total, and almost 25 percent of the automobiles sold in the United States were imported. A similar loss of the domestic market has occurred for the American steel industry. Today the United States depends on foreign sources for much of its basic needs in manufactured goods. To pay for these increased imports, the United States has shifted from being primarily an exporter of raw materials to an exporter of specialized manufactured goods such as aircraft, machinery, chemicals, and vehicles.

The emergence of a global economy has also resulted in the emergence of multinational corporations. Unlike earlier companies, these corporations are not economically tied to or dependent on any single country. Having manufacturing plants located in several countries and worldwide sales and distribution facilities, not infrequently these companies produce and sell most of their goods in countries other than the one in which their corporate headquarters is located. Unconstrained by national political boundaries these corporations can and do move their facilities from country to country in search of cheaper labor, lower taxes, and less demanding governmental regulations.

These recent changes in the world economic system would not have been possible without the development of international financing, which has made money available to capital-poor nations for economic development. In 1945 the World Bank and the International Monetary Fund were created to help war-ravaged Europe and Japan reestablish their industrial plants. These two institutions have played a pivotal role in the creation of the existing global economic system. The World Bank has been a major conduit for economic development loans to Third World nations. The World Bank's role in making loan money available to Third World countries has now been supplemented by numerous European, American, and Japanese banking houses that have become international financiers. Some banking practices have adapted to foreign traditions in interesting ways (see Box 17.1).

Loans provided to these capital-poor countries have allowed them to adopt high-cost technology more quickly and increase their economic productivity. With these funds Third World countries have constructed irrigation projects, expanded and modernized their trans-

portation and communication systems, developed or expanded port facilities, and, in some cases, developed their own manufacturing industries. In the past decade alone these loans have amounted to hundreds of billions of dollars. An underappreciated consequence of these loans is a stimulation of the exports of industrialized nations because most of these funds are used to purchase needed technology and equipment from Japan, Europe, and the United States. At the same time, most of the economic development projects funded by these loans have focused on increased production of raw materials needed by these same industrialized countries.

International financing adds another dimension to the increasing interdependence of nations. With Third World countries owing hundreds of billions of dollars in loans to industrial nations through international banks, the citizens of the industrial nations have a direct vested interest in the economic prosperity of these countries. American banks hold the largest single block of outstanding loans to Third World countries. For example, much of Mexico's national debt of $98 billion is owed to American banks. A default by Mexico would have a devastating effect on American banks and would result in tremendous financial losses to American investors and, ultimately, American taxpayers. In speaking of Mexico's loan debts, a Mexican minister for finance noted that when a country's debts are as large as those of Mexico, the country and the banks become in effect partners; that is, the banks cannot afford to let Mexico default. He might have gone a step further and stated that economically speaking, the United States and Mexico are now partners because the U.S. government ultimately guarantees these loans.

As discussed in this overview, neither the United States nor any other country in the world even approaches economic self-sufficiency. Virtually all peoples are integrated into the global economy. We depend on one another for critical energy fuels, raw materials, and particular categories of foodstuffs and manufactured goods. Without these imports we could not sustain our economy or even adequately provide food, clothing, and shelter for our population. In turn, other countries depend on us, both as a source for particular manufactured goods and foodstuffs and as a market for their products. Although some countries and regions may be more critical than others because they provide some particular essential goods or resources, all are important in maintaining the current global economic system. In the future the integration and interdependence certainly will become significantly greater. Given that we are all part of the single global system that evolved as a

## BOX 17.1

## THE BANKERS AND THE SHEIKS

During the Middle Ages in Europe the Catholic Church through its canon courts declared usury, or the charging of interest on loans, to be un-Christian. Thus Christians were prohibited from charging interest, and banking in medieval Europe was in the hands of Jews. During the late Middle Ages, Italian Catholics began founding banking houses and by clever semantics were able to circumvent the church laws against usury. An individual would be loaned money, interest free, for an unrealistically short period. When the loan was not repaid within this stated time, which it seldom was, the bankers charged "damages."

The Islamic religion also prohibits usury. However, Islam differs in a number of significant ways from Christianity. The Koran is not merely a book of religious teachings but also is a codified legal system called the sharia. Courts in traditional Islamic countries use the Koran as the basis for legal rulings and function as what are sometimes called *Islamic courts.* The Koran prohibits usury by any Muslim.

The law courts in much of the Arab world—Saudi Arabia, Kuwait, Bahrain, and the United Arab Emirates—are Islamic courts. Thirty years ago this fact had little international significance. Relatively poor, these countries had lit-

tle need for financial transactions and banking institutions. With the discovery of oil and the rapid development of this region starting in the 1960s, a need for such institutions quickly developed. A number of European and American banking houses, such as Citibank and Chase Manhattan, opened Middle Eastern branches. Not only did they manage the vast flow of dollars changing hands through the sale of oil and the purchase of imports, but they also began loaning money to local Arab entrepreneurs who organized companies to profit from this economic boom.

Like the medieval Italian bankers, they developed semantic ways of circumventing the Islamic prohibition against usury. The word *interest* was never used in loaning money. Instead, these banks charged Islamic borrowers "administrative fees" or "loan initiation discounts." By 1986 it was estimated that the various world banks had between $8 and $9 billion in loans to

Saudi Arabian companies alone. This system worked well as long as oil income kept rising and all parties made handsome profits. In the 1980s the price of oil began to decline, and in early 1986 the price collapsed, falling from $28 a barrel to (at one point) under $10 a barrel.

As their income from oil plunged, governments began to slow payments to government contractors and suppliers. Arab companies with a cash flow problem quickly fell behind on loan payments to banks. Many Arab businessmen suddenly rediscovered their religion. A flood of Arab companies and individuals quickly took the banks to court, charging them with usury. These courts correctly found the bank guilty of usury under Islamic law.

In the summer of 1986 a number of international banks cut back on their Middle Eastern operations. Citibank reduced its offices in Bahrain and the United Arab Emirates; Chase Manhattan closed its Jordanian branch. The issue has yet to be resolved. Western banking practices conflict with Islamic law, yet the oil-rich Arab states need such practices. Arab governments realize this need, but the question remains: How can Western banking institutions be accommodated under Islamic law? ✦

consequence of the expansion of European peoples and ideas, enlightened self-interest as well as humanitarianism demand that we understand and respect those with cultural heritages different from our own.

## Demographic Changes

The postwar period has also been a time of rapid population growth. In the forty-year period from 1950 to 1993 the world population has jumped from only slightly

more than 2.5 billion to almost 5.5 billion. This population growth has not been equally as pronounced among all the world's peoples. The greatest increase has been in Africa, Asia, and Latin America. The population growth rate in Europe, North America, and the former Soviet Union during this period was well below the world rate. As a result, European peoples have declined from about 30 percent of the world's total population in 1950 to only about 20 percent, a factor that has contributed to the waning of European influence and power in the world.

The highest rates of population growth—those of Latin America, Asia, and Africa—are in the least industrialized regions of the world. Although the economic development of many of these regions has been significant, economic expansion has not kept pace with population growth. Thus this population explosion has created extreme economic and population pressures in many of the less developed rural regions of the Third World, contributing to outmigrations of peoples. (Chapter 19 discusses some anthropological insights on population growth.) As we have noted, mass movements of people are not new in history because migrations of populations came in the wake of European expansion. However, both the nature and the geographical direction of population movements since World War II differ from those of earlier periods. These earlier migrations were primarily movements of European and African peoples to the Americas, with secondary waves of European immigrants settling in portions of Oceania, Africa, and Asia and Asian immigrants being relocated in Asia or resettled in portions of Africa and Oceania. Since 1945 there have been two main patterns of human migration: (1) a worldwide phenomenon of rural-to-urban migration and (2) a migration of Third World peoples to the industrialized countries of Europe and North America.

During the nineteenth and early twentieth centuries the development of major urban centers was associated with industrial economies. Increasing demand for industrial workers had been the primary factor in the growth of cities. In industrialized societies this trend toward urbanization has continued. In addition, major urban centers have emerged in nonindustrialized Third World countries. Just before World War II about 50 percent of the total population of the United States and Europe was urban, compared with only about 8 to 10 percent for Africa and Asia and 25 percent for Latin America. Today about 75 percent of Americans and 70 percent of Europeans are city dwellers. However, the urban populations of Asia and Africa have jumped to between 25 and 30 percent and in Latin America the urban population has increased to more than 60 percent. The growth rate of urbanization has thus been highest outside Europe and North America. In fact, the world's five most rapidly growing cities are located in nonindustrialized nations: Bandung (Indonesia), Lagos (Nigeria), Karachi (Pakistan), Bogotá (Colombia), and Baghdad (Iraq). In some of these cities the growth rate has been phenomenal. In the 1950s Bogotá had a population of only about 650,000; by 1990 its population was estimated at almost 5 million. Similar increases are common in many Latin American, Asian, and African nations.

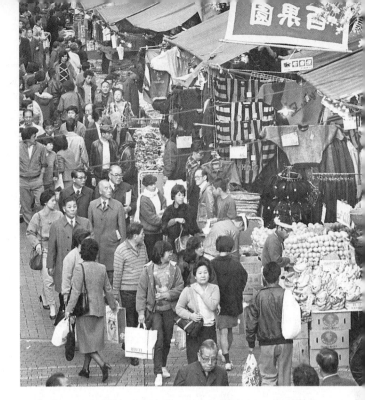

*With almost 40 million people living within a 100-mile radius of the Emperor's palace, Tokyo, Japan is one of the largest and most densely occupied cities in the world.*

Most Third World cities lack the large industrial complexes capable of employing the great masses of people migrating into them, but their small-scale industries, transportation services, and government jobs, although limited, offer greater economic opportunities than do the overcrowded rural regions of the adjacent countryside.

Most migration has been within countries, but a growing trend has been toward international migration. Most evident has been the migration from the nations of Latin America, Asia, and Africa to the highly industrialized countries of North America and Europe. As their industrial economies expanded during the 1950s and 1960s, many Western European countries began experiencing labor shortages. West Germany initiated a "guest-worker" program to actively recruit foreign laborers, first in southern Europe, Italy, and Spain and later in Yugoslavia and Turkey. Concurrently, French factories began recruiting Arab workers from their then North African colonies, particularly Algeria. In the 1950s England began experiencing an influx of West Indians from its possessions in the Caribbean. In the 1960s a wave of Pakistani and Indian immigrants also settled in

England. Other Western European countries experienced a similar phenomenon, although usually on a smaller scale.

By the early 1970s, when the economic growth of Western Europe began to slow, large non-European communities were well established in most of the major cities. When West Germany ended its guest-worker program in 1974 it had hosted 2.5 million foreign workers, a number equal to over 10 percent of its total labor force. Through various means the West German government tried to repatriate these guest workers and their families but failed. France, England, and other Western European countries have considered stricter immigration laws to stop the continuing influx of African and Asian workers, but the number of new immigrants is increasing despite tighter controls. In 1985 alone an estimated 150,000 additional immigrants entered Western Europe. In 1986 Western Europe, out of a total population of 238 million about 16 million were legal immigrants and an additional 1 million were illegal immigrants, most from Asia and Africa. As a result, Western European countries, which once had relatively homogeneous populations, are now home to a number of culturally and ethnically diverse peoples.

This change in patterns of human migration is equally evident in the United States, a country peopled primarily by Old World immigrants and their descendants. Since World War II, about 25 percent of American population growth has been the result of immigration.

Migration patterns to the United States have changed dramatically in the postwar period (see Figure 17.3). In the 1950s well over one-half the immigrants to the

United States were still coming from Europe; the second largest group, about one-third, were coming from Latin America. In the 1960s the flood of immigrants began to increase. From only about 300,000 persons per year in the 1960s the number of immigrants jumped to more than 400,000 per year in the 1970s and to more than 700,000 per year in the 1980s. As the number of immigrants increased, the origin of the immigrants shifted markedly. Proportionally, the number of Latin-American immigrants remained about the same, and European immigration declined. The major increase change was in the number of Asian arrivals, from less than 10 percent of all immigrants in 1950 to more than 40 percent by the 1980s. As a result, between 1980 and 1990 the number of Asian Americans more than doubled, from 3.5 million (1.5 percent) to almost 7.3 million (2.9 percent), whereas the number of Latin Americans increased almost 50 percent, from 14.5 million (6.4 percent) to more than 22 million (9 percent). These figures are only for legal immigrants; if the number of illegal immigrants could be added, the shift would have been much greater, since most of these immigrants are Asians or Latin Americans. Large and ever-growing communities of Chinese, Vietnamese, Cambodians, Laotians, Koreans, Asian Indians, Arabs, Iranians, Mexicans, Guatemalans, Colombians, Salvadorans, and Peruvians immigrants—to name just some—are appearing in the cities of the United States. Thus the ethnic diversity of the U.S. population is increasing.

Although Europe and North America have been the primary destinations for most international migrants,

**FIGURE 17.3**
**Immigrants to the United States**

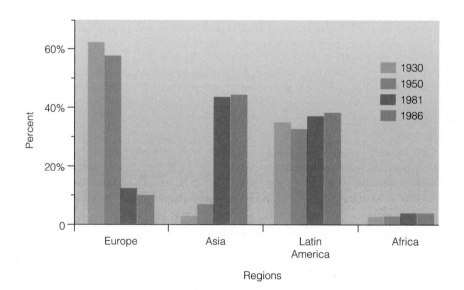

other regions with high income, labor shortages, or both have experienced major influxes of immigrants. Many of the oil-rich Arab countries—Libya, Saudi Arabia, Kuwait, Quatar, Oman, and the United Arab Emirates—have recruited foreign workers from India, Pakistan, Bangladesh, and Egypt and from among Palestinian refugees. Indeed, in some of the smaller of these countries foreign workers outnumber native Arabs. Thus the population of the world is in constant flux.

In the not too distant past white missionaries took Christianity and European culture to the peoples of the Americas, Africa, Asia, and Oceania. Although Christian missionary work continues, today we also find Islamic mosques in such cities as Berlin, Paris, London, and New York, and Hindu gurus find converts among European peoples in both Europe and North America. Before World War II small pockets of European peoples were found scattered throughout the cities of Africa and Asia. Today enclaves of newly arrived Turks, Arabs, Africans, Asians, and Latin Americans are scattered throughout the cities of Western Europe and North America.

This massive migration of peoples has alleviated some of the economic and population pressures in many Third World countries. At the same time, like it or not, it is bringing peoples from extremely diverse cultural backgrounds into direct daily contact with one another.

## Political Fragmentation

The postwar era has been characterized by increased political fragmentation. Although the precise number varies, depending on how one defines an "independent" or "autonomous" country, at the beginning of World War II there were about sixty countries in the world. Most of Asia, Africa, and Oceania was divided between European colonial empires. As the era of colonialism came to an end after the war, the number of politically independent countries increased rapidly. Between 1946 and 1980 eighty-eight new countries were carved out of the colonial empires of Europe. The recent collapse of the Soviet Union and Yugoslavia has resulted in the creation of eighteen new countries. From only about 80 countries in 1945 the number of independent countries has grown to almost 200.

The emergence of these new countries has forever changed the face of global politics. Before the war European leaders, consulting only among themselves, controlled the political destiny of the world's peoples. Even Japan was considered a second-level power. As non-European countries have increasingly emerged as

*The Hare Krishna movement and many other non-Western religions have found converts in the United States and Western Europe during the past few decades.*

economic and even military powers, non-European leaders have to come to play an ever-expanding role in world politics. (Chapter 18 expands on this discussion of political fragmentation.)

## CONSEQUENCES OF AN INTERDEPENDENT WORLD

As stated earlier, the world we live in today is not the world of our grandparents. This is true at both the individual level and the national level.

For the individual the consequences of recent changes are both direct and indirect. Urbanization is resulting in increased daily contact between individuals from diverse ethnic and cultural backgrounds. In cities throughout the world people are finding that employers and employees, customers and vendors, landlords and tenants, doctors and patients—in other words, individuals whose actions affect the quality of their everyday lives—are increasingly individuals with whom they do not share a common cultural heritage. Certainly there has always been diversity in American cities; but when our grandparents thought of ethnic diversity, they thought primarily about the differences between Irish, Italians,

Poles, Germans, Russians, Swedes, and so forth. Although there were some cultural differences between these groups, they shared a basically common cultural tradition. Today these new immigrant groups are from Asia, Africa, Latin America, and the Middle East, people with whom most Americans do not share a common cultural tradition. Thus greater awareness of and tolerance for cultural differences are increasingly necessary parts of our lives.

These changes have important consequences at the individual level, but it is at the national level where the consequences of these changes become greatest. First, the economic interdependence of the world's peoples requires a steady flow of manufactured goods, foodstuffs, and raw materials from other countries. Because virtually no region of the world is economically self-sufficient, disruption in the steady flow of this exchange could conceivably have catastrophic economic repercussions. The vulnerability of the United States and its dependence on other countries for critical resources were made clear in 1973 when the Arab oil-producing countries embargoed shipments of oil to the United States for six months in retaliation for American support of Israel. The result was a major shortage of petroleum products that created lines at gasoline stations throughout the country. The primary threat to this global trade network is political conflict that has the potential to cut trade in particular items. Population pressures and related economic pressures increase the possibilities for political conflict. Whether we want to view the existing and potential problems of the world in a humanistic way or look at it with pragmatic self-interest, the answers are the same. The turning to desert of portions of Africa and the resulting problems of starvation are not simply African problems; these are problems of the world community. Economic development projects in Latin America or Africa or Asia serve the needs not only of the peoples of these particular regions but also of the global economy.

What is the value of anthropology to me? Why should I study the cultural institutions of people from some other region of the world? The reason is simple. These "strange and exotic" people no longer live half a world away; they live in your city, your neighborhood, and maybe next door. They may soon be your schoolmates, your colleagues, your customers, or your employer—if they are not already. You depend on these people, directly or indirectly, for much of the food you eat, the clothes you wear, the tools you use, the gasoline that powers your car, and, possibly, the car itself. You in turn have to sell, either directly or indirectly, to these same people goods or services so that you can afford to buy what they produce. In the modern world there is no escape from other peoples. In the highly interdependent world that is rapidly evolving the understanding of and toleration for other peoples' cultural values, norms, and traditions will be a necessity for living.

In the world today there are two dangerously contradictory trends in the directions of human history. One is the global economy and the ever-increasing economic interdependence of the world's peoples that we have just discussed. The other is toward political fragmentation, which we have only mentioned. Nationalism and ethnic conflict are escalating rapidly. If nationalism continues to escalate unchecked, there is the very real possibility that it will destroy the global economy and with it the economic well-being of every people in the world. In the next two chapters we examine the nature of ethnic conflict and the factors that serve to inflame these conflicts.

## SUMMARY

The post–World War II period has been a time of tremendous economic, political, demographic, and sociocultural growth and change. The two important features of this period have been the emergence of a highly interdependent global economic system and the political fragmentation that ensued as the colonial empires were dismantled and "new" countries were created.

During the past half century a rapidly growing economic interdependence between the various nations and regions of the world and a shift in world economic and political power have taken place. Before World War II, with the exception of Japan, the world was both economically and politically controlled by individuals of European ancestry—people from the United States, England, Germany, France, and so forth. Thus important decisions were made by a relatively small group of leaders who shared what were basically common sets of values, norms, and beliefs. With European political and economic dominance of the world rapidly waning, this is no longer the situation. In the increasingly complex global political and economic climate of today, important decisions now frequently involve agreements between leaders with quite different sets of cultural values, norms, and beliefs. The economic and political conditions of the world necessitate a far greater degree of cross-cultural understanding and tolerance than ever before in human history.

Certainly we would not argue that tolerance and understanding of cultural differences can solve all the world's difficulties. However, many problems in the world today are the result of cultural intolerance and misunderstandings. Anthropologists and anthropological theory are well suited to understanding and arbitrating these problems and to showing why we all ought to show more respect for one another's rights and opinions.

## Suggested Readings

Bodley, John H. *Anthropology and Contemporary Human Problems*. Menlo Park, Calif.: Cummings, 1976.
> *Provides a good overview of many contemporary world problems from an anthropological perspective.*

Hepner, George, and Jesse O. McKee. *World Regional Geography: A Global Approach*. St. Paul: West, 1992.
> *This cultural geography text provides an excellent overview of the contemporary regional trends in economic development, population growth, and ethnic issues.*

Stravrianos, L. S. *The World Since 1500: A Global History*. 4th ed. Englewood Cliffs, N.J.: Prentice-Hall, 1982.
> *The last part of this history text contains an excellent overview of twentieth-century history. Particularly interesting are the author's discussions of the rise of nationalism and the end of the colonial world.*

Wolf, Eric, and Edward Hansen. *The Human Condition in Latin America*. New York: Oxford University Press, 1972.
> *Although slightly dated, this study still provides important insights into the problems of contemporary Latin America.*

For suggested readings concerning contemporary ethnic, population, and economic issues, see suggested readings for chapters 18 and 19.

## CHAPTER 18

# ETHNICITY IN THE MODERN WORLD

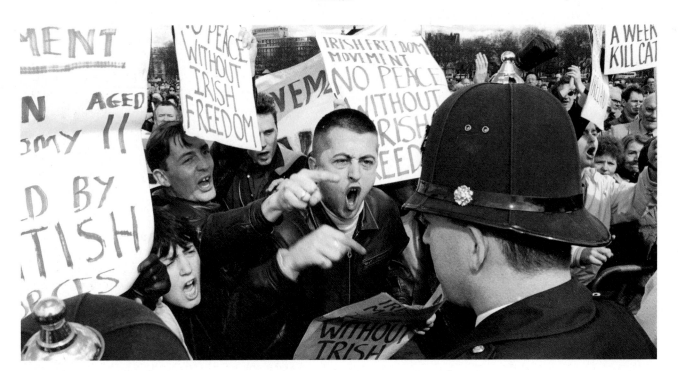

Members of the Irish Freedom Movement demonstrate in London against the continued British presence in Northern Ireland.

## CONTENTS

Every day there are reports of ethnic conflicts or wars someplace in world. On the nightly news we see pictures and hear accounts of half-destroyed cities and villages, of refugee camps, of women and children who are starving, and of the number of people who have been killed. The faces may be black or white or brown; after a while they all look the same. The new set of pictures may be from Bosnia or Armenia, the Sudan or Ethiopia, Guatemala or Afghanistan, but they are all the same. We hear of another bombing by the Irish Republican Army in Northern Ireland or England, of another killing of a Palistinian by an Israeli soldier in Gaza, and of another stabbing of an Israeli by a Palistinian in Tel Aviv or Jerusalem. No place is safe. Neo-Nazis in Germany attack foreigners. There are ethnic riots in Los Angeles, and the World Trade Center in New York City is bombed. New words like "ethnic cleansing" and "failed state" have become part of our vocabulary. As the level of violence escalates in the world, we can only wait and wonder where the next terrorist bomb will explode and what peoples will constitute the next group of refugees.

As we discussed in chapter 17, the global trade that has emerged has resulted in an ever-increasing economic interdependence among the peoples of the world. At the same time, ethnic conflicts have escalated and seem likely to increase. One could argue that ethnic conflict is the most potent political force in the modern world. It threatens not only the political stability of many nations but possibly the global economy as well.

In this chapter we address several questions: (1) What is an ethnic group? (2) Why is ethnicity such a powerful political force in the modern world? and (3) What has been and can be done to try to resolve ethnic conflicts?

## ETHNIC GROUPS

Over the past two decades the terms *ethnic* and *ethnicity* have become part of our everyday vocabulary. We frequently hear and use the terms *ethnic food, ethnic vote, ethnic conflict, ethnic clothes, ethnic neighborhood,* and *ethnic studies*. In the 1960s, anthropologists began studying ethnicity as a distinct social phenomenon, and since that time the literature on ethnicity has proliferated. Part of the increased scholarly interest in ethnic groups came as a result of Nathan Glazer and Daniel Moynihan's study (1963) of ethnic groups in New York City. They found that "in the third generation, the descendants of the immigrants confronted each other, and knew they were both Americans, in the same dress, with the same language, using the same artifacts, troubled by the same thing, but they voted differently, had different ideas about education and sex, and were still, in many essential ways, as different from one another as their grandfathers had been" (13). These findings contradicted the idea of the American melting pot. Ethnic differences were far more resilient and significant than had been believed.

What is an ethnic group? First it is necessary to realize that all peoples, not just minority populations, have a feeling of ethnicity and an ethnic group identity. In essence, an **ethnic group** is a named social category of people based on perceptions of shared social experience or ancestry. Members of the ethnic group see themselves as sharing cultural traditions and history that distinguish them from other groups. There is in ethnic group identity a strong psychological or emotional component that divides the social world into the categories of "us" and "them." In contrast to social stratification (discussed in chapter 14), which divides and unifies people along a series of horizontal axes on the basis of socioeconomic factors, ethnic identities divide and unify people along a series of vertical axes. Thus ethnic groups, at least theoretically, crosscut socioeconomic class differences, drawing members from all strata of the population.

Before discussing the significance of ethnic differences and conflicts in the modern world, we need to examine the varying dimensions of ethnic group identity, including (1) the situational nature of ethnic group identity, (2) the attributes of ethnic groups, (3) the fluidity of ethnic group identity, and (4) the types of ethnic groups.

*Protesting treatment of Native Americans, members of the American Indian Movement (A.I.M) occupied Wounded Knee, South Dakota, by force in 1973.*

## Situational Nature of Ethnic Identity

One of the more complicating aspects of ethnicity is that an individual's ethnic group identity seldom is absolute. A particular individual may assume a number of different ethnic identities, depending on the social situation. For example, in the United States an individual may simultaneously be an American, a Euro-American, an Italian American, and a Sicilian American. The particular ethnic identity chosen by an individual varies with the social context. When in Europe or among Europeans he or she would assume an ethnic identity of American in contrast to German, French, or Italian. In the United States the same individual might assume an identity of Euro-American as opposed to African-American or Native American. Among Euro-Americans, the person might take the ethnic identity of Italian American as opposed to Irish American or Polish American. When among Italian Americans the individual might identify himself or herself as Sicilian American, as opposed to an Italian American whose family came from Rome, Naples, or some other region of Italy.

The situational nature of ethnic identity demonstrates what some have called the **hierarchical nesting** quality of identity. A particular ethnic group forms part of a larger collection of ethnic groups of like magnitude or social significance. In turn these ethnic groups may collectively form still another, higher level of ethnic identity, which may in turn be nested in still another higher level of ethnic identity. Thus ethnic identity does not simply divide the world into categories of us and them but into varying hierarchically ranked categories of us and them.

## Attributes of Ethnic Groups

Two main attributes help to define and identify an ethnic group: (1) an origin myth or history and (2) various ethnic boundary markers.

**ORIGIN MYTH.** Each ethnic group is the product of a unique set of social and historical events. The common or shared historical experiences that serve to unite and distinguish the group from other groups and give it a distinct social identity constitutes the group's **origin myth.** By *myth* we do not mean to imply that the historical events did not really happen, or that the group is not what it claims to be. We mean only that these particular experiences serve as the ideological charter for the group's common identity and provide the members with a sense of being different from other people. Origin myths play an integral part in creating and maintaining ethnic group identity: They define and describe the origin and collective historical experiences of the group.

Not all historical events are equally important. Origin myths make selective references to historical events. Wars and conflicts with other peoples frequently are emphasized, since they clearly distinguish us from them. The origin myth imbues the group's members with feelings of distinctiveness and, often, superiority in relation to other groups. What makes an origin myth so powerful is that their mythic themes and concepts are embedded in virtually every aspect of the popular culture of the people: stories (written and oral), songs, dances, games, music, theater, film, and art. So pervasive are these mythic images in the everyday lives of the people that they are learned passively rather than consciously. Thus all the members of the group are well versed in the basic tenets of the group myth, and in the minds of most, these ideas become an unquestioned "truth." In larger, more sophisticated groups the origin myth also takes the form of a written, purportedly objective history that is formally taught in schools. American history as taught in elementary and high school is not merely the objective, factual history of a geographical region; it is also the story of the American people. Thus it serves as the officially sanctioned origin myth of the American ethnic group. Similarly, English,

French, Japanese, and Russian history as taught in their schools is the "authorized" origin myth of those groups.

When you realize that history as taught in schools in fact is the collective origin myth of the group, then you realize the significance of including or excluding a particular subgroup of the population. Using American history as an example, we can see how a number of historical events play a critical role in the emergence and definition of a distinctively American ethnic identity. Among these events are the landing of the *Mayflower,* the American Revolution, the Civil War, the westward expansion, and the world wars. Certain historical groups, such as cowboys and cavalry, are used as embodiments of American ideals and identity. Americans are the descendants of the various peoples who collectively participated in these and other group-defining events. Thus it is not surprising that every American subgroup is sensitive to their portrayal in these events. Thus to African-Americans, it is important that American history, as taught in the public schools, acknowledge that the first man to die in the American Revolution was an African-American, that African-Americans fought as soldiers in the Revolutionary and Civil Wars, that a high percentage of cowboys were African-Americans, and that African-American cavalrymen played an important part in winning the West. Similarly, the public acknowledgment and recognition that their groups were active participants in some, if not all, of the major events of American history are equally important for Polish Americans, Italian Americans, Irish Americans, Chinese Americans, and other immigrants in a nation of immigrants. It is inclusion in the collective origin myth that truly legitimates a people's status as members of the group.

**ETHNIC BOUNDARY MARKERS.** Every ethnic group has a way of determining or expressing membership. Overt factors used to demonstrate or denote group membership are called **ethnic boundary markers.** Ethnic boundary markers are important not only to identify the members to one another but also to demonstrate identity to and distinctiveness from nonmembers. Because they serve to distinguish members from all other groups, a single boundary marker seldom is sufficient. A marker that might distinguish one ethnic group from a second group may not distinguish it from still another group. Thus combinations of markers commonly are used. Differences in language, religion, physical appearance, or particular cultural traits serve as ethnic boundary markers.

As we saw at the end of chapter 4, speech style and language use serve as symbols of personal identity: We send covert messages about the kind of person we are by how we speak. Language, therefore, frequently serves as an ethnic boundary marker. The native language of an individual is the primary indicator of ethnic group identity in many areas of the world. In the southwestern United States, Hopi and Navajo members are readily distinguished by their language alone. However, just because two populations share a common language does not mean they share a common identity, any more than the fact that two populations speak different languages means that they have two distinct identities. For example, the Serbs and Croats of what was Yugoslavia speak Serbo-Croatian. They are, however, distinct and historically antagonistic ethnic groups. Conversely, a person may be Irish and speak either Gaelic or English as his or her native language. The German government grants automatic citizenship to all ethnic German refugees from Eastern Europe. A difficulty in assimilating these refugees is that many speak only Polish or Russian. Thus one does not have to speak German to be an ethnic German.

Like language, religion may serve as an ethnic boundary marker. The major world religions such as Christianity, Islam, and Buddhism encompass numerous distinct ethnic groups, so that religious affiliation does not always indicate ethnic affiliation. But in many cases religion and ethnic group more or less correspond. The Jews may be categorized as either a religious or an ethnic group. Similarly, the Sikhs in India constitute both a religious and an ethnic group. In still other situations religious differences may be the most important marker of ethnic identity. As we mentioned earlier, the Serbs and Croats speak the same language; the most important distinction between these two groups is that the Serbs are Eastern Orthodox and the Croats are Catholic. Conversely, the Chinese ethnic identity transcends religious differences: a person is still Chinese whether he or she is a Muslim, Christian, Taoist, Buddhist, or Marxist atheist.

Physical characteristics, or phenotypes, can also (at times) indicate ethnic identity. It is impossible to identify Germans, Dutch, Danes, and other northern European ethnic groups by their physical characteristics. A similar situation is found in those regions of the world in which populations have been in long association with one another. Thus physical characteristics do not distinguish a Zulu from a Swazi, a Chinese from a Korean, or a Choctaw from a Chickasaw Indian. However, with the massive movements of people, particularly over the

*Conflict between ethic Germans and immigrant workers and refugees has been growing. Here German police in Rostock use water guns and tear gas to disperse a mob attacking a home for refugees.*

past few hundred years, physical characteristics have emerged increasingly as a marker of ethnic identity. Members of the three major ethnic groups in Malaysia—Malays, East Indians, and Chinese—are readily distinguishable by their physical appearance. The significance or lack of significance of physical characteristics in ethnic identity may also vary with the level of ethnic identity. The American identity includes almost the full range of human physical types. However, at a lower level of identity—Euro-American, African-American, and Native American—physical characteristics do serve as one marker of ethnic identity. Yet within these groups physical characteristics alone cannot be the only marker. Some Native Americans physically appear to be Euro-Americans or African-Americans, and some African-Americans would be identified as Euro-Americans or Native Americans on the basis of physical appearance alone.

A wide variety of cultural traits, clothing, house types, personal adornment, food, technology, economic activities, or general life-style may also serve as ethnic boundary markers. Over the past 100 years a rapid homogenization of world material culture, food habits, and technology has erased many of the more overt cultural markers. Thus today you do not have to be a Mexican to enjoy tacos, an Italian to eat pizza, or a Japanese to have sushi for lunch. Similarly, you can dine on hamburgers, the all-American food, in Japan, Oman, Russia, Mexico, or most other countries in the world. Cultural traits

remain, however, the most important, diverse, and complex category of ethnic boundary markers. For the sake of brevity, we will limit our discussion to one trait—clothing.

Clothing styles have historically served as the most overt single indicator of ethnic identity. In the not too distant past almost every ethnic group had its own unique style of dress. Even today a Scottish-American who wants to overtly indicate his ethnic identity wears a kilt, and a German American may wear his *lederhosen.* Similarly, on special occasions Native Americans wear "Indian clothes" decorated with beadwork and ribbon-work. These are not the everyday clothing of these people, and they are worn only in social situations in which they want to emphasize their ethnic identity. In many regions of the world ethnic clothes are still worn every day. One of these regions is highland Guatemala. In that region clothing, particular women's clothing, serves to readily identify the ethnic affiliation of the wearer. Guatemalan clothing styles actually indicate two levels of ethnic identity. If a woman wears a *huipil,* a loose-fitting blouse that slips over the head, it indicates that she is a Native American. Non–Native American women, called *Ladinas,* dress in western-style clothes. The style, colors, and designs on the huipil further identify the particular Native American ethnic group she is from: Nahuala, Chichicastenango, Solola, or one of the other hundred or so Native American groups in highland Guatemala.

## Fluidity of Ethnic Groups

Ethnic groups are not stable groupings of people, since (1) ethnic groups vanish, (2) people move between ethnic groups, and (3) new ethnic groups come into existence.

During the past 500 years numerous ethnic groups have vanished. Massachusetts, Erie, Susquehannock, and Biloxi were not originally place names but the names of now extinct Native American ethnic groups. Still other ethnic groups in Asia, Africa, Oceania, Europe, and the Americas have vanished as well. Extinction of an ethnic group seldom is biological extinction. In most cases the members of one group are merely absorbed into the population of a larger ethnic group. The Tasmanians of Australia are typical of what happened to many smaller ethnic groups. Numbering at most 5,000 when the British began colonizing the island of Tasmania in 1802, the population was so ravaged by wars and massacres that only a handful existed by 1850, and the Tasmanians as a viable ethnic group had ceased to exist. In 1869 the last full-blooded Tasmanian man died and in 1888 the last full-blooded woman died. However, even today mixed-blood descendants of the Tasmanians can be found among the Australian population.

Both individuals and communities can and do move between ethnic groups. During the sixteenth and seventeenth centuries French Protestants, called *Huguenots,* fled persecution in France and settled in large numbers in England and the English colonies in North America. These people quickly became absorbed into the English population. Over the past 200 years Americans have absorbed numerous immigrant populations.

**Ethnogenesis** refers to the emergence of a new ethnic group. Ethnogenesis usually occurs in two ways: (1) a portion of an existing ethnic group splits away and forms a new ethnic group, or (2) members of two or more existing ethnic groups fuse, forming a new ethnic group.

Probably the most common cause of ethnogenesis is the division of an existing ethnic group. At one time the Osage, Kansa, Omaha, Ponca, and Quapaw Indians of the central United States were a single ethnic group. The origin myths of these peoples tell how at different times portions broke away until there were five distinct groups. In the 1700s small groups of Creek Indians began moving south into Florida, where they eventually developed a distinct identity as the Seminole. Similarly, as Bantu-speaking peoples spread through central and southern Africa, they became separated, and new ethnic groups formed. As the Spanish Empire in the Americas disintegrated during the early 1800s, new regional ethnic identities (such as Mexican, Guatemalan, Peruvian, and Chilean) began emerging among the Spanish-speaking peoples in that region. In 1652 the Dutch began settling near the Cape of Good Hope in southern Africa. These people eventually developed their own distinctive dialect of Dutch, called *Afrikaans,* and their own identity, Boers (see Box 18.1).

In other cases members of two or more ethnic groups fuse and a new ethnic identity emerges. In England the Angles, the Saxons, and the Jutes fused and became known as the English. The original Euro-American ethnic group was not the result of a split among the English people but rather the result of a fusion of English, Dutch, German, Scots, Irish, French Huguenots, Scotch-Irish, and other European settlers residing on the coast of North America. Most African-American groups in the Americas are the result of the fusion of numerous distinct African groups. Intermarriage between French traders and Native Americans in Canada resulted in the emergence of the Metis. Under their leader Louis Riel the Metis in 1870 rebelled against the government of Canada. Similarly, in South Africa the Cape Coloured, people of mixed Dutch and Khoikhoi ancestry, are socially and politically distinct from both whites and Africans. The Cape Coloureds are an excellent example of how new ethnic categories often arise as a result of economic forces and political mobilization (see Box 18.1).

*Afrikaner extremists in South Africa protest the movement for shared power with Black Africans.*

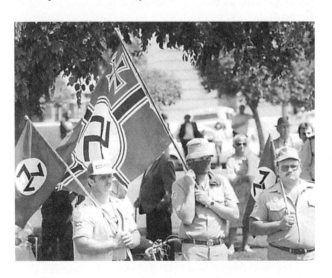

An American tourist who spends an afternoon window-shopping in one of Johannesburg's downtown malls might be startled to come upon numerous shops filled with African handicrafts of the finest quality from every part of the African continent. Why, this tourist may ask, would white South Africans who decorate their homes with these artifacts be so taken with what they call "Africanity"? A pronounced interest in African ethnicity seems strange in a system that legitimizes racism and oppresses people of African origin. Not only are ethnic categories rigidly regulated by the state, but separate national identities distinct from that enjoyed by the White minority have also been imposed on people of African origin. This is called *apartheid,* or "separate development." People of European ancestry are supposed to develop industrial lifestyles, while people of African ancestry are forced by law to develop within their own tribal areas where they are expected to maintain traditional lifestyles.

The system of apartheid developed out of early twentieth century events and laws, but it was not legally implemented until the Afrikaner-dominated Nationalist party came to power in 1948. Afrikaners are the offspring of Dutch settlers who originally came to South Africa in 1652. They conquered the African inhabitants and later came into conflict with the British over political hegemony for South Africa's gold and diamond mines. Afrikaners were originally fundamentalist Christian farmers who even today maintain an origin myth based on a biblical interpretation that views blacks as the errant descendants of Ham, in need of control and salvation. This view legitimizes a position of superiority over nonwhite peoples. The emergence of the Afrikaner ethnic identity—which includes a distinct language with Dutch, German, French, Malay, Portuguese, English and African elements—is itself a response to nineteenth-century indus-

## BOX 18.1

# THE EMERGENCE OF COLOURED ETHNICITY IN SOUTH AFRICA

Mary Howard
OHIO WESLEYAN UNIVERSITY

trialism and British imperialism. Often referred to as the "White Tribe of South Africa," Afrikaner people believed ethnic solidarity to be the keystone for an Afrikaner nation and control over South Africa's mineral resources, urban industries, and African labor.

British colonists who first arrived in 1820 were less identified with mobilization for independence and the creation of a distinct South African nation. Instead, their interests lay in maintaining ties with Britain to secure their economic self-interest. The Afrikaners (also known as the *Boers*) were defeated by British troops in the Boer War of 1899–1902, and the Union of South Africa was formed in 1910.

Afrikaners gained control of Parliament in the 1948 elections. They enacted legislation that (1) classified every person according to race; (2) established *Bantustans,* or homelands, for people classified as black; (3) restricted people into group areas outside the industrial centers, which were divided along racial lines; (4) developed job classifications that maintained white privilege; (5) began a pass system for influx control of black labor so that migration and settlement of Africans around urban areas would occur only when corporations could use their work; and (6) instituted a vast array of security legislation that has resulted in numerous declarations of emergency, arrests, tortures, and murders of black protesters. This legalized segregation is what is meant by apartheid.

The arbitrary racial divisions created by the Race Classification Act of 1950 are white, Asian, Bantu, and coloured [*sic*]. Japanese businessmen were recently given "honorary white" status for sound economic reasons, which was soon followed by a similar shift in the status of people of Chinese ancestry. Presently, 17 percent of the population (about 5.5 million) are whites who are themselves split into two groups—the original Dutch Afrikaner settlers and the more recent British immigrants. Eight hundred thousand people are Asian descendants of the Indian laborers who first came to South Africa in 1860. The majority population (16 to 17 million) are classified as Bantu-speaking black Africans from such indigenous groups as Swazi, Tswana, Sotho, Zulu, Ndebele, and Xhosa. No black is considered a citizen of South Africa and no black can vote for the South African government. Instead, every black person is supposed to be a citizen of his or her "nation," or one of the ten Bantustans that loosely corresponds to each individual's ethnic origins.

Like most Native American reservations, land allocated to the Bantustans is of poor quality and far from resources and urban centers. Over 70 percent of South Africa's population are supposed to live in these areas, which make up only 13 percent of all South African territory. This has had disastrous consequences for the health and well-being of the majority of black South Africans, whose infant and child mortality rate in the Bantustans and incidence of tuberculosis in the black townships rivals the very poorest nations in the world. In contrast, whites enjoy the world's highest living standard, based largely on rich mineral resources mined by a cheap and oppressed black labor pool. These injustices have resulted in the formulation of numerous black resistance movements, such as the African Na-

*continued on next page*

tional Congress, which have been struggling for an end to white minority rule even before the beginning of the twentieth century.

Caught between black and white conflict are about 5.5 million people presently classified as coloured. They are the result of over 400 years of close proximity of the "races" in spite of various legislation against interracial sexual relationships and marriage. The emergence of the official racial category coloured is closely related to the "divide and conquer" objectives of the ruling white class, while coloured self-identity was in part a product of ethnic mobilization to maintain or improve relative social positions. The fluidity of ethnic identity boundaries is especially apparent in the case of South Africa's Cape Town coloured population. These boundaries have constantly shifted in response to political, social and economic circumstances, as the following brief history testifies.

Until the turn of the twentieth century, the term *coloured* referred to all non-Europeans. At the time there had been a definite class of poor whites, and ethnic divisions were blurred by class divisions in areas where poor whites and coloured lived together. Many of the coloured were artisans, skilled laborers, and petty traders. Some were able to achieve advanced education and a relatively high standard of living. During the Victorian era, when notions of social Darwinism and eugenics reached South Africa, upper-class whites developed humanitarian concerns about poor whites and saw miscegenation as a peril to the survival of white supremacy. These concerns resulted in extensive improvements in the working and living conditions for poor whites, while coloured people began to be seen as a sign of the dangers of racial contamination. Coloureds became regarded as the illegitimate offspring of a mixing of European "civilization" and African "savagery," although many of them were better off and more educated than poor whites.

However, because of their claim to European ancestry, coloureds were thought to be superior to Africans. Coloureds therefore had little to gain from an identification with Africans and "passing for white" remained a possible escape route for many lighter-skinned Coloureds.

A 1901 urban plague epidemic forced segregation of whites away from impoverished rat-infested areas in the cities. Coloureds resisted forced removal from their urban homes and formed an African Peoples Organization that excluded Africans. This organization sought to advance their economic interests and to gain assurance that the segregation measures then being imposed on Africans would not be extended to coloureds. By 1905 the coloured ethnic identity in the Western Cape Province was established. This identity was the result of white efforts to maintain their own privileges combined with coloured efforts to maintain their distinctiveness from oppressed blacks.

When the Nationalist party came to power in 1948, racial categories were reconstituted into the four present groupings. Even more effort was placed on uniting all Afrikaners, regardless of class. In 1950, with the passage of restrictive legislation such as the Immorality Act (which forbad sexual relations and marriage between the races) and the Group Areas Act (which forced people of each race classification to live in governmentally designated areas), light-skinned coloureds could no longer easily pass for white. Instead, the Nationalist party tried to foster in the coloureds a sense of distinct ethnic pride in being coloured and to prepare them for segregated relocation into coloured townships. Afrikaners also stripped coloureds of direct representation in Parliament so that neither their proximity nor their votes would constitute a threat to white rule. These actions disenfranchised the coloureds from whites and fed into a growing identification with the African struggle,

even though understandably their participation was not always welcomed by blacks.

In efforts to co-opt coloured interests with white economic power, the government did not compel coloureds to carry passes, nor did it regulate them with influx control legislation. The Nationalist party also enacted an employment preference policy that favored Coloureds so that "passing for coloured" became as important to Africans as "passing for white" had once been for coloured.

An unrelenting assault on black squatter settlements during the 1950s, 1960s, and 1970s kept alive coloured fears of being relocated. Eventually such fears were realized when residents of District Six in Capetown were forced to relocate outside the city. This event intensified the ambiguity many coloured people felt in choosing between participation in the white system to prevent further impoverishment or in the black struggle to eliminate a racist regime.

In 1981 a tricameral parliamentary system was introduced that gave coloureds and Asians a vote, but only in matters pertaining to their own affairs. Most of them, to protest the exclusion of blacks, boycotted the referendum that endorsed the changes. However, this token representation has served to further fragment coloured opposition to the blatantly racist policies of South Africa. Many coloureds are now very visible in nonracial liberation organizations composed of persons from all four classifications. In the wake of the release of Nelson Mandela from prison, the hopes of South Africans opposed to apartheid have risen, but the fragmentation sown by long-standing purposeful efforts to align some disenfranchised members to the system while exploiting the rest seems destined to result in violence. Such is the legacy of European colonialism in South Africa. ✦

SOURCE: Goldin (1987).

## Types of Ethnic Groups

From our discussion and examples so far, it should be apparent that the term *ethnic group* covers a range of social groupings. In general, ethnic groups fall into two main categories: national and subnationals.

A **nationality** is an ethnic group with a feeling of **homeland,** a geographical region over which they have exclusive rights. Implicit in this concept is the assumption of an inherent right to political autonomy and self-determination. In contrast, *subnationalities* lack a concept of a distinct and separate homeland and the associated rights to separate political sovereignty and self-determination. A subnational group sees itself as a dependent and politically subordinate subset of a nationality.

Although it is easy to define the difference between ethnic nationalities and subnationalities, sometimes it is far more difficult to classify particular groups. The ethnic groups in the United States demonstrate some of the difficulties in classification. With some ethnic groups there is no doubt about their classification. Italian Americans, German Americans, Polish Americans, Scottish Americans, and Irish Americans are all subnational groups. At a higher level of identity, the same is true for African Americans. None of these groups has a concept of a distinct and separate geographical homeland within the United States. Hence they are subnational groups who together with many other groups collectively constitute the American ethnic nationality.

There are other ethnic groups within the United States whose status is not as clear. What is the status of Native American groups such as the Navajo, the Hopi, the Crow, the Cheyenne, the Cherokee, and the Osage, to name only a few? These groups have a concept of homelands within the United States. They also have histories quite distinct from that of other Americans. In recent years they have been asserting increased political sovereignty and self-determination within their reservations (homelands). Although there is disagreement, many Native American individuals and groups still see themselves as distinct nationalities. The U.S. government does recognize most American Indian groups as national groups with collective legal and political rights. No other ethnic groups in the United States have officially recognized governments and limited rights of self-determination. There is also some question about the ethnic status of Spanish-speaking peoples in the southwestern United States. Until the mid-nineteenth century Texas, New Mexico, Arizona, and California

were part of Mexico. The United States acquired this region through military conquest. Most of the native Spanish-speaking people in this region think of themselves as Mexican Americans or Spanish American, a subnational group. There is, however, a small group who see themselves as "Mexicans" living in a land that is rightfully part of Mexico, a region they call "Atzlan."

The distinction between nationality and subnationality is important because of their different political implications. As we shall see, the demands of subnational groups for equal rights and treatment have long been a source of conflict. But the demands of nationalities for independence and sovereignty in a region carved out of an existing country create a political time bomb.

## THE PROBLEM OF STATELESS NATIONALITIES

It is difficult for most Americans to understand the causes and bitterness of ethnic conflict in other parts of the world. We think of *nationality* and *nation* as being one and the same. An American is any person who is a citizen of the United States. Most of us think of ourselves as Americans first and secondarily as Irish, Italian, or Chinese Americans. This mind-set about the meaning and significance of ethnicity is due mainly to our history as a nation of immigrants—with the exception of Native Americans, immigrants renounced their claims to their national homelands when they came to the New World. For the most part, the ethnic groups in the United States are subnationalities, not nationalities. Thus, from our common perception, a Russian is a person from Russia, a Nigerian is a citizen from Nigeria, and so forth. Falsely equating country of origin with ethnic nationality, we view ethnic conflicts in other regions of the world as if they are comparable to conflicts between subnational groups within the United States. Ethnic problems within a country are thought to be the result of social or economic discrimination—resolvable and reparable by reforms—and their political significance is minimized. However, the ethnic conflicts in most countries are not between subnational groups but between distinct nationalities.

The ethnic conflicts in Northern Ireland and in Israel and Palestine have proved particularly bitter. In 1922, after several centuries of British colonial domination and periodic rebellions by the native Irish, the Irish Free State (now the Republic of Ireland) was established. However, not all of Ireland was given independence. In

*The ethnic riots in Los Angeles that followed a jury's acquittal of four police officers on trial for the beating of Rodney King showed the potential ethnic problems in the United States.*

the seventeenth century, to control the Irish, the British evicted Irish farmers from the northernmost portion of the island and colonized the region with Scottish Presbyterians, who became known as the *Scotch-Irish*. The Scotch-Irish did not identify themselves as Irish and had no desire to become part of an independent Ireland. Recognizing the wishes of the Scotch-Irish, at independence the British partitioned the island. The northern six counties became Northern Ireland and remained part of the United Kingdom. Many Irish did not and do not accept the legality of this partitioning of Ireland. To them Northern Ireland is part of the Irish homeland and thus should be part of the Republic of Ireland. Since 1968 the Irish Republican Army, a secretive guerrilla army that is illegal in the Republic of Ireland, has been actively waging a war with the object of reuniting Northern Ireland with the Republic of Ireland. Since 1968 bombings, ambushes, and assassinations have claimed the lives of more than 2,200 persons, and no end appears in sight. The news media frequently report the problems in Northern Ireland as conflict between the British and the Irish or between Catholic and Protestants; in reality it is neither. The root of the problem is the conflicting claims of two rival and hostile nationalities: the Irish and the Scotch-Irish. The Scotch-Irish have emerged over the past 400 years as a distinct nationality who claim the northern part of Ireland as their homeland. In contrast, the Irish see the area as an integral and inalienable part of the Irish homeland.

After an absence of almost 2,000 years the Jews began returning to their historic homeland in Palestine in 1882. During the early twentieth century Jewish settlements in Palestine grew, and in 1948 the state of Israel was unilaterally proclaimed by the Jewish settlers. For the past forty-five years conflict between Israelis and Palestinians has been constant, varying only in the intensity and form of violence. The problem is similar to that in Northern Ireland, in that two nationalities—Israelis and Palestinians—claim the same geographical region as their legitimate homeland. As in Northern Ireland, most of us understand the conflict as being caused by disagreements and hatred between religious groups—Jews and Muslims. And as in Northern Ireland, it is impossible to resolve this conflict to the satisfaction of both nationalities, so conflict between Israelis and Palestinians continues with no resolution in sight.

These two conflicts vividly illustrate the strength of nationalist sentiments. In both cases we see groups of educated, rational human beings who are willing to sacrifice their lives and economic well-being in unending conflicts for what they consider to be their nationality's legitimate rights.

Such conflict between rival nationalities is more common in the modern world than most of us realize. To understand the magnitude or potential magnitude of this problem, one need only realize that the world is divided into less than 200 countries and between 3,000 and 5,000 distinct ethnic nationalities. As a result, the populations of most countries encompass a number of distinct nationalities. China officially recognizes fifty-six distinct nationalities. Some estimates are as high as 300 ethnic nationalities in Indonesia. Ethiopia has at least 70 nationalities. Only a handful of countries are peopled by members of a single nationality and are thus ethnically homogeneous.

The ethnic nationality problem is further complicated because current political boundaries frequently divide members of a nationality and their historic homeland. For example, Hungarians are found not only in Hungary but large numbers also live in the adjacent portions of

Romania and Serbia. Somalis live not only in Somalia but also in the adjacent Ogaden portion of Ethiopia. Thus the world is filled with ethnic groups who do not fully recognize the legitimacy of "their" central government and who aspire or may potentially aspire to have political autonomy.

For the most part the nationality problems in most countries were not created by the nationalities themselves. The current political boundaries for most of the world are legacies of European colonialism and expansion (see chapter 6). During the nineteenth century, the European powers divided most of the geographical regions and peoples of the world among themselves. In 1884–1885 at the Berlin Conference, European leaders sat at a table and with pens and pencils drew lines on a map of Africa, dividing the resources and peoples of that continent among themselves. Through this agreement the English, French, Germans, Belgians, and other European powers assumed sovereignty over lands they had never traveled and over peoples who had never seen a white man. Nor was Africa the only continent to have boundaries imposed by Europeans. The national boundaries of most of the world were drawn by Europeans for their own interest with little regard for the interest of any indigenous peoples or the boundaries of the ethnic groups affected. As a result, most European colonial possessions were a polyglot of ethnic groups, many of whom had long histories of hostilities toward one another. In other instances an ethnic group found its land and people divided between two or more European colonies. To make matters worse, colonial powers frequently moved people from one colony to another to supply labor, introducing still other ethnic groups to new areas. For example the British settled Indian laborers in Burma (Myanmar), Malaya (Malaysia), Fiji, Sri Lanka, Kenya, Uganda, South Africa, Trinidad, and British Guiana.

The end of the colonial period did not end the ethnic conflicts in the world but only signaled the beginning of the problems. As European powers granted independence to their colonies they made little attempt to redefine political boundaries. In most cases these newly independent countries had precisely the same boundaries and ethnic composition as the former colonies. Because these political divisions were imposed by European military power, some scholars have termed these former colonies **artificial countries** (see Figure 18.1). In most cases the basic colonial administrative and governmental structure was maintained after independence; the major departure from the colonial period was that native officials replaced European officials. However, not all ethnic groups were equally represented in these new governments, and most former colonies quickly came under the domination of one or two of the more powerful ethnic groups. Thus in many instances European domination was replaced by domination by one or another "native" ethnic group. With this in mind, the political problems endemic in much of the Third World become more comprehensible.

India is a prime example of ethnic problems in the postcolonial period. Consisting of several hundred distinct ethnic groups as well as major religious divisions, India did not exist—and never existed—as a unified country before British domination (see Figure 18.2). As independence approached in the 1940s, hostilities between rival Muslim and Hindu factions became so intense that British officials decided that a unified, independent India was an impossibility. They decided that India had to be divided into two countries: India (predominantly Hindu) and Pakistan (predominantly Muslim). The borders of these new countries were drawn by the British. The problem was the lack of clear geographical boundaries separating these groups; in many regions the populations were mixed Hindu and Muslim. An East Pakistan and a West Pakistan were carved out on either side, separated by 1,000 miles of what was to be India. After the official announcement of the boundaries massive migrations began as millions of Muslims and Hindus found themselves on the wrong sides of the boundary. These migrations were stimulated by fanatics on both sides, who massacred Muslims living in what was to become India and Hindus in what was to be Pakistan. Some estimate that as many as one million people were killed in these riots. The grant of actual independence to the two countries in 1947 made the situation worse because neither side was satisfied with their geographical boundaries. The new Indian army occupied the largely Muslim region of Kashmir, and war quickly broke out between the two countries. The first India-Pakistan war ended in 1949, with Kashmir occupied by India.

The creation of two separate states out of British India addressed—but did not solve—only one of the region's problems. Immediately after independence the Naga people in India's easternmost Assam province revolted and demanded an independent Nagaland. This Naga secessionist movement is still active, and for more than forty-five years periodic bloody clashes have occurred between Naga rebels and Indian authorities. More recently a Sikh separatist movement emerged, demanding an independent homeland in Punjab. The violent tactics of the Sikh nationalists resulted in the Indian army's

## FIGURE 18.1
### Ethnic Groups and National Boundaries in Africa

The boundaries of most African countries do not correspond with the territories of ethnic groups.

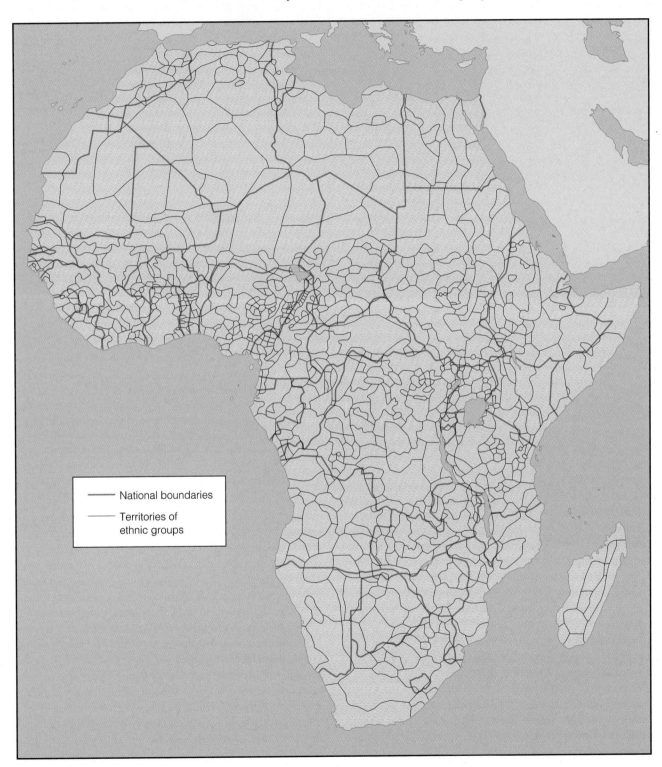

— National boundaries
— Territories of ethnic groups

## FIGURE 18.2
### Language Regions of South Asia

Some of the ethnic boundaries of India are reflected by these language regions.

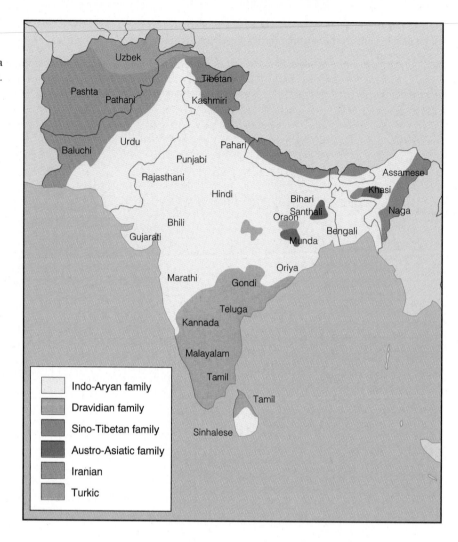

attacking the holiest Sikh religious shrine, the Golden Temple in Amritsar, in 1984. Later that year two Sikhs assassinated Indira Gandhi, the prime minister of India, causing more violence between Sikhs and Hindus. In 1990 violence again broke out in Kashmir. Muslim leaders are demanding either a separate nation or unification with Pakistan. As if India's problems with its religious-ethnic minorities were not sufficient, the Hindu majority is becoming increasingly hostile to non-Hindu minorities. In 1993 Hindu radicals destroyed a sixteenth-century Muslim mosque in northern India, claiming that it had been built on the site of an early Hindu temple. The destruction of the mosque led to a series of riots that left almost 2,000 dead. The internal religious-ethnic problems of India are increasing, not subsiding.

Pakistan has also experienced ethnic difficulties. Although both Pakistans were Muslim, there were major ethnic differences between the two. East Pakistanis were predominantly Bengalis. West Pakistan was more heterogeneous ethnically but dominated by Urdu-speaking peoples. Although West Pakistan had a smaller population, the capital was located there after independence in 1947, and the Urdu peoples gained dominance in the government and the military. In West Pakistan a separatist movement emerged among the Baluchi, who sought an independent Baluchistan. However, it was with the Bengalis in East Pakistan that the major conflict emerged. Although the Bengalis were economically exploited and discriminated against by the Urdu, it was not until the government attempted to impose the Urdu language in the schools of East Pakistan that the situation came to a head. In 1971 the East Pakistanis revolted and, after a short but bloody war aided by India, succeeded in establishing the state of Bangladesh.

Bangladesh is experiencing its own internal ethnic problems. Even before independence from Pakistan, Bengali settlers had begun occupying land in the Chittagong hills, displacing the indigenous tribal peoples. After independence, with official encouragement, the flow of Bengali settlers increased, causing the tribal peoples to rebel and demand local autonomy. The government has refused to halt the settlements, and periodic killings and massacres are continuing. In the realm of ethnic conflict today's victims can quickly become tomorrow's villains.

Similar secessionist movements have occurred and are still occurring throughout the old colonial world.

✦ Burma includes a dozen or more distinct ethnic groups. Immediately after independence from Britian in 1948 Karen and Shan peoples declared their freedom from Burma and revolted. Other ethnic groups soon followed the lead of the Karen and Shan. Today, more than forty-five years later, the Burmese army is involved in an inconclusive war with secessionist armies of ten different ethnic groups.

✦ In 1960 Nigeria became independent. In 1967 the Ibos, seeing Nigeria increasingly controlled by the Yoruba and Hausa peoples, seceded and established the Republic of Biafra. Three years of bloody war followed before the Ibos were militarily overwhelmed.

✦ Burundi became independent in 1962, and political conflict developed between the Tutsi and the Hutu; in 1972 this conflict culminated in the slaughter of about 200,000 Hutu.

Nationalist separatist movements are also active in the southern Sudan, the island of Mindanao in the Philippines, and in Sri Lanka—just to name a few of the most important movements. Certainly, it is facile to lay all the blame on colonialism for these and other conflicts in the postcolonial era. But it is undeniable that violence between ethnic nationalities, each believing its political and territorial claims are legitimate, is one of colonialism's most unfortunate and long-lasting legacies.

Not all the ethnic conflicts have been or are confined to the old colonial world. For example, the Kurds (who

*Hindu fundamentalists in India have become increasingly intolerant of the Muslim minority in the country. Here Hindu militants gather in Ayodhya before destroying the Muslim mosque in the background.*

**FIGURE 18.3**
**Kurdistan**

The Kurdish area and the proposed boundaries of an independent state of Kurdistan.

*Following the Slovenian declaration of independence in 1991, the Serbian dominated Yugoslavian Federal Army invaded the new country in an attempt to reestablish control.*

live in the mountainous regions of Turkey, Iraq, Iran, Syria, and the Soviet Union) have had an active separatist movement since the 1960s (see Figure 18.3). At different times they have fought the Turks, the Iraqis, and the Iranians. In 1950 China invaded and occupied Tibet, a region that the Chinese consider part of China. A Tibetan revolt in 1959 was crushed, but conflict is again escalating as Tibetan Buddhists seek political autonomy under the Dalai Lama, their spiritual leader.

Today some of the most violent ethnic conflicts are in Europe and the former Soviet Union. In the early 1990s Yugoslavia disintegrated as the republics of Slovenia, Croatia, Bosnia, and Macedonia proclaimed their independence. Yugoslavia was reduced to only two of the former six republics: Serbia and Montenegro. Hundred of thousands of ethnic Serbs found themselves living in Croatia and Bosnia. Supported by the Serb-controlled Yugoslavian army, Serb nationalists in Croatia and Bosnia rebelled, took control of regions in both republics, and demanded unification with Serbia. With more than 100,000 dead and more than one million homeless, the war in Bosnia has been the bloodiest and most destructive war in Europe since World War II and no end is in sight. Many fear that the war in Bosnia might spread to the Kosovo province of Serbia and the republic of Macedonia and may even ignite a war throughout the Balkans that could potentially involve Greece, Albania, Bulgaria, and Turkey. Many Europeans remember that World War I started in Bosnia. Similar ethnic wars have broken out in several republics of the former Soviet Union, and the potential for ethnic conflict both within and between these republics exists (See Box 18.2).

This is only a sampling of armed nationalist conflicts. Nationalist movements are difficult to defuse. In most cases the recognized national governments lack the military resources to totally defeat them. Even when a government has overwhelming resources, such as the British in Northern Ireland, guerrilla wars are difficult to win decisively. As a result, few separatist movements have been extinguished. In some cases the central governments have either disintegrated or lost control over most of the country. This situation exists in Liberia and Afghanistan. In other cases the central governments have adopted policies of geographical containment and lessening of direct conflict. A graphic example of this approach is in Western Sahara, formerly Spanish Sahara. In the early 1970s Spain committed itself to a policy of independence and self-determination for its colony. However, in 1976, before independence was achieved, Morocco occupied the northern portion of the region, claiming it was historically part of Morocco. In 1979 Morocco occupied the southern portion of the region. The Spanish did not resist the Moroccan occupation. However, the local Sahrawi population rejected Moroccan domination, formed the Polisario Front, and initiated a guerrilla war. Unable to defeat the guerrillas but yet unwilling to withdraw, the Moroccan government partitioned the region with a 2,500-kilometer-long sand "wall" equipped with electronic devices to detect movements; the purpose of the wall was to separate the portion Morocco controlled from the area they did not control. In 1989 the Moroccan government agreed to a referendum sponsored by the United Nations, but the status of Western Sahara has yet to be resolved. Almost yearly the number of unresolved ethnic conflicts increases and the number of peoples and regions affected widens. There are about 150 ongoing armed conflicts in the world today, and 80 to 90 percent of these conflicts would be classified as nationalist movements.

Central governments as a whole have been unsuccessful in achieving total military victories over separatist groups, but nationalist separatist groups themselves seldom have been successful in achieving political victories.

Bangladesh was recognized by the United Nations only because it was a *fait accompli,* backed by the overwhelming military support of India. In contrast, the United Nations was extremely slow to extend recognition to Slovenia and Croatia. Only when it appeared that Yugoslavia might militarily intervene did the United Nations act and then only in hopes of preventing a war. Under the military protection of the United Nations the Kurdish people in northern Iraq have proclaimed their independence and organized their own republic. However, while protecting them from the Iraq military, neither the United Nations nor any other country has formally recognized the new Kurdish state. The reason is simple. If an independent Kurdish state is created in northern Iraq, it would encourage Kurdish nationalists in Turkey, Iran, and Syria. With an active Kurdish separatist movement in its country, Turkey is adamantly opposed to the creation of any Kurdish state, and neither the United States nor the United Nations will challenge Turkey on this issue. The recent problems of chaos and starvation in Somalia have been limited to the southern portion of the country. When the central government of Somalia disintegrated in 1991 the leaders in the north declared their independence and established their state of Somaliland. Although Somaliland is politically stable, it has yet to be granted recognition by any country. The United Nations and the Organization of African Unity have taken the position that northern and southern Somalia will "remain" united and act as if no government exists in the north.

One may well ask why separatist governments seldom are extended official recognition. In Chapter 1, Article 1, of the Charter of the United Nations the right of a people to self-determination is recognized. The United Nations also recognizes the sovereignty and territorial integrity of the existing states. Thus recognition of a secessionist group would be considered intervention in affairs of a sovereign state. Other governments have also pledged themselves not to recognize separatist states. In 1964 the Organization of African Unity adopted the policy that "the borders of African States on the day of independence constitute a tangible reality," and thus they firmly oppose any changes in the political boundaries of Africa. The real, unstated reason is that almost every country in the world has one or more minority nationalities that either have or potentially may develop an independence movement. Thus both formal and informal agreements are made among the existing countries of the world to maintain the current political status quo.

The most significant political event of the early 1990s has been the collapse of the Soviet Union and its division into fifteen countries (see Fig. 18.4). In many ways the Soviet Union serves as a microcosm of the ethnopolitical problems besetting the world. Just before its collapse the Soviet Union encompassed almost 290 million people and more than 100 distinct ethnic nationalities. Although ethnic Russians constituted a slight majority (about 52 percent), there were more than twenty-three minority nationalities with populations in excess of one million people.

The Soviet Union was, politically speaking, nothing more than the Russian Empire under a new name, with Lenin, Stalin, and other Communist leaders being the political heirs of Czar Ivan IV. It was Ivan, also known as "the Terrible," who laid the foundations of the empire in the sixteenth century by solidifying the political hold of the czar over the Russian people. In the centuries that followed subsequent czars and their armies extended their political control beyond the lands of the Russian people. In the seventeenth century Russian frontiersmen known as the Cossacks overran and conquered the tribal peoples of Siberia, extending the boundaries of the empire all the way to the Pacific Ocean. During the same period Russian armies began extending the boundaries of the empire west and south, incorporating other Slavic and non-Slavic peoples—Finns, Latvians, Estonians, Lithuanians, Poles, Ukrainians, Bylorussians, and others. The ethnic composition of the empire was further diversified during the eighteenth century when the czar invited German farmers to settle on some of the newly won lands. Finally, during the nineteenth century, Russian armies pushed into central Asia, bringing numerous Muslim peoples into the empire.

BOX 18.2

# COLLAPSE OF THE SOVIET UNION

In March of 1917 the revolt against the czar began. The three years that followed were a period of internal wars and political chaos. It was not until 1920 that the Communists eliminated the counterrevolutionaries and solidified their control. During this period numerous ethnic nationalities had taken the opportunity to escape Russian domination. The Finns, Estonians, Latvians, Lithuanians, Georgians, Armenians, Azeris, and Bylorussians established their own countries. The Moldavians seceded and politically united with their close kin, the Romanians. With the support of the allied powers, the Polish regions of Russia, Germany, and Austria were joined to create a new Poland.

The new Communist rulers of Russia worked feverishly to rebuild the "empire." Soon they were able to reestablish control over Georgia, Armenia, Bylorussia, and Azerbaijan and group them into what was now called the Soviet Union. In 1939 the Soviets signed a secret nonaggression pact with Nazi Germany, and in September they joined the Germans in attacking and partitioning Poland. In November 1939 they invaded Finland, but the Finns were successful in halting their advance. In March of 1940 they militarily occupied the Moldavian portion of Romania and quickly reintegrated it into the Soviet Union. In June 1940 they invaded and annexed Estonia, Latvia, and Lithuania. Thus, by the end of June 1940, the Communists had reannexed to the Soviet Union all the lands of the czar with the exception of Finland. The invasion of the Soviet Union by Germany in 1941 proved only a temporary reversal, since Soviet troops "liberated" these regions near the end of World War II, and their reannexation was not questioned. The other allied powers even agreed to the redrawing of the boundaries of postwar Poland to correspond with Soviet territorial claims.

The Soviets created a political structure that superficially gave political recognition and "autonomy" to at least the major national minorities within the Union. The Soviet Union was divided into fifteen "union republics," one for each of the major ethnic nationalities: Russia, Byelorussia, Ukraine, Georgia, Armenia, Estonia, Latvia, Lithuania, Moldavia, Azerbaijan, Kazakhstan, Uzbekistan, Kirghizia, Tajikistan, and Turkmenistan. Five of these "union republics" included regions called "autonomous republics" for smaller nationalities. Altogether there were twenty "autonomous republics." Sixteen of these autonomous republics were in the Russian Republic, those for the Ossetians, Tatars, Yakut, Chechen-Ingush, and twelve other groups. Five of the union republics had still other, smaller ethnic political units called "autonomous oblasts." The best known of the eight oblasts are Nagorno-Karabakh (an Armenian ethnic region in the Azeri Republic of Azerbaijan) and Yugo Ossetian (an Ossetian ethnic region in the Georgian Republic). In addition, the Russian Republic had six very small ethnic regions called "nationality okrugs." Thus about forty-five of the largest nationalities within the Soviet Union had some form of political recognition.

Although every level of ethnopolitical unit had its own formal government, there was no meaningful local autonomy. Nor were these various re-

*continued on next page*

## FIGURE 18.4
Republics and Divisions of the former Soviet Union

| | | | | | | |
|---|---|---|---|---|---|---|
| International boundaries | 1. | Karel'skaya A.S.S.R. | 8. | Bashkirskaya A.S.S.R. | 15. | Abhazskaya A.S.S.R. |
| | 2. | Komi A.S.S.R. | 9. | Kalmytskaya A.S.S.R. | 16. | Nakhichevanskaya A.S.S.R. |
| | 3. | Mordovskaya A.S.S.R. | 10. | Dagenstanskaya A.S.S.R. | 17. | Karakalpakskaya A.S.S.R. |
| A.S.S.R. boundaries | 4. | Chuvashskaya A.S.S.R. | 11. | Checheno-Ingushskaya A.S.S.R. | 18. | Tuvinskaya A.S.S.R. |
| | 5. | Mariyskaya A.S.S.R. | 12. | Severo-Osetinskaya A.S.S.R. | 19. | Buryetskaya A.S.S.R. |
| | 6. | Tatarskaya A.S.S.R. | 13. | Kabardino-Balkarskaya A.S.S.R. | 20. | Yakutskaya A.S.S.R. |
| | 7. | Udmurtskaya A.S.S.R. | 14. | Yugo-Osentinskaya A.O. | | |

gions the exclusive homes for the designated ethnic group. Members of different ethnic groups moved or were moved between ethnic regions. This was particularly true for Russians. Large Russian minorities were found in most of the fourteen other union republics. In fact, it was not uncommon for resident Russians to control the political bureaucracy of other republics.

Political recognition did not mean that the Soviet government encouraged ethnic differences. Any overt demonstration of ethnic pride or nationalism was ruthlessly crushed. The Russian language was taught in the schools, and local cultural traditions were suppressed. This suppression was particularly marked in the Islamic regions of central Asia, where Islamic schools and mosques were closed and many religious leaders were shot or imprisoned. This intolerance toward cultural and religious dissidents was not limited to larger, potentially dangerous nationalities. For example, the Yokuts, a reindeer-herding people of Siberia who numbered only a few hundred thousand, also suffered. In the 1920s and 1930s their herds were collectivized, their language and cultural activities suppressed, and their religious leaders shot.

*continued on next page*

The Soviet Union was the "Russian Empire" under a new name, and regardless of what was publicly stated by political leaders in Moscow, members of the other nationalities recognized that they were under Russian domination. Given this feeling of Russian domination, the events of the past few years should not have surprised us. The political chaos in the Soviet Union in the early 1990s once again gave the minority nationalities the opportunity to regain their independence, and thus there was a repeat of what happened in 1917 and 1918.

The disintegration of the Soviet Union into fifteen new nation-states has not ended the ethnic problems of the region but rather intensified them. Ethnic problems exist both within and between the new states. More than eighty of the smaller nationalities have yet to achieve political independence. In other cases a portion of the population of one of the fifteen nationalities who do have their own nation-state resides within the boundaries of another state. Fully 25 percent of the total population within the fifteen republics belongs to a minority national group.

The disintegration of the Soviet Union has increased the nationalist aspirations of many of the eighty or so smaller national groups. Nationalist separatist movements have already emerged among the Tatar and Chechen peoples in Russia. The Ossetian peoples (Yugo Ossetia) in Georgia have rebelled, seeking to be politically reunited with the Ossetian peoples in Russia. Thus we see a second wave of nationalist movements emerging.

The most potentially dangerous ethnic problems are between, not within, the fifteen new states. A destructive war is already raging between the Armenians and the Azeris over Nagorno-Karabakh. However, it is the twenty-five million Russians living in the fourteen non-Russian republics who may create the great threat to peace. In some countries ethnic Russians constitute 30 to 40 percent of the population. What is going to happen to these Russian minorities? Local nationalists are openly hostile to Russian residents and want them to return to Russia. In Estonia nationalists have tried to deny resident Russians any political rights by imposing stringent residency and language (ability to speak Estonian) requirements for citizenship. Fearing reunification with Romania, the Russian and Ukrainian residents of Moldavia have rebelled and proclaimed the independent Dniester Republic. In Tajikistan and some of the other central Asian republics Russian residents have been attacked and murdered. In Kazakhstan, militarily the most powerful of these republics, 37 percent of the population (more than six million people) is Russian, and the northern portion of the republic is almost exclusively occupied by Russians. Russian and Kazahk are both official languages of the republic. Some believe that the Kazakh leaders are trying to strengthen their positions before moving against the Russian minority. The fear is that the Russians might succeed and unite northern Kazakhstan with Russia.

The leaders of the Russian Republic have recognized the problem facing the Russian minorities in the other republics and proclaimed that their rights will be protected. On a limited scale the Russian army has already intervened to protect the Russian residents of Moldavia and Tajikistan as well as the Ossetians in Georgia. The complicating factor is the rebirth of the Cossacks. The Cossacks were free Russian peasants who lived on the borders of the empire. Organized as paramilitary communities under their own leaders, they saw themselves as the protectors of the Russian people and the Eastern Orthodox Church. Disbanded by the Communists, military units are being reorganized in many of the Cossack communities. Cossack volunteers have already joined the Russian secessionists in the fighting in Moldavia, and several hundred other Cossacks have joined the Serbs (also Eastern Orthodox) in Bosnia fighting the Muslims. What would happen if an ethnic cleansing program against Russians occurs in Kazakhstan, Uzbekistan, or some other former Soviet republic? There can be little doubt that the Russian army would be forced to intervene.

We have mentioned only a few examples of ethnic conflicts within the former Soviet Union. The *Moscow News* in 1992 compiled a list of seventy-nine existing or potential ethnic conflicts. What makes the situation in the former Soviet Union more dangerous than the situations in most similar regions of the world is the presence of vast quantities of not only modern conventional weapons but also nuclear weapons at military bases throughout the republics. The potential for ethnic conflict and bloodshed on a massive scale exists within the former Soviet Union. You might well ask, Other than for humanitarian reasons, why should we be concerned about our former enemies? The answer is simple. It is doubtful that large-scale ethnic wars could be confined within the boundaries of the fifteen republics. These wars would quickly spill over into the Middle East and Eastern and Western Europe. Even if these wars could be contained, the republics of the former Soviet Union are the world's largest producers of oil, producing 20 percent of the total world supply. These same republics supply the peoples and industries of Western Europe with most of their natural gas. Thus large-scale conflicts in this region would have a devastating effect on the global economy. ✦

## RESOLVING ETHNIC CONFLICT

How can such deep-rooted conflicts be resolved? The most obvious solution is to divide the country, giving the dissatisfied nationality their land and independence and allowing them to establish their own country or merge with another country. However, central governments have always been highly reluctant to surrender their territorial claims. As Burma, the Sudan, and many other countries have shown, they would rather fight a long, destructive, and inclusive war than officially recognize the independence of a rebellious nationality. This stance is taken partly because governments fear setting a precedent. As a result, most ethnic conflicts have been resolved—and future solutions will probably have to be sought—within the existing political structure.

Historically, such internal solutions to ethnic issues have taken two forms: (1) ethnic homogenization of the population through the elimination of rival ethnic groups and (2) the political accommodation of ethnic groups.

### Homogenization

**Ethnic homogenization** is the process by which one ethnic group attempts to eliminate rival ethnic groups within a particular region or country. Historically, ethnic homogenization has taken one of two main forms: (1) **ethnic cleansing** or (2) **assimilation.**

The term *ethnic cleansing* entered our vocabulary in reference to the warfare in the republics of what was formerly Yugoslavia. Ethnic cleansing is the physical elimination of an unwanted ethnic group or groups from particular geographical areas. It involves the use of genocide and/or relocation.

**Genocide** is the deliberate and systematic attempt to physically destroy the members of the rival population. The objective may be the total destruction of the group, the reduction of their numbers, or a stimulus for the surviving members of the group to migrate. Regardless of the actual objective, the process is the same: the indiscriminate slaughter of men, women, and children of the targeted ethnic group.

Today when we think of genocide we think of the recent events in Bosnia or of the killing of millions of Jews and Gypsies by the Germans during World War II, but genocide has been a recurrent event in human history. Only the magnitude of the killing has varied. In the late 1970s and early 1980s thousands of Native

*After World War II millions of ethnic Germans living in Poland and Czechoslovakia were forced from their homes.*

Americans were massacred by the Guatemalan army. The Turks instituted a policy of systematic killing of Armenians during the early years of this century. During the colonial period the English, Dutch, French, Spanish, Portuguese, Belgians, and Germans were periodically guilty of genocide. Incidents of genocide are found even in American history, beginning with the slaughter of the Pequots of Connecticut in 1637 and ending with the massacre of more than 150 Sioux at Wounded Knee, South Dakota, in 1890. Genocide has been and still is a far too common response to ethnic conflict and rivalry.

**Relocation** is the forced resettlement of an unwanted ethnic group in a new geographical location. The forced relocation of the target population may be in conjunction with genocide, as in Bosnia, or separate from it. Sometimes the unwanted group is forced outside the boundaries of the country, becoming what today we term *refugees*. In other cases an ethnic group is forcibly moved to a new area within the boundaries of the state, where it is assumed that they will pose less of a problem. After World War II the boundaries of much of Eastern Europe were redrawn. That portion of Germany located east of the Oder River was given to Poland, and seven million German residents were forcibly evicted. At the same time, Czechoslovakia evicted almost three million resident Germans from their homes (see Figure 18.5). After independence many East African countries expelled many East Indians who had settled there during the colonial period. In American history Native Americans were regularly relocated as the frontier moved west, thus "solving" the Indian problem for white settlers and

FIGURE 18.5
Relocation of Ethnic Germans after
World War II.

Direction arrows indicate the transfer,
eviction, or flight of ethnic Germans.
Figures are in thousands of people.

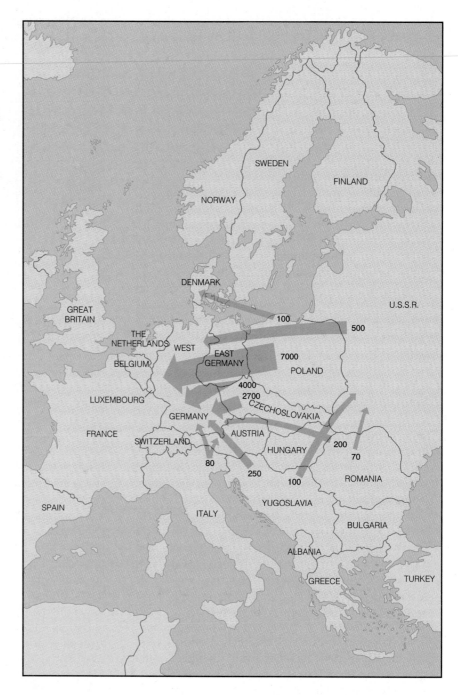

the U.S. government. The largest and best known of these relocations occurred in the 1830s, when the Five Civilized Tribes were forced to move (along the so-called Trail of Tears) from their homes in the southeastern states to what is today Oklahoma. Most indigenous tribes of the United States experienced similar resettlement programs. In Bosnia and Croatia the main objective of the Serbs is the relocation of the Croat and Muslim families. The killings, rapes, and destruction are the tactics used to cause them to abandon their homes. In this case there is no designated place for these people to go, and thus hundreds of thousands of refugees are attempting to find refuge in other European countries and Turkey.

**Assimilation** is the social absorption of one ethnic group by another, dominant one. Assimilation may be total, in which the ethnic identity of one group is lost, or partial, in which one ethnic group assumes a subordinate identity. Assimilation may be either forced or passive.

**Forced assimilation** occurs when the government adopts policies designed to deliberately and systematically destroy or change the ethnic identity of a particular group. The ultimate objective usually is the total absorption of the group into the dominant ethnic group. A key target of forced assimilation policy is the elimination of ethnic boundary markers: language, religion, modes of dress, and any cultural institution that readily distinguishes the population. If these boundary markers are destroyed, the group loses much of its social cohesiveness. For example, until recently the Bulgarian government pursued a policy designed to assimilate its Turkish population. Turks were not free to practice their Islamic religion, and they were forced to speak Bulgarian in public and adopt Bulgarian names.

One of the best examples of forced assimilation was the United States's Indian policy in the latter part of the nineteenth and early twentieth centuries. Federal Indian policy attacked Native American ethnic identity from several directions. Reservation lands, which were owned communally, were broken up, and the land was allotted (deeded) to individual members of the tribe. The objective was to destroy community or village life. Many ceremonies, such as the Sun Dance and peyote religion, were made illegal. Traditional or hereditary tribal leaders were not recognized, and tribal governments were either dissolved or reorganized along an American political model. People who worked for the government commonly were forced to cut their hair and wear "citizens" (western-style) clothes. Native American children were taken from their families and placed in boarding schools, where they were forbidden to speak their native language, had their hair cut, were made to dress in citizens' clothes, were taught Euro-American technical skills, and were indoctrinated with Euro-American Christian values and attitudes.

Assimilation need not be the result of a conscious official policy to solve an "ethnic problem" by incorporating the population into the cultural mainstream. Another form, called **passive assimilation**, occurs without any formal planning or political coercion. Unless strong social barriers prevent assimilation, social and economic forces frequently result in more dominant ethnic groups absorbing the members of less powerful groups with whom they are in contact. The dominant ethnic group does not necessarily have to be the larger, but it must be the most socially prestigious and

*Overt ethnic boundary markers usually are the main targets of forced assimilation policies. This is the same Native American before and after attending an Indian school founded by the government.*

economically powerful group. Many of the governments in Latin America have historically followed a laissez-faire policy toward Native American groups. Guatemala has not had a policy of forced assimilation. In Guatemala the primary differences between Ladinos and Native Americans are not biological but social and cultural, and people who are ethnically identified as Native Americans are socially and economically discriminated against. As a result, more ambitious and educated Native Americans frequently have abandoned their native languages, dress, and life-styles (ethnic boundary markers) and reidentified themselves as Ladinos. During the past 100 years the Native American population in Guatemala has decreased from about 75 percent of the total population to less than 50 percent; passive assimilation is the primary cause of this decrease.

## Accommodation

An alternative to ethnic homogenization is some form of political **accommodation** that formally recognizes and supports the ethnic and cultural differences of the population. A number of multinationality countries have adopted this strategy of formalized ethnic pluralism. For instance, Canada has two main nationalities: Anglo-Canadians (English-speaking) and French-Canadians (French-speaking). Both English and French are formally acknowledged as official languages. Although Quebec is the only province in which French-Canadians are the majority, French-speakers are found throughout the other, predominantly Anglo-Canadian provinces. Belgium also has two major national groups: the Flemish (Dutch-speakers) and the Walloons (French-speakers). Both Flemish and Walloon are official languages of Belgium, and although internal political boundaries closely correspond to ethnic boundaries, neither group is recognized politically. Spain has four main linguistic ethnic groups: Spanish, Galitian, Catalinian, and Basque. Although Spanish is still the official language of Spain, since 1980 both the Basques and the Catalonians have had local political autonomy.

In the cases of Canada, Belgium, and Spain the number of distinct nationalities is limited. Other countries have confronted far more complex ethnic mixes. The two most ambitious attempts to create functioning multinational states have been those of the Soviet Union and Yugoslavia. The Soviet Union encompassed more than 100 national groups (see Box 18.2)

Yugoslavia had eight major nationalities: Serbs, Croats, Muslims, Slovenians, Montenegrins, Macedonians, Hungarians, and Albanians. Separate republics have established for the Serbs, Croats, Montenegrins, and Macedonians. Although no separate republic was created for the Muslims, they were the largest group in the ethnically mixed republic of Bosnia. The Albanians and Hungarians were given autonomous provinces within the republic of Serbia. Yugoslavia was organized as a confederacy, and a great deal of local autonomy was given each of the republics.

## Resolution

Having looked at the various means by which peoples have attempted to resolve ethnic differences, we can now examine the results. What are the results of ethnic cleansing? No American can deny that ethnic cleansing does not work. You need only to look about you. How many Native American faces do you see? Yet America was once entirely Native American. American Indian peoples were massacred and the defeated survivors driven steadily westward to lands considered less desirable. Today most Native Americans survive in small, scattered communities in the plains, deserts, and mountain states.

Setting aside the moral issues, ethnic cleansing seldom is a permanent solution. Except for very small groups, rarely has one ethnic nationality been successful in destroying another. Even though it may be greatly reduced in number, the targeted group usually survives. The history of genocidal attacks by the other group becomes an integral part of the origin myth of the victimized group and thus serves to strengthen—not weaken—their identity. Genocide also creates hatred and distrust between groups that can persist for generations after the actual event and make future political cooperation between the groups difficult, if not impossible.

Relocation also produces mixed results. As in the case of genocide, the forced removal of a people becomes part of their origin myth and serves to strengthen their cohesion and identity. Removal of a people from their homeland in no way negates their claims to the lands they lost. Four hundred years after the Irish were evicted from Northern Ireland the Irish Republican Army is fighting to reclaim this portion of the lost Irish homeland. The Jews were expelled from Jerusalem in the first century A.D. and dispersed over Europe, North Africa, and the Middle East. Yet the past century has seen their return to Israel and the reclaiming of their homeland. The collective memory of a nationality is long. Old wrongs seldom are forgotten, and lost homelands are never truly relinquished.

Assimilation—whether passive or forced—is not always effective. There is no question that throughout history smaller groups have been absorbed by larger groups. Assimilation usually is a slow and uncertain process. As we discussed, in Guatemala, Native Americans have slowly declined as a percentage of the total population over the past 100 years. We might therefore assume that passive assimilation has proved effective in this case. However, considering absolute rather than relative population, we find that the Native American population actually increased from one million to about four million during the same period. The main problem with passive assimilation, then, is that population growth often creates new members as fast as or faster than former members become assimilated. Another problem is that many peoples do not want to give up their ethnic identity; if they did, forced assimilation would not be necessary. The forced assimilation policies in the United States were equally unsuccessful in regard to Native Americans. Loss of language, material culture, and other cultural institutions that functioned as ethnic boundary markers did not destroy ethnic identity or group cohesiveness because new cultural institutions and ethnic boundary markers soon emerged to replace the old. From a population of only about 250,000 in 1890 the Native American population of the United States has risen to more than 1.5 million today, and the major political demands are for greater tribal sovereignty and self-determination on Native American lands.

So genocide, relocation, and forced or passive assimilation may be effective to a greater or lesser degree, but each, under most circumstances, does not truly resolve ethnic problems. More often they postpone the formulation of workable policies and are even counterproductive—they worsen rather than alleviate conflicts. Besides these "pragmatic" considerations genocide and forced assimilation are so morally abhorrent that few modern governments would admit to pursuing such policies. Relocation, likewise, poses ethical dilemmas; most groups are moved against their will, and some other nationality must be relocated to make room for the migrants. In the modern world there is nowhere to relocate to without violating some other group's rights. Finally, as we have seen, passive assimilation usually is slow and its result uncertain: Many nationalities want to maintain their traditions and refuse to give up their identity.

Political accommodation is the only practical and morally acceptable solution. But how well does it work,

and what are the problems in maintaining a multinationality state? Although the vast majority of countries encompass two or more national groups, few have attempted to politically accommodate multiple nationalities. Most countries are controlled by a single nationality that politically and economically dominates the other nationalities and holds the country together by force or the implied threat of force.

In an effort to understand the problems of political accommodation we are going to examine the recent history of three such states: Canada, Yugoslavia, and Czechoslovakia. (In Box 18.2 you can read about a fourth, the Soviet Union.) Canada remains a united country as the leaders of both English- and French-speaking Canadians struggle to find a political solution to their ethnic problem. Czechoslovakia peacefully split into the Czech Republic and Slovakia in January 1993. The disintegration of Yugoslavia into six republics in 1991 and 1992 has resulted in a series of bloody ethnic wars. Each of these three cases tells us something about the volatility and problems enherent in multinationality states.

Canada originally was settled by French colonists during the seventeenth century. The British gained control of portions of eastern Canada in 1713, after Queen Anne's War. French settlers were expelled and replaced by British colonists. In 1763, after the French and Indian War, the British took control of the rest of French Canada. Under the Quebec Act of 1774 French settlers were granted the right to have their own language, religion, and civil laws. After the American Revolution large numbers of American loyalists settled in Canada, which greatly increased the resident English-speaking population. In 1867 the Dominion of Canada was created and the policy of accommodation was continued, with both French and English being recognized as official languages.

In the 1960s a separatist movement emerged among the French-Canadians in Quebec. The main catalyst for this movement was demographic changes. Originally a small minority, the English-speaking population in Canada grew rapidly during nineteenth century. The twentieth century has seen an acceleration of this trend. Most immigrants to Canada during the twentieth century chose to adopt English, not French, as their language, thus adding to the English-Canadian population. At the same time, the birthrate of French-Canadians has declined. Thus the French-Canadians see themselves as constituting an ever-smaller percentage of the total population. French-Canadian separatism is thus not the result of personal animosity toward English-Canadians but rather the collective fear of being overwhelmed by the shear number of English-speakers, the loss of their language, and the erosion of their cultural distinctiveness. In the 1976 elections the Parti Québécois, the separatist party, won control of the government of Quebec and the next year made French the official language of the province. However, in a 1980 referendum in Quebec voters rejected separation from Canada. Although 60 percent of the people in Quebec voted against separation in 1980, the issue was not resolved.

Although opposing separation from Canada, the majority of French-Canadians remained concerned about the potential loss of French culture and identity. In 1987 the Meech Lake Agreement was negotiated. This agreement would have given Quebec constitutional rights that could be used to preserve the French language and culture. The agreement had to receive the unanimous approval of all the provinces. Two English-speaking provinces rejected the agreement in 1990. In another attempt at reaching a political compromise, a new agreement, called the Charlottetown Accord, was reached in 1992. This new agreement would have weakened the powers of the central government and recognized Quebec as a "distinct society." It also would have permanently given Quebec 25 percent of the members of the House of Commons. Submitted to a national referendum in October 1992, the Charlottetown Accord were soundly rejected, even by the people of Quebec. Yet the basic issue remains, and the Parti Québécois, no longer in power in Quebec, is calling for another referendum on independence for Quebec. Can a workable solution be found for Canada, or will it eventually disintegrate?

The early 1990s saw the demise of two multinationality states: Czechoslovakia and Yugoslavia. Both had similar histories: They had been created by the Allied Powers after World War I; they had attempted politically accommodation for their different nationalities and were controlled by Communists since the end of World War II; they disintegrated once democratic institutions evolved.

Czechoslovakia was created in 1919 out of a portion of what had been the Austro-Hungarian Empire. It was a two-nationality state that combined both the Czech ethnic regions of Bohemia and Moravia and the Slovak ethnic region of Slovakia. Linguistically, culturally, and socially, the Czechs and Slovaks are closely related peoples. Although rivalry exists between the two peoples, there was no history of any major hostilities or wars between them. Yet in January of 1993, by mutual agreement, the country peacefully split into the Czech Republic and the Republic of Slovakia. It was the smaller nationality, the Slovaks, who initiated the division, despite the fact that separation would be to their economic disadvantage. The industrial heart of Czechoslovakia was always in Bohemia and Moravia. Prague, the national capital, was in Bohemia. In terms of political and economic power as well as education, the Czechs had always dominated the country. Not surprisingly, many Slovaks thought that the Czechs treated them like their poor country cousins. It was ethnic pride, not ethnic hostility, that led to the breakup of the country.

In the dismantling of the Austro-Hungarian Empire after World War I, a new country was also created in the Balkans. Yugoslavia was to be the most ethnically diverse of the central European countries and included within its boundaries Slovenians, Croats, Serbs, Bosnian Muslims, Macedonians, Montenegrins, Hungarians, and Albanians. Unlike other European countries, Yugoslavia had no ethnic majority group. Originally a kingdom, the country was overrun by the Germans during World War II. The local Communist partisan forces under Marshal Tito were able to liberate the country with little direct outside assistance. After the war Tito created a new political structure for the country in which every ethnic would have at least some local autonomy. The country was divided into six republics: Slovenia, Croatia, Serbia, Bosnia, Montenegro, and Macedonia. Within the republic of Serbia two autonomous provinces were created: Kosovo, in which the majority of people were Albanians, and Vojvodina, which had a large Hungarian population. The national capital, Belgrade, was also the capital of Serbia. The army was also dominated by Serbs. With 36 percent of the total population, the Serbs were the largest national group, followed by the Croats (20 percent), the Bosnia Muslims (9 percent), the Slovenes (8 percent), the Albanians (8 percent), the Macedonians (6 percent), and the Montenegrins (3 percent). Members of the other ethnic groups complained that the Serbs acted as if Yugoslavia was "their" country. After Tito's death in 1980 the office of president rotated among the presidents of the six republics (see Fig. 18.6).

The history of the Balkans is a history of long and bloody wars between the various ethnic groups. A particularly deep hatred exists between the Croats (Catholics), the Serbs (Eastern Orthodox), and the Bosnian Muslims. Genocide has been common, and at one time or another each has massacred members of the other group. During World War II almost two million Yugoslavians died, and more were killed by members of rival ethnic groups than by Germans.

## FIGURE 18.6
### Republics and Autonomous Provinces of Yugoslavia

The individual republics and autonomous provinces more or less correspond with the territories of major ethnic groups.

In June 1991 Slovenia and Croatia declared their independence, with Slovenia leading the way. The wealthiest and best educated of the nationalities, the Slovenians believed that the poorer republics of the country were inhibiting their economic development. The Croats seceded for both economic and nationalistic reasons. With Slovenia and Croatia gone the ethnic balance in the remainder of Yugoslavia shifted. Serbs now constituted a majority in what remained of Yugoslavia—the country was now a de facto Serb state. In the fall of 1991 Macedonia declared independence, and in early 1992 the Bosnians voted for independence.

So far there has been major fighting only in Croatia and Bosnia. Croatia has an 18 percent Serbian minority population. Unable to tolerate political domination by the Croats, the Croatian Serbs rebelled, demanding that the areas in which they lived be politically joined to Serbia. The situation in Bosnia was different. With a population consisting of 43 percent Muslim, 31 percent Serbs, and 17 percent Croats, Bosnia had no ethnic majority. Once again the resident Serbs rebelled. Historic hatreds aside, there were two main reasons for the rebellion of the Bosnian Serbs. The Bosnian Muslims are better educated and more prosperous than the local Serbs, creating economic jealousy. In addition, the birthrate among the Muslims is higher than that of the Serbs. Thus there was the expectation that in the future the Bosnian Muslims would become the majority, and Bosnia would be an Islamic country.

By examining these three cases we can see some of the problems that exist in multinationality states, even under the best of conditions. The very presence of two or more nationalities within a country creates the potential for political volatility. Historic hatreds between groups increase the potential for conflict and political division. To be successful, political accommodation requires the creation and maintenance of a social, political, and economic balance between the groups. Members of all groups have to feel a collective social equality with members of other groups. They cannot think that their language or cultural institutions are being threatened or eroded by those of another group. Politically, they have to believe that their collective political rights are secure. Finally, no group can feel that their collective economic well-being is inhibited or that they are collectively being exploited by other groups. No country has ever existed with a perfect social, political, and economic balance between nationalities. Some social, political, and economic differences and inequalities between nationalities always exist. However, these differences and inequalities must not be of such magnitude as to threaten any particular ethnic group and all must believe that political unity is to their mutual benefit. The problems faced by multinationality countries is not in their initial creation but in their maintenance over time.

The factors that most seriously threaten the political stability of multinationality countries are (1) differential rates of population growth and (2) relative differences in economic development between the constituent nationalities. If the population of one nationality grows more rapidly than that of another, it threatens the existing social and political balance of the country. The nationality or nationalities whose relative populations are declining may think that their social and cultural institutions are being threatened. They may also think that their collective political influence will decline. Regional differences in resources may result in significant changes in the relative economic status of the different nationalities. Changes in relative economic power can be translated into shifts in relative political power. Attempts to redistribute or divide the new wealth of one nationality among the other nationalities within the country can result in a feeling of exploitation.

The evolving global economy requires close cooperation between countries and nationalities. Rising nationalism directly threatens the global economy. Although we cannot change our basic human feelings, we can more clearly understand those factors that serve to unleash ethnic emotions, and attempt to minimize them. In the next chapter we discuss the critical issues of population growth and world hunger.

## SUMMARY

In this chapter we have discussed the nature of ethnic groups and their significance in the world. Every individual, not just members of minority populations, belongs to an ethnic group and has an ethnic identity. An ethnic group is a named social grouping of people based on what is perceived as being shared ancestry, cultural traditions, and history. Ethnic group identity divides the world into categories of "us" and "them."

An individual's ethnic group identity seldom is absolute, but changes with social context. An individual may assume various hierarchically ranked identities. This characteristic is called the *hierarchical nesting quality* of identity.

There are two main attributes of an ethnic group. Every ethnic group has an origin myth or "history" that describes the common or shared historical experiences that created the group. Every ethnic group also has ethnic boundary markers that make its members identifiable. Ethnic boundary markers may include language, religion, physical characteristics, and other cultural traits such as clothing, house types, personal adornment, food, and so on.

There are two distinct types of ethnic groups. An ethnic nationality is an ethnic group with a feeling of homeland and the inherent right to political autonomy. An ethnic minority is any subnational ethnic group. An ethnic minority does not have a feeling of a separate homeland or of an inherent right to political autonomy.

Much of the conflict in the world today is between ethnic nationalities. There are between 3,000 and 5,000 ethnic nationalities in the world but only about 200 separate countries. Most countries in the world are multinationality countries, and much conflict is the result of nationalities wanting to establish their own independent countries.

There is no simple or easy solution to ethnic conflict. Genocide, relocation, and forced assimilation are not only immoral but history shows that they seldom solve ethnic problems. Passive assimilation is a slow and uncertain process. Attempts by governments of multinationality states to accommodate cultural differences and nationalistic aspirations are not always successful. Ethnic conflict is and will be a major destabilizing factor in world politics for some time to come. So far the citizens and even governments of militarily powerful Western nations have not come to grips with the threat of nationalism.

## KEY TERMS

| | |
|---|---|
| ethnic group | artificial countries |
| hierarchical nesting | ethnic homogenization |
| origin myth | ethnic cleansing |
| ethnic boundary markers | genocide |
| ethnogenesis | relocation |
| nationality | forced assimilation |
| homeland | passive assimilation |
| subnationalities | accommodation |

## SUGGESTED READINGS

Bodley, John. *Victims of Progress.* 2d ed. Palo Alto: Mayfield Publishing, 1982.
> A very readable book that is a good overview of tribal peoples in the modern world, with emphasis on how they are being destroyed by industrial civilization.

Burger, Julian. *Report from the Frontier: The State of the World's Indigenous Peoples.* Cambridge, Mass.: Cultural Survival, 1987.
> A general survey of the plight of indigenous peoples of the world.

Carmack, Robert, ed. *Harvest of Violence.* Norman: University of Oklahoma Press, 1988.
> This collection of twelve original essays is concerned with the war in Guatemala during the late 1970s and early 1980s, and how the war effected and involved the native Maya communities.

De Vos, George, and Lola Romanusci-Ross, eds. *Ethnic Identity: Cultural Continuities and Change.* Palo Alto: Mayfield Publishing, 1975.

> *A collection of fourteen important essays (with a conclusion) covering a variety of ethnic issues. A number of European, Asian, African, and American ethnic groups are examined.*

Eder, James F. *On the Road to Tribal Extinction: Depopulation, Deculturation, and Adaptive Well Being Among the Batak of the Philippines.* Berkeley: University of California Press, 1987.

> *During the twentieth century the Batak have become increasingly integrated into the Philippine economy. This has had far-reaching effects on the Batak sociocultural system and has resulted in an erosion of their ethnic identity.*

Foster, Charles, ed. *Nations Without States.* New York: Praeger, 1980.

> *This collection of essays covers ethnic conflict and nationalist movements among Western European peoples such as the Scots, Welsh, Basques, Brittons, Corsicans, and Catalans.*

Friedlander, Judith. *Being Indian in Hueyapan.* New York: St Martin, 1975.

> *An excellent and readable study of Native American identity in rural Mexico.*

Grobsmith, Elizabeth. *Lakota of the Rosebud.* New York: Holt, Rinehart and Winston, 1981.

> *This is one of the best studies available on a contemporary Native American community in the United States.*

Handler, Richard. *Nationalism and the Politics of Culture in Quebec.* Madison: University of Wisconsin Press, 1988.

> *An excellent introduction to French-Canadian nationalism. This text examines the growth and changes in nationalism in terms of ideology.*

Horowitz, Donald. *Ethnic Groups in Conflict.* Berkeley: University of California Press, 1985.

> *This study examines ethnic conflict on a global basis. It has a good discussion of theory of conflict, examples of conflict, and strategies for conflict reduction.*

International Work Group for Indigenous Affairs. *The Naga Nation and Its Struggle against Genocide.* Copenhagen: International Work Group for Indigenous Affairs, No. 56, 1986.

> *A survey of the historical background and contemporary problems of the Naga people of India, who have had an separatist movement for more than forty years.*

Urban, Greg, and Joel Sherzer, eds. *Nation-States and Indians in Latin America.* Austin: University of Texas Press, 1991.

> *A series of excellent articles on the varying relationships between Indians and non-Indian populations in Mexico, Colombia, Brazil, Panama, Ecuador, and other Latin-American countries.*

Verdery, Katherine. *Transylvania Villagers: Three Centuries of Political, Economic, and Ethnic Change.* Berkeley: University of California Press, 1983.

> *The Romanian region of Transylvania is occupied by German, Hungarian, and Romanian peoples. This study examines the social, political, and economic changes that have affected three nationalities and their relationships with one another over the past 300 years.*

## CHAPTER 19

# ANTHROPOLOGY AND TWO WORLD PROBLEMS

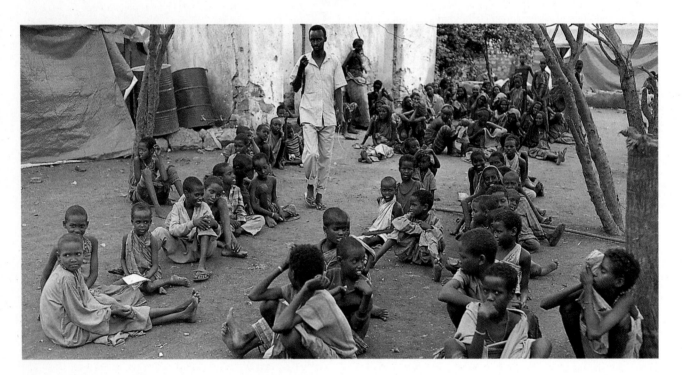

*A World Vision feeding center in Baidoa, Somalia. Recent famines in the Horn of Africa and other regions are not caused simply by population growth, drought, or natural disaster.*

**CONTENTS**

In addition to rising nationalistic aspirations and ethnic conflicts, numerous other problems confront the world today. Two of the most important, the related problems of population growth and chronic hunger, are the focus of this chapter. We choose population and hunger as topics for two reasons. First, most citizens of the industrialized countries misunderstand them and their causes. Second, new insights on both problems have been contributed by anthropological fieldwork and comparative studies.

Both population growth and hunger beset mainly the lesser developed countries (LDCs), which collectively are called the Third World. (Undernourishment besets children in many inner cities of North America as well.) Many citizens of the more developed industrial countries believe that population increase is mainly caused by the fact that people in the Third World prefer large families because of their cultural values. In this view, the value parents (especially, it is thought, fathers) place on having lots of children might have been adaptive in the past, but today—under the changed conditions of the modern world—it is irrational. One goal of this chapter is to challenge the common notion that having lots of children is irrational under the conditions faced by poor, rural families in the Third World.

Furthermore, many people believe that population growth and hunger are causally related in the following way. Because people in the Third World have so many children, their countries are faced with shortages of land, fertilizers, and other food-producing resources, which leads to large-scale, chronic hunger. In this view, chronic hunger is mainly caused by a shortage of food, and this shortage in turn is caused by ever-increasing population numbers. In short, population increase causes hunger. Our second goal in this chapter is to show that other factors are at least as important as population growth in causing hunger in the Third World. These other factors include the structure of both the world economy and the economies of the nations in which most hungry people live.

Our most important aim in this chapter, then, is to challenge the ideas that many of our readers have about these two problems—ideas that have been fostered by the news media and other sources. We hope you will be critical the next time you hear someone bemoan the "fact" that Third World people are "breeding themselves into starvation."

Finally, a word of warning: Population growth and hunger are complex and variable. Complex because there is no simple reason for them or universal solution to them. Variable because they hit some countries and regions harder than others. We do not pretend to cover this complexity or variability but only to present enough information to make you think about these problems in a new way—and, we hope, to stimulate you to action.

## POPULATION GROWTH

One of the most important worldwide problems of modern times is the phenomenal increase in the earth's population. Many people who have not studied this subject believe that human numbers have been increasing steadily for millennia. We who live in the twentieth century just happen to live in a time when human numbers have finally reached a critical point and threaten to exceed the capacity of the earth to support them.

In fact, today's high population growth rates are a recent phenomenon, at least on a global level. Around the time of Christ there were 250 to 300 million people on earth. By the mid-nineteenth century there were one billion. By 1930 human numbers had reached 2 billion; by 1960, 3 billion; by 1974, 4 billion; by 1986, 5 billion; by 1993, 5.5 billion (see Figure 19.1). To drive home the point that high rates of worldwide population growth are historically recent, note that it took the human population 200,000 to 300,000 years to number one billion; about eighty years to reach two billion; thirty years to reach three billion; fourteen years to reach four billion; and only twelve years to reach five billion. By the year 2000 the human population will probably increase to 6.2 billion.

It is therefore only in the past 100 years that the earth's population has been increasing at high rates. What has changed in the past century that accounts for this increase?

If we exclude the effects of migration, the rate of growth of a population depends on its excess of births over deaths, that is, on its fertility and mortality rates. So population growth is caused by some combination of

FIGURE 19.1
Growth of World's Population

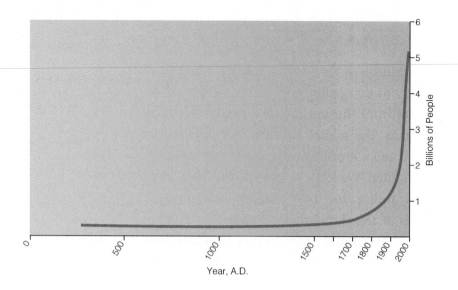

falling death rates and rising birthrates. (See below for definitions of these and other terms used in this section.)

## POPULATION TERMINOLOGY.

birthrate (crude birthrate): number of births per 1,000 persons per year

death rate (crude death rate): number of deaths per 1,000 persons per year

infant mortality rate: number of deaths of children under the age of one per 1,000 children under the age of one per year

total fertility rate: number of children born to an average female during her entire reproductive life

One possible cause of population growth is the increased supply of food made possible by modern technology, which could lower mortality, raise fertility, or both. But contrary to many people's beliefs, improved nutrition is not an important cause of recent population growth. It is most unlikely that rural people in the LDCs, where most of the growth is occurring, eat better than they did, say, a century ago. In fact, countries with the highest rates of population growth usually have the most serious hunger problems. The poorest residents of nations such as Somalia, Sudan, Ethiopia, Mali, and Chad suffer chronic hunger. Yet the populations of sub-Saharan African countries grew at an average annual rate of 3.1 percent between 1980 and 1990. In contrast,

the citizens of the industrialized market economies (all of Western Europe plus Canada, the United States, Japan, Australia, New Zealand, Israel, Singapore, and Hong Kong) are well nourished. Yet their populations increased at an average annual rate of only 0.6 percent between 1980 and 1990. So the mere fact that a population eats well does not mean that its women will have more children; indeed, in the modern world it is the relatively more malnourished people who usually have the most children. Some factors other than better nutrition are contributing to worldwide population growth.

Most demographers (experts who describe and analyze human populations) agree that improvements in public health and medical care are the main reason for twentieth-century population growth. Vaccinations against smallpox, typhoid, yellow fever, cholera, and other diseases that often are fatal have lowered death rates. The spread of diseases such as dysentery and tuberculosis has been reduced by drugs and public health measures. Pesticide sprayings have reduced the numbers of mosquitoes and other insects that carry malaria and bubonic plague. Physicians and other medical personnel carry scientific treatments for illness into most parts of the world.

Improved public health and medicine affect population growth by reducing mortality: more infants survive into adulthood, or more adults live longer, or both. The former is probably the most important way in which medical science has reduced mortality because the infant mortality rate in almost all LDCs began to decline significantly after World War II. Both infant mortality and death rates continue to fall today. For example, in the low-income countries of sub-Saharan Africa and southeast and south Asia infant mortality rates fell from 145 to 92 between 1965 and 1990. Between them China and India have nearly 40 percent of the world's people. In China the infant mortality rate fell from 90 to 29 between 1965 and 1990; in India, it fell from 150 to 92. Crude death rates, likewise, have fallen. Between 1965 and 1990 death rates fell in sub-Saharan Africa from 23 to 16, in China from 10 to 7, and in India from 20 to 11.

In comparison, most developed industrialized countries have infant mortality rates of 10 or less and crude death rates of between 9 and 11. People in industrialized nations also live longer—life expectancy is around seventy-five years, compared with only around fifty in sub-Saharan Africa.

So, despite medical progress, the LDCs lose far more of their infants and children to malnutrition and disease; they have higher crude death rates; and their life expectancies are lower. Nevertheless, their populations are growing at an average of about 2 percent (closer to 3 percent in sub-Saharan Africa and the Middle East), whereas the developed countries' overall rate of population increase is well under 1 percent.

The reason is that developed countries have lower fertility rates than LDCs. An average Japanese, British, or North American woman has 1.7 children during her lifetime, whereas an average Nigerian woman has 6.0, a Kenyan woman has 6.5, a Pakistani woman has 5.8, and an Indian woman has 4.0. In the past couple of decades birthrates also have fallen in the LDCs, but death rates have declined even faster, so their populations continue to grow.

In summary, population growth has accelerated rapidly in the past century. Worldwide progress in medicine and public health, not greater availability of food, is mainly responsible. It is occurring mainly in the LDCs today because birthrates are not falling as fast as death rates.

What insights do anthropologists offer on this complex problem? To answer this question we must first consider the adverse effects of population growth.

## Consequences of Population Growth

Many undesirable effects are caused by high population growth rates. Some consequences are global—they affect everyone on earth, regardless of whether they live in an overpopulated region. For example, it has been suggested that the cutting of large amounts of tropical forest for cultivation to feed more people may have significant impacts on the earth's climate, raising its temperature enough to affect ecosystems and agriculture in unknown ways.

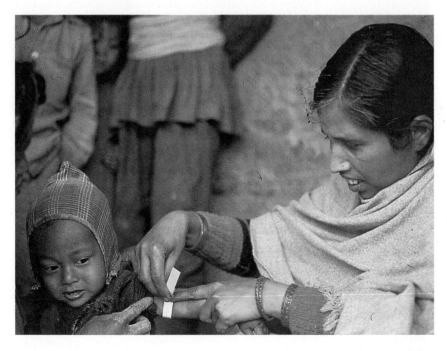

*Improved public health and medical care have led to falling death rates in Third World regions. This child in Nepal receives an immunization.*

Americans already know one way population growth in one country, Mexico, affects their own nation—thousands of Mexicans cross the border in pursuit of the jobs and income that their nation cannot provide, due partly to population growth (see Chapter 17). Dense and growing population aggravates resource scarcity in Central American countries such as El Salvador and Guatemala, contributing to discontent, political instability, and even civil war.

For such practical as well as humanitarian reasons we all should care about worldwide population growth because it threatens the whole world ecologically, economically, and politically. The issue here is not the global consequences of population growth but its adverse effects on those very people and nations who are having "too many children." What are some of these consequences?

Population growth contributes to environmental problems. More people consume more resources of all kinds, so the production of food, wood, minerals, energy, and clean water will have to grow. In turn, this increased exploitation of nature means environmental deterioration—pollution, soil erosion caused by overgrazing and more intensive land use, habitat destruction for other living things, deforestation, urban sprawl, and so forth are accelerated by increasing numbers of people.

Economic problems also are magnified in countries with high population growth. The higher the population growth rate, the more children as a proportion of the total population will be alive, so the country must devote more of its resources to education and other things that "unproductive" children require. Further, when all these children grow up and become potentially productive adults, at least some of them will enter the labor force. Many will be unemployed, and even those who find work will suffer low wages because there will be so much competition in the labor market.

Finally, many social and political problems are related to overpopulation. To escape rural poverty, many people born on farms migrate to cities, where they add to crime rates, produce housing shortages, create problems of sewage disposal and water supply, and so on. Increases in human numbers contribute to political conflicts, insurrections, and civil wars as different ethnic groups, regions, classes, and parties compete for their slice of a shrinking pie.

Enough has been said to make the point: Population growth is harmful to most LDCs. And, indeed, most governments have policies designed to curb fertility through educating couples in family planning and providing them with contraceptive devices to prevent conception. For example, realizing the probable disastrous long-term effects of continued population growth, in the late 1970s the Chinese government initiated a policy of allowing a family to have only two children. In the 1980s a controversial one-child policy was instituted.

*If population increases, environmental exploitation also grows to provide more people with resources, including wood from the Brazilian rain forest.*

Women apply for a child-bearing permit for the right to bear their only child, and those who become pregnant for a second time are subjected to intense social, political, and economic pressure to have abortions. Yet, despite the policies of their governments and the harmful effects of population growth, citizens of the LDCs continue to have large families, often rejecting birth control even when it is widely and freely available.

This seems to be a paradox. An average North American family is able to afford more children than an average Nigerian family. Canadians and Americans have more money to house, feed, clothe, educate, and otherwise provide for their children. Yet they have only two or three, whereas the Nigerian family averages six or seven. And this is the most puzzling thing about high fertility: It continues despite its adverse consequences for those very nations that are experiencing it and whose citizens are causing it—the LDCs.

Why do these people continue to have so many children? Are Indians, Nigerians, and El Salvadorans too ignorant to realize that they cannot afford to support so many children? Can't they see the strain that all these children put on their nation's educational, health, and agricultural systems? Don't they realize that when all these people grow up, their economies will have to supply jobs for them? Isn't the refusal of couples in these countries to practice birth control even when condoms, pills, and intrauterine devices are available a perfect example of their backwardness and ignorance?

Not at all.

## Costs and Benefits of Children: North America

We as Canadians and Americans have no trouble seeing ourselves as making conscious choices to create our own family sizes. We decide whether or not to get pregnant based on how we weight our desire for children against the conditions of our personal lives. One factor that affects our decision is our cultural ideas (norms) about the proper and socially acceptable number of children. True, some of us want more children than others, but most of us would agree that eight is too many. So we fear that people will laugh at us or think us socially irresponsible or foolish if we have "too many."

North American cultural norms surrounding family size are important, but they are not the only factors that influence the number of children we have. (Besides, the norm of family size itself responds to other conditions.)

Population growth leads many rural people to migrate to cities in search of a better life. Urban crowding, unemployment, and housing shortages often result, as seen in this shanty town in Rio de Janeiro, Brazil.

Other factors that influence our reproductive choices include the following.

✦ *Occupational and spatial mobility.* Many young couples do not know where they will be or how they will be earning a living in the next few years. They want children someday but are too unsettled and lack the income to start their family right away. If most couples postpone pregnancy until their midtwenties or thirties, a lower completed average family size results than if most women begin child-bearing earlier.

✦ *Women's employment.* Many women want a career and perceive that numerous children will interfere with this goal. A husband may want four children, but the wife wants her career, so they settle for two.

✦ *Monetary costs.* Children are an economic liability to most couples in a twentieth-century industrial society. Many bills—for food, housing, doctors, clothing, transportation, insurance, education, day care, and babysitting—increase with the number of children. So when a young couple read in a newspaper that it costs more than $100,000 to raise a child, not including college, they decide that one or two is quite enough. Nor are children likely to contribute much economically to their parents as they grow older—retirement plans, social security, and, recently, IRAs are expected to provide most of the income of elderly people.

✦ *Social burdens of children.* Modern society offers numerous social and recreational outlets, which serve as alternatives to devoting one's time and energy to children. A couple may know some friends who have hardly left their house since their baby was born, and they have no desire to be so tied down.

None of this implies that North American couples always have the number of children they choose. Some have an "accident" and wind up with more children than they want or with a child sooner than they had planned. And the preceding considerations, to some extent, are class and race biased—they apply more to well-educated, middle-income whites than to blacks and Hispanics, for example. But we do make reproductive choices, and the result of them—barring infertility and so forth—is that we have about the number of children we desire. (Couples who want two children only rarely wind up with four, for instance, even allowing for unplanned pregnancies.)

There are other factors that North American couples consider, of course. But notice the main overall feature of the considerations just listed: They are all things that will affect the deciding couple personally. Reasons such as, we're too unsettled, we can't both pursue our careers fully, we will have less money to spend on ourselves, we won't be able to go out as often—these are the general kinds of influences people consider. They consider the benefits and costs of having or not having children, or of having so many and not more children, to *themselves*. They do not worry much about whether their children will increase the burden on the American educational system, or increase the unemployment rate twenty years in the future, or contribute to society's expenditures on public waters and sewers, or overload the nation's farmlands. That is, for the most part they do not concern themselves with the *societal consequences* of their reproductive decisions. They do what they think is best for themselves.

## Costs and Benefits of Children: LDCs

Curiously, although we know we make reproductive decisions, many of us think people in the LDCs do not

do so. They seem to us to reproduce blindly, perhaps because "their culture values children," so they "have no choice." And, also curiously, although most of us do not take the societal consequences of our reproductive choices into account, for some reason we expect people in the LDCs to be more altruistic.

Part of our error comes from our failure to put ourselves in their shoes—to grasp the conditions of their lives that lead them to bear more children than we do. Just because children are an economic liability in a highly mobile, industrialized, urbanized, monetarized society does not mean that they are a liability everywhere. Many demographers argue that rural people in the LDCs have high fertility not simply because their culture leads them to like children but because children are economically useful. Village-level ethnographic studies conducted since the 1960s suggest that children do indeed offer a variety of material benefits to their parents in the LDCs.

One study was done by Indian anthropologist Mahmood Mamdani, who analyzed why a family planning program failed to reduce the birthrate in seven Indian villages. The villagers, it seemed, accepted the birth control pills offered by the staff of the program, but many did not take them. The reaction of the program's administrators was like that of many outsiders when local people do not respond in the way experts believe they should: They blamed the ignorance and conservatism of the local people. To the experts, the benefits of lowered fertility seemed obvious. The amount of land available to village families was already barely adequate, so by reducing the size of their families, villagers could stop the fragmentation of land that was impoverishing them each generation.

The village's parents did not see it that way. They believed that it was to their benefit to have many children—especially sons. Most advantages revolved around having extra labor to work the family land—labor for which they did not have to pay. By having many sons, villagers also hoped to send one or more of them to the city, where they would earn cash that the family could use to buy more land. Acquiring more land—rather than having fewer children—was the way individual village families believed they could best solve their personal resource-scarcity problems.

Children offer similar benefits to their parents in other LDCs. On the densely populated Indonesian island of Java, parents do not have to wait for their children to grow up to acquire the benefits of their labor. Children aged six to eight spend three to four hours daily in tending livestock, gathering firewood, and car-

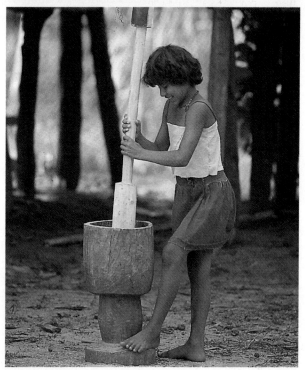

*People in the low fertility developed countries often fail to realize that children are economically beneficial in the developing countries. Clockwise from upper left: a young*

*Peruvian boy spins wool while watching his family sheep and alpaca; a Korean boy prepares to sell wares at a market; an Amazonian girl pounds food; an Ethiopian lad helps with oxen.*

ing for their younger siblings. By the time they are fourteen girls work almost nine hours a day in child care, food preparation, household chores, handicrafts, and other activities. Most of the labor of children does not contribute directly to their family's cash income or food supply, so it is easy to see how outsiders might conclude that children are unproductive. However, children accomplish many household-maintenance tasks that require little experience and skill, which frees the labor of adult family members for activities that do bring in money or food. Ethnographer Benjamin White sug-

gests that large families are more successful economically than small families in Java.

Similar findings have been reported by ethnographers working in rural Nepal, Bangladesh, Samoa, and the Philippines. Unlike suburban and urban North Americans, farming families in the LDCs use much of the time of even young children productively. As children grow older they are used to diversify the economic activities of a household, earning cash themselves or performing subsistence work that frees their parents for wage labor. In many regions adult children migrate to a city or to a developed country, where they send cash back to their parents and siblings. Such remittances make up 50 percent of the total cash income of Western Samoans and also are important in Ghana, Nigeria, Burkina Faso, India, Mexico, and much of the Middle East.

In most parts of the world children also serve as the major source of economic support in their parents' old age because rural villagers lack pension plans and social security. As Stanley Freed and Ruth Freed have pointed out, in many parts of India parents prefer to bear two or three sons to ensure themselves of having one adult son to live with them, in case one son dies or moves elsewhere.

In addition to the value of children's labor, remittances, and old age security, many other factors encourage rural families in the LDCs to have many children, including

✦ relatively high rates of infant mortality, which encourage parents to have "extra" children to cover possible deaths of their offspring;
✦ extended families, which spread out the burden of child care among other household members, thus reducing it to individual parents;
✦ low monetary cost of children compared with ourselves, partly because many necessities (such as housing and food) are produced by family labor rather than purchased; and
✦ the fact that the labor tasks women commonly are assigned are not as incompatible with child care as wage employment (see chapter 12).

Such factors mean that children are perceived (probably correctly) as both more valuable and less costly than they are among ourselves. We should not assume that couples in the LDCs are too ignorant to understand the costs of having many children or to appreciate the benefits of small families. Nor should we think that they are prisoners of their "traditional cultural values," which have not changed fast enough to keep up with changing conditions. We should rather assume that they make reproductive decisions just as we do. We should seek to understand the economic and other conditions of their lives that lead them to *want* many children. We then will understand why the simple availability of family planning advice and contraception so often has little effect on fertility—ignorance and lack of birth control technology were not the problems in the first place.

As we have seen, rising human numbers certainly contribute to the resource shortages faced by the LDCs today. One of the resources in shortest supply is one of the things people cannot do without: food. Most North Americans see malnutrition and overpopulation as two sides of the same coin. In the popular view the "fact" that there are "too many people" in the world is the major reason that there is "too little food to go around." And the solution to world hunger is "more food," that is, increased production by the application of modern mechanized agricultural methods. In the next section we shall try to convince you that neither the problem ("too many people") nor the solution ("more production through better technology") is this simple. (Box 19.1 argues that "too much consumption" is a greater cause for alarm than "too many people" for resource depletion of many kinds.)

## WORLD HUNGER

The situation in Somalia in 1992 and 1993 is only the most recent and heartbreaking case of famine. Worldwide, tens of millions of people are undernourished to some degree. In the early 1990s major hunger problems existed in parts of the southern Sudan, Mozambique, Ethiopia, Chad, Bolivia, Peru, Bangladesh, and numerous other nations. Children under the age of five are hit especially hard, dying either from malnutrition or from illnesses that well-nourished children could fight off.

*Young children are most likely to be malnourished and to suffer the most during famines.*

As we have discussed, one consequence of the growing world population is environmental deterioration and depletion of the earth's resources. More people mean more consumption of energy, more forests removed to cultivate land and provide living space, more minerals and other raw materials exhausted, and so on.

So far, so true. But this is not far enough. Fossil fuels, forests, minerals, water, and other resources can be depleted either because there are more people or because some people grow more affluent and consume them at a growing rate. Contrary to popular belief, population growth is not the major reason for the rapid exhaustion of global resources and is not the cause of most environmental problems. The high and growing standards of living of the developed countries are more responsible for the depletion of global resources than are the increasing populations of the LDCs.

This point is most conveniently made for energy consumption, which is a good measure of overall resource consumption. The amount of energy a person consumes can be expressed in kilocalories, and because we know how many kilocalories are locked up in a kilogram of oil, we can compare energy consumption using kilograms of oil equivalent. According to the World Bank's *World Development Report 1992,* an average citizen of an industrial market economy used about 5,158 kilograms of oil equivalent in 1990. An average sub-Saharan African used only about 103 kilograms of oil equivalent. The 1990 per capita energy consumption of some familiar countries is shown on the following list, broken down into the categories of low income, middle income, and high income. Note how much higher the per capita energy consumption of the high-

*BOX 19.1*

# POPULATION OR CONSUMPTION?

income countries is than that of the other two categories.

*Low income*

Ethiopia, 20

Bangladesh, 57

Kenya, 100

Nigeria, 138

Honduras, 198

India, 231

*Middle income*

Peru, 509

China, 598

Turkey, 857

*Resource depletion and other environmental problems are caused by high levels of consumption in the developed countries as well as by increasing numbers of people in the LDCs. This is a Texas oil refinery. Which countries use the greatest amount of oil per capita?*

Brazil, 915

Mexico, 1,300

*High income*

Spain, 2,201

Japan, 3,563

France, 3,845

Australia, 5,041

United States, 7,822

Canada, 10,009

These figures for per capita energy consumption show how much more important high consumption levels are than high population growth rates as a cause of worldwide resource depletion. An American family of four consumed about 31,000 kilograms of oil equivalent in 1990. An average Mexican family of five consumed 6,500; an average Chinese family of five consumed 3,000; a Kenyan family of eight consumed 800; a Bangladesh family of seven consumed 400; an Ethiopian family of ten consumed 200. The small American family, therefore, used 4.8 times more energy than the larger Mexican family, 10 times more than the Chinese family, 34 times more than the Kenyan family, 78 times more than the Bangladesh family, and 155 times more than the Ethiopian family.

As described in chapter 17, the world economy is a single interdependent system. The oil, minerals, soil, and other nonrenewable natural resources used by the economies of the developed countries, therefore, has global consequences: The consumption habits of the rich nations are *partly* responsible for the depletion of resources on a global scale. Is "their" growing population as much to blame for resource depletion as "our" consumption habits? ✦

*SOURCE:* World Bank 1992.

In this section we discuss twentieth-century conditions that have contributed to the (perhaps unprecedented) scale of worldwide malnutrition. We examine some of the problems of trying to feed the world with mechanized agricultural methods. And we suggest some anthropological insights on the problem.

## Scarcity or Inequality?

Two major explanations commonly are offered for hunger and starvation in the LDCs. The first is the one most people believe. It holds that hunger is mainly caused by too many people chasing too few resources. Poor countries like India, Bangladesh, Peru, Ethiopia, and El Salvador simply have too many people to be supported adequately by their land area, this argument runs. With so many people on the edge of starvation, natural disasters such as drought reduce food production enough to lead to massive famine. So the periodic outbreaks of starvation in these already overpopulated countries have natural causes: The famines in Bangladesh in the 1960s, in the Sahel in the early 1970s, and in Ethiopia in the 1980s were all popularly thought to be caused by lack of rain, for example.

According to this explanation, hunger and starvation are caused by overpopulation combined with natural disasters. (Ethnic conflicts and the breakdown of established political institutions also are major causes of famine, as recent events in Ethiopia, the Sudan, and Somalia remind us.) Overpopulation creates chronic undernourishment, which turns into periodic outbreaks of starvation when crop diseases, insect pests, droughts, or political instability inevitably strike. This argument holds that food, water, land, and other life-sustaining resources are absolutely scarce—that is, there is not enough food, land, or water to go around in a country or region. We therefore call it the **scarcity explanation of hunger.**

The major alternative to the scarcity explanation may be called the **inequality explanation of hunger.** It holds that resources are not in fact absolutely scarce: that is, there is enough productive capacity in the land of practically every nation to feed its people an adequate diet. The reason for hunger is not overpopulation, drought, war, or any other short-term catastrophe that reduces the availability of food for people. At least these factors are not the main ones responsible for hunger. Instead, the reason is the long-standing unequal access to land, water, and other resources required to feed people. Some people are poor because of the way their national economy, and the global economy as a whole, allocates resources, according to the inequality explanation.

*The scarcity explanation holds that insufficient land, water, and other food-producing resources are available to feed ever-increasing numbers of people. These Somali men are digging a trench for irrigation.*

*The inequality explanation holds that the global economy allocates land and other food-producing resources on the basis of ability to pay rather than need. Where will the pineapples produced on this large Colombian plantation go?*

In essence, the global economy allocates resources on the basis of ability to pay rather than on need. For example, if wealthy North American consumers want coffee and sugar, they have the ability to pay for it. So wealthy and politically powerful landowners in Central America will devote their land to coffee and sugarcane plantations because these crops bring the most profit. These products will be exported, and the profits will be invested in enterprises that bring the greatest future monetary returns, regardless of the need of Central American peasants for farmland to feed their families.

As often is the case with competing explanations for some phenomena, these two are not entirely alternatives. Scarcity explanations are correct to the extent that, all else equal, the amount of land available per capita is reduced by population growth. Likewise, the amount of food available is reduced if drought, insects, or other natural disasters reduce yields or force some land to be taken out of production. It is hard to see how these statements could be wrong.

But they could be right and still tell only part of the story. The hunger story is more complex than "too many people" or "not enough rain." Hunger is created by human institutions as much as by natural conditions. For example, at a growth rate of 3 percent a year a population will double in less than twenty-five years. Does this mean that in twenty-five years everybody will have only half the amount of food? Of course not. Land that formerly was underused will be brought into fuller production; more labor-intensive methods of cultivation can bring higher yields per acre; people can change their diets and eat less meat; and so on. People will adjust

their cultivation methods, work patterns, eating habits, and other behaviors to the new conditions.

Or rather, they will adjust if they have access to the resources they need to do so. And this is a large part of the problem in many LDCs: it is not *just* that there are too few resources but that too few people own or control the resources available. In their books *Food First* and *World Hunger: Twelve Myths* Francis Moore Lappé and Joseph Collins question what they call "the myth of scarcity." They claim that every nation could provide an adequate diet for its citizens if its productive resources were more equitably distributed.

A further discussion of the evidence that inequality is as important as scarcity in explaining hunger around the world is outside the scope of this text. Here we can only examine briefly one country, El Salvador, in which anthropologist William Durham analyzed in detail the scarcity versus the inequality explanation of hunger and other manifestations of poverty.

Durham notes that El Salvador appears to be a perfect example of the scarcity explanation of hunger and poverty. In 1892 the country had a population of about 700,000; by 1983 more than five million people were living there, giving a population density of about 650 per square mile. (To compare with two countries considered overpopulated, China's 1983 density was under 300 and India's under 600. The United States's density is about 65.) Indications of El Salvador's overpopulation include widespread deforestation; widespread erosion and environmental devastation caused by intensive cultivation of marginal lands; and declining food production per capita, accompanied by a marked increase in food imports since about 1950. These characteristics are exactly what we would expect to find in a country whose population has outgrown its land resources.

But a closer look reveals that population growth is only part of the reason for the poverty of most of El Salvador's people. Although it is true that production of basic foods (notably maize, beans, and rice) has declined since 1950, total agricultural production has kept pace with population increase. Food production per capita has declined not because the country's land has become filled up with people, but because much of the land that could be used for food is in fact planted in export crops (coffee, cotton, sugar). By the 1960s land devoted to exports averaged more than 40 percent of all the land under cultivation in the country. Almost as much land was devoted to coffee as to maize, the principal food crop for El Salvador's rural peasants.

Producing coffee rather than food might not be so bad because by selling coffee the peasantry can earn money, which they can then use to buy food. But most of the coffee is not produced by peasants, notwithstanding North American coffee drinkers' images of Juan Valdez making a better life for his family by "selling only the finest beans."

To see why, we must first understand that land ownership in El Salvador is unequally distributed. Almost one-half the farms are under one hectare (2.5 acres) and are worked by peasant families mainly for daily subsistence. Only 1.5 percent of the farms are more than fifty hectares, and these 1.5 percent of all "farmers" hold nearly one-half the total farmland of the country. This concentration of land in the hands of a wealthy minority goes back to the colonial era and so is not a recent development. But it has worsened: In 1950, 39 percent of El Salvador's agriculturally active population was landless or land-poor (owned less than one hectare); in 1971 the proportion of landless or land-poor people had risen to 51 percent.

Now most of the food in El Salvador is produced by small farmers. Farms of less than five hectares account for only 16 percent of all the agricultural land in the country, yet they produce 58 percent of El Salvador's maize. Conversely, large farms of more than 100 hectares account for 48 percent of all the productive land, yet they produce only 19 percent of the maize. As for coffee, the 85 percent of small farmers who own less than five hectares of land produce only 8 percent of the coffee. The 0.9 percent of farms over 100 hectares produce 51 percent of the coffee, most of which is exported. In short, unless Juan Valdez is a large land-

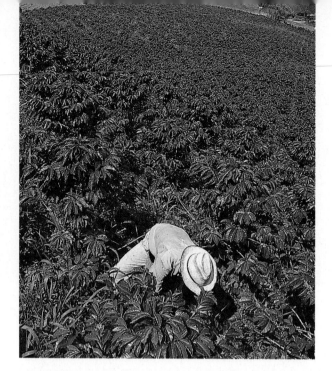

*Coffee, sugar, bananas, and other tropical fruits produced for export are usually grown on large plantations owned by a relatively few wealthy families. This is a coffee plantation in Colombia.*

owner, he is not likely to produce enough coffee beans to escape poverty.

Durham also presents evidence indicating that the larger the size of a farm, the more likely its land is to be underutilized. Small farmers use their land more fully: Farmers with less than one hectare cultivate 81 percent of their land annually, whereas farmers with more than fifty hectares cultivate less than 35 percent of their land. Nearly one-half the land of farms over fifty hectares was used for grazing, mainly of cattle. We already have seen why this is an inefficient way to use land that is cultivable (Box 7.1) if farmers are interested in maximizing the amount of food produced on an area of land. (If farmers are interested in maximizing the amount of money they can earn from the land, then cattle may be the most efficient use because wealthy El Salvadoran urbanites and North American fast-food chains can afford to pay for beef.)

Durham concludes his analysis of hunger and poverty in El Salvador with two points:

First, we find that food is scarce not because the land is incapable of producing enough for the resident population, but rather because large areas have been under-utilized or dedicated to the production of export crops. Second, we find that land is scarce not because there is too little to go around, but rather because of a process of competitive exclusion by which the small farmers have been increasingly squeezed off the land—a process due as much to . . . land concentration as to population pressure. (1979, 54)

There is no denying that population growth contributes to the hunger and poverty that victimize the peasantry of El Salvador and many other LDCs. But neither should we conclude that "too many people" is *the* problem, or that the scarcity explanation is sufficient. Population growth always occurs within a political and economic context, and this context greatly influences the degree to which poor people can adjust to it.

The combination of population growth and increasing land concentration is doubly devastating. Even if they manage to hang on to their land, the poor will get poorer if their numbers grow. If their increased poverty makes it necessary for them to borrow from the wealthy, to sell part of their land to raise cash, or to work for low wages to make ends meet, they are likely to grow poorer still. This "double crunch" is precisely the experience of the rural poor in many LDCs.

Still, to use a popular metaphor, a rising tide raises all ships. Income and assets are unequally distributed in the developed countries as well, yet most developed countries have raised the nutrition levels of their poor through poverty programs made possible by technological progress. True, as farm productivity has grown, people have benefited unequally, but everyone has in fact benefited. Can't increased productivity made possible by capital investment in modern technologies solve the world hunger problem?

## Is Technology Transfer the Answer?

A commonly proposed solution for world hunger is to apply modern scientific know-how and technology to areas in which agriculture is still technologically underdeveloped. This solution seems simple: Thanks to agricultural machinery, plant breeding, modern fertilizers, pest control methods, advances in irrigation technology, and so on, the developed countries have solved the nutrition problem for most of their people. We have developed science and technology and applied it to agriculture. The LDCs need only adopt our know-how and technology to solve their hunger problems. In this view, the main thing hungry countries need is a transfer of our food production technology.

There are many problems with the **technology transfer solution.** We can touch on only a few. First, as we saw in our discussion of shifting cultivation in chapter 8, many of the methods developed for application in temperate climates fail miserably when transported to the tropics, where most hungry people live. This is largely because of the profound differences between tropical and temperate soils and climatic conditions.

Second, many experts doubt that so-called high-tech solutions to food problems are appropriate to economic conditions in the LDCs. Labor is much more available than capital in these nations, so to substitute technology (machinery, herbicides, artificial fertilizers, etc.) for labor is to waste a plentiful factor of production in favor of a scarce one. Besides, those who need to increase production the most—the poorest farmers—are those who can least afford new technology. And borrowing money for new investments involves risks because many small farmers who borrow from rich landowners lose their land if they default.

Third, although it seems paradoxical, it may not be in the interest of poor farmers for land to become *too* productive. In countries such as Mexico many poor families get all or part of their food and cash by renting marginal lands from wealthy landowners. When technological improvements raise yields, the landlord may decide to use the land for cash crops, and the poor will be forced off the land altogether. On the Indonesian island of Java many rural peasants do not own enough land to feed their families, so they must seek short-term work in the fields of rich landowners. When "green revolution" crop varieties were introduced to west Java in the 1960s, big landowners used the wealth made possible by increased yields to purchase tractors and rice-milling machines. Richard Franke argues that this reduced rural wages and forced some poor farmers into the cities.

Fourth, new technologies often come as a package deal. For instance, new crop varieties usually require large amounts of water, pesticides, and fertilizers to do well. Small farmers must adopt the whole expensive package for success. The expense, combined with the logistics of long-term supply of each element of the package in countries with uncertain transportation and political regimes, makes many farmers wary of innovations.

Fifth, agricultural experts from the developed world often report problems of "resistance" by peasant farmers. Sometimes peasants cling tenaciously to their traditional crops, varieties, and methods of cultivation even when genuine improvements are made available to them. This famed cultural conservatism of peasants seems downright irrational to many technical experts.

But some anthropologists who have conducted village-level fieldwork offer an alternative interpretation of peasant resistance to change. Living in intimate contact with local people, sometimes fieldworkers are able to perceive problems the way peasants do. Subsistence farmers barely feeding their families cannot afford to drop below the minimum level of food production it takes to survive. Traditional crops and varieties give some yield even when uncontrollable environmental forces are unfavorable because over the generations they have adapted to local fluctuations of climate, disease, and pests. The new ones might not fare as well. Because the consequences of crop failure are severer for a poor subsistence farmer than for a well-off commercial farmer, they minimize risks by using tried and true crop varieties and methods. Peasant cultural conservatism thus may be a sound strategy, given the conditions of peasant lives.

For these and other reasons, many of the agricultural technologies and methods that have increased agricultural productivity in the developed countries do not achieve the same results elsewhere in the world. Later in this chapter we discuss some of the alternatives to technology transfer—alternatives that build on the technologies and methods traditional farmers already know. First, we look at mechanized agricultural technologies from a comparative perspective. Such a comparison suggests that modern mechanized agriculture requires too much energy to be adopted on a worldwide scale.

## Comparative Perspectives on Food and Energy

In chapter 8 we noted that the major feature of mechanized agriculture, as we called our own system of cultivation, is the substitution of inanimate sources of energy for the energy of human labor needed to create and maintain an artificial community of domesticated plants. In Box 8.2 we showed that food production systems can be compared on the basis of (1) their **labor efficiency**, or the number of calories of food energy obtained per unit of human labor, and (2) their **energetic efficiency**, or the number of food calories obtained ("output") per calorie of energy "input." Energetic efficiency includes as an input the energy of human labor, toolmaking, fuels, animals, fertilizers, and so on. It includes as an output the energy of the food produced.

We need to note that using energy output-input ratios as a measure of efficiency is not entirely satisfactory because foods have varying amounts of protein, vitamins, and minerals as well as energy. However, calories are the only available comparative measure of how much nutritive value is locked up in a wide variety of foods. In the following discussion *calories output* should be interpreted to mean roughly the amount of food produced.

To see the enormous difference between the labor efficiency of mechanized agriculture and the preindustrial systems described in chapter 8, we compare the approximate number of calories obtained per hour of labor actually spent producing food. As shown in Table 19.1, for example, North American rice grown using mechanized methods is 150 to 250 times more labor-

TABLE 19.1   Labor Efficiencies of Preindustrial and Mechanized Agriculture

| CULTIVATION SYSTEM | LABOR EFFICIENCY | |
| --- | --- | --- |
| | Kcal./ Man Hour[a] | Kcal./ Kcal. Labor[b] |
| *Preindustrial Systems* | | |
| Swidden dry rice | 2,600–4,500 | 17–30 |
| Other tropical horticulture | 6,000–7,200 | 40–48 |
| Intensive wet rice, China | 9,600 | 64 |
| *Mechanized Agriculture* | | |
| Rice, U.S.A. | 670,000 | 4,467 |
| Maize, U.S.A. | 900,000 | 6,000 |
| Cereals, United Kingdom | 730,000 | 4,867 |

[a]Number of calories locked up in the food produced per hour of farm labor.
[b]Number of calories contained in the food produced per calorie of energy expended by the farm laborer. The figures in the column assume that a farm laborer expends a mean of 150 calories per hour of work.
SOURCES: Calculated from data in Leach (1976) and Pimentel and Pimentel (1979).

*These mechanical harvesters add to the productivity of farmland and farm labor, but they and other agricultural machinery require a large input of energy. Could this energy-intensive technology be the solution to the world food problem?*

efficient than tropical rice grown under shifting cultivation; maize grown in North America is roughly 130 times more labor-efficient than maize grown in the tropics using horticultural methods.

Table 19.1 contains only data on the labor that food producers actually spend working in the swidden plot, rice field, or modern farm; that is, it includes only on-farm labor. The labor spent making tools, producing fertilizers, and on other activities needed to produce crops is not included in the table, nor is the time spent processing, preparing, and cooking the harvest. The significance of these omissions become apparent later.

Table 19.1 documents the much praised productivity of mechanized agriculture—one person working on a mechanized farm produces much more food than a preindustrial farmer. This high level of labor efficiency on the modern farm means that one farm worker produces enough food to feed roughly sixty to seventy persons in the United States and Great Britain. The same is true, as we like to brag, about yields per acre using mechanized methods—new crop varieties, chemical fertilizers, proper irrigation, and other technical inputs produce remarkable yields, which potentially means that more people can be supported from an acre of land than ever before.

Those who champion the export of modern technology as a means to allay hunger in other nations point to numbers like these. Other numbers paint a more pessimistic picture of the possibilities of solving the world food crisis by diffusing our mechanized methods around the world.

No farming method can produce something out of nothing. If modern methods conserve labor and have high yields per acre, some things other than labor and land are being put into our food system to gain our outputs. These somethings are fertilizers, pesticides, herbicides, water, tractors, and so forth. Technology substitutes for labor and makes land more productive—this is what we mean by *mechanization*.

But energy is required to manufacture and operate farm equipment, to produce and apply fertilizers and chemicals that control pests and weeds, and so on. Electricity and fossil fuels (oil, natural gas, and coal) are used at various stages of production. It is not just farmers and land that produce our food—it is farmers plus land plus wood plus steel plus energy plus a multitude of other materials. In fact, the energy of human labor (farm workers) is only a fraction of 1 percent of the total energy required to produce our food. We must treat nonhuman energy as an input to food production in mechanized agriculture. (Nonhuman energy is also an input for preindustrial cultivation systems, but there human labor energy represents a high percentage of the total energy input.)

How much energy does mechanized agriculture require? A lot. Several studies in the 1970s documented that food production in Great Britain and the United States is enormously energy intensive.

*A major reason for the low energetic efficiency of modernized food systems is that so much land is devoted to producing food that is fed to livestock on feedlots like this one.*

To consider the United States first, David Pimentel and his associates estimated the amount of energy consumed in producing various crops. From these figures they made estimates of total energetic efficiency, that is, the ratio of the energy contained in the harvested crop (energy output) to the total energy required to produce it (energy input) using mechanized agriculture. For example, in 1975 corn (maize) had an energetic efficiency of about 2.9, meaning that 2.9 calories of corn were harvested for every calorie of energy used to manufacture, apply, and operate the fertilizers, pesticides, machinery, and so forth used in corn production. If you compare this 2.9 ratio for *total* energetic efficiency with the 6,000 ratio for *labor* efficiency for corn given in Table 19.1, you can see the degree to which inanimate energy substitutes for labor in mechanized agriculture. To give a better feeling for how much energy is required, Pimentel and associates estimated that to raise one acre of corn in the United States in 1970 required the energetic equivalent of eighty gallons of gasoline. We pay a price for our productivity—our farms use prodigious amounts of energy.

This is not the end of the agricultural energy story. The ratio of 2.9 makes it appear that we still come out ahead, getting almost three calories of food from each calorie of total energy we use in production. In fact, we come out way behind—it takes more energy to produce our food than we get out of the food. Why? Partly because most of the agricultural output of our country is fed to livestock, which spend much of their eating lives in feedlots rather than open rangeland. As mentioned in Box 7.1, more than 90 percent of the grains, legumes (especially soybeans), and other vegetable protein produced by American farmers was fed to livestock in 1975. We consumed this vegetable protein indirectly in the form of milk, eggs, poultry, pork, beef, and other animal products. But in passing it through the bodies of animals we lost most of it to their respiration and wastes.

So the total energetic efficiency of our farm production is low because we use energy-intensive methods to cultivate our crops and because we feed so many of our crops to livestock. But we have not discussed the other energy it takes to get our food from farm or feedlot to our dinner tables. And we don't just mean transportation. Much of our food is processed. It is refined (e.g., sugar, flour), canned, frozen, cut up, and placed in containers. The steel, aluminum, glass, paper, plastics, and other products used in processing and packaging take energy to produce. We buy almost all our food in commercial stores and restaurants, where more energy is consumed in freezing, cooling, and cooking it. When we take it home we store much of it in our electric-powered refrigerators before we cook it on our electric or gas stoves.

In short, between the time the food leaves the farm and the time it enters our mouths, more energy is used to transport, process, package, preserve, and prepare it. Energy experts Carol Steinhart and John Steinhart estimated the amount of energy used by our total *food system,* that is, in all the various energy inputs on farms, in processing, and in commercial and home refrigeration and cooking. They found that on-farm inputs (energy consumed before the crop leaves the farm) are only 25 percent of the total energy expended in our entire food system. The remaining 75 percent was divided about equally between processing and home or commercial uses. For 1970 the Steinharts concluded that about nine calories of energy (input) are required to get one calorie of food (output) into our mouths. This gives an energy output-input ratio of 1:9, or 0.11.

Now we shall consider Great Britain. In 1976 Gerald Leach estimated the overall energetic efficiency of British mechanized agriculture. He found that about three calories of energy were needed by British farmers to produce one calorie of food energy. As in the United States, the major reason for this low efficiency is the cultivated crops fed to livestock. Only 13 percent of Britain's cultivable land is planted in crops that are fed directly to people; the remaining 87 percent produces wheat, barley, oats, and other forms of fodder for sheep, cattle, pigs, and poultry. Considerable energy and land savings could be made in both the United States and Great Britain if we ate less meat, eggs, and milk, or if our ranchers, hog farmers, and poultry producers reduced the amount of time livestock spend in feedlots.

Leach also estimated the amount of energy required to transport, process, package, sell, refrigerate, and cook food in Great Britain. He concluded that the overall energetic efficiency of Great Britain's food system is about 0.14: Seven calories of energy are required to get one calorie of food energy into British mouths.

The energy required to run our food system is a significant proportion of the total energy we consume for all household and industrial purposes (e.g., heating and cooling homes and buildings, producing steel and lumber). Eric Hirst found that the American food system used about 12 percent of the national energy supply in 1963, and the proportion increased to 16 percent in the 1970s, according to David Pimentel and Marcia Pimentel. Similarly, Leach estimated that putting food on British tables required almost 16 percent of the total energy consumed in that country.

This information should interest all of us. Knowing that at least half the energy used on farm is fed to

*A lot is done to most of our food between the time it leaves the farm and enters our mouths. It is processed, frozen, and packaged. These inputs must also be counted as part of our entire food system, and they too require considerable energy inputs.*

livestock might affect our eating habits. Aside from the personal health benefits of reducing red meat consumption, patriots could save their nations considerable energy by eating more protein-rich vegetable foods and less beef. Knowing that almost 40 percent of the energy required to put food on our tables is used in processing, packaging, and transporting might encourage us to forgo energy-intensive frozen and canned foods in favor of fresh vegetables and fruit.

Our purpose—and the reason we began this discussion of the energy requirements of our food system—is to question whether mechanized agriculture can feed the world. Table 19.2 contains a comparison of the energy output-input ratios for horticulture, intensive agriculture (using draft animals), and mechanized agriculture (using artificial fertilizers, machinery, fuels, insecticides, and so forth). It shows only the energy used on farm, including human labor, seeds, tools, fertilizers,

**TABLE 19.2  Comparative Energetic Efficiencies, On-Farm Inputs Only**

| CULTIVATION SYSTEM | CROP | O/I RATIO[a] |
|---|---|---|
| *Horticulture*[b] | | |
| Tsembaga (Papua New Guinea) | Mixed roots | 18 |
| Southeast Asia, Tanzania | Rice | 14–23 |
| Africa (various regions) | Mixed roots | 23–61 |
| Africa, Mexico, Guatemala | Maize | 14–38 |
| *Intensive agriculture*[c] | | |
| Chinese village (1935–1937) | Wet rice | 41 |
| Mexico, Guatemala | Maize | 4–5 |
| *Mechanized agriculture*[d] | | |
| Great Britain, U.S. | Maize | 2–3 |
| Great Britain, U.S. | Wheat | 2–3 |
| California, Japan | Rice | 1.5–2.5 |
| United States | Sorghum | 2 |
| United States | Soybean | 4 |

[a]Energy output/input ratio, or energetic efficiency, defined as the calories of food produced per calorie of energy input.
[b]In this table we define horticulture as the absence of the animal-powered plow. In all the systems included, human labor constituted over 90% of the total energy inputs.
[c]Defined as systems including significant energy inputs derived from animals. In Mexican and Guatemalan corn farming, oxen provided about five times more energy inputs than human labor, which explains the low O/I ratio.
[d]Inputs include mainly energy used to manufacture machinery, herbicides, pesticides, and fertilizers; to power equipment and transportation; and to dry grain. Human labor is an insignificant (far less than 1%) input to all except rice produced in Japan, where human labor is 11% of the total energy input.
SOURCES: Leach (1976); Pimentel and Pimentel (1979).

and animal or machine power if relevant; the energy needed for transporting, processing, packaging, cooking, and other after-farm activities is not included.

As evident from the data in Table 19.2, preindustrial cultivators have energy-efficiency ratios on the order of about 15 to 50:1, depending on crop, local conditions, and specific methods. Mechanized agriculture has output-input ratios of around 2 to 4:1. So preindustrial cultivation systems use seven to ten times less energy per amount of food produced.

The energy of food processing (e.g., grinding corn into tortillas) and preparation (e.g., cooking) is not included in the ratios of Table 19.2 because to our knowledge no studies exist that take these energy inputs into account in preindustrial systems. As we have seen, in the food systems of the United States and Great Britain, the after-farm energy inputs make up a high proportion of the total energy in our food system, greatly lowering its overall efficiency to about 0.11 and 0.14. If we want to compare total food systems, we must lower the ratios for preindustrial cultivators to make the comparison with our own food system meaningful. Because most of the energy input of horticulturalists and intensive agriculturalists is in the form of human labor, lowering the ratios by 50 percent seems reasonable. This would give total energetic efficiencies of around 7 to 25:1 for the preindustrial systems. (Lowering the ratios by two-thirds still gives ratios of 5 to 17:1. Lowering them by 90 percent—a preposterous adjustment—still means that 1.5 to 5 calories of food energy are produced for every calorie of total energy input in preindustrial food systems.)

Compare these output-input ratios with the food systems of the United States and Great Britain. Instead of 7 to 25:1 our ratios are about 0.11:1 (United States) and 0.14:1 (Great Britain). Preindustrial food systems are probably about 50 to 200 times more energetically efficient than the modern food systems some people want to replace them with!

To point out that mechanized agriculture requires a lot of energy is not to claim that people should not use it. It does, however, lead us to consider one of costs of adopting mechanized technologies that we might otherwise overlook. Taking the high energy costs into account also leads us to consider whether there are alternative agricultural methods available—methods that are productive yet avoid some of the high energy requirements and other problems associated with modern agriculture. Some agricultural scientists have recently been conducting research on such alternatives.

## Agricultural Alternatives

Beginning in the 1980s, increasing numbers of agricultural scientists have been taking another look at traditional farming practices, that is, methods of cultivating the soil that have been used for decades or centuries by the people living in a particular region. In the past technical experts in agricultural development often derided traditional farming methods, which they viewed as inefficient and overly labor intensive. But today there is increasing awareness of the benefits of traditional methods.

This awareness stems partly from the failure of so many agricultural development programs for the Third World. It also stems partly from the environmental movement that began in the developed countries in the 1970s, which called attention to the negative environmental impacts of mechanized agriculture. In addition to the high energy requirements of mechanized agriculture discussed in the previous section, some of the farming practices commonly used in the developed countries cause environmental problems. Such problems include water pollution from fertilizer runoff, poisoning of farm workers and wildlife from agricultural chemicals, soil erosion from failure to rotate crops, and increasing resistance of insects because of exclusive reliance on pesticides.

In addition to negative environmental impacts, many technologies, such as machinery, pesticides, herbicides, and fungicides, are too expensive for traditional farmers to afford. Sometimes they are inappropriate or uneconomic to use on the small plots that are characteristic of farms in many parts of the world. They may be unfamiliar to local people, who understandably are reluctant to abandon proven cultivation methods for alternatives they perceive to be riskier.

Considerations such as these led some agricultural scientists in the 1980s to ask, Are there *viable* alternatives to mechanized agricultural technologies and practices? Some experts believe that there are. The main goals of such alternatives are minimization of negative environmental impacts, affordability to small farmers, reliance on technologies and resources that are locally available, adaptation to local environmental conditions, and long-term sustainability (Gliessman and Grantham 1990, 201–2).

Over the centuries traditional farming systems evolved that meet many of these goals. Increasingly, agricultural scientists and development agencies look at traditional agriculture not as a system that should be replaced but as a set of farming techniques that they can learn from. Much research on this topic is ongoing; here we can present brief descriptions of only two of the specific traditional methods that are promising: intercropping and resource management.

**INTERCROPPING.**    One method used by traditional farmers in many parts of the world (in the tropics especially) is intercropping, also known as multiple cropping or polyculture. In contrast to monoculture, intercropping involves the intermingling of numerous crops in a single plot or field. It has been practiced for centuries by shifting cultivators (see chapter 8), whose plots usually contain dozens of crops and varieties.

Although the fields that are intercropped look untidy, this method offers several benefits. Most of the benefits stem from the diversity of crops growing together in a relatively small space. Many plant diseases and pests attack only one or a few crops, so if there is a diversity of crops, yields may still be good despite an outbreak. In regions where water supply is a problem and rainfall is erratic, some crops suffer during droughts but others will still produce a harvest. The varying growth patterns and root structures of diverse crops have useful ecological benefits: Erosion is low because more of the soil is covered, and sun-loving weeds are suppressed by the shade of the crops themselves.

Traditional farmers in some parts of the world have learned over the centuries that many crops grow as well or better when planted together. Leguminous crops, such as beans, peas, and peanuts, take nitrogen (a necessary plant nutrient) from the air and store it in their roots. Intercropping legumes with crops that need lots of nitrogen can increase yields. This is done in Mexico and Central America, where traditional farmers have long intercropped corn, beans, and squash. The stout corn plants provide support for the bean vines to climb, and the ground-hugging squash plants keep the soil covered. African farmers intercrop sorghum with peanuts and millet with cowpea with similar benefits.

**TRADITIONAL RESOURCE MANAGEMENT PRACTICES.**    In many parts of the world traditional farmers actively take steps to control the plant species that are growing in areas that, to outsiders, look "wild" or "abandoned." They are, in other words, managing their resources so that they can continue to use them indefinitely. Two brief examples illustrate these management practices.

The Kayapó of the Xingu river basin of Brazil farm in the forest by shifting cultivation. According to anthropologist Darrell Posey, who has worked among the Kayapó for years, the Kayapó manage the forest carefully. One of their traditional practices is the creation of "islands" of forest in deforested areas. They move composted soil made from termite and ant nests and vegetation into open areas and transplant crops and other useful plants. The created and managed environment provides plant foods, medicines, and building materials and attracts some of the animals hunted by the Kayapó.

The Lacandon Maya of the state of Chiapas in southern Mexico practice slash-and-burn. Although the staple crop is corn, a variety of other crops are planted in the cleared fields, including several tree species that yield fruits. Lacandon farmers clear and plant new plots frequently, but they do not simply abandon a plot once its main crops are harvested. Rather, they return to it for many years to harvest the long-lived fruit trees and other species they planted. Even while the natural forest is regrowing, the Lacandon continue to make use of the land. They manage their fallowing fields and thus integrate their exploitation of the land with the natural process of forest regeneration.

We have presented some of the reasons many scientists and others concerned with agricultural development are reconsidering traditional agriculture. It is all too easy to romanticize traditional farmers, to think that they really have had the answers all along and that only recently have so-called experts been forced to pay attention. This view, too, is simplistic: In all likelihood, solutions to the food crisis will require a mixture of traditional and modern technologies. It is, however, encouraging that the knowledge and methods embedded in traditional agricultural adaptations are being taken seriously by the World Bank and other institutions in a position to make critical decisions.

There is an old saying that those who want to spread Western agricultural technologies around the globe are fond of quoting: "Give a boy a fish and you'll feed him for a meal; teach a boy to fish and you'll feed him for a lifetime." In other words, "we" need to teach "them" how to grow food, rather than simply being generous with our food aid. However well-meaning this sentiment may be, much evidence suggests that most hungry people already know how to fish, and that their unsophisticated bamboo rods can serve them quite adequately. What they need most is access to a productive pond.

In chapters 17 through 19 we have looked at the modern global system and some of its implications for the world's peoples. We have seen that the nations and regions of the world are interdependent economically, and we have discussed some of the implications of this interdependence. We have seen how the historical (and largely colonial) creation of political boundaries contributed to conflicts between ethnic nationalities and other groups, who often have inherently conflicting claims over territories and other resources. We have suggested that two of the major problems of the modern world—population growth and chronic hunger—often are misunderstood by those of us who live in developed countries. We have indicated that the cultural knowledge of traditional farmers themselves is more sophisticated and relevant to farming in their own environment than some outside experts credit them with. We end *Humanity* with a consideration of some of the last groups of people to maintain themselves as communities *relatively* independent of the world system.

## SUMMARY

This chapter provides anthropological insights on two contemporary world problems: population growth and hunger. High rates of worldwide population growth are a recent phenomenon. High growth rates are caused mainly by advances in medicine and vaccines and by widespread improvements in public health facilities. These advances have reduced death rates and increased life spans in most countries, but in underdeveloped regions birthrates are still relatively high.

Population growth has many unfavorable consequences for those very nations that are experiencing it. It contributes to serious environmental problems, low economic productivity, urban sprawl and shantytowns, political conflicts, and even war. This is the main paradox of population growth: The high fertility of a country's citizens is mainly responsible for it, yet their high fertility contributes to many of their nation's problems.

But having many children is not a simple product of ignorance or irrational cultural conservatism. The fertility rate is a response to the overall economic conditions and cultural climate in a country. This is shown by how North American couples choose how many children to have. Our low fertility is a rational response of couples to the conditions of our personal lives. In deciding how many children they want, most modern couples consider the personal, not the societal, costs and benefits of children.

High fertility in the LDCs likewise is a consequence of the overall economic and social environment that constrains reproductive behavior. Ethnographic studies suggest that children are a net economic asset rather than a liability in the rural areas of the Third World. Children are productive family members at a young age. They seek jobs with local people, supplementing the family income. When older, they go to the cities or to foreign countries and send money back home. They provide old-age security for their parents. Under such conditions high fertility exists because large families are beneficial.

Population growth is popularly believed to be the major cause of world hunger. This is the scarcity explanation of hunger, which holds that overpopulation results in chronic malnutrition and periodic massive starvation. The alternative is the inequality explanation. It holds that land and water resources are in fact satisfactory to provide an adequate diet for the whole world. Hunger is caused by the way the local and world economies allocate resources—on the basis of ability to pay rather than of need. Durham's study of El Salvador illustrates that the two explanations are compatible: Population growth contributes to hunger by increasing the scarcity of food production resources, yet prevalent inequalities in access to productive resources aggravate the scarcity and prevent people from adjusting to it.

Technology transfer is the best viable solution to hunger in the LDCs, according to many. But there are numerous obstacles to exporting modern methods and machinery; reasons to think that a simple transfer of technology will not work well in the tropics; many cases in which such a transfer has harmed the poorest families; and good reasons to think that such a solution is undesirable and perhaps impossible. The most basic reason is that modern mechanized agriculture requires prodigious amounts of energy. Although mechanized agriculture is enormously labor-efficient, its energetic efficiency is much lower than that of preindustrial cultivation systems. Ethnographic studies suggest that preindustrial food systems are about 50 to 200 times more energetically efficient than our own. Given these comparisons of energy requirements, it is difficult to envision how modern mechanized agriculture could solve the world food crisis.

## KEY TERMS

scarcity explanation of hunger

inequality explanation of hunger

technology transfer solution

labor efficiency

energetic efficiency

## SUGGESTED READINGS

Bodley, John H. *Anthropology and Contemporary Human Problems* 2nd ed. Menlo Park, Calif.: Cummings, 1985.
 *A good place to start in glimpsing the relevance of anthropology to modern problems. Provides insights on war, poverty and hunger, and environmental destruction.*

Foster, Phillips. *The World Food Problem.* Boulder: Lynne Rienner Publishers, 1992.
 *Covers technical information on undernutrition and discusses some of its causes. Also has a lengthy section on policy issues.*

Franke, Richard W., and Barbara H. Chasin. *Seeds of Famine: Ecological Destruction and the Development Dilemma in the West African Sahel.* Montclair, N.J.: Allanheld, Osmun, 1980.
 *A well-documented study of the Sahelian drought and famine, arguing that planners and the international economy were as much responsible as natural disasters.*

Gupte, Pranay. *The Crowded Earth: People and the Politics of Population.* New York: Norton, 1984.
 *Overview of the social, economic, and political dimensions of population growth and control.*

International Bank for Reconstruction and Development. *World Development Report 1992.* New York: Oxford, 1992.
 *One of the World Bank's annual reports on the state of the world economy. The statistical tables in the back of the report provide a wealth of information on population, economic growth and trade, international debt, health, and education.*

Lappé, Frances Moore, and Joseph Collins. *Food First: Beyond the Myth of Scarcity.* New York: Ballantine, 1977.

————. *World Hunger: Twelve Myths.* New York: Grove, 1986.
 *Two books that argue against the scarcity explanation of hunger and provide evidence and analysis in favor of the inequality explanation.*

Leach, Gerald. *Energy and Food Production.* Guildford, Surrey: IPC Science and Technology Press, 1976.
 *A comprehensive yet brief study of energy use in the food system of the United Kingdom.*

Pimentel, David, and Marcia Pimentel. *Food, Energy and Society.* New York: Wiley, 1979.
 *A study of the energy requirements of producing various crops, livestock, and fish in the United States. Processing and transportation energy uses are also estimated.*

Wrigley, E. A. *Population and History.* New York: McGraw-Hill, 1969.
 *Traces the history of human population, concentrating on Europe.*

Wrong, Dennis. *Population and Society.* New York: Random House, 1977.
 *A short text on demography.*

# THE SURVIVAL OF INDIGENOUS PEOPLES

A Yąnomamö thatches a roof. The physical and cultural survival of Yąnomamö and millions of other indigenous peoples is threatened.

**CONTENTS**

Throughout this book we have emphasized the cultural diversity of humanity. How much of this diversity will persist into the future? Since 1500, as Westerners have spread themselves and their way of life around the world, non-Western technologies, economic systems, kinship and marriage forms, political organizations, and religious traditions have been destroyed deliberately or have withered and died. As a result, there is less cultural diversity in the twentieth century than there was in the nineteenth; if current trends continue, there will be still less in the twenty-first century.

We conclude *Humanity* with a discussion of the disappearance of preindustrial ways of life. We also close as advocates for the rights of native peoples to preserve their cultural systems, if that is their choice.

## INDIGENOUS PEOPLES TODAY

*Indigenous* may be used to refer to any people who have resided in a region for many centuries. By this definition, the Germans of Germany, the Irish of Ireland, and the Chinese of China are indigenous. However, as the phrase **indigenous peoples** usually is used today, it refers to "culturally distinct groups that have occupied a region longer than other immigrant or colonist groups" (*Cultural Survival Quarterly*, Spring 1992, 73). So defined, there are around 600 million indigenous people in the modern world. Among them are the Native American peoples of North, Central, and South America; the Australian aborigines; the Sami (formerly known as the Lapps) of northern Europe; the so-called "tribal" cultures of mainland and southeast Asia; and numerous ethnic groups of Africa.

Indigenous people most often survive as enclaves within a larger nation. The government controlled by the dominant ethnic group of these nations usually claims to have ultimate control over the land and other resources of the indigenous people who live within the officially recognized national borders. For many indigenous peoples in effect the colonial world still exists. Lacking effective political autonomy and being so small as to make physical resistance futile, their remaining lands are constantly threatened by the wider society. Too often their ways of life are being destroyed because more numerous and powerful ethnic groups consider indigenous cultures anachronisms and barriers to national progress and development.

The question of the legal rights of indigenous peoples first became an issue with Columbus's landfall in the Americas. Did the native peoples of the Americas—or for that matter any indigenous people—have any inherent rights to their land, resources, or political autonomy? These questions were debated in Spain. Although legal particulars differed from one colonial power to another as well as over time, a basic consensus was reached early in the colonial period. An indigenous people did have some rights based on prior occupancy. However, more "civilized" peoples could unilaterally claim jurisdiction over them and make use of land and resources that were either not utilized or underutilized by them. Civilized peoples had both a right and an obligation to uplift indigenous peoples and act in their "best interest." This responsibility was the so-called whiteman's burden concept. Civilized peoples also had the right to travel and trade wherever they wanted without any interference from indigenous peoples. Finally, if an indigenous people resisted, then the civilized people had the right to use military force against them. These attitudes were well expressed by a colonial official in German Southwest Africa in justifying the Herero War of 1904, a war in which more than 100,000 Herero died.

The native tribes must withdraw from the lands on which they have pastured their cattle and so let the White man pasture his cattle on these self-same lands. If the moral right of this standpoint is questioned, the answer is that for people of the cultural standard of the South African Natives, the loss of their free national barbarism and the development of a class of workers in the service of and dependent on the Whites is primarily a law of existence in the highest degree. For a people as for an individual, an existence appears to be justified in the degree that it is useful in the progress of general development. By no argument in the world can it be shown that the preservation of any degree of national independence, national prosperity and political organization by the races of South West Africa would be of greater or even of equal advantage for the development of mankind in general or the German people in particular than that these races should be made serviceable in the enjoyment of their former territories by the White race (quoted in Bodley 1982:55).

*The caption on this print reads: "An Indian Welcome on Charles River." Post-Columbian encounters between Native Americans and Euro-Americans led to the biological extinction, relocation, or assimilation of most indigenous peoples of the Americas.*

Thus racism, ethnocentrism, and social Darwinist ideas about the inevitability and desirability of progress provided the moral justification for the treatment of indigenous peoples.

Such attitudes and policies affected the governing of most indigenous peoples in the colonial possession of European nations. When independence came to Asian and African countries in the twentieth century, the political and economic leaders of many of the new nations adopted similar attitudes and policies. As discussed in chapters 17 and 18, the modern boundaries of most existing countries are legacies of European colonization in the sixteenth through the early twentieth centuries. In many cases the political and legal systems of these countries are also Western-derived or heavily Western-influenced. Such attitudes, governmental policies, and legal concepts often are the basis for the treatment of indigenous peoples and other ethnic groups within a Third World nation itself. In fact, if one wants to understand what is happening to most remaining indigenous peoples in the world today, one can start by reexamining American Indian policy during the nineteenth and early twentieth centuries. In Brazil, Peru, Indonesia, the Philippines, and elsewhere the same introduction of new diseases, genocide, relocation,

forced assimilation, and appropriation of land and resources of the smaller indigenous groups by the politically dominant ethnic groups is taking place.

Modern governments in Latin America, Africa, and parts of Asia face serious economic, political, and social problems—problems that were created by the history of their incorporation into the worldwide economic and political system. Many governments—including those democratically elected—are under pressure from their dominant ethnic group to pursue policies that lead to the displacement or assimilation of the indigenous peoples whose territories lie within their national boundaries. In many countries aspiring to modernization indigenous people living in remote, "undeveloped" regions are forced to move aside in the interest of what the dominant ethnic group sees as the "greater good" of their nations.

Sometimes this greater good consists of opening up undeveloped areas to settlers. Indonesia has long had a plan to resettle peasants from overpopulated Java onto its outer islands, now claimed to be underpopulated (whatever that means) by indigenous shifting cultivators. Although often considered a modernized nation, Brazil has some of the poorest people in the world living in its northeastern area. It also is one of the few countries left with a frontier—the vast tropical rain forest of Amazonia. In the 1970s Brazil constructed highways intended to open up Amazonia to resettlement and to mineral, timber, grazing, and agricultural exploitation. One-third of Brazil's Native American tribes have disappeared since 1900, and many others have lost most of their lands to outsiders.

One people who are threatened by the opening up of Brazil's Amazonian frontier is the Yąnomamö, mentioned in chapters 2 and 10. Until the early 1970s most of the approximately 9,000 Yąnomamö were relatively isolated from outside influences. In 1974 the Brazilian government constructed a road through the southern part of Yąnomamö territory. Workers involved in forest clearing and road building introduced new diseases such as influenza and measles, and in some regions as many as one-half the Yąnomamö died during epidemics. Dirt airstrips constructed during the 1980s also made Indian territory accessible to Brazilian gold prospectors. In the late 1980s thousands of gold seekers—most of them impoverished—poured into the area in search of wealth. By early 1990 as many as 45,000 prospectors had invaded Yąnomamö traditional lands and extracted gold worth an estimated one billion dollars.

The government's National Indian Foundation is charged to protect Brazil's Native American peoples and territories from invasion and plunder, but it has been unable to control violence against the Yąnomamö and other indigenous groups. Brazil's former president announced plans to evacuate the miners using military aircraft, forcibly if necessary. But the prospectors protested the policy and threatened guerrilla-style resistance, leading the government to reverse its position early in 1990. President Fernando Collor de Mello—since removed from office himself—ordered the landing strips destroyed in March of 1990 to reduce future access. But it may already be too late for the Yąnomamö, who have already lost rights to 70 percent of their territory in Brazil. Deaths caused by new diseases and violence are almost certain to continue.

Another common justification for the neglect of the territorial rights of indigenous peoples is the desire to improve a country's balance of trade. The Philippines, Indonesia, Zaire, and other countries earn foreign exchange by leasing rights to harvest timber from their tropical hardwood forests to multinational companies, although much of the "unexploited" forest is needed as fallow by indigenous shifting cultivators. Debts owed to foreign banks and international lending agencies encourage some nations to open up their hinterlands to resource development, pushing their indigenous inhabitants aside. In countries such as Brazil, Mexico, and Argentina minerals, cattle, timber, vegetables, coffee, and other exports are sold to Europe and North America to earn foreign exchange to help pay off international debts.

*As demand for products grows in the worldwide economy, companies move into remote areas home to indigenous peoples. This is an iron ore strip mine in Brazil.*

As these and numerous other cases show, many still consider it legitimate to take land from those who have lived on it for centuries. Racism and social Darwinism are not as fashionable as official justifications as they once were. But new rationalizations exist for the forced removal and exploitation of the territories of indigenous peoples: "developing" the whole country; solving "national problems" by providing lands to peasants and making payments on debts owed to foreign banks and international lending institutions; and making the countries' products "competitive" in international markets.

The indigenous people who remain in living cultural communities are learning to protect themselves through political action. In increasing numbers indigenous peoples around the world are fighting attempts to dispossess them of their access to traditional territories and resources. Many are resisting efforts to assimilate them into the cultural mainstream of their nations. They are publicly objecting to racist and ethnocentric attitudes about their beliefs and customs.

One people who are resisting are the Kayapó. In the 1980s the government of Brazil sought World Bank funding for the construction of two enormous hydro-electric dams on Amazon River tributaries. Eighty-five percent of the land that would have been flooded belongs to one or another indigenous Indian population. Organized by leaders of the Kayapó tribe, members

*Today indigenous people are organizing themselves politically to resist further encroachments on their resources and ways of life, as illustrated by this aboriginal rights group in Brisbane, Australia.*

of twenty-nine Brazilian Indian groups protested the dams. In early 1988 two Kayapó leaders traveled to Washington with anthropologist Darrell Posey to speak against the project to officials of the World Bank and to U.S. congressional authorities. When the World Bank deferred action on the loans, Brazil brought charges against the three protestors under a law that forbids "foreigners" from engaging in political activity harmful to the nation. The courage and sophistication of the Kayapó and other members of threatened communities illustrate how indigenous peoples are organizing themselves to acquire the political power to fight various "developments."

In early 1990 the Colombian national government recognized the land rights of various indigenous tribes to half of the Colombian Amazon. Supposedly the territory will belong to the Indian communities forever and sale to outsiders is prohibited. Whether the government's motives are entirely humanitarian or part of an effort to control illegal drug trafficking and left-wing guerrillas is not clear, but this is a hopeful sign for Colombia's Amazonian peoples.

## VANISHING KNOWLEDGE

Despite the increased political sophistication of indigenous peoples around the world and the protests of concerned citizens in many countries, there is no doubt that preindustrial cultures are in danger of extinction. Even if the people themselves survive the onslaughts of lumbering, mining, damming, grazing, and building, their way of life is liable to disappear. Most people would agree that genocide is a crime of the highest degree. But destruction or alteration of a culture is another matter—is it not possible that indigenous people themselves would be better off if they joined the cultural mainstream of their nations?

Yes, many peoples do want to acquire formal education, get jobs, improve their living standards, and generally "modernize" their societies. For many peoples and for many individuals within an indigenous culture, contact with the wider world offers them new opportunities and new choices. Young people especially are attracted by the material goods, entertainments, new experiences, and sheer variety of activities found in towns and cities. They should have these opportunities and these choices. But indigenous peoples and their ways of life often are overwhelmed by forces over which they have no control. It is not that most indigenous peoples are given the opportunity to carefully weigh the options available to them, so that they make informed choices about whether it is best for them to preserve or modernize their ways of life. Today, as in the past, their traditions are disappearing more often because powerful national governments want to open up their territory or because private entrepreneurs or corporations want to exploit their resources.

Anthropologists are especially concerned with the rights of indigenous peoples for several reasons. First, because of our interest in cultural diversity, we are more aware of what has happened to non-Western cultures in the past several centuries than are most people. Second, we identify with indigenous peoples partly because so many of us have worked among them. Third, our professional training gives us a relativistic outlook on the many ways of being human, so we can appreciate other peoples' customs and beliefs as viable alternatives to our own. Finally, the fieldwork experience often affects our attitudes about our own societies—deep immersion into other cultural traditions leaves some of us not so sure about our commitment to our own.

Whether one is an anthropologist or not, one can appreciate the rights of any group of people to have their lives, property, and resources secure from domination by powerful outsiders. The most important factors in considering the rights of indigenous peoples to be left alone are ethical ones. Do not people everywhere have the right to live their lives free from the unwanted interference of those more powerful and wealthier than themselves? Does any government, regardless of its "problems," have the right to dispossess people from land they have lived on and used for centuries? Is the demand of citizens in Japan, Europe, North America, or anywhere else for wood, minerals, meat, electricity, or other products a sufficient justification for relocating a people or taking land away from them? (Our American readers who follow politicians' statements about human rights violations in Iran, Iraq, China, Bosnia, and other countries might wonder why they have so little to say about the rights of indigenous peoples.)

Surely, most of us can agree on the answers to such questions. Ethical concerns for the social and material welfare of indigenous peoples, combined with a respect for other ways of being human, are the primary reasons for granting them their rights to survive as living communities. But if the ethical arguments alone are not compelling, there are other arguments. These arguments are analogous to those of ecologists worried about the extinction of natural species.

Plants and animals live in communities, and the species that make up a community are interrelated.

Again and again, removal of one species has been shown to affect other species of the community, often in harmful ways. Ecologists tell us that the maintenance of ecological communities may depend on a certain minimum level of species diversity. Each species therefore is important to other species besides itself. Further, when a plant or animal becomes extinct the information carried in its genes likewise disappears. This lost information may have practical value to humanity—in the treatment of disease, for example. So each species contains information that may be valuable to humans, and we may be unable to recover this information once it is lost.

Analogously, the long-term welfare of all humanity may be jeopardized by the reduction in the cultural diversity of our planet. And we do not mean merely that our lives will be less rich if there are no "natives" left to appear on new National Geographic Society TV specials. The knowledge found in the cultural traditions of indigenous peoples is useful to all humanity. The rest of the world, including the West and the social, economic, and political elites of other nations, has much to learn from indigenous peoples and their cultures. We conclude this book with a small sample of some of the knowledge indigenous peoples have already contributed to the world, beginning with medical treatments.

## Medicines We Have Learned

The medical knowledge of indigenous peoples provides one practical reason why we should care about the preservation of their cultures. Preindustrial peoples around the world use the plants that occur naturally in their habitats to treat medical ailments. Their primitive remedies often have genuine medical value. In fact, we originally learned about many of the most important drugs we use today from preindustrial peoples.

We can only provide a few examples of the useful medicines discovered by preindustrial peoples that now have worldwide significance. Numerous other instances may be found in *Medical Botany*, by Walter H. Lewis and Memory P. F. Elvin-Lewis.

Malaria remains a debilitating, although usually not fatal, sickness in tropical and subtropical regions. Its main treatment is quinine, a component of the bark of the cinchona tree. Europeans learned of the value of quinine in the seventeenth century from Peruvian Indians.

The Madagascaran periwinkle has long been used in folk medicine to treat diabetes. Researchers first became interested in the plant as a substitute for oral insulin, but it seems to have little value for this purpose. However, during the course of their investigation, scientists discovered that extracts from periwinkle yielded dramatic successes in treating childhood leukemia, Hodgkin's disease, and some other cancers. Drugs based on the plant—notably vincristine and vinblastine—remain the major treatments for these otherwise fatal diseases.

Muscle relaxants are important drugs to surgeons. A popular one is curare, made from the chondodendron tree. Taken in large amounts, curare can paralyze the respiratory organs and lead to death. This property was recognized by South American Indians, who used it as arrow poison for hunting birds, monkeys, and other game and from whom medical science learned of the drug's value.

The ancient Greeks and several North American Indian tribes used the bark of willows for relief from pain and fever. In the nineteenth century, scientists succeeded in artificially synthesizing the compound that today we call *aspirin*.

There is no way of knowing how many plants used by surviving indigenous peoples could prove to be medically effective. The potential is great. According to pharmacologist Norman Farnsworth, about one-fourth of all prescribed drugs in the United States contain active ingredients extracted from higher plants. The world contains more than 250,000 species of higher plants. Although as many as 40,000 of these plants may have medical or nutritional values that are undiscovered by science, only about 1,100 of these have been well studied. Botanists and medical researchers are coming to realize that indigenous peoples already have discovered, through centuries of trial and error, that certain plants are effective remedies for local sicknesses and diseases. The future value of their medical wisdom to all of humanity is largely unknown but probably great.

## Adaptive Wisdom

Many preindustrial peoples have lived in and exploited their natural environments for centuries. Over their history they have selected those crops and varieties that grow and yield well in the conditions of their local habitat. They have learned to control insect pests and diseases that attack the plants on which they depend and to do so without the need for expensive and often polluting artificial chemicals. They often have learned how to make nature work for them with minimum deterioration of their environments. They have, in short, incorporated much adaptive wisdom into their cultural traditions.

This is not to say that preindustrial peoples always live in harmony with their environments. Such opinions are part of civilized humanity's image of the noble savage. This romantic image reflects our desire for an existence that contrasts with our own more than it represents the realities of preindustrial peoples' relations with nature. Still, given the variety of existing cultural systems, there certainly are adaptive lessons to be learned from surviving indigenous peoples. Following are a few possible benefits that all humanity might gain by preserving the ecological knowledge of indigenous peoples.

**PRESERVATION OF CROP VARIETIES.** In all cultivation systems natural selection operates in the fields. Like wild plants, domesticates are subject to drought, disease, insects, and other natural elements, which select for the survival of individual plants best adapted to withstand these hazards. In addition, domesticates are subject to human selection. For example, crop varieties most susceptible to drought or local diseases are harvested in smaller quantities than drought- and disease-resistant varieties. Perhaps without knowing it, the cultivator replants mainly those varieties best adapted to survive the onslaughts of drought and local diseases. This "tuning" of plant varieties to the local environment, with all its hazards and fluctuations, goes on automatically so long as the domesticates harvested from the fields are replanted in the same area. Thanks to the unintentional and intentional selection by hundreds of generations of preindustrial cultivators around the world, each species of crop (e.g., beans, potatoes, wheat) evolved a large number of *land races,* or distinct varieties adapted to local conditions.

Over the course of human history several thousand species of plants have been used for food but less than a hundred of these were ever domesticated. Of all the plants that have been domesticated, today only a handful provide significant amounts of food for the world's people. In fact, a mere four crops—wheat, rice, maize, and potato—provide almost one-half the world's total consumption of food.

Since around 1950 plant geneticists and agricultural scientists have developed new varieties of wheat, corn, rice, and potatoes that are capable of giving higher yields if they receive proper amounts of water and fertilizers. These new strains were developed by crossing and recrossing native land races collected from all over the world. The aim was to achieve a "green revolution" that would end world hunger by increasing production (see chapter 19). Most new varieties are hybrids, which means that farmers must receive a new supply of seeds yearly from government or private sources.

Ironically, having been bred from the genetic material present in their diverse ancestors, the new strains threaten to drive their ancestors to extinction. As the seeds of artificially bred varieties are planted by farmers in Asia, Africa, and the Americas, the traditional varieties—the land races that are the product of generations of natural and human selection—fall into disuse and many have disappeared.

Why should we care? Increasingly, agricultural experts are realizing the dangers of dependence on a few varieties. If crops that are nearly identical genetically are planted in the same area year after year, a new variety of pest or disease eventually will evolve to attack them. The famous Irish potato famine of the 1840s was directly related to the genetic uniformity of the potato because all the potatoes in Ireland were apparently descended from only a few plants. More than a million people died as a result of the potato blight and a million more immigrated to North America. The United States has also suffered serious economic losses: The corn blight of 1970 destroyed about 15 percent of the American crop. Losses would have been less severe had most American farmers not planted a single variety of corn.

Many plant breeders are alarmed at the prospect of losing much of the genetic diversity of domesticated plants. Today they are searching remote regions for surviving land races that contain genes that one day might prove valuable. (The seeds are stored in seed banks for future study.) They have been well rewarded— although no one knows how much of the genetic diversity of crops such as wheat and corn has already disappeared.

The knowledge of indigenous peoples is an important resource in the effort to preserve land races. In many parts of the world—the Andes, Central America, Amazonia, the Middle East, and elsewhere—cultivators still grow ancient varieties of crops. They know where these varieties yield best, how to plant and care for them, how to prepare them for eating, and so on. In the Andes mountains, for instance, hundreds of potato varieties survive among the Quechua Indians as a legacy of the Inca civilization. Many have specific ecological requirements, and some are even unique to a single valley. Research is now under way to determine how well specific land races will grow in other areas, to help solve food supply problems elsewhere. It is important to

preserve the genetic information encoded in these varieties for future generations. Indigenous peoples who still retain the hard-won knowledge of their ancestors and who still use the often-maligned "traditional crop varieties" are important informational resources in the effort to save the genetic diversity of crops on which humanity depends.

**"UNDISCOVERED" USEFUL SPECIES.** In addition to their familiarity with local crop varieties with potential worldwide significance, many indigenous peoples cultivate or use crop species that currently are unimportant to the rest of the world. One example is amaranth, a grain native to the Americas that was of great importance to the Indians in prehistoric times. The great Mesoamerican civilizations made extensive use of the plant in their religious rituals. This led the Spanish conquerors, in their anxiety to root out heathenism, to burn fields of amaranth and prohibit its consumption. Otherwise, it—like maize, potatoes, beans, squash, and other American crops—might have diffused to other continents. Amaranth remains an important food to some indigenous peoples of highland Latin America, who retain knowledge of its properties and requirements. Its unusually high protein content might someday make it valuable to the rest of the world.

Other crops used by native peoples have the potential to become important elsewhere. Quinoa, now grown mainly in Peruvian valleys, has twice the protein content of corn and has long been recognized as a domesticate with great potential. The tepary bean, now grown mainly by the Papago Indians of the American Southwest, can survive and yield well under conditions of extreme drought, which might make it cultivable in other arid regions of the world. Another legume, the winged bean, has long been cultivated by the native peoples of Papua New Guinea, and it has recently helped nourish people in fifty other tropical countries.

Humans use plants for more than food. Indigenous peoples have discovered many other uses for the plants found in their habitats. Scientific researchers today are attesting to the validity of much native knowledge about the use of plants as sources of fuel, oils, medicines, and other beneficial substances, including poisons. Forest peoples of Southeast Asia use the toxic roots of a local woody climbing plant as a fish poison. The root is so powerful that a mixture of 1 part root to 300,000 parts water will kill fish. From the indigenous tribes, scientists learned of the toxicity of these roots, which allowed them to isolate the rotenoid that now is used as an

*This market in Cuzco, Peru shows the great variety of crops (here potatoes) grown by traditional farmers. The potential loss of this variety may have worldwide consequences.*

insecticide spray for plants and as dips and dusting powders for livestock.

When botanist Alwyn Gentry learned that the seeds of a vine (*Fevillea pedatifolia*) serve as candles for the Campa Indians of eastern Peru, he subjected them to laboratory analysis. The seeds turned out to have among the highest oil content ever reported for any plant. The researchers believe that these plants "may be capable of becoming some of the most productive sources of vegetable oil yet discovered in the world" (Gentry and Wettach 1986, 177–78).

Scientists no doubt will rediscover many other useful plants that today they know nothing about—if the tropical forests in which most endangered plant species are found last long enough. Their task will be easier if the original discoverers—indigenous peoples—are around to teach them what their ancestors learned.

## Cultural Alternatives

There is another kind of practical lesson we might yet learn from surviving indigenous peoples. Industrialized humans have developed technologies that discover, extract, and transform natural resources on a scale undreamed of a century ago. To North Americans and to many other citizens of the developed world, *progress* is almost synonymous with "having more things." Yet whether our economies can continue to produce ever-increasing supplies of goods is questionable. Many of us are frightened by the thought that economic growth might not continue or might even be negative. The widespread foreboding that we will be forced to accept a stagnation or even a decline in our levels of material consumption no doubt contributes to the interest today's undergraduates have in fields that will probably yield high incomes.

But humanity survived for many thousands of years without TVs, VCRs, BMWs, CDs, and PCs. Billions of people throughout history lived under conditions many modern people consider backward, with consumption levels we consider minimal. As we have seen in previous chapters, there is little evidence to suggest that their lives typically were as nasty, brutish, and short as often portrayed. Indeed, native peoples around the world more often were the victims rather than the beneficiaries of what we call progress (chapters 17 and 18).

In a sense, we all are victims of the mentality of progress—of that restless desire to earn more and to have more. If the industrial bubble does not burst in our lifetime, most of us who live in the developed world will spend our lives in continuous effort to maintain or increase our consumption of goods. We will do so despite the fact that we can never catch up with the Joneses because there will always be other Joneses whom we have not yet caught. We will do so despite the fact that our efforts will never be sufficient to get us all we want because no one can consume goods as fast as companies can turn them out and advertisers can create new desires for them. We will do so despite the fact that many of our marriages and families will be torn apart by the effort and many of us will suffer psychologically and physically from stress-related disorders. Sadly, most of us pursue our dollars and goods unthinkingly because we remain ignorant of any alternative way of living.

The world's remaining indigenous peoples provide us with such alternatives. They do not and did not live in a primitive paradise. Subjugation of neighboring peoples (chapter 8), exploitation by the wealthy and powerful (chapters 9 and 14), degradation of women (chapter 12), warfare (chapter 13), and other ideas and practices many of us find abhorrent existed among some preindustrial peoples, just as they do today. Yet we also often find other cultural conditions that some of us long to recover: closer family ties, greater self-sufficiency, smaller communities, more personal and enduring social relations, and "more humane," "more moral" values.

No anthropologist can tell you whether life is better or worse in preindustrial communities; indeed, we cannot agree on the meaning of *better*. We do know that humanity is diverse. We know that this diversity means that human beings—ourselves included—have many alternative ways of living meaningful and satisfying lives. In the end, it is these cultural alternatives provided by indigenous peoples that might have the greatest value to humankind.

Perhaps a people themselves are the only ones qualified to judge the quality of their lives, to decide what it will take to lend meaning and dignity to their existence. We hope to have convinced you that there are many ways of being human. We hope you have learned to appreciate some of the alternative ways of living experienced by various human populations. We hope you will agree that some of these alternatives are worth preserving, both in their own right and for the long-term well-being of all humanity. And we hope you will become informed about what you can do to help preserve some of these alternatives by writing to the organizations listed at the end of this chapter.

*Indigenous peoples remind us that there are many ways of being human.*

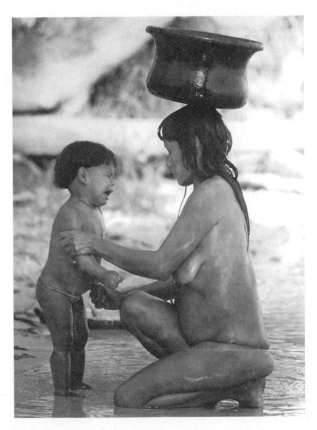

## SUMMARY

As European influences and industrial economies swept the world during the past few centuries, the lives of indigenous peoples were dramatically altered. Many tribal groups have disappeared altogether because of deliberate genocide or introduced diseases. Many others are threatened with relocation, reduction of their traditional lands and resources, and loss of their cultural autonomy through assimilation.

Rationalizations for policies harmful to the interests of indigenous peoples have changed since the colonial era, but many modern governments continue to violate their rights. Common official justifications for such violations include resettling people from overpopulated to "underpopulated" areas; lumbering and mining operations; developing energy resources; producing crops and livestock for internal and external markets; improving trade balances; and paying off debts owed to international lending agencies and multinational banks.

As a result of these and other pressures, the cultures of many surviving preindustrial peoples are in danger of destruction. Ethical considerations alone are a sufficient reason these peoples should be allowed to remain in their communities, on their traditional lands, living in the ways of their ancestors, if that is their choice. Pragmatic considerations also are important because these people still retain a vast body of knowledge—knowledge that is of great potential value to all humanity.

Science already has adapted several important medicines and treatments from indigenous peoples. Many other plants with medical value probably will be discovered, if the tropical forests and the cultural knowledge of their indigenous inhabitants last long enough.

Adaptive wisdom is also to be found in the traditions of indigenous peoples. Land races of important crops still survive and might contain genetic materials from which useful foods might someday be bred. Crops that today are used primarily by indigenous peoples—such as amaranth, quinoa, tepary bean, and the winged bean—might eventually have worldwide significance. Nonfood plants used by indigenes are also important as insecticides, oils, fibers, and other products.

Finally, indigenous people provide us with alternative cultural models that should reduce our anxieties about the likelihood of eventual decline in our material living standards. The diversity of the human species shows that we can live meaningful and wholly satisfying lives in the future without the technologies and huge quantities of consumer goods we now consider necessary to our economic welfare. The remaining preindustrial cultures allow us to see that there is more than one narrow road to personal fulfillment, cultural health, and national dignity and prestige.

## KEY TERM

indigenous peoples

## SUGGESTED READINGS

Bodley, John. *Victims of Progress.* 3d ed. Palo Alto, Calif.: Mayfield, 1990.
> *A very readable book that is a good overview of tribal peoples in the modern world and how they are being destroyed by industrial civilization.*

Burger, Julian. *Report from the Frontier: The State of the World's Indigenous Peoples.* Cambridge, Mass.: Cultural Survival, 1987.
> *The best general survey of the plight of indigenous peoples. This study contains good recent histories of the relations between indigenous peoples and governments in most major regions.*

Chalk, Frank, and Kurt Jonassohn. *The History and Sociology of Genocide.* New Haven: Yale University Press, 1990.
> *Comprehensive study of genocide. Describes twenty tragic cases and contains an outstanding bibliography.*

Davis, Shelton H. *Victims of the Miracle: Development and the Indians of Brazil.* Cambridge: Cambridge University Press, 1977.
> *A study discussing economic development in Brazil and the resulting destruction of Indian communities.*

Denslow, Julie Sloan, and Christine Padoch, eds. *People of the Tropical Rain Forest.* Berkeley: University of California Press, 1988.
> *Written for the general public, this edited work is a broad introduction to both indigenous and recent peoples living in the tropical forests of Latin America, Asia, and Africa. Many of the articles are concerned with destruction of the forest by modern development. Some discuss what can be learned from indigenous peoples about developing the forest in manner than is sustainable.*

Harrison, Paul. *The Greening of Africa,* London: International Institute for Environment and Development, 1986.
> *Shows how indigenous cultivation systems and scientific ecological principles can be integrated to alleviate Africa's food shortages.*

International Work Group for Indigenous Affairs, comp. *The Naga Nation and Its Struggle against Genocide*. International Work Group for Indigenous Affairs Document no. 56. Copenhagen, 1986.

> *A survey of the historical background and contemporary problems of the Naga peoples of India, who have had an independence movement for more than forty years.*

Jorgensen, Joseph, ed. *Native Americans and Energy Development II*. Washington D.C.: Anthropology Resource Center, 1984.

> *An excellent collection of papers examining energy development and American Indian communities.*

Paine, Robert. *Dam a River, Damn a People?* Copenhagen: International Work Group for Indigenous Affairs, 1982.

> *A study discussing the effects of a hydroelectric project in Norway on the indigenous Lapp, or Sami, population.*

Scudder, Thayer. *No Place to Go: Effects of Compulsory Relocation on Navajos*. Philadelphia: ISHI, 1982.

> *A study containing a short history of the Navajo-Hopi land dispute, together with a study of the effects of removal on the Navajo families.*

Suzuki, David, and Peter Knudtson. *Wisdom of the Elders*. New York: Bantam Books, 1992.

> *Lucid (although often romanticized) overview of how preindustrial cultures view nature and their relation to it. Sees many parallels between "scientific" and "native" knowledge of nature.*

Turnbull, Colin. *The Mountain People*. New York: Simon and Schuster 1972.

> *A highly readable account of what happened to the Ik, a foraging people of Uganda, when the government appropriated most of their hunting territory for a national game reserve.*

Weyler, Rex. *Blood of the Land: The Government and Corporate War against the American Indian Movement*. New York: Vintage, 1982.

> *A polemical attack on the U.S. and Canadian governments and corporate development of Indian resources.*

**The best sources of information concerning contemporary problems among indigenous peoples are the newsletters, bulletins, pamphlets, and monographs published by various support organizations such as the following:**

Anti-Slavery Society, 180 Brixton Road, London SW9 6AT, U.K.

Cultural Survival, Inc., 53A Church Street, Cambridge, MA 02138

Cultural Survival Canada, 1 Nicholas Street, Suite 420, Ottawa, Ontario K1N 7B7

Cultural Survival U.K., 4 Albion Place, Galena Road, Hammersmith, London W6 OLT

International Workgroup for Indigenous Affairs, Fiolstraede 10, DK-1171 Copenhagen K, Denmark

Minority Rights Group, 379 Brixton Road, London SW9 7DE

Survival International, 310 Edgware Road, London W2 IDY

World Council of Indigenous Peoples, 555 King Edward, Ottawa, Ontario K1N 6N5

# GLOSSARY

## A

**accommodation**  The creation of social and political systems that provide for and support ethnic group differences.

**acculturation**  The cultural changes that occur whenever members of two cultural traditions come into contact.

**adaptation**  Process by which organisms develop physical and behavioral characteristics allowing them to survive and reproduce in their habitats.

**affines**  In-laws, or people related by marriage.

**age set association**  A formally organized and named group including all males or females of about the same age.

**ancestral cults**  A type of communal cult centered around rituals performed to propiate a kin group's ancestors.

**animism**  Belief in spiritual beings.

**anthropological linguistics**  Subfield that focuses on the interrelationships between language and other aspects of a people's culture.

**apocalyptic revelation**  A revelation in which the prophet predicts the end of the world.

**applied anthropology**  Subfield whose practitioners use anthropological methods, theories, and concepts to solve practical real-world problems; practitioners often are employed by a government agency or private organization.

**arbitrariness (conventionality)**  Refers to the fact that the meanings of words and other kinds of symbols have no inherent or necessary relationship to the physical properties of the symbols themselves.

**archaeology**  The investigation of past cultures through excavation of material remains.

**artificial countries**  Multinationality countries created by external powers; usually applied to former colonies.

**assimilation**  The merging of the members of one ethnic group into another, with the consequent abandonment of the former group's identity.

**authority**  The recognized right of an individual to command another to act in a particular way; legitimate power.

**avunculocal residence**  Couples live with or near the mother's brother of the husband.

## B

**balanced reciprocity**  The exchange of goods considered to have roughly equal value; social purposes usually motivate the exchange.

**band**  A small foraging group with flexible composition that migrates seasonally.

**big men**  Political leaders who do not occupy formal offices and whose leadership is based on influence, not authority.

**bilateral kinship**  Kinship system in which individuals trace their kinship relations equally through both parents.

**bilocal residence**  Postmarital residence is with either the wife's or the husband's parents, according to choice.

**biological determinism**  The idea that biologically (genetically) inherited differences between populations are important influences on cultural differences between them.

**biome**  A large geographic region with similar climate, vegetation, and soils throughout.

**biopsychological functionalism**  A variety of functionalism asserting that cultural elements exist to fulfill the physical and psychological needs of individuals.

**bound morpheme**  A morpheme attached to a free morpheme to alter its meaning.

**brideservice** Custom in which a man spends a period of time working for the family of his wife.

**bridewealth** Custom in which a prospective groom and his relatives are required to transfer goods to the relatives of the bride to make the marriage valid.

# C

**cargo cults** Melanesian revitalization movements in which prophets claimed to know secret rituals that would bring wealth (cargo).

**carrying capacity** The maximum number of people a region can support, given its resources and the way humans exploit them.

**caste** Stratification system in which membership in a stratum is in theory hereditary, strata are endogamous, and contact or relations between members of different strata are governed by explicit laws, norms, or prohibitions.

**chiefdoms** Centralized political systems with authority vested in formal, usually hereditary, offices or titles; exchange in such systems is often organized by redistribution.

**child-rearing practices** Methods by which infants and children are nurtured, supported, and enculturated.

**child-care compatibility hypothesis** The hypothesis that some economic tasks are assigned to women mainly because they are most compatible with pregnancy, nursing, and child care.

**civilization** A form of society in which many people live in cities.

**clan (sib)** A named unilineal descent group, some of whose members are unable to trace how they are related, but who still believe themselves to be kinfolk.

**class** System of stratification in which membership in a stratum can theoretically be altered, and intermarriage between strata is allowed.

**classifications of reality** Ways in which the members of a culture divide up the natural and social world into named categories.

**cognatic descent** Form of descent in which relationships are traced through both females and males.

**cognatic descent group** A group of relatives created by the tracing of relationships through both females and males.

**collective understandings** The component of cultural knowledge that allows communication and interaction to occur by means of symbolic language, gestures, behaviors, and other means.

**communal cults** Cults in which the members of a group cooperate in the performance of rituals intended to benefit all.

**comparative methods** Methods that tests hypotheses by systematically comparing elements from many cultures.

**comparative perspective** The insistence by anthropologists that valid hypotheses and theories about humanity be tested with data from a wide range of cultures.

**composite bands** Autonomous (independent) political units consisting of several extended families that live together for most or all of the year.

**conflict theory of inequality** Theory holding that stratification benefits mainly the upper stratum and is the cause of most social unrest and other conflicts in human societies.

**consanguines** "Blood" relatives, or people related by birth.

**consultant (informant)** A member of a society who provides information to a fieldworker, often through formal interviews or surveys.

**controlled historical comparisons** A methodology for testing an hypothesis using historic changes in societies.

**court legal systems** Systems in which authority for settling disputes and punishing crimes is formally vested in a single individual or group.

**courts of arbitration** Court systems in which sanctions imposed are designed more to restore harmonious relations between parties than to punish.

**courts of regulation** Court systems that use codified laws, with formally prescribed rights, duties, and sanctions.

**cross-cultural comparisons** A methodology for testing an hypothesis using a sample of societies drawn from around the world.

**cross cousins** Offspring of siblings of different sex.

**Crow kinship terms** Associated with matrilineal descent; in this system paternal cross cousins are called father or father's sister, while maternal cross cousins are called son or daughter if ego is a male, and niece or nephew if ego is a female.

**cult** Organized practices and beliefs pertaining to interactions with and control over supernatural powers.

**cultivation** Planting, caring for, and harvesting domesticated plants.

**cultural anthropology (ethnology)** The subfield that studies the way of life of contemporary and historically recent human populations.

**cultural construction of gender** The idea that the characteristics a people attribute to males and females is culturally variable, not biologically determined.

**cultural identity** The cultural tradition a group of people recognize as their own; the shared customs and beliefs that define how a group sees itself as distinctive.

**cultural integration** The interrelationships between the various components (elements, subsystems) of a cultural system.

**cultural knowledge** Information, skills, attitudes, conceptions, beliefs, values, and other mental components of culture that people socially learn during enculturation.

**cultural materialism** A modern theoretical orientation holding that natural resources, overall environment, technology, population size and density, and other material things are the major influence on cultural systems and change.

**cultural relativism** The notion that one should not judge the behavior of other peoples using the standards of one's own culture.

**cultural universals** Elements of culture that exist in all known human groups or societies.

**culture** (as used in this text) The socially transmitted knowledge and behavior shared by some group of people.

**culture shock** The feeling of uncertainty and anxiety an individual experiences when placed in a strange cultural setting.

# D

**descent** The tracing of kinship relationships back to previous generations.

**descent group** A group whose members believe themselves to be descended from a common ancestor.

**dialect** A regional or subcultural variant of a language.

**diffusion** The spread or transmission of cultural elements from one people to another.

**diffusionism** A theoretical orientation, popular around the turn of the century, that studied the spread of cultural traits from one region to another; assumed that most cultural features are "borrowed" rather than independently invented.

**displacement** Ability of language users to converse about things remote in time and space, including things that do not exist and events that never occurred.

**distribution** The relative share of income, property, and culturally valuable resources possessed and consumed by individuals or groups in a society.

**division of labor** The patterned assignment of specific productive and economic activities (tasks) to individuals and groups in a society.

**domestic group** Individuals, usually relatives, who reside together in a single household.

**domestication** The process by which people control the distribution, abundance, and biological features of certain plants and animals, in order to increase their usefulness to humans.

**dowry** Custom in which the family of a woman transfers property or wealth to her upon her marriage.

**dry land gardening** A type of horticulture in which aridity is the major problem that cultivators face.

# E

**ecclesiastical cults** Highly organized cults in which a full-time priesthood performs rituals believed to benefit believers or the whole society; occur in complex societies.

**economic system** Patterned and organized behaviors by which people produce, distribute, and consume material goods.

**egalitarian society** Form of society in which there is little inequality in access to culturally valued rewards.

**enculturation** The transmission (by means of social learning) of cultural knowledge to the next generation.

**endogamous rules** Marriage rules requiring individuals to marry some member of their own social group or category.

**energetic efficiency** The number of calories of energy obtained per calorie of total energy input.

**Eskimo kinship terms** In this system mother's and father's siblings are called aunt and uncle, while their children are called cousins. English kinship terminology is of the Eskimo type.

**ethnic boundary markers** Any overt characteristics that can be used to indicate ethnic group membership.

**ethnic group** A named social group based on perceptions of shared ancestry, cultural traditions, and common history that culturally distinguish that group from other groups.

**ethnic homogenization** The attempt to create a single ethnic group in a particular geographical region.

**ethnocentrism** The attitude or opinion that the morals, values, and customs of one's own culture are superior to those of other peoples.

**ethnogenesis** The creation of a new ethnic group identity.

**ethnographic fieldwork** Collection of information from living people about their way of life; see fieldwork.

**ethnographic methods** Research methodologies used to describe a contemporary or historically recent culture.

**ethnography** A written description of the way of life of some human population.

**ethnohistoric research** The study of past cultures using written accounts and other documents.

**ethnohistory** See ethnohistoric research.

**ethnology** The study of human cultures from a comparative perspective; often used as a synonym for cultural anthropology.

**exchange** Transfer of goods or rights to goods between individuals or groups.

**exogamous rules**  Marriage rules prohibiting individuals to marry a member of their own social group or category.

**extended family**  A group of related nuclear families.

**extended household**  A group of related nuclear families that live together in a single household.

# F

**factors of production**  The labor, technology, and natural resources used in producing goods.

**fertility maintenance hypothesis**  The hypothesis that females do not usually perform strenuous tasks because such tasks may decrease their child-bearing potential.

**feud**  A method of dispute settlement in self help legal systems involving multiple but balanced killings between members of two or more kin groups.

**fieldwork**  Ethnographic research that involves observing and interviewing the members of a culture to describe their contemporary way of life.

**foragers (hunter-gatherers)**  Populations that rely on wild (undomesticated) plants and animals for their food supply.

**forced assimilation**  The social absorption of one ethnic group by another ethnic group through the use of force.

**forensic anthropologists**  Physical anthropologists who identify and analyze human skeletal remains.

**form of descent**  How a people trace their descent from previous generations.

**free morpheme**  A morpheme that can be used alone.

**functional theory of inequality**  Theory holding that stratification is a way to reward individuals who contribute most to society's well-being.

**functionalism**  Theoretical orientation that analyzes cultural elements in terms of their useful effects to individuals or to the persistence of the whole society.

# G

**general evolution**  Leslie White's approach to cultural change, which holds that improvements in technology and energy capture power cultural development.

**generalized reciprocity**  The giving of goods without expectation of a return of equal value at any definite future time.

**genocide**  The deliberate attempt to eliminate the members of an ethnic category or cultural tradition.

**grammar**  Total system of linguistic knowledge that allows the speakers of a language to send meaningful messages and hearers to understand them.

**group marriage**  Several women and several men are married to one another simultaneously.

# H

**Hawaiian kinship terms**  In this system mother's and father's siblings are called mother and father, while their children are called brother and sister.

**hierarchical nesting**  Occurs when an ethnic group is part of a larger collection of ethnic groups, which together constitute a higher level of ethnic identity.

**historic archaeology**  Field that investigates the past of literate peoples through excavation of sites and analysis of artifacts and other material remains.

**historical materialism**  Karl Marx's theory that changes are caused by development of the forces of production and the conflicts resulting from the opposed interests of classes.

**historical particularism**  The theoretical orientation holding that each culture is the unique product of all the influences to which it was subjected in its past.

**holistic perspective**  The assumption that any aspect of a culture is integrated with other aspects, so that no dimension of culture can be understood in isolation.

**homeland**  A geographical region over which a particular ethnic group feels it has exclusive rights.

**horticulture**  A method of cultivation in which hand tools powered by human muscles are used and in which land use is extensive.

**human variation**  Refers to physical differences between human populations; an interest of physical anthropologists.

# I

**idealism**  A contemporary theoretical orientation holding that cutural knowledge and behavior patterns are largely independent of the material conditions of life; claims that each culture must be analyzed separately, on its own terms, and mistrusts cross-cultural comparisons.

**ideology**  (narrow meaning of the term) Ideas and beliefs that legitimize and thus reinforce inequalities in stratified societies.

**interviewing**  Collection of cultural data by systematic questioning; may be structured (using quesionairres) or unstructured (open-ended).

**incest taboo**  Prohibition against sexual intercourse between certain kinds of relatives.

**independent invention**  The development of similar ideas or behavior among two or more peoples who have never had contact with one another.

**indigenous peoples**   Culturally distinct peoples who have occupied a region longer than peoples who have colonized or immigrated to the region.

**individualistic cults**   Cults based on personal relations between specific individuals and specific supernatural powers.

**inequality**   Degree to which individuals, groups, and categories differ in their access to rewards.

**inequality explanation of hunger**   Notion that hunger is not caused by absolute scarcity but by the unequal distribution of resources and how these resources are used.

**influence**   The ability to convince people they should act as you suggest.

**initiation rite**   A rite held to mark the sexual maturity of an individual or a group of individuals of the same sex.

**innovation**   The creation of a new cultural trait by combining two or more existing traits.

**intellectual/cognitive functions of religion**   The notion that religious beliefs provide explanations for puzzling things and events.

**intensive agriculture**   A system of cultivation in which plots are planted annually or semiannually; usually uses irrigation, natural fertilizers, and (in the Old World) plows powered by animals.

**interpretive anthropology**   The contemporary theoretical orientation that analyzes cultural elements by explicating their meanings to people and understanding them in their local context.

**Iroquois kinship terms**   In this system father's brother is called father, and mother's sister is called mother, while their children are called brother and sister. Father's sister is called aunt and mother's brother is called uncle, while their children are called cousins.

# K

**key consultant (informant)**   A member of a society who is especially knowledgeable about some subject, and who supplies information to a fieldworker.

**kin group**   A group of people who culturally conceive themselves to be relatives, cooperate in certain activities, and share a sense of identity as kinfolk.

**kin terms**   The words (labels) that an individual uses to refer to his or her relatives of various kinds.

**kindred**   All the bilateral relatives of an individual.

**kinship terminology**   The way a people classify their relatives into labeled categories, or into "kinds of relatives."

# L

**labor efficiency**   Number of calories of energy obtained per time unit of human labor.

**law**   A kind of social control characterized by the presence of authority, intention of universal application, obligation, and sanction.

**levirate**   Custom whereby a widow marries a male relative (usually a brother) of her deceased husband.

**lexicon**   The words that occur in a language.

**life chances**   An individual's opportunities to achieve rewards proportional to his or her talents, diligence, and other personal qualities.

**life cycle**   The changes in expected activities, roles, rights and obligations, and social relations individuals experience as they move through culturally defined age categories.

**limited-purpose money**   Money that may be used to purchase only a few kinds of goods.

**lineage**   A unilineal descent group larger than an extended family whose members can actually trace how they are related.

**linguistics**   The scientific study of language.

# M

**market**   Exchange by means of buying and selling, using money.

**marketplace**   Location where buyers and sellers meet for the purpose of acquiring goods and making money.

**market principle**   Term used to describe exchanges of goods and services at a price determined by supply and demand.

**marriage alliances**   The relationships created between families or kin groups by intermarriage.

**materialism**   The theoretical orientation holding that the main influence on human ways of life is how people acquire resources from their environment.

**matrilineal descent**   Form of descent in which individuals trace their primary kinship relationships through their mothers.

**matrilocal residence**   Couple live with or near the wife's parents.

**mechanized agriculture**   Cultivation system in which machinery powered by oil, gasoline, electricity, and other inanimate energy sources provide the major energy inputs to farms.

**modal personality**   Within a single society, those personality elements that are most common.

**monogamy**   Each individual is allowed to have only one spouse at a time.

**morpheme** A combination of phonemes that conveys a standardized meaning.

**morphology** The study of the units of meaning in language.

**multimedia potential** Property of language that allows messages to be communicated through many mediums, including sound waves and written symbols.

**multipurpose money** A money that can be used to purchase a very broad range of goods and services.

**myths** Stories that recount the deeds of supernatural powers in the past.

# N

**nationality** An ethnic group which claims a right to a discrete homeland and to political autonomy and self-determination.

**natural selection** Charles Darwin's theory that competition, predation, disease, and other natural forces favor the survival and reproduction of the most fit individuals in a population.

**negative reciprocity** Exchange motivated by the desire to obtain goods, in which the parties try to gain all the material goods they can.

**neolocal residence** Couples establish a separate household apart from both the husband's and wife's parents.

**nomadism** Seasonal mobility, often involving migration to high-altitude areas during the hottest and driest parts of the year.

**norm** Shared ideals and/or expectations about how certain people ought to act in given situations.

# O

**Omaha kinship terms** Associated with patrilineal decent; in this system matrilineal cross cousins are called mother and mother's brother, while patrilineal cross cousins are called son and daughter if ego is a female and niece and nephew is ego is a male.

**origin myth** The collective history of an ethnic group that defines which subgroups are part of it and its relationship to other ethnic groups.

# P

**paleoanthropologists** Physical anthropologists who specialize in the investigation of the biological evolution of the human species.

**parallel cousins** Offspring of siblings of the same sex.

**participant observation** The main technique used in conducting ethnographic fieldwork, involving living among a people and participating in their daily activities.

**passive assimilation** The voluntary social absorption of one ethnic group by another ethnic group.

**pastoralism** Adaptation in which the needs of domesticated animals for naturally occurring pasture and water greatly influence the settlement and movements of herders.

**patrilineal descent** Form of descent in which individuals trace their most important kinship relationships through their fathers.

**patrilocal residence** Couples live with or near husband's parents.

**patterns of behavior** The behavior that most people exhibit when they are in certain culturally defined situations.

**patterns of cooperation** Recurrent ways in which many people coordinate their labor to make some task or activity more efficient or successful.

**peasants** Rural people who are integrated into a larger society politically and economically.

**personality** Conscious and unconscious modes of thought, motivation, and feeling that guide the behavior of a person.

**phoneme** The smallest unit of sound that the speakers of a language recognize as distinctive and meaningful.

**phonology** The study of the sound system of language.

**physical (biological) anthropology** The subfield that studies the biological aspects of humankind.

**polyandry** One woman is allowed to have multiple husbands.

**polygamy** Multiple spouses.

**polygyny** One man is allowed to have multiple wives.

**postmarital residence pattern** Where a newly married couple go to live after their marriage.

**prehistoric archaeology** Field that uses excavation of sites and analysis of material remains to investigate cultures that existed before the development of writing.

**priest** A kind of religious specialist, often full-time, who officiates at the rituals of ecclesiastical cults.

**primatologists** Those who study primates, including monkeys and apes.

**procedural law** The structured manner in which a breach of the law is adjudicated or resolved.

**production** Activities that transform the energy and raw materials in the environment into want-satisfying goods.

**productivity** Property of language that allows its speakers to send an infinite number of novel messages.

**prophet**  A person who claims to have dreams or visions in which he or she received a message from a supernatural power.

**psychological functions of religion**  The emotional satisfactions people derive from religion.

# R

**ranked society**  Society in which there are a fixed number of statuses (e.g., titles, offices) that carry prestige, and only certain individuals are eligible to attain these statuses.

**reasonable man model**  A model used in legal reasoning that basically asks, How should a reasonable individual have acted under these circumstances?

**reciprocity**  The transfer of goods for goods between two or more individuals or groups.

**recombinable elements**  Property of language by which the total grammatical system is composed of phonemes and morphemes that can be combined in various rule-governed ways to convey diverse meanings.

**redistribution**  The collection of goods or money from a group, followed by a reallocation to the group by a central authority.

**relocation**  The forced removal of the members of a particular ethnic group from one geographical region to another.

**revelation**  A message that a prophet claims to have received from a supernatural power.

**revitalization movement**  A religious movement explicitly intended to create a new way of life for a society or group.

**rights of access**  How rights to exploit or use particular resources are allocated to individuals and groups.

**rite of passage**  A public ceremony or ritual recognizing and marking a transition from one group or status to another.

**ritual**  Organized and stereotyped symbolic behaviors intended to influence supernatural powers.

# S

**scarcity explanation of hunger**  Holds that there is not enough land, water, and other resources to feed all the people of a country or region an adequate diet.

**secular ideology**  An ideology that does not rely on the will of supernatural powers but justifies inequality on the basis of its societywide benefits.

**self-help (ad-hoc) legal systems**  Informal legal systems in societies without centralized political systems, in which authorities who settle disputes are defined by circumstances of the case.

**semantic domain**  A class of things or properties that are perceived as alike in some fundamental respect; hierarchically organized.

**sexual division of labor**  The kinds of productive activities (tasks) that are assigned to women versus men in a culture.

**shaman (medicine man)**  Part-time religious specialist who uses his special relation to supernatural powers for curing members of his group and harming members of other groups.

**shamanistic cults**  Cults in which special individuals (shamans) have relationships with supernatural powers that ordinary people lack.

**shifting cultivation (slash-and-burn, swidden)**  Type of horticulture, most common in the tropics, in which short periods of cultivation of a plot alternate with long periods of fallow.

**simple bands**  Autonomous or independent political units, often consisting of little more than an extended family, with informal leadership vested in one of the older family members.

**social control**  Mechanisms by which the behavior of individuals is constrained and directed into acceptable channels, thus maintaining conformity.

**social distance**  The degree to which cultural norms specify that two individuals or groups should be helpful to, intimate with, or emotionally attached to one another.

**social functions of religion**  The effects of religion on maintaining the institutions of society as a whole.

**social learning**  The process of learning by means of imitating or communicating with others.

**society**  A territorially distinct and largely self-perpetuating group whose members have a sense of collective identity and who share a common language and culture.

**sociolinguistics**  Specialty within cultural anthropology that studies how language is related to culture, and the social uses of speech.

**sodalities**  Formal institutions that cross-cut communities and serve to unite geographically scattered peoples; may be based on kin groups (clans or lineages) or on non-kin-based groups (age grades or warrior societies).

**sorcery**  The performance of rites and spells for the purpose of causing harm to others by supernatural means.

**sororate**  Custom whereby a widower marries a female relative of his deceased wife.

**specific evolution**  Julian Steward's evolutionary approach, which holds that many aspects of a culture result from the population's adaptation to its local environment.

**state**  A centralized, multilevel political unit characterized by the presence of a bureaucracy that acts on behalf of the ruling elite.

**status of women** How women are treated and regarded because of their gender, particularly the degree to which females are subordinant to males, participate equally in valued activities, and are allowed access to important positions and other rewards.

**stereotypes** Preconceived mental images of a group of persons that biases the way they are perceived and how their behavior is interpreted.

**stratified society** Society with marked and usually heritable differences in access to wealth, power, and prestige; inequality is based mainly on unequal access to productive resources.

**strength hypothesis** The hypothesis that many widespread patterns in the sexual division of labor are explained by superior male strength.

**structural functionalism** The variety of functionalism that assumes that cultural features fulfill the needs of societies for orderly relations, minimal conflict, conformity, and so on.

**structuralism** A modern theoretical orientation holding that cultures are the product of unconscious processes of thought and reason.

**subculture** Cultural differences characteristic of members of various ethnic groups, regions, religions, and so forth within a single society or country.

**subnationalities** A subgroup within a larger nationality, which lacks the concept of a separate homeland and makes no claim to any inherent right to political autonomy and self-determination.

**substantive law** Refers to the actual types of behavior that are categorized as illegal, together with the appropriate sanctions imposed.

**surplus** The amount of food (or other goods) a worker produces in excess of the consumption of herself or himself and his or her dependents.

**symbols** Objects, behaviors, and so forth whose culturally defined meanings have no necessary relation to their inherent physical qualities.

**syntax** The rules by which morphemes and words are combined into sequences to form meaningful sentences.

# T

**technology-transfer solution** Notion that developing nations can best solve their hunger problems by adopting the technology and production methods of modern mechanized agriculture.

**tone languages** Languages in which changing voice pitch within a word alters the entire meaning of the word.

**totemism** A form of communal cult in which all members of a kin group have mystical relations with one or more natural objects from which they believe they are descended.

**trial-and-error learning** The process of learning by means of experimenting with behaviors and repeating only those behaviors that bring a net return.

**tribe** Autonomous political unit encompassing a number of distinct, geographically dispersed communities that are held together by sodalities.

**tribute** The rendering of goods (typically including food) to an authority such as a chief.

# U

**uniformitarianism** The geological theory that features of the earth result from imperceptible, steady, gradual processes.

**unilineal descent** Descent through "one line," including patrilineal and matrilineal descent.

**unilineal descent group** A group of relatives all of whom are related through only one sex.

**unilineal evolution** The nineteenth-century theoretical orientation that held that all human ways of life pass through a similar sequence of stages in their development.

**universal grammar** Noam Chomsky's idea that at a deep level the grammar of all languages exhibits fundamental similarities.

# V

**values** Shared ideas or standards about the worthwhileness of goals and lifestyles.

**vision quest** The attempt to enlist the aid of supernatural powers by intentionally seeking a dream or vision.

# W

**Whorf-Sapir hypothesis** The idea that language profoundly shapes the perceptions and world view of its speakers.

**witchcraft** The use of psychic powers to harm others by supernatural means.

**world view** The way a people interpret reality and events, including how they see themselves as relating to the world around them.

# REFERENCES

## Chapter 1

**Subfields of Anthropology**
The information on the percentages of anthropologists represented in each of the four subfields is taken from American Anthropological Association (1991).

**Perspectives of Cultural Anthropology**
The zoologist who tried to explain why humans are allegedly pair-bonded is Morris (1967).

## Chapter 2

**What is Culture?**
Tylor's definition of culture is from Tylor (1871, 1).

**A Formal Definition of Culture**
The distinction between trial and error and social learning is from Boyd and Richerson (1985) and Pulliam and Dunford (1980), who also discuss the advantages of social learning. The material on the Yąnomamö and Semai is drawn from Chagnon (1983) and Dentan (1968), respectively.

**Cultural Knowledge**
The symbolism of the Ndembu milk tree is discussed in Turner (1967). The Hanunoo plant classification example is taken from Conklin (1957). Information on Navajo witchcraft comes from Kluckhohn (1967). Reichel-Dolmatoff (1971) describes shamanism among the Tukano.

**Cultural Knowledge and Behavior**
Brinkerhoff and White (1985, 309) report the American adultery rate.

**Biology and Culture**
Extended coverage of cultural universals is in D. Brown (1991).

## Chapter 3

**Some Properties of Language**
From Hockett (1960).

**Grammar**
The examples on Thai aspiration and Nupe tones are from Fromkin and Rodman's (1988) excellent text. We thank our colleague Lamont Lindstrom for the Tannese example illustrating syntax.

**Universal Grammar**
The information used in the discussion of child language acquisition is from Aitchison (1985), Fromkin and Rodman (1988), and Moskowitz (1985). The interview with Noam Chomsky was conducted by Gliedman (1985).

**Language and Culture**
Tyler (1969) provided the American farmer's classification of livestock. On color terms, see Berlin and Kay (1969). We consulted Frank and Anshen (1983) and Lakoff (1975) in preparing the material on sexist usages in American English. D. Brown (1991) has a concise discussion of the Whorf/Sapir hypothesis.

**The Social Uses of Speech**
See Farb (1974) and Trudgill (1983) on male and female speech and on Javanese "levels" of speech. Chagnon (1983) discusses the Yąnomamö name taboo. We thank Kathryn Meyer of Ohio Wesleyan University for help with the example of Japanese honorifics.

## Chapter 4

**Unilineal Evolution**
Unilineal evolutionary theory is best known from the works of Tylor (1865, 1871) and Morgan (1877).

**Historical Particularism (ca. 1900–1940)**
The best source on Boas is a collection of his articles (1966). See Harris (1968) for a critique of particularism.

**Functionalism (ca. 1920–1950)**
Biopsychological functionalism is set forth in Malinowski (1960). Radcliffe-Brown (1922, 1965) presents the structural-functional theory.

### Later Evolutionary Approaches
On general evolutionism, see L. White (1949, 1959). Specific evolutionism is derived from Steward (1955).

### Modern Materialist Approaches
On dialectical materialism, see Marx (1967, 1970). Cultural materialism is described in Harris (1977, 1979, 1985).

### Modern Idealist Approaches
See Lévi-Strauss (1963a, 1963b, 1966) on structuralism. Good sources on interpretive anthropology are Geertz (1973, 1980) and Shweder and Levine (1984).

## Chapter 5

### Ethnographic Methods
The discussion of how to evaluate a particular historical account was influenced by Naroll (1962). See also Hickerson (1970) on ethnohistoric methods. Sahlins (1981) discusses the Hawaiian interpretation of Captain Cook's visit. See Fogelson (1989) for a discussion of interpretation of historical events. The discussion of suicide in the Trobriand Islands is derived from Malinowski (1926). The problems of collecting genealogies among the Yanomamö are recounted by Chagnon (1983, 18–20).

### Ethnological Methods
The cross-cultural test of the sorcery and social control hypothesis is from B. Whiting (1950). See Adams (1982 and 1988) for an excellent example of what can be done with historical data. Data on matrilineal and patrilineal societies are from Bailey (1989).

## Chapter 6

### Culture Change
The concepts of innovation and invention are from Barnett (1953). Foster (1962) has a good discussion of why particular changes are accepted or rejected by a society.

### The World in 1500
General data on the world in 1500 was taken from Stavrianos (1982), Wolf (1982), Braudel (1979a and 1979b), Abu-Lughod (1989), and Levenson (1992). Regional data was taken from Murdock (1959), Lipsky (1962), Davidson (1969), Grove (1971), Robinson (1967), McVey (1967), Kolb (1971), Eickelman (1989), Oliver (1989), Steward and Faron (1959), Wagley (1968), Wolf and Hansen (1972), Szwed (1970), Kehoe (1981) and Price (1979).

### The World since 1500
The most important single source used was Stavrianos (1982). Secondarily, information was drawn from E. Wolf (1982) and—for the period from the fifteenth through the eighteenth centuries—from Braudel (1979a, 1979b). Information on the general effects of Old World contact on Native American populations was drawn primarily from Crosby (1972) and Thornton (1987). Data on the demographic effects of contact on Native American populations are from Dobyns (1976). For specific information on historic changes among North American Indians, see Leacock and Lurie (1971). Historical data on Africa and the African slave trade were from Davidson (1961, 1969) and Oliver and Fage (1962). Data on the effects of New World cultigens on Africa are based primarily on Miracle (1966, 1967). Statistics on foreign workers in Europe were drawn from Zanker (1986) and data on foreign data came primarily from Russell (1986). Information on slave raids on Easter Island is taken from Goldman (1970) and Heyerdahl (1958). Statistics on the number of Europeans in India during the 1920s is from Mayo (1927).

## Chapter 7

### Biomes
Based on Ehrlich, Ehrlich, and Holdren (1977, 144–59).

### Foragers
Dobyns (1983) provided some of the information on the distribution of foragers in North America used to draw the map. On Hadza, see Woodburn (1968). On Cheyenne see Hoebel (1978). On Netsilik, see Balikci (1970). On the Western Shoshone, see Steward (1938, 1955). On !Kung band organization, see Lee (1979). The material on the Northwest Coast Indians was taken from Ferguson (1984), Piddocke (1965), and Suttles (1960, 1962, 1968). The data on time spent in foraging among the !Kung comes from Lee (1968, 1969, 1979). The information on labor time in industrialized nations is compiled by Minge-Klevana (1980). More comparative information on work hours among foragers is found in Sahlins (1972) and Cohen (1977).

## Chapter 8

### The Advantages of Domestication
Information on plant and animal domestication is from Fagan (1986).

### Cultivation
On the advantages and disadvantages of cultivation, see Cohen (1977).

### Horticulture
Sources used to draw the North American portion of the map on the distribution of horticulture are Dobyns (1983) and Doolittle (1992). See Bradfield (1971) on dry land gardening among the Western Pueblo. Material on shifting cultivation is from Geertz (1963), Conklin (1957), Rappaport (1968), Freeman (1970b), and Ruddle (1974). The process of intensification is best described in Boserup (1965).

### Intensive Agriculture
Differences between extensive and intensive agriculture are set forth in Boserup (1965) and Grigg (1974). Material on intensive agriculture in the New World is drawn from our general knowledge and from Donkin (1979). Quantitative data on the labor requirements of intensive agriculture are found in Boserup (1965, 1970), C. Ember (1983), and Minge-Klevana (1980). Geertz (1963) describes Javanese wet

rice, and Grigg (1974) discusses how continued high productivity in wet rice paddies is possible. The Sinhalese material is from E. Leach (1968). E. Wolf (1966) is a good source on peasants. On peasant revolts, see E. Wolf (1969).

### Pastoralism
Porter (1965) discusses the subsistence risk reduction benefit of pastoralism. Schneider (1981) shows the negative relation between the distribution of the tsetse fly and cattle pastoralism in Africa. On the Basseri, see Barth (1961). A short source on the Karimojong is Dyson-Hudson and Dyson-Hudson (1969).

## Chapter 9

### Exchange
The three forms of exchange are presented in Sahlins (1972). Malinowski (1922) describes Trobriand *wasi*. The Maring discussion is from Rappaport (1968) and Peoples (1982). Alkire (1977) and Sahlins (1958) describe tribute in Micronesia and Polynesia, respectively. See Neale (1976) on money. Schneider (1981) describes some African monies. Pospisil (1978) discusses the uses of Kapauku money. Bohannan (1955) describes Tiv exchange spheres. On Philippine *suki*, see W. Davis (1973). Mintz (1961) discusses Haitian *pratik*.

### Control in Economic Systems
Dyson-Hudson and Smith (1978) present a model of territoriality. The description of kin-group control is greatly adapted from Sahlins (1972). Chiefly control is taken from Service (1962, 1975) and Fried (1967). Moore (1958) provided much of the information on the Inca.

## Chapter 10

### Marriage: Definitions and Functions
The material on Nayar marriage is from Gough (1959).

### Marriage: A Cross-Cultural Perspective
Inuit (Eskimo) polyandry is described by Kupferer (1988). Goldstein (1987) describes Tibetan polyandry and its advantages to husbands and the wife. The 50 percent American divorce rate is reported in Brinkerhoff and White (1985, 302–3). Chagnon (1983) discusses the importance of marriage alliances among the Yąnomamö. Kuper (1963) describes Swazi bridewealth. See Lee (1976) on !Kung brideservice. See Goody and Tambiah (1973) and Harrell and Dickey (1985) on dowry.

### Postmarital Residence Patterns
The frequencies of different residence patterns are as reported in Pasternak (1976, 44). Among those who have discussed the influences on residence patterns are Ember and Ember (1971, 1972), Goody (1976), and Pasternak (1976), but none of them should be held responsible for the ideas presented in this section.

### Family and Household Forms
Murdock (1949) showed how forms of postmarital residence produce various forms of the family and household. Paster-

nak, Ember, and Ember (1976) suggest an economic hypothesis for why extended families exist.

## Chapter 11

### Unilineal Descent
Data on the frequencies of patrilineal and matrilineal descent are from Divale and Harris (1976). Firth (1936, 1965) describes the functions of Tikopian lineages and clans. See Eggan (1950) on Hopi matrilineal descent.

### Cognatic Descent
Cognatic descent in Polynesia is discussed in Firth (1968), Howard and Kirkpatrick (1989), and Oliver (1989). Material on the Maori *hapu* is from Firth (1959). The Samoan *'aiga* is described in M. Ember (1959), Holmes and Holmes (1992), and Oliver (1989).

### Bilateral Kinship
Material on Iban kindred are from Freeman (1968, 1970).

### Influences on Kinship System
Sources for this discussion are Aberle (1961), Divale (1974), Divale and Harris (1976), C. Ember (1974), Ember and Ember (1971), and Ember, Ember, and Pasternak (1974).

### Classifying Relatives: Kinship Terminologies
Aberle (1961) and Pasternak (1976) provide statistical data on the correlation between forms of kinship and terminological systems.

## Chapter 12

### Cultural Construction of Gender
The Hua material is from Meigs (1988, 1990).

### The Sexual Division of Labor
Table 12.1 was put together from data in Murdock and Provost (1973). On female hunting among BaMbuti pygmies and Agta, see Turnbull (1962) and Estioko-Griffin (1986), respectively. On the possibility that strenuous exercise inhibits ovulation, see Graham (1985). The child-care compatibility hypothesis is from Brown (1970a). The discussion of why female contributions to subsistence tend to decline with intensification uses information in C. Ember (1983); Martin and Voorhies (1975); Boserup (1970); Burton and White (1984); and White, Burton, and Dow (1981).

### The Status of Women
The general discussion relies on di Leonardo (1991), Leacock (1978), Morgen (1989), Rosaldo and Lamphere (1974), Quinn (1977), and Sacks (1982). The suggestion that women's status improves with age in most cultures is from J. Brown (1988). Information on the Iroquois is from Albers (1989) and J. Brown (1970b). The idea that women's control over key resources frequently leads to high overall status is discussed in Sanday (1973, 1981). Yoruba material is from Barnes (1990). Schlegel (1972) and Whyte (1978) discuss why matrilineality and matrilocalility tend to give women high status, all else equal. Information on Chinese wives is

from M. Wolf (1972) and our general knowledge. Material on the effects of overall societal complexity on women's status is synthesized from Goody (1976), Boserup (1970), Whyte (1978), and Sacks (1982).

## Chapter 13

### Forms of Political Organization
The definitions and ideas concerning political structure were influenced by Steward (1955), Service (1962), Cohen and Service (1978), Krader (1968), and Fried (1967). Ethnographic examples were taken from the following sources: Comanche from Hoebel (1940) and Wallace and Hoebel (1952), and Tahiti from Goldman (1970).

### Social Control and Law
For the basic definition of law as well as many of the concepts about legal systems, we relied upon Hoebel (1954), Pospisil (1958), Fallers (1969), Bohannan (1968), Newman (1983), and Gluckman (1972, 1973). Ethnographic examples were taken from the following sources: Comanche from Hoebel (1940), Cheyenne from Llewellyn and Hoebel (1941), Nuer from Evans-Pritchard (1940), Jivaro from Harner (1973a), and Barotse from Gluckman (1972, 1973).

## Chapter 14

### Systems of Equality and Inequality
The classification of societies into egalitarian, ranked, and stratified was proposed by Fried (1967). Woodburn (1982) discusses the reasons for the egalitarianism among foragers. The material on Tikopia is from Firth (1936). Berreman (1959) noted the similarity of race relations in the American South to a caste system.

### Castes in Traditional India
The Indian caste system and its relationship to Hinduism are discussed in Dumont (1980), Hiebert (1971), Mandelbaum (1971), and Tyler (1973).

### Classes
Natchez stratification is covered in Swanton (1946). Material from the subsection on stratification in the United States is drawn from information given in Domhoff (1983), Avery *et al.* (1987), Joint Economic Committee (1986), Mischel and Bernstein 1993, and U.S. Bureau of the Census (1992).

### Maintaining Inequality
The Hawaiian religion is described in Valeri (1985).

### Theories of Inequality
The functionalist theory was first proposed by Davis and Moore (1945). Conflict theory goes back to Marx (1967, original 1867), but a clearer version appears in Marx (1975). Dahrendorf (1959) and Lenski (1966) discuss conflict theory.

## Chapter 15

### Defining Religion
An excellent recent summary of *mana* is Shore (1989). The idea that Judeo-Christian myths provides a world view con-

ducive to environmental destruction is taken from Lin White (1967).

### Theories of Religion
The Trobriand magic example is from Malinowski (1954). Frazer's intellectual theory is from Frazer (1963). Geertz (1965) argues that religion provides meaning. Malinowski (1954) argued that magic and religion serve to alleviate anxieties during times of stress and uncertainty. Kwaio pollution is described in Keesing (1982). The theory that ritual behavior creates social solidarity goes back to Durkheim (1915). The cross-cultural study indicating the association between supernatural punishment and inequality is from Swanson (1960, 166).

### The Sphere of Supernatural Intervention
Ethnographic data are from Turner (1967; Ndembu), Rasumssen (1979; Inuit), Moore (1957; Naskapi), Malinowski (1922; Trobriands), and Frigout (1979; Hopi).

### Supernatural Explanations of Misfortune
The distinction between imitative and contagious magic is taken from Frazer (1963). Fortune (1932) describes Dobu sorcery. The witchcraft examples are from Kluckhohn (1967; Navajo), Wilson (1951; Nyakyusa), Evans-Pritchard (1976; Zande); Offiong (1983; Ibibio), and Middleton (1965; Lugbara). Kluckhohn (1967) hypothesizes that Navajo witchcraft beliefs reduce overt, socially disruptive hostilities.

### Varieties of Religious Organization
Wallace (1966) formulated and named the kinds of cults. The vision quest material is from Lowie (1954, 1956). Harner (1973b) describes Jivaro shamanism. Middleton (1965) describes the Lugbara ancestral cult. The idealist interpretation of totemism is from Lévi-Strauss (1963b).

### Revitalization Movements
A general description of cargo cults is in Worsley (1968). Lawrence (1964) describes the Garia cults. On Handsome Lake's movement among the Seneca, see Wallace (1969). Stewart (1980) describes peyotism among Native Americans.

## Chapter 16

### Personality and Culture
Winthrop (1991) provided the definition of personality used in this section. The configurational or thematic approach to culture and personality was elegantly stated in Benedict (1934). DuBois (1944) describes Alorese child-rearing practices and their effects on adult personality. Rohner (1975) conducted the cross-cultural test of the notion that parental rejection during childhood tends to be associated with certain adult personality traits. The social systems model of the relation between personality and the cultural system comes from the work of Kardiner (1945) and is modernized and explicitly formulated by Whiting (1977). Figure 16.1 is drawn from Whiting (1977), but substantially modified to make it compatible with the terminology and concepts developed in chapters 7 through 15 of *Humanity*.

### Age Categories and Age Sets

The information on Hidatsa age sets is from Lowie (1954). Material on the Swazi is from Kuper (1963). Hanson (1988) discusses the idea that age sets function as mechanisms for organizing warfare in decentralized societies.

### Life Cycle

The Cheyenne concept of abortion is from Llewellyn and Hoebel (1941). See Jenness (1932) and Hoebel (1954) for a discussion of Eskimo infanticide. The description of the Osage child-naming rite is based on LaFlesche (1928). The material on whether Samoan young women do or do not experience all the stresses and strains typical of American adolescents is based on Mead (1928) and Freeman (1983). The information on New Guinea beliefs about feminine pollution and male initiation rituals is taken from Meggitt (1970–Enga) and Newman and Boyd (1982–Awa). The data on the Tucuna girl's puberty rite are from Ninuendaju (1948). Wallace and Hoebel (1952) provided the information on the treatment of the elderly among the Comanche. On the Inuit treatment of the elderly, see Hoebel (1954). Data on abandonment and parricide among subarctic peoples are drawn from Vanstone (1974) and Jenness (1932). Robertson (1987:335) reports the history of the now-customary American retirement at age sixty-five.

## Chapter 17

Most of the historical data used was from Stavrianos (1982). Most of the general economic and population data were drawn from Hepner and McKee (1992) and Jackson and Hudman (1990). Data on the changing magnitude of world trade were obtained from Rostow (1978), while data on the economies of particular countries were taken from Stamp (1973), The World Bank (1982) and the CIA (1993). Additional information was taken from current news reports in the *Washington Post* and the *Christian Science Monitor.*

## Chapter 18

There is a vast body of literature in anthropology and sociology on ethnicity and related issues. Our ideas on the nature and significance of ethnicity have been most strongly influenced by the studies of Frederick Barth (1958 and 1969), Joan Vincent (1974), Bud B. Khlief (1979), Nathan Glazer and Daniel Moynihan (1963 and 1975), John Bennett (1975), Robert E. Norris (1990), Joseph Himes (1974), DeVos and Romanusci-Ross (1975), Ronald Cohen (1978), Sol Tax (1967), Edward Spicer (1961), Bernard Nietschmann (1989), Donald Horowitz (1985), and Richard Jackson and Lloyd Hudman (1990). For discussions of international legal and political issues, see Gudmundur Alfredsson (1989) and Lee Swepton (1989). For additional data concerning particular ethnic groups and historical events, we have drawn on a number of sources: Charles Foster (1980), John Bodley (1982), Joseph Opala (1987), Eric Wolf (1982), L. S. Stavrianos (1982), Basil Davidson (1968), Robert Carmack (1988), Alice B. Kehoe (1981), John T. McAlister (1973), Dale Eick-

elmen (1989), Richard Handler (1988), and Richard Price (1979) as well as basic reference sources, discussions with colleagues and even with students from Saudi Arabia, Oman, Bangladesh, Indonesia, and Malayasia. In addition, one of the authors spent the summer of 1988 in Yugoslavia and the summer of 1989 in Guatemala collecting data on ethnic identity and conflict. For information on current ethnic conflicts we have had to rely upon current new reports from the *Washington Post* and *Christian Science Monitor.* Information on potential regions of ethnic conflict within the former Soviet Union is from *The Moscow News* June 15–28, 1992.

## Chapter 19

### Population Growth

The data on world population growth are from Ehrlich, Ehrlich, and Holdren (1977, 182–3). Information on population numbers, mortality rates, birthrates, and growth rates from modern nations is taken from the tables compiled in the statistical Annex of World Bank (1988). The economic interpretation of high fertility in seven Indian villages was given by Mamdani (1973). Data on large Javanese and Nepalese families appear in B. White (1973) and Nag, White, and Peet (1978). Nardi (1981, 1983) and Shankman (1976) discuss the importance of remittances. Freed and Freed (1985) discuss why Indian couples feel they need more than one son.

### World Hunger

The inequality explanation of hunger is stated and defended in laypersons' terms in Lappé and Collins (1977, 1986). The El Salvadoran data are reported and analyzed in Durham (1979). The discussion of the effects of the "green revolution" on Javanese peasants is from Franke (1974). Johnson (1971) discusses risk minimization among peasants. The quantitative data on the labor and energetic efficiency of various food systems are compiled from information given in Pimentel et al. (1973, 1975, 1980), Hirst (1974), G. Leach (1976), Pimentel and Pimentel (1979), and Steinhart and Steinhart (1974).

### Agricultural Alternatives

The potential value of traditional farming methods for the modern world is described in volumes by Altieri (1987) and Wilken (1987). The advantages of intercropping and other traditional methods are covered in Innis (1980), Gliessman and Grantham (1990), and Harrison (1987). Traditional resource management is covered by Alcorn (1981) and Posey (1983, 1984, 1985). Nations and Nigh (1980) discuss the potential of Lacandon Maya shifting cultivation.

## Epilogue

### Indigenous Peoples Today

For the best general discussion of the evolution of European attitudes to indigenous peoples see Berkhofer (1978). Germany's policies toward the Herero are discussed in Bodley (1982). S. Davis (1977) discusses the impact on indigenous tribes of Brazil's efforts to develop the Amazon Basin. Specific material on the plight of the Yąnomamö is from *Newsweek* magazine (April 9, 1990:34) and from the Commission for the Creation of the Yąnomami Park (1989a, b), published in *Cultural Survival Quarterly*. The experiences of the Kayapó are recounted by T. Turner (1989).

**Vanishing Knowledge**
The examples of medicines we have learned about from indigenous peoples are taken from Lewis and Lewis (1977). Farnsworth (1984) argues that many more plants will be discovered to have medical uses. A good discussion of the insights of "traditional medicine" is in Fabrega (1975). The discussion of the erosion of the genetic diversity of major food crops is from our general knowledge and Harlan (1975). The material on amaranth is from Sokolov (1986). An informative discussion of the many uses of tropical forest plants is Myers (1984). Gentry and Wettach (1986) report on the oil-bearing vine among the Campa.

# BIBLIOGRAPHY

Aberle, David F.
1961   "Matrilineal Descent in Cross-cultural Perspective."
In Matrilineal Kinship, edited by David M. Schneider and
Kathleen Gough, 655–727. Berkeley: University of California Press.

Abu-Lughod, Janet L.
1989   Before European Hegemony. *The World System A.D.
1250–1350.* New York: Oxford University Press

Adams, Richard N.
1982   Paradoxical Harvest. Cambridge: Cambridge University Press.
1988   "Energy and the Regulation of Nation States." Cultural Dynamics 1:46–61.

Aitchison, Jean
1985   "Predestinate Grooves: Is there a Preordained Language 'Program'?" In Language: Introductory Readings,
edited by Virginia P. Clark, Paul A. Eschholz, and Alfred F.
Rosa, 90–111. New York: St. Martin's Press.

Albers, Patricia C.
1989   "From Illusion to Illumination: Anthropological
Studies of American Indian Women." in Sandra Morgen,
ed., 1989, pp. 132–170.

Alcorn, Janice
1981   "Huastec Non-crop Resource Management." Human
Ecology 9: 395–417.

Alfredsson, Gudmundur
1989   "The United Nations and the Rights of Indigenous
Peoples." Current Anthropology 30:255–59.

Alkire, William H.
1977   An Introduction to the Peoples and Cultures of
Micronesia. 2nd ed. Menlo Park, CA.: Cummings.

Allen, Michael
1984   "Elders, Chiefs, and Big Men: Authority Legitimation and Political Evolution in Melanesia." American Ethnologist 11:20–41.

Allworth, E., ed.
1977   Soviet Nationality Problems. New York: Columbia
University Press.

Altieri, Miguel A.
1987   Agroecology: The Scientifc Basis of Alternative Agriculture. Boulder, Colo.: Westview Press.

American Anthropological Association
1991   1990 Survey of Anthropology PhDs. Washington,
D.C.: American Anthropological Association.

Avery, Robert B., Gregory E. Elliehausen, and Arthur B.
Kennickell
1987   "Measuring Wealth with Survey Data: An Evaluation
of the 1983 Survey of Consumer Finances." Paper presented
at the 20th Congress of the International Association for
Research on Income and Wealth, Rocca di Papa, Italy.

Bailey, Garrick
1989   "Descent and Social Survival of Native Horticultural Societies of the Eastern United States." Paper presented at the American Anthropological Association meetings, Washington, D.C.

Balikci, Asen
1970   The Netsilik Eskimo. Garden City, N.Y.: Natural
History Press.

Barnes, Sandra T.
1990   "Women, Property, and Power." in Peggy Reeves
Sanday and Ruth Gallagher Goodenough, eds., 1990, pp.
253–280.

Barnett, Homer
1953   Innovation: The Basis of Cultural Change. New York: McGraw-Hill.

Barth, Fredrik
1958   "Ecologic Relationships of Ethnic Groups in Swat, North Pakistan." American Anthropologist 60:1079–89.
1961   Nomads of South Persia. Boston: Little, Brown and Company
1969   Ethnic Groups and Boundaries. Boston: Little, Brown and Company.

Bateman, Rebecca
1990   "Africans and Indians: A Comparative Study of the Black Carib and Black Seminole." Ethnohistory 37:1–24.

Benedict, Ruth
1934   Patterns of Culture. Boston: Houghton Mifflin Company.

Bennett, John, ed.
1975   "The New Ethnicity: Perspectives from Ethnology."
1973 Proceedings of the American Ethnological Society. St. Paul, Minn.: West Publishing Co.

Berch, Bettina
1982   The Endless Days: The Political Economy of Women and Work. San Diego: Harcourt, Brace, Jovanovich.

Berkhofer, Robert F. Jr.
1978   The White Man's Indian: Images of the American Indian from Columbus to the Present. New York: Knopf

Berlin, Brent, and Paul Kay
1969   Basic Color Terms—Their Universality and Evolution. Berkeley: University of California Press.

Berreman, Gerald D.
1959   "Caste in India and the United States." American Journal of Sociology 66:120–127.

Bertelsen, Judy S. ed.
1977   Nonstate Nations in International Politics: Comparative System Analyses. New York: Praeger.

Blalock, H. M., Jr.
1962   "Occupational Discrimination: Some Theoretical Propositions." Social Problems 9:240–247.

Boas, Franz
1966   Race, Language and Culture. New York: Free Press (original 1940).

Bodley, John H.
1982   Victims of Progress. 2nd ed. Palo Alto, CA: Mayfield Publishing Company.

Bohannan, Paul
1955   "Some Principles of Exchange and Investment Among the Tiv." American Anthropologist 57:60–70.

1968   Justice and Judgement Among the Tiv. London: Oxford University Press.

Boserup, Ester
1965   The Conditions of Agricultural Growth. Chicago: Aldine.
1970   Woman's Role in Economic Development. New York: St. Martin's.

Boyd, Robert and Peter J. Richerson
1985   Culture and the Evolutionary Process. Chicago: University of Chicago Press.

Bradfield, Maitland
1971   The Changing Pattern of Hopi Agriculture. Royal Anthropological Institute of Great Britain and Ireland Occasional Paper, no. 30. London: Royal Anthropological Institute.

Braudel, Fernand
1979a   The Structures of Everyday Life: Civilization & Capitalism 15th–18th Century, Vol. 1, New York: Harper & Row.
1979b   The Wheels of Commerce: Civilization & Capitalism 15th–18th Century, Vol. 2, New York: Harper & Row.

Brinkerhoff, David B. and Lynn K. White
1985   Sociology. St. Paul: West Publishing Company.

Brown, Donald E.
1991   Human Universals. New York: McGraw-Hill, Inc.

Brown, Judith K.
1970a   "A Note on the Division of Labor by Sex." American Anthropologist 72:1073–1078.
1970b   "Economic Organization and the Position of Women among the Iroquois." Ethnohistory 17:131–167.
1988   "Cross-Cultural Perspectives on Middle-Aged Women." in Cultural Constructions of 'Woman', edited by Pauline Kolenda, pp. 73–100. Salem, Wisc.: Sheffield.

Burger, Julian
1987   Report From the Frontier: The State of the World's Indigenous Peoples. Cambridge MA: Cultural Survival Inc.
1990   The GAIA Atlas of First Peoples. New York: Anchor Books

Burton, Michael L. and Douglas R. White
1984   "Sexual Division of Labor in Agriculture." American Anthropologist 86:568–583.

Callender, Charles, and Lee M. Kodrens
1983   "The North American Berdache." Current Anthropology 24:443–90.

Carmack, Robert, ed.
1988   Harvest of Violence. Norman: University of Oklahoma Press.

Central Intelligence Agency
1993  The World Factbook 1992. Washington, D.C.: Gvo-
ernment Printing Office.

Chagnon, Napoleon A.
1983  Yąnomamö: The Fierce People. 3rd ed. New York:
Holt, Rinehart and Winston.

Coakley, Jay J.
1978  Sport in Society. St. Louis: C. V. Mosby.

Cohen, Mark Nathan
1977  The Food Crisis in Prehistory. New Haven and
London: Yale University Press.

Cohen, Ronald
1978  "Ethnicity: Problem and Focus in Anthropology."
In Annual Review of Anthropology vol. 7, 1978, edited by
Bernard Siegal. Palo Alto: Annual Reviews Inc.

Cohen, Ronald, and Elman Service
1978  Origins of the State: The Anthropology of Political
Evolution. Philadelphia: Institute for the Study of Human
Issues.

Cohen, Ronald, and John Middleton, eds.
1970  From Tribe to Nation in Africa. Scranton, Penn.:
Chandler Publishing Company.

Cohen, Theodore F.
1987  "Remaking Men." Journal of Family Issues 8:
57–77.

Commission for the Creation of Yanomami Park (CCPY)
1989a  "The Threatened Yanomami." Cultural Survival
Quarterly 13:45–46.
1989b  "Brazilian Government Reduces Yanomami Territory by 70 Percent." Cultural Survival Quarterly 13:47.

Conklin, Harold C.
1957  Hanunoó Agriculture. FAO Forestry Development
Paper, no. 12. Rome: Food and Agriculture Organization
of the United Nations.

Crosby, Alfred W.
1972  The Columbian Exchange. Westport, Conn.:
Greenwood.
1986  Ecological Imperialism: The Biological Expansion of
Europe, 900–1900. Cambrige: Cambridge University
Press

Dahrendorf, Ralf
1959  Class and Class Conflict in Industrial Society. Berkeley: University of California Press.

Davidson, Basil
1961  The African Slave Trade: Precolonial History 1450–
1850. Boston: Atlantic-Little, Brown.
1969  Africa in History. New York: Macmillan.

Davis, Kingsley, and Wilbert E. Moore
1945  "Some Principles of Stratification." American Sociological Review 10:242–49.

Davis, Shelton H.
1977  Victims of the Miracle. Cambridge: Cambridge
University Press.

Davis, William G.
1973  Social Relations in a Philippine Market. Berkeley:
University of California Press.

DeMallie, Raymond J.
1983  "Male and Female in Traditional Lakota Culture."
In The Hidden Half: Studies of Plains Indian Women, edited by Patricia Albers and Beatrice Medicine, 237–65.
Lanham Md.: University Press of America.

Denig, Edwin Thompson
1961  Five Indian Tribes of the Upper Missouri, edited by
John Ewers. Norman: University of Oklahoma Press.

Dentan, Robert Knox
1968  The Semai: A Nonviolent People of Malaya. New
York: Holt, Rinehart and Winston.

DeVos, George, and Lola Romanusci-Ross, eds.
1975  Ethnic Identity: Cultural Continuities and Change.
Palo Alto: Mayfield Publishing Co.

di Leonardo, Micaela, ed.,
1991  Gender at the Crossroads of Knowledge. Berkeley:
University of California Press.

Divale, William T.
1974  "Migration, External Warfare, and Matrilocal Residence." Behavior Science Research 9:75–133.

Divale, William T., and Marvin Harris
1976  "Population, Warfare, and the Male Supremacist
Complex." American Anthropologist 78:521–38.

Dobyns, Henry F.
1976  Native American Historical Demography: A Critical
Bibliography. Bloomington: Indiana University Press.
1983  Their Number Become Thinned. Knoxville: University of Tennessee Press.

Domhoff, G. William
1983  Who Rules America Now? Englewood Cliffs, N.J.:
Prentice-Hall, Inc.

Donkin, Robin
1979  Agricultural Terracing in the Aboriginal New
World. Tucson: University of Arizona Press.

Doolittle, William E.
1992  "Agriculture in North America on the Eve of Contact: A Reassessment." Annals of the Association of American Geographers 82:386–401.

Douglas, Mary
1966    Purity and Danger. Middlesex, England: Penguin.

DuBois, Cora
1944    The People of Alor. Minneapolis: University of Minnesota Press.

Dumont, Louis
1980    Homo Hierarchicus: The Caste System and Its Implications. Chicago and London: University of Chicago Press.

Durham, William H.
1979    Scarcity and Survival in Central America. Stanford CA: Stanford University Press.

Durkheim, Emile
1915    The Elementary Forms of the Religious Life. London: George Allen and Unwin Ltd.

Dyson-Hudson, Rada, and Eric Alden Smith
1978    "Human Territoriality: An Ecological Reassessment." American Anthropologist 80:21–41.

Dyson-Hudson, Rada, and Neville Dyson-Hudson
1969    "Subsistence Herding in Uganda." Scientific American 220:76–89.

Edwards, Harry
1971    "The Myth of the Racially Superior Athlete." The Black Scholar 3:16–28.
1973    Sociology of Sport. Homewood, IL: Dorsey Press.

Eggan, Fred
1950    Social Organization of the Western Pueblos. Chicago: University of Chicago Press.

Ehrlich, Paul R., Anne H. Ehrlich, and John P. Holdren
1977    Ecoscience: Population, Resources, Environment. San Francisco: W. H. Freeman.

Eickelman, Dale F.
1989    The Middle East: An Anthropological Approach. Englewood Cliffs, N.J.: Prentice-Hall, Inc.

Ember, Carol
1974    "An Evaluation of Alternative Theories of Matrilocal Versus Patrilocal Residence." Behavior Science Research 9:135–149.
1983    "The Relative Decline in Women's Contribution to Agriculture with Intensification." American Anthropologist 85:285–304.

Ember, Melvin
1959    "The Nonunilinear Descent Groups of Samoa." American Anthropologist 61:573–577.

Ember, Melvin and Carol R. Ember
1971    "The Conditions Favoring Matrilocal Versus Patrilocal Residence." American Anthropologist 73:571–594.

1972    "The Conditions Favoring Multilocal Residence." Southwestern Journal of Anthropology 28:382–400.

Ember, Melvin, Carol R. Ember, and Burton Pasternak
1974    "On the Development of Unilineal Descent." Journal of Anthropological Research 30:69–94.

Estioko-Griffin, Agnes
1986    "Daughters of the Forest." Natural History 95: 36–43.

Evans-Pritchard, E. E.
1940    The Nuer. Oxford: Clarendon.
1976    Witchcraft, Oracles, and Magic among the Azande, abridged edition. Oxford: Clarendon Press.

Ewers, John
1955    The Horse in Blackfoot Indian Culture. Bureau of American Ethnology, Bulletin 159, Washington, D.C., U.S. Government Printing Office.

Fabrega, H., Jr.
1975    "The Need for an Ethnomedical Science." Science 189:969–75.

Fagan, Brian M.
1986    People of the Earth. Boston: Little, Brown and Company.

Fallers, Lloyd A.
1969    Law Without Precedent. Chicago: University of Chicago Press.

Farb, Peter
1974    Word Play. New York: Alfred A. Knopf.

Farnsworth, Norman R.
1984    "How Can the Well Be Dry When It Is Filled with Water?" Economic Botany 38:4–13.

Farrer, Claire
1987    "The 1931 Mescalero Apache Field Project: Review and Response in Reconstructing the Past." Anthropology Newsletter 28:3–4.

Ferguson, R. Brian
1984    "A Reexamination of the Causes of Northwest Coast Warfare." In Warfare, Culture, and Environment, edited by R. Brian Ferguson, 267–328. Orlando, Florida: Academic Press.

Figler, Stephen K.
1981    Sport and Play in American Life. Philadelphia: Saunders College Publishing.

Firth, Raymond
1936    We, The Tikopia. Boston: Beacon Press.
1959    Economics of the New Zealand Maori. 2d editon. Wellington: Government Printer.
1965    Primitive Polynesian Economy. New York: Norton.

1968   "A Note on Descent Groups in Polynesia." In Kinship and Social Organization, edited by Paul Bohannan and John Middleton, pp. 213–223. Garden City, N.Y.: The Natural History Press.

**Fogelson, Raymond D.**
1989   The Ethnohistory of Events and Nonevents. Ethnohistory 36:133–47.

**Fortune, Reo**
1932   Sorcerers of Dobu. New York: E.P. Dutton.

**Foster, Charles R., ed.**
1980   Nations Without a State: Ethnic Minorities of Western Europe. New York: Praeger.

**Foster, George**
1962   Traditional Cultures: and the impact of technological change. New York: Harper & Row.

**Frank, Francine and Frank Anshen**
1983   Language and the Sexes. Albany: State University of New York Press.

**Franke, Richard W.**
1974   "Miracle Seeds and Shattered Dreams in Java." Natural History 83:10–18, 84–88.

**Frazer, Sir James George**
1963   The Golden Bough, abridged edition. Toronto: The Macmillan Company (original 1911–1915).

**Freed, Stanley A., and Ruth S. Freed**
1985   "One Son Is No Sons." Natural History 94:10–15.

**Freeman, Derek**
1968   "On the Concept of the Kindred." In Kinship and Social Organization, edited by Paul Bohannan and John Middleton, pp. 255–272. Garden City, N.Y.: The Natural History Press.
1970   "The Iban of Western Borneo." In Cultures of the Pacific, edited by Thomas G. Harding and Ben J. Wallace, 180–200. New York: Free Press.
1983   Margaret Mead and Samoa. Cambridge, Mass.: Harvard University Press.

**Fried, Morton**
1967   The Evolution of Political Society. New York: Random House.

**Frigout, Arlette**
1979   "Hopi Ceremonial Organization." In Southwest, edited by Alfonso Ortiz, 564–76. Handbook of North American Indians, vol. 9. Washington, D.C.: Smithsonian Institution.

**Fromkin, Victoria, and Robert Rodman**
1988   An Introduction to Language. 4th ed. New York: Holt, Rinehart and Winston.

**Gentry, Alwyn H. and Richard H. Wettach**
1986   "Fevillea—a New Oil Seed from Ancient Peru." Economic Botany 40:177–85.

**Geertz, Clifford**
1963   Agricultural Involution. Berkeley: University of California Press.
1965   "Religion As a Cultural System." In Anthropological Approaches to the Study of Religion, edited by Michael Banton. Association of Social Anthropologists Monographs, no. 3. London: Tavistock Publications.
1973   The Interpretation of Cultures. New York: Basic Books.
1980   Negara. Princeton, N.J.: Princeton University Press.

**Gliedman, John**
1985   "An Interview With Noam Chomsky." In Language: Introductory Readings, edited by Virginia P. Clark, Paul A. Eschholz, and Alfred F. Rosa, 366–75. New York: St. Martin's Press.

**Gliessman, Stephen, and Robert Grantham**
1990   Agroecology: Reshaping Agricultural Development. In Lessons of the Rain Forest, edited by Suzanne Head and Robert Heinzman. San Francisco: Sierra Club Books. pp. 196–207.

**Gluckman, Max**
1972   The Ideas in Barotse Jurisprudence. Manchester: Manchester University Press.
1973   The Judicial Process Among the Barotse. Manchester: Manchester University Press.

**Glazer, Nathan, and Daniel P. Moynihan**
1963   Beyond the Melting Pot. Cambridge: Harvard University Press.

**Glazer, Nathan, and Daniel P. Moynihan, eds.**
1975   Ethnicity: Theory and Experience. Cambridge: Harvard University Press.

**Goldman, Irving**
1970   Ancient Polynesian Society. Chicago: University of Chicago Press.

**Goldin, Ian**
1987   "The Reconstitution of Coloured Identity in the Western Cape." In The Politics of Race, Class, and Nationalism in Twentieth Century South Africa, edited by Shula Marks and Stanley Trapido, 156–81. Reading, MA: Longman Group UK Limited.

**Goldstein, Melvyn C.**
1987   "When Brothers Share a Wife." Natural History 96(3):38–49.

**Goodenough, Ward H.**
1961   "Comment on Cultural Evolution." Daedalus 90:521–28.

Goody, Jack
1976    Production and Reproduction. Cambridge: Cambridge University Press.

Goody, Jack, and S. J. Tambiah
1973    Bridewealth and Dowry. Cambridge: Cambridge University Press.

Gough, E. Kathleen
1959    "The Nayars and the Definition of Marriage." Journal of the Royal Anthropological Institute 89: 23–34.

Graham, Susan Brandt
1985    "Running and Menstrual Dysfunction: Recent Medical Discoveries Provide New Insights into the Human Division of Labor by Sex." American Anthropologist 87:878–82.

Grigg, David
1974    The Agricultural Systems of the World. Cambridge: Cambridge University Press.

Grove, A. T.
1971    Africa South of the Sahara. Oxford: Oxford University Press.

Handler, Richard
1988    Nationalism and the Politics of Culture in Quebec. Madison: University of Wisconsin Press.

Hanson, Jeffery R.
1988    Age-Set Theory and Plains Indian Age-Grading: A Critical Review and Revision. American Ethnologist 15:349–64.

Harlan, Jack R.
1975    "Our Vanishing Genetic Resources." Science 188:618–21.

Harner, Michael J.
1973a    The Jivaro. Garden City, NY: Doubleday-Anchor.
1973b    "The Sound of Rushing Water." In Hallucinogens and Shamanism, edited by Michael J. Harner, 15–27. London: Oxford University Press.

Harrell, Stevan, and Sara A. Dickey
1985    "Dowry Systems in Complex Societies." Ethnology 24:105–120.

Harris, Marvin
1968    The Rise of Anthropological Theory. New York: Thomas Y. Crowell.
1977    Cannibals and Kings. New York: Random House.
1979    Cultural Materialism. New York: Vintage Books.
1981    America Now. New York: Simon and Schuster.
1985    Good To Eat. New York: Simon and Schuster.

Harrison, Paul
1987    The Greening of Africa. New York: Penguin.

Hart, C. W. M. and Arnold R. Pilling
1979    The Tiwi of North Australia. New York: Holt, Rinehart, and Winston.

Hassrick, Royal B.
1964    The Sioux: Life and Customs of a Warrior Society. Norman: University of Oklahoma Press.

Hepner, George F. and Jesse O. McKee
1992    World Regional Geography: A Global Approach. St. Paul: West

Heyerdahl, Thor
1958    Aku-Aku. Chicago: Rand McNally & Company.

Hickerson, Harold
1970    The Chippewa and Their Neighbors: A Study in Ethnohistory. New York: Holt, Rinehart and Winston.

Hiebert, P. G.
1971    Konduru: Structure and Integration in a Hindu Village. Minneapolis: University of Minnesota Press.

Himes, Joseph S.
1974    Racial and Ethnic Relations. Dubuque, Ia.: Wm. C. Brown Company.

Hirst, Eric
1974    "Food-Related Energy Requirements." Science 184:134–38.

Hockett, Charles D.
1960    "The Origin of Speech" Scientific American 203:88–96.

Hoebel, E. Adamson
1940    The Political Organization and Law-ways of the Comanche Indians. American Anthropological Association, Memoir 54.
1954    The Law of Primitive Man. Cambridge: Harvard University Press.
1978    The Cheyennes. 2d ed. New York: Holt, Rinehart and Winston.

Holmes, Lowell D. and Ellen Rhoads Holmes
1992    Samoan Village Then and Now. 2d edition. Fort Worth: Harcourt Brace Jovanovic College Publishers.

Horowitz, Donald L.
1985    Ethnic Groups In Conflict. Berkeley: University of California Press.

Howard, Alan, and John Kirkpatrick
1989    "Social Organization." In Developments in Polynesian Ethnology, edited by Alan Howard and Robert Borofsky, pp. 47–94. Honolulu: University of Hawaii Press.

Innis, Donald Q.
1980    "The Future of Traditional Agriculture." Focus 30:1–8.

Jackson, Richard, and Lloyd E. Hudman.
1990a  Cultural Geography: People, Places and Environment. St. Paul, Minn.: West Publishing Company.

Jackson, Richard H. and Llyod E. Hudman
1990b  World Regional Geography: Issues for Today. New York: John Wiley & Sons

Jenness, Diamond
1932  The Indians of Canada. Ottawa: National Museum of Canada.

Johnson, Allen W.
1971  "Security and Risk-Taking Among Poor Peasants: A Brazilian Case." In Studies in Economic Anthropology, edited by George Dalton, 143–50. American Anthropological Association Special Publication, no. 7. Washington, D.C.: American Anthropological Association.

Joint Economic Committee
1986  The Concentration of Wealth in the United States: Trends in the Distribution of Wealth Among American Families.

Kahn, J., et al, eds.
1979  World Economic Development. Boulder CO: Westview

Kahn, Lawrence
1991  "Discrimination in Professional Sports: A Survey of the Literature." Industrial and Labor Relations Review 44:395–418.

Kammer, Jerry
1980  The Second Long Walk, The Navajo-Hopi Land Dispute. Albuquerque: University of New Mexico.

Kardiner, Abram
1945  The Psychological Frontiers of Society. New York: Columbia University Press.

Keesing, Roger M.
1976  Cultural Anthropology: A Contemporary Perspective. New York: Holt, Rinehart and Winston.
1982  Kwaio Religion. New York: Columbia University Press.

Kehoe, Alice B.
1981  North American Indians: A Comprehensive Account. Englewood Cliffs, N. J.: Prentice-Hall, Inc.
1989  The Ghost Dance. New York: Holt, Rinehart and Winston.

Khlief, Bud B.
1979  Language as Identity: Toward an Ethnography of Welsh Nationalism. Ethnicity 6 (4): 346–57.

Kluckhohn, Clyde
1967  Navaho Witchcraft. Boston: Beacon Press.

Kolb, Abert
1971  East Asia. London: Methuen and Co. Ltd.

Krader, Lawrence
1968  Formation of the State. Englewood Cliffs, N.J.: Prentice-Hall.

Kuper, Hilda
1963  The Swazi: A South African Kingdom. New York: Holt, Rinehart and Winston.

Kupferer, Harriet J.
1988  Ancient Drums, Other Moccasins: Native North American Cultural Adaptation. Englewood Cliffs, N.J.: Prentice-Hall, Inc.

La Flesche, Francis
1928  "The Osage Tribe: Two Versions of the Child-Naming Rite." 43rd Annual Report of the Bureau of American Ethnology, 1925–1926, 23–164. Washington, D.C.: Government Printing Office.

Lakoff, Robin
1975  Language and Woman's Place. New York: Harper & Row.

Lappé, Frances Moore
1982  Diet for a Small Planet. New ed. New York: Ballantine Books.

Lappé, Frances Moore, and Joseph Collins
1977  Food First. New York: Ballantine Books.
1986  World Hunger: Twelve Myths. New York: Grove Press.

Lawrence, Peter
1964  Road Belong Cargo. Manchester: Manchester University Press.

Leach, E. R.
1968  "The Sinhalese of the Dry Zone of Northern Ceylon." In Economic Anthropology, edited by Edward E. LeClair, Jr., and Harold K. Schneider, 395–403. New York: Holt, Rinehart and Winston (original 1960).

Leach, Gerald
1976  Energy and Food Production. Guildford: IPC Science and Technology Press for the International Institute for Envrionment and Development.

Leacock, Eleanor
1978  "Women's Status in Egalitarian Society: Implications for Social Evolution." Current Anthropology 19:247–75.

Leacock, Eleanor, and Nancy Lurie, eds.
1971  North American Indians in Historical Perspective. New York: Random House.

Lee, Richard B.
1968  "What Hunters Do for a Living, or, How to Make Out on Scarce Resources." In Man the Hunter, edited by

Richard B. Lee and Irven DeVore, 30–48. Chicago: Aldine.
1969 "!Kung Bushman Subsistence: An Input–Output Analysis." In Environment and Cultural Behavior, edited by Andrew P. Vayda, 47–79. Garden City, N.Y.: Natural History Press.
1979 The !Kung San. Cambridge: Cambridge University Press.

Lenski, Gerhard E.
1966 Power and Privilege. New York: McGraw-Hill.

Levenson, Jay A. ed.
1992 Circa 1492: Art in the Age of Exploration. New Haven and Washington D.C.: Yale University Press and The National Gallery of Art

Levinson, David, and Martin J. Malone
1980 Toward Explaining Human Culture. New Haven, Conn.: HRAF Press.

Lévi-Strauss, Claude
1963a Structural Anthropology. New York: Doubleday.
1963b Totemism. Boston: Beacon.
1966 The Savage Mind. Chicago: University of Chicago Press.

Lewis, Oscar
1941 Manly-hearted Women Among the South Piegan. American Anthropologist 43:173–87.

Lewis, Walter H., and Memory P. F. Elvin-Lewis
1977 Medical Botany. New York: John Wiley and Sons.

Lipsky, George
1962 Ethiopia: Its People, Its Society, Its Culture. New Haven: Human Relations Area Files Press.

Little, Michael A., and George E. B. Morren, Jr.
1976 Ecology, Energetics, and Human Variability. Dubuque, Iowa: Wm. C. Brown Company.

Llewellyn, Karl and E. Adamson Hoebel
1941 The Cheyenne Way. Norman: University of Oklahoma.

Lowie, Robert H.
1954 Indians of the Plains. Garden City, N.Y.: American Museum of Natural History.
1956 The Crow Indians. New York: Holt, Rinehart and Winston (original 1935).

Malinowski, Bronislaw
1922 Argonauts of the Western Pacific. New York: E. P. Dutton and Company, Inc.
1926 Crime and Custom in Savage Society. London: Rutledge and Kegan Paul.
1954 Magic, Science and Religion. Garden City, N.Y.: Doubleday and Company, Inc.
1960 A Scientific Theory of Culture and Other Essays. New York: Oxford University Press (original 1944).

Mamdani, Mahmood
1973 The Myth of Population Control: Family, Caste and Class in an Indian Village. New York: Monthly Review Press.

Mandelbaum, David G.
1970 Society In India. 2 vols. Berkeley: University of California Press.

Martin, M. Kay, and Barbara Voorhies
1975 Female of the Species. New York: Columbia University Press.

Marx, Karl
1967 Capital. Volume 1. New York: International Publishers (original 1867).
1970 A Contribution to the Critique of Political Economy. New York: International Publishers (original 1859).
1975 Wages, Price and Profit. Peking: Foreign Languages Press (original 1898).

Mayo, Katherine
1927 Mother India. Harcourt, Brace & Company.

McAlister, John T., ed.
1973 Southeast Asia: The Politics of National Integration. New York: Random House.

McVey, Ruth T., ed.
1962 Indonesia. New Haven, Conn.: Human Relations Area Files Press.

Mead, Margaret
1928 Coming of Age in Samoa. New York: Morrow.

Medicine, Beatrice
1983 "'Warrior Women': Sex Role Alternatives for Plains Indian Women." In Hidden Half: Studies of Plains Indian Women, edited by Patricia Albers and Beatrice Medicine, 267–75. Lanham, MD.: University Press of America.

Meggitt, Mervyn
1970 "Male-Female Relationships in the Highlands of Australian New Guinea." In Cultures of the Pacific, edited by Thomas G. Harding and Ben J. Wallace, 125–43. New York: Free Press.

Meigs, Anna S.
1988 Food, Sex, and Pollution: A New Guinea Religion. New Brunswick, N.J.: Rutgers University Press.
1990 "Multiple Gender Ideologies and Statuses." In Peggy Reeves Sanday and Ruth Gallagher Goodenough, eds., 1990, pp. 99–112.

Middleton, John
1965 The Lugbara of Uganda. New York: Holt, Rinehart and Winston.

Minge-Klevana, Wanda
1980 "Does Labor Time Decrease with Industrialization? A Survey of Time-Allocation Studies." Current Anthropology 21:279–98.

Mintz, Sidney W.
1961   "Pratik: Haitian Personalistic Economic Relationships." Proceedings of the American Ethnological Society, 54–63. Seattle: University of Washington Press.

Miracle, Marvin P.
1966   Maize in Tropical Africa. Madison: University of Wisconsin.
1967   Agriculture in the Congo Basin. Madison: University of Wisconsin.

Mishel, Lawrence and Jared Bernstein
1993   The State of Working America 1992–93. Economic Policy Institute Series. Armonk: M.E. Sharpe.

Moore, Omar Khayyam
1957   "Divination—A New Perspective." American Anthropologist 59:69–74.

Moore, Sally Falk
1958   Power and Property in Inca Peru. New York: Columbia.

Morgan, Lewis Henry
1877   Ancient Society. New York: World Publishing.

Morgen, Sandra, ed.
1989   Gender and Anthropology: Critical Reviews for Research and Teaching. Washington, D.C.: American Anthropological Association.

Moskowitz, Breyne
1985   "The Acquisition of Language." In Language: Introductory Readings, edited by Virginia P. Clark, Paul A. Eschholz, and Alfred F. Rosa, 45–73. New York: St. Martin's Press.

Murdock, George Peter
1949   Social Structure. New York: The Free Press.
1959   Africa: Its People and Their Culture History. New York: McGraw-Hill.
1967   Ethnographic Atlas. Pittsburgh: University of Pittsburgh Press.

Murdock, George P., and Caterina Provost
1973   "Factors in the Division of Labor By Sex: A Cross-Cultural Analysis." Ethnology 12:203–225.

Myers, Norman
1985   The Primary Source: Tropical Forests and Our Future. New York: W. W. Norton and Company.

Nag, Moni, Benjamin N. F. White, and R. Creighton Peet
1978   "An Anthropological Approach to the Study of the Economic Value of Children in Java and Nepal." Current Anthropology 19:293–306.

Nardi, Bonnie
1981   "Modes of Explanation in Anthropological Population Theory." American Anthropologist 83:28–56.
1983   "Goals in Reproductive Decision Making." American Ethnologist 10:697–714.

Naroll, Raoul
1962   Data Quality Control—A New Research Technique. New York: The Free Press.

Nations, James, and Robert Nigh
1980   "The Evolutionary Potential of Lacandon Maya Sustained-Yield Tropical Forest Agriculture." Journal of Anthropological Research 36:1–30.

Neale, Walter C.
1976   Monies in Societies. San Francisco: Chandler and Sharp.

Newman, Katherine S.
1983   Law and Economic Organization: A Comparative Study of Pre-Industrial Societies. Cambridge: Cambridge University.

Newman, Philip L., and David J. Boyd
1982   "The Making of Men: Ritual and Meaning in Awa Male Initiation." In Rituals of Manhood: Male Initiation in Papua New Guinea, edited by Gilbert Herdt, 239–85. Berkeley and Los Angeles: University of California Press.

Nietschmann, Bernard
1988   "Third World War: The Global Conflict Over the Rights of Indigenous Nations." Utne Reader (Nov./Dec.):84–91.

Ninuendju, Curt
1948   "The Tucuna." In Handbook of South American Indians, vol. 3, edited by Julian Steward, 713–25. Handbook of South American Indians: The Tropical Forest Tribes. Bureau of American Ethnology Bulletin 143. Washington, D.C.: U.S. Government PrintingOffice.

Norris, Robert E.
1990   World Regional Geography. St. Paul, Minn.: West Publishing Company.

Offiong, Daniel
1983   "Witchcraft Among the Ibibio of Nigeria." African Studies Review 26: 107–24.

Oliver, Douglas L.
1989   Oceania: The Native Cultures of Australia and the Pacific Islands. Honolulu: University of Hawaii Press.

Oliver Roland, and J. D. Fage
1962   A Short History of Africa. Baltimore: Penguin.

Oliver, Symmes C.
1962   Ecology and Cultural Continuity as Contributing Factors in the Social Organization of the Plains Indians. University of California Publications in American Archaeology and Ethnology 48(1).

Opala, Joseph
1987   The Gullah. Freetown, Sierra Leone: United States Information Service.

Pasternak, Burton
1976 Introduction to Kinship and Social Organization. Englewood Cliffs, N.J.: Prentice-Hall, Inc.

Pasternak, Burton, Carol R. Ember, and Melvin Ember
1976 "On the Conditions Favoring Extended Family Households." Journal of Anthropological Research 32:109–23.

Peoples, James G.
1982 "Individual or Group Advantage? A Reinterpretation of the Maring Ritual Cycle." Current Anthropology 23:291–309.

Piddocke, Stuart
1965 "The Potlatch System of the Southern Kwakiutl: A New Perspective." Southwestern Journal of Anthropology 21:244–64.

Pimentel, David, et al.
1973 "Food Production and the Energy Crisis." Science 182:443–49.
1975 "Energy and Land Constraints in Food Protein Production." Science 190:754–61.
1980 "The Potential for Grass-Fed Livestock: Resource Constraints." Science 207:843–48.

Pimentel, David, and Marcia Pimentel
1979 Food, Energy and Society. New York: John Wiley and Sons.

Porter, Philip W.
1965 "Environmental Potentials and Economic Opportunities—A Background for Cultural Adaptation." American Anthropologist 67:409–20.

Posey, Darrell
1983 "Indigenous Ecological Knowledge and Development of the Amazon." In The Dilemma of Amazonian Development, Emilio Moran, ed. Boulder, Colo.: Westview Press.
1984 "A Preliminary Report on Diversified Management of Tropical Forest by the Kayapó Indians of the Brazilian Amazon." Advances in Economic Botany 1:112–126.
1985 "Indigenous Management of Tropical Forest Ecosystems: The Case of the Kayapó Indians of the Brazilian Amazon." Agroforestry Systems 3:139–158.

Pospisil, Leopold
1958 Kapauku Papuans and Their Law. Yale University Publications in Anthropology, no. 54.
1978 The Kapauku Papuans of West New Guinea. 2d ed. New York: Holt, Rinehart and Winston.

Price, Richard, ed.
1979 Maroon Societies: Rebel Slave Communities in the Americas. Baltimore: Johns Hopkins University.

Pulliam, H. Ronald, and Christopher Dunford
1980 Programmed to Learn. New York: Columbia University Press.

Quinn, Naomi
1977 "Anthropological Studies on Women's Status." Annual Review of Anthropology 6:181–225.

Radcliffe-Brown, A. R.
1922 The Andaman Islanders. Cambridge: Cambridge University Press.
1965 Structure and Function in Primitive Society. New York: Free Press.

Rappaport, Roy
1968 Pigs for the Ancestors. New Haven: Yale University Press.

Rasmussen, Knud
1979 "A Shaman's Journey to the Sea Spirit." In Reader in Comparative Religion, edited by William A. Lessa and Evon Z. Vogt, 308–11. New York: Harper & Row.

Reichel-Dolmatoff, Gerardo
1971 Amazonian Cosmos. Chicago: University of Chicago Press.

Robertson, Ian
1987 Sociology. 3d ed. New York: Worth.

Robinson, Harvey
1967 Monsoon Asia: A Geographical Survey. New York: Praeger.

Rohner, Ronald P.
1975 They Love Me, They Love Me Not: A Worldwide Study of the Effects of Parental Acceptance and Rejection. New Haven, Conn.: HRAF Press.

Rosaldo, Michelle Z., and Louise Lamphere, eds.
1974 Women, Culture, and Society. Stanford: Stanford University Press.

Rostow, W. W.
1978 The World Economy: History and Prospect. Austin: University of Texas.

Ruddle, Kenneth
1974 The Yukpa Autosubsistence System: A Study of Shifting Cultivation and Ancillary Activities in Colombia and Venezuela. Berkeley: University of California Press.

Russell, George
1986 "Easing into an Era." Time (July 14). 44–5.

Sacks, Karen
1982 Sisters and Wives. Urbana: University of Illinois Press.

Sahlins, Marshall
1958 Social Stratification in Polynesia. Seattle: University of Washington Press.
1972 Stone Age Economics. New York: Aldine Publishing Company.

1981  Historical Metaphors and Mythical Realities: Structure in the Early History of the Sandwich Island Kingdom. Ann Arbor: University of Michigan Press.

**Sanday, Peggy R.**
1973  "Toward a Theory of the Status of Women." American Anthropologist 75:1682–1700.
1981  Female Power and Male Dominance. Cambridge: Cambridge University Press.

**Sanday, Peggy Reeves and Ruth Gallagher Goodenough, eds.**
1990  Byond the Second Sex. Philadelphia: University of Pennsylvania Press.

**Sapir, Edward**
1964  "The Status of Linguistics as a Science." In Edward Sapir, edited by David G. Mandelbaum, 65–77. Berkeley: University of California Press (original 1929).

**Schlegel, Alice**
1972  Male Dominance and Female Autonomy. New Haven, Conn.: HRAF Press.

**Schneider, Harold K.**
1981  The Africans. Englewood Cliffs, N.J.: Prentice-Hall.

**Scudder, Thayer**
1982  No Place To Go: Effects of Compulsory Relocation on Navajos. Philadelphia: ISHI.

**Service, Elman R.**
1962  Primitive Social Organization: An Evolutionary Perspective. New York: Random House.
1975  Origins of the State and Civilization. New York: W. W. Norton.

**Shankman, Paul**
1976  Migration and Underdevelopment: The Case of Western Samoa. Boulder, Colo.: Westview Press.

**Shore, Bradd**
1989  "Mana and Tapu." In Developments in Polynesian Ethnology, Alan Howard and Robert Borofsky, Editors, pp. 137–173. Honolulu: University of Hawaii Press.

**Shweder, Richard A., and Robert A. LeVine, eds.**
1984  Culture Theory: Essays on Mind, Self, and Emotion. Cambridge: Cambridge University Press.

**Sokolov, Raymond**
1986  "The Good Seed." Natural History 95:102–105.

**Spicer, Edward, ed.**
1961  Perspectives in American Indian Culture Change. Chicago: University of Chicago Press.

**Stamp, L. Dudley**
1973  A Commercial Geography. 9th ed. London: Longman.

**Stavrianos, L. S.**
1982  The World Since 1500: A Global History. 4th ed. Englewood Cliffs, N.J.: Prentice-Hall.

**Steinhart, Carol, and John Steinhart**
1974  Energy: Sources, Use, and Role in Human Affairs. North Scituate, Mass.: Duxbury Press.

**Steward, Julian H.**
1938  Basin-Plateau Sociopolitical Groups. Bureau of American Ethnology Bulletin 120.
1955  Theory of Culture Change. Urbana, IL: University of Illinois Press.

**Steward, Julian, and Louis Faron**
1959  Native Peoples of South America. New York: McGraw-Hill.

**Stewart, Omer C.**
1980  "The Native American Church." In Anthropology on the Great Plains, edited by W. Raymond Wood and Margot Liberty, 188–96. Lincoln, Neb.: University of Nebraska Press.

**Suttles, Wayne**
1960  "Affinal Ties, Subsistence, and Prestige among the Coast Salish." American Anthropologist 62:296–305.
1962  "Variations in Habitat and Culture on the Northwest Coast." In Man In Adaptation: The Cultural Present, edited by Yehudi A. Cohen, 128–41. Chicago: Aldine.
1968  "Coping with Abundance: Subsistence on the Northwest Coast." In Man the Hunter, edited by Richard B. Lee and Irven DeVore, 56–68. Chicago: Aldine.

**Swanson, Guy**
1960  The Birth of the Gods. Ann Arbor: University of Michigan Press.

**Swanton, John R.**
1946  The Indians of the Southeastern United States. Bureau of American Ethnology Bulletin, no. 137. Washington, D.C.

**Swepton, Lee**
1989  Indigenous and Tribal Peoples and International Law: Recent Developments. Current Anthropology 30:259–64.

**Szwed, John F., ed.**
1970  Black America. New York: Basic Books.

**Tax, Sol, ed.**
1967  Acculturation in the Americas. New York: Cooper Square Publishers.

**Thornton, Russell**
1987  American Indian Holocaust and Survival: A Population History since 1492. Norman: University of Oklahoma Press.

Tischer, Henry L.
1990   Introduction to Sociology. 3d ed. Fort Worth, Tex.: Holt, Rinehart and Winston.

Trudgill, Peter
1983   Sociolinguistics. Middlesex, England: Penguin.

Turnbull, Colin M.
1962   The Forest People. New York: Simon and Schuster.

Turner, Terence
1989   "Kayapo Plan Meeting to Discuss Dams." Cultural Survival Quarterly 13:20–22.

Turner, Victor
1967   The Forest of Symbols. Ithaca, NY: Cornell University Press.

Tyler, Stephen A., ed.
1969   Cognitive Anthropology. New York: Holt, Rinehart and Winston.

Tyler, Stephen A.
1973   India: An Anthropological Perspective. Pacific Palisades, Calif.: Goodyear Publishing Company.

Tylor, Edward B.
1865   Researches into the Early History of Mankind and the Development of Civilization. London: J. Murray.
1871   Primitive Culture. London: J. Murray.

United States Bureau of the Census
1992   Statistical Abstract of the United States 1992. Washington, D.C.

Urban, Greg and Joel Sherzer eds.
1992   Nation-States and Indians in Latin America. Austin: University of Texas.

Valeri, Valerio
1985   Kingship and Sacrifice: Ritual and Society in Ancient Hawaii. Chicago and London: University of Chicago Press.

Van den Berghe, Pierre
1979   Human Family Systems. New York: Elsevier.

Vanstone, James W.
1974   Athapaskan Adaptations: Hunters and Fishermen of the Subarctic Forest. Chicago: Aldine.

Vincent, Joan
1974   The Structuring of Ethnicity. Human Organization 33:375–79.

Waddell, Eric
1972   The Mound Builders. Seattle: University of Washington Press.

Wagley, Charles
1968   The Latin American Tradition: Essays on the Unity and the Diversity of Latin American Culture. New York: Columbia University Press.

Wallace, Anthony F. C.
1966   Religion: An Anthropological View. New York: Random House.
1969   The Death and Rebirth of the Seneca. New York: Vintage Books.

Wallace, Ernest, and E. Adamson Hoebel
1952   The Comanches: Lords of the South Plains. Norman: University of Oklahoma.

Weyler, Rey
1982   Blood of the Land. New York: Vintage Books.

White, Benjamin N. F.
1973   "Demand for Labor and Population Growth in Colonial Java." Human Ecology 1:217–36.

White, Douglas R., Michael L. Burton, and Malcolm M. Dow
1981   "Sexual Division of Labor in African Agriculture: A Network Autocorrelation Analysis." American Anthropologist 83:824–49.

White, Leslie
1949   The Science of Culture. New York: Grove Press.
1959   The Evolution of Culture. New York: McGraw-Hill.

White, Lynn
1967   "The Historical Roots of Our Ecologic Crisis." Science 155:1203–1207.

Whiting, Beatrice
1950   Paiute Sorcery. Viking Fund Publications in Anthropology 15. New York.

Whiting, John W. M.
1977   "A Model for Psychocultural Research." In Culture and Infancy, edited by P. Herbert Leiderman, S. R. Tulkin, and A. Rosenfield, 29–49. New York: Academic Press.

Whitworth, John McKelvie
1975   God's Blueprints: A Sociological Study of Three Utopian Sects. Boston: Rutledge and Kegan Paul.

Whyte, Martin King
1978   The Status of Women in Preindustrial Societies. Princeton, N.J.: Princeton University Press.

Wilken, Gene C.
1987   Good Farmers: Traditional Resource Management in Mexico and Central America. Berkeley: University of California Press.

Wilson, Monica
1951   Good Company. Oxford: Oxford University Press.

Winthrop, Robert H.
1991   Dictionary of Concepts in Cultural Anthropology. New York: Greenwood Press.

Wolf, Eric
1966   Peasants. Englewood Cliffs, N.J.: Prentice-Hall.

1969   Peasant Wars of the Twentieth Century. New York: Harper and Row.
1982   Europe and the People Without History. Berkeley: University of California Press.

**Wolf, Eric R., and Edward C. Hansen**
1972   The Human Condition in Latin America. New York: Oxford University Press.

**Wolf, Margery**
1972   Women and the Family in Rural Taiwan. Stanford, Calif.: Stanford University Press.

**Woodburn, James**
1968   "An Introduction to Hadza Ecology." In Man the Hunter, edited by Richard B. Lee and Irven DeVore, 49–55. Chicago: Aldine.

1982   "Egalitarian Societies." Man 17:431–51.

**World Bank**
1982   World Development Report 1982. New York: Oxford.
1992   World Development Report 1992. New York: Oxford.

**Worsley, Peter**
1968   The Trumpet Shall Sound. New York: Schocken Books.

**Zanker, Alfred**
1986   "Europe's Immigration Battles." U.S. News and World Report (March 31). 25–27.

England/English, 94, 116, 118, 119, 121, 122, 123, 164, 371, 377, 378, 380, 401, 405, 413, 425–428
Eskimo (see Inuit)
Estonia/Estonians, 398, 400
Ethiopia, 106, 111, 121, 383, 391, 392, 412, 418, 419, 420
Euro-Americans, 121, 128, 215, 253, 371, 384, 386, 403
Europe/Europeans, 106–108, 113, 120, 123–127, 152, 155, 175, 215, 266, 273, 274, 376, 377, 378, 379, 380, 412, 435, 437

## F

Far East (see East Asia)
Fiji, 113, 123
Finland/Finns, 398
Flemish, 404
France/French, 116, 118, 119, 121, 281, 371, 377, 378, 380, 401, 405, 419
French-Canadians, 404, 405–405

## G

Galitians, 404
Garia, 343, 345
Genieri, 164
Georgia/Georgian, 398, 400
Germany/Germans (see also West Germany), 121, 123, 364, 371, 372, 380, 383, 385, 398, 401, 433
Ghana, 418
Great Britain (see England)
Greece (ancient), 357, 438
Greece (modern), 397
Gros Ventre, 58
Guatemala/Guatemalans, 378, 383
ethnic clothing, 386, 387, 401, 404, 405, 414
Gullah (see also African-Americans), 126–127
Gypsies, 401

## H

Hadza, 138, 140, 147, 191, 302
Haiti, 190, 197
Hanunoo, 30, 159
Hausa, 395
Hawaiians, 94, 113, 123, 313
Hidatsa, 355, 366
Honduras, 419
Hong Kong, 371, 373, 374, 412
Hopi, 56, 233–234, 235, 247, 271, 330, 350, 385
Hua, 251–253
Huguenots, 387

Hungary/Hungarians, 391–392, 404, 406
Huron, 241
Hutterites, 26
Hutu, 395

## I

Iban, 159, 238–239
Ibibio, 333
Ibos, 395
Inca (see also Peru), 165, 195–196, 198, 286, 312, 313, 340
India/Indians, 106, 108–109, 112, 119, 122–123, 128, 136, 162, 206, 215, 267, 305–307, 312, 313, 340, 371, 377–378, 379, 385, 386, 392, 394, 397, 401, 413, 414, 416, 418, 419, 420, 421
Indo-China, 371
Indonesia, 162, 281, 352, 391, 416–417, 423, 434, 435
Inuit, 140, 147, 210, 302, 330, 364
Iraq, 377, 396–97
Iran/Iranians, 378, 396–397
Ireland/Irish, 379, 383, 385, 390–391, 397, 404, 433, 439
Iroquois (see also Seneca), 241, 269–270, 271
Israelites (ancients), 80–81, 211
Israel/Israeli (modern), 380, 383, 385
origin of, 391, 401, 404, 412
Italy/Italians, 371, 374, 377, 379

## J

Japan/Japanese, 58, 109, 122, 155, 202, 266, 267, 313, 335, 340, 371, 372, 374, 375, 379, 380, 385, 412, 413, 419, 437
Java (see also Indonesia), 58, 119, 160
Jews as ethnic group (see Israel/Israeli)
Jivaro, 291–292, 338

## K

Kanem-Bornu, 110, 118
Kapauku, 187
Karen, 395
Karimojong, 170, 174–175, 176, 193
Kayapo, 429, 436
Kazakhstan/Kazakh, 170, 398, 400
Kenya/Kenyans, 413, 419
Khoisan (see also ikung), 110
Kikuy, 34
Kirghizia, 398
Kiowa, 115, 344
Kongo Empire, 110, 117, 118
Korea/Koreans (see also South Korea), 109, 378, 385

Kosraen, 46–47, 50
ikung (see also Khoisan), 103, 142–144, 145, 146–47, 164, 180, 191, 302, 336
Kurds, 395–396, 397
Kuwait, 376, 379
Kwaio, 328
Kwakiutl (see also Northwest Coast), 351–352

## L

Lacandon, 429–430
Laos/Laotians, 378
Lapps (see also sami), 169–170
Latin America/Latin Americans, 125–126, 175, 376, 377, 378, 379, 380, 404, 434, 439
Latvia/Latvians, 398
LDCs, lesser developed countries (see Third World)
Liberia, 121, 397
Libero-Americans, 127
Libya, 379
Lithuania/Lithuanians, 398
Luba, 110
Lugbara, 333, 339
Lunda, 118

## M

Macedonia/Macedonians, 396–397, 404, 406–407
Madagascar (see also Malagasy), 111, 437
Mali, 412
Malagasy (see also Madagascar), 111
Malaitans, 345
Malaya/Malays (see also Malaysia), 122, 371, 386
Malaysia (see also Malaya), 386
Manns, 345
Maring, 159, 164, 182, 193
Maori, 123, 237
Masai, 172, 251
Maya, 70, 165, 166, 340
Melanesia, 113, 120, 123, 186, 202, 342–343, 345, 346, 355
Mesoamerica, 112, 114, 439
Meti, 387
Mexico-Mexicans, 116, 152, 158, 161, 375, 378, 386, 387, 390, 414, 418, 419, 423, 429, 435
Micronesia, 112, 120, 123
Middle East (see also Arabs), 108, 152, 158, 171, 215, 273, 380, 413, 418, 439
Moldavia/Moldavians, 398, 400
Monomatapa, 110, 117, 118
Montenegro/Montenegrins, 396, 404, 406–407
Morocco, 397
Mozambique, 418

## N

Naga, 392
Naskapi, 330
Natchez, 307–308
Native Americans, 113–117, 125–126, 128, 371, 384, 385, 386, 387, 390, 403, 405, 433, 434, 438
Navajo, 9, 30, 91, 333, 334, 358, 385
Nayar, 203, 205, 220, 241
Ndembu, 29, 330, 362
Nepal, 417
Netherlands, 116, 122, 123, 127, 371, 385, 387, 401
Netsilik (see also Inuit), 140–141, 145, 336
New Caledonia, 123
New Guinea, 113, 123, 359–361
New World, 106, 152, 153, 154, 160, 168
New Zealand, 113, 123, 412
Nigeria/Nigerians, 8, 377, 395, 413, 414, 418, 419
North America/North Americans, 31, 33, 53–54, 57–58, 136, 155, 183, 184–185, 187, 192, 212, 217–218, 224, 226, 235, 238, 254–255, 266, 312, 324–325, 330, 335, 352, 353, 372, 376, 377, 378, 379, 411, 413, 415–416, 417, 418, 421, 424–425, 430, 435, 437, 440–442
North Borneo, 371
Northern Ireland (see Ireland/Irish)
Northwest Coast, 144–145, 147, 302
Nuer, 170, 290–291, 292
Nupe, 47–48
Nyakyusa, 333, 356

## O

Oceania, 112, 120, 123, 168, 213, 371, 377
Old World, 106, 152, 154, 160, 165
Oman/Omani, 110, 112, 117, 379, 386
Osage, 91, 344–345, 357, 366, 386
Ossetians, 398, 400

## P

Pacific (see Oceania)
Pakistan/Pakistani, 377, 379, 392, 394–395, 413
Palestine/Palestinians, 379, 383, 391
Papago, 440
Papua New Guinea (see also New Guinea), 440
Peguots, 401
Peru (see also Inca), 112, 114, 152, 195
Peru/Peruvians (modern), 378, 387, 418, 419, 420, 434, 440
Philippines, 119, 190, 197, 281, 371, 395, 417, 434, 435

Plain Indians, 114, 115, 213, 256–257, 336, 337, 344
Poland/Polish, 380, 398, 401
Polynesian, 112, 120, 123, 237
Portugal/Portuguese, 114, 116–117, 119, 121, 371, 401
Pueblos (see also Hopi and Zuni), 91, 158
Pygmies (see also Ba Mbuti), 110

## Q

Quapaw, 344
Quatar, 379
Quechua, 439

## R

Russia/Russians, 119, 126, 281, 371, 380, 386, 398–400

## S

Sahrawi, 397
Salvadorans (see El Salvador)
Sami (see also Lapps), 433
Samoa/Samoans, 123, 237, 358–359, 417
Sarawak, 371
Saudi Arabia, 376, 379
Scotch-Irish, 391
Semai, 24–25
Seminoles, 126–127, 386
Seneca (see also Iroquois), 343–344, 346
Serbia/Serbs, 385, 396–397, 400, 402, 404, 406–407
Shan, 395
Shoshone (see also Western Shoshone), 115
Siberia, 110, 127, 398, 399
Sikhs, 385, 392, 394
Singapore, 373, 374, 412
Sinhalese (see also Sri Lanka), 163, 164
Sioux, 256, 401
Slovakia/Slovaks, 405, 406
Slovenia/Slovenians, 396, 397, 404, 406–407
Somalia/Somali, 111, 392, 397, 412, 418, 420
Songhai, 110, 118
South Africa, 387, 388–389
South Asia (see India)
South Korea (see also Korea), 373, 374, 375
Southeast Asia, 109–110, 152, 161, 162, 168, 202, 213, 440
Soviet Union (see also Russia), 376, 379, 396, 397, 398–400, 404
Spain/Spanish, 49–50, 57, 113–114, 116–117, 119, 371, 377, 401, 404, 433, 439
Sri Lanka (see also Ceylon), 395
Sub-Saharan Africa (see also Africa), 110–112, 116–119, 121–122, 158, 213, 273, 274, 341, 412, 413, 419

Sudan, 383, 395, 401, 412, 418, 420
Swazi, 170, 214, 355–356, 366, 385
Sweden/Swedish, 380
Syria, 396–397

## T

Tahitians, 251, 285–286
Taiwan, 373, 374
Tajikistan, 398, 400
Tamil, 122
Tannese, 345
Tasmanians, 113, 123, 386
Tatars, 398, 400
Thai, 47, 48
The Americas, 106, 112, 113–117, 120–121, 152, 263–264, 377
The Horn (see also Ethiopia and Somalia), 111
Third World, 411, 416–418, 419, 420, 421, 423, 428, 430–431, 434
Tibet/Tibetans, 210–211, 396
Tipokia, 232–233, 234, 247, 303–304, 319
Tiv, 187, 197
Trobriander, 89, 181, 326–327, 330
Tswana, 170
Tuareg, 171
Tucuna, 361
Tukano, 30
Tungus, 170
Turkey/Turks, 377, 379, 396, 397, 401, 402, 403
Turkmenistan, 398
Tutsi, 395

## U

Ukraine/Ukrainians, 398, 400
United Arab Emirates, 376, 379
United Kingdom (see England)
United States (see also North America), 14, 44–45, 164, 223, 274–275, 301, 308–312, 313–316, 319, 355, 359, 364, 373–375, 377, 378, 380, 384–385, 390, 405, 412, 415–416, 419, 425–428, 438, 439
Uzbekistan, 398, 400

## V

Vietnam/Vietnamese, 47, 378

## W

Walloons, 404
West Germany (see also Germany), 377, 378
West Indians, 377
Western Sahara, 397
Western Samoa (see Samoa)

Western Shoshone, 141–142, 145, 147, 191, 302

# Y

Yakut, 398, 399
Yana, 58

Yanomamö, 24–25, 58–59, 91–92, 211–212, 214–215, 251, 336, 435
Yoruba, 271, 396
Yugoslavia, 377, 379, 385, 396–397, 404, 405, 406–407
Yukaghir, 58
Yukpa, 159

# Z

Zaire (see also Congo), 435
Zande, 333, 334, 335
Zulu, 59, 212, 312, 385
Zuni, 351–352

# SUBJECT INDEX

systems of control over, 190–196
use of by foragers, 138–145
revelations, 342
revitalization movements, 342–345
rights of access, 137, 192, 193, 156, 191,
196, 216, 302
among !Kung, 143–144
among pastoralists, 173–174
in horticulture, 157
rite of passage, 363
defined, 357
*see also* initiation rites
rituals, 233, 234, 284, 323, 325–326, 327,
328, 329, 330, 331, 341, 342

# S

scarcity explanation of hunger, 420–423
secondary features, 77
secular ideologies, 313–314
*see also* ideologies
self-help legal systems, 289–292
semantic domain, 54–55
serial monogamy, 211
sexual division of labor, 175, 204, 219,
254–266
among foragers, 137
cross-cultural patterns in, 258, 25
(table)
hypotheses about, 258, 263
in horticulture, 156
intensive agriculture and, 263–266
shaman, 30
*see also* shamanistic cults
shamanistic cults, 336, 337–338
shifting cultivation, 30, 157, 158–160, 182,
423
among Kayapó, 429
among Lacandon Maya, 429–430
sickness
and shamanism, 337–338
*see also* illness; disease
Sikhs, 392–394
simple bands, 282
slash and burn
*see* shifting cultivation
slave trade, 116, 117–118, 121
social classes, 307–312
among Natchez, 307–308
and supernatural sanctions, 330
in United States, 308–312
*see also* stratification; stratified societies
social control, 281
defined, 287
witchcraft and sorcery and, 335
*see also* law; legal systems; court systems
social distance, 183
social functions of religion, 328–330
social learning, 23

social solidarity, 329
social systems model, 352–355
society, 25, *passim*
sociolinguistics, 57–60
sociological interpretations of witchcraft,
334–336
sodalities, 284–285
age sets as, 355
sorcerers
*see* sorcery
sorcery, 287, 331
accusations of, 332
and social control, 96–97
as a political weapon, 332–333
interpretations, 333–336
sororal polygyny, 209
sororate, 212
specialization
in chiefdoms, 285–286
in Indian caste system, 306–307
*see also* civilizations; states
specific evolution, 75
spirit helpers, 337, 338
sports, 38
and African Americans, 36–37
stages, 68–70, 71–72
state control, 194–196, 196
states, 286–287, 292
court systems of, 295–296
ecclesiastical cults and, 340–342
*see also* state control
status of women, 266–277
ethnographic record and, 268–270
influences on, 270–276
stereotypes, 90
stratification
and women's status, 273–276
in the United States, 308–312
*see also* castes; social classes; stratified societies
stratified societies, 301, 304–305, 319
*see also* castes; social classes
strength hypothesis, 262
structural functionalism, 73, 74–75
structuralism, 81, 82
subculture, 26
subnationalities, 390
substantive law, 288
supernatural beings, 323, 326, 330
supernatural forces, 323–324, 326
supernatural intervention, 330–331
supernatural powers, 323–347 *passim*
surplus, 145, 165, 286
in intensive agriculture, 163–165
swidden
*see* shifting cultivation
symbolic equation, 331–332
symbols, 29, 83, 182, 327, 334
in rituals, 325
syntax, 45, 49–50

# T

taboo, 58–59, 311
taboos
among Hua, 252
*tabu,* 286
taxes, 184, 194, 195
in colonial regions, 121, 122
technology, 68–69, 83, 105, 106, 131, 135, 153,
154, 156, 158, 188, 190, 193, 266, 316
among Netsilik, 140
in agriculture, 423–424, 425-430
in general evolution, 75–76
in idealist approaches, 79–81
in materialist approaches, 77–79
in specific evolution, 76–77
in transportation, 372
of shifting cultivators, 158–159
technology transfer solution, 423–424
theoretical orientations, 65–85
tone languages, 47–48
totem
*see* totemism
totemism, 231, 339–340
trade, 106, 182–183, 212, 240
in Old World, 111–112
with Africa, 117
with Asia, 119–120
*see also* world trade
trade partnership, 181
traditional resource management practices,
429–430
trance, 337
trial-and-error learning, 23
tribes, 284–285
incipient courts among, 292–293
tribute, 185–186, 194, 196, 316, 341

# U

uniformitarian theory, 67
unilineal descent, 225–229, 229, 236, 246
defined, 227
forms of, 227–229
groups, 229–232
*see also* descent, kinship
unilineal evolution, 68–70, 371
unilineal evolutionists, 71–72
universal grammar, 50–51
urbanization, 379

# V

values, 12, 28–29, 32, 74, 185, 296, 328,
334, 418
and behavior, 33
for large families, 411, 418
vision quest, 336–337

## Chapter 8

150, Courtesy of Michael Whalen. 151, © Tony Stone Worldwide. 154 (UL), Courtesy of Garrick Bailey. 154 (UR), © Jeffrey L. Rotman/Peter Arnold, Inc. 154 (LL), Anthro-Photo File. 154 (LR), © David Cavagnaro/Peter Arnold, Inc. 157, © Jeffrey L. Rotman/Peter Arnold, Inc. 159, Courtesy of Lamont Lindstrom. 161, Ahmed/David R. Frazier Photolibrary. 163, Ronald A. Liss/Peter Arnold, Inc. 166, © Robert Frerck/Woodfin Camp & Assoc. 167, United Nations (Photo No. 137151). 168, United Nations (Photo No. 123536). 170, United Nations. 171, United Nations. 174, United Nations.

## Chapter 9

178, Courtesy of Garrick Bailey. 179, © Eastcott/Momatiuk/Woodfin Camp & Assoc. 180, © Stan Washburn/Anthro-Photo File. 181, Courtesy of Lamont Lindstrom. 185, © Blair Seitz 1988/ Photo Researchers, Inc. 189 (all), Courtesy of Garrick Bailey. 192, Anthro-Photo File. 195, Culver Pictures, Inc.

## Chapter 10

200, Anthro-Photo File. 201, © Von Meiss-Teuffe/Photo Researchers. 202, © Bruno P. Zehnder/Peter Arnold, Inc. 203, Anthro-Photo File. 204, Anthro-Photo File. 207, © Homer Sykes/Woodfin Camp & Assoc. 210, Anthro-Photo File. 211, © Andy Bernhauf/Photo Researchers. 213, © Malcolm S. Kirk/Peter Arnold, Inc. 214, © Sabine Weiss/Photo Researchers. 216, © Sabine Weiss/Photo Researchers. 218, Anthro-Photo File.

## Chapter 11

222, Anthro-Photo File. 224, © Mark Gamba. 225, © Schuler/Anthro-Photo File. 230, © Tony Stone Worldwide. 231, Courtesy of James Peoples. 238, © Israel Talby 1991/Woodfin Camp & Assoc. 239, © Penny Tweedie 1986/Woodfin Camp & Assoc. 240, Anthro-Photo File.

## Chapter 12

250, Courtesy of James Peoples. 254, © Jeff Greenberg/Peter Arnold, Inc. 255, © Malcolm S. Kirk/Peter Arnold, Inc. 260 (UL), © John Paul Kay/Peter Arnold, Inc. 260 (UR), © Lindsey Hebberd 1990/Woodfin Camp & Assoc. 260 (ML), © Blair Seitz/Photo Researchers. 260 (MR), © Alain Evrard/Photo Researchers. 260 (LL), Anthro-Photo File. 260 (LR), © Stan Wayman/Photo Researchers. 261 (UL), © George Holton/Photo Researchers. 261 (UR), Anthro-Photo File. 261 (ML), Courtesy of Garrick Bailey. 261 (MR), © Hamilton Wright/Photo Researchers. 261 (LL), Anthro-Photo File. 261(LR), © Porterfield-Chickering/Photo Researchers. 262, United Nations. 263, United Nations. 264, United Nations. 267 (UL), United Nations. 267 (LR), © Douglas Mason 1992/Woodfin Camp & Assoc. 269, © 1992 Stock Montage. 271, R. Krubner/H. Armstrong Roberts, Inc. 273, Anthro-Photo File. 275, Courtesy of James Peoples. 276, © Connie Freer/Peter Arnold, Inc.

## Chapter 13

280, Courtesy of Garrick Bailey. 283, Courtesy of Thomas Gilcrease Institute of American History of Art, Tulsa, Oklahoma. 290, Anthro-Photo File. 293, Anthro-Photo File.

## Chapter 14

300, Peter Arnold. 303, © David Austen/Tony Stone Worldwide. 304, Bradley Smith. 306, © Bernard Wolff/Photo Researchers. 307, Peter Arnold. 309, Peter Arnold. 311 (LL), Courtesy of James Peoples. 311 (LR), Bob Daemmrich/The Image Works. 315, © Barbara Burns/Photo Researchers. 317, © Gerhard Gscheidle/Peter Arnold.

## Chapter 15

322, Norman Prince. 324, United Nations. 326, Anthro-Photo File. 329, © BIOS (A. Compost)/Peter Arnold. 331, © Loren McIntyre/Woodfin Camp & Assoc. 337, Anthro-Photo File. 340, Courtesy of Lamont Lindstrom. 341, Courtesy of James Peoples. 343, Courtesy of Lamont Lindstrom. 345, Courtesy of Thomas Gilcrease Institute of American History of Art, Tulsa, Oklahoma.

## Chapter 16

348, © N. Chagnon/Anthro-Photo File. 350, Anthro-Photo File. 351, Courtesy of Garrick Bailey and James Peoples. 354, United Nations (Photo No. 136487). 356, United Nations (Photo No. 148660). 358, United Nations (Photo No. 79816). 361 (UL), Courtesy of David Boyd. 361 (LR), Anthro-Photo File. 362, Anthro-Photo File. 363, Courtesy of John R. Wilson. 364, United Nations (Photo No. 152132). 365, United Nations (Photo No. 149065).

## Chapter 17

368, © Vanessa Vick/Photo Researchers. 370, United Nations (Photo No. 132862). 372, Anthro-Photo File. 373, United Nations (Photo No. 133558). 377, The Bettman Archive. 379, The Bettman Archive.

## Chapter 18

382, Reuters/Bettman. 384, UPI/Bettman Newsphotos. 386, AP/Wide World Photos. 387, AP/Wide World Photos. 391, Reuters/Bettman. 395, Reuters/Bettman. 396, Reuters/Bettman. 401, AP/Wide World Photos. 403, Smithsonian Institution.

## Chapter 19

410, © Bruce Brander/Photo Researchers. 413, Anthro-Photo File. 414, © Luiz C. Marigo/Peter Arnold. 415, © Charles Trainor/Photo Researchers. 417 (UL), © Mark Gamba. 417 (UR), © Martha Cooper/Peter Arnold. 417 (LL), Peter Arnold. 417 (LR), © Martha Cooper/Peter Arnold. 418, United Nations (Photo No. 154267). 419, United Nations (Photo No. 131437). 420, © Michael S. Yamashita/Woodfin Camp & Assoc. 421, © Carl Frank/Photo Researchers. 422, © Carl Frank/Photo Researchers. 425, © Michael Hart 1991/FPG. 426, © Mark Burnett/Photo Researchers. 427, UPI/Bettman.

## Epilogue

432, Anthro-Photo File. 434, © 1992 Stock Montage. 435, © Stephanie Maze/Woodfin Camp & Assoc. 436, Anthro-Photo File. 440, H. Armstrong Roberts. 441 (LL), © David R. Frazier Photolibrary. 441 (LR), © Stan Wayman/Photo Researchers.